The
American
IDEA OF
SUCCESS

by
RICHARD M. HUBER

PUSHCART

This book is for Suzanne, Cintra,
Dickie, and Casilda

CONTENTS

1 | Money . . . Status . . . Fame . . . *1*

2 | The Heritage *10*

3 | Schoolbooks and Journalists *23*

4 | ". . . Religion Demands Success" *42*

5 | "Money Getters Are the Benefactors
of Our Race" *62*

6 | A Message to Garcia *79*

7 | The Gospel of the Character Ethic *93*

8 | Why the Ambition to Succeed? *107*

9 | "The Mind Is a Magnet" *124*

10 | "Poverty Is a Mental Disease . . . ." *145*

11 | "To Think Success Brings Success" *165*

12 | "Day by Day, In Every Way, I Am
Getting Better and Better" *177*

13 | Keeping Up with the Joneses *186*

14 | "A Kill-Joy! He Was the Most Popular
Dinner Guest in Jerusalem!" *196*

15 | Don't "Soak 'Em . . . . Serve 'Em" *210*

16 | How To Win Friends and
Influence People *226*

17 | "I'm Talking About a New Way
of Life" *251*

18 | Sources of a New Way of Life—
and Its Perils *272*

CONTENTS

19 | The Search for Power   *295*

20 | The Power of Positive Thinking   *314*

21 | "I Don't Care How Weak or Small
You Are . . . ."   *341*

22 | The Failure of Success   *357*

23 | Politics   *380*

24 | "Beware of the Man Who Rises to
Power from One Suspender"   *402*

25 | "A Different Drummer"   *424*

26 | Bitch Goddess or Coy Mistress?   *448*

Acknowledgments   *458*

References and Bibliography   *459*

Index   *547*

FOREWORD
TO THE 1987 EDITION

The first edition of *The American Idea of Success* began with a report from the novelist James Michener. It was the late 1960's and Michener was lamenting the plight of the successful father confronted by his questioning children. Militants were demonstrating in the streets, the war in Vietnam was lacerating the unity of the nation, and hippies were blowing marijuana smoke in the face of the middle class dream of success.

Michener reported from the late 1960's that many a father had spent a lifetime making money only to find himself powerless to answer the philosophical probings of his children. They were demanding why he did it, what good did he get out of it. What did he have to show for the rat race, except two cars and a comfortable house.

Now, two decades later, that same father might well gather his children around him for a current heart-to-heart. No one is saying, the father might begin, that you are selling out — you're buying in. And I agree with you that Adam Smith's famed eighteenth century observation rings true for us today: "It is not from the benevolence of the butcher, the brewer, or the baker that we expect our dinner, but from their regard to their own interest. We address ourselves not to their humanity but to their self-love, and never talk to them of our own necessities but of their advantages." In our own Age of the Entrepreneur, the father continues, perhaps social justice will trickle down from the supply-side. No doubt a free society stays strong by protecting unequal rewards earned by the market-driven evaluation of profits. And, alas, if you must be reduced to a demographic statistic, upscale is better. The good life does indeed consist of the good things in life.[1] *

---

* References for the 1987 Foreword are found on page 546.

But the father might feel compelled to press on and ask his children: Is there not more to life than a Ferrari? Of course, success has always been measured by possessions. But there are the things of the spirit which are important, too; what your forebears used to call 'true success.' And there are all kinds of dangers to your soul along the route to success. So you might want to take a look at this book — *The American Idea of Success.* It's full of seasoned ideas about what the people who came before you in this country had to say about getting ahead in the world. And it's about all kinds of dilemmas that each generation must confront with its own set of answers. Your birthright as part of the American experience carries with it the responsibility to understand your heritage. This book may help you to avoid the hollow confession in T.S. Eliot's *Four Quartets:* "We had the experience but missed the meaning..."[2]

In the late 1960's Michener's college-age children challenged the philosophy of parents who had committed their lives to the pursuit of success. Most kept on hustling during the period, but were forced to question their assumptions. And this happened not so much because of the disruptive war in Vietnam. Protests against the establishment would have taken place most probably without the war. The four-lettering assaults on authority were strongly demographic.

The Baby Boom generation, in all its massive power, struck at America's deepest beliefs. The Baby Boomers did to the philosophy of success, when old enough to think for themselves, what they had done to the diaper business, popular music, and pre-marital sex — transformed the institutions through which they were passing by challenging the authority of traditional values.

Born in the decades after World War II, between 1946 and 1964, the Boomers represent an awesome one-third of the total population. While the Yuppies, the young upwardly mobile professionals, represent a small percentage of the entire generation, they often articulate the mood of their generation. And as they become Muppies, middle-aged upwardly mobile professionals, they are increasingly occupying the positions of power in the society.

The Boomers in the 1980's, spearheaded by the Yuppies, are putting the energy of their numbers into an admiration for the drive to get on in the world. *The New York Times* confirmed in 1986 what others had been reporting: "Success and money are more fashionable and sought after than they have been since the 1950's." It wasn't only the Boomers who were in favor of hustling. A reliable poll took the measure of college freshmen in 1985. Compared to 44 percent in 1967, 71 percent stated that it was essential or very important to be "very well-off financially." In 1967, student interest in "developing a meaningful philosophy of life" stood at 83 percent. In 1985 interest had sunk to 43 percent. As critic John Gross observed: "Gossip columns and glossy articles increasingly give the impression that money has become more sexy than sex."[3]

And it wasn't just men now competing for the prizes. Women wanted to play — not for jobs and raises, but careers with promotions to power and prestige. Defining work as a career rather than a job stimulates ambition because self-esteem is measured by promotional achievement. No more was female self-esteem defined so predominantly by finding a husband and bearing him children. The price women have had to pay for competing with men on the job is to endure the additional burden of measuring personal worth by occupational achievement. At the same time, many women remain obedient to the mandate of catching a husband, having babies, and nurturing the family.

The invasion of women into the marketplace in the 1970's and 1980's to compete with men, and each other, for the rewards of success has been one of the most significant revolutions in the American experience. Many were Boomers, and along with men of their generation, they quickly jettisoned their 1960's antiestablishment reputation. A new name surfaced and stuck fast like an offensive leech — the "me" generation.

The success-driven executive in the "me" generation was said to be self-indulgent rather then family-building, me-centered rather than compassionate. He or she is self-absorbed in faddish consumerism rather than community-conscious about the poor, the aging, and the less fortunate. The "me" generation was accused of a self-seeking materialism barren of impulses toward self-giving idealism.[4]

The "me" generation, and its attending liberation movements, is shaped by forces that all Americans of every age are experiencing. What has been happening in American society is the acceleration of a trend which is driven by massive technological forces sustained by that most enduring of American values — the sanctity of the individual. The individual is becoming the center of society, free to be, free to choose, increasingly released from traditional restrictions and formal identifications.

No longer is the family the center of society. It is the individual within the structure of the family that is the focus. The wife-mother has broken the tyranny of gender over role and is free to explore the risks and rewards of achievement in the marketplace. As the roles men and women play become less gender-specific, the husband can give way to feelings of nurturing without shame. Flirtations with androgyny may be viewed as an expansion into human fulfillment or a decline into societal decay. However it is perceived, the question — what does it mean to be a man and what does it mean to be a woman — is no longer defined in the comforting certitudes of rigidly assigned roles.

For adolescents, always a time of torment, the self is increasingly required to define the self. The teenager is offered the range to define himself or herself as an individual rather than establishing that identity largely through family status and traditions. As parents lose control over the information that shapes their children, teenagers are moulded more by peers, television, and school than the continuing immediacy of family, relatives, and the church.

Americans still may describe themselves as Protestants, Roman Catholics, or Jews, Republicans or Democrats, old family or more recently arrived, but formal identifications increasingly succumb to informal associations. Just as gender becomes less a determinant of identity, so does chronological age. People are recognized to age at differing rates and often to grow less like each other the older they become.

Stimulating expectations, multiplying options, America as an advanced industrial society increasingly demands that the individual choose. Sex by choice for the unwed, even death by choice for the terminally ill, are options which previously were severely punished. Accelerating the rush troward the self as the center of society is the search for self-awareness and emotional fulfillment through the insights of psychotherapy.[5]

The challenge for the "me" generation, and for all of us who are heirs to the individual-centering forces of our society, is to wrestle anew with the philosophical issues of our forebears. What is the justification for becoming a success? Can I do good to society by getting the good things of life for myself? Are there limits to ambition? What about honesty? Is success the highest goal in life?

How to make the selfishness of the self contribute to the general welfare while preserving the decency of the achiever is what the idea of success has been all about since its inception in the early years of the American experience. The idea of success for much of our history has been about this responsibility. In our own age so assertive of rights, there are not so often proclamations about our responsibilities.

Richard M. Huber

Washington, D.C.
April 1987

FOREWORD

As the 1960s drew to a close, James Michener commented: "Many a father who has spent the years from 22 to 52 in a mad race to accumulate now finds himself powerless to answer his children who ask, 'Why did you do it, Pop? What good did you get out of it? What have you to show for the rat race except two cars and three picture windows?' These are terrifying questions to throw at a man in his 50s. . . ." [1]

Questions of this nature are easy to ask and difficult to answer. One purpose of this study is to explore the meaning of success for each of us as individuals. "Philosophy," a Peter De Vries character has lamented, "is the attempt to pick at a wet knot with boxing gloves." The wet knots that this study has tried to untangle are the same old cosmic problems that thinkers have been wrestling with since men could reason. But for the man in the street heading for work, cosmic problems get down to earthy specifics: What should be the goal of my life, how do I reach it, and what justification is there that this is the right thing to do? Is this goal the highest good? [2]

The other purpose of this study is to explore the meaning of success in the broad American experience. Some have found a kind of meaning in cursing the 'bitch-goddess success.' Yet understanding a civilization must begin with the recognition that its parts are sensitively interrelated. Castigating the bitch goddess and yet cherishing the democratic forces which created her is as superficial as defining a social force in terms of its abuses. When examining the role of success in American life, our story is limited to white individuals with middle-class values and excludes the South, for reasons given elsewhere.

The book begins with a chapter defining success and then analyzes self-help literature from Benjamin Franklin to Dale Carnegie and Norman Vincent Peale. What did these philosophers of the marketplace think was the way to get ahead and the justification for doing so? Next, dissenting critics attack the views of these success writers while political conservatives rush to their defense. Moving through this clash of opinions is an analysis of the causes and consequences of the success drive. My objective is to examine the success complex from different angles of vision, using whatever disciplines are necessary to do so.

The number of success books and magazine articles is enormous from the seventeenth century to the present time. This study is in part a distillation of that literature. The works analyzed establish general principles for achievement and are not instruction handbooks for specific occupations. Every reader must judge for himself which principles for success are most valid in the light of his own experience.

How to live? What to live for? Every society offers its own set of answers. This adventure into values has tried to probe for an American set of answers from the viewpoint of one idea. The thoughtful young who question, as they should, the traditional values of their society may well discover that answers have a way of twisting themselves into uneasy dilemmas. The reader himself must judge with what mind and spirit Americans over a whole series of generations have lived with their dilemmas.

Richard M. Huber

Princeton, N. J.
March 1971

1

MONEY...STATUS...FAME...

What is success? In America, success has meant making money and translating it into status, or becoming famous.

Success was not earned by being a loyal friend or good husband. It was a reward for performance on the job. It is not the same thing as happiness—which is how you feel. Success was brutally objective and impersonal. It recorded a change in rank, the upgrading of a person in relation to others by the unequal distribution of money and power, prestige and fame. Yet, success was not simply *being* rich or famous. It meant *attaining* riches or *achieving* fame. You had to know where a man began and where he ended in order to determine how far he had come.

How high did one have to rise to be judged a success? One measurement was to do better than your father by holding a job of higher pay or prestige. A man who retired with a gold watch as a bank clerk would more likely be thought of as a success if his father had been a dishwasher than a corporation president. The son of a very successful man, who had the advantages of money and contacts, was also at a disadvantage in being judged a success in his own right when measured against his father. Another measurement of success was having substantially a better job or making more money at the end of your working life than at the beginning.

Success could never be precisely measured, whether by the intergenerational mobility of son over father or the intragenerational rise to a better job and a higher income. However, it did

1

have to be recognized by other people. "American success must be recognized success," explained Ralph Barton Perry, "not by the God of Things as They Are, but by one's neighbors." Recognition was the nerve of success—recognition measurable in money or applause. "The vital roots of the American spirit," Harold Laski perceived, "are either the building of a fortune or the building of a reputation which makes you held in esteem by your neighbors." [1]

Was success the same for everyone? Suppose one twin brother entered business and the other the ministry, was the definition of success the same for both? The race for success was like a track meet, but you had a choice of running on one of two tracks. You could choose one track and work for profit, or the other and work at a non-profit job. For the twin brother in a profit job there was no ceiling on the amount of money he could make. Compensation was opened-end. On this private pay scale, business success, as we have indicated, was the accumulation of wealth, translated into status, or the achievement of fame.

The twin brother entering the ministry was working at a non-profit job on the public pay scale with a ceiling on the amount of money he could make. Compensation was closed-end. The non-business success of this twin was not defined by money but by rank related to an institution or by public prominence.

Whether the job was for profit or non-profit determined the track, not whether a person was a professional man or a businessman. Certain professional men, lawyers, physicians, architects, dentists, were businessmen. They did differ from businessmen because of their long years of training, admission procedures to practice, self-policing, adherence to enforceable codes, and a presumed correspondence of interests with their clients beyond the exchange of money. But self-employed professionals were essentially businessmen because they operated an office, charged a fee, deducted overhead from gross profits, and ended with a net, fluctuating profit for the year. Whether self-employed, or salaried executives in a corporation, they were operating on an opened-end, private pay scale and were judged accordingly.

In non-profit jobs, examples of professionals on the public pay scale whose achievements were judged by non-business success would be a physician who worked at a research institute, an attorney who became a judge, a public school teacher, a scholar or an army officer. Included with these occupations were non-profit jobs in the local, state, and federal government. The criterion for judging their success was not money but rank, though obviously the higher the rank the higher the pay. As the well-loved John XXIII of peasant origins said four months after his elevation to the papacy: "Well, here I am—at the end of the road and the top of the heap." [2]

The general outranked the major, the archbishop was superior to the priest, but lesser ranks could always be catapulted into the recognized success of public prominence. If both our twins entered the public school system, the one who became a superintendent was a bigger success as far as the public was concerned than the one who taught tenth grade Spanish. But if the Spanish teacher developed a course which received wide public acclaim, Hometown, U.S.A., might well consider him a success equal to or greater than his brother.

Success is relative. Rank is related to the prestige and power of an institution. A seasoned Episcopalian priest in charge of a large, wealthy church was viewed somewhat differently from the shepherd of a small parish with little influence. An associate professor at Harvard made it in bigger terms than a full professor of the same age at Crestfallen U. A judge of the state supreme court was viewed differently than a local magistrate. In the non-profit, closed-end, public pay scale, occupational success was measured by rank related to an institution or by public prominence. The fact that the higher rank on the totem pole of the institution was paid more only indicated that money usually talks, though in muted tones in a non-profit atmosphere.

There was a type of success *within* the universe of the institution or profession about which the general public was unaware. The emblems of what might be called institutional or professional success could apply both to the profit-oriented professional man as well as his public pay scale colleagues. These emblems consisted of positions in professional societies, awards and prizes, and invitations to speak or exhibit. Success within the universe of the institution or profession did not depend on the consumer's ability to pay or the public's giving or withholding applause. It was awarded by the esteem and approval of the individuals within that universe.

Though different criteria were used to measure business and non-business success, they were constructed on the same theory. An individual generally became a success in the degree to which he contributed to the success of the business or institution that paid him. A business operation was a success in the degree to which it made a profit. Therefore, those individuals who most effectively and responsibly helped the company make money were rewarded with bigger salaries. A university, for example, was a success to the degree in which it gained prestige. Therefore, those individuals who most effectively helped the university achieve this prestige were rewarded with promotion to a higher rank. The prestige of a university was established, not by the teaching process of conveying knowledge, but by published research which contributed to it. Therefore, those "teachers" who advanced in rank were often chosen, not on the basis of their competence in teaching, but on the basis of their contribution to knowledge through published research. And that is why university teaching is probably the only profession in which you can become a success without satisfying the client.

Success within one pay scale was not generally compared with success in the other. A judgment oft-expressed about American values fails to distinguish between the cultural definitions of business and non-business success. Two observers of the American scene have insisted that "if Marilyn Monroe has a much larger income than Einstein did—and she has—it is a sign that as a whole we want, or value, her services more than his." Society rewarded Marilyn Monroe and Albert Einstein in different ways. Because a popular entertainer earned more than a disinterested scientist, it did not necessarily follow that society placed a higher value on the one who received the higher pay. Money did talk, but the universe of discourse was within the pay scales, not between them.[3]

The public did not compare the achievements of a university

professor and a manufacturing executive, the objectives of a minister with a sales manager, the earnings of a federal judge with a corporation lawyer. *Within* each pay scale, or more precisely, within the same occupations of each pay scale, such comparisons were made. Thus, the success of one manufacturing executive might be compared with another, the rank of one judge in relation to another. But could one say that a manufacturing executive making $100,000 a year was either more or less successful than a federal judge earning $30,000 a year?

This distinction prevents us from falling into the error of assuming that *Who's Who in America* was a balanced record of those who succeeded. *Who's Who in America* has been heavily weighted with names from the public pay scale since its first volume in 1899. The editors were gripped by an almost indecent passion for professors and educators as well as those in civil, military, and religious occupations. The best chance for being enthroned within the crimson covers of *Who's Who in America* was to enter a non-profit occupation.[4]

A cynic once remarked that "a man is a success if he can make more money than his wife can spend." The rejoinder might be: "Yes, and a woman is a success if she can find such a man." A wife took not only the name of her husband, but also her rate of mobility from him. However, one did not speak of a housewife as a "success." A housewife didn't get promoted. There was no way of measuring her achievement.

The cultural definition of success was the same for a woman as a man in American society if the woman competed with the man in the world of work. There was a difference in degree, however. The distance between where a woman careerist began and ended need not have been so far as the distance traveled by a man. Often a woman careerist was judged a success with less achievement because it was generally recognized that she had bigger obstacles to overcome competing in a man's world. When women embarked on a "career," they might use their femininity to get ahead, but "getting ahead" was measured in the same terms as a man. They were both competing for the rewards that success conveys.

For writers, musicians, and many creative people, business

and non-business success had its counterpart in popular and critical success. If the novelist or composer competed in the marketplace for the consumer's dollar or acclaim, he was judged by his ability to make money or achieve popular fame. His business success was measured by the royalty checks for his books or the box office receipts for his performance. He was judged on the private, opened-end, profit pay scale. His work answered first the question: "Will it sell?" then "Is it any good?" On the other hand, if the criterion was his contribution to artistic truth or merit, his non-business success was measured by a different reference group—the approval of his peers or respected critics. He was judged on the public, closed-end, professional non-profit pay scale. Many artists and writers were a popular success and also enjoyed critical acclaim, but the judgments about them were arrived at independently. Because a book sold did not necessarily indicate it was any good. For a book to be of high quality was no guarantee that it would sell.

"Every one knows," reported John C. Van Dyke in 1908, "that success with the great masses spells money." August B. Hollingshead, after studying a small Midwestern town in the 1940s, announced: "To be sure, other cultural factors enter the picture, but in this acquisitive, success-dominated ideology the primary criterion of 'social worth' is measured in terms of dollars." Success has meant business success for most Americans. For the balance of this study, unless qualified, success will mean business success on the private pay scale track, though some observations will be relevant to non-business success.[5]

We have maintained that the cultural definition of business success was the attainment of wealth, translated into status, or the achievement of fame. But why the emphasis on status? Because if success was motion upwards, it was not the making of money that put one into motion but its use. America was a nation of social climbers. "Bettering oneself" had to be socially recognized by translating money into status.[6]

America's favorite folk tale—'rags to riches'—tells only part of the story. The jump from poverty to riches was also the ascent from rags to respectability. But crossing the tracks with so gigantic a leap was rare. The more usual and slower climb was from a city slum to a better part of the city or to the foothills of a suburban development, thence, perhaps in a later generation, to a slightly more commanding hill. The process was the translation of an economic class position derived from making money to a social class position which was partially established by the spending of it. It was economic achievement becoming social achievement.

The American status system was pluralistic. There was no nationally recognized titled nobility. There was no city in America, like London or Paris, which gathered to itself supreme power financially, politically, and intellectually. If New York City was the financial hub and liked to think of itself as the cultural center, Washington, D.C., was the nation's capital and the undisputed political center. The thirteen colonies which joined together into a union, and the thirty-seven states that followed, were not provinces bowed into submission. They were self-respecting regions with a deep pride in their states and burgeoning towns. Each town or city constructed its own status structure. When the breadwinner made his pile, little or big, he translated it into status in his community. If he was indifferent or obtuse to the clues, his wife probably was not. If both husband and wife couldn't care less, their children would be rare indeed who did not respond to the ranking proclivities of their peers.

The conversion of pelf into possessions and possessions into position became more exquisite the higher one climbed the social class ladder. The impoverished valued money for its own sake. The middle-class with discretionary income used money symbolically. Things were no longer simply things but stood for something. A roof over your head became less important than the neighborhood and address which identified the roof; money as the power to purchase became proportionally less important than the prestige of the occupation in which the money was made; parties were not simply events but represented stages in the advancement toward a social goal; the finery of personal transportation, a carriage or an automobile, took its place beside many other salutes to achievement; education was not just education but was exalted by the special stature of the school or college; a child was not only an object to be loved and fed but a living extension of one's aspirations and values.

In a family's climb upward in the status system of its community, people played a crucial role. Ben Hecht once remarked that "success requires us to change our friends, as does failure." What better way was there of measuring the pace of keeping up with the Joneses than by getting ahead of the Browns by getting in with the Smiths? A favorite lubricating introduction to the "right" people was through a charity. If a charity was a worthy cause in search of money, the parvenu was a living donation in search of a charity. Charities were higher status people exploiting lower status people in order to uplift the poor. It was a social class milking an economic class for an underprivileged class.[7]

Translating occupational achievement into status was the procedure for moving up within the middle class. To ascend into the summits of the upper class meant reshaping the cash register of a Dun & Bradstreet rating into a social register of birth and breeding. Old family and old money became crucial elements. Walter Bagehot has observed that "the possessors of the 'material' distinctions of life . . . rush to worship those who possess the *im*material distinctions." "Getting ahead" meant acquiring immaterial distinctions of taste and manners, bearing and speech. This is one reason why the better novels about success, from Henry James and Edith Wharton through F. Scott Fitzgerald to J. P. Marquand, focus not on how to make money but how money is exploited to establish a position in society.[8]

If the sins of the parents are visited on the children, so too are the virtues of their status. A man's success was deepened and widened if his children or grandchildren associated with and married into a higher class than the one into which he was born. A successful man who knew the importance of family advancement, as well as individual achievement, was the father of President John F. Kennedy. "From the beginning, Joe knew what he wanted—money and status for his family," recalled an intimate of the 1930s. "He had the progenitor's sense; to him, his children were an extension of himself." [9]

"One of the central elements in life," said playwright Arthur Miller, "is the driving need of people to define themselves, not merely as individuals, but also in terms of a function they can respect." We have tried to answer the question, What is success?, but there are other questions more interesting and revealing. How have Americans felt about success? What meanings did they assign to it? Why should one try to be a success and how should one go about it? Was making money or becoming famous the *summum bonum* of life? In Dostoyevsky's *The Brothers Karamazov,* the Grand Inquisitor declared: "For the secret of man's being is not only to live but to have something to live for. Without a stable conception of the object of life, man would not consent to go on living. . . ." Or as Nietzsche perceived: "Once one is clear about the 'why?' of one's life, one can let its 'how?' take care of itself." [10]

We shall now examine in American popular thought the "how" of success and the "why" which encouraged it. "Persons of all qualities and all professions make their court to money," trilled an early success writer, "the gaining of which, as if it were the great Diana of the world, is the chief mark they aim at, in all their undertakings. And therefore to inform 'em how they may catch this coy mistress and embrace her in their own arms, must needs be a very pleasant art." Whether success was a "coy mistress" or a "bitch goddess" depended on who was taking her measure. No doubt many would like to embrace the mistress and strangle the bitch at the same time. Certain critics will later in the study articulate the impulse to strangle her. Now let us unfold the yearning to embrace her. We begin by setting the background and then sketching in the heritage to the middle of the nineteenth century. [11]

2

THE HERITAGE

The idea of success was a force which drove men on to build America. At the center was the individual. Self-confident in his God-given rights, he entered a free world of expanding opportunities. How he seized upon three thousand miles of virgin land and bounteous natural resources to develop those opportunities into the most productive nation the world has ever known has for many always been the thrill of the American achievement.

In America, making money had dignity. Here was no mere plundering operation, as in feudal cultures, no apologetic backsliding of an aristocracy, as in eighteenth-century England. The American sought money as he loved his wife or worshipped his God, sure that every extra dollar permitted him a higher tilt of his head.

In the beginning the words were freedom and opportunity. The bold ones who crossed an ocean to a new land in Colonial times were eager to make the most of it. Those who pulled up roots for the new land were generally more ambitious and adventurous than the stay-at-homes. Decade after decade shiploads of middle- and working-class Europeans spilled onto the east coast of America, dissatisfied in one way or another with things at home and anxious for a fresh start to get ahead in the new world.[1]

Under American conditions, swiftly and clearly, there developed a hunger for wealth. It was not the sensuous hunger

of an oriental potentate, but a moral hunger fed on the awareness that one's self-esteem depended on results. Free of the
ascribed inequalities of Europe, the American soon relied on
wealth as a criterion of recognition. The means to success were
equally functional. If the pioneer was to land feet first on the
frontier and not go under, he had to keep at it, work hard, and
save his money. The farmer's day was a long day, and America
was a nation bound to the soil. The Revolution was fought by a
country in which nineteen out of twenty people were farmers.
For those who were urban rather than agrarian capitalists, the
same qualities were mandatory for anything more than mere
survival. It was a scarcity economy demanding frugality and
hard hours of toil.[2]

The early Colonists were children of the Renaissance and
Reformation. Theirs was a self-assertive age which had rebelled
against the disapproval in the Middle Ages of getting ahead by
competition in business. Indeed, what had been considered a
vice in the Middle Ages—the making of a profit through the
exchange of goods—had in the Colonists' economic system
become a virtue. That it was a virtue was assured by the doctrines of Puritanism. The economic system which encouraged
the accumulation of wealth was capitalism. Religion worked
in harness with economics toward the goal of individual success.
Religious values encouraged and justified economic behavior.
    In the later seventeenth and early eighteenth centuries no one
spoke with greater authority for the religious interpretation of
what we have termed the character ethic than Cotton Mather.
A New England divine of great influence and power, Mather
spoke for God while saturating the idea of success in Calvinism
and the Old Testament. He introduces us to the Puritan concept
that every Christian has two callings. In the general calling,
Mather instructed his flock, a good Christian should "serve the
Lord Jesus Christ and save his own soul in the services of
religion. . . ." In his personal calling, a Christian should have a
"particular employment by which his usefulness in his neighborhood is distinguished." In his personal calling, or what we would
call a job, a Christian should spend most of his time in "some

settled business . . . so he may glorify God by doing of good for others and getting of good for himself." Unless disabled by infirmities, a man without a job is "unrighteous" towards his family, community, and country, as well as being open to temptations from the Devil. "Every man ordinarily should be able to say, 'I have something wherein I am occupied for the good of other men.' " [3]

Many of the pressures of our own day to get ahead lay heavy upon those early immigrants and their children—except the hand of God increased the pressure. In Proverbs, Mather pressed on, it is written: " 'He becomes poor who dealeth with a slack hand, but the hand of the diligent maketh rich.' Such lessons are so frequent in the Book of God that I wonder how any man given up to slothfulness dare look into his Bible. . . . Come, come, for shame, away to your business. Lay out your strength in it, put forth your skill for it. . . . 'Solomon, seeing that the young man was industrious, he made him a ruler.' I tell you with diligence a man may do marvelous things. Young man, work hard while you are young; you'll reap the effects of it when you are old. Yea, how can you ordinarily enjoy any rest at night if you have not been well at work in the day? Let your business engross the most of your time." [4]

Mather saw a dangerous paradox. Laziness is a sin, but hard work, greedily motivated, and the fruits of hard work, unplucked for pious uses, may lead to a greater sin. "The business of your personal calling" must not "swallow up" your general calling. With a vivid image Mather caught the nature of a properly balanced life. The Christian in his two callings is like a man in a boat rowing toward heaven. If he pulls only one oar (either the spiritual or the worldly one), he "will make but a poor dispatch to the Shoar of Eternal Blessedness." You should pull hard on the oar of worldly achievement, but do not neglect the oar of your soul and its salvation through union with Jesus Christ. Row always in the fear of God and strive to be holy and diligent in both your callings. (Mercifully, however, it is true that "the poorest labourer among you all, tho' of a low degree on earth, may be of an high account in heaven.") Say your prayers, be faithful to God, and remember that "at no time of the day may we expect that our business will succeed without God's blessing. . . . All will fall out as God shall order it." [5]

In essays of power and persuasion, Mather forged the links between success and God. He asks us to consider "what we are told in Deut. 8. 18., 'Thou shalt remember the Lord thy God, for 'tis he that gives the power to get wealth.' " Mather observes that the reverse is also true. It is God who denies us the power to become rich. But, we ask, if this be so, what control have we over our own destiny? Is God's control over our fortunes subject to divine whim, or can we influence God to act favorably towards us? Mather replies that if we serve God faithfully in both our callings, say our prayers twice a day, obey the Sabbath, stay honest, and liberally disburse our income to pious uses as a steward of the Lord, then God will smile favorably upon us. "By these things you will obtain the blessing of God upon your business." If we fail, probably we have displeased God by being dishonest, gluttonous, unthankful, or full of pride. It is God, then, who controls our fortune, but by thought, word, and deed we can influence God to exercise his control in our favor. At the same time, however, we should never forget that material things are not only ephemeral but can corrupt the soul. The highest success is measured by our treasures in heaven. [6]

Wherever Calvinism, or the Biblical ideas which it expressed, stamped their mark, the message was similar. Puritanism in America was a modified expression of the Calvinist branch of Protestantism. Though some religious leaders denounced Calvin, Puritanism was especially strong among the Presbyterians, Congregationalists (Reformed), and Methodists. The Quakers were no friends to Puritan theology, but they endorsed Calvin's implicit support of capitalism. In Philadelphia, William Penn tried to teach his children that "Diligence is [a] Virtue useful and laudable among Men: It is a discreet and understanding Application of one's Self to Business; and it avoids the Extreams of Idleness and Drudgery. It gives great Advantages to Men. . . . It is the Way to Wealth." Cultivate the virtues of frugality, industry, prudence, order, and honesty, the ideology counselled, worship God and live in his image, and he will bless you with material prosperity which you can regard as a visible sign that you are living "in the Light." [7]

If the Philadelphia Quakers emphasized order and a benevolent compassion for the poor more strongly than did the Boston Congregationalists, they were no less insistent on the intimate relation between religion and worldly affairs. While the getting of wealth was exalted, the ancient dilemma that the fruits of one's labors could rot on the tree of virtue was recognized. An extravagant passion for accumulation should be checked lest it destroy individual rectitude and tempt some to forget that their purpose was to erect temples of holiness and righteousness in the new land. [8]

There was nothing uniquely American in all this. The idea of success was not produced by the frontier or by any other indigenous environmental force. America has always been a part of Western Civilization, with a particular indebtedness to English culture. Similar forces and ideas which shaped the means and goal of success in England operated in the new land. The colonies often lagged twenty or so years behind the mother country in painting, architecture, and furniture design. No such obedient imitation enslaved the idea of success. When the intellectual baggage of the colonists was unpacked in the new land, the idea of success took on its own independent existence. It paralleled, but did not imitate, developments in the mother country.

Cotton Mather and William Penn were drawing upon a two-hundred-year tradition of popular writing on the subject. The middle classes were on the move in England and they did not find themselves wanting in either advice or justification. In the eighty years after Elizabeth's accession to the throne in 1558, more than twenty works were printed which were devoted to success. Their message was the same—"put money in thy purse" by hard work, frugality, and the like. The tradesman who thrilled to Shakespearean adventures of warriors and kings could read in books of lesser art about the righteousness of material gain and count himself no less noble. From Hugh Latimer through William Perkins to Richard Baxter of the later seventeenth century—clergymen all—came the moral assurance, at once comforting but filled with possibilities of guilt, that one served God by laboring ceaselessly in an earthly calling.[9]

When the theology-dominated seventeenth century gave way to the Enlightenment of the eighteenth, the presentation of success literature in England shifted with the times. Western Civilization was breaking out of its intellectual strait jacket and pouring its released energy into exciting discoveries based on reason and science. There was a neo-classic concern for clarity, balance, and a delight in epigrams and aphorisms. The style of British success books swung into line with the prevailing literary fashion. Any tradesman with touches of elegance in his pen and a few fresh comments on life could satisfy his longing to be a writer. In a confusion of extended titles, gross plagiarism, and pirated editions, a sort of inter-library loan of ideas operated. They thieved from one another after the fashion of the time, plundered the rich storehouse of life about them, invoked a nimble classical allusion whenever possible—and often ignored the Bible as a source of authority.[10]

In America, it was the eighteenth century which produced the most influential success apostle in the history of the American experience. In his writings on success, which were to be handed down by Americans from generation to generation, Benjamin Franklin took the position that wealth was the result of virtue. In his own life, and in other writings less influential, Franklin reflected the eighteenth-century patrician view that virtue was the result of wealth. A man of many parts, it is Franklin the success writer who is important for establishing the American heritage of the success idea.

Benjamin Franklin made a fortune in his own lifetime—then expanded it by telling others how he did it. He started on the road to success by writing about it. There was little that was original in his contribution. He did not link into new connections ideas which were swirling about in the air. As we have indicated, his bourgeois ideology had been sold wholesale in England long before his time and diffused to America where it already had a grip on the mind of the colonists. It was Franklin's significance, as the ideal eighteenth-century bourgeois, that he swept together into a number of writings the thinking of a nation. This was altogether fitting and proper, for unlike England, with its diversity of classes, America *was* a rising middle class to which this doctrine offered a wider appeal. The colonists were eager to get ahead in a nation on the make. When the time came, they broke away from the mother country to prove it.[11]

"The supreme symbol of the American spirit is Benjamin Franklin," Harold Laski has maintained, "for he made a success of all that he attempted. . . . In his shrewdness, his sagacity, his devotion to making this world the thing that a kindly and benevolent soul would wish it to be, Franklin seems to summarize in a remarkable way the American idea of a good citizen." He was a hard-driving businessman, sage philosopher, pioneer scientist, inventor of a stove and an arm for retrieving books from high shelves, founder of a college, sire of three children (one illegitimate), representative of his country to France, a steady hand at the Constitutional Convention—the list seems endless. His accomplishments were fantastic even for an age which could boast a considerable number of great men. The emperor by popular acclaim of the character ethic, so crafty a manipulator and so shrewd a self-promoter was Franklin that success writers have served him up as a model in our own age of persuasion. A man of action as well as ideas, it was typical of his versatility that toward the end of his life, when the gout and stone had him down, he longed for "a balloon sufficiently large to raise me from the ground. . . being led by a string held by a man walking on the ground." [12]

One episode in his life, which he tells on himself, is particularly significant for American popular thought. The scene pictures a seedy youth strolling up Market Street in Philadelphia munching a great puffy roll of bread and convulsing his future wife by his ludicrous appearance. Described by Franklin with relish and pride, it remains to this day the most vivid and popular pictorial symbol of the social origins of the self-made man in America.[13]

Franklin was both a mirror of his own age and a tutor to succeeding generations. That part of his writings which has exerted the most influence on popular thought and stimulated the widest appeal was devoted to success. The first was *The Way to Wealth*, a compilation of Poor Richard's maxims setting down the proper procedures for making money. Most of the sayings were freely borrowed, for Franklin was heir to a long tradition of writing on this subject. The second was his *Autobiography*, a case study of the first, which describes how an earnest young man employs these maxims to emerge "from the poverty and obscurity in which I was born and bred, to a state of affluence and some degree of reputation in the world. . . ." [14]

What qualities should an ambitious youth cultivate in order to get ahead? Franklin exalts two. The first is *industry:* ("Early to bed, and early to rise, makes a man healthy, wealthy, and wise." "Then plough deep, while sluggards sleep, and you shall have corn to sell and to keep.") The second is *frugality:* ("A fat kitchen makes a lean will." "Rather go to bed supperless than rise in debt.") Conversely, idleness and extravagance produce their own results: ("Laziness travels so slowly, that poverty soon overtakes him.") The means and the goal were crisply stated in *Advice to Young Tradesmen:* "In short, the way to wealth, if you desire it, is as plain as the way to market. It depends chiefly on two words, *industry* and *frugality;* that is, waste neither *time* nor *money,* but make the best use of both." [15]

To these cardinal virtues, eleven more were added in the *Autobiography:* temperance, silence, order, resolution, sincerity, justice, moderation, cleanliness, tranquillity, chastity, and humility (the latter being added to the original list after a Quaker friend "kindly informed" Franklin that he was generally thought proud, overbearing, and insolent in conversation). Always a practical man, Franklin went on to explain more specifically how these virtues might be achieved. He drew up a lined chart with the days of the week at the top and the virtues on the left-hand side. Each week he concentrated on one virtue and would ruthlessly fail himself by a black mark on the days that he did not measure up to the self-examination. In this manner, he reported, one could go through a complete course in thirteen weeks, and four courses in a year. [16]

There is compulsion in Franklin's efforts to purge himself of any vices which might hinder his ascent in the world. There is a sense of overwhelming duty in his intense dedication. It is not simply expediency or naked self-interest which propels him forward. He is burning with a moral conviction that a good person *should* and *must* drive himself without mercy until the little chart stands clean of black marks. And his chart was there for everyone. He ignored the importance of luck, contacts, family influence, and native intelligence. The start was equal for all.[17]

To tie Benjamin Franklin too closely to Puritanism, as some have done, is to slip over a significant point of distinction. Both Mather and Franklin were in the same boat, but one was rowing for the "Shoar of Eternal Blessedness" while the other was making for a different port. Both agreed that cultivating certain ascetic virtues led to wealth, but Mather justified it primarily as a way of worshipping God. Franklin also justified it as a means to a final end, but an end less concerned with religious implications. These ends were the leisure which money provided to enable him to do what he wanted in life, such as an opportunity for humanitarianism or enough leisure to study.[18]

The distinction is revealed in the concept of the stewardship of wealth. Mather charged that every man should give at least a tenth part of his income to the service of God and the relief of the miserable. Franklin's benevolence was primarily secular. For Franklin it was all quite simple. "Poverty often deprives a man of all spirit and virtue: 'Tis hard for an empty bag to stand upright. . . ." Since being poor is undesirable, train yourself in the qualities that make money. The justification for accumulating wealth is utilitarian and instrumental. It is a way to moral perfection, but not necessarily a way to worship God. One can use wealth to become healthy and wise, or to do good to others. But the final ends are up to every individual. In other words, what Franklin did was to preserve the means and immediate goal of wealth of Puritanism, but then went on to diminish its theological sanction by emphasizing a utilitarian justification. The consequence may have been unintended, but the result was that any man lacking in religious convictions could make money and still consider himself virtuous.[19]

Franklin did, of course, believe in the existence of God and the power of Providence to intervene in the affairs of mankind. He immediately confessed in the opening pages of his autobiography that "now I speak of thanking God, I desire with all humility to acknowledge that I owe the mention'd happiness of my past life to his kind providence, which led me to the means I us'd and gave them success." It is true, *"God helps them that help themselves,"* but "do not depend too much upon your own *Industry,* and *Frugality,* and *Prudence,* though excellent Things, for they may all be blasted without the Blessing of Heaven. . . ." [20]

Franklin was in accord with the Puritan belief that God was a means to success, but broke with the tradition at that point. Success was a visible sign of God's favor, but the wealth that success brought was not primarily justified as a way of worshipping God. It was justified, in the ideology of the Enlightenment's emphasis on the environment, because it benefited mankind and because it gave the individual the opportunity to become virtuous in whatever way he wished to define that term. Franklin catches this feeling in an anecdote. A friend of his who was a preacher was coming to Philadelphia and had no lodgings. When Franklin offered accommodations at his house, he reported that the minister replied that "If I [Franklin] made that kind offer for Christ's sake, I should not miss of a reward. And I returned, 'Don't let me be mistaken; it was not for Christ's sake, but for your sake.'" Benevolence, then, was to be done in the name of a secular humanitarianism with man as the final purpose, not a ritual faith in God. Making money was justified because it made this possible and simply because it was easier to be virtuous with a full pocketbook than an empty one.[21]

From a philosophical viewpoint, Franklin's contribution to the American heritage of the success idea was to invigorate what we have termed the secular interpretation of the character ethic. The tradition he represented cut the cables holding the idea of success to its religious anchor and sent it drifting into a sea of pragmatism.

One difficulty in understanding this great man is that for generations Americans quite naturally assumed that Franklin and Poor Richard were the same person. This impression was encouraged by the *Autobiography,* a lopsided account of his life. But the way Franklin actually lived his life and the way he said he lived it were not at all the same. In living his life, money for Franklin was obviously a means to an end. Money meant freedom, and freedom meant, among other things, leisure. Without money and the free time of leisure, how could one play the eighteenth-century gentleman of intellectual pretensions? The sage of Philadelphia longed to play the Enlightenment's model of the cultivated patrician, which is to say he followed the classic Greeks in their conception of the *summum bonum* in life. Franklin would have nodded approval to Aristotle's definition of happiness in *The Nicomachean Ethics:* "The active exercise of the mind in conformity with perfect goodness or virtue." [22]

But it was Franklin the tough-minded bourgeois, not the cultivated patrician, who spoke directly to the needs of the American people. Franklin's success advice for popular consumption was composed in the spirit of a frontier pragmatist more interested in means than ends. In the *Autobiography* and *The Way to Wealth,* he does not reflect on what the final goals in life should be. In certain obscure places in his writings he did state that success has ruined many a man and that avarice could never lead to happiness. But compared to many writers of the nineteenth century who publicly instructed ambitious young men on how to get ahead, he appears to be a shallow materialist disinterested in the dangers of materialism and what the final goals in life should be.[23]

From a symbolic viewpoint, Benjamin Franklin's influence was immense. The *Autobiography* kindled the fires of ambition in countless numbers of young men. He was not only America's first famous self-made man, but has remained, since the eighteenth century, the supreme symbol of the poor boy who made

good. He represented the hope of rising in the world, the thrill
of identification with the saga of rags to riches, the pride in a
country where getting ahead was based on individual effort.
Through the image of Benjamin Franklin, all America, by
reason of hard work and diligence, not only stood before kings,
but dined with one of them. Franklin's father would have liked
that. He frequently recited to young Ben a proverb of Solomon's
which reechoed down the corridors of the next century as a loud
favorite of success writers: "Seest thou a man diligent in his
business? He shall stand before kings; he shall not stand before
mean men." [24]

Because Franklin was a business success as well as a founding father of the Republic, he became that rare kind of hero
suitable for occupational emulation as well as emotional devotion. And there always seemed to be more of the American
in him than Washington or Jefferson. While Washington was
remote and formidable and Jefferson a kind of well-bred intellectual of political theory and national expansion, Franklin was
common, intimate, cozy, and practical.

Unlike most heroes in America, Benjamin Franklin was his
own best public relations agent. The first in the tradition of successful men who told their own story, Franklin was the Johnny
Appleseed of the idea of success. The author of a best-selling
almanac and the most popular autobiography in American
literature, he cast his seeds across the meadows of the American
mind. He became, as Hawthorne noted, "the counsellor and
household friend of almost every family in America." Perhaps
there is some validity in the claim, made towards the end of
the nineteenth century, that *The Way to Wealth* had been
printed and translated more often up to that time than any other
work from an American pen. For Franklin was not only a tutor
to those who actively aspired to success; he was a mentor to
whom other writers on the subject went to school.[25]

As America moved into the nineteenth century, two basic
themes were already running through the character ethic. Both
themes expressed agreement about the means to money-making,
but disagreed on the justification. Cotton Mather, and the more
religious writers, justified the accumulation of wealth primarily

as a way of glorifying God. Benjamin Franklin, and those of a more secular persuasion, justified success by a philosophy which owed little or nothing to divine sanction. The great German scholar, Max Weber, had assumed that by Franklin's time the "religious basis" of "Puritan worldly asceticism . . . had died away." But, in fact, throughout the history of the nineteenth century a religious as well as a secular basis for the character ethic was vigorously supported. The overwhelming majority of success writers made their choice between one or the other of these philosophical positions.[26]

3

SCHOOLBOOKS AND JOURNALISTS

Success writers of the nineteenth century were philosophers of the marketplace. They both directed and reflected popular thinking. But the issues they wrestled with for the common people were the same as those pondered by the more highbrow sages of intellectual thought: Who am I? What should I do with my life? Why should I do it? Before the full impact of the Industrial Revolution vastly accelerated the volume of success literature around the middle of the nineteenth century, a doctrine of values had already begun to take shape.

Where better to begin to explore the values of a society than in schoolbooks for the young? The contents are rigidly standardized to conform to adult prejudices; the lessons carefully chosen to shape a child into the kind of citizen he ought to be. In the long, dog-eared tradition of schoolbooks, from *The New England Primer* and Webster's 'Blue Back Speller' to Muzzey's textbook on American history, none exerted a more incisive impact on American values than McGuffey's 'Eclectic Readers.' To mid-twentieth-century children following the ramblings of Dick and Jane, an old lady of ninety confessed in 1951: "We held them in our childish and youthful hands and read with a pleasure beyond my words to express." [1]

The American West literally went to school to William Holmes McGuffey, the Pennsylvanian Presbyterian of Scottish descent who started life a whiz at memory work and went on to become a professor and university president. The first five

'Electic Readers' were published between 1836 and 1844 and the sixth was issued in 1857. They were constantly revised and passed through edition after edition. Over 122,000,000 copies have been sold, with the peak years falling in the 1870s and 1880s. One student has concluded that from 1836 to 1900 at least half the school children of America were inspired by the pages of McGuffey's Readers. The 'Eclectic Readers' reflected the thinking of a nation, not only in their wide acceptance, but because they were typical of the message other schoolbooks and children's stories were teaching in little red schoolhouses spread out across the land.[2]

The McGuffey Readers expressed three great traditions of American thinking. First, their political conceptions were based on the conservative heritage of Alexander Hamilton, John Marshall, and Daniel Webster. Second, the theology of John Calvin prevailed, while the character ethic of hard labor, industry, and thrift was glorified. Third, the older Hebraic-Christian tradition of the brotherhood of man under the fatherhood of God was emphasized. This was the great achievement of these schoolbooks. On the one hand, the aggressive virtues of the character ethic were demanded of the children. At the same time, they were commanded to follow Christ with kindness, gentleness, and good will. This defense of opposite virtues was the great achievement of the McGuffey Readers. No doubt these children went on in later life to wrestle, as countless others before and after them, with the terrible dilemma of this double command.[3]

God had his eye on everyone, especially little children, taught the McGuffey Readers, and nothing pleased him more than diligence and hard work. In tightly structured tales, the good boys who obeyed the character ethic carried home the prize, while the bad boys (in these books, more thoughtless than wicked) were left empty-handed. In "Waste Not, Want Not," Ben saves a piece of whipcord while brother John destroys his. This bit of frugality enables Ben, not long afterwards, to win the archery contest by replacing his broken bow string with the piece of whipcord. John's bow string had broken too, but his whipcordless condition brings him down to defeat. But John is a good boy at heart, and without sour grapes he is willing to punch home the moral: "I'll take care of how I waste any thing, hereafter." What about failure? It clearly was the fault of the individual in a land where "the road to wealth, to honor, to usefulness, and happiness, is open to all, and all who will, may enter upon it with the almost certain prospect of success." [4]

Could schoolchildren of the nineteenth century go out into the world and grow rich with a good conscience? The McGuffey Readers assured them that making money was a moral duty sanctioned by divine decree. At the same time it had a practical justification. Wealth could be put to good use once it was made. The Second Reader of 1844 was certain that *God gives a great deal of money to some persons, in order that they may assist those who are poor.* Is money-making the highest goal in life to which one should aspire? No, for while the acquisition of wealth was a worthy goal, 'true success' must be measured by different criteria, for instance, the development of a noble character.[5]

How different from our own day was the message of those nineteenth-century schoolbooks! Church and state supported one another in a great conservative defense of their fundamental principles. The three R's are an inadequate metaphor. It was really the four R's—Reading, Writing, Arithmetic, and Religion. Honesty was the best policy, thrift a virtue, hard work a duty, and material achievement a righteous goal in life.[6]

To assure an orderly transition from schoolhouse to counting house, a halo of Protestant clergymen encircled the young men of nineteenth-century America. To the youth of the 1840s Henry Ward Beecher directed his *Lectures to Young Men.* That was long before Beecher rocked the nation in the 1870s. In that decade he was accused by his best friend of adultery. A hung jury raised millions of eyebrows in a thrill of scandalous horror, for Henry Ward Beecher was a very important man from a very important family. While his sister, Harriet Beecher Stowe, was writing *Uncle Tom's Cabin* in the 1850s, he was on his way to becoming the most outstanding pulpit orator of his day. Beecher was a sentimentalist in an age of tearful novels. Emotionally excitable and exuberantly childish, he was, in the opinion of

Sinclair Lewis, "a combination of St. Augustine, Barnum, and John Barrymore." From his pulpit at the Plymouth Congregational Church in Brooklyn, he captivated his congregation and on wide lecture circuits became the most conspicuous clergyman in nineteenth-century America.[7]

Thirty-one years old and just ten years out of Amherst, Beecher had reached some conclusions about the nature of success. Published in 1844, *Lectures to Young Men* was hailed as a 'must' by a profusion of favorable notices and was continually reissued in new editions and reprints. "Beware!" is what Beecher and his clerical colleagues shouted in such tracts. With images aflame and cadences throbbing with emotion, the thirty-one-year-old pastor issued fearful warnings against gambling, loose women, dishonesty, liquor, horse racing, and the theater. What he did like was hard work. "If a young man has no higher ambition in life than riches," he lectured, "Industry—plain, rugged, brown-faced, homely clad, old fashioned Industry, must be courted." Avoid speculation, he counselled, shun public offices by which the indolent are paid only a small pittance anyway, and count yourself fortunate if you do not inherit money. Your best investment is the honest sweat from your brow. Beecher clinched his argument with the Biblical promise: *"Seest thou a man diligent in his business, he shall stand before kings, he shall not stand before mean men."* [8]

"When justly obtained, and rationally used, riches are called a gift of God, an evidence of his favor, and a great reward," Beecher assured his young men. Then he plunged into the real religious problem and came up with a solution. *But* "when gathered unjustly, and corruptly used, wealth is pronounced a canker, a rust, a fire, a curse. There is no contradiction, then, when the Bible persuades to industry, and integrity, by a promise of riches; and then dissuades from wealth, as a terrible thing, destroying soul and body. Blessings are vindictive to abusers, and kind to rightful users;—they serve us, or rule us. Fire warms our dwelling, or consumes it. Steam serves man, and also destroys him. Iron, in the plough, the sickle, the house, the ship, is indispensable. The dirk, the assassin's knife, the cruel sword and the spear, are iron also. The constitution of man, and of society, alike evinces the design of God. Both are made to be happier by the possession of riches;—their full development and perfection are dependent, to a large extent, upon wealth. Without it, there can be neither books nor implements; neither commerce nor arts, neither towns nor cities." [9]

The rich man does not dwell in a land of milk and honey however. On every side dangers lurk in the shadows. To speed the young man along the road to riches, Beecher set up six warnings. First, do not get the idea that riches necessarily confer happiness, or that poverty equals unhappiness. There is a type of poverty that reaps its treasures from usefulness to others. If you have worked hard and are still poor, do not scorn your lot but know that "there is often in the hut more dignity than in the palace; more satisfaction in the poor man's scanty fare than in the rich man's satiety." If you become wealthy, remember that the rich man's happiness flows from his benevolence to society. Second, anyone who is in a hurry to be rich "hath an evil eye" which tempts ruin. "When God sends wealth to *bless* men he sends it gradually like a gentle rain. When God sends riches to *punish* men, they come tumultuously, like a roaring torrent, tearing up landmarks and sweeping all before them in promiscuous ruin. Almost every evil which environs the path to wealth, springs from that criminal haste which substitutes adroitness for industry, and trick for toil." Third, God's law commands that you do not covet. "He whose heart is turned to greediness, who sweats through life under the load of labor only to heap up money, and dies without private usefulness, or a record of public service, is no better, in God's estimation, than a pack-horse,—a mule,—an ass; a creature of burden, to be beaten, and worked and killed, and dragged off by another like him, abandoned to the birds and forgotten. HE IS BURIED WITH THE BURIAL OF AN ASS! This is the MISER'S EPITAPH—and yours, young man! if you earn it by *covetousness!*" [10]

Fourth, "I warn every aspirant for wealth against the infernal canker of selfishness. It will eat out of the heart with the fire of hell, or bake it harder than a stone." Fifth, beware of dishonesty. "Whenever you have exerted all your knowledge, all your skill, all your industry, with long continued patience and without success, then, it is clear, not that you may proceed to employ trick and cunning, but that you must STOP. God has put before you a bound which no man may overleap." Finally, anyone who extorts the poor, the miserable, the ignorant is an avaricious villain. In short, Beecher warned the young men of his day: Travel the road to riches, but beware lest you tumble into the deep, black hole of avarice and plummet straight to hell.[11]

Until the middle of the nineteenth century the success message was most frequently cast in the form of an essay, address, or sermon. The success piece often joined other essays as a book on the theme of ethical values. The fictional tale and the moral tract were particular forms which Timothy Shay Arthur used with effectiveness. Arthur is best known for his lost-weekend tract about *Ten Nights in a Bar-Room, and What I Saw There.* Satirical irreverence towards *Ten Nights'* melodramatic fulminations against the ravages of booze has furnished enough vaudeville jokes to tickle a hundred audiences into laughter. "Father, dear father, come home with me now!" was at one time a maudlin tune with enough spoof in it to sadden the troubled heart of any temperance leader. But it should be pointed out that the laughter was not at Arthur's expense. The take-off was not on the novel but on the play of the same name which was written by another. Though a sermonizing and sentimental novel, *Ten Nights* is not funny. The characterization is sharp, the pace swift, and the structure is always under control. Arthur's specific success tales and tracts are hardly ambrosia for sensitive literary tastes, but they have a kind of brilliance which rests on the achievement of accomplishing what they set out to do.

The grandson of a Revolutionary officer, Timothy Shay Arthur was born into a large family of limited means. At the age of eight he was taken from New York State to Baltimore and enrolled in a public school. A dull lad, his teacher thought, so he was taken from school and apprenticed to a watchmaker. During the day he learned about watches; at night he read hungrily. The combination injured his eyesight, so he forgot about watches, and after a while declared himself for the literary life. A friend of Edgar Allan Poe and the literary elite of Baltimore and Philadelphia, he edited a succession of publications, and by the end of his life had authored some one hundred works. Many of them were moral tales and tracts devoted to educating sinners against the evils of drink. One brute statistic which would have shattered the pedagogical confidence of his old teacher was that Arthur alone was responsible for over five per cent of all volumes of fiction published in the 1840s.[12]

Where There's a Will, There's a Way, which appeared in the early 1850s, is a good example of Arthur's plots, simple but competently executed. During hard times, Harker (the one to emulate) and Wilson (for contrast) are laid off their jobs. Harker bustles about town, taking whatever work is available; Wilson is too proud to slave at menial tasks until business picks up. On a slow day, Harker and Wilson wander down to the Battery where Harker hits upon the plan of rowing people out to the ships anchored off-shore. He rents a boat for a dollar and the first day clears seven dollars. Pretty soon he is the owner of three boats, rowing one himself and hiring out the other two. Wilson, needless to say, has been sauntering listlessly about the streets. With trade revived, the enterprising Harker sells his boats, adds the sum to his savings, and sets himself up in business. Everything prospers for Harker in his venture. As for Wilson—he's working for Harker. How did Harker do it? He just kept reminding himself: "Where there's a will, there's a way."

In sundry tracts and tales Arthur ranged over the issues of the success idea. *True Riches or Wealth Without Wings* are not money and material things, but moral and intellectual treasures stored up on this earth. *A Way to be Happy* is *not* to retire from business into the relaxed pleasures of leisure, but to work hard right up to the last moment in some useful employment. *Retiring from Business* brings to a prosperous manufacturer disaster and unhappiness and provides Arthur the opportunity to discuss at length "the law of reciprocal benefits." Linking the eighteenth-century economic theories of Adam Smith to the twentieth-century doctrine of service, Arthur argues that a healthy, able man is morally bound to labor on and on, because he has an obligation to serve usefully those who are in their own way laboring to serve him. *How to Attain True Greatness* hammers home this favorite theme: the motivation as well as the justification for ambition should be the desire to be useful and serve others. Settling down into a heart-to-heart via the essay form, Arthur's *Advice to Young Men* is this: with society under the direction of an all-wise Providence, "whoever seeks to secure the common good most effectually secures his own." [13]

America and the idea of success were fitting together like 4th and July. The nation was on the threshold of fantastic material expansion. Applied science was beginning to exploit a birthright of bounteous natural resources. The tyranny of distance was being solved by the railroad, the need for power by coal, and the necessity of strong materials by iron and steel. The machine age was changing the face of America on a foundation of ready capital, a domestic market, fresh waves of immigration more concerned with economic opportunity than political and religious liberty, plenty of land and food, and a government sympathetic to the entrepreneur.

Throughout the latter half of the nineteenth century, from population to annual savings, statistics indicated that America was pushing ahead. Boasted Andrew Carnegie, the immigrant boy from Scotland, as he poured out his love for the new land: "The old nations of the earth creep on at a snail's pace; the Republic thunders past with the rush of the express. The United States, [in] the growth of a single century, has already reached the foremost rank among nations, and is destined soon to outdistance all others in the race." Before the century had closed, in the quantity and value of her products, America had become the first manufacturing nation of the world, and in national wealth had surged ahead of Great Britain, then at the height of its power under Queen Victoria.[14]

Just after the Industrial Revolution hit with full force in the middle of the nineteenth century, the old gave way to the new by violence. The nation turned against itself, fought a war of contending interests, and finally declared itself for industrialism and the businessman. Down went the South in defeat, its economy smashed, its political power dissipated. With the support of the western farmers, the financial-manufacturing East translated a military victory into an economic triumph by means of political legislation. After acts favorable to the new order of the North had been pushed through Congress, businessmen settled back into the support of a freewheeling economy and a denunciation of any attempts to regulate it by discontented agrarian and laboring groups. It was a swift shake-up in the political power structure of America.[15]

The Civil War marked the contrasts between the South and the rest of the nation. This study has excluded the South for good reasons. Up North and out West the idea of success had taken hold. It was a goal pursued in the city, not on the farm. The idea of success concentrated, in the beginning, in a mercantile-commercial world. Later, it embraced manufacturing and finance. In values and action, heritage and economy, the North was ready for quick expansion during the last half of the nineteenth century. The South, on the other hand, was shattered by economic disintegration and hurt pride. With its crumbling plantation economy and predominantly agrarian values, it was in no condition to compete with applied science and technology.

There were other factors which made the South distinct from the rest of the nation. The criteria of success were different where the goal of aspiration was slave ownership and the possession of a landed estate. With its romantic enchantment with the past and reverence for family background, the South refused to exalt so passionately the self-raised man. As one correspondent briskly commented in the first decade of the twentieth century: "Blood counts far more down here than it does in many other places. . . ." To extend beyond our time period for a moment, in the decades following World War I, southern literature and drama swung from the poles of sentimentality over fair maidens, chivalrous gentlemen, magnolias, mint juleps, and Rastus, to a violence based on an authoritarian relationship to the Negro, or to the psychological disasters inherent in a pride of caste and the decadence of ancestor worship. These moods reflected the agonies endured by a society at war with itself.[16]

Though wrenching changes in recent decades have left their mark on southern values, the one hundred years since the Civil War for most of the nation has been a drama of the present; for the South, the century was an epilogue to a tragedy. Genteel poverty for some time after the Civil War was almost a badge of honor, the more so if you were wealthy before the conflict. Lack of money was a positive sacrifice for the Cause. The eagerness to become a success by making money was blunted. The connection between money and social class position was ruptured. The white, well-born Southerner not only looked forward to the past; the past lived in him. What was this southern 'differentness'? It contained values which were counterproductive to industrialism. Comforted by a Lost Cause and a Plantation Legend, southern 'differentness' was expressed in a European deference for social distinctions, graciously formed manners between men and women and children and adults, a smouldering mood of defeat, anxieties about the Negro and the meaning of work, tribal customs and dialects, the fantasies of both suffering as the victim and surviving as an executioner. However similar the South may have been to the nation in other respects, too many generalizations about success do not comfortably correspond to the southern experience or its values. We have, therefore, omitted a consideration of the South from this study.[17]

There were propagandists in the South in the decades following the Civil War who did work hard at giving dignity to the new industrial-financial order. The task was not easy. C. Vann Woodward has pointed out how the lives of those men driven by the profit motive "had to be invested with a glamour that would evoke emulation, their destination recognized as 'success,' and the changes they wrought be regarded as 'progress.' Indeed it was important that the meaning of life be discovered in the vicissitudes and triumphs attending the competitive struggle for business profits." Henry W. Grady, Georgia journalist and vigorous leader of the new order, hit the aristocratic-worshipping

South where it hurt. Self-made men, he insisted, "have sunk the corner stone of the only aristocracy that Americans should know." It was a new way of life for the South that these apostles of the new order were preaching.[18]

In the North and West it was a way of life that had already sunk deep roots. In the period after the Civil War opinion leaders in most areas of American society, as well as success writers, lovingly nourished the values which supported and expressed the Industrial Revolution. The last half of the nineteenth century witnessed the final triumph of a middle-class way of life over patricians of landed property and older fortunes. The common man had threatened this aristocracy of land and commerce in the first half of the nineteenth century. Common men, who had become uncommonly wealthy, moved in and took over in an explosion of bourgeois baroque during the Gilded Age. It is important to remember that the change in the power structure of America was celebrated in the name of the common man. It was the triumph of Jacksonian democracy over Jeffersonian aristocracy. The fact that this new ruling group later became a Hamiltonian plutocracy should not dim the luster of its spirit. Indeed, in feeling it was far more democratic than the spirit of colonial America.

The heart of this democratic feeling and the new power group of manufacturing-financial wealth was peculiarly American—the self-made man. *The* ideal career in America was the poor boy who struggled unaided against overwhelming odds to the top of his occupation. In politics, it was symbolically defined as the distance between a log cabin and the White House. In the arts and professions, it was from obscurity to fame. Best of all was *the* supreme achievement in the uphill battle—from rags to riches. The final accolade to such a triumph was this—that the money so laboriously piled up be given away to good works.

Why was it that America was more consciously profuse than Europe in her praise of the self-made man? "The instinctive flush of sympathy and pride with which Americans listen to such a story [of a self-made man]," Bliss Perry has explained, "is far more deeply based than any vulgar admiration for money-making abilities. No one cares whether such a man is rich or poor. He has vindicated anew the possibilities of manhood under American conditions of opportunity; the miracle of our faith has in him come true once more." His very success, the Kluckhohns explained, was a "dramatic vindication of the American way of life and an invitation to identification and emulation." [19]

The poor boy who made good was a powerful weapon to fight a haughty European air of social and artistic superiority. He was a symbol of America's contribution to the world—the free man improving himself and his position in a land of freedom and opportunity. A man of action, not of ideas, he rose by his own efforts, unaided by contacts, family, or blood. He was, in fancy and in fact, a living denial of those romantic European tales which assumed that a talented person in the lower ranks must somehow be a kidnapped or stray scion of noble birth. At the same time he was praised, not for the advantages of being born into poverty, but for his persistence in fighting his way out of it. [20]

The self-made man was celebrated because he was a source of hope and pride. The American was also logically compelled to honor and respect him because wealth was not simply an isolated end-product providing certain comforts in life. It possessed a deeper meaning as the measure of a man's worth. When "wealth is considered as an index of character," perceived Ralph Barton Perry, "then the deeper the depths of poverty from which the possessor has risen, the greater the obstacles over which he has triumphed, the less he has profited by the favor of fortune, the more creditable his wealth. The man of humble origin, surrounded in his youth with every possible disadvantage of lowly station, of ignorance, of material deprivation, or even of ill health, who has through the pure power of his moral will ascended to the summit of affluence, is the paragon and model of youthful aspiration. His prosperity is accepted without resentment, and applauded by his admiring contemporaries." [21]

The applause swelled into a roar in the sweep of American history after the Jacksonian period. The political managers of William Henry Harrison shrewdly recognized this when they invoked the insights of a social class interpretation in the election of 1840 to play up the supposed log cabin background of their candidate. But it so happened that the businessman, not the politician, rode in on the crescendo of praise to the self-made man. When the Industrial Revolution created opportunities for swift ascent, the talented flocked to the sources of power. The businessman was to enjoy for a long time to come some of the fruits which the ministry tasted in the seventeenth century and the statesman in the eighteenth century.[22]

The Jeffersonian concept of leadership based on an aristocracy of virtue and talents was beaten down by a Jacksonian belief that anyone could rule. And as the politician's prestige plummeted, Jefferson's chosen people of God, the farmers, remained, of course, 'the backbone of America,' but, after all, really only hicks and hayseeds. Agrarian America was slipping into the limbo of a remembrance of things past. "The modern nobility," proclaimed financier Henry Clews, "springs from success in business," while a choir of apostles sang in unison the reverent melody. The businessman had moved front and center on the stage of American life. A sensitive intellectual, Henry Seidel Canby, looking back over the 1890s, tried to spotlight the values of his home town. The B's, C's and D's were given out, he remembered, to a public-spirited citizen, brilliant conversationalist, or deeply religious person. A++ was reserved for "a first-rate business man with all that implied." [23]

Harold Laski has contended that "in no previous civilization has the business man enjoyed either the power or the prestige that he possesses in the United States. . . . The great business man in the United States has an aristocratic status comparable to that of the landowner or the soldier or the priest in pre-capitalist Europe." When the agrarians gave their mighty heave for power at the end of the nineteenth century, William Jennings Bryan wanted everyone to know the proper name for his supporters. "We come to speak," he declared in his Cross of Gold speech, "for the broader class of business men," which he defined as the workers in the cities, country-town attorneys and merchants, miners, and farmers.[24]

No holy spot, however, has ever been made of the birthplace

or tomb of a businessman. The reason is that few businessmen, self-made or otherwise, were raised to the stature of what we might call a Model of Devotion. Models of Devotion, like the dutifully admired Washington or the beloved Lincoln, secured their prestige from public service. They represented a way for the nation, particularly schoolchildren, to cherish certain ideals (freedom, democracy, the ante-bellum South, national patriotism, goodness) as flesh and blood symbols for abstract ideas, places, or things. The businessman, on the other hand, was an Image of Aspiration, a figure to be equalled or excelled in terms of occupational achievement. Whenever the businessman did emerge as a Model of Devotion, it was because he symbolized a major contribution to the national welfare, for example, Henry Ford and his role in developing the magic of mass production. Noble politicians were named statesmen, able soldiers were called military leaders, but there was no equivalent escalation of occupational prestige for the businessman. About all he could do was give away his money and hope to be praised with a non-business classification, i.e., a philanthropist.[25]

The business journalist, a new type of success writer, was determined to set the record straight. He sung to the lives of businessmen hymns of praise no less reverential than the exaltation of statesmen and military leaders in history textbooks.

Business journalists began to increase sharply in numbers as America moved from an agrarian to an industrial economy. Emerging as a long-term growth occupation in the 1840s, throughout the nineteenth century they polished the image of the rising merchant, industrialist, and financier to a glamorous sheen. The job was clearly defined. It was to be of service, in the words of Philadelphia's Edwin T. Freedley, "to those for whom I entertain a higher respect than for any other class of men in the world—I mean the active, intelligent business men of the country—and especially to those who are fitting themselves for business pursuits." [26]

Freedley in the 1850s, and cohorts like Freeman Hunt, publisher of a magazine for merchants and businessmen in New York City, were claiming that the successful businessman rightfully belonged to the upper class. They were talkers and writers who were proving that the merchant "may also be a gentleman and a scholar, as well as an honest and kind-hearted man." In short, the man who made a fortune by selling goods was not a dumpy bourgeois, but a gentleman of taste, education, and refinement. It was a magnificent battle for prestige and social position—until the blood of a Civil War was spilled, as well as printer's ink, in their behalf.[27]

In the bourgeois revolutionary camp, men of action marched forward to seize economic and political power. Close behind followed the men of ideas, the Intelligence Force, justifying and ennobling the conquering heroes and their weapons of business capitalism. There was unity on fundamental principles. These writers were allies; they borrowed freely from one another. Freedley confessed that *Hunt's Merchant Magazine* was "the most valuable periodical for the business man ever published in any country." When Hunt plucked his best from the back issues of his magazine in 1856 and joined them into *Wealth and Worth,* he praised Freedley's book. At the same time he could not resist the comment that it was difficult to quote from because their ideas were so similar. "Mr. Freedley has had the good taste," the master explained, "to avail himself of our labors by liberal extracts." [28]

While the quality and shape of this literary cake might differ from writer to writer, the taste was the same. None of them could individually claim to be the master chef. The recipe for making money was quite simple, according to Freedley. To be charitable to the destitute is a religious duty. But in order to be charitable, one has to have something to be charitable with. Hence, "to get money" is a religious duty. There is also an added incentive—to be independent. Although "the *getting* of money, and the proper *use* of money" are distinct, the two are related. On the one hand, no one has "any moral right to limit his exertions by his wants." Under the proper limitations of man-made laws, the moral law, and the laws of honor, every man should work to pile up as much treasure on earth as he can. On the other hand, he has no "natural right" to keep all he gets. Thus, his justification for making money is the independence it offers, plus the comforting realization that it enables him to be charitable and therefore obedient to the will of the Creator. The *way* to get this money is not by attending college. Indeed, Freedley suggests that college is more liable to ruin than help you. The best alma mater is the counting house. Back this training up by six essential habits of business—industry, arrangement, calculation, prudence, punctuality, and perseverance—and you are well on your way to a fortune.[29]

For Freeman Hunt, diligence in business and a fervent religious spirit supported one another. The same divine authority required that man attend to both. A religious spirit was a means to success, but at the same time it was wrong to feign religion just to make a sale. The proper and effective means to success were as rigid as geometry: self-reliance, perseverance, honesty, caution, frugality, punctuality, and similar qualities. Above all, don't be in too much of a hurry. The gradual increase of wealth is more auspicious than sudden accumulation. Citing the observations of a contemporary magazine, Hunt pointed up the differences between Europe and America. In Europe there are distinctions of blood, title, or inherited rank. In America, however, "there remains but one basis of social distinction, namely, wealth. . . . In society at large, gradations of social position are measured by stock-certificates, rent-rolls, and bank-accounts." But be not deceived, for 'true success' is not material success. 'True success' is the "peace of mind which springs from right impulses and which promises a serene future," "the proper and harmonious development of those faculties which God has given us," and the virtues which an individual has had to develop in order to accumulate wealth.[30]

The rags to riches romance was fondly told by the business journalists. Matthew Hale Smith in his *Bulls and Bears of New York,* published in the 1870s, was certain that the laws of the universe are not more unbending and regular than the law of success in Wall Street. Industry, honesty, perseverance, sticking to one thing, invariably lead to success in any reputable calling." His report that "there are wealthy men in New York, who began life picking up rags in the street," touches off a chain reaction of success stories, like the rag picker who built his occupation

into a mighty wholesale supplier for paper-makers, or the penniless widow and her sons who started making sugar goodies in the
kitchen of their house and made the firm so respected that the
Queen of England became a patron of their candy house. Newsboys, humble glue-makers, stableboys, milk-peddlers all parlayed
their lowly beginnings into positions of prominence and wealth
by the get-rich-slow-but-sure methods of hard work and honesty.
After plucking biographical anecdotes from the lives of 800 or
so eminent men and putting them together into another book,
Smith concluded that their lives "all tell the SAME STORY.
Without character there is no permanent success." [31]

There was a time in the American past when certain legal
holidays automatically set in motion a tidal wave of oratory
rolling from coast to coast. Hymns of praise were sung to
Washington and Lincoln on their birthdays (no less celebrated
was Lee in the South), voices swelled with pride on the Fourth
of July, while the last Thursday in November was the day to be
thankful. For success oratory, the big holiday was graduation day.
It fell usually in the month of June, in a country where a student
could be graduated into life with a diploma representing every
conceivable type of instruction. It was a time for looking forward
to future's hopes, not to the glories of the past. Upon the
shoulders of the commencement speaker rested the assignment
of guiding young men and women from their ivory towers of
theory into the realities of life.

Educators honored very important people with the task. While
some commencement orators spoke easily of current events and
public policy, others took a firm grip on their own values and
plunged into one of the most difficult speeches of their lives.
Such an oration was delivered by James A. Garfield in 1869 to
the graduating students of a Washington business college. As
applause rose to meet his words, the future President of the
United States spoke of his sincere interest in youth, blasted those
colleges which taught only classical learning as an "absolute
failure" in preparing young men and women for the practical
business of life, admonished the ambitious never to work for the
government civil service, and then settled down to tussle with

the title of his address, *Elements of Success.* "Let me beg you, in the outset of your career," he said, "to dismiss from your minds all idea of succeeding by luck. . . . A pound of pluck is worth a ton of luck." Be self-reliant, he charged, develop within yourselves "surplus power" to make a name and/or fortune for yourself. Turn poverty to an advantage, for "nine times out of ten the best thing that can happen to a young man is to be tossed overboard, and compelled to sink or swim for himself. In all my acquaintance, I have never known one to be drowned who was worth the saving. (Applause.)" Pointing a proud finger of comparison to England, Garfield opened the door of social class equality and opportunity for all to enter. "The strata of our society resemble rather the ocean, where every drop, even the lowest, is free to mingle with all others, and may shine at last on the crest of the highest wave. This is the glory of our country. . . ." [32]

Two years after the ending of the Civil War, the President of Packard's Bryant & Stratton Business College in New York underestimated the subject and the speaker. An hour before the visiting lecturer was to begin, not only were all one thousand seats occupied, but the lecture rooms "were crowded almost to suffocation," and people were being turned away at the door. The students who had missed out requested another performance. The address was to be repeated at Cooper Union's spacious hall with a comfortable seating capacity of twenty-five hundred persons. A half-hour before time, the place was jammed, "every seat was taken, and finally, every inch of standing space, while hundreds went away who could not be accommodated." The speaker? Horace Greeley. The subject—success. [33]

The editor of the *New York Tribune* was always positive: "Young men, I would have you believe that success in life is within the reach of every one who will truly and nobly seek it." Integrity, frugality, a new approach, persistence—these are the qualities that make for success. And here is a moral duty. "I do hold," he charged, "that thrift, within reasonable limits, is the moral obligation of every man; that he should endeavor and aspire to be a little better off at the close of each year." With soaring praises to opportunity, Greeley concluded that

America was destined "to bound forward on a career of prosperous activity such as the world has not known." [34]

But Horace Greeley's ringing command, "Go West, young man, and grow up with the country," pressing from the editorial columns of the *New York Tribune* in favor of the homestead law, sounded no echo in the pages of success literature. As the nation went on swashbuckling its way to material greatness in the decades following the Civil War, a different kind of opportunity was beckoning.

4

"... RELIGION DEMANDS SUCCESS"

For thirty years after the Civil War there were two great areas of opportunity in America. One was agrarian, with its expanding frontier pushed forward by farmers moving West. The other was urban, with its promise of mercantile, industrial, and financial gain. In the universe of the success idea, the soundest course was generally to cultivate your own garden, stay on the farm, and make the best of it. But if this proved impossible, get off the farm and into some business. Success writers did not advise their readers to strike out for the frontier. Their frontier was not on the land but in the ever-expanding towns and cities. It was up from the asphalt, not up from the sod. The pot of gold was waiting in the city or town, not at the end of some western rainbow.[1]

To fill the aspiring with inspiration and instruction, an ocean of advice from rolling presses and lecture platforms flooded the mind of America. Success was powerful box office. Lecture halls rang with the gospel, pastors in pulpits offered the security of religious sanction (and the insecurity of religious duty), schoolbooks taught it, novelists discovered its best-selling appeal, an army of journalists and hack writers cashed in on its inspiration, while successful businessmen struggled to reveal how it was done, or how they wanted the public to think it was done. From tracts, magazine articles, books, speeches, biographies, and autobiographies, there was an abundance of inspiration to excite the nation's mind with dreams of urban gold.

In the thirty-five years following the Civil War, three success writers towered high above their colleagues. The three became a success by talking or writing about success. These monarchs of their trade were all New England born, graduates of Ivy League colleges, and ordained (though not necessarily practicing) ministers in respectable Protestant denominations. They expressed the values of their age with a simplicity so dramatically exciting that they kindled the fires of ambition in millions of hearts wherever they were heard or read.

The first of the monarchs is better known, for his name became synonymous with success. To be called "an Horatio Alger hero" in America has been a badge of distinction. Occasionally, however, the accolade was jumbled into confusion. An "Horatio Alger hero" was not shaped in the image of Alger but rather in the image of the fictional heroes in his novels. The "Horatio Alger hero" symbolized respect for the self-made man and faith in equality of opportunity. As a symbol, it stood for a poor boy of lower-class origins, with no advantages except his own sterling character, who rose to the top by his own abilities and efforts. The symbol has often been modified over the years to raise the starting point of the hero to the middle class. It has been broadened to include a fervent hymn to a freedom of enterprise system which encouraged the ascent to fame and fortune. But in essence it has always remained the story of a boy who started somewhere near the bottom and worked his unassisted way to the top. The symbol of an "Horatio Alger hero," as it came to be used in the twentieth century, differed, as we shall see later, from the real heroes in an Alger novel.

Alger exerted his impact during the latter part of the nineteenth century and the early decades of the twentieth, but it was not until 1947 that anyone got around to exploiting him into an organized symbol. The American Schools and Colleges Association was "concerned about the trend among young people towards the mind-poisoning belief that equal opportunity was a thing of the past. . . ." Each year a number of men "who by their own efforts had pulled themselves up by their bootstraps in the American tradition" received their Horatio Alger Awards. As the scrolls or plaques were handed out, it was a time for reaffirming equality of opportunity and the American way of life under the freedom of enterprise system. "I'm beginning to feel a fellow hasn't got a chance in this country," cracked David Sarnoff on one of these occasions, "unless he starts as a newsboy." Not all the award-winners started from scratch, however. Pepsi-Cola's Walter S. Mack, Jr., had to struggle up from Harvard; elder statesman Bernard Baruch was not exactly born into poverty; and did Grover Whalen's prosperous father really keep his elegant son in rags? No matter. The rags-to-riches Horatio Alger hero was a bootstrap symbol which could be stretched to include young men who 'came up the hard way' by overcoming such obstacles as earning their way through college. It was the adaptation of a classical American myth (in the academic sense) to changes in the preparation for achievement.[2]

Alger's literary output was in volume extraordinary, in content monotonous. He wrote approximately 100 novels, most of them on the theme of success. The figure should give pause to his "I've read 'em all" 'nostalger' fans, but maybe if you've read one, you *have* read them all. Beginning just after the Civil War with his eighth book and first smash-hit success novel, *Ragged Dick* (1868), and continuing to his death in 1899, Alger's nervous pen poured out novels at the rate of three or four a year. Sales mushroomed into the millions, and though Alger lived quite comfortably, he never acquired great wealth from his works. Approximately sixty different publishers issued his books. Alger's appeal had peaked before World War I, and what was left of it by the irreverent 1920s was further damaged by the depression 1930s. Styles in juvenile fiction had begun to swing toward the mechanized adventures of the likes of Tom Swift. For today's teenager, the thrifty straight arrows in Alger's novels are as hopelessly old-fashioned as great-grandfather must seem.[3]

What kind of a man was Horatio Alger, Jr.? Most of the references to Alger's life written after 1928 are filled with errors.

The encylopedic and standard accounts, spanning some forty years, have all taken as their source an inaccurate biography of Alger by Herbert Mayes, published in 1928. Mayes, himself a classic 'Horatio Alger hero,' was born in a New York tenement and went on to become the brilliant editor of *Good Housekeeping* and *McCall's*. He based important parts of the biography on Alger's private diary, which would have been revealing, except it was Mayes, not Alger, who wrote Alger's diary. If Mayes had dug deeper into the sources, he would have uncovered a bigger story than any fantasy forged into a diary. Horatio Alger, Jr., without very much of a doubt, was a homosexual.[4]

What are the facts? He was the eldest of five children, born in 1832 and raised in small towns surrounding Boston. His father, a Harvard graduate, was a Unitarian minister. Horatio was a sickly child, a momma's boy, who was tutored part of the time at home. He went on to Harvard, worked his way through, and graduated Phi Beta Kappa with the class of 1852. For the next fourteen years he tutored other boys, taught school, traveled to Europe, wrote quite a bit, and became an ordained Unitarian minister, more to please his father than himself. In 1866 he left his ministerial position at the Unitarian Church in Brewster on Massachusetts' Cape Cod and took off for New York City. Two careful bibliographers of Alger's works, Frank Gruber and Ralph Gardner, suggest that Alger left the formal ministry because of a dedication to writing and Gardner adds that Alger was probably thankful when the parish committee decided not to reappoint him. But another sad reason is written in one-hundred-year-old church records now stored in a Cape Cod bank vault.

"We learn from John Clark and Thomas S. Crocker [two boys]," a special parish investigating committee reported in 1866, "that Horatio Alger, Jr. has been practicing on them at different times deeds that are too revolting to relate. Said charges were put to the said Alger and he did not deny them. He admitted that he had been imprudent and considered his connection with the Unitarian Society of Brewster dissolved." Another committee was immediately formed to send a letter to Unitarian headquarters in Boston communicating the feelings of an "outraged community": "That Horatio Alger, Jr. who has officiated as our Minister for about 15 months past has recently been charged with gross immorality and a most heinous crime, a crime of no less magnitude than the abominable and revolting crime of unnatural familiarity with *boys*. . . . Whereupon the committee sent for Alger and to him specified the charges and evidence of his guilt which he neither denied or attempted to extenuate but received it with apparent calmness of an old offender—and hastily left town on the very next train for parts unknown. . . ." The crime, the committee charged, "is too revolting to think of in the most brutal of our race. . . ." [5]

Guilty he no doubt was, but brutal he was not. So this gentle, little man scarcely more than five feet in height, frail and sensitive, went off to New York City to befriend with a generous hand the street urchins of the Newsboys' Lodging House and write them and their city, the city itself, into the American Dream. For thirty years until his death in 1899, he lived in New York, now and then traveling or summering in South Natick, Massachusetts and Old Orchard, Maine. He became famous, moved in the better social circles as befitted a Harvard graduate of the time, and lived a comfortable life as a shy, increasingly rotund little bachelor—but always he returned to the world of the street gamins with a kind word and a helping hand. "Holy Horatio" needed them as much as they needed him.

Alger's fictional heroes started poor and finished rich. That is why they were a success. As we noted earlier, an "Horatio Alger hero" in American mythology came to mean a self-made man. But the Horatio Alger hero as a symbol differed from "our hero" in an Alger novel in several respects. First, the heroes in the novels are teenagers, not adults. They are really self-made boys. Second, not all of Alger's fictional heroes started in rags. One type begins as a lower-class, uneducated, slum child. He is an orphan, abandoned, or the son of a widowed mother. But the social origins of another type of hero is much higher. He is a middle-class, educated, country lad. His family is in reduced financial circumstances because of a dead, absent, or failure father. Third, "our hero" did not end up fabulously rich.

What he did achieve was a respectable appearance with proper manners, a solid job (generally in a mercantile establishment), a healthy income, and a promising career. He had successfully made the transition, both economically and socially, into the world of small business and was on his way to greater fame and fortune.[6]

Fourth, the careers of Alger's fictional heroes often surge quickly ahead by that gimmick which has always been the bugaboo of all non-fiction success writers—luck. Ragged Dick, who longs to chuck his bootblack's box for better things, rescues a child who has tumbled from a ferryboat. The grateful father (who just happened to be an employer in the kind of job Dick wants) hires the plucky lad in his counting house and starts him on the way to fame and fortune. Phil, the Fiddler, has been forced to play the violin in the streets of New York for his tyrannical padrone. Fleeing from the padrone, Phil fiddles on his own. Getting nowhere, he drops exhausted in a snowdrift on a cold Christmas Eve. At this juncture, a physician plucks his half-frozen body from the snowdrift and takes him home. It happens that this physician is not only wealthy and prominent, he also lost his only child on Christmas four years ago. Phil is happily adopted and set up for life. In *Luck and Pluck,* John Oakley's rightful inheritance is restored to him by the recovery of a will kept hidden by his wicked stepmother.[7]

Luck, in a good many of Alger's novels, is a stranger whom the young hero helps in some manner, a stranger, fortunately, who is in some position to reciprocate with funds or a promising job. As Henry and Katherine Pringle have detected: "No Alger hero was so silly as to rescue anybody with less than an AAA rating in Dun and Bradstreet." Although this luck gimmick is an exciting solution to a crisis, it is not the message that Alger works hard to convey. Central to most plots are the hard facts that the boy deserved the break, that he had prepared himself through goodness, hard work, and perseverance to seize the opportunity when it arrived. Whatever came his self-reliant way by chance was used to the best of his ability to advance his own career.[8]

Alger cherished a particular affinity for the self-explanatory alliterated title: *Do and Dare, Brave and Bold, Luck and Pluck, Strive and Succeed, Fame and Fortune, Slow and Sure.* Many of his heroes (so reminiscent in feeling of nineteenth-century genre painting) end up a living recitation of the boy scout creed. Many are like Harry Walton in *Bound to Rise,* "a broad-shouldered, sturdy boy, with a frank, open face, resolute, though good-natured." [9]

Amidst all the manly wholesomeness and moral preaching, it is important to remember that these tales of success identification were not unreal adventures of pirates and cowboys but lessons in vocational education. Alger was a tutor to that great migration of ambitious country boys who broke home ties to seek their fortune in the city. Every novel on this theme was an exciting guidebook teeming with colorful, minute descriptions about living and working in the nearest great metropolis. How many country boys Alger pulled into the city is unknown, but it is certain that after reading his novels they went there better prepared to confront the shock of its bustling life swarming with chiselers and urchins, loafers and drunkards. No wonder the novels were gobbled up by barefooted farm boys sneaking a few minutes in the hayloft to read the next chapter or by dreamy delivery boys loafing through a quiet moment at the village store.

Alger's tales do dash along at a fast clip. But, as Russel Crouse warns, if you pick up an Alger novel with "any idea that you are about to sit down for a swig of nectar with one of the gods, your literary taste may be permanently impaired." What you will find are false leads, clumsy construction, unbalanced structure, and shallow characterization. Alger's characters are about as one-dimensional as the 'goodies' and 'baddies' in a standard comic strip. Although his newsboys and other heroes err and stray now and then like lost sheep, they are shortly yanked back to goodness by the long crook of righteousness. The 'baddies' were the enemies of social democracy, economic justice, and an honest ambition to get ahead; for example, social-class snobs, the money-hungry squire foreclosing the mortgage, idlers, cheats, bullies, and greedy oppressors of the poor. But the 'goodies' included not only the sacrificing mother and the determined-to-do-good-and-make-money son. This category embraced perhaps the real heroes of Alger's novels—the wealthy merchants, lawyers, and businessmen whom the rapidly upward mobile boy was determined to be like.[10]

A look at Alger's unconscious through the plots of his success novels is tempting—just so long as one admits that the pieces of the puzzle can be arranged to show more than one picture. One standard Alger tale contains the following: An adolescent of good character whose father is dead, absent, or a failure, a mother dependent on her son, a manly rescue by the hero rewarded by an elderly benefactor, then the arrival of the son in the nick of time with funds to rescue from the villainous squire his admiring mother's mortgaged home. We know now that when Alger himself was a dreamy, sickly twelve years old, his father became involved in debt and his land assigned. A mortgage was held by a local squire. Was Alger identifying with the rescuing hero, claiming the elderly benefactor as a father surrogate, then playing the son who saved his mother's home by lifting the mortgage? Or was Alger, with homosexual undertones, identifying himself with the benefactor of the little boys? Or did his fantasies permit him to play both roles—mother's rescuing hero and the kindly benefactor? [11]

It must be said for Horatio Alger, Jr., that he knew a good thing when he found it. He made three forays into the field of 'non-fiction.' All these were biographies about statesmen and cast in the same mould. James A. Garfield, Abraham Lincoln, and Daniel Webster were resolute, honest young men, born to poverty and humble beginnings, who overcame obstacles and temptations, and drove on to win their way to achievement. For Presidents Garfield and Lincoln, the route led from log cabin to White House. These two biographies prominently exploit the log cabin and bare feet themes in American mythology. The opening lines in both books point up the symbolism which in American mythology borders on a kind of environmental determinism. The Garfield biography begins: "From a small and rudely-built log-cabin a sturdy boy of four years issued, and looked earnestly across the clearing to the pathway that led through the surrounding forest. His bare feet pressed the soft grass. . . ." The Lincoln story opens on this scene: "Three children stood in front of a rough log-cabin in a small clearing won from the surrounding forest. The country round about was wild. . . ." In such surroundings were great men reared! [12]

Alger's promise to American youth was summed up in the closing pages of the biography of Daniel Webster. "No poor boy who reads his life need despair of becoming eminent," vowed Alger, "for he can hardly have more obstacles to overcome than the farmer's boy, who grew up on the sterile soil of New Hampshire, and fought his way upward with unfailing courage and pluck." When he celebrated Lincoln's rise from humble beginnings, Alger captured the purpose of his own life's work—a purpose which declared the existence of opportunities for all in America: "I know of nothing more wonderful in the Arabian Nights than this." [13]

The second great success writer who flourished from the 1860s through the 1890s, William Makepeace Thayer, was a master of the biographical form. As a way of expressing the success idea, the biographical form enjoyed decided advantages. The 'real-life' story of a well-known man soaring from obscurity to fame or from humble beginnings to great wealth was dramatic. The biographical form for success writers was a one-way street. Seldom did they dwell on the story of a man moving in the other direction. The drama of this route was reserved for 'serious' novelists and scholars. The theory of the success writers was similar to that of the teacher of the arts. It is more effective to instruct the young artist to emulate good painting, music, or literature than to learn by the mistakes of inferior work. These teachers held up successful men to be emulated and used the failures occasionally for purposes of contrast.

Before the middle of the nineteenth century the most popular form of success literature was the essay or tract. An essay required only pencil and paper. Biography demanded research. It was not until the Gilded Age that success writers really had enough research material relevant to their own times. Before that time there existed a few Peter Coopers and John Jacob Astors. The Gilded Age was adding a fresh supply of self-made men every decade. Their careers were interpreted as a living statement of the character ethic. The biographical form was not limited to the chronological evolution of a man's life. Biographical anecdotes from the lives of famous men were selected to support moralizing advice. Theories make dull reading, ideas are fatiguing, but ideas expressed through and by real-life people in a setting of romance and action are alive with the warmth of human interest. Non-fiction success writers whose works sold the most copies used biographical anecdotes, both as a technique to entertain their readers and as evidence to support their instructions.

William Makepeace Thayer, along with Horatio Alger, Jr., were in the nineteenth century the best-known and most widely read writers of juvenile literature expressing the success theme. Both were college graduates (Brown and Harvard), natives of Massachusetts, and sometime preaching parsons in their own Massachusetts churches (Congregational and Unitarian). Their lives were interrupted by a departure from the organization of the church, and they both died within the closing two years of the nineteenth century. But their personalities and careers were distinct. Alger fled from the world of adult parishioners to the urchins of New York City; Thayer left his pulpit because of throat trouble. Both were men of busy pens, but Alger's favorite medium was the novel, while Thayer relied on biographical "facts" to enforce his message.

William Makepeace Thayer was born into the topside of New England's middle, but not upper, class. He was a direct descendant of a seventeenth-century Massachusetts family and the son of a hat manufacturer. His mother was a frustrated intellectual who stimulated in her son a love for education and things of the mind. After graduation from Brown, he taught school for awhile, studied theology, and was a preaching minister until 1857, part of the time at Edgartown on Martha's Vineyard Island. He edited a number of magazines, twice served as a member of the Massachusetts General Court, and admirably filled the job of Secretary of the State Temperance Alliance. Teacher, minister, temperance leader, knitted together by a propensity to write— Thayer was a natural for the success field. Novels he considered debilitating and never read them. When he hit upon the biographical form, a suitable vehicle was found to carry his children's sermons.[14]

One use of the biographical form by Thayer was the life of a great man. Most of the books emphasized a 'from–to' struggle from bottom to top. The publishers got five of them out in what they called the "Log Cabin to White House Series." In his titles Thayer took Washington from a farm house, Garfield from a log cabin, Lincoln from a pioneer home, and Grant from a tannery, and then settled them all triumphantly in the White House. Benjamin Franklin, who somehow managed to qualify for the series, went simply "From Boyhood to Manhood." This series, particularly abroad where it was widely translated, did much to strengthen folklore about American chief executives. In all his works, Thayer insisted that the facts revealed that the first step to success was the development of character in the early part of life. You cannot reap greatness, he reiterated, unless you have sown the elements of character as a youth. By character he meant a combination of qualities expressed by a Christian life and the character ethic. Thayer's comment on a colleague's juvenile biography of Washington caught the spirit of his own work: "The virtues are taught both by precept and example, and the vices are held up in all their deformity to warn and save. Religion, too, receives its just tribute, and wears the crown of glory." [15]

Another use of this form was the biographical package containing the lives of a dozen or more of the famous and wealthy. This type eliminated superfluous detail and got right down to the business at hand. A variation on this form used these short biographies to point up a particular aspect of success. In *Turning Points in Successful Careers*, Thayer gave instructions in how opportunity does its knocking. "The favorable opportunity presents itself," he lectured, "and the observant and aspiring behold and seize it, and move on to fortune; while the indifferent and shiftless let it slip, and thereby invite failure." The lives of fifty men and women are sketched out in proof, and from Shakespeare's *Julius Caesar* a pet quotation of success writers is cited to cement the point:

> There is a tide in the affairs of men,
> Which, taken at the flood, leads on to fortune;
> Omitted, all the voyage of their life
> Is bound in shallows, and in miseries. . . .[16]

To place a finger on the precise turning point from mediocrity to success, with all the staggering variables involved, would cause the boldest social scientist to quiver with indecision. Thayer went to it with courage running high. The turning point for George William Childs, wealthy Philadelphia editor and publisher, was a decision at the tender age of fourteen to leave the Navy and work in a book store. "All that followed," Thayer concluded, "was but a divine leading on to fortune." For Peter Cooper, the big moment was the day he put his capital into a glue factory. It was God's Providence that burned up Leland Stanford's library of law books and started him in the direction of California and railroad building. When Horace Brigham Claflin turned his back on Latin and Greek, "the choice between college and store made him manager of the largest drygoods house in the world." The crisis in Alexander Stewart's life came when he quit teaching and took over a drygoods store in order to save his investment. One might wonder if a turning point was not another name for luck. But for Thayer this was no problem. Fires and shaky investments were merely part of Providence. When Thayer was maneuvered into a tight spot, he always fell back upon God to rescue him. For example, good little boys do not run away from home. But when young Ben Franklin recklessly evacuated from Boston, "his rash deed was overruled for good by a wise Providence." In short, as Thayer put it: "Man deviseth his own way, but the Lord directeth his steps." [17]

An effective variation on the biographical form was a number of crisp essays on various phases of success, illustrated by anecdotes from the lives of the great and famous. *Ethics of Success: A Reader for the Higher Grades of Schools* told schoolchildren what their values ought to be. It took 108 chapters from "Self-Reliance" and "Perseverance" to "Character as Capital" and "The Tobacco Habit" to fit out a complete set of values and rules for behavior. In a distinctly pre-Dewey conception of

education, principal Albert G. Boyden stated in his introduction
that *Ethics of Success* was designed to help the teacher inspire
students with "that noble purpose which overcomes all difficulties
in the way to success. To inspire that purpose . . . is the highest
achievement of the teaching art." [18]

Thayer drove immediately to the point in his chapter "How
to Achieve Success." This was the answer: "Each one possessed
character, a noble purpose, ability to do, courage to dare, industry, perseverance, and patience, or waiting for results. Whatever
other qualities they possessed, these led the van and controlled
all." No sensible man, he went on, could "embrace the popular
delusion about luck. It had nothing to do with the triumphs
of the great and good in the past, and it can have nothing to do
with the triumphs of this class in the future." If a handy slogan
was necessary, it could all be summed up under the three words,
"tact, push, and principle." By "tact," however, Thayer did not
mean skill in human relations. He meant the practical execution
of ideas, a blending of one's talents for pragmatic ends. In short,
"common sense on the alert is tact." [19]

Thayer believed that money is a noble object to pursue, *if* it is
accumulated honestly and not made the sole end of life. Once a
fortune is made, he exhorted the schoolchildren, there is an
obligation to give some of it away. On no point was he more
insistent than this. Praise never graced a miser in his pages.
Praise was reserved for the wealthy who played God's steward
to the community. Now some misguided souls think, he went on,
that religion should be limited to the Sabbath. Not so. "A greater
mistake was never made, for religion requires the following very
reasonable things in secular affairs, namely: that man should
make the most of himself possible; that he should watch and improve his opportunities; that he should be industrious, upright,
faithful, and prompt; that he should task his talents, whether
one or ten, to the utmost; that he should waste neither time nor
money; that duty, and not pleasure or ease, should be his
watchword. And this is precisely what is demanded of employers
and employed in shops and stores. Religion employs all the just
motives of worldly wisdom, and adds thereto those higher
motives that immortality creates." In one final, crashing chord,

Thayer ended his symphony to the utility of religion and the justification for wealth. "Indeed," he commanded, "religion demands success."[20]

The third monarch of the success idea in the last half of the nineteenth century lived a verbal marathon which must hold some kind of record in the annals of oratory. He played the same theme in a lecture delivered over 6,000 times. (If one were to lecture *every* night in the year for fifteen years on the same topic, this man's record would still not be equalled.) It was the most popular speech ever given in America on the single theme of opportunity. From the proceeds of the lecture mushroomed a large university. *Acres of Diamonds* mined a fortune for the Baptist minister named Russell Conwell.

Russell Herman Conwell was as big and exuberant as his message. His was no Algerine escape from life into a literary dreamworld, no back-sliding into fantasies he could only marvel at. He drove himself with the vigor of a man who wanted to make history, not write about it. His favorite occupation, he once chortled, was "living," and no man ever worked at it with such huge enjoyment. A good man, his heart was as generous as his friendly smile, vibrant voice, and hearty handclasp. He was America's greatest salesman of opportunity.[21]

Russell Conwell was born in 1843, a lower-middle-class farm boy from the Berkshire Hills of Massachusetts. Around home everyone worked endless hours, worshipped together at family prayers, and worried about the mortgage. His parents kept up a lively interest in current affairs which fed his bright, imaginative mind. At the age of fifteen, tired of scratching a living from the rocky land and dreaming of better things, he ran away and worked on a cattle ship to pay his passage to Europe. A few years later he entered Yale, earning his own way while taking the law and academic courses together, and then left for the Civil War two years later an agnostic. College life among all the rich young gentlemen had been a pretty humiliating experience for this shabbily dressed poor boy. But the sharp contrasts between rich and poor which he saw at Yale did not drive him into an embittered criticism of the *status quo*. And when wealth finally poured in upon him, most of it was dedicated to providing educational opportunities for poor boys like himself.

After the Civil War and a Lieutenant Colonelcy, Conwell moved around the United States and Europe, practicing law, writing, editing, fiddling in politics and community affairs, buzzing in and out of countless activities. In the late 1870s he entered the ministry, a decision which stemmed from his conversion in a Civil War hospital tent. From that point he rose steadily, and in 1881 started building Philadelphia's Grace Baptist Church into the huge Baptist Temple, put up to house the throngs that poured in to hear his sermons. Using the folksy approach, according to an *American Mercury* contributor in the 1920s, "he transferred the hearty informality of the middle-class fireside into the worship of the Almighty. The Protestants of the Gilded Age, accustomed to worshipping God on hard benches and in high, starched collars and frock coats, accepted the new idea of being jolly and informal about the business with the glad relief of a flapper chucking her corset." The church board had made Conwell "a sporting proposition in regard to salary. The church had paid a salary of eight hundred dollars: every time he doubled the membership they would double his salary. To the man who had worked his way through school peddling Ridpath's 'Life of John Brown' from door to door in New England, the offer was good as a gold mine. His commissions mounted so rapidly that when he reached ten thousand all hands piped a halt, and ten thousand dollars remained his salary for the rest of his days." From a group of volunteer teachers and students meeting in the basement of Conwell's church grew Temple University, a huge plant dedicated to educating working-class people. Benefiting from the pastor's love of organization, more than 100,000 students had studied there at one time or another up to his death in 1925. His other great charitable monument was the founding of three hospitals for which he was largely responsible. Here was one of the few clergymen in America who ever made (rather than married or inherited) enough money to practice in bulk what he preached at length about the doctrine of stewardship.[22]

Somewhere in it all he found time for the rhythmical obligation of sermons, compiling a grab bag of lecture subjects, and putting together over thirty books on unrelated topics from the *History of the Great Fire in Boston, November 9 and 10, 1872* to *Effective Prayer*. For the Republican party he wrote campaign biographies of Grant, Hayes, Garfield, and Blaine. His quick, retentive mind could sometimes finish the entire job in three or four weeks. But the arena in which Conwell joyfully performed, in which he rose to considerable fame and fortune, was talking. At cattle shows and picnics, funerals and sewing circles, Conwell learned his trade, warming up for the most spectacular phase of his career. Like all popular lecturers, he was an actor whose appetite grew on the applause it fed upon. For almost thirty continuous years, he delivered two lectures every three days in the decades before the automobile, the radio, and motion pictures carried entertainment to the people. He sent laughter and inspiration rippling through chilly tents and overheated auditoriums, and in the temples of Chautauqua he was the high priest of success. With his ordination to the ministry in 1879, the urge to stand before crowds and the desire to do good were triumphantly united. There was a kind of satisfaction reserved for few in this life in the *Acres of Diamonds* phase of his career. Delivering the speech over 6,000 times, his voice was heard by millions. The several millions of dollars he made from this single lecture filled his own heart with the joy of acknowledged success. His double satisfaction was found in turning over all of it to poor boys to get an education, and finally, in raising up a large university for a testament to that ideal. As he scratched the name of another poor boy off his list —a list that added to a total of some 10,000 names, the slights and snubs were softened that once at Yale had hurt so terribly.[23]

Listening to this tall, heavy-set spellbinder on the Lyceum and Chautauqua circuits must have been an experience. Conwell would talk for two hours to a kind of people unspoiled by our contemporary surfeit of electronic entertainment. He would start out in a friendly, conversational manner, warming up to all age groups in his audience until they were responsive to every phrase and gesture. Then anecdotes and illustrations would pour forth, translating abstract ideas into stories with human interest, each tagged with a clear moral. "His gestures were exquisite pantomime," two historians of the lecture circuit explained. "Even the great Ralph Parlette, who could convulse his audience with the crook of a finger, was a tyro by comparison. When Conwell mentioned an old man, he *was,* by faultless suggestion, a raddled oldster, hobbling and senile. Again, he would mince along with eyebrows raised and head aslant, a rich man's son, or sit, half leering, on a park bench, presumably lost in thought but his roving eye all too obviously intent on the pretty ankles tripping by." [24]

Acres of Diamonds sparkled with enthusiasm for life's opportunities and the possibilities for success in everyone and in every situation. Conwell was convinced that materialism meant progress, that getting rich equalled the measure of a man's worth. From an incredible memory he could introduce supporting biographical sketches or personal reminiscences to meet the changing demands of every appearance. As he talked his way around the country from the 1870s into the 1920s, specific advice pointed up local conditions and references to current events were kept up to date. But the core of the message remained the same.

Acres of Diamonds begins with a story within a story. Conwell explains that he was jogging down the banks of the Tigris and Euphrates Rivers on a camel led by an old Arab guide. The guide told him this story. There once lived in ancient Persia a wealthy and contented farmer by the name of Ali Hafed. One day an old priest visited him. The old priest talked about diamonds—their value, what luxuries they could buy, the power they commanded. That night Ali Hafed went to bed a discontented man. He feared he was poor. When the passion had finally worked through him, Ali Hafed "sold his farm, collected his money, left his family in charge of a neighbor, and away he went in search of diamonds." After wandering through Asia and most of Europe, a wretched man in rags, he threw himself into a great tidal wave that came roaring through the pillars of Hercules, and he drowned. Now the man who purchased Ali Hafed's farm one day led his camel into the garden to drink. As the camel nosed the cool water, the new owner of the farm noticed a flash of light from the white sands of the brook. He picked up the stone and took it into the house. A few days later the old priest came for a visit, recognized the stone as a diamond, and together they rushed to the garden brook. As they stirred the white sands with eager fingers, gems of great beauty and value flashed in the sunlight. Thus, concluded the old Arab guide, was discovered "the diamond-mine of Golconda, the most magnificent diamond-mine in all the history of mankind. ... Had Ali Hafed remained at home and dug in his own cellar, or underneath his own wheat fields, or in his own garden, instead of wretchedness, starvation, and death by suicide in a strange land, he would have had 'acres of diamonds.' " [25]

The symbol launched, Conwell rushed on to tell one story after another about the poor fools who sold their backyards in search of better things, and along with it a fortune in oil, gold, or silver. But "unless some of you get richer for what I am saying to-night my time is wasted," multimillionaire Conwell observed, so he sharpened the symbol into concrete, specific evidence. "Now then," he boomed, "I say again that the opportunity to get rich, to attain unto great wealth, is here in Philadelphia now, [or wherever he was speaking] within the reach of almost every man and woman who hears me speak to-night, and I mean just what I say. ... There never was a place on earth more adapted than the city of Philadelphia to-day, and never in the history of the world did a poor man without capital have such an opportunity to get rich quickly and honestly as he has now in our city." [26]

Lest any in the audience be apathetic about such exciting prospects, Conwell could shock them out of their complacency. "I say that you ought to get rich, and it is your duty to get rich," he thundered. "Money is power, and you ought to be reasonably ambitious to have it. You ought because you can do more good with it than you could without it. Money printed your Bible, money builds your churches. ... I say, then, you ought to have money. If you can honestly attain unto riches in Philadelphia, it is your Christian and godly duty to do so. It is an awful mistake of these pious people to think you must be awfully poor in order to be pious." Conwell's generosity was extravagant, but his doctrine of retribution in this world was as harsh as the Old Testament's Jehovah. "While we should sympathize with God's poor—that is, those who cannot help themselves—let us remember there is not a poor person in the United States who was not made poor by his own shortcomings, or by the shortcomings of some one else. It is all wrong to be poor, anyhow." [27]

There are some things higher than gold in this world of ours, he continued. Love, for example, "is the grandest thing on God's earth, but fortunate the lover who has plenty of money. Money is power, money is force, money will do good as well as harm. In the hands of good men and women it could accomplish, and it has accomplished, good." The Bible does *not* tell us that 'money is the root of all evil.' It does state an absolute truth: " 'The love of money is the root of all evil.' He who tries to attain unto it too quickly, or dishonestly, will fall into many snares, no doubt about that. The love of money. What is that? It is making an idol of money, and idolatry pure and simple everywhere is condemned by the Holy Scriptures and by man's common sense. The man that worships the dollar instead of thinking of the purposes for which it ought to be used, the man who idolizes simply money, the miser that hordes his money in the cellar, or hides it in his stocking, or refuses to invest it where it will do the world good, that man who hugs the dollar until the eagle squeals has in him the root of all evil." Conwell advised his listeners to carry their religion into business. In fact, "the foundation of godliness and the foundation principle of success in business are both the same precisely." Both are based on reciprocal benefits. The businessman receives a fair profit for satisfying a need.[28]

It was not for the poor, but for the sons of the rich that Conwell expressed the most pity. "I pity the rich man's son," he mused sadly. "He can never know the best things in life." Only the self-made man can thrill to the sense of independence reserved for those who have made their own way. The best way to do it is to find out what people need, and then fill the need. Above all, don't go into politics. "Young man," he glowered from the platform, "won't you learn a lesson in the primer of politics that it is a *prima facie* evidence of littleness to hold office under our form of government?" Remember this, he moved to his conclusion: "Greatness consists not in the holding of some future office, but really consists in doing great deeds with little means. . . . To be great at all one must be great here, now, in Philadelphia." [29]

Horatio Alger, Jr., William Makepeace Thayer, and Russell H. Conwell were the most popular spokesmen for the promise of urban success during the last half of the nineteenth century. Behind them stood legions of supporters echoing their advice. But they were only commentators. What did the businessman himself, the image to be emulated, have to say about success?

"MONEY GETTERS ARE THE BENEFACTORS OF OUR RACE"

Americans who had succeeded did not often explain how it was done. Yet now and then, through an autobiography, essay, or personal interview, the nation could go to school directly to the respected source. Most nineteenth-century businessmen were as stony to public opinion as our contemporary corporate managers are sensitive to it. But by the turn of the century, as certain elements in the success idea came under increasingly harsh attack, some men of success agreed to interviews or took pen in hand with a special purpose. They not only told how it was done; they seemed more anxious to justify the doing of it.

One of America's early pollsters on success offered 'scientifically' acquired evidence. In 1883, twenty years before Nathaniel C. Fowler tried the same thing, Wilbur F. Crafts put together in *Successful Men of To-Day and What They Say of Success* the replies from some five hundred prominent men to eight questions. Biographical sketches provided additional evidence. Crafts, a scholar, minister, and specialist in Sunday-school work, appealed to the certitudes of the scientific method.

Most of the returns pleased him, except one. Some judge had dared to reply that chance and circumstances were the most important elements of success. "That is not true," Crafts fumed, "as I have the documents to prove. It is the worst kind of a lie—a half truth. It has just enough truth to make it dangerous. ..." Crafts was certain that character controlled circumstances.

But he was quick to admit that certain things over which we have no control are helpful. "A country environment of pure air, plain food, regular out-door work, early sleep, and freedom from cigarettes and saloons, gives the farmer boy an advantage ... when, in young manhood, he comes to the city to enter upon a commercial or professional life." Though the city boy is raised in a more intellectually stimulating environment, his country cousin more than matches him in "physical and moral pre-eminence. Sound *morals* in a sound body is the watchword of success." [1]

Fortunate is the child born into poverty, Crafts claimed. "Seventy-three per cent of our successful men belonged to families so poor that they had to work most of the time out of school hours, which to these boys were generally few. . . . Seventy per cent of all my correspondents entered upon business between the ages of thirteen and seventeen." They succeeded, however, not because of a lack of education, but in spite of it. No one should turn down an education if possible, but everyone should get in the habit of working very early in life. Though rural origins, an early job, and good mothers were significant, Crafts was certain that in the end, men make circumstances. The best inheritance that you can have is a pure character and determination. "Whether a boy is from farm or city, rich or poor, weak or strong, talented or not, will and work are sure to win. Wishes fail, but wills prevail." [2]

Yet success means nothing, Crafts insisted, unless God is part of our lives. "Religion pays 'a hundredfold in this life, and in the world to come life everlasting.' In history we see many a man who was diligent in his earthly business standing before kings; in heaven we shall see all those who were diligent in our Father's business standing before the King of kings. Yes, *it pays, it pays* to serve God." But the payoff is not only in heaven. "In every legitimate business true religion is a positive helper. It is frequently mentioned as one of the secrets of success in the replies which I have received from prominent men. . . . Most of the suffering poor are the victims of vice. Most of the well-to-do are those who have been in a large degree loyal to the laws of God." There is no better source of advice for success than the

Bible. "Business success and failure is one of its chief topics.
. . . In the heart of the Bible lies the business man's own book—
Proverbs. There is hardly a maxim of business success that was
not suggested by it." This intimacy between business and religion works both ways. To the brethren, Crafts advised: "We
are not only to conduct our earthly business on Christian principles. The church . . . ought to be managed as a great business
corporation, in which men are junior partners with God." [3]

What is success? "Doing your best is success," the Brooklyn
clergyman replied confidently. This is a duty. "Over both departments of our business, the earthly and the heavenly, in each of
which we are called to glorify God and do good to men, let us
write,

GOD EXPECTS EVERY ONE TO DO HIS BEST."
And "if you are called as God's stewards to acquire money-
power . . . to use for the good of humanity, do your best in that."
Follow the mottoes of John Wesley:

> " 'Make all you can honestly;
> Save all you can prudently;
> Give all you can possibly.' "

Be God's steward and know that "wealth consecrated to the
fatherhood of God and the brotherhood of man is twice blest;
the poor rise up to call it blessed, and it has the blessing of the
Lord, which maketh rich and addeth no sorrow with it; but gold
without God, and bank-notes which have not beneath their
rustle the throbbing of a Christian heart, are like a millstone
hanged about the soul to sink it in the depths of despair." [4]

There has always been a strong strain in American culture
that goals be justified in moral terms. What impact did the
morally disturbing concept of evolution have on the idea of success? Most of us are pretty well adjusted now to the shock of
Darwinian evolution. But from the latter decades of the nineteenth century to the Scopes trial in the mid-1920s, Darwin's
1859 bombshell, *Origin of Species,* shook the American mind,
from highbrow to lowbrow, disturbing comforting beliefs about

every man's conception of himself, his relation to his fellow man, and his relation to God.

What is Social Darwinism? Many nineteenth-century intellectuals were intrigued by the theory of evolution and the use of 'scientific' allusions from the natural world. They adapted Darwin's biological conclusions about the origin and survival of species to the society of mankind. Progress, claimed the Social Darwinists, results from an evolutionary process in which the fittest survive in a struggle for existence by natural selection. Social Darwinists used this doctrine to strike at arguments for government intervention to regulate business. Government regulation of business would meddle with the process of evolution. The results would be disastrous. An unregulated, free-wheeling economy was an assurance of progress just as the unregulated, natural laws of evolution lead to a higher order. Let the government meddle with the economy and you interfere with what must inevitably work out for the best.

How could Social Darwinism be used to justify success? If the laws of evolution are unbreakable, then the fittest, or most successful, must have survived in a struggle for existence by a process of natural selection. And if the laws of evolution work for progress and a better America, then to have emerged as a wealthy man in this contest must be a sanction for success. Not only do the biological laws of growth operating on the earth among all living things justify it, but the successful man is the best man because he has proven to be the fittest in a constant struggle for survival with his fellow man.

Many students of the Gilded Age have erroneously argued that successful businessmen subscribed to just such an argument. Richard Hofstadter has made this observation about America after the Civil War: "With its rapid expansion, its exploitative methods, its desperate competition, and its peremptory rejection of failure, post-bellum America was like a vast human caricature of the Darwinian struggle for existence and survival of the fittest. Successful business entrepreneurs apparently accepted almost by instinct the Darwinian terminology which seemed to portray the conditions of their existence." Social Darwinism, Joseph J.

Spengler has commented, "well suited the climate of opinion of a burgeoning Age of Gilt and Mammon that was witnessing the integration of the economy and the rise of the captain of industry. An outstandingly successful business man was hard put to find a philosophical basis for his *apologia pro vita mea* more satisfactory. . . . " Thomas C. Cochran and William Miller have stated that "from the Civil War to the New Deal, businessmen explained themselves to the 'public' " in terms of Herbert Spencer, the English philosopher and most influential exponent of Social Darwinism.[5]

An important distinction must be made between businessmen justifying their own personal success and, on the other hand, defending the uncontrolled growth of large impersonal corporations. There is some evidence, though hardly overwhelming, that businessmen invoked Social Darwinism to defend a *laissez-faire* economy, consolidation, and the elimination of competitors. A rare but oft-quoted expression was offered by John D. Rockefeller, Jr., to the Y.M.C.A. at Brown University: "The growth of a large business is merely a survival of the fittest. . . . The American Beauty rose can be produced in the splendor and fragrance which bring cheer to its beholder only by sacrificing the early buds which grow up around it. This is not an evil tendency in business. It is merely the working out of a law of nature and a law of God." But in most cases when Social Darwinism was advanced in support of large-scale organizations, it was put forward by the spokesmen for business interests, especially lawyers, rather than by businessmen themselves.[6]

There is slim evidence indeed that businessmen justified their own personal success by Social Darwinism. The case rests pretty much on the writings of Andrew Carnegie. In an age of silent businessmen Carnegie voiced his opinions so frequently and at such length that one might reasonably suspect that his views were unrepresentative. In addition to sounding sometimes more like a reforming intellectual than a nineteenth-century entrepreneur, the ghostly fingers of literary assistants were always shaping the steelmaster's magazine articles and books. Because he was so articulate and prolific, Carnegie's literary legacy has been working harder since he died than when he was alive carrying the load of businessmen's thinking for interpreters of the Gilded Age.

From the viewpoint of the success idea, Andrew Carnegie is a mutation unrepresentative of the species businessman. He is included in this study for two reasons. First, he gives us a clear look into the mind of one businessman who analyzed his way to two separate justifications for money-making. Second, since one of his arguments is based on Social Darwinism, he provides us with an opportunity to suggest some possible explanations why the argument was unusual and why Social Darwinism was avoided as a justification for personal success.[7]

Andrew Carnegie was an impoverished middle-class boy from Scotland who came to America, worked on a before-dawn to after-dusk shift at an age when most boys today are in the eighth grade, became an industrialist and financier, made hundreds of millions of dollars, and then gave most of it away. He was driven by a compulsion to succeed. He wanted to get ahead not only because he had been poor and didn't like it, but for the sake of success itself by which he judged himself as a man, and no doubt for the sheer adventure of it. But the tension was always there, more tightly drawn than in most men. He had to justify his life in moral and humanitarian terms. The tension was probably increased by the knowledge that his wealth was built on the fierce competitive drive which he instilled in his senior employees and associates. It was deepened by memories of political radicalism to which his Scottish family had offered leaders for generations. Protest was bred into the family. When the immigrant boy from Scotland fought his way above the crowd, the tradition did not die. He protested against himself. The hunger for justification is revealed in a memorandum in telegraphic style he wrote to himself in 1868:

> Thirty-three and an income of $50,000 per annum! By this time two years I can arrange all my business as to secure at least $50,000 per annum. Beyond this never earn—make no effort to increase fortune, but spend the surplus each year for benevolent purposes. Cast aside business forever, except for others. Settle in Oxford

and get a thorough education, making acquaintance of literary men—this will take three years' active work—pay especial attention to speaking in public. Settle then in London and purchase a controlling interest in some newspaper or live review and give the general management of it attention, taking a part in public matters, especially those connected with education and improvement of the poorer classes. Man must have an idol—the amassing of wealth is one of the worst species of idolatry—no idol more debasing than the worship of money. Whatever I engage in I must push inordinately; therefore should I be careful to choose that life which will be the most elevating in its character. To continue much longer overwhelmed by business cares and with most of my thoughts wholly upon the way to make more money in the shortest time, must degrade me beyond hope of permanent recovery. I will resign business at thirty-five, but during the ensuing two years I wish to spen   the afternoons in receiving instruction and in reading systematically.[8]

This fascinating self-analysis exposes the sense of guilt that has always smoldered in the idea of success. Carnegie's confession is really a secular treatment of the old dilemma. On the one hand, he knew himself so intimately that "whatever I engage in I must push inordinately." On the other, he was fearful that "to continue much longer overwhelmed by business cares and with most of my thoughts wholly upon the way to make more money in the shortest time, must degrade me beyond hope of permanent recovery." His rudderless wanderings, like some ship lost in the seas of philosophy, finally anchored in a secure haven. But a haven from the storms of materialism was not found by retreating to the towers of Oxford. The degrading concentration on making money was averted by justifying it. In short, instead of saving his "character" by ceasing to make money, Carnegie made a double rescue. He continued to make money and preserved his "character" by glorifying the accumulation of wealth. The doctrine was developed fully in 1889 in an article for the *North American Review*. Widely debated, particularly in England and America, the doctrine was soon known as the Gospel of Wealth.

Focusing on the points most relevant to our discussion, this was Carnegie's famed Gospel of Wealth. In a highly competitive and individualistic economic system based on the security of private property, he argued, some men accumulate great fortunes by their superior talents. The price society pays for this is great. Castes are rigidly formed, and employers and employees become strangers and distrustful of one another. Under the law of competition, employers are forced to economize by holding down wages. This causes friction. "But the advantages of this law are also greater still, for it is to this law that we owe our wonderful material development. . . . While the law may be sometimes hard for the individual, it is best for the race, because it insures the survival of the fittest in every department." This is the first part of Carnegie's justification.[9]

In the second part, Carnegie meets the problem of the unequal distribution of wealth resulting from this beneficial system. He solves the problem of the very rich and the poor by charging the successful man to give away his money during his lifetime. "This, then, is held to be the duty of the man of Wealth: First, to set an example of modest, unostentatious living, shunning display or extravagance; to provide moderately for the legitimate wants of those dependent upon him; and after doing so to consider all surplus revenues which come to him simply as trust funds, which he is called upon to administer, and strictly bound as a matter of duty to administer in the manner which, in his judgment, is best calculated to produce the most beneficial results for the community—the man of wealth thus becoming the mere agent and trustee for his poorer brethren, bringing to their service his superior wisdom, experience, and ability to administer, doing for them better than they would or could do for themselves." Carnegie concluded that even the man of wealth who leaves his money to charity, but fails to administer it himself, departs from this world without honor: " 'The man who dies thus rich dies disgraced.' " [10]

The second part of the gospel of wealth was a happy solution to Carnegie's dilemma. The problem, as he saw it in another place, was this: "How is the struggle for dollars to be lifted from the sordid atmosphere surrounding business and made a noble career?" The answer was brilliantly to the point: "Acting in accordance with this advice, it becomes the duty of the millionaire to increase his revenues. The struggle for more is completely freed from selfish or ambitious taint and becomes a noble pursuit. Then he labors not for self, but for others: not to hoard, but to spend. The more he makes, the more the public gets. His whole life is changed from the moment that he resolves to become a disciple of the gospel of wealth, and henceforth he labors to acquire that he may wisely administer for others' good. His daily labor is a daily virtue." This is a secular treatment of the stewardship of wealth principle. It is a passionate but representative statement echoed by countless success books.[11]

Carnegie's 1889 essay "Wealth" caused a sensation on both sides of the Atlantic, but not because of its familiar stewardship principle. Here was a millionaire saying that society must pay a great price for its millionaires, even though the price is material growth. Here was a man of fabulous wealth actually cheering on the government to a heavy taxation of large estates. Indeed, this American businessman was really wondering in his own mind whether the sacred rights of property extended beyond a man's lifetime. "Men who continue hoarding great sums all their lives, the proper use of which for public ends would work good to the community, should be made to feel that the community, in the form of the state, cannot thus be deprived of its proper share. By taxing estates heavily at death the state marks its condemnation of the selfish millionaire's unworthy life. It is desirable that nations should go much further in this direction. Indeed, it is difficult to set bounds to the share of a rich man's estate which should go at his death to the public through the agency of the state, and by all means such taxes should be graduated, beginning at nothing upon moderate sums to dependents, and increasing rapidly as the amounts swell. . . ." For those defenders of success who later cried out against a rate of inheritance taxation far less confiscatory than the steelmaster recommended, Carnegie had a ready answer to their protest: "Nor need it be feared that this policy would sap the root of enterprise and render men less anxious to accumulate, for to the class whose ambition it is to leave great fortunes and be talked about after their death, it will attract even more attention, and, indeed, be a somewhat nobler ambition to have enormous sums paid over to the state from tneir fortunes." [12]

It hardly seems likely that Carnegie's peers in the fraternity of millionaires jubilantly tossed their homburgs in the air over these particular views. There is little evidence that they rushed to that other unrepresentative argument of the steelmaster's established in the first part of his justification for success. In the steelmaster's opinion, America owed its material progress to the law of competition, because "it insures the survival of the fittest in every department."

The seminal philosopher of Pragmatism, Charles Peirce, has commented: "The conviction of the nineteenth century is that progress takes place by virtue of every individual's striving for himself with all his might and trampling his neighbor under foot whenever he gets a chance to do so. This may accurately be called the Gospel of Greed." Peirce may be right. The businessman might have been secretly convinced that progress consisted in trampling one's neighbor under foot. Many did viciously crush their competitors and were contemptuous of the public welfare and the consumer. If, however, we take what businessmen said was true, or wanted the public to think was true, which is all we really have evidence for, it is apparent that businessmen took the position that progress resulted from every individual striving for himself—but not by trampling his neighbor under foot. Destroying others was not said to be the way to become a success and most certainly no justification for it. Occasionally businessmen might justify the uncontrolled growth of large impersonal corporations in terms of Social Darwinism. Rarely did they justify their own success in these terms.[13]

What were the reasons for the businessman's rejection of

Social Darwinism as a justification for the accumulation of wealth? First, the real struggle in life was not supposed to be with other people but with oneself. The successful man was the ascetic who beat down and finally triumphed over his own worst tendencies. Second, Social Darwinism is a totally selfish philosophy which assumes that man is no more altruistic than a panther on the prowl. It is amoral and negative. The successful man may have survived because he was the fittest in a struggle for existence by natural selection, but in the Social Darwinist process of proving himself the fittest, he doesn't do anything *for* anybody. Indeed, if naturally pursued to the extremes of biological analogy, he crushed other men like some jungle beast destroying his less powerful adversary. Now all this might have been a tantalizing intellectual exercise for professors, lawyers, and various intellectuals, both conservatives and reformers, depending on the purpose for which they were invoking biological allusions, but for the businessman whose *own* life needed justifying, there was understandably less enthusiasm for viewing his own success in terms that could easily be translated into a jungle blood bath.[14]

Social Darwinism, in the third place, is hardly a justification for a businessman who is defending himself against sharp criticism. Throughout this period businessmen were trying to raise their calling to the dignity of a profession. Fourth, for Christians, and most of these men thought of themselves as such, it is difficult to glorify being fittest if it meant that you were doing unto your neighbor what you would not appreciate him doing to you. If you were making money, it could easily be reasoned that your neighbor was making less or was even destroyed financially because you were waxing successful. The idea of success took this stand: Every man who soars to the top pulls countless others up a notch and contributes to their success. He also contributes to the success of society. "Money getters," said P. T. Barnum, "are the benefactors of our race. To them, in a great measure, are we indebted for our institutions of learning and of art, our academies, colleges and churches."[15]

Though we have been centering our position on the justification for personal success, it is also doubtful that business men were in the habit of justifying the growth of their corporations in terms of Social Darwinism. What happened when John D. Rockfeller, Jr., made his famous crack in the mid-1900s about the American Beauty rose? "The saddest words that have been written in this generation," fretted one troubled minister, "were spoken before Brown University by a young man who is to inherit one of the greatest fortunes in this country. They were spoken in defense of the trusts. Listen to them: 'The American Beauty rose can be produced in all its splendor only by sacrificing the early buds that grow up around it.' The rose has 1,000 buds and in order to produce the American Beauty the gardener goes around it with a knife and snips 999 in order that all the strength and beauty may be forced into one bloom. In his economic argument, this young man brutally tells the working classes that 999 small business men must be snuffed out of existence in order that his American Beauty, the trust, may be produced." The Episcopal Bishop of Michigan struck hard. He called Rockefeller "a young scion of greed and wealth, possessed of more wealth than ideas." But the good Bishop erred in implying that the younger Rockefeller was short of ideas. No more than eight years out of Brown University, the younger Rockefeller perhaps had forgotten that he was no longer an undergraduate privileged to comment about life with the detached objectivity of an academic intellectual free to play with ideas in search of the truth. It is doubtful that the younger Rockefeller nourished again such a metaphor or cultivated publicly the philosophy from which it grew.[16]

Finally, Social Darwinism implies limited opportunity. The philosophy of the success idea could not possibly conceive of people struggling for existence amidst so much opportunity.

In summary, the impact of Social Darwinism on the idea of success was negligible. Paid spokesmen for specific business interests, such as lawyers and ghost writers, and 'impartial' savants, for instance professors and assorted intellectuals, may have used Social Darwinism to defend a *laissez-faire* economy, business consolidation, and the elimination of inefficient competitors. Businessmen themselves may have invoked Social Darwinism occasionally to defend the triumph of large-scale, impersonal business organizations, though it was decidedly foolish public relations. Rarely did they use it to justify their own personal success. The solid body of professional success writers, whether working within the character ethic, or within later developments in the success idea, did not affirm or deny Social Darwinism. They ignored it. It is a fair guess, however, that the philosophy would have seemed repulsive to them. The heart and mind of the success idea stood in total opposition to the spirit of Social Darwinism. The tone of success books was not tooth and fang. The spirit was Christian and humanitarian. Success writers based their justification on safer and more noble foundations—on the Bible and Christian ethics, not on the *Origin of Species* and the law of the jungle.

It was the wealthiest millionaire of his age, and at one time the most hated businessman in America, who returned to the world a succinct, representative statement of the character ethic. John D. Rockefeller, Sr., started life as a bookkeeper and ended by floating America's first mighty trust on an ocean of oil. A genius at organizing competitors out of business, he piled up a fortune of close to one billion dollars. Such wealth never changed the basic nature of this reticent bookkeeper, who found such pleasure in adding a column of figures and coming up with the correct answer. Rockefeller shivered at what he called "generalities" as a good accountant dreads imprecision. His succinct comments, though they do not include every point in the character ethic, should replace Andrew Carnegie's in any anthology of this period which pauses long enough to reflect accurately on the character ethic interpretation of the success idea by a businessman.[17]

In a rare interview, during the summer of 1906, he recited parts of the success creed. Mr. Rockefeller, what do you think the chances are for young men today? "There never were greater opportunities for young men in America than are offered here on every side to-day." Well, what about the growth of trusts? "I deny emphatically the assertion that opportunity has been restricted or individual effort stifled by reason of the growth of the trusts. On the contrary, the trusts have opened wider avenues and greater opportunities to the young men of to-day than those of any other generation ever enjoyed. . . . In the enlarged field which consolidation and concentration have created, there is no possible limit to the success which an ambitious young man may achieve." Do you think the poor boy stands much of a chance in the race for success? "The poor boy is in a position of impregnable advantage. He is better off than the son of the rich man, for he is prepared to do what the latter will not do, or rarely so; that is, plunge in with his hands and learn a business from the bottom. It is to them, the sons of hardy Americans, that we look to carry into the future the progress of the present. The future, with all of its infinite possibilities, is in their hands."

Perhaps so, but what about education? "Education is also a tremendously important factor—the technical school particularly—in making the upward course of the earnest, willing-to-work young man straight and clear." Would you elaborate on that point? "I think a college education is a splendid thing for a boy; but I would not say that it is absolutely necessary. I hadn't the advantage of a college education; but I had a good mother and an excellent father, and I like to feel that whatever I may have lost through failure to secure a college education I made up through my home training. It is in the home circle that the character of a boy is formed. There he imbibes those principles which will follow him all through life. The home training gives him something that he can never get at college; but at the same time I am not decrying the advantages of a college education, and I should say that wherever it is possible a boy should have it. Better than a college education, however, is the training that a boy gets in the technical schools that have sprung up all over the country. This is an age of specialization. There is an unceasing demand on every hand—in the mining industries, the railroads, the industrials, the mills, and the factories—for men with special, technical knowledge that will enable them intelligently to take up the important work that is going on. Here is a great advantage that the boy of fifty years ago didn't enjoy. Now one may enter a school and learn in his youth many of the things that the hardest kind of labor was needed to teach in bygone days. He gets the technical knowledge that enables him to begin a long way ahead of the boy of fifty years ago."

Mr. Rockefeller, who would you say has the advantage, the boy raised in the city or on the farm? "The atmosphere of the farm, I think the history of our famous men has shown, is a great beginning for a man. But it does not follow that a city-bred boy has not equal opportunities. I suppose that, after all, much depends upon the boy himself in this case. But whether born in city or country, a boy must ever be careful to avoid the temptations which beset him, to select carefully his associates and give attention at once to his spiritual side as well as to his mental and material sides." What exactly do you mean by "spiritual side"? "Religion is one of the great moving forces of the world. No man can neglect its teachings and hope to be a completely rounded out man." What score do you put on money? "Don't conceive the vain notion that wealth is everything. No man has a right to hoard money for the mere pleasure of hoarding. . . . Every man owes a debt to humanity, and in accordance with the manner in which he discharges that debt will he be judged." Would you be more specific on that point? "Do all the good that you can. Be generous and charitable in your attitude toward your neighbors. It will cost you nothing, and you will reap a rich reward."

You have given freely of yourself on how to be a success, Mr. Rockefeller, and have emphasized a number of qualities necessary and helpful to making money. Would you care to say a few words in conclusion? "Yes, decidedly, the opportunities for the young American boy are greater to-day than they have ever been before; and no boy, howsoever lowly—the barefoot country boy, the humble newsboy, the child of the tenement—need despair. I see in each of them infinite possibilities. They have but to master the knack of economy, thrift, honesty, and perseverance, and success is theirs." [18]

Two points in Rockefeller's testament require comment. One concerns education. The standard advice on education, from both businessmen and professional success writers, was to skip college, start work earlier, and learn through self-education. A liberal arts college preparation was not only useless, it might do you positive harm. Toward the close of the nineteenth century the success idea began to admit the value of a college education, but not a liberal arts education. A college education was not *necessary* for success, but training in a technical, business, commercial, or vocational college should prove to be helpful. Rockefeller reflects this change in attitude. As the founder of the University of Chicago, he was more than usually sympathetic to a liberal arts type of education, though he did make it clear that a technical education offered greater leverage for rising to the top.

The other point which requires comment is Rockefeller's justification for success. In the above article he only hinted at the stewardship principle; elsewhere he was more specific. While some businessmen rooted their stewardship in a secular philosophy, Rockefeller, an ardent Baptist, grew his in religious soil. Speaking of the University of Chicago, he said: "The good Lord gave me the money, and how could I withhold it from Chicago?" "I believe the power to make money is a gift of God . . . ," he declared, "to be developed and used to the best of our ability for the good of mankind. Having been endowed with the gift I possess, I believe it is my duty to make money and still more money, and to use the money I make for the good of my fellow man according to the dictates of my conscience." In another place he paraphrased the influential principle of John Wesley, the eighteenth-century founder of Methodism: *"I think it is a man's duty to make all the money he can, keep* [i.e. save] *all he can, and give away all he can."* [19]

In his autobiographical reminiscences published in 1909, John D. Rockefeller, Sr., summoned the word which future businessmen were to find so useful: "The man will be most successful who confers the greatest service on the world." For Rockefeller, service meant not only fulfilling the wants of people. He included under its meaning the doctrine of systematic and intelligent philanthropy to get at causes rather than effects and to help others to help themselves. Whether it was to justify his own success, or promote good public relations, this steward of God gave away during his lifetime a half billion dollars.[20]

6

A MESSAGE TO GARCIA

During the 1890s and the first decade of the twentieth century, the character ethic version of the success idea began to take on a defensive tone. The misnamed "Gay Nineties" at the end of the century was filled with strikes, Populist rumblings of agrarian discontent, and the contrast between extremes of wealth lavished on extravagant parties and extremes of poverty endured in filthy slums. When the Muckrakers struck at the trusts in the early years of the new century as a restriction on the opportunity of all Americans to get ahead, certain traditional themes in the success idea were reasserted in defense of conservative economic principles. As we saw in the preceding chapter, John D. Rockefeller, Sr., reflected this defensive tone. When asked whether the trusts had restricted opportunity, Rockefeller insisted that the reverse was true. The trusts had opened up wider avenues and greater opportunities for all.

The most famous piece of success literature written with conscious intent to defend propertied interests was dashed off after supper one night in 1899 by a retired soap salesman turned self-conscious bohemian. It was a tract honoring self-reliant perseverance. Elbert Hubbard wrote it, and he called it *A Message to Garcia*. Tom Paine's tract, *Common Sense*, had inflamed the colonists with ambitions for independence, while Karl Marx's manifesto challenged the foundations of Western Civilization. Next to Benjamin Franklin's *Way to Wealth*, *A Message to Garcia* was the most effective and widely distributed tract in the history of success literature.

Elbert Hubbard was the product of an Illinois farming community of five houses, a church, a general store, and a blacksmith shop. The son of a hard-working, but impoverished, eccentric country doctor, he grew up with the Bible, farming chores, spelling bees, and a hungry mind. Hubbard possessed a spark of initiative. As sales manager of a soap company, he devised a plan to entice the public into selling his soap. The housewife bought soap on credit from the manufacturer at the retail price. She then sold it to anyone she could for the same price. The payoff for the housewife was in premiums good for anything from bric-a-brac to bureaus, depending on the amount of sales. A fresh idea at the end of the nineteenth century, it made the soap manufacturer a multi-millionaire.

Then Hubbard wrote a novel which was accepted for publication. Business was not enough for him after that. "He wanted more out of life—to write, to teach, to influence others toward a greater good. He wanted fame, to win recognition from his fellows in the world of intellectual achievement." At the age of thirty-six he sold out his share of the soap business and began a new life to feed the hungers of his mind. Harvard was selected. After that experience he had nothing but scornful contempt for the groves of academe. His departure from Cambridge was speeded by a crack from one of his professors that he was wasting his time trying to become a writer. The rest of Hubbard's life was spent running up a bibliography as long as a Chinese scroll.[1]

The qualities that made Elbert Hubbard a prosperous soap salesman—his showmanship, business acumen, driving energy —did the same for him as editor, writer, publisher, and lecturer. In fact, what he longed for as a salesman of soap was a soapbox. When he turned literary at the halfway mark of his career, he scrambled aboard his soapbox with all the glee of an actor long deprived of a stage. He edited and contributed to his own magazine, *The Philistine*, wrote advertising copy for handsome fees, profited from an arrangement with Hearst newspapers, which reprinted what they fancied from his daily output, played to packed houses on the lecture circuit, and served as business adviser for a number of important concerns. Further entrepreneurial and aesthetic energies were poured into the Roycroft Shops which produced, among things, furniture, wrought-iron work, hammered metals, molded leather, and hand-woven rugs. An important part of this production plan, established in 1895 at East Aurora, New York, was a bookbindery and printing press which turned out arty books and spread the message of the Roycroft idea. At the heart of this message was an arts and crafts' faith in hand fabrication, with a return to the aesthetic principles of the Middle Ages. Hubbard first heard the message from William Morris and was enchanted by the idea of defeating the evils of the Industrial Revolution with goods handmade by sensitive artisans. The Roycroft Shops were a way of releasing his creative faculties and satisfying his impulse for self-expression. Since they operated more in the spirit of capitalism than Morris's socialism, he enjoyed the further delights of running the show himself. It was *la vie de Bohème,* but not the obscurantist, art-for-art's-sake kind. The 'sage of East Aurora' wanted to educate the sensibilities of the public by a kind of aesthetic journalism and self-conscious art. With typical American dash, what he succeeded in doing was to reverse the process of William Morris and convert art into industry.[2]

Elbert Hubbard's hair spilled down to his shoulders, but the bohemianism was a gesture of showmanship and individualism, not a blanket protest against middle-class values. He used to refer to himself as "a businessman with a literary attachment." Sympathetic to both business and the arts, he tried to create prose and *objets d'art* in praise of both—and this in a period when the businessman and the intellectual were drifting further and further apart. His 170 *Little Journeys* to the homes of the great and famous took his readers over thresholds from those of Jesus of Nazareth to John B. Stetson, maker of hats. In many of these *Little Journeys,* and in his works on success, Hubbard made it quite clear that his bohemian inclinations were not a revolt from bourgeois values. His was a philosophy of the joy of hard work well-done, a philosophy which dignified initiative, self-reliance, and dogged individualism, qualities which guided his own life. Fra Elbertus, as he drolly called himself, was genuinely hated by a healthy number of people. With Mencken-like slashes, he hacked away at the traditions of mighty institutions, like colleges and churches, chortling all the while with a kind of arrogant irreverence. His flippancy knew many forms, such as lending a hand to seventeen definitions of "success" from "the accomplishment of one's best" to writing "your name high upon the outhouse of a country tavern." [8]

Out of the complexity of this man's heart and mind came *A Message to Garcia*. Hubbard said that his son had sparked the idea. "Bert" Hubbard was maintaining that the real hero of the Spanish-American War was Lieutenant Andrew S. Rowan, who was ordered by President McKinley to fight his way across Cuba with a vital message to General Garcia, head of the Cuban Insurgents. "It came to me like a flash," Hubbard recalled. "Yes, the boy is right, the hero is the man who does the thing—does his work—carries the message." An hour later the piece was done. It appeared casually in the March 1899 issue of *The Philistine* and was run without a head, so little did he think of it. The preachment caught fire. The entire issue of *The Philistine* was exhausted in three days. Orders poured into the Roycroft Press. Then George Daniels of the New York Central Railroad really started the ball rolling. He wired for a price on 100,000 copies in pamphlet form, with a railroad advertisement on the back. Hubbard figured it would take him two years to do the job with his limited facilities, so he gave Daniels permission to print the homily in any way he saw fit. Daniels gritted his teeth and went to the job of supplying the demand, "if it takes the entire Twentieth Century to accomplish it." In all, the New York Central distributed over 1,000,000 copies of the sermon, sandwiched between appropriate advertising for the railroad. A guess is that Hubbard's tract reached 40,000,000 copies, with translations into some forty or fifty languages and dialects. It popped up in odd places. In the war with the Russians in 1904, the Japanese found copies in the enemy's knapsacks. Not to be outdone, the Japanese translated it into their language and by order of the Mikado, a copy was given to every man in the employ of the Japanese government. It was a jackpot, and, particularly for Hubbard, a soapbox, which most success writers could only dream about.[4]

A Message to Garcia was a bare fifteen hundred words. For the purpose intended, its tight structure was to the point. Most of Hubbard's journalism was shabby, and his novels were terrible, but his technique in this piece was effective. After a very brief account of Rowan's mission to Garcia, the preachment shifts to a scolding of the "imbecility of the average man—the inability or unwillingness to concentrate on a thing and do it. Slip-shod assistance, foolish inattention, dowdy indifference, & half-hearted work seem the rule. . . ." Now and then Hubbard returns to the phrase, "a message to Garcia," which symbolizes getting a job (any job) done efficiently with a minimum of fuss and bother. He explained that the article was written at the end of a long, trying day supervising the Roycroft Shops. The bitterness of a frustrated employer flowed like acid from his pen: "You, reader, put this matter to a test: You are sitting now in your office—six clerks are within call. Summon any one and make this request: 'Please look in the encyclopedia and make a brief memorandum for me concerning the life of Correggio.' Will the clerk quietly say, 'Yes Sir,' and go do the task? On your life he will not. He will look at you out of a fishy eye and ask one or more of the following questions: Who was he? Which encyclopedia? Where is the encyclopedia? Was I hired for that? Don't you mean Bismarck? What's the matter with Charlie doing it? Is he dead? Is there any hurry? Shan't I bring you the book and let you look it up yourself? What do you want to know for? And I will lay you ten to one that after you have answered the questions, & explained how to find the information, and why you want it, the clerk will go off and get one of the other clerks to help him try to find Garcia—and then come back and tell you there is no such man. Of course I may lose my bet, but according to the Law of Average I will not. Now if you are wise you will not bother to explain to your 'assistant' that Correggio is indexed under the C's, not in the K's, but you will smile sweetly and say, 'Never mind,' and go look it up yourself. And this incapacity for independent action, this moral stupidity, this infirmity of the will, this unwillingness to cheerfully catch hold and lift, are the things that put pure Socialism so far into the future. If men will not act for themselves, what will they do when the benefit of their effort is for all?"

Hubbard then tosses some words of compassion to the employer: "We have recently been hearing much maudlin sympathy expressed for the 'down-trodden denizen of the sweatshop. . . .' Nothing is said about the employer who grows old before his time in a vain attempt to get frowsy ne'er-do-wells to do intelligent work; and his long, patient striving with 'help' that does nothing but loaf when his back is turned." Day after day the employer must constantly weed out the incompetent. "Self-interest prompts every employer to keep the best—those who can carry a message to Garcia."

When we are doing our pitying, Hubbard warmed to his final point, "let us drop a tear, too, for the men who are striving to carry on a great enterprise, whose working hours are not limited by the whistle, and whose hair is fast turning white through the struggle to hold in line dowdy indifference, slip-shod imbecility, and the heartless ingratitude, which, but for their enterprise, would be both hungry and homeless. Have I put the matter too strongly? Possibly I have; but when all the world has gone a-slumming I wish to speak a word of sympathy for the man who succeeds—the man who, against great odds, has directed the efforts of others, and having succeeded, finds there's nothing in it: nothing but bare board and clothes. I have carried a dinner pail and worked for day's wages, and I have also been an employer of labor, and I know there is something to be said on both sides. There is no excellence, per se, in poverty; rags are no recommendation; and all employers are not rapacious and high handed, any more than all poor men are virtuous. My heart goes out to the man who does his work when the 'boss' is away, as well as when he is at home. And the man, who, when given a letter for Garcia, quietly takes the missive, without asking any idiotic questions, and with no lurking intention of chucking it into the nearest sewer, or of doing aught else but deliver it, never gets 'laid off,' nor has to go on a strike for higher wages. Civilization is one long anxious search for just such individuals. . . . The world cries out for such: he is needed, and is needed badly—the man who can carry a message to Garcia." [5]

Elbert Hubbard's 1899 tract was well-timed. The Populists had just shaken the propertied interests of the country, Thorstein Veblen's *Theory of the Leisure Class* was invigorating the attack from the Left, Edwin Markham was laying bare the exploitation of labor and "the world's blind greed" in *The Man with the Hoe*, while Henry Demarest Lloyd's *Wealth Against Commonwealth* had pointed the way for the Muckrakers of the coming decade. It was a case of the best defense relying on an aggressive offense, though *A Message to Garcia* would kindle faint enthusiasm among today's labor-management experts.

During the 1890s and 1900s reformers from all sides, in every area of thought, were challenging the assumptions of the success idea. Religion, too, embraced its variety of reforming solutions for a better tomorrow. Through the social gospel movement, Protestantism responded most sensitively to the dislocations of American society caused by the Industrial Revolution. Human beings were fighting one another as workers and employers, families were going hungry in stinking tenements, children were slaving from sunrise to sunset in depressive working conditions. The social gospel movement is accurately described by its name. Its solution was to apply the teachings of Jesus revealed in the Gospels of the New Testament to the social problems torturing urban, industrial America. Some leaders, avowed socialists, struck at the profit motive as subversive of Christian ethics; others held to the capitalistic system, seeking to correct its evils yet retain its advantages. The Reverend Lyman Abbott, like the progressive movement in politics during the 1900s, stood for a compromise. He was enthusiastic about the promise of industrial capitalism, but certain that it would never be realized without economic regulation and a spiritual regeneration. A liberal politically and theologically, he is a magnificent example of pro-gressivism filtered through the clerical mind of Protestantism. Believing that people ought to get ahead and make money, he blessed the idea of success with the ethical teachings of Jesus.[6]

Lyman Abbott built his life on compromise—the democratic, not opportunistic kind. He refused to handcuff himself to ex-treme dogmatists. "My sympathies have been for the most part neither with the radicals nor with the reactionaries, but with the progressives in every reform," he happily confessed towards the close of his life. "I have been an evolutionist, but not a Darwinian; a Liberal, but not an Agnostic; an Anti-slavery man, but not an Abolitionist; a temperance man, but not a Prohibitionist; an Industrial Democrat, but not a Socialist." Born in 1835, Abbott's early years were spent in the New England of his seventeenth-century ancestors. The family still worshiped in double Sunday services—the afternoon meeting ending in time so the men could hurry home to milk the cows. His father, Jacob Abbott, was a Congregational minister of some substance, who compounded a love of teaching with the lucrative joys of writing 180 books, mostly juvenile fiction instructing children in ethics, science, travel, and history. Much of the father brushed off on the son, who carried old Jacob's ideas to their logical conclusions. Graduating from New York University after the family had moved to New York City, he practiced law for a few years, then responded to his youthful dreams for a life in the ministry. Ordained in 1860, he preached during the 1890s in Henry Ward Beecher's Plymouth Congregational Church, and finally descended from the pulpit to devote his prolific energies to editing the *Outlook,* a powerful instrument of Progressivism enthusiastically dedicated to the respectable re-forming of Theodore Roosevelt.[7]

The story of Lyman Abbott is that of a bright young man who broke away from fundamentalist, Puritan, conservative New England into the exciting whirl of ideas that carried America towards reform in the first decade and a half of the twentieth century. In his theology, God was not a King to be feared, but a Father who was love; man did not fall into depravity, but was ascending from a previous animal order; salvation was not the rescue of the elect from a world lost to sin, but the transformation of free men into a life with Christ. In his warm, hopeful religion, Abbott made his peace with Darwin. Evolution was not a struggle for existence with the fittest surviving, but a process which explained the perpetual growth of life from a lower, more simple stage to a higher, more complex one. Down the line of fresh ideas which were striking at the foundations of conservative America, Abbott made his compromises, holding firmly to what he believed to be the good and true, rejecting the antiquated and false.[8]

With his ascetic face, flowing white beard, and beaklike nose poised above the crowd, Lyman Abbott was no ivory-tower theologian. All around him industrial America was doing things to people which stirred him to righteous anger. "An industrial system which produced poverty in a land of wealth, and hunger in a land of plenty," he declared, "which incited to crime and begot criminals, invited needless disease, bred pestilence and multiplied deaths, which robbed men and women of their homes and which robbed children of their fathers and mothers, their education, and their play hours, was an unjust and intolerable system." Rejecting both a free-wheeling economy and state-owning socialism, he stumped for Progressivism's faith in the regulation of business, and expressed his own trust in the healing power of Christ's teachings applied to industrial problems. Abbott was the religious spokesman for reform-minded, middle-of-the-road Progressivism in the forty years following Appomattox. What he had to say about the idea of success reflected that thinking.[9]

"The ambition to succeed may be and always ought to be a laudable one," Abbott asserted in 1882 in *How To Succeed*. "It is the ambition of every young man for himself, and of every parent for his child. It is emphatically an American ambition; at once the national vice and the national virtue. It is the mainspring of activity; the driving-wheel of industry; the spur to intellectual and moral progress. It gives the individual energy; the nation push. It makes the difference between a people that are a stream and a people that are a pool; between America and China. It makes us at once active and restless; industrious and overworked; generous and greedy. When it is great, it is a virtue; when it is petty, it is a vice." Petty ambition is a desire to win the emblems and tokens of success, he went on. "True success is achievement. . . . Every man who leaves his home, his village, his nation better for his thoughts and deeds has succeeded; every man who has not, has failed." On the other hand, "the notion, borrowed from paganism, that the price of eternal wealth is earthly poverty, and the price of eternal happiness earthly wretchedness, has no warrant in Christ's teaching." In fact, the precepts of the New Testament contain the most practical instructions in how to make money. "There is no chart of sailing directions so good to steer by for the port of success as those to be gathered from the instructions of Jesus of Nazareth. The golden rule is a good rule to do business by. . . . The successful business men, from the days of Abraham—who started in life as a poor emigrant and amassed an enormous wealth of herds and flocks and servants—to those of our own day, have achieved their success by studying not how they could squeeze the most out of their fellow men, but how they could achieve the greatest service by their commercial abilities." [10]

In 1910, Abbott expressed in greater detail his interpretation of Christ's attitude toward making money. "Jesus Christ was one of the men who think that it is right to be rich. He did not condemn wealth. On the contrary, he approved of wealth; he approved of the accumulation of wealth, and he approved of the use of accumulated wealth to accumulate more wealth. He did this in a well-known parable [of the talents]. . . . I am aware that we have spiritualized this parable; and we have done well to spiritualize it. But the parable is none the less true without a spiritual interpretation; its direct and immediate meaning is true as well as its indirect and spiritual meaning. Jesus never condemned thrift or industry or the accumulation of property. What Jesus did condemn was making the accumulation of property an end in life. . . . To Jesus accumulation was not wrong. But to accumulate for the sake of accumulation was both sin and folly. It was making the man the servant of things, not things the servant of man." Chiding those who misquote out of context, Abbott wanted to make certain that the words of Jesus were not mangled on this point. "Jesus did not say, 'Lay not up for yourselves treasures upon earth.' He said, 'Lay not up for yourselves treasures upon earth *where moth and rust doth corrupt and where thieves break through and steal.*' And no sensible American does. . . . What Jesus condemned was hoarding wealth; he never condemned possessing it or using it for the benefit of society. . . . The great mass of American wealth is active; it is serving the community, it is building a railway to open a new country to settlement by the homeless; it is operating a railway to carry grain from the harvests of the West to the unfed millions of the East. . . . Not having wealth and using it for the world's betterment, but hoarding it unused, Jesus condemned." Why? Because hoarding and acquisition for its own sake inevitably carried with it indifference and neglect, if not oppression, of the poor. It not only wronged others, but wronged the man who was bent on acquisition for its own sake. " 'What shall it profit a man if he gain the whole world and lose his own life' " does not mean: what's the advantage of getting this world and losing another. This teaching should not comfort those "who think the other world is so uncertain that a world in the hand is worth two in the bush." What Jesus meant was this: what's the good of getting things in this world if you lose yourself in the process? [11]

Lyman Abbott's Progressivism led him into a faith in the effectiveness of government intervention to free the clogged channels of opportunity. He placed a particularly heavy emphasis on the evils of materialism. In the essentials, however, his conception of success was similar to his more conservative colleagues in the ministry. All heads could nod in comfortable unison when Abbott asserted simply: "All things are right if they are contributing to character; all things are wrong if they are not contributing to character." At the same time Abbott reflected two changes in emphasis that were taking place in the justification for success during the 1890s and 1900s. One paral-

leled a widespread shift in theological interest from the Old to
the New Testament in these decades. He explored Christ's New
Testament teachings in greater measure than the nineteenth
century in order to bless the success idea. The other change in
emphasis pointed the way with the big word for the coming
generation of success writers: "In effect Jesus said to his
disciples: 'I do not condemn the use of the world, but use it in
service; I do not condemn the acquisition of wealth, but acquire
it for service; I do not condemn the exercise of power, but
exercise it for service.' " [12]

From Lyman Abbott to William ("Godliness is in league with
riches.") Lawrence, the right-wing Episcopal Bishop of Massachusetts, the best friend the idea of success ever had in the
nineteenth century was the solid body of Protestant clergymen.
If they did not outwrite others, they collectively outtalked
everyone else on the subject. From the Civil War to World War
I, Protestantism supported the controlling groups that were
surging into power throughout urban America. [13]

Like the response of religion to change in any society, Protestantism had at least three choices in this period. It could
attack, tolerate, or support the transition to an industrial economy. If the major Protestant denominations attacked the strong
economic forces that were sweeping to victory, they would ultimately be forced to withdraw from society and decline into sects
without influence. If they tolerated any and all economic
behavior without standing for what is right and wrong, they
would grossly compromise their ideals. It is easy to be cynical
about the response of the major denominations. Propertied
interests supported religion by donating funds, serving on church
governing bodies, and paying lip service to its teachings. In a
quid pro quo, clergymen often seemed to place property rights
above social justice. In the 1890s and 1900s particularly, there
was wide-ranging disagreement among clergymen about the
best methods for achieving a Christian society. A few favored
government ownership, some government regulation, while
others clung to the status quo. But these were methods which
depended on political viewpoints, liberal or conservative, Demo-

cratic or Republican. Specific solutions to economic problems were not, and never had been, a central concern of success literature. Even in the defensive decades of the 1890s and 1900s, clergymen who were writing success literature stuck to advice on how to make money and the proper attitude towards its accumulation and distribution. The central issue for religion was not government intervention into business but divine intervention into the souls of men. Their concern was not with government regulation but self-regulation of sinful temptations. They were not politicians seeking immediate solutions to specific problems but theologians interpreting the Scriptures to clarify ancient dilemmas. With enlarged opportunities sharpening the hunger for wealth, the age-old struggle between God and Mammon had become more perilous.

The clergymen of the major Protestant denominations did not sell out to powerful propertied interests in power during this period. Indeed, compared to the fuzzy thinking of clergymen in our day about the propriety of money-making, they offered sensible answers to the problem of reconciling God and Getting On. Of course there were exceptions and sharp degrees of emphasis. But judged by the values of the nineteenth century, the clergy not only reasserted the obligations of successful men and placed checks on the sin of runaway greed, but lambasted illegal practices and those businesses which contributed nothing to the general welfare. The clergy wanted to help Americans benefit from materialism. At the same time most of them were always fighting for God against Mammon in a timeless struggle for the souls of men. A critic today can protest that achievement through hard work is a virtue with ethical proportions, and he can scoff at such a naive faith in character and self-discipline. It is only snide to repudiate the sincerity of most nineteenth-century conservative clergymen. Their faith was the faith of the world they were raised in. Most Protestant clergymen were not hypocrites. They poured blessings by the bucketful on the virtuous duty of accumulating wealth. Seldom did they urge Americans to get ahead without adding strict words of caution about the perils of drowning in materialism.

Curiously enough, it was not the major denominations of

Protestantism which sold out to Mammon, but a cluster of smaller sects which we shall consider later. But first, let us tie together the loose strands and see if there is some pattern in the design of the success idea in nineteenth-century America.

7

THE GOSPEL OF THE
CHARACTER ETHIC

Every religion has its annual ceremonies. Year after year devout Christians reenact Christ's birth, death, and resurrection, never grow bored, but are refreshed by the renewal of faith. With the same eagerness to announce the good news, the gospel of success was preached as an unending reaffirmation of an American faith.

The apostles of this faith, a mighty army of success writers and lecturers, almost entirely Protestant in background, ventured forth to teach Americans how to get ahead. They were not economists but philosophers, not technical advisers on production methods but poets of inspiration singing about the meaning of America. They tried to give answers to ancient problems that are ever new: What should be the goal of my life? How can I attain that goal? How can I be sure that this is the social, economic, and moral right thing to do?

What we have witnessed is the unfolding of a classic American myth. In current academic usage, a myth runs deeper than a legend and is not necessarily a falsehood. "A myth," suggests psychoanalyst Rollo May, is "man's way of expressing the quintessence of his experience—his way of seeing his life, his self-image and his relations to the world of his fellow men and of nature. . . ." A myth carries "an element of ultimate meaning which illuminates but reaches beyond each individual man's concrete experience." [1]

93

The myth of the idea of success, hovering between dream and reality, had an enormous impact on the development of American Civilization. It offered instructions on the means to wealth (intertwined with certain standard observations about the nature of American society), ventured a definition of 'true success' while criticizing unbridled materialism, and then concluded by justifying material success.

By no later than the 1830s the idea of success had settled down into a formula. The component parts of this formula varied in the order of their presentation and the emphasis given to each. With a few changes, which we shall point up, the character ethic version of the success idea was remarkably static throughout the nineteenth century and into the early part of the twentieth century. Wars and depressions could come and go, but every generation which wrestled anew with the how and why of success came up with the same answers.[2]

However, the consistency of the success message during this period did not indicate an insensitivity to fundamental social and economic conditions. Success books were eagerly read because they were relevant to America's stage of economic growth at that time. Our contemporary personality ethic of Dale Carnegie's *How to Win Friends and Influence People* would have been no more relevant to nineteenth-century America than it is to the stage of economic growth of many developing countries. For a future premier of Burma to translate, as he did, that volume into his native tongue is to fail to take advantage of the value equivalent of that concept in Keynesian economics called the multiplier effect. A nation gets a 'bigger bang for the buck' by investing in a steel plant than an equivalent expenditure in, say, training doctors or lawyers. The consequences of success literature are involved in what we might term a value multiplier effect. But the value multiplier effect exerts its greatest impact only when the content of the success literature is most sensitively related to the national stage of economic growth. For a country moving into industrialization, the character ethic should help to stimulate individual ambition, encourage confident self-reliance, and dignify the self-discipline of hard work and deferred gratification. Thus, the carloads of paperback success books (or anthologies) which might be shipped to developing countries, if one recognizes the importance of values, should not be by Dale Carnegie but by the Freeman Hunts and the Russell Conwells. Developing countries today, like America in the nineteenth century, do not need the personality ethic's golden smile but the character ethic's nose to the grindstone.[3]

What is the gospel of the character ethic? To the question "how can I get on in the world?" came an answer which echoed the heritage of Cotton Mather and Benjamin Franklin: "Industry, honesty, perseverance, sticking to one thing, invariably lead to success in any reputable calling." The way to wealth was by building within yourself specific personal virtues. The qualities of character which appear over and over again are industry or hard work, frugality or thrift, perseverance or resolution, initiative, sobriety, punctuality, courage, self-reliance, patient plodding, and honesty. Negation of these virtues spelled certain failure. A speculating, get-rich-quick attitude was sharply criticized as not practical. It was Longfellow's observation which moved heads to an affirmative nod:

> The heights by great men reached and kept
> Were not attained by sudden flight,
> But they, while their companions slept,
> Were toiling upward in the night.[4]

The attitude toward social and economic conditions and the relevance of these conditions to youthful aspirations was unchanging. There was always an abundance of opportunity. It was plentiful where you were. It was not necessary to go elsewhere to find it, except in the case of a farm boy. The farm boy should move to the town or city only after exhausting all the possibilities for advancement near his home.

Chances for success were not influenced by environment or heredity, though there were several exceptions. Aspirants with rural origins and a good mother possessed greater environmental advantages at the start. Another advantage was to be born into poverty. The worst curse was to be the son of a rich man. If you were poor, you would be forced to overcome obstacles. This would build your character and give you self-respect, which few sons of the rich could enjoy. As for luck, there was no such thing. If there was something similar to it, like contacts and influence, in the long run, they made no difference at all. All anyone had to do was to realize that he used only one fraction of his potential and follow the proper means. Success could then be his, because in America everything depended on the individual and everyone had within him the potential for making money.

Self-education yielded profitable returns, but all success advisers agreed that a formal education was not necessary. Many writers considered a college education a positive hindrance, and some thought it fatal. At the same time, the idea of success was expanding towards the end of the nineteenth century to include a more favorable attitude towards higher education. But education had to be practical in the form of business, commercial, technical, or vocational colleges. The liberal arts curriculum was useless. Worse than that, it could curb or cripple the ascetic qualities of self-denial necessary to get ahead.

There were differences with respect to brains and intelligence. Most writers slipped over this means without mentioning them or denied that they were important. But a few emphasized brains, and occasionally even raised them to a level equal with such qualities of character as hard work or frugality.

The success idea during the Gilded Age did not represent a greedy hunger for wealth. It never stood for that and to assume that it once did is to misunderstand the counterbalancing spirit of American idealism. Most success writers, whether of a religious or secular persuasion, denounced the worship of Mammom. There was great variety, however, in the amount of space and vigor devoted to warnings against materialism and the threat that success might destroy the very qualities that made it possible. But the theme of evil and disaster inherent in the love of money was strong and continuing in the success idea. Not only were brakes clamped on runaway greed; wealth itself was seldom cherished as the final goal in life. The goals that success writers espoused almost always bounced back and forth between two types of success. The first was generally money; the second was final, ultimate, or 'true success.' 'True success' was happiness, the joy of living, developing yourself by doing your best with the faculties that God has given you, leading a self-respecting life with a noble character, peace of mind, service to others, or the love and respect of family, friends, and community. Whether 'true success' and material success were a contradiction or simply a natural tension between opposites depended on the individual success writer. Some writers put together an entire book on how to make money and then concluded at the end, in a kind of backsliding into idealism, that money was not the object of their instructions at all. Others recognized the natural tension between 'true success' and material success. They tried to hold this tension in healthy balance by sanctioning money-making, but only if it did not become the sole end in life and if the money was put to good purposes once it was made.

Warnings against greed reach back to antiquity. Given the power by Dionysus to turn everything he touched to gold, King Midas nearly starved to death until Dionysus allowed him to wash away his power in the Pactolus River. Consuming can consume the consumer; possessions possess the possessor. In the American experience the immediate source of vigilance against material gain as the sole end and purpose of life was religion. Christianity, especially Puritan Protestantism, dominated American values. Observed Matthew Hale Smith, sometime minister turned lawyer, lecturer, and journalist: "Whoever writes the history of our merchant, mechanical, or agricultural life, must write the history of religion." Even though an American writer was indifferent to religion, he could not escape the ethics of Christianity upon which the ideals of surrounding institutions and values were based. To make success and immediate self-interest the sole end of life was worldliness, a one-way ticket to hell and damnation. American culture was materialistic; it was also Christian. "For what shall it profit a man," asked the Saviour, "if he shall gain the whole world and lose his own soul?" [5]

This clash between materialism and idealism in the American spirit is expressed in the deep need to justify success. More than most societies, Americans yearn to justify their behavior in moral terms. In the nineteenth century success writers were always justifying the accumulation of wealth as socially, morally, and economically the right thing to do. It was not a rationalization but a justification based on a moral construct that making money was a good thing. It was what one ought to do. It was good, not only because it built character within the individual, but also enabled the successful man to contribute funds to the general welfare of the community and the nation. The philanthropic argument was the most important. You had to make good in order to do good. This was the moral reasoning of the steward-ship of wealth.

The doctrine of the stewardship of wealth, drawing from the Scriptures, was a fusion of Cotton Mather's belief that wealth glorified God with Benjamin Franklin's warm faith that money should be used in a humanitarian way. It was Puritanism blended with the eighteenth-century Enlightenment. The line is straight and clear. "I will remind rich men," advised Cotton Mather some one hundred and fifty years before the Civil War, "of the opportunities to 'do good,' with which God, who gives power to get wealth, has favoured and enriched them. . . . Sirs, you cannot but acknowledge that it is the sovereign God who has bestowed upon you the riches which distinguish you." The rich are a steward to the Lord, he instructed, and should give at least a tenth of their income for pious uses and the relief of the miserable. Just as rich men owe their original success to God, so will He intervene to help those who fulfill the obligations of stewardship. "They who have conscientiously employed their tenths in pious uses, have usually been remarkably blessed in their estates, by the providence of God. . . . They have been re-warded with remarkable success in their affairs, and increase of their property." [6]

Without quite so precise a percentage for God and philan-thropy, this was the foundation upon which the nineteenth century constructed its religious justification. To make money was a good thing because God wanted you to make it, it was evidence of God's favor, and you could do good with it after it was made. The secular interpretation simply bypassed God and took the position that money was justified on humanitarian grounds. It could be given away to help others after it was made. This was the stewardship of wealth. As a justification, it was honored by Peter Cooper. At its worst, it was fouled by Daniel Drew.

There were two changes of emphasis in the justification for success during this period. In both the religious and secular interpretations, the concept of service began to challenge the stewardship principle in popularity in the 1890s and the first decade of the twentieth century. In the religious interpretation, the Old Testament quotations were giving way to a justification for success based on the New Testament teachings of Christ.

There are implications which bear analysis. In a society which professed and called itself Christian, the idea of success stood solidly for what was morally good. Indeed, dishonesty and sinful behavior of any sort was considered not only ignoble but also an impractical way to make money. Pragmatically, it was not supposed to pay off. Those men who somehow amassed a fortune by crooked means were either scorned as unworthy exemplars of right conduct or ignored. Making money was a holy thing. From the pulpit and religious tracts came the reassuring advice that God wanted you to be rich, that the way to be rich was to cultivate a right character—and prayer. Indeed, prayer itself was a means to success in a culture which believed that God could and did intervene in the affairs of men.

Because it was a force for morality, the success idea rejected Social Darwinism as a justification for achievement. Perhaps successful men of this period did believe, with or without Darwinian theories, that progress came through the triumph of those best fitted to survive in a struggle for existence. But businessmen and writers on the subject claimed that the justification for wealth was *not* climbing over the fallen bodies of others, but struggling against the evil in oneself and then going on to some kind of moral triumph. They rested their case on the

Bible and philanthropic results, not on the *Origin of Species*.

Anti-intellectualism was inherent in the idea of success. Ambitious youths were advised to study and read, but the emphasis was on moral character, not learning and reason. Things of the mind had to be utilitarian. As we have stated, towards the close of the nineteenth century, when higher education was advised with greater frequency, the college had to be technical and vocational. The classical curriculum of the humanities was considered useless. While anti-intellectualism was inherent in the success idea, the strictures against a formal college education might also be explained by the quality of readership. A success writer who made higher education a requirement for achievement would forfeit the uneducated part of his audience. Also, the hero was the self-made man who never did think very much of the college man anyway—or at least he said he never did.

The purpose of the character ethic was not to produce a pious monk with a halo of virtues revolving around penitence, humility, and meekness. Neither was it to rear a chivalric knight with the qualities of bravery, loyalty, and honor. The goal was to produce a man of wealth—but not an inhuman money-making machine. This was a great achievement of the character ethic. It managed to offer sensible means to the attainment of wealth, and at the same time declared itself for the Ten Great Beatitudes through the definition of 'true success' and the justification for material success. The character ethic fused the Book of Proverbs and the Sermon on the Mount into a workable philosophy.

If the philosophy was workable, were these bourgeois virtues functional in practice? Was this actually the way to get ahead? The answer, to an extent, is yes. The nineteenth-century way to success was to start a business, expand it in competition with others, and then drive on with it as high as one could go. An enterprising individual generally owned the property with which he worked. His status and income were determined by the qualities he himself put into the firm. The success of the firm was the measure of his own success. The bourgeois virtues of perseverance and thrift functioned in the world of the small entrepreneur.[7]

There are several variables in the success story as myth which are intriguing. The hero was a poor boy, often just off the farm or a recent boat from Europe. With very little education, he went to work at an early age, started at the bottom, overcame what was known as "obstacles," and by moral virtues rose in the world unaided, except for such fortuitous variables as a farming birthplace or a good mother. This was the traditional story which flourished in the last half of the nineteenth century and was carried into the twentieth, not only by inspirational writers, but even by distinguished historians who were inclined to portray the typical business tycoon of the Gilded Age as a lower-class poor boy of foreign or rural origins.[8]

The respect for rural origins and a good mother entangled the character ethic in a contradiction. Was there really equal opportunity in America when country boys with a good mother had the jump on their city-bred cousins? And wasn't it a contradiction of equal opportunity to assert that poor boys had an advantage over rich men's sons? Of course the success idea was constantly laboring the assertion that there was equal opportunity for everyone to get ahead. Whimpering about the advantages of others, adverse economic conditions, or the grip of fate was no excuse for not moving forward.

Yet, did a poor boy of rural origins with a "good mother" really have an advantage over a rich, city-bred kid without one? Well, in the first place, if it were true that numerically more poor boys from rural origins became a success, it would not prove them better, for there were more of them. In the second place, the country boy might have pushed ahead of the city-reared boy, not because he was born in the country, but because he had enough initiative to leave the country and move to the city. Still, one can't help wondering.

What the character ethic meant by "poor" between the middle decades of the nineteenth century and the early decades of the twentieth was not the debasing poverty of the city as we think of it. They were thinking of a literate, middle-class boy brought up on a farm, or in a small town, in which the family had to struggle to make ends meet. What a boy does learn on a farm is business management. Unlike the factory worker or rich man's son, he is occupationally involved from an early age in developing those qualities which success writers considered essential.

The evidence, if any, to support the importance of the mother, or the father, in creating ambition in a child we shall save for the next chapter when we set the success idea more deeply into its historical context.

The idea of success was dedicated to what might be called a-great-man-in-the-process-of-becoming-great interpretation of history. Here was no class conflict. The folk hero was the self-made businessman and the practical inventor, not the politician or military campaigner. Presidents of the United States and famous statesmen were held up as models, but entering politics to make a living was looked upon very unfavorably. Politics was sanctioned, however, as a non-paying gesture of civic responsibility. The gospel of get-ahead in the nineteenth century had little or no respect for paid politicians. The power was in Wall Street, not Washington.

The idea of success was always democratic, but in different periods it was associated with varying types of democratic feeling. In the eighteenth and early nineteenth centuries, the idea of success was anti-aristocratic rather than conservative. It exalted the self-made man of business over the landed gentry. In 1832 Henry Clay, on the floor of the United States Senate, expressed the first known recorded use of the designation "self-made men." Clay argued that manufacturing industries run by self-made men were more democratic than the aristocratic cotton plantations based on Negro slavery. The success idea had a Jacksonian faith in the common man and in a fluid class system of achieved, not ascribed, status.[9]

After the middle decades of the nineteenth century, the idea of success, while no less democratic, became conservative. It stood solidly for the *status quo* and the old American values which had carried the nation on to progress and better things. By implication, there was no need for governmental meddling.

Not by luck or contacts did a man rise in the world, but by personal qualities within himself which he had fought hard to develop. The battle was waged by the individual against his own worst tendencies and was won without hurt or damage to his fellow man. In an equal and fair struggle, some were capable enough to win the prize. They deserved to be on top. As stewards of God, or secular humanitarians, they had distributed their wealth to good works. Always there was an abundance of opportunity for anyone who would awaken the sleeping qualities within himself. The environmental interpretation was ignored. The society, the environment, the system was never at fault. Always the pressure centered on the individual. He alone could savor the sweet pleasures of triumph; he alone must taste the bitterness of defeat. A favorite Shakespearean quotation was from *Julius Caesar:*

> The fault, dear Brutus, is not in our stars,
> But ourselves, that we are underlings.

The idea of success, then, was anti-aristocratic and democratic in the early nineteenth century. But it became conservative after the Civil War. If it seems like a contradiction to label an idea both democratic and conservative at the same time, that is because liberalism, rather than conservatism, has often appeared to express more faithfully the spirit of democracy.

By the ironical twists of history, what was used to challenge the *status quo* in agrarian America developed into an implied, and sometimes outright, defense of the *status quo* in industrial America. But a distinction should be made between the *effect* of the success idea and the *intent* of its apostles. After the 1860s the effect of the idea in every case was conservative. But the intent of success writers was politically indifferent. Most success writers did not argue for or against the reformer's policy of using the government to assist discontented groups. Their purpose was to tell aspiring young men how to make money. Excursions into the salutary or disastrous policies of the immediate administration were no concern of theirs. They were not conscious of defending any particular social or economic class in America, not even the wealthy class. If that had been their purpose, they obviously would not have so sharply struck at an important segment of that class—the sons of the rich.

The political uses of the success idea depended on the intent of the user. In the late 1890s and 1900s the success idea did add to its conservativism a tone of defensiveness, particularly on the point of equal opportunity in relation to the growth of trusts. In those years the success idea was consciously exploited to defend propertied interests, most frequently by businessmen and their paid spokesmen. The bulk of success literature, however, was written without intent to make political propaganda. At the same time the effect of the success idea was to defend freedom of enterprise by describing a condition of equal opportunity where achievement depended on the individual and required no assistance from the government to rectify disadvantageous economic conditions.

While the political effect of the success idea was conservative, its philanthropic consequences were liberal. Many rich men did heap up their fortunes by swindles and the exploitation of human and natural resources. But to the credit of certain rich men in America, or their public-relations advisers, it can be said that they held to the honor of the stewardship theory. The larger foundations set up by the Rockefeller, Carnegie, Guggenheim, and Mellon families, and more recently by the Fords, to cite only a few, were living monuments to good works. Hundreds of smaller foundations have made their contribution. (Many have also grossly abused their trust.) The rich in America in less formal ways have given away a greater percentage of their income to charity and philanthropy than equivalent elites in Europe or Asia.[10]

In the absence of fixed titles and in the presence of a fluid social class system, it was astonishing that the plutocracy in America should have developed a sense of *noblesse oblige*. It was precisely in this feeling of obligation to give generously that successful individuals in America differed from their European peers. The run of successful businessmen in Europe never gave away anywhere near so great a percentage of their fortune. What makes this large—and small—scale philanthropy peculiarly American was the democratic spirit in which part of these huge sums were given to help others get ahead.

The monied elite in America in its ideals (but less so in practice, of course) have believed that the less fortunate in the world should have the opportunity to rise above the station to which they were born. The deeper meaning of the phrases "vested interests" and "entrenched wealth" were the natural result of conflicting economic groups which James Madison understood with particular clarity. But the phrases, and their meaning, do not imply aristocratic barriers thrown up against the admission of others into the inner circle, but merely the protection of the interests of those who are in it. It might seem foolish, if not suicidal, that the rich should give huge sums to scholarships, fellowships, libraries, and educational institutions for the benefit of all. These vehicles of mobility could be used by ambitious young men to challenge their power and replace the superior position of their families and children. To be a success a man often had to beat down others, but once he made the grade, there was a democratic pride in whatever help he could give to less fortunate young men who were eager to repeat the process. It was a particularly democratic form of *noblesse oblige* that the English aristocracy, with their tradition of public service, and the Continental elite, with their class rigidity, could never understand.

The wealthy in America, on the other hand, have seldom been known to hide their light of generosity under a bushel of obscurity. The stewardship principle was a liberal means to a conservative end. It was, indeed, not only good public relations, but also served to weaken discontented challenges to the *status quo* by boosting ambitious young men into the ranks of the privileged.

The idea of success, in the various elements of its formula, was indeed functional. But what of the man who was a failure? Would he not be inclined to support political radicalism in order to redistribute the wealth? Though poverty was said to indicate a lack of moral fiber, the idea of success was functional because it was also merciful. In 'true success,' the man whose level of achievement fell far below his level of aspiration could find solace. After all, 'the best things in life are free.'

8

WHY THE AMBITION TO
SUCCEED?

Max Lerner has ventured that America ranks with "Greece
and Rome as one of the great distinctive civilizations of history."
Much of what is distinct in that civilization, for better and for
worse, is contained in the values and conditions which nourished
the idea of success. Why were Americans ambitious to become
a success? Why was it, as one foreign commission observed in
1903, that "restless ambition is almost universal"? [1]

The most important element in the foundation of American
Civilization was not economic, political, or ethnic. It was religious. Nowhere is the importance of Puritan-Protestantism more
apparent than in explaining why Americans were ambitious
to succeed. The Christian goal of the Middle Ages was to know
and do the will of God. "The traditional social teaching upheld
the virtues of meekness and contentment and tried to minimize
the competitive spirit." Although ambition was not entirely
smothered, one was expected to do his duty in the station of life
to which it shall please God to call him. The Christian goal of
Puritan-Protestant America was also to know and do the will
of God—except man's understanding of God's will had changed.
The quest for grace became a quest for wealth. If, as Gunnar
Myrdal perceived, "Americans worship success," it was because
Americans from early in their history worshiped a God which
they were confident wanted them to be a success.[2]

The consequences of this conviction were immense. In a

productive economy, the quality of human resources has always been more important than the quantity of natural resources. It is the flame of values within human resources which ignites natural resources into productive wealth. Every society has the same essential range of activities. But every society differs in the importance attached to those activities. In America, the most important activity has been making a living. This has been true, not because making a living was exalted for its own sake, but because it was surrounded with a cluster of values which increased its symbolic significance. People are ambitious when they work for a reward, e.g., money or the inner satisfaction of achievement. But they are far more ambitious when work itself is endowed with a high value. It is the sacred realm which endows secular work with value. The irony is that the spiritual controls the material. It is not the material which enslaves the spiritual.[3]

All societies pursue certain objectives which they define as saintly. Yet some societies, like America, ended up wealthy by pursuing what they believed was saintly. Other societies remained in poverty. The fatalism of the Islamic religion discouraged ambition. The mysticism of Hinduism, Buddhism, and Confucianism deprecated rather than encouraged self-assertion in this world. Religion was counterproductive to industrialism.

In America, the religion of Puritan-Protestantism encouraged man to be productive. Piling up a fortune was a way of worshipping God and a visible proof of His favor. As Erich Fromm has pointed out, this ethic "supported the feeling of security and tended to give life meaning and a religious sense of fulfillment. This combination of a stable world, stable possessions, and a stable ethic gave the members of the middle class a feeling of belonging, self-confidence, and pride." [4]

Puritan-Protestantism was the mainspring of creative tension. Some societies attempt to dissolve tension into harmony. The American spirit strung tight the tension between man and his God (sin and salvation), between man and himself (aspirations beyond achievement), between man and man (competitive conflict for self-assertive superiority), and between man and nature (mastery). It was a psychic tension within the individual which was generally, but not always, released for purposeful action. When the middle class, economically radical and politically conservative, was given the creative tools of applied science, the result was an Industrial Revolution far more significant than any political revolution before or since.

If Puritan-Protestantism ideologically supported productive personal qualities, it may also have psychologically helped to mould such qualities into its believers. How did Puritan-Protestantism build in entrepreneurial traits of initiative, self-reliance, and risk-taking? It stressed a direct relation between man and God. Every man was his own priest. He confronted God in free prayer with individual responsibility for his own destiny. The achievement of grace was a personal achievement between God and the self. The eye of God never winked at indiscretion. The sinner-saint, in a kind of moral bookkeeping, was in charge of his own ledger. In this freer Reformation approach of a God by the people, there were always the risks imposed by the responsibility of individual decision-making.

Protestantism took much of the mystery out of life and replaced it with a set of problems. Mystery was an insufficient explanation for a world capable of rational mastery. Education was necessary for all class levels and all occupations, for in the Bible was written the word of God. But more important than the stress on literacy was a process of thinking which forced the individual to seek his own answers.

That most Protestant denominations were democratic rather than authoritarian in their government is important. But the psychological consequences are the key point. Rather than a priestly intermediary standing between man and God within an authoritarian framework, which might have led to passive dependency, Protestantism stressed individual decision-making with no intermediary between man and God. This process translated itself into decentralized individual decision-making in secular affairs. The authority and responsibility lodged in the individual in religious matters accentuated the confidence to exercise authority in secular affairs. Such an individualistic mindset did not look to authority for guidance but to internalized standards. The burden of private judgment with respect to sin was carried over to an acceptance of the burden of private judgment in business, a confidence in oneself to make decisions, to innovate, to act.

The price that was paid for Puritan-Protestantism was emotional sterility. The character ethic was part of a sixth sense which froze the other five. The absorption in a goal of striving-becoming rather than sensuous-being led to a tight suppression rather than joyful expression of the senses. The result was a restraint on deep feelings, an inhibition of passion, a fear of ecstasy.

What is important about this aspect of Puritan-Protestantism for our purposes was not its guilt-ridden obsession with sex as sin. Nor are we concerned with pointing out that it was the nineteenth-century Victorian puritans in their uptight obsession with respectability, not the colonial Puritans, who overlaid sex with the hypocrisies which infuriated later generations. Nor must we necessarily echo the scholarly corrective that the colonial Puritans really liked sex, however guilty they may have felt about the temptations of the flesh. What we are emphasizing are the *denial* of feelings and the consequent release of emotions for productivity. To be aesthetically overwhelmed by beautiful paintings and music, gourmet food, and perfume, to give way to emotions aroused by caressings of the flesh means that the environment is acting on you rather than you on the environment. It means that external stimuli, aesthetic and sensual, are in control of your feelings. Aesthetes do not generally make good ascetics. Theologically, worldly pleasures were wicked. Psychologically, they dominated. And if there was anything that the success idea wanted its practitioners to be, it was to be in control. The way to control one's environment was to smother feelings.

This foundation of religious values and their psychological consequences was strengthened by other causal forces which help to explain why Americans were ambitious to be successful. Puritanism struck at laziness with the stick of guilt; capitalistic values tempted ambition with the carrot of self-interest. By the end of the eighteenth century, reaching for the carrot was not only for the good of the self but for the good of all. Adam

Smith pronounced the doctrine that the justification for the unregulated pursuit of one's own self-interest was the generally unintentional promotion of the public welfare. Economic doctrine had swung into line with religious convictions. Puritanism and Adam Smith had bequeathed to a nation a good conscience in the making of money. You promote the public good by promoting your own good.[5]

Doctrines of economic and political individualism encouraged the ambition to get on. What the rights of the voter were to political democracy, the achievement of the self-made man was to economic democracy. Individualism was encouraged by an optimistic belief that one could rise in the "land of opportunity." ("You can't keep a good man down.") "America," hymned Emerson, "is another word for Opportunity." The Statue of Liberty echoed the promise:

> 'Give me your tired, your
> poor,
> Your huddled masses yearning to breathe free,
> The wretched refuse of your teeming shore.
> Send these, the homeless, tempest-tost to me,
> I lift my lamp beside the golden door!'

Since 1886 the Statue of Liberty has held high her torch and has come to symbolize the promise of opportunity as well as the reality of freedom.[6]

A growth factor in opportunity was mobility, the willingness of people to migrate. Opportunities did not make America. It was people taking advantage of the opportunity to uproot themselves geographically and strike for a fresh start. Equally important was the way in which the land was taken up. Across three thousand miles the land was settled and exchanged by an independent middle class of small property owners and not by a landed gentry overseeing baronial estates worked by dependent wage earners.

Whenever the cherished hope of opportunity was in danger, deeply felt liberal movements responded with ideas and action to preserve it. Strong planks in the platforms of Jacksonian Democracy, Populism, Progressivism, and the New Freedom were hammered out with the intent of abolishing privilege and reopening the clogged channels of upward mobility. The old fear that America was going the way of Europe tugged at the heart in these times. "What this country needs above everything else," Woodrow Wilson declared in 1913, "is a body of laws which will look after the men who are on the make rather than the men who are already made." The belief in opportunity and concern for its preservation explains to some extent why the socialist doctrines of the redistribution of wealth experienced such difficulty in catching hold of the American mind. "Capitalism, in the long run, will win in the United States," H. L. Mencken predicted, "if only for the reason that every American hopes to be a capitalist before he dies." [7]

In the American open class system, status was attained by achievement rather than by ascription. No titles or legal safeguards protected an individual from skidding into an inferior class position within his own lifetime. At the same time he was not formally denied entrance into a superior status. In the absence of a feudal tradition, primogeniture, entailed property, a noble, peasant or proletarian class, the life of the American was spent on an escalator capable of moving in both directions. This fluid class system was a vertical expression of the mobility factor in the American experience, just as its horizontal expression was the readiness to migrate across space onto the land and into the cities and then into the suburbs. It was restless motion with a purpose—moving out towards opportunity and up towards achievement.

Every generation in America has had its nose pressed against the windowpane, dreaming above its station—and encouraged to do so by the values of the society. In Europe a deference towards those whose station was above was compensated for by a haughtiness towards those whose position was below. "It is impossible for an Englishman to open his mouth," moaned George Bernard Shaw, "without making some other Englishman hate or despise him." Class accents can be erased, but in France and Germany deference is built into the very structure of the language. Is the person spoken to a superior to be addressed with the "you" of *vous* in French or *Sie* in German?

Or is he an inferior to be addressed with the "you" of the French *tu* or German *Du?* If the American class system was quite unlike the classless society that so many patriotic apologists claimed, it was so different from Europe and Asia's more formal and rigid class systems to make the contrasts meaningful.[8]

Running through all these causes, both expressing and intensifying them, was the competitive nature of American culture. "From the very beginning, American life was competitive from the top downward," D. W. Brogan has commented. "There was no real stability, no real security for anyone. . . ." Where people in other cultures might break down under the pressure, Americans did their best work under the lash of competitive conditions. With respect to the emotional development of the self, competition has been viewed less favorably. Karen Horney has remarked that "it is so deeply ingrained in all of us that everybody wants to get ahead of the next fellow, and be better than he is, that we feel these tendencies to be 'natural.' But the fact that compulsive drives for success will arise only in a competitive culture does not make them any less neurotic. Even in a competitive culture there are many people for whom other values—such as, in particular, that of growth as a human being —are more important than competitive excelling over others." [9]

One of the shaping influences for this competitive drive was the school system. The purpose of education in the seventeenth century was to serve religion. By the nineteenth century education had itself become a religion with its own belief and faith. The belief was that a democracy could function only on the foundation of an educated citizenry capable of making decisions in the light of the American tradition. The faith was in education as an escalator to lift one's children to a higher economic and social position.

If free education for all was a meal ticket, one of its massive functions was to assimilate the children of foreign-born parents into the basic values of American culture. In some societies a child learns through subtle cues that he has a given place in the social order. In America, the child was taught that his place could be higher than his parents'. In encouraging the child to be a success, school teachers reflected the values of their middle-class society. Designed to arouse the competitive drive in children was a whole battery of marks, prizes, and degrees from the first grade through high school which measured how a student stacked up against his schoolmates. Competitive grading in academic, athletic, social and extracurricular activities was designed to prepare a student to be willing to fight it out in a world where vigorous competition was justified. What instilled ambition in a child was a process of thinking in which achievement was measured by a recorded reward. After graduation, the measurable reward was simply shifted to money.

Success may be written $ucce$$. Contributing to ambition was the nature of the success goal. Money is objective and impersonal. Unlike a noble title, anyone can acquire it. Unlike professional rank, it can be acquired quickly—and lost even more swiftly. Money does not possess quality, only quantity. It has no intrinsic value but only what is assigned to it. The paradox, of course, is that to which we assign the most worth is in itself worthless. Money is without prejudice. It speaks with the universal tongue of clinking coins and rustling paper. We worship it as the "almighty dollar" and loathe it as "filthy lucre." [10]

The passion to possess money may grow out of deep emotional conflicts, reaching back to those early years when a child begins to understand the connection between money and power. He learns how to get money from his parents, the torment of both wanting to spend now and to save for later, the awful perception that parents are not a cornucopia of coins and therefore not omnipotent, and the invidious comparison that some kids are richer than he is. How a child handles these emotional conflicts helps to establish his attitude towards money as an adult. An example familiar to everyone is the tightwad. The tightwad may appear to be money-hungry, but in reality he is love-hungry. Most of these stingy, compulsive non-spenders, reports William Kaufman, "were deprived in their early lives of love and affection, and experienced poverty, punishment and regimentation. Symbolically, money represents the love, affection and security which they never had and for which they have an insatiable craving." [11]

Early orthodox psychoanalytic literature equated money with filth. The basis of the irrational ways of behaving about money is the symbolic equation: money = feces. The origin of the possession of money as an end in itself is established during infantile development—especially in toilet training. Freud suggested that certain traits of character are modified by the sexual excitement experienced by the infant in the anal region. Others have contended that what is significant about the infant undergoing toilet training is the attitude of the person in charge of the toilet training. A rigid, anxious woman demanding strict regularity of action will incorporate into the child different personality characteristics than one more relaxed and casual about the child's elimination of excrement.

The key to the adult's attitude toward the possession of money is related to his experience as a child in deciding between two monumentally pleasurable choices—holding on or letting go. Fenichel has explained: "Anal eroticism has so much greater significance in the desire to accumulate possessions than oral or genital eroticism [because] in the anal sphere holding back and accumulating can afford an experience of erogenous pleasure." "If 'to hold' is retained as one's life pattern," suggests Knight, "then he may be dominated by the trait 'to have and to hold.' Thus, gold becomes a symbolic replacement for excrement. . . ." [12]

Ferenczi has traced the stages by which the child ultimately makes the connection between excrement and money. The first stage is the feces itself, manipulated as a toy, followed by moist mud (deodorized *dejecta*), then on to sand, pebbles, marbles to finally coins. Money is "nothing other than odourless, dehydrated filth that has been made to shine. *Pecunia non olet* [Money doesn't smell]." Whatever form money assumes, Ferenczi concludes, paper money or common stocks, "the enjoyment at possessing it has its deepest and amplest source in coprophilia,"—the love of dung. [13]

A more obvious insight about the nature of the success goal

as money is that there is no fixed point of achievement. When made of money, compared to institutional rank, the ladder of success is a topless ladder. Money was also the measure of a man's worth. One hundred years ago Thomas Nichols wondered: "Why the universal and everlasting struggle for wealth? Because it is the one thing needful; the only secure power, the only real distinction. Americans speak of a man being *worth* so many thousands or millions. Nowhere is money sought so eagerly; nowhere is it so much valued. . . . The real work of America is to make money for the sake of making it. It is an end, and not a means. . . . Talleyrand said America was a detestable country, where a man was ready to sell a favorite dog. I think the habit of fixing a price to everything may have misled the diplomatist. A man might be very unwilling to sell his dog; but he would be very likely to describe him as worth so many dollars. . . . Everything, whether for sale or not, has a money value. Money is the habitual measure of all things." [14]

"Things" were the measure of men on the private pay scale track in America. Yet, "No people in the world give their money away with greater ease," declared the British observer, Geoffrey Gorer. To the muckraker Lincoln Steffens it was a mystery "how Europeans ever came to say that Americans worship money when they [Europeans] sell everything for money—the state, honors, business, the arts. . . ." All the world loves money for its power to buy the comforts of life. In America, money has been primarily a symbol. It was a way of keeping score.[15]

Money-grubbing in America took on added dimensions. In a highly mobile society stressing individual responsibility, there were few concrete standards by which a man might be judged. "The motive that really predominates, now as in the past," concluded Charles Horton Cooley in 1899, "is essentially social and moral, it is the desire to be something in the minds of others, to gain respect, honor, social power of some sort." Money is the symbolic equivalent of medals on the chest of the soldier, favorable reviews in scholarly journals, or the achievement of high office. But is the motive only "to be something in the minds of others"? What we think we are is shaped by what we imagine other people think of us. How a man does in his work helps to establish a man's image of himself. The deeper drive beyond money and fame is the motive to prove one's worth to oneself. If success is externally judged, it is internally driven by the need for self-regard and self-respect. Success is the affirmation of self-esteem and the confirmation of self-worth.[16]

All these causal forces help to explain why it was that Americans were ambitious to be a success. Success writers added another variable—a "good mother." Was there any validity in their emphasis? If a parent at all, why not the father? An almost forgotten episode in the history of American painting makes the point.

One of the most popular paintings in late nineteenth-century America (perhaps *the* most popular by a resident artist) was not a scene depicting democracy or national patriotism but a leave-taking between a mother and her departing son. The painting touched something deep in the American experience during these decades. When Thomas Hovenden's "Breaking Home Ties" was exhibited for the first time at the 1893 Columbian Exposition in Chicago, the crowds were so great that several times the carpeting in front of the picture had to be replaced. At the center of the painting stands the mother, wearing a long, white apron, with her son. Off to either side the family is grouped in a somber mood while a man, perhaps the father, is moving toward the door with the boy's small bag. The mother places both her hands on her son's shoulders and gazes at him. He is carrying the hopes of the family to the city. His exit will mark the entrance to a new life. In the mother's gaze at her son, her posture, determination, and repressed emotion, there lives the Puritan-Protestant mother of agrarian late nineteenth-century America. One feels that the crucial psychological inputs that the departing son will take with him are not from the father, off to one side, but from this "good mother" as the son finally breaks dependency ties with his home.

Every success aspirant is like a tree with deep rootage in his childhood and broad leafage in his culture. Childrearing is universal, but childrearing practices are particular to each culture. Adults are the way they are because as children they had parents who psychologically conditioned them in particular ways. These psychological inputs may appear to be individual, but they are largely culturally conditioned. People are the way they are not simply because of their mothers and fathers, but because their mothers and fathers stressed the special values of their class, ethnicity, and religion. If we are the builders of our success, the architects are those endless psychological inputs which begin from the moment we are born. Childrearing is complex. But if we restrict ourselves again to the "Americanized," non-Southern, white middle class, there are some insights that can be offered about the role of the American family and childrearing practices in relation to ambition.

The child in America represented another chance for the parents. Parents deprived themselves in order to give their child, especially the male child, "a good start" in life. This deprivation was also a bargain. The son "measured up" to the sacrifices that made the start possible by making a place for himself in the world which the parents could vicariously share. Margaret Mead has commented that from the day of birth a child was valued in comparative terms. In a fast-moving urban world in which the son participated in activities remote from his father's experience, the parents were forced to judge their offspring by a rating scale keyed to other children rather than by inner qualities or absolute standards. In this way the child soon learned that the love and approval of his parents were determined by his performance in the competitive world of other children: "We can recognize that yearning for achievement which is planted in every American child's breast by his mother's conditional smile." Deep within the traditions of the American family, Mead has further suggested, there burned an eagerness for the son to surpass the father. In a culture in which there were so many second and third generation Americans, the passion for assimilation and achievement was intense.[17]

How did parents create a strong need for achievement in their child? We often refer to the ladder of success, but a more functional image from this angle of vision is a rope of success.

To climb a rope, a child must let go of one hand and hang perilously for a moment while he reaches up to seize the rope with the other hand. At an early point in his life the male child learns that he must not be like his mother who bore him and mothered him but like his father. Later on, he must break dependency ties with his parents, especially his mother, if he is to be mobile. If he seizes the rope possessively and will not let go with one hand to reach up, he will not climb.

To instill a need for achievement in a child, some researchers favor a happy family background while others emphasize an unhappy family setting. David McClelland, stressing the happy family milieu, has isolated several key factors in childrearing. The parents must expect great things of their child. They must set high standards of achievement, be warmly encouraging of his performance, and the father must not be dominating and authoritarian.[18]

Bernard Rosen also stresses a happy family setting. Both parents are involved, but the main force in creating a need for achievement is the mother. The father is most effective when he encourages in his son independence and self-reliance. Fathers "tend to beckon from ahead rather than push from behind." The mother may be more demanding and express greater disapproval for poor performance. This may be because the mother is perceived as imposing her *standards* on the boy while the dominating father is perceived as imposing *himself* on the son. Growing up in a family which creates a strong need for achievement in the son may be seen as an endless cycle of psychological mechanisms for motivation. The parents impose standards and goals for the boy to achieve. When he succeeds, they are warm in their approval. The mother is more demanding that standards be met while the father encourages independence. Higher goals are set as the child moves towards greater autonomy with a built-in impetus to excel. The result is often a child who derives an immense amount of satisfaction for a job well-done. He is keyed to accomplishment.[19]

The way parents and children interacted with each other helps to explain why sons developed a strong need for achievement. What were the sources of these childrearing practices in the United States? They came from the values that the parents held about life. These values were shaped by religion, specifically the dominant and enduring ethos of Puritan-Protestantism. But the Puritan ethos did not exist in a vacuum. It constantly interacted with social and economic conditions. The development of childrearing practices is another example of new world conditions modifying old world institutions.

Early Americans inherited the Elizabethan family structure. Mother, father, children, maiden aunts, and sometimes nieces, nephews, cousins—all lived under one roof. The male head was the unquestioned legal boss, and the children were brought up to be obedient and dependent. Under new world conditions this Elizabethan family was transformed. What emerged was a mobile unit restricted to parents and children. The distribution of power dissolved into a greater equality, raising the importance of women, diminishing the power of the male head, and increasing the independence of the children. Where aggression and independence had been held in check, it was released. Children began to be weaned earlier, fed on schedule, cradled and swaddled less. Individualism and independence were encouraged and a more permissive attitude adopted toward aggression. As the Elizabethan extended family stressing obedience and group responsibility shifted to the American nuclear family emphasizing self-reliance and individualism, there came into being that bane of the entire globe—the detestably undisciplined American child. But this kind of child, in American eyes, was not so much undisciplined as forthright, self-reliant, risk-taking, and confident of his own powers. He could survive under wilderness conditions. He could strike out for the cities mushrooming across the continent, able to make his own way independent of his parents.[20]

Though success writers were not scientifically trained, they knew, both from experience and from reading the biographies of great men, that what they termed "a good mother" was crucial in the development of an ambitious child. One suspects that what they meant was a literate woman who set standards for her son, encouraged him to meet those standards, taught him to read and write, defended him against a father who might be oppressively dominant, and when the time came for him to get married, shoved him out of the nest to earn his own way and raise his own family. No doubt in many cases she projected her own secret ambitions onto his personality. This mother was not an illiterate, lower-class, peasant-oriented woman living in a stratified society where females were abundant. She was a literate, American, middle-class, Protestant mother in a mobile society where a shortage of women made her indispensable to a man because he could not survive as a civilized human being without a wife. There is just enough truth in the precept to make it interesting that "the hand that rocks the cradle rules the world."

To summarize these studies and additional points in other studies which emphasize a happy family setting: The child receives early independence training leading to an attitude of responsibility, the mother is more dominant in childrearing than the father, present gratification is deferred for later objectives, the child learns to consider people instrumentally rather than emotionally, and there is greater involvement with parents or other adults and less with the child's peers.[21]

It is in the misery, rather than the joy, of growing up that psychoanalysts have located a neurotic rather than a healthy ambition. Analysts have found the origins of certain kinds of high aspirations and mobility drives in an unhappy childhood of wounded self-esteem, parental rejection, or unjust punishment with favoritism shown for a brother or sister in a setting of clashing interpersonal family relationships. The background of typical self-made men, concluded Alfred Messer, "had little in the way of parental love and support and were almost totally devoid of the emotional satisfactions that are part of an ordinary childhood. The only thing they were sure of was their ability to work; this they did with fanatical vigor and dedication. The self-made man who has had inadequate mothering and fathering has difficulty envisioning himself as a worthwhile individual. He attempts to make up for his feeling of worthlessness by constantly 'proving' his importance. . . . He has created a world in which his own performance and accomplishments are the mainstays of his identity." [22]

Many men in the chariot race for success were not the drivers but the driven. They were not chasing simply money or fame or status so much as the satisfaction of needs which were of deep psychological importance to themselves. It was psychic income that was being earned as well as the bigger house and car.

On a cosmic level it could be argued that Western Civilization's material accomplishments represent a massive overcompensation to an ego wounded by: Copernicus's proof that the earth is not the center of the universe, Darwin's then shocking revelation that man is distantly related to the apes rather than to an Adam and Eve made in the image of God, and Freud's exposé that we are in the grip of instinctual drives too frightening to contemplate.

On the emotional level of individual experience, some success hunters were obsessed by a work ethic because of hidden self-hatred, unresolved guilt feelings, or a compulsion to self-assertion. Others were driven by the need to compensate for feelings of inadequacy or inferiority. Some were incestuously testing their potency in the womb of business affairs. Many successfully sublimated their energies into productive or creative work, but others were torn by inner conflicts—an aggressive ambition contending with a need for childish dependence and love.

If some men owed their success to their neuroses, others were doomed to failure by their emotional disorders. As Samuel J. Warner has observed: "Anxiety has *drive* properties: it impels us to do something in order to keep its level down to certain limits." Anxiety drives some men towards achievement and others into defeat. To become a success, one has to risk the verdict that one may be inferior. Self-defeating mechanisms against anxiety may flow out of a glorified conception of the self with grandiose aspirations or a denigrated view of the self with stunted goals. Everyone has a quota of suffering that he must fill. The quota in the self-defeating neurotic is an insatiable demon. It monstrously feeds on self-defeating mechanisms and then regurgitates to feed the thing it has fed upon, producing an incestuous self-perpetuating mechanism for defeat. The demon is a wound that never mends, a sickness that never heals, a sorrow that lies too deep for tears. The cure is the very free will the sickness enslaves. The cure is the courage through self-awareness to confront the demon who feeds upon failure and self-imposed mediocrity under layers and layers of self-deception.[23]

Who is right? Does a happy or unhappy family setting create ambition in a child? The answer may be that both are correct. Ambition is still ambition whether it has healthy or neurotic origins. If many psychoanalysts have stressed neurotic drives, that is only because the patients they analyzed were suffering from emotional disorders. The stimulants for achievement may be healthy or neurotic, psychological or cultural. They may occur in childhood or adolescence. What is certain is that they emerge out of the complex fusion of many variables. It makes a difference in personality disposition if the child has brothers or sisters, whether he is the eldest or youngest, what kind of father-figures were available in addition to the real father, whether the parents felt they were upward or downward mobile, and what the influences were outside of the family, such as peer group interaction. We must also be aware that subjective feelings about rejection are not the same as objective facts. And the aspiration to achieve is not synonymous with the willingness to behave in a way which will achieve mobility. Heraclitus was a wise man in his humility: "You would not find out the boundaries of soul, even by travelling along every path: so deep a measure does it have." Yet the success idea of the nineteenth century was wise in one particular: You may take the boy away from his mother, but you can never take the mother out of the boy.[24]

9

"THE MIND IS A MAGNET"

The first serious challenge to the character ethic came toward the close of the nineteenth century. The competitor was New Thought. It struck at individual character as the only path to the accumulation of wealth. The way to get rich, asserted New Thought writers, was to think your way to wealth by the power of your mind.

New Thought was a religious movement, similar in many ways to Christian Science, devoted primarily to healing the sick in mind and body. Its point of departure was the proposition of Phineas P. Quimby, the founder of mental healing in America: "Disease being in its root a wrong belief, change the belief and it will cure the disease. By faith we are thus made whole." [1]

Since you are divine and one with God, by thinking you are one with God, you cannot be sick because God cannot be sick. New Thought developed a wing of success writers who picked up the limitless proposition and put it this way: Since you are divine and one with God, by thinking you are one with God, you cannot be poor, because God cannot be poor. Poverty being in its root a wrong belief, change the belief and it will cure the poverty. By faith we are thus made prosperous. If you will put yourself in tune with the infinite, your power of positive thinking can be your guide to confident living and bring you health, happiness, and prosperity.

Though the name New Thought is unfamiliar to most people, the message should be familiar. In 1948 and 1949, *A Guide to*

Confident Living stayed among the top ten non-fiction best sellers. In 1953 and 1954, more people walked into bookstores and purchased *The Power of Positive Thinking* than any other non-fiction book—except Western Civilization's all-time best seller, which enjoyed the additional advantage of a revised standard version. Norman Vincent Peale, and lesser luminaries from Emmet Fox to Ernest Holmes, were sustaining a fifty-year tradition which has largely been ignored in histories of American thought.[2]

New Thought is a label for a theological viewpoint around which groups varying in size and name are organized. Some names are restricted to a single, local organization, while others knit together local groups into a regional or national network. Many of these groups, such as Divine Science, Home of Truth, Church of the Truth, and Institute of Religious Science, are affiliated with the voluntary, loosely organized International New Thought Alliance. Others, like Unity and Psychiana, are not members. The International New Thought Alliance is actually a federation embracing most of the more important and larger groups, outside of the Christian Science Church, which teach a metaphysics of practical idealism.[3]

It is not the number of people who belong to its organized groups but the influence of New Thought as a mental attitude that is impressive. At the turn of the century, the psychologist William James became fascinated by the " 'Mind-cure movement' . . . which has recently poured over America and seems to be gathering force every day." In the years around World War I, it was estimated that from 300 to 400 New Thought centers were operating in the United States and Canada, while possibly a million people might have been influenced by its doctrines in the United States. One observer in this same period reported that owners of several religious bookstores were forced to sweep older theological books from two or three sections of their shelves and fill them with New Thought literature. He was "surprised to find travelling salesmen in the Pullman sleeping cars talking about this matter among themselves and reading books along this line. I have been amazed, in offices of certain business men whom I thought forever immune against religious literature of any kind, to see lying upon their desks little booklets bearing unmistakably the ear marks of the New Thought philosophy." By World War II, leaders of the movement were estimating that from fifteen to twenty million people in America were being influenced by New Thought teachings.[4]

As a point of view, a way of looking at reality, New Thought has exerted its most extensive influence through public lectures and writings which have not necessarily been labeled as such. For over half a century, best-selling authors have borrowed freely from New Thought ideas but have not formally identified their works as part of the movement. One of the earliest was Ralph Waldo Trine's *In Tune with the Infinite,* a title which reflects the subject matter. Cutting through New Thought's metaphysical fog with a style of grace and beauty, Trine steered a middle course between the extremes of mental healing and the drive to accumulate material possessions. Launched by the editors of Bobbs-Merrill in 1897, *In Tune with the Infinite* has sold over a million and a half hardbound copies. Its universal appeal has been marked as favorite reading at one time or another by sundry notables from Queen Victoria and Henry Ford to screen star Janet Gaynor. The Prince of Wales was so impressed that he presented a copy to his father as a birthday present, while the editors of *Publishers' Weekly* risked the observation in the early 1930s that "there is probably no foreign writer whose books are more widely known throughout Germany than those of Trine." [5]

The diversified denominational appeal of *In Tune with the Infinite* helps to support this interpretation about American Protestantism: it is difficult to determine what people believe about religion from figures which give the number of communicants in various denominations and sects—assuming those figures are accurate. For it is one of the interesting characteristics of American Protestantism that there is a wider theological diversity *within* many of the major denominations than *between* them. Theologically liberal Episcopalians, Presbyterians, or Methodists are often closer in their religious beliefs than they are to the more fundamentalist inclined brethren in their own denominations. It is also difficult to determine the degree of orthodox religious belief because of Protestantism's doctrine of the priesthood of all believers, which in practice has offered the individual a wide range of freedom to seek out his own God. The belief of Protestants is further confused because socio-economic factors are heavily influential in determining denominational affiliation. The conclusion is tempting that Protestants end up in a particular denomination more for social class than for theological reasons. Major denominational institutions seem to suffer a similar lack of precision in matters of faith. The only major Protestant schism since 1840, containing large numbers of people, has not been for religious but because of economic and political differences. Even though the Baptists, Methodists, and Presbyterians gave their differences over slavery an ethical interpretation, the split was not theological, but economic and political.[6]

American Protestants, therefore, can easily accept what they wish out of the New Thought philosophy and continue to worship in their own churches. Indeed, New Thought meetings are often held at times other than Sunday mornings in order to avoid a conflict with the services of established churches. The pervasiveness of the movement is reflected in packed auditoriums, fast-selling magazines, and books which are not designated as New Thought by their commercial publishers. Because of its loose organization, lack of discipline, and vast literature, the more popular writers within the movement have been able to blend their ideas into the stream of American thought—something not possible for Christian Science with its centralized, authoritarian organization.

New Thought has been sensitive to the climate of opinion. The sharp rise of medical competence during the twentieth century, coupled with an increase in anxiety-producing factors, seems to have swung the balance of New Thought's therapy away from the cure of organic diseases to nervous and mental disorders, kindling a renewed interest since World War II. In 1949 one careful student of minority religious movements re-emphasized the point that New Thought's "influence is enormous and there is nothing to indicate that it is in any way decreasing. On the contrary, it seems to be extending its influence, directly or indirectly, upon the life of the American people." During the 1950s and 1960s there was abundant evidence to support the accuracy of that prediction. To understand this phase of the success idea today, it is necessary to examine the tradition from which it grew.[7]

Phineas Parkhurst Quimby was the founder of mental healing in America and the pioneer of Christian Science and New Thought. Born in 1802 the son of a blacksmith, Quimby spent his entire life in New England in an unselfish search for a way to cure the sick. With a total of no more than six weeks of schooling and an undersized 125 pounds of nervous energy, he shifted from clock-making to mesmerism when he discovered he had a special talent in hypnosis. In 1843 he traveled through New England with an impressionable youth named Lucius Burkmar. Quimby's technique was to throw Lucius into an hypnotic trance. While under the hypnotic sway of Quimby, Lucius could apparently diagnose the diseases of sick people and prescribe the proper medicines. After further experimentation, Quimby discovered that Lucius's diagnosis was identical with what the patient believed to be his own disease, or what someone else present at the time believed. What did this prove? For Quimby, it proved that Lucius was only a mind reader, that the disease must be in the mind of the patient. Quimby was on to something. In 1847 he gave up Lucius and mesmerism for mental healing.

Quimby was completely unselfish in his explorations into the psychosomatic causes of disease. A warm-hearted, generous man without personal ambition, he tried to fill his patients with his own passionate conviction that disease was in the mind. He sat in sympathy by the sick while his piercing black eyes and depth of concentration helped them to understand that "man is made up of truth and belief; and, if he is deceived into a belief that he has, or is liable to have a disease, the belief is catching, and the effect follows it." Life for all of us, he counseled, is what we make it by our attitudes and beliefs.

Quimby was convinced that he had rediscovered Christ's method of healing. In this sense the treatment was spiritual, since he tried to awaken within the patient his birthright of divine power. But he took no unique credit for himself. Deserting his former role as a hypnotist, he did not try to control his patients' minds. He considered himself merely an agent revealing that the power of curing was the divine wisdom in all of us accessible through intuition.[8]

A quick way to fan a hot disagreement with New Thought disciples is to suggest that Christian Science had very much to do with the formulation of their theology. They prefer to see Quimby as the original storehouse, with his ideas enriched by borrowings from idealistic philosophers down through the ages. This is not entirely accurate. The more prominent teachers of New Thought, who set the pattern of later philosophical ideas, were dissenting Christian Scientists. Though New Thought did develop as an independent line from Quimby distinct from Christian Science, it was deeply influenced by rebels who kept breaking away from Mary Baker Eddy's authoritarianism. In many respects twentieth-century New Thought became a modified Christian Science. Not only was Quimby the common source of both, but Christian Science was being fed into New Thought theology through apostates from Mrs. Eddy.[9]

In the decades following Quimby's death in 1866, religious mental healing split into two main lines of development. One line was developed by Mary Baker Patterson, later Mary Baker Eddy, who clamped a tight vise of authority on therapeutics by establishing the Christian Science Church. The New Thought line was extended through the Swedenborgian minister, Warren Felt Evans, who unintentionally hurried mental healing into wealth-getting by bolstering Quimby's ideas with the Hegelian principle that thought is a creative force, the greatest creative force in the world.

In what way do Christian Science and New Thought differ? As is often the case in such matters, those who seem to outsiders to be the most similar ideologically are often the most bitter enemies. New Thoughters scorn Christian Scientists as corrupters of the pioneering Quimby. Like Protestants and Catholics in all lands, apostates from one church to the other are tenderly embosomed when they have awakened to the true faith at last.

Though to an outsider Christian Science and New Thought seem practically indistinguishable, they differ sharply in two areas. Christian Science is closely organized and rigidly centralized with a unified doctrine and an absolute discipline over its practitioners. In matters of faith, the absolute idealism of Christian Science denies the existence of matter and the reality of suffering. The New Thought movement consists of independent sects loosely organized and is unified very casually in doctrine. Centering authority in no book or person, it permits the individual to roam freely in the world's literature and to develop his own beliefs. In matters of faith, the restrained idealism of New Thought does not deny the existence of sickness, sin, and poverty, but asserts that these evils can be overcome by right thinking.[10]

The principal explanation why Christian Science did not embrace the success idea is its tight discipline. Anyone drifting in that direction would have been crushed by the Mother Church in Boston. If the urge to drift was overpowering, a potential success writer could quietly slip over into New Thought. He would find there affectionate and understanding company.

Jumbled together in the growing New Thought movement were patients of Quimby, apostates from Christian Science, and students of both. Toward the end of the 1880s these groups began to branch out into the philosophies of the past. They found lots of idealism in the world's philosophies to support and develop their therapeutic teachings. Following the neo-Platonist line in Western Civilization's running battle over the duality of mind and matter, they were convinced that matter was contained in mind rather than mind subordinated to matter.

In American thought, the natural connection was made with Emerson and the Transcendentalists. In Europe, they turned to Coleridge's transcendental intuition, Wordsworth's pantheism, Hegel's pan-logism, Berkeley's idealism, to Kant and to the great body of works on Christian mysticism. From India, there was the influence of Buddhism expressed in theosophy, while swamis revealed the mysteries of Vedanta philosophy from New Thought lecture platforms. Others connected New Thought's therapeutic teachings with spiritualism or mediumship. Though

New Thought leaders never seem deterred by abstruse metaphysical soarings, they permitted the complex simplicity of the American philosopher Emerson to speak to them most frequently and persuasively.[11]

The new discipline of psychology exerted its own impact beginning in the 1890s. Psychology lent a dignified, scientific air to success writers who delighted in the jargon of "subconscious mind," "unconscious," and "suggestion," and it helped them to buck up New Thought into a more optimistic philosophy stressing affirmation, attraction, and the right mental attitudes to achieve the heart's desire. Throughout the twentieth century, psychology had an immense influence on mind-power religious success writers as they fought "inferiority complexes" with "psychosomatic" facts, took their own plunges into the "unconscious" following the lead of Freud, and emerged somehow with God intact.[12]

What was new about New Thought? It surrounded mental healing, which was practiced by the Medes and Persians, with a theology of religious idealism, as old as Plato, and then injected it with the scientific dignity of psychology. Its newness was contained in America's most distinctive contribution to intellectual thought—pragmatism. New Thought's religious pragmatism offered a view of life which guaranteed sick people health, poor people riches, and troubled people happiness.[13]

The New Thought movement caught fire in the 1880s. In the late 1880s there were indications that its doctrines could be applied to wealth-getting. As a name, New Thought was adopted around the middle of the 1890s, and after that it came to designate more and more the religious mental healing movement outside of Christian Science.

The movement spread from its birthplace in Boston to gatherings with an independent origin in the larger metropolitan areas of the Middle and Far West. It gathered strength in auditoriums, halls, and theaters, study clubs, mothers' meetings, and training classes, in centers and circles, and in magazines with a brief and extended existence. It was a woman's kind of religion. As the movement swept toward the Middle and Far West, many of the pioneer workers were women, while after 1890 there were probably more leaders among women than men. Unlike most religions in America, New Thought did not discriminate against the ladies, but offered them responsible positions of leadership. It was, too, such a downy way to achieve your heart's desire, and it offered such wonderful rewards. Chortled Effie (Barnhurst) Kaemmerling: "Not for anything that could be offered me would I go back to what I was two months ago. The one fault I can find is that my throat and chest have so rounded out that my clothes no longer fit." [14]

After the first flutterings of excitement at organizing for the Truth, there followed the inevitable decline in some centers. That was the time for vigorous action. Miss Leila Simon reported the deplorable situation in Cincinnati in 1912, and what she did about it: "I found the New Thought Temple Society struggling along without a leader, disorganized, inharmonious, with forty-seven members on the roster, about one half of which were active. They were without adequate funds, and found difficulty in paying the small expense of $30.00 per month rent for a hall for Sunday services. . . . New Thought in Cincinnati had neither recognition nor standing in the community. It was thought to consist of long-haired men and short-haired women; who were queer, erratic, crazy folk. Today we have nine hundred members, call out an audience of fifteen hundred, own property amounting to $26,000.00, besides having more than $3,500.00 in the bank. We have gained the respect of all Cincinnati, and number among our members the most cultivated and prominent men and women of the city." [15]

After the organization of local groups came the conventions which began to meet annually in typical American style. In 1915 the first Congress of the International New Thought Alliance met to recognize in name what already had existed in fact. Two years later the leaders moved toward greater unanimity as they hammered out a Declaration of Principles which affirmed, among things, that "he who trusts in the divine return, has learned the law of success." American leaders stumped foreign lands to further the cause, and their books were translated into foreign languages. As a principle, rather than denomination or sect, the movement spread in strength to England, France, Australia, and other nations. In England the history of the movement's popularity did not differ essentially from its development in the United States, except that it was known as the Higher Thought. Christian Science first kindled interest among the public, then individuals and groups drifted apart to set up their own independent branches.[16]

In London during World War I, a consulting engineer turned therapeutist was telling Her Majesty's soldiers that "there is no limit to this apparent effect of thought. If you are certain enough that you are dead, you are dead instantly. . . ." The Happy Thought Coffee House of Honolulu, Hawaii, with a touch of the Social Gospel unnatural for this religion, was providing refreshing meals and baths for human derelicts and spiritual sustenance in the form of New Thought literature. The volunteers working in the Happy Thought Coffee House would no doubt have agreed with the International New Thought Alliance, though it is doubtful if their indigent guests did, that "thought is the most powerful force in the world. It constructs all cities, all works of art, all machinery, all invention, all institutions and all states. . . . It literally builds the body, molds the features, forms the character, controls the health, shapes the circumstances, and makes the fortune and the happiness or unhappiness of the individual." [17]

There were critics standing at the ready to puncture New Thought's soaring balloon of metaphysical semantics. Years of practice slashing at the Christian Scientists had honed a sharp edge to their knives. They hacked away mostly at the medicine men of drugless healing, but took their cuts, too, at the success wing—calling the whole business and its purveyors "absent treatment quacks," "metaphysical hash," "commercial cunning," "intensely ignorant," "inordinately egotistic," "medieval magic and miracle mongering," "the spook of the middle ages ludicrously gibbering." Many doctors were willing to admit that mental therapeutics could help in the cure of functional neuroses and nervous disorders, but would have balked at the report of one observer: "Twenty years ago I heard Mrs. Julius Dresser, the mother of Horatio, say, at a public meeting, that 'through the power of thought even nails may be digested and poisons swallowed with impunity.' " After the poor fellow had clogged his intestines with nails and the poison had eaten into his stomach, what then? A properly instructed New Thoughter would point out that the poor fellow did not hold the appropriate thought with sufficient clarity and tenacity.[18]

When the United States Government finally took action, relying on a source of power more tangible than mind, a tidal wave of fear thoughts must have flooded through the world of mental therapy. It was a tidal wave which wrecked Helen Wilmans' New Thought paradise at Sea Breeze on Florida's east coast. Helen Wilmans was a forceful, energetic woman who probably saw in the power of the mind a way to even up the score with the physical supremacy of the male. It worked, at least, on her landlord in the days before she founded her lucrative courses in "mental science." Having just quit her newspaper job, Helen Wilmans tells us that in a blush of freedom, she dashed off an article on the subject of "I." The landlord, whose usually sodden face had recently appeared on an errand about her rent-paying potential, read "I" and then, suddenly, his face became "illuminated, and for the moment actually beautiful." "I" did more than lift the landlord's face; "I" opened the landlord's pocketbook. He offered to lend his tenant $20,000 to start her own newspaper.[19]

Everything was balmy at Sea Breeze, Florida, as Helen Wilmans grew rich from the sales of *A Conquest of Poverty,* a buck-up autobiographical account of how she did it. What wrecked everything were her correspondence courses of absent treatment. "Have you not heard that through the power of *right thinking* you can be healed of every form of disease whether it be physical or mental?" she advertised. "This is a fact, and you can be healed in your own homes while the healer is hundreds of miles away. Distance is no hindrance to thought. . . . It [thought] goes from the brain of the healer to the brain of the patient and corrects the error existing there, so that the patient gets well." The United States Government was not impressed. It indicted Helen Wilmans for fraudulent use of the mails. The

Supreme Court later reversed the decision, but it was too late. She died impoverished, her spirit broken, her business ruined.[20]

It takes an initiate to pick his way through the metaphysical fog which often surrounds New Thought's sunshine philosophy. Since New Thought is not a denomination or an organization, but a body of affiliated believers, there is a natural urge towards theological diversity. This diversity is increased, not only by the freedom of every believer to shape his own opinions, but also by the continual reexamination of New Thought in the light of sympathetic philosophies. The following represents at least a solid core of agreed fundamentals.

New Thought begins with a Principle of Being in the universe. The Principle, or God, is present everywhere and in everything, all-powerful and all-wise. It is non-material and absolutely unlimited. This Principle is Pure Spirit. And the essence of Spirit is Mind. Therefore, the Principle is Universal Mind. Its substance and power is mental. Since the Principle is all-powerful, present everywhere, and all-wise, and because It is Mind, then everything everywhere is Mind. Since nothing exists but this One Principle, then man must necessarily be an emanation, expression, or manifestation of this One Principle. Like the Principle, whose power is mental, the only real power of man must be mind power. Therefore, every individual's power is determined by his ability to express this indwelling power of the mind.

How is it possible for this theology to assure us health, happiness, and prosperity? Since every individual's power is his ability to express this indwelling power of the mind, then what we are is determined by our mental attitudes. Our character, our health, our degree of success is determined by the thoughts we hold in our minds. Therefore, thinking the proper thoughts, using the divine power of our minds will result in the realization of our desires.

New Thought did not stop at defining the relation of man to his God and to himself. Like all religions, it defined the relation of man to his fellow man and to the universe. Since we all are expressions and manifestations of the One Principle, then we are not separate one from another but all One Substance, One Spirit, One Mind. The knowledge of this creates love in our hearts for one another. The Golden Rule then becomes—do unto your neighbor *not* as you would have him do unto you, but as you would do unto yourself, because your neighbor is yourself as part of the One Principle, the one whole in life. A hopeful, optimistic religion, New Thought capped its philosophy by seeing man as the result of God's evolutionary method of creation. Man is ever looking upward, onward, and forward to a higher stage of spiritual evolution in which the Divine Essence is continually unfolding within himself. Since man's soul is one with the Principle, it must live on after death because spirit is indestructible.[21]

Perhaps this faith will be clearer by comparing it to certain doctrines of more orthodox Christianity. New Thought denies the duality of man and God or the need for a priestly intermediary, because God and man are one. The vicarious atonement of Jesus Christ is unnecessary, because the only separation of man from God could be in thought. Further, New Thought contends that the allegory of Adam and Eve and the apple is false in meaning. God could never have condemned man for seeking to be wise, that is, for seeking to be more like God.[22]

The guilt-filled agony of moral struggle which racked the character ethic dissolves under the warmth of New Thought's philosophical sunbeams. The depravity of man in his original sin is replaced by natural goodness and infinite perfectibility. The doctrine of grace is not earned as a gift from God, but is a birthright and a natural heritage. Godlets are we! All we must do is to plug into the divine power plant and our bodies will refresh themselves with health, our lives bubble over with happiness, and our pocketbooks expand with the plumper paychecks of success.

Prentice Mulford began to express the possibilities in the 1880s. If the power of thought could make you healthy, why couldn't it make you rich? Earlier New Thought leaders had pointed the way, but Mulford was the pivot who swung mind power to success. He was the first writer of popularity and influence to promise the world, in a large part of his works, that "TO THINK SUCCESS BRINGS SUCCESS."

"Your every thought is a force, as real as a current of electricity is a force," he declared. "Set the magnetic power of your mind persistently in the desire and *demand* of the best of every thing; and the best will, by an inevitable and unerring law, eventually come to you." Mulford liked to fill the bottom of his pages with sharp reminders in bold letters that "THOUGHT IS FORCE," "GOD COMMANDS. MAN DEMANDS." (Indeed, the presence of mind is so powerful, so omnipresent, that "CLOTHING ABSORBS THOUGHT.") He popularized the slogan that "THOUGHTS ARE THINGS" with the power of bringing to you a comfortable house, a splendid coach with four fine bays, and servants to erase the grime of life. Though a pioneer in this phase of the success idea, he was never able to tune up his thoughts with sufficient force to win the luxuries of life for himself.[23]

Prentice Mulford was always a pioneer, but the kind that set out on one trail and soon shifted to another. He was born at Sag Harbor on Long Island in 1834 and died mysteriously in a small boat in Sheepshead Bay, Long Island, in 1891. Between the beginning and the end he lived a life that got to know about life. By the time he had reached the age of twenty-one, Mulford had failed in more jobs than most inhabitants of Skid Row manage in a lifetime. He then moved his base of operations 3000 miles to San Francisco by shipping out of New York on the clipper *Wizard*. When the *Wizard* at last nosed through the fog and slipped past the Golden Gate, the Captain was prepared to venture the opinion that Mulford's nautical abilities were considerably less than sufficient. It was an old story to the Sag Harbor boy now stranded in California. He began a life of drifting from job to job. As the cook for a whaling vessel out of San Francisco, he tortured the crew with one particular culinary atrocity of an "involuntary meat pie" produced by a mouse that fell into the biscuit dough. He drifted inland, lured by the gold fields, and ended up teaching school in a little church six hours a day to sixty children ranging from four to eighteen years of age. The copper fever seized him, then silver, but there was more fever than silver, and soon he was reduced to digging post-holes for a living.

At the age of thirty-one he finally hit upon his life's work as a comic lecturer, essayist, and journalist. During the late 1860s he joined that sharp-witted group of frontier humorists around San Francisco, which included, at various times, Mark Twain, Bret Harte, Ambrose Bierce, and Joaquin Miller. Mulford's delight was in puncturing the inflated elegance of life as portrayed in Eastern novels. And he was already taking his cuts at the character ethic's worship of hard work as a means to success. "The physical degeneracy of a portion of the American people is owing to an excess of industry," he ventured the heresy. "They have been overdosed by such maxims as—

> *Early to bed and early to rise,*
> *Makes a man healthy, wealthy and wise....*

My friends term me lazy. That does not trouble me. I laugh as I behold them rushing by, wearing out body and soul in the chase after dollars.... Therefore, as long as I can afford it, I shall choose the better part and be lazy." [24]

After sixteen dizzy, eccentric years in California, Mulford left a small heritage of sparkling frontier humor and set off for Europe on a trip financed by San Francisco businessmen. The purpose of the visit was "to advance by writing and talking the good and glory of California." It is true that Mulford returned to America with an English bride and nine dollars, but certain details in the story of his marriage are not established fact. It is rumored that Mulford's friend, Joaquin Miller, then in England, found Josie Allen, a girl with wistful eyes and soft, dark curls, starving on the London streets, that Mulford was enchanted by her and proceeded to play Henry Higgins to Josie's Eliza Doolittle, that some years after they returned to America, Josie became disenchanted with her husband's scanty income as a columnist on the New York *Daily Graphic,* and fell back into an old practice of posing in the nude for pin money. It is rumored also that the shock which helped Mulford to agree to a separation came when he innocently viewed her picture on the back of a pack of cigarettes.

After almost six years of trying to condense the local news of the day into one column, he became fed up with the eternal round of scandals, crimes, and accidents—the horrors of civilization that make news—and decided to make another break. In 1883 he built a small cabin in the New Jersey woods seventeen miles from New York City and settled down in Thoreauean isolation to recuperate and write. Out of this experience, and a stay in New England where he went to refresh himself at the Bostonian fountains of New Thought, came the published fruits of a philosophy which had intrigued him for years. The pamphlets he issued between 1886 and 1892 were bound together into six volumes under the title *Your Forces and How to Use Them*. They stand as the first solid emphasis on the achievement of success by mind power.

The pamphlets say a lot about Prentice Mulford—and the kind of people to whom New Thought appealed. He was a man not given to exaltations about the dignity of labor. He was quiet, shy—abnormally shy—with sores of self-depreciation which festered with every failure. He simply could not assert himself. "I was called modest and retiring," he reminisced. "That was not it at all. I was cowardly, and thought almost every one I met who had a pretentious air was in some way to me unknown my superior." And yet he always had a great faith in his destiny, so he kept battling away at the insecurities, the fears, and the torments of inferiority. Like so many others from that day to this, he finally saw them all dissolve under the bright, cheery sunshine of New Thought.[25]

It was all simply a matter of law in the Mulfordian philosophy. "Success in any business or undertaking comes through the working of a law," he promised from his cabin in the New Jersey woods. "It never comes by chance. . . . You can, as you find out the law, make of yourself whatever you please." Like a tree which sheds its leaves or a bird its plumage, the first thing you must do is shake off your old thoughts. Striking at centuries of tradition, Mulford questioned the simple virtues of industry and frugality and denied that poverty was a training ground for the aspiring. But he did hold firmly to Ben Franklin's advice that 'honesty is the best policy.' Trickery and deceit can only lead to a diseased mind and body.[26]

Where is the key to unlock the treasure house? It is not in one's character, as centuries of success writers have insisted, but in thought. "Your thought is an invisible substance, as real as air, water, or metal. It acts apart from your body; it goes from you to others, far and near; it acts on them, moves and influences them. It does this whether your body be sleeping or waking. This is your real power. As you learn how this power really acts; as you learn how to hold, use, and control it,—you will do more profitable business, and accomplish more in an hour than now you may do in a week. . . . The mind is a magnet. It has the power, first of attracting thought, and next of sending that thought out again. . . . What kind of thought you most charge that magnet (your mind) with, or set it open to receive, it will attract most of that kind to you. If, then, you think, or keep most in mind, the mere thought of determination, hope, cheerfulness, strength, force, power, justice, gentleness, order, and precision, you will attract and receive more and more of such thought-elements. These are among the elements of success." [27]

On the other hand, "if you are thinking most of the time discouragement or anger, or any form of ill-temper, you are sending hundreds and thousands of miles away from your body this thought-element of discouragement, hopelessness, or anger, literally a part of your unseen self. It attracts, meets and mingles with the same thought-element similarly sent out by others (parts of such people). So it attracts you to them, your partners in misery. You hurt each other's health and fortune. A thought attracts thought of like kind. . . . Keep in mind the idea of force, 'go-ahead,' push, and you attract to you in element that which gives you force, push, and go-ahead." [28]

Mulford promised his readers that "to think persistent resolve, to think persistent push in your one aim and purpose,—to simply think it, and do nothing else,—will create for you a power as certain to move and effect results as the jackscrews placed under the heaviest building will move it upward. The power you so create of your mind and of unseen forces will work while you sleep. It will bring to you new devices, plans, and methods for moving your business forward. . . . The world pays best those who push." [29]

Mulford was firm about specific elements in the law. "There is possible a state of mind which, if permanently kept, will draw to you money, lands, possessions, luxuries, health and happiness." To gain this state of mind you must transport yourself into a mood of serenity, repose, and calm determination. If you start getting anxious, impatient, or angry about the thing, it won't work. However, if you feel the need of something, you increase the force of your demand for it. "A great deal of drawing power is set upon the thing demanded when you say, 'I demand this special thing because I need it; because it is right I should have it; because I feel that my ability to benefit first, myself, and next others will be increased by it.' " [30]

You must love your business, seek to manage it yourself with full responsibility, and exude confidence. Do not ignore your wife's intuitions and suggestions, for "the feminine eye, which, if rightly used and trained, will always see in advance farther than the masculine. . . ." Do not talk over your business secrets, or even think about them with any force, in a situation where your competitors may tune in on your thoughts. Above all, avoid failures. They can infect you with their diseased thoughts about poverty.[31]

The same power that enabled Christ to work miracles, "that same power exists in embryo in every mind or spirit. It can be, and is to-day, exercised in different channels. It brings to those who exercise it, though perhaps unconsciously, results in money and possessions. It does not work so quickly as with Christ. The results come more slowly; but the power which brings millions to Jay Gould is a spiritual power, a power working apart and often far from his body, and a power, which, like fire or electricity, unless used with the highest motive and for the good of all, will *certainly,* in time, bring great injury to those using it, either on this or the unseen side of their lives." [32]

Finally, the source of all our power in the means to success is "The Great Supreme Power, the Spirit of Infinite Good. . . . This Power will respond to every demand we make upon it.

For we are parts of it—parts of an Infinite life, and as you . . .
recognize . . . your relationship to the Supreme Power, you will
come to know that yours is the right to demand as much as
possible of this Supreme or Divine Power to be expressed through
you." [33]

What is the justification for success? Mulford did not tiptoe
around the issue. "There is no merit in being poor or in desiring
to be poor," he urged the hesitant, and gratified the successful.
"It is right and necessary that you should have the very best
of all this world's goods—of clothing, food, house, surroundings, amusements, and all of which you are appreciative; and
you should aspire to these things." To live a narrow, cramped,
and starved life is degrading. [34]

The stewardship of wealth doctrine was not Mulford's justification for success. He warned that it is a dangerous offense to
hoard money, not so much because the money should be given
away to help others, but because the purpose of wealth is to
provide the comforts, luxuries, and pleasures of life. What is
'true success'? 'True success' is the enjoyment of what success
brings you in terms of material possessions. "I mean by a 'one-
sided success' that success which gains wealth at the expense of
health," he explained, "and in its absorption for money getting
only, loses nearly all capacity to enjoy what money can bring."
You benefit too by spending, because it puts you in the proper
frame of mind for further acquisitions. [35]

Bizarre, even for New Thought, was Mulford's belief in a
series of reincarnations and "ghosts" who wander about after
shuffling off the mortal coil. The miser's parsimony would torment him beyond the grave, because he would see the wealth
he longed to possess before him, but could exercise no control
over it.

Mulford expressed enough additional heresies to chill a good
Calvinist as he contrived further reverse twists on the character
ethic's justification for success. Christ said: "It is more blessed
to give than to receive." Mulford pleaded that Christ's message
had been misinterpreted. It is not "more blessed to give than
to receive," Mulford insisted, and it most certainly is not better
for you as a person to do so. It is a sin and there is a penalty for

giving without a just return. It is a *sin* because you are encouraging another person to be selfish, you are preventing "another God or Goddess from maturing"; it is a *penalty* because the thoughts which could make you rich are sucked out of you by leeches whose only return is weakness. On the other side, it is just as bad to take and not give the same measure in return.[36]

This is "the law of justice and compensation," that you will injure yourself if you do a service to another without receiving its value in return. "The highest motive comes of the desire to benefit first ourselves in order to benefit others. . . . For it is a law of nature that you cannot be really and permanently benefited yourself without benefiting others." In short, by the law of compensation, we are justified in taking all we can sensibly and honestly. In giving, we should release our thoughts and material possessions only in proportion to a just return.[37]

"Undoubtedly to some the idea of giving so much love to self will seem very cold, hard and unmerciful," Mulford admitted in an idea different in spirit, but reminiscent of Adam Smith's 'invisible hand.' "Still this matter may be seen in a different light, when we find that 'looking out for Number One' as directed by the Infinite is really looking out for Number Two and is indeed the only way for permanently benefiting Number Two." [38]

But there was one terrifying final problem. In praying, Mulford's advice was to "demand" wisdom from the Supreme Power to know what to ask for. Then you should "ask imperiously but ask in a willing mood for what the Supreme Power sees best for you." But suppose we will not defer to the Supreme Power and pray in this manner: " ' I want what I demand anyway, I defer to no higher wisdom; I don't care if what I want is an injustice to others or not. . . .' " What then? Who controls the power? Is the Supreme Power merely a gigantic pipe organ on which anyone who learns the technique of silent demand can play his own tune, or can the Supreme Power call the tune? Who is the *real* God—man or the Supreme Power? In all his hours of contemplation, Mulford never emerged with a consistently decisive answer, though in his zeal for man's exaltation he often sounded as if anyone with the proper method could demand whatever he wished and receive it. He was positive, however, that if a demand were made over the wishes of the Supreme Power, and answered, it would prove to be a curse, not a blessing.[39]

The *New York Times* front-paged Prentice Mulford's mysterious death in 1891 and noted that he was "well known in the newspaper world from this city to San Francisco." It must have been a mystery to his California friends why he switched from deflating man's pomposity by satirical jabs to inflating man's ego by New Thought metaphysics. But here was one way, was it not, for Mulford, and countless others, to smother their insecurities, their fears, and their uncontrollable urges towards self-depreciation? With the cooperation of the Supreme Power, they were finding their natural birthright of health, happiness, and prosperity. And if we can take him at his ghostly word of reincarnation, Prentice Mulford is no doubt at this very moment standing by New Thought success writers throughout the nation, clucking to them like some mother hen, as they carry on in that great tradition in which he was first, and for a popular and influential time, foremost.[40]

10

"POVERTY IS A MENTAL DISEASE. . . ."

New Thought was flourishing in the 1900s and 1910s. A variety of popular writers were experimenting with the "new" way to riches and were flooding the market with books, pamphlets, and magazine articles which promised wealth, as well as health. During these years it was a great *coup* for New Thought when it captured one of America's most famous advisers on success in life. Orison Swett Marden, editor of *Success* magazine, author of over forty-five books on the subject, presents us with one of the most interesting intellectual challenges in the entire history of the success idea.[1]

Marden published his first book on the subject of success in 1894. Contrary to most references to Marden, he was a bitter critic of material success in this book, and in many books that followed. It was not until New Thought began to seep into his writings in the mid-1900s that he can be considered a success writer, i.e., a writer who establishes general principles for the accumulation of wealth. Until New Thought exerted its impact, Marden wrote books reflecting a pure character ethic—except that the goal of hard work and perseverance was not money, but the 'true success' of character. If anything, Marden was a 'true success' writer when he advocated character as the means. He was a maverick from the literary tradition of material success in which he is frequently, and incorrectly, placed as an important spokesman.

Orison Swett Marden could not have struggled through a more dramatic early life if he had invented it. The only blemish marring an otherwise fine success story background was the deficiency of a good mother. She died when he was three years old. Despite the absence of this asset, his life, at least until his early forties, does make an inspiring story of a man of action determined to improve himself and to rise in the world.

He was born in 1850 into the hard land and harsh winters of New Hampshire, just across the valley from the great Stone Face of the White Mountains. After his mother's death, his father, a big, strong fellow, was determined to keep his three children together. He forced a living from the soil, hunted and trapped the abundance of game in the forest, went without a "hired girl" to save money, and did all the housework, cooking, and the making of clothes for his family. One day in the woods he accidently sprang a tree-trap heavy enough to crush a large bear. In constant pain from the injury, he continued the fight to provide for his family until death mercifully relieved him from the struggle.

Young Orison was seven years old when his father died. In the hands of a guardian who turned out to be both unkind and unjust, he was soon "bound out" to work until he had finally served five different families in the backwoods of New Hampshire. The first family considered him an outsider. The daughters were permitted the privilege of taunting and abusing the "hired boy," while the parents whipped him upon the slightest provocation. From the humiliation of this existence he moved to the gloom of a Baptist minister's farm in Woodstock. In Elder Strong's childless parsonage, young Orison had no friends his own age to play with, never had enough to eat, and worked from twelve to fourteen hours a day.

It was Orison's bad fortune to relive a similar story through five successive families—days of toil, nights of loneliness, intermittent schooling, abuse and insults. In the Baptist church there was no solace. The theology of the 1850s and 1860s frightened and repelled him—a factor which helped to convert him, as so many others his own age, to New Thought in later years. Jonathan Edwards' terrifying images of humans as loathsome spiders eternally sizzling in the hands of an angry God over the fires of Hell, Marden defiantly recalled, "was the sort of sermon I used to hear every Sunday when I was a boy. Ministers felt it was their duty to picture in the most frightful manner possible the horrors of eternal punishment. Those terrible pictures of the 'lake of fire' in which 'lost souls' suffered tortures forever and forever with no respite, without hope of redemption, were burned into my very soul. Many a night, for years, I would cry myself to sleep for fear that I had committed the unpardonable sin, and that I, too, might burn in hell for all eternity." [2]

Convinced that a heavy chain of unjust abuses was strangling his opportunities for self-improvement, the fourteen-year-old-boy finally decided to make a break. One Sunday he stole away from church after the morning sermon, gathered together a few personal belongings, and hit the open road. His hopes were soaring and the future seemed limitless. The limitless future soon began to blur into an endless round of chores at the saw mill where he found employment. Nursing his freezing feet in the attic, Orison read during odd moments whatever he could lay his hands on. Then, suddenly, he chanced upon a book which reinforced his determination for self-improvement. Samuel Smiles' *Self-Help,* Britain's big nineteenth-century success book, "was a perpetual delight to me," Marden fondly remembered in words frequently applied by others to his own works, "and I treasured it as if it were worth its weight in diamonds, reading and re-reading the precious pages until I had almost committed them to memory." [3]

Self-Help kindled in Orison two ambitions. He was getting nowhere in an isolated, narrow environment. "The stories of poor boys climbing to the top so thrilled and inspired me that I then and there resolved to get out of the woods—to get an education at any cost—and to make something of myself!" The book also "filled me with the hope that some day, perhaps, I might be able to do something that would stimulate and encourage poor American boys like myself to develop and make the most of all the powers God had given them. In fact, I even then conceived the bold idea that I might in the future write something that would help others!" [4]

The race to the top began with education. Before he finished, the race had become an educational marathon, the more exhausting because he worked his way through every institution. He started by persuading his guardian to send him to a New Hampshire preparatory school for one term. With an Horatio Alger, Jr., twist, he gained the support of General Luther McCutchins, known for his kindness to boys working their way through school, who also gave him a job in the summer. Emerging from the New Hampshire wilderness, Orison struggled to keep up with the more advanced and polished students at two private schools, started his own successful school for younger children during one year, and then during another, managed to force into line a group of boys who had carried their previous teacher out of the schoolhouse and even intimidated him with pistols. (He was engaged not "to teach books, but to keep order.") A genial, cheerful fellow with an entrepreneurial flair, Marden helped to pay his way through school by running a barber shop (a tonsorial massacre for his first customers), and during the summer by serving in a hotel, an experience he drew upon the following year to start the first of his popular student eating clubs.[5]

At the age of twenty-three he moved into higher education and began collecting academic degrees with a passion. After a year at Andover Theological Seminary, he switched to Boston University and by the age of thirty-two had been awarded the following academic accolades: a Bachelor's degree from Boston University (1877); a Bachelor of Oratory and a Master's degree from Boston University (1879); an M.D. from the Harvard Medical School (1881) and an LL.B from Boston University's Law School (1882). Doing double duty academic work did not interfere with his income. By the end of his college years at Boston, he had saved nearly $20,000. It was enough to send him on an extensive continental tour of Europe with sufficient capital left over to get down to the business at hand.

By 1892 the orphan boy from the New Hampshire mountains had risen to the rank of hotel magnate. At one time four hotels in three different states were under his control. Drawn by the Nebraska boom in the early 1890s, he invested heavily in real estate at Kearney. Well, it seemed like there just wasn't anything that could stop "Lucky Marden," a nickname his classmates had begun to call him at Boston University—except bad luck.

It all came at the same time. A succession of disasters struck like sledgehammers. The disasters began with a persistent drought which dried up the farm land of Nebraska and shriveled the fortunes of her citizens. One of his important hotels burned to the ground and with it over five thousand pages of manuscript into which the prosperous entrepreneur had been pouring his thoughts on success. The people from Kearney and businessmen from Omaha raised $8,000 to persuade him to stay on, but the financial cyclone that started whirling in Kearney seemed bent on destroying him. A hotel off the coast of Florida which he partly owned had been reduced to ashes, and not long afterwards cyclone Marden swept across the continent to Block Island where fire destroyed some four or five hundred bathing houses. The next season five cases of smallpox were sufficient to quarantine the hotel. In 1893 the sometime hotel magnate managed Chicago's Park Gate Hotel during the Columbian Exposition, and then, heavily in debt from the series of disasters, he decided to call it quits.

A crackerjack hotel man, Marden had overextended himself in a boom period and been hit simultaneously by a depression and, ironically, by hard luck. Perhaps there is some truth in what his old friend, Frank Munsey, prophesied: "If Doctor Marden had not written his first book he would have been a millionaire. He had a genius for hotel making." Unlucky Marden might well have accumulated sufficient capital as a popular and efficient manager of hotels to gain ownership and build his fortune once again. But Marden had been nursing for thirty years the dream of a fourteen-year-old boy. He wanted to become the Samuel Smiles of America.[6]

Deeply in debt, he carried his dream to Boston, ignored the paradox of writing about success after he had failed, and polished off the manuscript he had rewritten since the disastrous fire at Kearney. Perhaps he was more competent to write it now, for he had run the ladder of fortune in both directions during his forty-four years of struggle and hard work. Houghton-

Mifflin made Marden's dream of some thirty years come to life in 1894. They never regretted it. *Pushing to the Front: Or, Success Under Difficulties* got off to a fast start with twelve printings the first year and kept on going. Of over forty-five books, large and small, which Marden later published, none was ever so popular. It has been translated into some twenty-five languages. By the mid-1920s nearly one million copies had been sold in Japan alone. "Among ourselves we often call it the Japanese Bible," a visitor told one American and added a surprising comment on the Russo-Japanese War of 1904–1905, "Didn't you know that it was that book which gave us the courage to resist the Russian encroachments?" [7]

In the United States the response to Marden's works was enthusiastic. President McKinley said of *Pushing to the Front* "It cannot but be an inspiration to every boy or girl who reads it, and who is possessed of an honorable and high ambition." Judge Ben Lindsey of Denver's Juvenile Court confessed: "I have been inspired, cheered, encouraged, helped, and uplifted, as, I am sure, thousands of others have been by your gospel and your message. What a joy it must be to know how you have helped, cheered, and encouraged others! I always keep your books on my desk in the court room." From homes to libraries, court rooms to class rooms, Marden was considered a force for good. Educators, usually no friends of materialism, were particularly enthusiastic rooters, and for a reason, as we shall soon see.[8]

Bringing order out of the chaos of Marden's works reveals one of the most interesting stories in the history of the success idea. His massive production must be considered as it evolved, for in the early years of his literary life he was as heretical, in his own way, as Andrew Carnegie. The story begins with *Pushing to the Front* in 1894, a good example of his works to the middle of the 1900s.

The author's zest for his subject radiates from every page of *Pushing to the Front*. Ranging over the whole history of Western Civilization from the Greeks to Stephen Girard, Marden buttressed his message with concrete biographical evidence. "The world is hungry for life, more life," he once lectured to young writers, "it is interested in realities, in human experiences, in human struggles. There is nothing that interests man like man. . . ." He could personify any abstract idea with endless anecdotes borrowed from other success writers, and from the biographies of the great and famous. Marden's mind brimmed with examples which would have been the envy of, as he was the heir to the fame of, William Makepeace Thayer, then moving toward the sunset of his career.[9]

Part of Marden's philosophy was solidly within the gospel of the character ethic. Opportunities were abundant, to be born into poverty was a blessing, unremitting toil and perseverance were the keys to achievement, and rarely does luck play a part.[10]

The balance of Marden's advice, rather than standard success fare, is actually a criticism of important elements in the character ethic. He sometimes embraced Social Darwinism. The competitive struggle for existence, he ventured the heresy, is a warning that "as a rule every great success in the money world means the failure and misery of hundreds of antagonists." [11]

If this was heresy, his attitude toward the success goal was grounds for excommunication. Success writers usually defined 'true success' in non-materialistic terms and then went on to blast money-making *if* it became the sole end in life. When these obligations had been fulfilled, they got down to the business at hand—how to make money and the justification for it. Not Marden. IIe did illustrate with biographical anecdotes how hard work and perseverance could lead to a higher salary. But that was not his primary purpose. He kept trying to prove that "a great check-book can never make a great man . . . that he who would grasp the key to power must be greater than his calling, and resist the vulgar prosperity that retrogrades toward barbarism; that there is something greater than wealth, grander than fame; that *character is success,* and *there is no other.*" There was only one success and that was "true success." [12]

Marden agreed with most success writers that avarice was the real threat to character. There is, of course, nothing inherently sinful in riches by themselves. But he questioned whether it was possible for anyone to pile up wealth and not be avaricious. "Christ, who said to his disciples, 'Verily I say unto you, that a rich man shall hardly enter into the Kingdom of Heaven,' well understood the moral degeneracy that almost inevitably attends the struggle for great wealth. Somehow, in spite of many examples to the contrary, the race for thousands, and then millions, often strangles nobility of character and tarnishes the soul of honor." It was this continual hammering at the almost inevitable moral degeneracy of the struggle for wealth which places Marden outside the ranks of America's success writers in the early years of his literary life. And he meant what he said. One test of his sincerity is that he offered no justification for the accumulation of wealth.[13]

The productive years from *Pushing to the Front* in 1894 to the middle of the 1900s saw a reworking and elaboration of the message Marden felt himself destined to tell the world.[14] He held consistently to character as the means to achievement and virtually ignored any justification for the accumulation of wealth.[15] Often forced into the position of measuring achievement in the business world, he softened his blows against materialism and spoke with greater affection of higher salaries. After sending his reporters out for heart-to-heart talks with the nation's great men, he charitably concluded that it was not the goal which spurred on successful men, but "the pleasurable exercise of the chase." [16] Occasionally, in certain books, he would go along with the success tradition and assure his readers that "it is no sin to be rich, nor to wish to be rich; the mistake is in being too eager after riches." More frequently, he would bitterly assail even the wish to be rich as too dangerous. In every case, a bigger salary in itself was only one way of developing the highest ideal—a strong, virtuous character.[17]

After ten years of it, when the city editor was ready to shout: "What we need around this place are some new clichés," Marden pulled a switch. The switch in his whole concept of the success idea was triggered by New Thought. It occurred in the middle of the 1900s.

Some ten years before this shift in his thinking, however, Marden had come to a decision. Letters were pouring in expressing appreciation for the inspiration of *Pushing to the Front*.

What his message needed was the circulation of a magazine. Though his books were selling, he was still heavily in debt and trying to squeeze enough money out of the royalties to stay alive and purchase control of the plates of his first bonanza with Houghton Mifflin. After two years of badgering possible supporters of the magazine, he finally persuaded Louis Klopsch, publisher of New York's *Christian Herald*, to put up the capital with Klopsch retaining the controlling shares of stock. The magazine's name was to be just one word. *Success*, self-made at last in 1897, had its credo. It was to stand for "the only real success in life—the complete development of the man, of the woman, that God made, for service to mankind, and for making a life as well as making a living." [18]

While "the Doctor," as he was affectionately called around the office, was electrifying his staff with the wonderful opportunities in life, *Success* went on to top a 300,000 circulation and a staff of 200 employees. "The Doctor" worked out a plan for triple remuneration. He placed his editorials in the magazine, reworked them into book form, and then had them published by a house set up for that purpose in which he owned a large share. To replenish his storehouse of biographical anecdotes, he sent his reporters out to interview the great and famous, printed them in the magazine under the reporter's by-line, and then edited them into book form, frequently without proper acknowledgment. Theodore Dreiser was a favorite free-lance reporter. Not long after knocking out inspirational interviews for Marden in order to eat, Dreiser settled down to write *Sister Carrie*—a novel about the heartbreaking descent of a man into failure and the rise of his wife to fame.[19]

At the peak of his magazine's popularity in 1905, the hustling editor found time to fall in love. He was fifty-five; Miss Evans was just out of her teens, a slender, well-bred Kentucky girl who was studying voice in New York for the concert stage. Perhaps recalling that *"weak men wait for opportunities, strong men make them,"* Marden started "overcoming obstacles." With equal portions of grit, grip, and pluck, the love-struck editor pursued the youthful Miss Evans to Paris where he laid siege, until she at last laughingly reasserted the power of the pursued female over the pursuing male. "Well, I suppose I'll have to marry you," Miss Evans refreshed an old standby with her charm, "to get rid of you!" [20]

Settled snugly in Glen Cove, Long Island, with a wife who considered her husband "an intellectual giant," it looked as if the orphan boy from New Hampshire had finally made it. But an ill wind was blowing once again. About 1904, *Success* began running articles attacking business trusts and privileged power —articles which increased in fury over the years. The muckrakers bored from within until they seized control of the magazine, restricting Marden to the editor in charge of inspiration. *Success* had become something of a split personality. Then the attacked struck at the attackers. While the muckrakers were running articles critical of big business, a wounded banker called in the demand notes, creditors stampeded, and in 1911, *Success* failed. For the second time, Marden went down with heavy financial losses.[21]

He had to try for a comeback. Too often had the idea been expressed that the test of a man was his courage in struggling up from defeat. Following the maxim, "If at first you don't succeed, try, try again!," he kept turning out books from Glen Cove and busied himself with plans for a new magazine. Just like the crucial moment in his early education, an Alger-like gimmick turned the trick. Frederick C. Lowrey, a leading Chicago businessman, benefactor of struggling youngsters, and a strong rooter of the old magazine, put up the capital. There was to be no muckraking nonsense this time. The *New Success* was launched in 1918, and kept on going several years beyond the editor's death in 1924.

As editor of an inspirational magazine from 1897 to 1924 (except for the years from 1911 to 1918), just about every conceivable kind of literature on the subject crossed Marden's desk. He responded to it in his writings with seismographic sensitivity. But the copy which made his needle of editorial interest quiver was New Thought. As he began to associate with New Thought groups in New York, and the manuscripts on mind power flowed across his desk, more and more of his writings became saturated with the new power. Though there were earlier indications, the shift was more apparent from the middle of the 1900s. It took about ten years for New Thought to conquer Marden. From about the middle of the 1910s to his death in 1924, the greater percentage of his total writings were devoted to mind power. But at the same time he kept up a strong dissenting minority. Many books were rehashes of the character ethic, while others mixed hard work with thought power in uneven proportions.[22]

The introduction of New Thought set off a cause-effect relationship in Marden's concept of the success idea. Whenever the caress of New Thought smothered the character ethic, it ended in a kiss of death for Marden's vigorous anti-materialism. The purpose of New Thought for Marden was to make money. Naturally, with such a goal, he found himself offering a justification for material success. It was an ideological chain reaction which operated with a kind of uncanny scientific precision. The more New Thought he poured into a book, the more materialistic the content.

Marden not only indicates the impact of New Thought on the success idea; he clearly mirrors the ideology of wealth by religious mind power that New Thought writers were expressing in the first three decades of the twentieth century. Like most of his colleagues, he began with the certainty of divine law.

"Everything in man's life, everything in God's universe, is based upon principle—follows a divine law," Marden explained, "and the law of prosperity and abundance is just as definite as the law of gravitation, just as unerring as the principles of mathematics. It is a mental law. Only by thinking abundance can you realize the abundant, prosperous life that is your birthright; in other words, according to your thought will be your life, your supply, or your lack." [23]

The majority of people, he continued, are like the man who went out to water his garden, turned on the faucet, and then stepped on the hose. These people "are pinching their supply by stepping upon the hose through which plenty would come to them." [24]

The source of success power he called many names—Divine Mind, Omnipotent Source, Omnipotent One, All-Power, All

Supply, the great Fountain Head, the Creator, or simply God, though the latter, he mused, would more accurately convey the proper meaning if a second "o" were added. Shifting his images to keep in metaphorical tune with these various titles, Marden saw the tragedy of man as a failure to realize that he is made in the image of God. It is man's birthright to be like God and enjoy His powers, if man would only unite himself with the divine energy of the universe and be copartners with this creative power. "Health, abundance, success, happiness, a glorious, joyful living—these are the things the Creator intended for all his children." What you must do is "keep your supply pipes wide open by the consciousness of your oneness with the One, your connection with the All Supply." [25]

Happily, there were laws for unplugging clogged supply pipes to the Omnipotent Source. None was more supreme than the law that *"Like attracts like. . . .* It is an inevitable law, an inexorable principle, that everything attracts to itself everything else like itself. . . . The saying, 'Money attracts money,' is only another way of stating the law—'like attracts like.'. . . A Rockefeller, a Schwab, uses this law in a masterly way to amass a large fortune." [26]

How does the law of attraction work? "If you would attract success, keep your mind saturated with the success idea. . . . When you think success, when you act it, when you live it, when you talk it, when it is in your bearing, then you are attracting it." You must visualize success in your dreams, "even if you are only a humble employee, visualize yourself as the man you long to be; see yourself in the exalted position you long to attain, a man of importance and power carrying weight in your community." You must flood your mind with success thoughts, radiate success from your person. "Success is every human being's normal condition; he was made for success; he is a success machine, and to be a failure is to pervert the intention of his Creator." You must hold such positive thoughts that the vibrations from negative minds will find no response in you. Do these things and *"you can make yourself a success magnet."* [27]

The laws of divine supply, attraction, and visualization are supported by the law of affirmation. Marden advises us to emulate Walt Whitman and affirm by autosuggestion our right to wealth. "When giving a self-treatment, always get by yourself and talk to yourself in a firm, decided tone of voice, just as if you were speaking earnestly to some one else whom you wished to impress with the great importance of what you were saying. Addressing yourself by name, say: 'You are a child of God, and the being He made was never intended for the sort of weak, negative life you are leading. God made you for success, not failure. . . . You are perverting the great object of your existence by giving way to these miserable doubts of yourself, of your ability to be what you desire with all your heart to be. . . . The image of your Creator is in you; you must bring it out and exhibit it to the world. Don't disgrace your Maker by violating His image, by being everything but the magnificent success He intended you to be.' There is a tremendous achievement force, an upbuilding and strengthening power in self-assertion, in the asserting of the 'I am.' " [28]

It will help, Marden advised, to repeat daily the Twenty-third Psalm. Memorize the following lines of Ella Wheeler Wilcox, saying them to yourself with conviction:

> I am success. Though hungry, cold, ill-clad,
>   I wander for a while, I smile and say:
>   "It is but for a time—I shall be glad
>   Tomorrow, for good fortune comes my way.
>   God is my Father, He has wealth untold;
>   His wealth is mine, health, happiness and gold." [29]

The entry through which the laws of attraction and affirmation connect with the law of divine supply is our consciousness. Our conscious mind, in turn, is supported by our subconscious mind. The connection between the two should appeal to anyone so ambitious as to regret sleep's time-wasting demands. Your subconscious mind, Marden explained, "never sleeps, but is incessantly working on the suggestions it receives from the conscious or objective mind. . . . Your dreams will ultimately be expressed in your life." In Marden's means to success, you can get ahead twenty-four hours a day. By tapping the Infinite Mind with your subconscious mind, you can dream yourself into making your dreams come true. However, it is most important that you dictate the right message to your "invisible secretary." Your thoughts must be saturated "not with the things we hate and fear and worry about, but the things we long for and are striving to attain." [30]

Marden ended his advice on the techniques of success with a warning: Thought exerts an organic impact on the body. "Innumerable experiments have established the fact that all healthful, hopeful, joyous, encouraging, uplifting, optimistic, cheerful thoughts improve the cell life of the entire body. They are creative, while the opposite thoughts are destructive of cell life. . . . The brain cells are constantly bathed in the blood, from which they draw their nourishment, and when the blood is loaded with the poison of fear, worry, anger, hatred, or jealousy, the protoplasm of those delicate cells becomes hard and is thus materially injured." [31]

In summary, Marden's way to wealth was this: We connect with the law of Divine Supply, through the conscious and subconscious parts of our mind, by practicing the laws of attraction, affirmation, and visualization. In the process, we build up cells in our mind and body which help to carry us forward to success.

For some twenty years, from the mid-1900s to 1924, Orison Swett Marden switched back and forth between character and mind power as the means to success, frequently within the same book. Somehow, his favorite heroes of emulation, Charles Schwab, Thomas Edison, John Wanamaker, and Marshall Field, could be counted on to reflect either means. No amount of dexterity in this intellectual jugglery could conceal inconsistencies. But at the same time, the idea of success, no matter what the means, followed its own law of attraction by drawing to it certain logically consistent ideas. [32]

New Thought kept the success idea solidly in the conservative tradition. "There is plenty of everything all about us," Marden promised equal opportunity to all, "the great cosmic universe is packed with all sorts of beautiful, marvelous things, glorious riches, ready for our use and enjoyment." It little mattered that progressives were calling in this period for government intervention to control monopolistic restrictions on opportunity, that reformers were striking at the success idea's faith in equal opportunities for all with the new weapon of environmental determinism. Such high-brow speculations must have seemed to mind power enthusiasts poverty-saturated, negative-producing thoughts. They held aloft the rags-to-riches immigrant boy.[33]

The fault was still not in the stars but in Brutus. "Are you willing to go through life as a pigmy when there is something in you which even now is telling you that you can be a giant. . . ?" Marden asked. "Right where you are, no matter what your environment, what your disadvantages or handicaps, you have enough ability to make you a success in whatever you desire to do; to lift you out of lack and poverty and make you a millionaire." For Brutus, the pressure was still on him, only the relief this time was not more beads of sweat but more bolts of thought.[34]

The maverick days when Marden might wander from the success pack into Social Darwinism were over. "One of the most erroneous ideas that ever found entrance into the human brain is that there is not enough of everything for everybody, and that most people on the earth must be poor in order that a few may be rich. It had its origin in the pessimistic assumption that it is impossible for everybody to be wealthy or successful; in the thought of limitation of all the things which men most desire; and that, there not being enough for all, *a few must fight desperately, selfishly, for what there is,* and the shrewdest, the longest-headed, those with the most staying power, the strongest workers, will get the most of it. This theory is fatal to all individual and race betterment and it is absolutely false. The truth is, poverty is a mental disease. . . ."[35]

False, too, was that old bugaboo of all success writers. The trouble with most failures, Marden declared, is that "they waited for luck, waited for outside capital, for a boost, for influence, for a pull, for some one or something outside of them to help them. . . . Man is master of his own destiny. The power to solve his problems is right inside of him."[36]

The political implications were obvious. "Go among the very poor in the slums and you will find them always talking poverty, bewailing their fate, their hard luck, the cruelty and injustice of society. They will tell you how they are ground down by the upper classes, kept down by their greedy employers, or by an unjust order of things which they can't change. They think of themselves as victims instead of victors, as conquered instead of conquerors." [37]

If New Thought carried on the success tradition in its attitude toward opportunity and luck, it broke with that tradition on three specific points. The first break dissolved the asceticism of the character ethic. The second, challenged its ethical principles. The third, ignored the value of self-education.

The spirit of the character ethic was ascetic. It was a philosophy dripping with the sweat of drudgery and the backaches of labor, but each drop was holy, every ache blessed. The sons of rich men could never achieve the 'true success' of a strong character because they were not spurred on to earn a living. Fortunate is the lad born into the training ground of poverty and forced to fight his way out of it. "Poverty and hardship," hymned Marden, in the early years, "have ever rocked the cradles of the giants of the race. . . ." [38]

How different in its whole spirit and feeling is New Thought. The blessedness of drudgery becomes the curse of slavery; the training ground of poverty becomes a breeding ground of stingy thoughts. "I wish I could fill every youth with an utter dread and horror of it," Marden lashed out in an angry New Thought mood, "make him feel its shame, when preventable, its constraint, its bitterness, its strangling effect. . . . The Creator never made a man to be poor. There is nothing in his constitution which fits drudgery and poverty. Man was made for prosperity, happiness, and success. He was not made to suffer any more than he was made to be insane or to be a criminal. [39]

The world of the New Thought advocates is filled with sweetness and light, sugar and spice. It is all sweetmeats and sugarplums, lollipops and bonbons. You don't have to sweat and strain for necessities; just attract and affirm the luxuries. It was more than enough to sadden the stout heart of Ben Franklin's Poor Richard.

If saddened by the hedonism of New Thought's means, Poor

Richard would have been outraged by the ethics of some New Thought writers. Marden sometimes joined that group. When Poor Richard said: "Honesty is the best policy," success writers of all schools nodded agreement. Honesty was the *sine qua non* of success. But certain New Thought writers were more precise. "Now, a man's morals do not have anything specially to do with his money-making faculties," Marden shattered the personal virtues of the character ethic, "except that honesty is always and everywhere the best business policy. It is just a question of obeying the law of accumulation, the law that *like attracts like*. A very bad man may obey the law of accumulation, the law of attraction, and accumulate a vast fortune. If he is honest, his other defects and immoralities, his viciousness, will not hinder the working of the law. The law is unmoral—it is neither moral nor immoral." [40]

All success writers of the character ethic believed in the value of self-education. There was considerably less unanimity on the value of *formal* schooling, and even less on the necessity of it. However, towards the end of the nineteenth century, more and more success writers were taking the position that, if possible, it was a sensible decision to take advantage of formal training in a business college or a technical school. New Thought, on the other hand, virtually ignored education as a means to success, even self-education. Mental exercise for them was an entirely different kind of an affair. [41]

As we have seen, when Marden was working within the character ethic, he was not a representative success writer of that school. But when New Thought begins to fill his books, he becomes traditionally materialistic. Other elements of the success formula fall into place in proper balance. His anti-materialism in New Thought is a squeak, not a vigorous protest. And it is not directed against wealth itself, and its near inevitable degenerating influence, but only against the dangers of a complete absorption in money-getting. [42]

The success goal was quite simple for Benjamin Franklin and William Makepeace Thayer. The character ethic drew a clean, straight line from hard work to money. New Thought's line spiraled out from mind power to encircle not only money, but everything and anything your heart desired. "Is it a fault you wish to correct," Marden asked, "is it a talent or gift you desire to develop and improve; is it money, or friends, an education, success in any enterprise; is it contentment, peace of mind, happiness, power to serve, power in your work—whatever it is you desire, make it a bead in your rosary, pray for its accomplishment, think of it, work for its fulfillment and your desire will materialize." All you have to do is harmonize with the laws and "draw out of the unseen realms of supply whatever you will—knowledge, wisdom, power, health, wealth, happiness, success—the realization of all your hopes and visions." [43]

Humility is not a word which rests comfortably upon New Thought. It offered nirvana, not by extinguishing disturbing desires, but by satisfying them. It promised freedom from fear, anxiety, and worry. The character ethic had virtually ignored such psychological problems. In New Thought, it is not laziness or profligacy which holds people back, it is diffidence, doubts, and discouragement. "When you worry, *you maim and defraud yourself* . . . ," Marden exhorted and soothed at the same time, "worry, anxiety, lack of faith, self-depreciation, timidity, lack of self-confidence, these are all expressions of fear, and cannot exist in your mind for a moment in the presence of the courage-thought, the mental suggestion of fearlessness, self-confidence, self-reliance; the image of yourself as strong, resourceful, courageous, in touch with the infinite reservoir of divine power and energy that flows to you from your Source, the Omnipotent One, the Creator of the universe." [44]

In those early decades of the twentieth century, it was a fresh note in the idea of success; in the years after World War II, it was not quite so fresh, but very popular. Freedom from fear, worry, and anxiety equals peace of mind; peace of mind equals released powers for money-making. Joshua Loth Liebman's best-selling *Peace of Mind* in the years from 1946 to 1948 stopped at peace of mind; success writers like Norman Vincent Peale hurried on to the final materialistic equation. [45]

New Thought success writers did pause long enough at peace of mind, or what they also called happiness, to label it 'true success.' As far as we know," Marden mused, "rich people are no happier than poor people. With them it is largely a question of shifting anxiety and worry to other things." 'True success' is not the development of personal virtues, however. It is a mystical union with the All-Supply, an understanding that "our highest satisfaction, our highest enjoyment, our highest happiness, ever comes from within. Here is the fountain of all supply; here is where we touch God, the Source of all good; here is where we tap the divinity in the great within of us." [46]

In its justification for material success, New Thought joined the circumference of its philosophical circle. "Prosperity, or opulence, in the larger sense in which we use it," Marden concluded, "is everything that is good for us, an abundance of all that is beautiful, uplifting and inspiring in life. It is everything that will enrich the personality, the experience, the spiritual life." The justification for getting rich is that it lifts you out of the degradation of poverty. [47]

Orison Swett Marden bobbed along atop the currents of fashion, carried first in one direction, then in another, drifting with the strong tides in the success idea. When the tides were running strong for efficiency as a means to success in the early 1910s, he moved into a ready market with a 1913 book entitled *Training for Efficiency.*

When the American economy was on the verge of demanding a new approach, he met the need in 1921 with *Masterful Personality.* "YOU CAN COMPEL PEOPLE TO LIKE YOU!" Marden beamed. " 'It's the smile that boosts you up the ladder.' " How do you develop a masterful personality in order to win your fortune? The answer was a mingling of New Thought and a modification of the character ethic. First, catch the spirit of hustle and pep by keeping close to aggressive pushers on the way up to success. Second, practice the laws of attraction, affirmation, Divine Supply, and the mental chemistry of cell changes. Third, radiate magnetism by the law of visualization. Picture yourself as unselfish, interested in other people, gregarious, kind, generous, and tolerant. [48]

If the editor had lived on into the 1930s, he would have continued, no doubt, to fill his dictaphone daily with three to four thousand words. But his machine would not have received so naive a message as trying to change yourself. Always *au courant,* the new message would teach "applied psychology" to change, not yourself, but the other fellow's opinion of yourself.

If was apparent that the only thing capable of choking Marden's literary flow was death. With two million words of manuscript material awaiting publication, the end finally came in 1924. By that time "scores of people" had named their children after the great man. Thirty of Marden's works have been translated into both German and Spanish. "Altogether, his writings in book-form must have reached a total sale of 20,000,000 copies," H. L. Mencken mournfully estimated in 1926, "including 3,000,000 in twenty-five tongues other than English. . . . He remains today the most popular of American authors in Europe, and by immense odds. I have encountered translations of his books on the news-stands of remote towns in Spain, Poland and Czecho-Slovakia. In places where even Mark Twain is unknown—nay, even Jack London, and James Oliver Curwood—he holds aloft the banner of American literature. . . . How many false hopes he must have raised in his day!" [49]

It was in New Thought's Unity Church that his friends gathered for a memorial service to wish "the Doctor" well in the land of happier thoughts. On his arrival there, Marden may well have started to work on his plan for free "Prosperity Treatment Stations" run by the government. At the "Prosperity Treatment Stations," down-hearted Americans could recharge their tired batteries by hooking up with the Divine Dynamo. Specialists in mental chemistry would be on hand to help make contact with the All-Supply.[50]

11

"TO THINK SUCCESS
BRINGS SUCCESS"

New Thought for success was a religion of power drives. What kind of people did it appeal to? Why did it emerge at this point in American history? Mental healing was extended to wealth-getting in the late 1880s, principally through the influential work of Prentice Mulford. In 1897 Ralph Waldo Trine's *In Tune with the Infinite,* steering a dignified middle course between the extremes of mental healing and the drive to accumulate material possessions, introduced the message to a wider public. From that date, through the turn of the century and into the 1900s and 1910s, success by New Thought gained popular momentum. The forces which produced a market for this striking development in the success idea reach back into the latter part of the nineteenth century. The continuing popularity of mind power success advice throughout the twentieth century indicates that many of these causes were intensified, and augmented, in the Atomic Age until their combined pressure drove an astonishing number of people into experimenting with this theological panacea for their troubled, unhappy lives.

In the latter part of the nineteenth century many Americans endured a series of sharp blows which struck at their spiritual security. At the same time the accumulating effects of the Industrial Revolution hit America with full force. It was the linkage of these two factors—the threats to spiritual security and the impact of the Industrial Revolution—which helped propel

New Thought into a position of prominence in the history of the success idea. There were other reasons, of course—the heritage of Emerson and the Transcendentalists, the urge toward sectarian religion in America, writers who naturally flocked to a lucrative subject, the institutional assistance of the mental healing wing of New Thought, and the persistent attraction of any panacea for all troubles. But the timing of this development in the success idea would indicate that its popularity owes more to the forces which were challenging old ways of thinking and living.

The explorations of the natural sciences and the social sciences conspired to strike at old ways of *thinking* in the decades after the Civil War. Evolutionary theories, the study of comparative religions, and the disclosures of biblical scholarship challenged the certainties of the nature of the universe, the uniqueness of man, and the inerrancy of the scriptures. It was a time of dwindling faith and mounting skepticism as the scientific spirit cracked at the absolutes in which so many Americans had anchored their faith. Robbed of inherited beliefs which had brought inspiration and comfort, thousands of troubled people could no longer find solace in a God of wrath and justice, in a conception of man born automatically into sin, doomed to suffer in this world, and perhaps to roast eternally in the next.[1]

Shocks to old ways of *living* paralleled challenges to old ways of thinking. Many disruptive forces were concentrated in that crucial span of fifteen years from the mid-1880s to the turn of the century. Those years prepared an immediate market for New Thought and signaled the beginning of modern America as we know it. These forces were: a fading frontier with diminishing cheap farm land; a consolidation and concentration of the economy; a new type of immigrant from Central Europe, more difficult to assimilate into the culture; strikes, and the unequal distribution of wealth, with its envy and bitterness of class conflict; depressions which sucked the heart and spirit out of a man and scarred his wife and children; a government slow to awaken to its social responsibilities; resolute women scenting the bitter-sweet perfume of emancipation; the emergence of the United States as a world power; challenges to the family structure, the morals, and the whole institutional fabric of the nation. Added to these forces was the long-term shift in the economy and the population from an agrarian and rural to an industrial and urban society. Within the bigness and confusion of the thing, millions of bewildered people wandered in the anonymity of lonely cities. Amidst so many impersonal forces which bred fear and a lack of self-confidence, the anxious, wondering why Horatio Alger, Jr.'s, heroes could do it with even less advantages, were asking themselves: "What is wrong with me?" For them, the character ethic of hard work, perseverence, and frugality was just not the answer.[2]

The introduction of religious mind power into the success idea was not an historical accident. The above causes created needs which the character ethic left unsatisfied. In this concrete situation, the need was for an answer to a crumbling faith in the older theology, and for relief from the anxiety and the fear churning in an increasingly dislocated society.

To the challenges of science, New Thought responded with: "If you can't lick 'em, join 'em." The doctrine of evolution was absorbed by assuming that man was evolving into a finer spiritual nobility. Scholars in comparative religion turned out weighty tomes on Oriental theologies which New Thought leaders plundered for support of their faith. Perhaps the greatest *coup* of all was to deny a conflict between religion and science by asserting that the one supported the other, and even juxtaposing the two as the name of an organized New Thought group —Divine Science, although most Christians would deny that it was divine in the Christian sense, and not many scientists would admit that it was scientific. The challenges of science which could not be turned to advantage, as the higher criticism's testimony of certain blatant inconsistencies in the Scriptures, New Thought leaders simply ignored by diminishing the importance of the Bible.

A metaphorical analysis of the literature clearly indicates how New Thought writers transcended the ancient hostility of science and religion. Their images were drawn from physics, chemistry, psychology, and the applied science of industrialism.

"To recognize our own divinity, and our intimate relation to the Universal," said one writer, "is to attach the belts of our machinery to the powerhouse of the Universe." Psychology was enlisted as supporting evidence. For many thoughtful people, this new, burgeoning discipline, from Freud to Pavlov, struck at the heart of Christianity. How, it was asked, can an adult be responsible for sins decreed in childhood? New Thought never had to face the question. It ignored the taunts of psychology by denying the reality of sin. Psychological and psychoanalytic probings into the power of suggestion and the unconscious supported New Thought. Every patient risen from the couch was proof of the supremacy of the psyche (mind) over the soma (body). The cause of illness was psychosomatic. In New Thought we find a striking expression of the influence of psychology on American life and thought in the twentieth century —an influence which has extended from law and literature to marriage and morals.[3]

It was America's first great psychologist-philosopher who helped to lift the New Thought concept as a religion into some kind of intellectual respectability. William James was fascinated by what he called "the religion of healthy-mindedness," and was convinced that this new religion "must now be reckoned with as a genuine religious power.... They form a psychic type to be studied with respect." In *The Varieties of Religious Experience,* published in 1902, he was ready to say that "religion in the shape of mind-cure gives to some of us serenity, moral poise, and happiness, and prevents certain forms of disease as well as science does, or even better in a certain class of persons." Though William James reserved his enthusiasm for mental healing, success writers were quick to find encouragement and to share in the distinction as they evolved their own varieties of successful experience.[4]

A happy, optimistic religion, New Thought saw man, not depraved, but divine; worshiped a God, not on the seat of continual judgment, but a Principle everlastingly flashing bolts of success electricity. The traditional Christian tension of a moral struggle resolving into damnation or salvation became meaningless without a doctrine of good and evil. Since man was one with God, the Principle, man could not sin because God could not sin. The bookshelves of believers in New Thought held books, not about man's weakness and depravity, but works which glorified man's power and purity.

An economic interpretation of New Thought's appeal is vividly described in a personal reminiscence by Charles Hallinan. Hallinan was living in a suburb eight miles from "a raw, windy Western city." It was the late 1890s and a railroad was cut through from his suburb to the city where a plush, new department store had just been built. Then, suddenly, "there was scarcely a family which was not being pinched between the small, rigid income and the steadily rising prices. That department store played the very devil with our peace of mind. It multiplied enormously the apparent necessities of life, and brought the luxuries just without our reach. Now on this absorbing question, that of making ends meet, the four orthodox churches had nothing to say." The Episcopal, Presbyterian, Methodist and Baptist churches were holding aloof from the economic struggle.

"Then there came filtering into the suburb bits of a new and almost incredible gospel," Hallinan related. The name of this particular New Thought group was Christ Scientists, and it was careful to point out the distinctions between itself and Mrs. Eddy's church. Sunday services began in a private home and then settled down in a little auditorium in the suburban clubhouse. The chief exponent and sermonizer for Christ Scientists was Mr. Van Epps, a former Congregational clergyman and "a rather frail, agreeable gentleman who impressed everybody favorably, he seemed so intellectual and so free from the least trace of the charlatan." Mr. Van Epps became "easily the most quoted man in the town. At first, only the bolder or more restless spirits ventured out to hear him; it was an affair of some delicacy, since your presence at his church was quite likely to be reported at your own; but sooner or later a large proportion of the community had sampled 'New Thought,' and was deep in the discussion of it." A "sense of the cosmic process" led the plump Miss Fulton to join. Other souls rushed in burning with "a secret and romantic desire to recapture the spirit and the experience of the early Christians."

But "the thing which most deeply stirred our suburb was the frank and uncompromising way in which 'New Thought' addressed itself to our bread-and-butter problems, the problems posed for us by that amazing department store. 'New Thought' promised economic redemption in this world, and we were vastly more startled at that—really, I am measuring my words when I say this—we were vastly more startled at that than we were at the most lavish and specific assurances regarding salvation in the next. Remember, dear reader, as you loll gracefully on your dividends," Hallinan in 1920 recalled the mood of the late 1890s, "that for us the old order had changed, only yesterday, as it were; that the old traditional security, open to all thrifty, hard-working folks, had disappeared, and that in its place was a bewildering struggle to adjust rigid incomes to ascending prices. Not a pulpit in our suburb had addressed itself to this plebeian anxiety, this perpetual concern, until 'New Thought' came in. Given the right attitude of mind, said Van Epps (an attitude, I am explaining parenthetically, to be secured from him in twenty lessons for ten dollars, with an 'advanced course' of ten additional lessons for 'students and teacher'], and you could tap the boundless resources of the Universe. . . . Every Sunday morning he held up over our heads, in his frail scholarly hands, a vast cornucopia from which he poured out—bathing us in it—health, wealth, harmony, energy, abundant life. I want to give Van Epps his due—never in my life have I seen faces so transfigured as were the faces of those who left the secular atmosphere of that suburban clubhouse every Sunday morning."

The need in the idea of success which New Thought was meeting as America began to turn into the twentieth century is pinpointed by Hallinan. "Take Langdon, for example. He was the 'Western representative' for an Eastern 'concern'— happy nomenclature!—under a contract which ran for three years at a stretch. Every time it was up for renewal, Langdon and his wife went through a perfect hell of worry. They had been through five of them, and Langdon's head was gray at forty. Twice out of the five renewals he had succeeded in securing an increase in salary; twice he had been refused, coldly and flatly; and once, I believe, the unequal contest had ended in some sort of a draw."

"Langdon worshipped in the Presbyterian church, three pews behind us over to the right. He was counted a good churchman; I think he was clerk of the board, or something busy like that. But what, I ask you, did Langdon really care about 'muscular Christianity'? What did he care how many boys the minister taught to box? . . . The answer is that he didn't fundamentally care a straw, except possibly during the year following the renewal of his contract, when he was in such high spirits that he would have subscribed cheerfully to anything! Our whole suburb was made up of 'Western representatives,' of 'sales managers,' of 'chief clerks,' of struggling doctors and lawyers. Langdon's plight, in one form or another, was the common plight. When the spiritual Van Epps declared flatly that security and health and abundance were the privilege of all, he struck a chord to which every heart in our town thrilled." [5]

Though Hallinan does move us to compassion for his friends, the promise of Van Epps that "security and health and abundance were the privilege of all" was not translated into reality by the magic of New Thought. Hallinan himself soon gave it up as a bore, reflecting later that it was "a sort of department store religion, a vast hodge-podge of promise and half fulfillment, the shopper's El Dorado. . . ." Van Epps was preaching a form of self-seeking magic rather than self-giving Christianity. Like the witch doctor of primitive man, the New Thought convert resorted to a kind of magic which arrogantly sought to coerce God into granting his desires. But the sin, in the opinion of a more orthodox Christian or Jew, was even greater. The New Thoughter assumed that he himself was God. [6]

Success by religious mind power flourished in the 1900s and 1910s in response to certain cultural forces which had been gathering strength since the last decade and a half of the nineteenth century. The people it appealed to were not the character ethic's earnest young men but rather adults prosperous enough to afford faith in thought. The new market for success literature was solidly middle class in status and income, but lacked hardness of mind and toughness of character. The scrubbed and respectable seekers who fed on the literature and drank in the sermons were more, rather than less, privileged, mentally sloppy, rather than uneducated. As they pushed the sales of get-ahead books higher and higher, a part of the success idea was being transformed into a toasted marshmallow—a lovely golden brown on the outside, but soft and mushy at the center.[7]

As America moved through the early decades of the twentieth century, it was apparent that self-help brokers of New Thought were peddling a growth stock in a bull market. While the Van Epps settled in to work the metropolitan areas on a *vis-à-vis* basis, other success missionaries were satisfied with nothing less than the whole nation. The United States Post Office Department was ready to carry the message into the small towns. Their convenient services turned success by mind power into a mail order religion with a catalogue indexed for health, wealth, and happiness.

The correspondence course was one of the most lucrative packages in this post-office ministry. (Separate lessons always seemed like more for your money.) A large part of the literature emerged outside of the regular publishing channels. New Thought teachers were quick to establish an address from which they issued their own magazine, courses, pamphlets, and books. In San Francisco, Henry Harrison Brown's *Now,* and "Now Folk" publishing house, were spreading the word during the 1900s with *Dollars Want Me: The New Road to Opulence.* Brown worked a reverse twist on the law of attraction: "Say to the dollar, 'I do not need you. You need me. You are of no use until my brain and hand use you. You wish to be used. You come to me that you may be used. I do not need a dollar. Dollars need me.' "[8]

One of the grand old ladies in the rhythmical rise and fall of these publishing houses was Elizabeth Towne. The child of a prosperous lumber yard owner in Oregon and a mother who died when Elizabeth was nine, she played around with the rough workers at her father's saw mill on the banks of the Willamette, spent one year in high school, and was cutting out papeı dolls the month before she married at the age of fourteen. Always drifting in and out of debt, she began to practice and teach mental healing and soon recognized the more direct approach to wealth. "I went to filling myself up on *I-shall-be-wealthy* statements," Elizabeth specified for her readers the proper method. "Then suddenly it came to me one day that I was putting off my wealth to some future time. I must claim wealth NOW. Then I began to say, I AM *wealth*—I AM. I said it actually millions of times. And I tried to *imagine* it true, and to live up to it. When I had not money enough to buy a thing needed I consoled myself by calling it mine anyhow—as we used to do when we were children. When we needed something and I *did* have the dollar for it I *imagined* that dollar as one of a boundless store, and I spent it *willingly,* smilingly. . . . I took infinite pains to get into the *wealthy* attitude of mind over the spending of every five cent piece that went through my purse." [9]

Elizabeth's father, obedient to the law of divine supply, loaned his daughter some money to start a New Thought magazine. Holmes' poem ("Build thee more stately mansions, O my soul!") inspired the title. In 1900 she moved her two children and the *Nautilus* to Holyoke, Massachusetts, where she married William Towne, pausing just long enough en route for a divorce. A big woman, vigorous and impulsive, Mrs. Towne attracted to the *Nautilus* the New Thought poetry of Edwin Markham and Ella Wheeler Wilcox and expanded her publishing house into one of the most prosperous outlets for mental healing and success literature in the nation. [10]

When her husband and son took over many of the administrative duties, Mrs. Towne was ready to tackle some of the philosophical problems in the success idea. "Success is not money, nor is it fame," she explained in *Making Money: How to Grow Success,* but it "*includes the power to command money . . . coupled with a clear conscience and loving heart.*" The method must be ethical. When you think wealth into being, you must be certain to do it "*without thinking anything away from others.*" The justification is then established on the doctrine of service. "You desire wealth—money—the ability to gratify your desires," she chided the uplifters. "But you want to cling to your old affectation that money is filthy lucre and not as noble an object of effort as 'the good of mankind.' Oh, you dear dunce, *money* is the MEASURE of the good you can do mankind. Without money you can do nothing—but hire yourself out to some other man for bread and duds." [11]

Duncelike, too, are those who moan about opportunities. "It is what's IN a man which makes him a failure or a success. Pulls [*sic*], schools, bank accounts are less than 0. . . . The real truth is that every bit of money in the world is YOURS; just as every bit of blood in the body belongs to every individual cell." [12]

The way to get in touch with the Divine Supply is to keep "your goal everlastingly in sight by eternally affirming, affirming, AFFIRMING it. . . . Quit stating ANYTHING in the future tense. Say 'I AM beauty, joy, everything I want—I AM! I AM!' " Be neither a skinflint, nor a conspicuous consumer for the purposes of status. Be determined, concentrate on one thing at a time, and wash away all those nagging fears by flooding your mind with self-confident assertions. For a half hour or an hour, "sit straight and alert, take slow, full breaths, and picture money pouring into your purse. Get enthused over the picture and keep telling yourself it is real and the money is yours. But never permit yourself to wonder HOW the money is to come, or through whom. Simply picture it as coming to you from the All-Encircling Good. Feel just as tickled over it as you can." [13]

From India and the East came assistance. Many New Thoughters were fascinated by the breathing exercises of Yoga, using their own conception of this Hindu practice to assist the laws of affirmation and attraction. "One day it suddenly flashed across my mind that I AM THE SUN of God!" Elizabeth Towne joyously reported. (Previously she had made the mistake of trying to be a cold, sterile moon.) The center of this solar identification is the solar plexus. When this great nerve center, situated behind the stomach, is working properly, it radiates energy, just like the sun, sending vibrations through the nerve highways of the body. Since "BREATHING IS THINKING AND THINKING IS BREATHING," beware of fear-thoughts which shrivel the solar plexus. Flat on your back, in a relaxed, easy mood, breathe in, hold it, then exhale, repeating the exercise with a slow, steady rhythm. On the exhale cycle, pinpoint the goal by saying, "I AM *money*." [14]

Elizabeth Towne closed up shop in Holyoke, Massachusetts decades later in 1951. Words she wrote at the dawn of her career, over half a century before her death at the age of ninety-five in 1960, might stand as the memorial: "The grace of Good is with you all, dearies. Rise up and be what you desire to be." [15]

Success by religious mind power was based on laws. Wealth was yours simply by obeying the laws of attraction, visualization, and affirmation until you connected with the law of Divine Supply.[16]

What was the impact of New Thought on the success creed? It kept the success idea solidly in the conservative tradition. Opportunities were inexhaustible and luck unimportant, but the asceticism of the character ethic, and its glorification of poverty as a training ground, were sweetened by New Thought's philosophy of sugar and spice. Any strictures against materialism dissolved under the heated eagerness to explain the means to wealth, and, with less interest and intensity, its justification. 'True success' became something which accompanied material success, while the halo of Christian ethics which had protected the success idea for so long was stained by the disagreement on its necessity.[17]

For many people, unwilling to let go of the American dream and submerged by forces they could not understand, New Thought was a panacea. It offered confidence to the fearful, sanctuary to the guilt-obsessed, and soothed the anxious with the promise of an awakened, richly endowed self. The character ethic had never felt it necessary to dwell on self-confidence as a means to success. New Thought was stiffening the backbone of many a Casper Milquetoast two decades before it became a sign of sophistication during the 1920s to offer snap judgments about the "inferiority complexes" of others.

In the first three decades of the twentieth century, there was another route to success by mind power which we shall now explain. Unlike New Thought, God was not necessary. The 1920s were the years in which the secular interpretation of mind power most persuasively captured the imagination of the American people.

12

"DAY BY DAY,
IN EVERY WAY,
I AM GETTING BETTER
AND BETTER"

"I have read the philosophy of Coué," Henry Ford said thought-fully. "He has the right idea." Confided another devotee: "I would just as soon go without my breakfast as without my morning and evening autosuggestion." Émile Coué's self-hypnotic slogan, "Day by day, in every way, I am getting better and better," flashed across the idea of success in the early 1920s. It was a dramatic, widely publicized technique for mental healing which Americans quickly translated into a means to success.[1]

Like New Thought, many secular techniques for success by mind power began with the pursuit of health and were then applied to the pursuit of wealth. Unlike New Thought, success by secular mind power ignored any supernatural assistance from Divine Supply. The mighty fortress of secular mind power was psychology, or rather "applied psychology," for the American genius, as usual, exploited pure research for practical ends. Just as New Thought exploited the purity of God, so secular mind power put the psychology of the laboratory to work in the affairs of men. Especially in the 1920s, when Mencken-inspired intellectuals and a Victorian-rebelling generation declared an open season on church-baiting, secular success writers moved into a burgeoning market eased open for them by the psychological-religious enthusiasms of New Thought.

Success writers of secular mind power all agreed that something more than hard work and perseverance was necessary to get rich. To this end, they happily and carelessly chopped up the mind into parts, gave each a label, and then isolated one or more parts as the forces for success. William James' influential essays on the will and habit, for example, were constantly filtered through a sieve of materialism. In the character ethic, will was an expression of character, synonymous with determination: "Where there's a will, there's a way." In the world of applied psychology it became a mental muscle to be exercised.

For two dollars in 1918 you could take *The Success Course of Will-Culture and Concentration for Power and Success: I Will Be What I Will to Be.* If, by chance, you were dissatisfied with New Thought's theological reliance on an All Supply, this course was the answer. The will, as the most important element in thought, could be developed by deep breathing, concentration and attention exercises, and by the constant affirmation, in a sensible concern for first things first, of the phrase: *"I WILL to gain Strong Will-Power."* Want to impale a client with both "the Steady and Magnetic Gazes"? Sit calmly some six feet away from a sheet of white notepaper with a black spot drawn on it. Give it "the Steady Gaze" for a bit, then switch to the magnetic treatment by pouring "Strong Will into your gaze." Just to keep things interesting, "start with the Steady Gaze and count 10, then change to the Magnetic Gaze as above till you count 20, and in this way alternate the two gazes until 60 is reached. . . . By faithful and careful practice of the foregoing Gazing Exercises your eyes will increase greatly in brightness, beauty, and strength. You will be able to withstand with equanimity the most piercing gaze, while your own gaze will be one ever denoting Power of Will and Strong Personality." [2]

The Foster Correspondence Schools of Scranton, Pennsylvania, put it to their students in this way: "We are not appealing to you to educate yourself as education is generally understood, but to make yourself in will power and brain power a masterman. The question for you to decide is—Shall I remain a hewer of wood and a drawer of water for others, or shall I take the place among men that I am entitled to?" The course calmed any student fears of inferiority with assurances that "ninety per cent. of people at birth have about the same mental endowment." Making money is the result of a chain reaction. Concentration on the desire for success, by imagining the advantages of wealth and the miseries of poverty, will excite the emotions. Our aroused emotions will work through the will, which in turn becomes the active power for achieving our desires. Acquiring success-directed habits can help in developing will power. "Habit is character, and to acquire habits it is only necessary to persist in certain thoughts until thru repetition they become habits, by thinking in the right way a man can make himself whatever he wants to be." [3]

Psychoanalysts, like Freud, Jung, and Adler, soon had self-helpsters peering into the subconscious for clues to success. "Consciously we struggle to possess money and subconsciously we are struggling to be poor," explained the author of *Psychoanalysis: The Key to Your Success*. It all goes back to our childhood. We are dragged down by a "poverty complex," or a subconscious desire for poverty, because we remember such things as parents fighting over money, or mother reading how a rich man had as much chance of getting into heaven as a camel passing through the eye of a needle. The key to success is psychoanalysis. By psychoanalyzing ourselves, we can unlock the door into our subconscious and destroy the "poverty complex" by ripping away the façade which conceals these childhood urges. Furthermore, we must cease daydreaming and start acting. Daydreaming wastes the energy of our subconscious—a source of energy which should be harnessed for carrying us towards a concrete goal in life. For $2.98, a plain wrapper, and a money-back guarantee, Professor Eugene Victor Lagaren could teach you how to psychoanalyze yourself and others in order to "banish all fear, self-consciousness, timidity, nervousness, and all other forces which have caused you suffering, sorrow, and failure." [4]

In the 1920s, the Psycho-Phone offered excitingly new possibilities. "GET THE THINGS YOU WANT—WHILE YOU SLEEP," the Psycho-Phone Company advertised its unbeatable idea. "Are you only half alive, sickly in body, doing unpleasant work, beset with marriage problems, with never quite enough money to do what you want? . . . Change the impressions, convictions, suggestions, buried in your *unconscious mind,* and you can change your life!" One hundred and ninety dollars will get you what amounts to a victrola with a time clock and a batch of records. For a few minutes every hour the machine talks to you while you sleep. "The Psycho-Phone," the company explained, "is an automatic suggestion machine which reaches your unconscious mind while you are asleep and [while] your conscious mind, with its doubts, fears and objections, is in abeyance. Through liberating your unconscious powers you can make yourself over according *to your own specifications.* You can develop your power to get *money,* and the *things and conditions necessary to your highest development.*" For customers with delicate personal matters, there was a model which preserved secrecy by repeating suggestions in low tones. For customers with paper-thin walls, earphones were available.[5]

While such suggestion devices implied influences from an outside source, auto- (or self-) suggestion clearly were influences set in motion by oneself, upon oneself. (In New Thought this device was known as the law of affirmation.) Autosuggestion was psychology's most influential contribution to success by mind power.

One authority on the subject in the 1900s, Herbert A. Parkyn, agreed with the biblical proverb that "as a man thinketh in his heart, so is he." But Parkyn sharpened the maxim with up-to-date terms: "A man is what his auto-suggestions make him," or, "Change a man's auto-suggestions and you change the man." Like his fellow apostles, Parkyn advised the ambitious to repeat earnestly to themselves many times every day an optimistic, positive autosuggestion, such as, "I CAN and I WILL be successful in everything I undertake." The reasoning for it all was as simple as this: "In assuming that you are bound to be a success, that you are strong, determined, fearless; that you ARE a success . . . , your thoughts influence your actions, which in turn pave the way to success, and sooner or later you find yourself surprisingly confronted with your own brilliant achievements." [6]

By the early 1920s the nation was all set for a craze on autosuggestion. One magazine reported in November 1922 that "Day by day, in every way, I am getting better and better" had become "the stock phrase of the country almost overnight." The rhythmical lilt of the slogan helped, but the timing was propitious. Coué's reputation had spread from France, and England where he was "the most talked-of man in London." When he invaded America on a lecture tour in the early months of 1923, the press, from the better magazines to Sunday supplements, were ready for a story bubbling with novelty, controversy, and human interest appeal.

Coué himself was an asset. The short, thick-set chemist and apothecary with the waxed moustache was quietly convincing. His sharp brown eyes and kindly smile charmed friend and foe alike. Robert Littell, a reporter for the *New Republic,* knew Coué should be attacked by any decent political liberal, if for no other reason, perhaps, than that his reactionary movement tended to mutter away the necessity for protest. Mock Coué Littell did do, but he came away enchanted by the Frenchman, and like so many others, hypnotized by Coué's face. "The face of a dehydrated fox," Littell chuckled, but he could only muse at the end: "O wizened and solid and twinkling and inscrutable and shrewd and winning face, you might belong to the most honest station master in all of France." [7]

The technique which the good-natured Frenchman popularized was not entirely unfamiliar to Americans. Determined golfers, tormented by soaring divots, knew all about autosuggestion as they issued the silent self-command "keep your eye on the ball!" Tennis players soon learned that the quickest way to muddle the ball into the net was to fail to keep that command uppermost in mind. Every well-informed person was getting terribly sophisticated on how to jolly along his unconscious. Freud had more than the avant-garde plunging into the nether regions, while Watson was introducing the conditioned response amidst cocktail chatter and barbershop kidding about inferiority

complexes (everybody could boast one of those), fixations, re-
pressions, and inhibitions. Autosuggestion required no descent to
the couch, no psychoanalyst, and best of all, no expensive fees.
It was every man his own analyst with no messy exposures of
childhood traumas. Everything would be better if you just say so.

It was all based on one simple principle, according to Coué,
and good for any objective. Suppose we place a long plank, one
foot wide, on the ground, he explained. Everybody will be
capable of walking along the plank without stepping over the
edge. Imagine, then, the plank raised to the height of a cathe-
dral's towers. Who then could traverse the plank? You would
begin to tremble and in spite of every effort of your will, you
would be incapable of walking along the plank. Why? In the
first case, you imagined that you could do it; in the second,
you imagined that you could not, even though you were determined to do it through the use of your will. This was one of
many examples which proved to Coué that "it is always the
imagination which gains the victory over the *will*, without any
exception." (In mental healing, this principle meant that people
were sick only because they imagined they were sick.) "If you
persuade yourself that you can do a certain thing, provided this
thing be *possible,* you will do it however difficult it may be. If
on the contrary you *imagine* that you cannot do the simplest
thing in the world, it is impossible for you to do it, and mole-
hills become for you unscalable mountains." [8]

This was the procedure: "*As long as you live,* every morning
before getting up, and every evening as soon as you are in bed,
you must shut your eyes, so as to concentrate your attention,
and repeat twenty times following, moving your *lips* (that is
indispensable) and counting *mechanically* on a string with
twenty knots in it the following phrase: '*Every day, in every
respect, I am getting better and better.*' There is no need to
think of anything in particular, as the words '*in every respect*'
apply to everything." Though the public soon murmured the
phrase into an internal rhyme ("Day by day, in every way, I
am getting better and better"), the actual words were not important. Any forceful, positive slogan, narrowed to a more

specific objective, if desired, could do the job. When we repeat the slogan, our unconscious accepts the suggestion, transforms it into an autosuggestion, and the thing desired is realized. "Every thought entirely filling our mind becomes true for us and tends to transform itself into action." [9]

On his lecture tour, Coué soon recognized the most distinctive feature of the American mind. The French, he observed, are content to argue on the fundamentals of principle. The American mind, on the other hand, is teeming with plans to put the principle to work, "to carry the idea further even than the author of it may have conceived," and to discover "its practical adaptability to every-day life." In Cleveland, where the audience was particularly appreciative, the pragmatic urge brought the questioning around to: "Can auto-suggestion be adapted to business?" As Coué dwelled on the larger possibilities, he was further adapting, like so many success writers of mind power, principles originally designed for health to wealth-getting. [10]

" 'Man is what he thinks,' " Coué had declared in *Self Mastery Through Conscious Autosuggestion*. "The fear of failure is almost certain to cause failure, in the same way as the idea of success brings success, and enables one always to surmount the obstacles that may be met with. . . . Every one must set out in life with a very definite idea that he will succeed, and that, under the influence of this idea he will inevitably succeed. Not indeed, that he should quietly remain expecting events to happen, but because, impelled by this idea, he will do what is necessary to make it come true." Here was an activist, go-getting spirit which had a wider appeal for Americans than New Thought. In New Thought, it is quite possible to lounge around like a contented dog until you attract and affirm from the cupboard of Divine Supply a juicy bone onto your plate. With Coué's autosuggestion, you are, in the very spirit of the thing, a Stutz Bearcat roaring after your objective with an assist at the start from an extra fuel tank of autosuggestive slogans. [11]

This was precisely the mood that struck Coué on his lecture tour to the States in 1923. The American *"knows* he is going to succeed, and will let no obstacle check his march forward.

... The idea of success is in the blood of the nation, for the nation itself is a success—the most gigantic success history has ever recorded." Coué thought that Americans achieved this drive by a kind of national practice of autosuggestion initiated in childhood, and he was discerning enough to detect the importance of the comforting justification for success. "Always the American business man seems to have the notion firmly ingrained in his mind that he is working not only for himself but also for the nation, for his state and for his city." [12]

How, then, can we explain the appeal of Couéism? It was designed primarily, but not entirely, for mental healing. Filtered through the American mind, it became not only a system for health, but a general morale builder and a technique for success. To the extent that it was practiced seriously and consistently by a number of people, it can be explained by many of the causal forces which produced New Thought. But as a widely popular slogan which tickled the public's fancy, it was simply a fad. Half-serious, half-comic, it depended for its appeal, like most fads, on timing. The personal appearance of Coué, the nature of the slogan, the growing interest in psychology, all of these were buoyed on a wave of rolling prosperity. The reading public in 1923, for example, pushed Emily Post's *Etiquette* into the number one spot on the non-fiction best-seller list, and kept right on buying H. G. Wells' and Hendrik Willem Van Loon's cosmic outlines of human history and knowledge. Autosuggestion *á la Coué* promised a quick spurt in income; etiquette books encouraged status-jumping with a complete set of manners and knowledge outlines provided an arsenal of learned allusions designed to conquer any dinner party.[13]

No doubt, millions of people intoned "Day by day, in every way, I am getting better and better" with a confident assurance that they *were* getting better and better. Before the next craze of crossword puzzles sent the nation scurrying for its dictionaries, the jolly Frenchman had introduced a familiar phrase into American speech and sent some success writers of secular and religious mind power scurrying to clamber aboard the bandwagon. Asserted Elizabeth Towne from a New Thought viewpoint: *"God's love heals me NOW: every day, in every way, I realize it better and better."* [14]

Popular and occasionally diverting as mind power may have been, the character ethic held the center of the stage. It was still the predominant way to success. What was happening to this doctrine of hard work and perseverance in a world of rapidly changing social and economic conditions?

13

KEEPING UP WITH
THE JONESES

As America rollicked along in the 1920s, the prosperous businessman led the parade. More people were certain they wanted to be like him than anyone else. The businessman was not only "producing the goods," he was making money for himself. By the end of the decade Stuart Chase saw it this way: "Pecuniary standards make headway over all other standards. . . . Above all, the period has witnessed the emergence of the business man as the dictator of our destinies. . . . He has ousted the statesman, the priest, the philosopher, as the creator of standards of ethics and behavior, and has become the final authority on the conduct of American society." The businessman ran on a platform of prosperity, ignoring the criticisms of the muckraking 1900s, while soothing his angry opponents with a sharper understanding of public relations. Harold Laski has observed that "in no previous civilization has the business man enjoyed the power or the prestige that he possesses in the United States." The 1920s was his period of conscious triumph. "It was no accident that men like Mellon and Hoover and Morrow found their wealth an asset rather than a liability in public office," Frederick Lewis Allen remarked, "or that there was a widespread popular movement to make Henry Ford President in 1924. The possession of millions was a sign of success, and success was worshipped the country over." [1]

The 1920s cut new highways for the monied elite. In the

field of sports a Bobby Jones, Jack Dempsey, or a Babe Ruth was commanding both fame and wealth, while in the cinema a Douglas Fairbanks, Mary Pickford, or Rudolf Valentino was shoving the actor's prestige to heights which would have shocked earlier generations. As press agents began to realize the incredible possibilities of mass communication, such as radio, mass entertainment quite suddenly revealed a glistening new world of opportunities to get ahead. But for most Americans, who were incapable of playing championship golf, disinterested in swatting a baseball, or constitutionally opposed to bounding over insurmountable walls to rescue distressed maidens, the safest and most convenient avenue to wealth was business. Throughout it all, "the acquisition of money became the guiding obsession of the age," pronounced one student of the period, while another agreed that "it is doubtful if material success was ever worshipped more unreservedly." [2]

It was the 1910s and 1920s which endowed American speech with "keeping up with the Joneses." The phrase described an ancient game, but the choice of words was appropriately twentieth century. In the nineteenth century, the game was more dramatically played on a lavish level of consumption by the plutocracy keeping up with one another or by social climbing into the older families. In the twentieth century, everybody seemed to be playing the game in competition with the commonest name in America. How did we get this revealing phrase about American life?

In 1911 Irving Bacheller's *Keeping Up with Lizzie* set the stage. Sam Henshaw was in the grocery business and the father of a pretty, clever girl named Lizzie. Musing over the trend of events, the town's homespun philosopher, Socrates Potter, told this story: "Well, Sam began to aspire an' nothing would do for Lizzie but the Smythe school at Hardcastle at seven hundred dollars a year. So they rigged her up splendid, an' away she went. From that day she set the pace for this community. Dan [her beau] had to keep up with Lizzie, and so his father, Bill Pettigrew, sent him to Harvard. Other girls started in the race, an' the first we knew there was a big field in this maiden handicap. Well, Sam had been aspirin' for about

three months, when he began to perspire. The extras up at
Hardcastle had exceeded his expectations. He was goin' a hot
pace to keep up with Lizzie, an' it looked as if his morals was
meltin' away." So Sam upped the prices on his groceries. He
built a splendid new house, and the prices of his groceries
followed the progress of construction. Then it seemed to Socrates
Potter that everyone in town was selling their property and
borrowing cash to keep up with Sam Henshaw's Lizzie. "Then
one night the cashier o' the First National Bank blew out his
brains. We found that he had stolen eighteen thousand dollars
in the effort to keep up. That was a lesson to the Lizzie-chasers!
Why, sir, we found that each of his older girls had diamond
rings an' could sing in three languages, an' a boy was in college."

As struggling fathers sunk deeper into debt to keep up the
pace, Lizzie returned from Europe. "They've been six months in
Europe," Sam bubbled excitedly to Socrates. "Lizzie is in love
with it. She's hobnobbed with kings an' queens. She talks art
beautiful. I wish you'd come over an' hear her hold a conversation. It's wonderful." In a heart-to-heart talk, Socrates Potter
at last confided to Lizzie that her father was in financial difficulties. Taking the kindly philosopher's advice to "go back to
your old simplicity an' live within your means," Lizzie settled
down to work, cleverly managed her father's store, and finally
married Dan Pettigrew, who had taken up the simple life of
farming. (On an extensive and prosperous scale, however.)
People still tried to keep up with Lizzie, but now in terms of
modesty and simplicity, while Socrates Potter went on to show
the very, very rich in town that establishing orphanages was
one way out of boredom and a meaningless life of competing
for place.[3]

Lizzie's influence was not confined to the covers of a book.
She gave her name to the Model "T" Ford—thereafter known
affectionately as the "tin lizzie." Irving Bacheller, recognizing
a good thing when he created it, continued to use the title "Keeping up with" in a number of other stories. About this time (the
early 1910s) a struggling social climber, named Arthur "Pop"
Momand, was living at Cedarhurst, Long Island (country club,

maid, etc.), with bills ballooning to twice the size of his salary. He finally climbed off the treadmill, but amused by it all, submitted to H. H. McClure the idea for a comic strip. In 1913, "Keeping up with the Joneses" began its long career helping Americans to laugh, often painfully, at themselves. Tormented breadwinners, facing a mountain of unpaid bills, soon took up the phrase. Everyone understood that "keeping up with the Joneses" spoke volumes about the Smiths, who were battling for status with the Browns just down the street.[4]

"Keeping up with the Joneses" was determined by the things money could buy—the house you lived in, the luxury of a maid, the automobile you drove, your wife's clothes, the school or college your children attended. If you outstripped one group, you could move up to another and resume the battle. It was a game whipped to competitive intensity by what the French observer, Lucien Romier, saw in the 1920s as "the dominant and sometimes crushing obligation to make money" and "the certification of a man's social standing by his bank-account." What was behind this strong trend towards Jones-chasing in the 1920s?[5]

The causal forces we examined in an earlier chapter were at work, but at the center of the trend was the miracle of mass production. By the 1920s, most of the major technical problems of how to produce more and more goods at a cheaper price were on the way to a solution. An ancient, but now more vital problem, arose—how to sell what the machines were turning out at a quickening rate of acceleration. The era of the super-salesman was at hand. The fields of marketing, advertising, and public relations expanded to meet the needs of an economy shifting from a primary interest in production to an anxious concern for consumption. With a mixture of cunning and insight, advertisers brewed their potions of desire. Often playing up the effects of their products rather than their superior and inexpensive quality, they kindled longings to be desirable, rich, envied, or fashionable. Somehow it became terribly important to stay up-to-date with this year's model, to "maintain appearances," or simply to be free from trailing some offending olfactory residue. Salesmen were sent out to create new wants and a demand for their product. One English journalist, roving around the country, was astonished by it all: "No one is content with that station in life from which he started. Simplicity, thrift, the art of making a little go a long way, the cultivation of the fireside, have few votaries. The creation of new wants is one of the greatest of American industries, and is pursued with an energy, ingenuity and prodigality which makes European performances in the same line look childish." A rising standard of living for most urban groups, coupled with the delirious opium of installment buying and quick profits from stock market speculation, permitted more people to enter the thousand and one sophisticated skirmishes for status. When the 1920s generation felt the tingling excitement of breaking away from the Victorian propriety of their grandparents, "keeping up with the Joneses" was accentuated.[6]

What was the impact of all this on the idea of success? The 1910s and 1920s enlarged the opportunities of success through salesmanship. The success idea, dominated by the character ethic, shifted with the times. Breaking down "consumer resistance" demanded something more than just "perseverance." The salesman had to get up steam for his high-pressure delivery. Sales managers conceived ingenious methods for keeping up the pressure—the glorious triumphs of exceeding last year's quota, the calls to action reminiscent of locker room pep-talks before the big game, the contests that shamed the laggards, and the bonuses for every new aphrodisiac that fired a passion for their product. These were the days of the "go-getter" with the persistence of a pneumatic drill. The "self-starter's" attack was foot-in-the-door, the chatter was always fast, and the pen ever poised to close the deal. One "self-starter" later pictured his own experience: "I was running up and down the streets all day so fast you could shoot marbles on my coat tail. . . . Whenever someone at the Home Office had nothing else to do he would shoot us a 'PEP' wire. When things slowed up a little, some genius would hatch up a contest of some kind and then we would be under extra pressure from every direction sometime for weeks. The whole thing was enough to drive any one 'nuts.' . . ."[7]

In the era of high pressure selling, what was the advice of success writers to salesmen? The personal qualities necessary for closing a sale were the same as those vital to manufacturing, but enthusiasm, initiative, and perseverance were particularly stressed. In the 1910s and 1920s, qualities of character were still most important, but perseverance and industry were now known as hustle and pep.

One of the more popular stories reflecting this shift in emphasis was Peter B. Kyne's *The Go-Getter: A Story that Tells You How to Be One.* Cappy Ricks, owner of a West Coast lumber and shipping company, was having trouble finding a go-getter for his Shanghai office. On the scene appeared Bill Peck, a young veteran wounded in the war, whose eagerness and slick delivery finally landed him a job as a salesman in the company. When another Shanghai manager proved incompetent, Cappy Ricks decided that super-salesman Peck was the man for Shanghai—if he could win his "Degree of the Blue Vase." This was the examination leading to the degree: A little after one o'clock on Sunday afternoon, Cappy asked his innocent employee to purchase a blue vase and deliver it to him by eight o'clock that night before his departure by train for Santa Barbara. He had to have that vase for an anniversary present! With devilish ingenuity, Cappy had set a severe examination which was more like a perfect crime: the shopwindow exhibiting the vase was more than four blocks from the designated address; during the course of the afternoon the sign above the shop was changed from B. Cohen to B. Cohn and then back again (loyal Bill Peck thought *he* was going insane); a policeman was posted to guard the shop to prevent Peck from breaking the window; and he had to raise $2,000 on a Sunday afternoon in a town where he was unknown.

With his stump of an arm and lame leg aching with pain, Bill Peck finally obtained the blue vase. But it was past eight o'clock. In one final act of supreme go-getterism, Bill Peck clambered aboard a private plane, intercepted the train to Santa Barbara, flagged it down, and triumphantly delivered the blue vase to the astonished but delighted Cappy Ricks. "Bill, old boy, it was cruel—damnably cruel," Cappy confessed, "but I had a big job for you and I had to find out a lot of things about you before I entrusted you with that job. . . . You thought you carried into this stateroom a two thousand dollar vase, but between ourselves, what you really carried in was a ten thousand dollar job as our Shanghai manager."

It will be noted that Cappy's final exam for Bill Peck was not a test of Bill's competence at making policy decisions or his knowledge of business and finance. Neither was the purpose to learn how smoothly he could manipulate people. There was only one course of action and one answer, and Bill did it, and said it, more than once: "It shall be done!" [8]

William W. Woodbridge's short story, *"Bradford, You're Fired!": A Story of the Super-Self,* is another lesson for salesmen according to the 1910s and 1920s version of the character ethic. John Bradford, twenty-eight years old and a college graduate, was a failure. In less than three years, he had been dismissed from five jobs. This record didn't particularly alarm Bradford, because his was a philosophy of pleasure—"the having of a time, a big time! With a regular bunch of regular fellows." When the sales-manager caught him playing solitaire one afternoon in his hotel room, the axe fell for the sixth time. With *"Bradford, you're fired!"* still ringing through the hotel room, the unemployed dry-goods salesman numbly returned to his cards, then reviewed his philosophy of life, and finally went to work on a half filled bottle of whiskey. His mood shifted to self-pity, then resentment, and finally a determination to go tell the sales manager off. With half a bottle of whiskey inside of him, Bradford turned to the mirror, *"and then a strange thing happened, born perhaps of the distorted imaginings of a drink-crazed mind.* Instead of the reflection of *one* man, I saw *two* there in the tall mirror before me, *two* men, images of myself, and each of them looked me in the face. I stared amazed! And as I looked, I saw one of the figures turn to the other, and point his finger at the companion figure's face. Then I heard, as truly as I have ever heard anything, this strange incarnation of myself cry in a voice of force of conviction: 'Bradford, you're fired!' 'Fired?' whined the other, in a snivelling wail. *'Yes, fired! Get out of me! I'm through with you, now and forever. You're a failure, through and through. Go! You're my worst enemy. You're ruining my business, you're ruining my life. Bradford, you're fired!'* " As one Bradford faded from the glass, the other, the "*Super*-self," "turned and smiled into my eyes." At this juncture, the Bradford in the hotel room passed out.[9]

The next morning the battle was joined, "the fight for possession of that which I had never before realized man possessed —the *Super*-self. And to that cowering, slinking creature, that stood looking at me from the glass, I cried again: '*Bradford, you're fired!* I'm going to put another man on your job, and the man on the job will be my slave, and I will be a slave driver, for it takes a slave driver to make a success. *Bradford, you're fired!* Get out of me, now and forever, for there's a new man to take your territory, and I'm going to see that the new man makes good. For I'm going to *drive* that new man to success, I'm going to hound him, day after day, every minute of every day. And I'm going to *own* this other man, instead of his owning me. I'm going to be his boss, Bradford, and he will respect me and do my bidding. You're a failure, Bradford. You had your chance, and you fell down. So you've got to go—forever, you and your philosophy with you. I'm through with you. *Bradford, you're fired!*' " [10]

With his "*Super*-self" in control, Bradford finally talked his way into a job as a wagon driver for the Morton Drygoods Company. Knowing that "untiring energy, ambition, confidence, and a clean heart will win for any man," Bradford and his "*Super*-self" rose to the sales force. Orders came tumbling in, and his salary was raised. The final triumph was an offer to replace the sales manager who had fired him that afternoon in the hotel room. With a good word for his old boss and the last man (beside his "*Super*-self") who ever said: "*Bradford, you're fired!*," he declined the offer, for he had just accepted the salesmanagership of the Morton Drygoods Company. "And in this story of my rise, you may find the *secret of success*. If you have not succeeded, it is your *own* fault. First, realize that there is no success in life for you unless you are Boss. Be a *Boss*, a Man in Authority! Fire John Bradford, and put your *Super*-self

to work! Make your *Super*-self serve you—and Success is already within your reach. And when doubts and fears assail you,
remember the weaker man is no longer on your force. You are
the boss of your self, of the *Super*-self, the inner man who waits
to serve you. And what success has come to me in life is due
alone to this talisman:

'Bradford, you're fired!' " [11]

The kind of book Bill Peck or John Bradford might have
distributed to the budding go-getters of their offices was S. A.
Harrington's *Success Nuggets: "Pep" in Capsule Form*. A product of the Harrington Sales Engineering Company of Akron,
Ohio, *Success Nuggets*, in the words of the author, "is a rapid-
fire machine gun that shoots red hot, sizzling bullets of truth."
A diamond mine of "PEPOGRAMS" to open, perk up, or close
a sales meeting, *Success Nuggets* sparkles with inspiration:
"The BIG MEN of this country are ONLY average men
AROUSED.... Be a hard hitting, clean living, go-getter sort
of a sales person.... Success consists of one part inspiration
and four parts perspiration.... Hope-ology has given way to
hop-ology.... Success only comes to 'self-starters.' ... Put hustle
in the tussle.... The first essential of success is a dogged
determination to succeed." [12]

Harrington occasionally included the equivalent of personality
in his running pep talk, but the essence of his message was that
pep, enthusiasm, and dogged determination, which depended
on a man's character, were the basic necessities for success in
salesmanship. And so it was with the salesman's morning prayer:
"Now I get me up to work, I pray the Lord I may not shirk.
If I should die before to-night, I pray the Lord my work's all
right." In one of his suggested "CLINCHERS," Harrington
set down a model of high-pressure technique with the standard
props of a peremptory command for closing the sale and a
ready pen to mark it: "I appreciate your wish to grant my
proposition further consideration Mr. Blank," *Success Nuggets*
advised the go-getter to say, "but you are really better prepared
to give me your decision to-day than you will be at a later time."
Your judgment "tells you that this is a thing you ought to

do. . . . A good business executive gets all the essentials of a proposition, makes his decision promptly and ACTS. And that is just what you are going to do. Right here please. (Hand him the pen and place the order book before him.)" [13]

As bright-eyed and bushy-tailed thigh-slapping drummers roved the land, magazines and books on how to be a success exploited flashy typographical tricks and adopted a literary style of breezy, slam-bang sentences. With the total volume of success literature increasing in every decade, success apostles never permitted the nation to wonder about the proper means of getting ahead, for in America everyone else was said to be doing just that. From World War I to the Great Depression, America was whooping it up for a richer tomorrow and the idea of success was right in the middle of it.

For salesmen or accountants, engineers or expectant executives, the character ethic dominated the success idea in the 1910s and 1920s. There were other routes to success. Mind power we have already discussed. We shall explore in a later chapter such methods as astrology, graphology, and body building, which lured their own devotees. But it was the character ethic, in its religious or secular interpretation, which seemed to make sense to most Americans who stopped hustling long enough to take instruction. In the religious interpretation of the character ethic, no success merchant exceeded the fame of one prolific propagandist in the 1920s. He made it difficult to criticize the successful businessman without at the same time criticizing Jesus Christ.

14

"A KILL-JOY! HE WAS
THE MOST POPULAR DINNER
GUEST IN JERUSALEM!"

"Pick up any metropolitan newspaper—and hundreds through-out the country," George Seldes was fuming in the *New Republic* during the election months of 1938. "Almost every day there is a story about a man named Barton. Barton says, Barton suggests, Barton shakes hands, Barton laughs, Barton sneezes. It's Barton, Barton, Barton everywhere." A famed success writer in the 1910s and 1920s, popularizer of Jesus as a super-salesman, an advertising tycoon in the firm of Batten, Barton, Durstine & Osborn, congressman, candidate for the Senate, presidential timber in the late 1930s, Bruce Barton made a fortune out of specializing in human nature. Underneath his journalistic facility and advertising shrewdness burned a hard flame of ambition to get on in this world.[1]

It all began in Robbins, Tennessee, with a father who helps explain a great deal. William Eleazar Barton was the descendant of a soldier in the Revolutionary War and proud of it. An inde-pendent, thoughtful boy, William Barton rebelled against the hopelessness of his father's descent into poverty, ran away from home at the age of sixteen, worked his way through a small Kentucky college, rode as a circuit preacher out of a small church in Robbins, Tennessee, and then to better his position, went on to Oberlin Theological Seminary where he graduated at the top of his class at the age of twenty-nine. Tall, imposing, jovial with a passion for hard work and a flair for writing and preaching, he moved up the clerical ladder from one important Congregational church to another in New England and the Middle West. Along the way, he lectured at seminaries, found time to write something like sixty books, among them detailed, scholarly studies of Lincoln, edited a magazine and established himself as an influential and devoted servant of the church.[2]

Bruce Barton worshiped his father and caught the same spirit of enterprise and love of reading which made every meal an excursion into some stimulating topic of conversation. (Recalled Bruce years later: "We were not poor; we just didn't have any money.") It was a professional family which for generations had read books, talked about them, and sometimes added their own to fire the discussion. Bruce was a minister's son, and ministers' sons are something very distinct in America. "We show up so well," Barton once observed with just enough accuracy to make it interesting, "that any unprejudiced man will agree that all the money ever given to the church would have been well invested had it done nothing more than enable preachers to raise sons. . . . Not all of us make good, of course. A third of us go to the devil; another third float around in between; but the other third rule the world." It would be more precise, perhaps, to narrow the field to the sons of Presbyterian and Congregational ministers. Whenever Calvinism's stern demands bit deep, as in Woodrow Wilson, Henry Luce, Norman Thomas, Robert Hutchins, Adolf A. Berle, Jr., DeWitt Wallace, or John Foster Dulles, there was the moral earnestness, a mission—and often a destiny.[3]

Whether in politics, advertising, or writing about success, Bruce Barton could never lose that missionary zeal to search out his own destiny. His hopes for the idea of success can be defined in four missions. The first was to spur America's youth to achievement. "I hope I may never be guilty of writing anything intended to make poor people contented with their lot," he declared. "I would rather be known as one who sought to inspire his readers with *a divine discontent*." Bubbling with optimism and opportunity for all, Barton wanted to assure every young man of this fact: *"In America success is not the exception—it is the rule."* [4]

The second mission was an attempt to explain the distinctions between success and 'true success.' "It is easy to be hypocritical on the subject of money," he chided himself and his brothers of the uplift fraternity. "We have formed a habit of pretending publicly to despise money, while actually working our heads off to get more of it. We make speeches to young men advising them to 'seek the higher good,' and hurry straightway to our offices to make up for lost time. Let us have done with such hypocrisy. We are all out to make money; nor is there anything reprehensible in that fact." Pointing up the symbolic, rather than hedonistic significance of money in America, he confessed his delight at the possibility of piling up a mountain of dollars by writing a best seller, because "I shall be glad of the money as a measure of success." [5]

But Barton took a strong position on the philosophical limitations of materialism: "I like money. I hope to have more of it," he confessed. "But the common habit of measuring men by it, as though there were no other standard, makes me very weary." First, money is not omnipotent. It cannot magnify the pleasures of nature, neither can it improve one's health or increase the simple joys of life. For "he who has health, and a wife and children whom he loves, and work that is play, has gained already the best things in life. And money cannot add greatly to them; nor can the loss of it take them away." Second, money is a fearful thing, because "all through and underneath the scheme of things runs what Emerson termed the Law of Compensation." This law was Barton's understanding of justice. What is sown, shall be reaped; for something received, something must be given. "It is not 'money' that is the 'root of all evil,' as we often misquote, but *'the love* of money.'" Too much love of money demands its own pound of flesh. "Get money— but stop once in a while to figure what it is costing you to get it. No man gets it without giving something in return. The wise man gives his labor and ability. The fool gives his life." 'True success' is something both outside and within ourselves. It is to be up and doing, contributing something to the progress and happiness of the world. Within each one of us, its "measure consists not in wealth or titles, but in a man's own self-respect, his own deep-lying consciousness that he has, with the tools that were given him, done his level best." Money, fame, reputation, honors—all are ephemeral. Let a man invest "his life in the mastery and cultivation of his own best self, and he has laid up riches that cannot be lost." [6]

Whatever the strictures on wealth, in his own life this master of the uplift essay became a millionaire. Young Bruce started early. From the age of twelve to the age of fifteen he was dashing about as a part-time reporter on a local newspaper. A Phi Beta Kappa graduate of Amherst in 1907 and voted "the man most likely to succeed" by his classmates, he considered entering the University of Wisconsin on a fellowship to study history. "It seemed to me that few lives could be more attractive than that of a college teacher," he remarked brightly in the days when things must have been different. "To be paid for nine months of reading interesting books; and then to have three months in which to travel and to write, with a snug pension from Mr. Carnegie at the end—enough to pay the annual deficit on a chicken farm—who could ask more from life than this?" [7]

He decided to ask from life something different and thought he could find it in journalism. On and off for the next few decades he lived in the demanding world of the free-lance writer—editing some newspaper or magazine, popping up when least expected with a syndicated column, banging out novels on the Horatio Alger, Jr., theme, and always writing the crisp editorial, each one a shimmering moral wrapped up in a thought for the day. Bounding from one subject to another within the human interest arena, he shot up fast as a free lancer for over a half-dozen magazines, until the *American Magazine* was running a full-page picture of the thirty-two-year old young man in 1919, balanced by an autobiographical article. Around the offices of the *American Magazine* of this period, Bruce Barton was sure-fire. As one of editor John Siddall's favorite interviewers of the great, famous, and wealthy, he captured just the right spirit of inspiration and human interest appeal.

Unquestionably his most famous interview was with the President of the United States in 1926. Damned by Democratic Senator Bayard as a "press agent effort to sell the President personally to the country," and a " 'red herring' " to draw attention away from the smell of the Republican administration, the interview (with special permission for direct quotations) did manage to thaw out the chief executive with the old favorite interrogatives. "I think there is a better chance for boys to succeed now than there ever was before. . . . ," Calvin Coolidge answered firmly. "If he [a young man] wishes to earn money and go into business with the idea of accumulating a competence, there are more avenues open for that purpose than at any previous time. If he is desirous of securing what I should think is a true success, by performing a real service for his fellow men, from which the reaction will undoubtedly bring him a place in the estimation of his neighbors and a competence which will represent payment for his effort, I should say again that there are more opportunities than at any other time in history." The President was not ready to answer all the questions in the same mode, however. He was unwilling to admit that the sons of "well-to-do families" were handicapped by their background, though he felt it somewhat of a hindrance by removing the necessity for hard work. "I should hate to think," the Vermonter edged toward heresy with granite logic, "that for one generation to be a success was a necessary handicap on the succeeding generation." The one-time Vermont farm boy went on to deny that the country lad had an advantage over the city boy. But the conclusion to the interview was quite proper. He rejected luck as much of a factor in success, glowingly spoke of the absolute value of hard work, and remembered the healthy advantages which a sound marriage contributed to success.[8]

Bruce Barton was a big fellow with reddish hair and a square-jawed face chiseled into determination—a dynamo of energy. His mind was always throbbing with some new project which he executed with tremendous enthusiasm for a hard day's work. Always fearful of growing old and expanding about the middle, he was still working out three times a week in his fifties to keep fit. An avaricious reader and quick writer, he was driven by a yearning for self-improvement which he always managed to turn to self-advancement. His work was part of his religion. Out of the Puritanism in his heritage he believed that a good day's work was a day in the service of the Lord. No doubt idleness felt like a guilt-ridden burden. One of Bruce Barton's talents was empathy. He was sensitive to all the fears and the hopes, the yearnings and ideals of the American middle-class mind. Like Edgar Guest, he had the knack for retailing simple homelies. "I enjoyed your last editorial very much," one reader wrote in. "It's a funny thing, but I swear I could almost have written it myself. I've thought that very thing a hundred times, but I've never said it in just those words." [9]

The empathy was apparent when this leading retailer of values poured most of his energies into retailing products. With a few solid years of experience as a salesman before World War I, Barton had a hand in founding Barton, Durstine & Osborn (Batten was added in 1929 through a merger). Batten, Barton, Durstine & Osborn quickly moved into a leading position on Madison Avenue. Around the offices of B.B.D.&O., Barton was an engine of work, though frequently he idled down just long enough to take in a baseball game. A Niagara of sentimentalism, he could turn to flint when necessary, eager to puncture any inflated expense account. In later years, as "Mr. Big" of the more colorful hucksters, he would emotionally recall for his younger account executives "the good old days" when every advertising and public-relations campaign was an expedition into the unknown.[10]

Barton brought his own specialty to advertising—an insight into human nature. His basic advice for selling products and ideas?: "Say it simply, say it over & over, say it in one-syllable words." For evidence he pointed to the Lord's Prayer, the 23rd Psalm, and the Gettysburg Address—all models of brevity and simplicity, less than 500 words, and mostly one or two syllables. From 1937 to 1941, Barton was a Congressman from Manhattan's Republican "silk-stocking" district, and after less than two years, was voted one of its ten ablest members by fifty-three Washington correspondents. A Willkie man, but at

the same time a determined isolationist, he went down to defeat
as the New York Republican senatorial candidate in 1940 with
Franklin Roosevelt's mocking slogan of "Martin-Barton-and-
Fish" jangling in his ears. With a decent respect for Roosevelt's
own advertising genius, the defeated candidate later good-
naturedly observed that "Martin-Barton-and-Fish" was "one of
the most effective political slogans since 'rum, Romanism, and
rebellion.' " He died in 1967 at the age of eighty, but not before
suffering the sad loss of his wife and two of his three children.[11]

In his third mission, Bruce Barton offered various ways to
wealth. He drew on examples from his own life and experience,
interviews with successful men, and most of all, from biographies which he insatiably devoured and which have been the
cornucopia of illustrations for success writers since the nineteenth
century. But he occasionally recognized the magnitude of the
problem. "It is a disheartening thing that with all our increase
in knowledge we have learned so little about the reasons for
success or failure in the molding of human lives," he mourned.
"Shall we ever penetrate deeper into this most baffling of all
Nature's secrets?" Barton's own research into the problem convinced him that success was no accident, though he was prepared to admit that a good mother was a big advantage. "I am
in favor of mothers," he safely pronounced. "It is an interesting
thing to remember that the whole process of evolution has been
devoted to one single accomplishment—the development of a
mother. . . . Having made the mothers, Nature has never made
anything since. She considered her task complete." [12]

We need not linger with Bruce Barton's analysis of the means
to success except to point out that he emphasized particularly
hard work, concentration, honesty, faith, and prayer. Barton's
final mission, and the most important, was to justify the role
of business by surrounding the successful businessman with the
glory of Christ. Barton was convinced that business was a force
for good and was reforming the nation by raising the standard
of living. His main argument was based on a single concept: "A
great word has been added to the vocabulary of Business in
recent years. It is being overworked. . . . But the idea that the
word represents has come to stay. The word itself is SERVICE."

It is "the big new idea in modern business," though it is actually blessed by an ancient Christian tradition from which it was borrowed. It was this minister's son's greatest triumph that he helped to fill the gap left by the declining doctrine of the stewardship of wealth. The essence of that triumph was that he reaffirmed the concept of service in religious terms. In short, he placed the justification for success in the most secure of all places—heaven. And as we shall now see, he did so very much in the spirit of middle-class, middlebrow America in the 1920s.[13]

Heaven, because no one has ever been there and come back to tell about it, has always represented the vision of a longed-for ideal. Heaven has been a place which defined the deepest yearnings of an age. Indeed, one can be more certain about the nature of this world at any particular point in history than about the next world by analyzing what this world imagined the next world to be like. Heaven has ranged from a joyous place with pearly gates and material luxury to the more contemporary psychological view of peace of mind through a oneness with God. In the America of the 1920s, the go-getter's conception of heaven contained more self-starters than parlor lizards, more boosters than knockers. The boss of heaven, as Bishop Charles Fiske acknowledged, was "a sort of Magnified Rotarian." Naturally his clerical representatives on earth should run their churches like business organizations with the most up-to-date advertising techniques.[14]

In the year 1925 the nation snickered as science made a fool of William Jennings Bryan's fundamentalist interpretation of Genesis at the Scopes Trial. With rich irony, the year also witnessed the publication of a book by Bruce Barton entitled *The Man Nobody Knows*. It moved into the number four spot on the best-seller lists, and the next year had jumped to the top spot among best-sellers in the non-fiction field. The man Bruce Barton wanted everybody to know about was scarcely the same man as the Saviour of Charles M. Sheldon's famed late nineteenth-century novel, *In His Steps: 'What Would Jesus Do?'* In the hustle of Coolidge prosperity, the Jesus of the Gospel

according to Bruce Barton was much easier to emulate than
Sheldon's demanding model. *The Man Nobody Knows* was an
overpowering public-relations campaign written by a first-rate
account executive who had some knowledge of the subject
and years of journalistic experience. As far as the sales of the
book were concerned, he hoped that "every business man will
read it and send it to his partners and his salesmen." [15]

With knowledge so intimate that he might qualify as the thir-
teenth apostle, evangelist Barton set out to destroy the impression that Jesus was a physical weakling, a kill-joy, and a failure,
that he was a sissy, meek, and full of grief. "A physical weakling! Where did they get that idea?" he pointed to the Gospels.
"Jesus pushed a plane and swung an adze; he was a successful
carpenter. . . . A kill-joy! He was the most popular dinner
guest in Jerusalem! . . . A failure! He picked up twelve men
from the bottom ranks of business and forged them into an
organization that conquered the world." [16]

In this, his final mission, Barton did not begin with the
"typical" businessman and relate him to Christ. He reversed the
process and showed how Christ was eminently qualified as a
businessman. "Success is always exciting," he warmed to his
subject. "We never grow tired of asking what and how. What,
then, were the principal elements in his power over men? How
was it that the boy from a country village became the greatest
leader?" Jesus was a great executive, he went on, because of
his personal magnetism which commanded loyalty and respect,
his shrewd ability to pick men, and his vast patience in training
the organization that he had gathered together. He was an out-
door man, strong and healthy and full of the vigor of life. "And
for the proof of that assertion consider only four aspects of his
experience: the health that flowed out of him to create health
in others; the appeal of his personality to women—weakness
does not appeal to them; his lifetime of outdoor living; and the
steel-like hardness of his nerves." Barton was so persuaded by
this that he thought it about time that the worship of Jesus be
more masculine and that more reverence be shown to the forgotten Joseph, though he did not deny the importance of Mary.

Jesus was a sociable man, too. A wicked falsehood has come down through the ages that Jesus never laughed. The message of Jesus was that "God is supremely better than anybody had ever dared to believe. Not a petulant Creator . . . not a stern Judge . . . not a vain King . . . not a rigid Accountant . . . but a great Companion, a wonderful Friend, a kindly indulgent, joy-loving Father. . . ." The message of the Nazarene was bubbling with good cheer and joy. He liked to see people happy, and he certainly was no temperance leader. At the wedding feast, for example, Mary whispered to her son: "Son, the wine is gone." Jesus, glancing at his hostess ("already tears sparkled under her lids"), leaped immediately into action and saved the party from breaking up by changing the water into wine.[17]

Jesus' method Barton found particularly intriguing. He was so understanding of human beings and so effective with words that he could arouse interest and create desire—all in the same sentence. "Jesus knew how, and taught his followers how to catch the attention of the indifferent, and translate a great spiritual conception into terms of practical self-concern. Surely no one will consider us lacking in reverence if we say that every one of the 'principles of modern salesmanship' on which business men so much pride themselves, are brilliantly exemplified in Jesus' talk and work. The first of these and perhaps the most important is the necessity for 'putting yourself in step with your prospect.' " Any up-and-coming sales manager could profit by the technique the Nazarene used to call two men he wanted as disciples. They were fishermen, busy with their nets and thinking about the day's catch. Jesus did not cast his command in terms which might have jarred their thinking. He got in step with their train of thought and swung them into line. " 'Come with me,' " he beckoned as he put himself in step with his prospects, " 'and I will make you fishers of men.' " [18]

The Son of God captured public attention because "he recognized the basic principle that all good advertising is news." After the Messiah had produced one of his front-page stories, "can you imagine the next day's issue of the *Capernaum News,* if there had been one?

PALSIED MAN HEALED
JESUS OF NAZARETH CLAIMS RIGHT TO
FORGIVE SINS
PROMINENT SCRIBES OBJECT
'BLASPHEMOUS,' SAYS LEADING CITIZEN.
'BUT ANYWAY I CAN WALK,' HEALED MAN
RETORTS."

Jesus advertised himself, Barton continued, not by sermons, but by service. When he did lecture, it was in the form of parables which exemplify "all the principles on which advertising text books are written. Always a picture in the very first sentence; crisp, graphic language and a message so clear that even the dullest can not escape it.

TEN VIRGINS WENT FORTH TO MEET
A BRIDEGROOM

A striking picture and a striking head-line. The story which follows has not a single wasted word." Every advertising man ought to study these parables and understand the principles of their effectiveness. They are condensed, simple, sincere, and prove the necessity for repetition. And the finest example of all is the parable of the Good Samaritan—"the greatest advertisement of all time." [19]

In a chapter entitled "The Founder of Modern Business," Barton swept together certain key points in the idea of success and invoked divine authority for their support. Jesus said: "Wist ye not that I must be about my father's *business?*" What did he mean by "business," Barton asked. "To what extent are the principles by which he conducted his business applicable to ours? And if he were among us again, in our highly competitive world, would his business philosophy work?" The Redeemer's "recipe for success" Barton found in three statements. First, "whosoever will be great among you, shall be your minister, and whosoever of you will be the chiefest, shall be servant of all." Barton interpreted this to mean: "Whoever will be great must render great service." That is how George W. Perkins of the New York Life Insurance Company explained his own success: "We had a vision of extending the company's service throughout the world, of making it the finest, most useful institution of its kind. We made it that, and it made us rich." Though this doctrine is proclaimed as something quite modern, Barton observed, it is actually the way to success Jesus was preaching nineteen hundred years ago.[20]

Second, Jesus advised: "If you're forever thinking about saving your life, you'll lose it; but the man who loses his life shall find it." Barton interpreted this to mean: "Whoever will find himself at the top must be willing to lose himself at the bottom." Now this might seem impractical, Barton hurried on, "but look again! What did Perkins mean if it wasn't that he and his friends buried themselves in their great undertaking, literally lost their lives in it? And when they found their lives again, they were all of them bigger and richer than they had ever supposed they could be. Would such success have come to them" if they had been too concerned about their own self-interest?

Or take Henry Ford, Barton suggested. This was Ford's advice, based on his own experience: "Have you ever noticed that the man who starts out in life with a determination to make money, never makes very much? ... He may gather together a competence, of course, a few tens of thousands or even hundreds of thousands, but he'll never amass a really great fortune. But let a man start out in life to build something better and sell it cheaper than it has ever been built or sold before—let him have *that* determination, and give his whole self to it—and the money will roll in so fast that it will bury him if he doesn't look out." When Theodore N. Vail established the American Telephone and Telegraph Company, Barton concluded, "he gave everything he had—'threw his life into it,' as we say— 'lost his life in it,' as Jesus said. And it gave him back larger and richer life, and a fortune and immortality." Finally, Jesus said: "Whosoever shall compel thee to go a mile, go with him twain." For Barton, this meant: "The big rewards come to those who travel the second, undemanded mile." In short, "do more than is required of you, do twice as much." Over all these means to success, Barton concluded, is poised Jesus' practical affirmation: *"It is more blessed to give than to receive."* [21]

In his justification for business success, in addition to the appeal to service, Barton boldly struck out to link seven-

teenth-century Puritanism to twentieth-century Congregational-
ism. "Great progress will be made in the world," he contended, "when we rid ourselves of the idea that there is a
difference between *work* and *religious work*. We have been
taught that a man's daily business activities are selfish, and
that only the time which he devotes to church meetings and
social service activities is consecrated. Ask any ten people what
Jesus meant by his 'Father's business,' and nine of them will
answer 'preaching.' To interpret the words in this narrow sense
is to lose the real significance of his life. It was not to preach that
he came into the world; nor to teach; nor to heal. These are
all departments of his Father's business, but the business itself
is far larger, more inclusive. For if human life has any significance it is this—that God has set going here an experiment to
which all His resources are committed. He seeks to develop
perfect human beings, superior to circumstance, victorious over
Fate. No single kind of human talent or effort can be spared if
the experiment is to succeed. The race must be fed and clothed
and housed and transported, as well as preached to, and taught
and healed. Thus *all* business is his Father's business. All work
is worship; all useful service prayer. And whoever works whole-
heartedly at any worthy calling is a co-worker with the Almighty
in the great enterprise which He has initiated but which He can
never finish without the help of men." [22]

What did Barton mean by 'true success'? " 'There is a success
which is greater than wealth or titles,' [Jesus] says. 'It comes
through making your work an instrument of greater service,
and larger living to your fellow men and women.' " Material
success, Barton warned, is filled with many perils: "You know
men whose health is gone; men whose taste for reading and
music and art is gone. Men who have literally no interests in
life beyond the office which has become a mere treadmill
whereon their days are ground away. . . . This is not Jesus' idea
of what a life should be." [23]

The concept of service in Barton's universe, therefore, took
on a kind of omniscience. It was a definition of 'true success,'
and a means to material success. It was also a justification for
material success. *The Man Nobody Knows* was an attempt to do

two things. First, it glorified business and business success. Second, it tried to refresh Christian dogma. The technique was exaltation by association. It soaked the idea of success in the sanctity of the New Testament. The need it filled is measured by the following hard fact: In the year 1926, Americans purchased in book stores more copies of *The Man Nobody Knows* than any other current book of non-fiction.[24]

15

DON'T "SOAK 'EM....
SERVE 'EM"

From World War I through the 1920s, the idea of success was a powerful weapon in defense of conservatism. On and off for thirty years, reformers had been unsettling propertied interests by charging that equality of opportunity was a myth. Now was the time for conservatives to press on, to certify their values in the American credo. The success writer was only one voice in a chorus sung by Presidents of the United States and Supreme Court Justices down to elementary school textbooks.

Herbert Hoover believed that individualism, initiative, and equality of opportunity existed in his America of the 1920s, but that they must be vigilantly preserved if progress was to continue. "This ideal of individualism based upon equal opportunity to every citizen is the negation of socialism . . . ," Hoover explained as he accepted the Republican nomination for the Presidency in 1928. "It is as if we set a race. We, through free and universal education, provide the training of the runners; we give to them an equal start; we provide in the Government the umpire of fairness in the race. The winner is he who shows the most conscientious training, the greatest ability and the greatest character. Socialism bids all to end the race equally. It holds back the speedy to the pace of the slowest." Senator George Sutherland, soon to speak with the authority of a Supreme Court Justice, agreed that "the course of safety for society, as well as liberty for the individual, is to make and enforce laws which will keep free the gates of equal opportunity to all, compel an honest contest, and let the rewards for diligence fall where and how and in such measure as they may." From dog-eared textbooks, school children were learning that this was not only sound policy, but actual fact. For here was the land of economic opportunity, political freedom, and legal and social equality. Declared the author of *My Country: A Textbook in Civics and Patriotism for Young Americans:* "America is the one country in the whole world where each man has the same chance as every other man. Whether he was born in Ohio or in Italy does not matter. If he is brave and patient, not afraid of years of the hardest kind of work, he will win success and happiness." [1]

Beneath all the prosperity of the 1920s churned conflicts and contradictions, discontent and protest. Not every son was doing better than his father. There were declining occupations, such as farming, textiles, and coal mining; almost one-third of the nation's breadwinners received less than the $2,000 a year deemed adequate for the necessities of life; certain small segments of the population were disproportionately receiving huge chunks from the increasing national income for themselves; and by 1929, somewhere around one-half of retail sales were being transacted on credit. All along the line there yawned the usual crevices between the ideal and the real, between credo and fact. While "rugged individualism" was the honored theory, the benefits of cooperation through selected trade associations and associational activities began to appear irresistible. The nation's rock of conservatism, Herbert Hoover, was praising the personal qualities of a scouting frontiersman, and at the same time pushing some segments of the economy in a direction which would smooth the transition to the New Deal. Competition was a good thing—for the other fellow. Government intervention would drag freedom's own promised land down into decadence—unless it meant government intervention in your own favor by sympathetic politicians and administrators.[2]

Success writers tiptoed around these contradictions or drowned them in cheers for the *status quo.* As always, they were bursting with optimism, certain that there was plenty of oppor-

tunity for everyone, and convinced that success or failure depended on the individual, not on the environment. Most Americans must have agreed, for a napping government was just the
kind of government they kept in office.

The success idea as a weapon of conservatism was brandished
with the greatest flourish by the editor-publisher of a self-named
business magazine. With Scotch burr, and five feet, seven inches
of untidy chubbiness, B. C. Forbes bustled through the late 1910s
and the 1920s firing propaganda broadsides into the ranks of anyone who dared challenge the achievements of the American businessman. He probably wrote more inspirational life-stories of top
executives than anyone of his generation. An indefatigable free
lancer of the uplift essay, he also conducted for thirty years a
syndicated column for Hearst and other newspapers on business,
economics, labor, and finance. B. C. Forbes is his generation's
contender for the title of chief philosopher of business apolo-
getics. As such, he represents the counterpart of Bruce Barton
in the secular interpretation of the character ethic.[3]

Daily for Hearst, and twice a month for *Forbes,* his own
magazine, the columnist and editor sent out the message that
"business was originated to produce happiness, not to pile up
millions." He devoted his life to "humanizing" business. "Humanizing" business meant, among other things, persuading
executives to be more sensitive to the welfare of employees. He
was quick to chide business America for its reluctance to raise
wages, decrease hours, and improve working conditions. At the
same time he was not adverse to pointing out that a hike in labor's
wages came out of the consumer's pocketbook. Forbes was an
early welfare capitalist. Business must police itself. If it did
not, then some form of socialism would do the job in its own
way. This would be disastrous: "Under modern conditions business MUST be King. If it isn't, the nation languishes and dies.
... The nation that wins leadership in business puts itself in
the way of one day winning leadership in the arts and graces of
life, to say nothing of world politics. Leisure, culture, study,
research, all follow in the train of wisely-acquired wealth. Big
men are attracted by big propositions.... Today trade and

commerce, with their handmaidens, railroading and engineering, draw to them the flower of mankind." [4]

Forbes was an unofficial public-relations agent. Public relations likes to think of itself as a two-way street. It advises its client about the public response to a particular action; it interprets that client to the public. Most of Forbes' energies for "humanizing" were poured into interpreting to the public the achievements of business America. Much of his plea for America to understand and to be inspired by the glories of that achievement rested on the idea of success. To the reader reluctant to believe it, Forbes could hold up his own life as proof of his message. In the more than 500 life stories of businessmen that he wrote until death stayed his pen in 1954 at the age of seventy-three, none could surpass his own Horatio Alger rise. [5]

Bertie Charles Forbes was born in Aberdeenshire, Scotland, in 1880, the son of a Presbyterian country storekeeper and tailor who was short on funds, but long on children. One farming day young Bertie discovered that there was such a thing as a foreman who was paid more for being over other men: "That was the very first inkling I had in life that there was such a thing as rank. With all the determination my little soul could muster, I vowed that I wouldn't be a 'second man.' Indeed, I couldn't understand why anybody should be satisfied until he was a foreman." As a youngster he earned his first large sum by tramping three-quarters of a mile through the fields of Scotland before dawn to shine the shoes of visiting "Gentry" from England, there to enjoy the shooting. A mischievous, lively boy with a fertile mind, he taught himself Pitman shorthand, quit school at the age of fourteen and went to work for a newspaper. By a combination of brash, brilliance, and work, he started climbing journalism's ladder from the very bottom rung. [6]

Then rebuffed in love and twenty-one, he took off for South Africa and the Boer War. There he helped Edgar Wallace, the English author of detective thrillers, launch the Johannesburg *Rand Daily Mail* and learned the trade of special feature writing. "I was now drawing a rather large salary, was allowed to come and go as I pleased, and altogether had a pleasant, easy time," he recalled for the *American Magazine*'s inspirational pages.

"But I said to myself: 'Young fellow, this isn't the right kind of life for a youngster of less than twenty-four. You need to be bumped and buffeted about a whole lot more.' Throughout the world, the reporters of New York have the reputation of being the smartest that walk in shoe leather. European publications frequently print articles describing their amazing journalistic feats. I therefore concluded that the hardest school of all would be New York. So, having saved several thousand dollars, I visited a score of different countries to broaden my knowledge of the world and finally landed in New York." [7]

It was the year 1904, and Forbes didn't know Wall Street from Broadway. He got a job on the *Journal of Commerce*, became its financial editor, at the same time doubled as an editorial writer for the *Financial and Commercial Chronicle*, and from 1912 to 1916 was business and financial editor of the *New York American*. The hustling reporter learned a lot of things fast. One was that you had to know the rich, to gain "their respect, their confidence, and their friendship. In those days the great rendezvous in the evenings for financial people was the Waldorf-Astoria Hotel; so I quit my humble but comfortable ten-dollar-a-week boarding-house and went to live at the Waldorf. It cost me more than I was making; but I had saved money and felt that this would prove a good investment. And it did." He also mastered the fundamentals of his trade: "One thing I learned from writing for a large daily audience was that the simplest language registers best. Another thing was that human beings are more interested in human beings than in anything else in the world, and that if you can link the names, the personality, the achievements, the views and the advice of high authorities with business, money, investments, work, and other subjects in which most people are interested, then you have articles which are read just as eagerly by the wage earner as by the executive." Giving up the best-paid financial editorship in the United States, Forbes struck out in 1916 to launch his own magazine a year later which would deal with "people who do things, and with their doings; a publication that would strive to inject more humanity, more joy and more satisfaction into business, and into life in general." [8]

B. C. Forbes was one of the great interviewers in the history of success writing. From his early days in South Africa, when he quizzed a visiting member of the Japanese Imperial Family who was standing naked in a big washtub, to the pleadings and threats he used to squeeze autobiographical anecdotes from recalcitrant millionaires, Forbes mastered every trick known to the human-interest reporter. Like Bruce Barton, he wrote for the *American Magazine* (his peak years ran from 1917 to 1922), and received what was tantamount to a niche in its Hall of Fame by writing his own life story for editor John Siddall. Through magazines and newspapers he bombarded millions of Americans with calls to duty, and then happily reaped a triple remuneration by joining many of his essays into a series of books and publishing them himself.[9]

Forbes never tired of reporting on opportunity in America, and the kind of people that generally seized it. "Fruit is plentiful at the top of the tree," he pointed. "There are more $50,000-a-year jobs than there are $50,000-a-year men available to fill them." He had nothing but scorn and pity for rich men's sons: "Pampered sons of plutocrats may shine for a time in 'society,' but not in the world of affairs and of service unless they rip off their coats and get to work early and stay late. To be born with a golden spoon in the mouth is more of a handicap than a help in attaining worth-while success in this age. The Goddess of Success smiles more often upon the humble hard-worker than upon the high-born dilettante. Opportunity plays no favorites. The prizes are open to all. And never before were the prizes so big or so numerous." With a blizzard of statistics, Forbes could prove to you that "ninety per cent of America's business leaders began at the bottom. . . ."[10]

Many magazines and newspapers have a fund of fillers which they draw upon to cover blank spaces. The fund of fillers for *Forbes* magazine was the editor's imagination. His mind was a warehouse of aphorisms. When he couldn't locate the right maxim, he made one up. Many of his fillers were brief signposts pointing the way to success "along life's highways and byways." They are a *Poor Richard's Almanack* dressed up in a twentieth-century style: "ASPIRE—then perspire. . . . THE place for the 'knocker' is outside the door. . . . IS your boss entitled to regard you as an ass or an asset? . . . IT should be spelled Hop-por-tunity. . . . VIM wins. . . . DEVELOP pluck. LET the other fellow trust to luck. . . . THE fellow with the swelled head is pretty certain to be a pinhead. . . . TAKE the broom and sweep out Gus Gloom. . . . SWEAT or be swatted. . . . PUT the I CAN in Amer-i-can. . . . DON'T condemn all capitalists. You may be one some day. . . . THERE'S only one letter difference between l-e-a-r-n-i-n-g and e-a-r-n-i-n-g. . . . ANOTHER way of spelling success:—s-w-e-a-t. . . . THE capital you must depend upon most is this capital: I." [11]

In column after column Forbes expanded these epigrams into the way to wealth. Work, he recited, is "the sole ladder that leads to the Land of Success. . . . Enthusiasm is the steam which makes the engine go. . . . 'All things come to those who hustle while they wait.'. . . The fortunes of Rockefeller and Carnegie were founded by systematic saving of dollar after dollar." In addition to the usual strictures against speculation and dishonesty, Forbes broadened his secular character ethic to stress the power of intelligence, untouched by formal educational training. "The only caste recognized in America is not blood," he contended, "but brains. The prizes in this country are open to all. Most of them have been won by boys who began at the bottom, unhandicapped by inherited wealth—and unaided by superior educational advantages in many cases. . . . A romance of grit, sweat, perseverance—and success—could be written about almost every one of them. . . . Success has not been a matter of pure luck with these industrial giants. It has been mainly a matter of, first, work; second, work; third, work—with, of course, a plentiful mixture of brains, foresight and imagination." But more important in accumulating money is nurturing an attitude of service. You have to give satisfaction in order to get money.[12]

While Forbes was urging his readers on to higher incomes, he also issued warnings about where he was driving them. Too many ambitious men, he charged, sacrifice their family and health to the time-hungry obligations of business: "They reason that they can do better by their family by devoting their whole

time and energy to money-making affairs." Forbes recognized
that "they are anxious to give their wife and children a high place
in the social scale, and they figure that they can do this only by
the closest attention to business." It is the misfortune of such
men that "the Juggernaut of dollar-making has crushed out of
them every capacity for genuine enjoyment, every grace, every
unselfish sentiment and instinct." The wisest counsel to follow
is to hold your "striving for place and power . . . within bounds."
Then let your compassion overflow for the extravagantly rich
man who has sacrificed everything to make money. "If we
only knew the inner life of our multi-millionaires," he nodded
sorrowfully, "we would not make the mistake of envying them.
We would learn that an overdose of money is apt to be poison-
ous." [13]

What is, then, as Forbes titled it, "true-blue success"? It is
not money, because money is merely a means to happiness—
a final goal. "True-blue success" is measured by internal things
—friendships, an honorable reputation, self-respect, learning,
contentment, and joy of living. It is also external. "I have been
accused sometimes of emphasizing over-much dollar-success,"
Forbes began his denial. "As a matter of fact, here is, offhand,
how I would define success in a single sentence: Success is
finding, or making, that position which enables you to contribute to the world the very greatest services of which you are
capable, through the diligent, persevering, resolute cultivation
of all the faculties God has endowed you with, and doing it all
with cheerfulness, scorning to allow difficulties or defeats to
drive you to pessimism or despair." At the heart of his definition
of "true-blue success" was the principle of service. "In our own
land a generation and less ago," he chronicled, "enthusiasm
usually ran to money-making. To-day enthusiasm more often
runs to human service, to creating and building up useful enterprises, to bettering and extending the country's commerce, to
improving the lot of the rank and file, to raising the national
standard of education. . . . Success used to be spelt $UCCE$$—
dollars. Success is now coming to be spelt Service." [14]

Forbes criticized the methods of the businessman, but he
made it quite clear that his strictures were directed at the past.

The businessman was becoming more angelic as the years wore on. His justification for the high incomes of top executives was based on three convictions. First, he celebrated them as the "doers" who had built the nation's standard of living into a triumph of material conveniences. Second, he idealized the motives of successful men and thereby made motivation a justification: "To thoroughly relish work, there must be more than a purely selfish motive; there must be at either the front or the back of the mind an inspiration based on unselfishness, a desire to succeed for the pleasure or benefit it will mean for someone else.... Few of the world's conspicuously successful men have been animated solely by greed of gold." Finally, the concept of service was enlisted for triple duty (as a means to material success, a definition of "true success," and a justification for material success). "Business simply means performing some service which earns a reward," he developed the justification. "We have not yet reached the stage where those individuals or companies which serve most are always rewarded most generously: but we are rapidly progressing toward the ideal goal. The young man entering business who is anxious to succeed must recognize that his success will be in proportion to the value of the service he renders." In short, don't "Soak 'em.... Serve 'em." [15]

From the latter half of the nineteenth century, most success writers had tried to support their advice by empirical evidence. Through biographical anecdotes, polls, or the assertion of laws, the quest for certainty was pursued. Despite these efforts, they were still writing in the field of the humanities where value judgments affected their advice. In the second decade of the twentieth century, greater precision was sought by placing the success idea in the social sciences. In the factory and the office, the force which speeded this trend was called scientific management.

Scientific management, as a movement to increase production at decreased costs, began in the 1880s under Frederick W. Taylor. Success writers called it personal efficiency. They adopted the ·spirit, and some of the devices, of such industrial experts as Taylor, Henry L. Gantt, Morris L. Cooke—and

Frank B. Gilbreth, who carried the philosophy into his own family and hopefully assumed that children were cheaper by the dozen. In the factory, the worker was measured in relation to his machine. In efficiency success literature, the individual was taught how to conceive of himself as a machine. Like a machine, he could increase the quality and quantity of his work and therefore his income. He must learn to think in terms of a ratio between input and output, effort and results, expenditure and income. Though a stopwatch was not required, the principles of time and motion studies were adapted. To assist in a maximum of return for a minimum of expenditure, cost accounting principles, tests, and charts were included to check efficiency and record progress.[16]

In the early 1910s, scientific management was popularized in the press. By the World War I period, it had become something of a craze. Efficiency, as a word, was new. It became current in engineering during the latter half of the nineteenth century, and in business and economics from the beginning of the twentieth century. When it became popular in the early 1910s, many success writers eagerly adopted the word but neglected the philosophy behind it. One had to be efficient, as well as hard working and determined. (One writer in 1912 used it in the title of his book, probably as a selling point, and then scarcely mentioned the word or its concepts in the text.) By the middle of the 1910s, however, success writers were busy cashing in on the appeal of the new talisman with a more detailed analysis of its powers.[17]

Edward Earle Purinton was a pioneer in the field and the leading efficiency success writer during its period of adoption by the success idea in the 1910s. From 1914 to 1921, as Director of the Independent Efficiency Service, he kept the weekly *Independent* filled with articles. Through the "Efficiency Question Box," troubled readers could find advice on problems ranging from how to find a supreme talent to curing a nervous breakdown—the efficient way.[18]

What is the promise of efficiency? It is a "short cut to highest achievement," declared Purinton. It was in the "know how" that the efficiency success writers made their contribution. For instead of inspirational calls to work, they detailed meticulous instructions in *how* to work. In "A Day at the Office," Purinton guarantees that "not genius, nor influence, nor affluence, but a scientific work schedule, makes the great man or the great business. Whoever can order his own day can order his own destiny." He tells how a "scientific work schedule" can accomplish more work with less effort by standardization, routing, an organized plan, attention to health, and proper working conditions. At the end of the chapter a self-analytical test enables you to check your efficiency. Using the character ethic as a foundation, Purinton compares life to the construction of a house. Every building must rest on solid cornerstones. "The cornerstones in the lives of most great men," he asserts, "have been HEALTH, KNOWLEDGE, CHARACTER, INDUSTRY." [19]

Knowledge however, must be vocational. As Dean of the American Efficiency Foundation, Purinton suggested the following somewhat controversial piece of legislation: Why not pass "a law that a college which fails to prepare sixty per cent of its graduates for guaranteed self-support the first year after graduation shall be publicly censured and deprived of funds from the state or individual donors, until the required grade in monetary efficiency shall be attained by the curriculum? If I, being a parent of a youth of twenty or thereabouts, and having expended thousands of dollars on his college course, should find that he was not earning a good living six months after graduation—I would sue the college for the return of my money! Some day some father will do this." Less controversial was Purinton's rather routine presentation of the component parts of the success idea.[20]

During the 1910s and 1920s, the word "efficiency" kept indiscriminately popping up in success literature. For the few success writers who understood it as a system rather than a magic word, efficiency was a technique of self-organization. (Not many were so totally committed as Frederick W. Taylor, the founding father of scientific management. He died while winding his watch.) Scientific management promised maximum returns with a minimum expenditure of wasted effort and time.

Rating tables, charts, and schedules were devices to exploit to the fullest the character ethic's ancient emphasis on hard work, perseverance, and thrift. But the efficiency movement was more than simply a modification of the character ethic. It was hurrying the success idea into a dangerous new commitment. The old duty was to the personal virtues of the character ethic; the new commitment was to a clever learning of techniques. Instead of a plodding, ascetic attention to the growth of character, there was a system. The ancient virtues of the character ethic were moral absolutes, good in themselves; scientific management was relative, good only if it contributed to getting ahead. Taylor, for example, never drank liquor. He abstained, not because drink was morally wrong, but because he had scientifically concluded that liquor wasted his forces and was therefore inefficient. In the traditional gospel of the character ethic, liquor or laziness or indolence were morally wrong and their opposites were morally good. If hard work contributed to success, the results of it were secondary to the virtue of it. The drift of the success idea in succeeding decades was in the same philosophical direction as the efficiency movement.[21]

What impact did the 1910s and 1920s have on the character ethic? If we allow for a few variations, all the component parts of the success formula remained constant. Indeed, with the exception of the intense emphasis on service as a justification for success, the character ethic was *basically* the same in the Jazz Decade as in the Gilded Age.

Some variations are apparent. Beginning in the 1910s and flourishing in the 1920s, the qualities of initiative and perseverance were emphasized, particularly in books directed specifically at salesmen. Honored were pep, enthusiasm, and boosting; the ideal was the self-starter and go-getter. In these two decades, techniques borrowed from scientific management were adopted by success writers and called personal efficiency. The trend pointed to the 1930s and 1940s by indicating a breakaway from the moral absolutes of personal virtues which had been the foundation of the character ethic for so long.

Social Darwinism, as always, was rejected as a justification for success. With everyone hustling in the high pressure atmosphere of the 1920s, it might reasonably be assumed that Social Darwinism would creep into books on salesmanship. On the contrary, a traditional justification was that individual character was strengthened in battles which took place within oneself rather than with other people. The sales manager did not rise from the ranks by stepping on the faces of fellow drummers in his territory. A justification for success was *not* that he was fittest because he survived in a struggle for existence with other men, but because he provided better service to his buyers and to the public. Of course, this could be interpreted as a struggle for existence with the fittest surviving on the basis of service provided. But this would be distorting the feeling success writers were trying to get across. The tone of success books was not tooth and fang. The spirit was Christian and humanitarian.

Now and then in the 1920s, Americans stopped running long enough to wonder what it was all about. A burgeoning paycheck which blessed the home with a vacuum cleaner had its own excuse for being. But money and material things, even for the comfort of wife and children, left unsatisfied a deeper need in Protestant American culture. That need was to assign to work a self-giving as well as a self-seeking meaning. That is why one little word—"service"—was surrounded with such reverence.

Service was a grab bag concept. A manufacturer provided it when he made more and better products at a lower price. The sales department accomplished it when they distributed the products. Real estate and insurance salesmen, bankers and brokers, were doing it in their jobs. For business, profits were an index of service. For the individual, a measure of success was the amount of service rendered to the consumer, the community, or the nation. The professions were always supposed to have provided service, and it was not measurable in material terms. Now business was crowding in on the concept and using it far more than the nineteenth century as a justification for making money.

What lay behind this glorification of service? In the first place, the concept of service was a defense against attacks on business. In the literature of success, it began to challenge the stewardship principle in the 1890s and 1900s. By the 1910s, every loyal Rotarian knew that the proper function of the producer and the seller was to serve the consumer. So fervently did Rotary believe in this that they made the idea their motto: "He Profits Most Who Serves Best." By the 1920s service was the supreme justification—whether interpreted with secular support (as in B. C. Forbes) or a religious vindication now centered on the teachings of Christ rather than the Old Testament (as in Bruce Barton).[22]

Second, success writers were following the lead of a new philosophy spearheaded by the avant-garde of the business world. The Henry Fords and Edward Filenes were calling for a rising standard of living through mass production, mass distribution, and mass purchasing power with the purpose of service to the nation.[23]

Third, with the rise of corporations, labor unions, and the paternalistic state, it became increasingly difficult, and perhaps a bit arrogant, for the submerged individual to play the role of steward. The stewardship principle in the nineteenth century did not emphasize so strongly the advantages to the general welfare from the actual making of money. The nation benefited, after the money was made, in the form of gifts. The nature of ethics was personal. The twentieth century moved the process back a step and made ethics more public. Successful businessmen (in a trend which was accelerated in succeeding decades) spent less effort justifying their own careers and more time explaining the contributions of their factories and offices. As managers of corporations, which they neither owned nor legally controlled, they could defend their own high incomes by exalting the contributions of the businesses which they managed. Then the amount of salary that any top executive received was simply a yardstick of the contribution of the corporation he managed. If carried to an extreme, which it never was, this credo could relieve successful men from the obligation of dispensing personal funds to charitable organizations. They had already made their unselfish contribution to the world simply by making money. The amount of their income, in fact, was a measure of the service they had already contributed.

In the fourth place, there was strong historical precedent for it in economic theory. Adam Smith's theory of capitalism had emphasized that the general welfare was advanced by the pursuit of individual self-interest. For Adam Smith, however, it was not necessary, or even desirable, that the individual weigh his decisions by the scales of the public welfare. Modifying Smith's position, the doctrine of service insisted that the general welfare was consciously advanced by individuals who considered the welfare of the public before their own interests. The doctrine of service, then, at once denied and affirmed Smith's philosophy of capitalism. It denied that successful men were indifferent to the effects of their labor. At the same time, it affirmed the notion that individual effort collectively added up to the general welfare. As one English observer put it: "The American is honestly convinced that he is doing the chief part of a citizen's duty in pursuing business. Incidentally he may be making a fortune, but in the main he thinks of himself as developing the country, raising its standard of life, providing it with the things it wants at the lowest cost. His claim is generally conceded." [24]

Finally, the American religious tradition was sympathetic to it. Explained the visiting French economist, André Siegfried: "The idea of service, which has become so popular in America, springs from the Puritanical idea of wealth sanctified by labour. ... Money thus became not only the symbol of creative power, but a sort of moral justification. Efficiency was looked upon as a Christian virtue, and one could no longer separate what had been accomplished for God from what had been contributed to the development of the country. ... In the end, 'service' is the doctrine of an optimistic Pharisee trying to reconcile success with justice." At the same time, continued Siegfried, "such ethics have their purpose, for they advocate honesty, good manners, intelligence of the American, as well as his sincere idealism and kindliness. They are a marvellous expression of the practical ingenuousness." [25]

In the nineteenth century, the stewardship of wealth principle was assisted by the general idea of service as a justification for making money. As America moved through the twentieth century, the concept of service had to carry most of the load. It was astonishing that the whole concept of service did not collapse under the burden. Most success writers used it as a justification for making money. Some of them used it as a definition of 'true success.' Others claimed that it was the most effective means to material success. Some brushed aside a hunger for profit, power, or status, prestige, creativity, or adventure to claim that a passion for service was the motivation—all wrapped up in one tidy bundle and tagged "service." It was a "package deal" of comforting reassurances about their *raison d'être* for which most modern Americans must have felt grateful.

16

HOW TO WIN FRIENDS AND
INFLUENCE PEOPLE

It happened during the lean years of the depression. More so than ever Americans were searching for a key to success. The old one fitted no longer. The shift in the way to wealth from character to personality would have occurred without a depression, so strong were the forces working in its favor. The 1930s hastened a trend which had been on the move for several decades. The symbol which marked the transition was the publication in 1936 of a book by Dale Carnegie with the magnetic title *How to Win Friends and Influence People*. By that date, the success idea had decisively turned away from a belief in character as the most important means to wealth-getting—a belief which reached back over the centuries to colonial life, and further back to an earlier tradition in Europe.[1]

The personality ethic, a response to long-term social and economic forces, enjoyed its own intellectual heritage. What the personality way to success is, and how it developed, can be seen from a look at its heritage. The character ethic, of course, did not ignore the relationship of aspiring youth to other people. Most success books charged their readers to be courteous, polite, and well-mannered. Though they concentrated primarily on building the virtues of hard work and diligence into their readers, the character ethic did not neglect to point out that a sloppy, ill-mannered, and generally obnoxious youth had as much chance of getting ahead as a fingerless clerk in an accounting house. Seldom did a success book of the character ethic completely ignore the impression that one might make on other people. Most books mingled both schools of advice in unequal parts. Their classification is based on general emphasis. Up to the 1930s, the broad body of success literature was overwhelmingly character ethic in content and tone.[2]

In its references to the equivalent of personality, the character ethic drew largely from the type of etiquette manual which conceived of manners as an expression of character. Though there were etiquette books which were also success books, i.e., they offered instructions in how to accumulate wealth, most of them were more helpful to the parvenu who was straining to translate his wealth into social class status. This type of etiquette book, which the character ethic drew on, stressed that good manners were good morals, mandatory for any decent human being, and necessary for rising in the world. An aspiring youth should be courteous, polite, and well-behaved. Pleasant manners not only helped you get ahead. They were moral virtues in and of themselves.

Another type of etiquette book, more directly the heritage of the personality ethic, was sharply pragmatic in intent. There was less concern for manners as an expression of morals and character, more interest in the impression that manners would make on other people. Etiquette consisted of rules to be learned, courtesy possessed a cash value for its own sake and could be employed subtly to manipulate the other fellow.

Literature of this type begins no later than the time of the first courtier who pressured a favor from the King by seducing the Queen, and then recorded for less accomplished courtiers how he did it. But the immediate heritage of this type owes much to that suave eighteenth-century gentleman, that heartless polished column of marble, the elegant Earl of Chesterfield. In *Letters to His Son,* Chesterfield split morals from manners, instructed his illegitimate son in the art of duplicity, concentrated on the external graces for their own sake as a means of getting ahead, and filled his advice with the observation that "something or other is to be got out of everybody." Righteous Americans blasted Lord Chesterfield for his libertine principles, masquerading under a cloak of virtue, but when his more naughty precepts for self-advancement had been washed away by streams of editorial ink, *Letters to His Son,* in various cleansed editions, went on to become a best-seller in eighteenth-century America.[3]

Something of Chesterfield's craftiness, without his cynical amorality, is apparent in Benjamin Franklin. As noted in an earlier chapter, Franklin was the most important and influential success apostle of the character ethic. But he is also an ancestor of the personality ethic, and was frequently appealed to by preceptors in that school. Their source, however, was not the homilies of Poor Richard but the more sophisticated *Autobiography.*

Three autobiographical confessions in Franklin's life were particularly instructive for success writers of the personality ethic. First, Franklin thawed a cold enemy into a warm friend by purposefully asking a favor of the man. Second, in conversations with other people, he consciously appeared to be humble and tried to avoid dogmatic assertions. Third, always aware of what he *appeared* to be, Franklin, the printer, sometimes pushed a paper-laden wheelbarrow through the streets to impress other businessmen with his industriousness. Such confessions of shrewdness at impressing and handling other people may seem inconsequential, but in the ensuing discussion it will become apparent why success writers of the personality ethic responded to them with such enthusiasm.[4]

The part of the personality ethic which concentrated on the conscious manipulation of other people was enriched in the twentieth century by applied psychology. While Chesterfield and Franklin were playing it by ear, applied psychology scientifically laid down fixed rules. The personality school does owe something, as well, to the mind power ethic. In New Thought's religious means to success, the law of attraction, particularly when it was invoked to work on other people, had a strong manipulative quality about it. Secular mind power employed the psychological principle of suggestion to maneuver people into a receptive frame of mind. But in that part of the personality ethic which tried to influence and control the responses of other people, applied psychology exerted by far the most influence.[5]

The other category of literature, some of it advertising, which comprises the intellectual heritage of the personality ethic consists of the many techniques for a more charming presence and attractive physical appearance.

The social graces were efficiently exploited for pragmatic ends. Asserted the Sherwin Cody School of English in 1924: "Practically all the many formulas for success can be summed up in this simple principle: *You must be able to make other people do what you want.*" Sherwin Cody's correspondence course in grammatical English held up the ideal of those outstanding men whose words "bite like chisels into the brains of other people." With his high-domed forehead and close-cropped, pointed beard, Sherwin Cody gazed out at magazine readers in numberless advertisements and promised to teach them accurate spelling, correct grammar, and faultless pronunciation. No more embarrassing blunders now. It's just as if the master "himself were standing forever at your elbow." Fifteen minutes a day and you will express that "facility of speech which denotes the person of breeding and education!" [6]

After mastering correct English and developing a slick delivery, preferably through a public speaking course, the next step was to find something to say. It was all in Dr. Eliot's 'Five-Foot Shelf of Books,' a fifty-volume selection from the world's literature. The "Harvard Classics," the more formal name for Dr. Eliot's collection, contained "the essentials of a liberal education in even fifteen minutes a day" and enough material for a lifetime of conversation flashing with wit and wisdom. Musical advertisements like "They Laughed When I Sat Down at the Piano" do reveal something of the personality ethic's spirit, except that the expressed purpose of mastering the saxophone or piano is popularity, not money-making.[7]

Success writers of the character ethic did not ignore the advantages of a neat and well-scrubbed appearance. Cleanliness, after all, was next to Godliness in what is sometimes referred to as the bathtub interpretation of American values. But it was not until the 1920s, a decade before the triumph of the personality ethic, that the success idea began to exploit on a large scale physical attractiveness for financial gain. The source was primarily advertising, and the most familiar symbol is probably Lifebuoy soap. By 1936 Lever Brothers was reporting in national magazines the olfactory confessions of a wife who sniffed through to the reasons why her husband's sales record was collapsing: "He laughed at the idea that *he* could be guilty of 'B.O.' [body odor], but I got him to promise to use Lifebuoy —just to please me! . . . Once more his sales top all the rest at the office, so it's plain the trouble *must* have been 'B.O.'" Tuning in to a thousand fears in the nation's burgeoning office force, Lifebuoy later sent out over the radio the deep voice of a foghorn, moaning lugubriously: "BEEEE OOOO." With devilish ingenuity and commercial cunning, advertisers of other products increasingly continued to relate sundry sections and functions of the human body to success with a frankness heretofore restricted to the four walls of a doctor's office.[8]

During the first three decades of the twentieth century, the output of personality ethic success literature was abundant. Advice on how to manipulate other people and develop an attractive personal and physical appearance posed a threat to the supremacy of the character ethic. Much of the literature was directed at salesmen, coaching them in the step-by-step process of maneuvering customers from the first interview to the final closing of the sale.[9]

By the late 1920s and early 1930s, the "science" of handling people was reaching out to embrace those traditionally self-contained folk—the production-line men who manufactured the goods. Lamented in 1932 a professor of "Humanics" at Massachusetts Institute of Technology in *Problems in Human Engineering:* "The most common criticism of engineering graduates is not lack of skill in solving technical problems, but rather inability to get along with people." If engineering students study mechanics, reasoned the science-minded educators, clinging to the spirit of machine jargon, why not "humanics"? If electrical engineering, why not "human engineering"? These were necessary fields of study for engineers destined for managerial positions of power.[10]

*   *   *

The dam broke in 1936. That year Dale Carnegie published his monumental work in the history of the success idea. *How to Win Friends and Influence People* has sold more copies in America, excluding the Bible, textbooks, and manuals, than any other non-fiction book in the twentieth century. In the English language, the sales of the regular, clothbound edition have run to approximately 2,500,000 copies with 109 printings. The paperback edition has sold approximately 5,500,000 books with 89 printings, making a grand total of 8,000,000 copies in English alone. *How to Win Friends and Influence People* has been reproduced in over thirty languages and dialects, including Afrikaans, Gujarati, Punjabi, and Burmese.[11]

By clarifying the new-style means to success and setting it on a firm line, *How to Win Friends and Influence People* has exerted an immense impact on self-help literature in America. What sort of person wrote it? What kind of a man is responsible for creating a course in public speaking and human relations that has produced more than one million graduates?

It all began with a barefoot background in Maryville, Missouri, in 1888. Dale's father was a hard-working farmer and hog-breeder, but everything always seemed to go wrong. For six years every spring the One Hundred and Two River spilled its banks, destroying the fields of corn and hay, while the hogs died of cholera and had to be burned. Mule colts were broken to harness and then sold three years later for less than their original price. A newly purchased jackass walked into the barn, stepped on the other end of a loose board studded with long nails, and fell dead on the spot from a punctured stomach. Dale's mother was a devout Methodist who met each disaster with a stouthearted hymn and took her troubles to God.[12]

When Dale was about twelve, the family sold out and bought another farm three miles from the State Normal School at Warrensburg, Missouri. In 1904, close to sixteen years of age, Dale entered the freshman class at the State Normal School, which approximates the eleventh grade of high school in today's academic set-up. Too poor to board in town, he commuted each day by horseback, ashamed of his ill-fitting clothes, the poverty of the farm, and the ceaseless round of chores after school. But important influences were at work. He had the advantage of a good mother, the *sine qua non* of a success story background, and she cared about books. A teacher from his previous school came to live at the farm, owning a typewriter and using big words. A Chautauqua lecturer inflamed Dale with an autobiographical account of how he rose from a poor farm boy to a prosperous orator.

Dale quickly discerned which way was up at the State Normal School. There were two avenues to prestige—athletics and debating. Athletics was impossible. His mother had trained him in poetry recitals, so he plunged into debating. Drunk with eloquence, he declaimed to the horse as he bumped back and forth the three miles to school, to the cows in the field and to the pigeons in the barn. The first year he lost every debate. But he kept working at it. By his second year young Dale Carnegie was being hailed as one of the best speakers in college, and was coaching other students in elocution. His fellow students thought him egotistical. One prophet in the yearbook predicted: "Sure to win fame, makes all of us students think he can declaim." At the same time he was a likable fellow and was elected vice-president of his class. The yearbook also put these prophetic words into his mouth: "I will sit down now but the time will come when you will hear me." [13]

Quitting the State Normal School in 1908 after four years, two of which were roughly equivalent to college work, Dale hit the road to make some money. The first venture was a flop. He became a salesman for the International Correspondence Schools. His first, and last, sale was a course in engineering to a telephone repairman trapped on top of a telephone pole. He moved on from Alliance, Nebraska, to Omaha on a freight train, feeding and watering two carloads of wild horses in return for his passage. Armour & Company gave him a job selling bacon, soap, and lard in the Bad Lands of South Dakota. He did well, was offered an executive position with the company, but decided to take his $500 in savings to Boston and study oratory with the idea of becoming a Chautauqua lecturer. Persuaded by a minister to become an actor instead, he went to New York and enrolled in the American Academy of Dramatic Arts.

Dale was enchanted by the theater. In 1911 he toured the country as the assistant stage manager and filled the role of Dr. Hartley in *Polly of the Circus*. Howard Lindsay, that versatile man of the theater, later affectionately recalled those months with the touring company when both men were measuring their abilities. "Dale was quite a talker," Lindsay remembered. "I would not say that he had any gift of conversation; he didn't. He made speeches. At the dining table a knife or fork never impeded his gestures. I remember chiding him about this until he did put the silver down before bringing his hands into play to emphasize a point in his oratory. I remember giving him advice about the size of his collar and the kind of necktie that was appropriate. In the meantime I learned a great deal from him. He was a voracious reader and had a lively memory. He was a very hard worker. Not content with the $25 a week, which he was paid as a salary, he added to it by becoming a necktie salesman, carrying a heavy bag of samples and spending much time trying to persuade haberdashers to give him an order. As I recall, he didn't make enough to justify the amount of work he put in." [14]

Evidently Carnegie awakened to a similar conclusion about his talents as an actor. When the tour ended, so did his thespian career. Another crisis this time found him selling trucks for the Packard Motor Car Company, although his background had taught him nothing about motors, and he cared less. But there was one thing he did know—and enjoyed doing. He was twenty-four years old and it was 1912.

A new plan had come to him and he took it to the director of the Young Men's Christian Association at 125th Street in New York City. The director responded gloomily to the idea of a Y.M.C.A. course in public speaking, but in the interest of fellowship, invited the young man to come over the following Tuesday and make a speech, or do a stunt of some sort. Carnegie showed up and recited James Whitcomb Riley's "Knee-Deep in June," and "Giddyap, Napoleon, It Looks Like Rain," both to piano accompaniment. And that's how it all began. The director finally agreed to a night course in public speaking with Carnegie taking 80 per cent of the net.

By 1914 the Carnegie course was spreading to Y.M.C.A. branches in other cities and the sometime actor-salesman's income had jumped to $400 a week. Nights were spent teaching others how to speak; days were filled attending classes in how to write, until his inspirational articles began appearing in popular magazines. Things were really building as he moved around meeting important people, lining up Assistant Secretary of the Navy Franklin D. Roosevelt in 1916 to address a graduating class in Baltimore, and changing his name from Carnagey to Carnegie. It was, after all, absurd to rent space in Carnegie Hall and continue to spell your name differently from old Andrew.

World War I forced a hiatus. After the Army released him, Carnegie signed on to lecture for an overworked Lowell Thomas, who could not himself fill all the engagements of people who were eager to hear "With Allenby in Palestine and Lawrence in Arabia." He went on to become Thomas' business manager, and the years drifted by rich in travel and experience. With the manuscript of a novel called "Blizzard" tucked under his arm, Carnegie returned to the United States. "Blizzard" was given an icy reception by the publishers. No stranger to a crisis, Carnegie grabbed his bootstraps and started lifting. Patiently he began again in the field he knew best—instruction in public speaking. As his classes grew in size and number during the late 1920s and 1930s, he realized public speaking was only part of it. Americans were looking for a new way to success. Carnegie's answer was at first a brief talk, but as he gathered more information and experience, it grew into a full-scale lecture which he presented to his students of public speaking. He called the lecture "How to Win Friends and Influence People." Leon Shimkin of Simon and Schuster, a publishing house that kept a light burning all night, was in the course. He saw the possibilities, and Simon and Schuster put an expanded version between covers in 1936.

How can we explain the colossal sales of *How to Win Friends and Influence People,* outside of a well-timed interest in its approach and the perpetual promotion of Dale Carnegie and his students? There were readable books, as good, or better, which developed the same principles, e.g., a 1930 work entitled *Strategy in Handling People.* The answer lies in certain qualities of the book and the man who wrote it.[15]

First, Carnegie knew what he was talking about from personal experience. Out of his laboratory of human relations, with students as guinea pigs, he produced in 1926 a two-volume textbook on public speaking which has held steady sales through several editions. (The textbook concluded its advice with reprints of two classics of the character ethic, Russell Conwell's *Acres of Diamonds* and Elbert Hubbard's *A Message to Garcia,* plus a mind power essay by James Allen entitled *As a Man Thinketh.*) He had gone to school to the precursors of the personality ethic, particularly the works on psychology of H. A. Overstreet, William James, and Alfred Adler. Perhaps the most important influence was H. A. Overstreet's *Influencing Human Behavior* (1925) which contains most of the principles of applied psychology advanced by Carnegie in his book. An experienced writer of inspirational articles, he had tested his pen with *Lincoln the Unknown,* a sentimental biography of the great man, and *Little Known Facts about Well Known People,* brief sketches on the theme of the self-made man. For material of this type, Carnegie drew upon scores of personal interviews from Marconi to Clark Gable. He explained that he had "hired a trained research man to spend one and a half years in various libraries reading everything I had missed, plowing through erudite tomes on psychology, poring over hundreds of magazine articles, searching through countless biographies, trying to ascertain how the great men of all ages dealt with people." Such labor was hardly necessary, however. His predecessors in the personality ethic had dug out most of the stories and incorporated them in their own books.[16]

A second explanation for its sales lies in the quality of the book itself. *How to Win Friends and Influence People* is a model success book of the personality ethic. Always practical, insistently driving toward the goal of manipulating others, it races along in a fast-paced, clipped, almost abrupt style of writing, making a point, rounding it out, and then hammering the point home with a concluding statement in bold letters at the end of each chapter. The reader is spared the effort of digging out the theme, because the book is constructed in outline form.

Biographical anecdotes are the guts of most success books. Incidents in the lives of the great and famous serve as supporting evidence, sustain a narrative drive (of an episodic type), and warm the message with color and human interest. But while the character ethic mostly confined itself to impersonal documentations of the living and the dead, the personality ethic was fond of reporting directly from personal interviews. Frequently the stories were about little men who had grown into bigger, more prosperous men by applying a particular principle of human relations. Best of all, however, were personal interviews with the biggest men and women. With obvious pleasure, Carnegie reported his parleys at the summit of success, reverently sprinkling his pages with the intimacy of "I spent an afternoon with Mary Pickford...," or "Charles Schwab told me his smile had been worth a million dollars." A new tendency, too, was to get very personal and reveal incidents from the author's own life. Carnegie invokes the personal confession with regularity and effectiveness. How good it is to share his misery, feeling so frustrated as we do; how satisfying to witness his toe-stepping stupidities, recalling ourselves in similar circumstances; how appreciative we are to hear teacher's lecturish tones replaced by humble confessions of personal blunders. And if he can triumph over all, so then can we.[17]

Finally, the spirit of the book pulls readers to it. Every effective success book must be optimistic and inspirational. It is a tract urging the reader to action. Down on the farm, Mother Carnagey always longed for Dale to be a missionary, and in his own way he turned out to be just that. He writes about getting along with people with the same kind of religious fervor as an evangelist exhorting his congregation to cleanse itself of sin and embrace the Saviour. But the route the barefoot boy from Missouri passionately extols is not from sin to salvation, but his own path from poverty to riches. For Carnegie, wisdom begins with the knowledge of how to deal successfully with people and life ends with the practical achievement of worldly success.

Lowell Thomas introduces *How to Win Friends and Influence People* with a soaring hyperbole significantly entitled, "A Short-Cut to Distinction." Carnegie continues in the preface with promises of immediate touchdowns in the game of life. "Men are frequently astonished at the new results they achieve," he reports quite accurately. "It all seems like magic." None of the character ethic's hard asceticism here, but magical shortcuts more similar to the mind power ethic. Carnegie and his colleagues of the personality ethic did not ignore those qualities of character so cherished by the nineteenth century. They simply shoved them aside for the practical gimmick. Reported Carnegie:

> I once interviewed Jim Farley and asked him the secret of his success. He said, "Hard work," and I said, "Don't be funny."
>
> He then asked me what I thought was the reason for his success. I replied: "I understand you can call ten thousand people by their first names."
>
> "No. You are wrong," he said. "I can call fifty thousand people by their first names." [18]

Carnegie promises to help you win many things, desirable in themselves, for example, self-confidence and popularity. But they become essentially a means to increasing your income. "Dealing with people is probably the biggest problem you face, especially if you are a business man," Carnegie assures us. "Yes, and that is also true if you are a housewife, architect, or engineer." Research studies have proved that "even in such technical lines as engineering, about 15 per cent of one's financial success is due to one's technical knowledge and about 85 per cent is due to skill in human engineering—to personality and the ability to lead people." [19]

The shaky ones, unsteady of their ability, Carnegie encourages with a pet quotation of twentieth-century success writers of any persuasion. Said the psychologist-philosopher William

James: "Compared to what we ought to be, we are only half awake. We are making use of only a small part of our physical and mental resources. . . . The human individual . . . possesses powers of various sorts which he habitually fails to use." [20]

The first step in tapping our unused powers is to understand the problem. Since the problem is people, Carnegie and his colleagues introduced into the success idea a different concept of the nature of man. The problem for the character ethic was not people, but the individual's own inner resources. The biggest obstacles to be overcome were laziness and profligacy which dragged the individual down to failure. Now the big obstacles were not in the individual himself, though he must overcome his agonies of fear, but in the responses of other people.

For Carnegie, and success writers of the personality ethic, what is man? The answer is not flattering. "When dealing with people," Carnegie warns us, "let us remember we are not dealing with creatures of logic. We are dealing with creatures of emotion, creatures bristling with prejudices and motivated by pride and vanity." Man is filled with a number of insistent wants which he seeks to satisfy, e.g., food, sleep, and sexual gratification. But there is one craving which is seldom gratified. "It is what Freud calls 'the desire to be great.' It is what Dewey calls the 'desire to be important.'" This longing for a feeling of importance drove Rockefeller on to amass unspent millions. It compels all of us to own material things in competition with one another.[21]

Craving an ego-oriented feeling of importance, man is maneuverable, *if* we remember one cardinal principle. "There is only one way under high Heaven to get anybody to do anything. Did you ever stop to think of that? Yes, just one way. And that is by making the other person want to do it. Remember, there is no other way." What about altruism? The principle still holds. That $100 gift to a charity gave us a good feeling which gratified our egoistic wants. An autobiographical anecdote reifies the idea. "I go fishing up in Maine every summer. Personally I am very fond of strawberries and cream; but I find that for some strange reason fish prefer worms. So when I go fishing, I don't think about what I want. I think about what they want. I don't bait the hook with strawberries and cream. Rather, I dangle a worm or a grasshopper in front of the fish and say: 'Wouldn't you like to have that?' Why not use the same common sense when fishing for men?" But in this gospel the hook is hardly covered with the bait of the New Testament. Carnegie's disciples must learn to cover their hooks with lures enticing to the egocentric nature of man. The lures are specific and numerous.[22]

How to Win Friends and Influence People is divided into six parts, five of which are relevant to success. Part One (with the Preface) sketches Carnegie's concept of man. Parts Two, Three, and Four contain specific psychological principles, called "rules," and Part Five discussess the art of letter-writing. Carnegie once remarked that the *examples* he invokes to support his psychological principles for success are "typical of the experience of thousands of other men." The *principles* he advocates are also included in hundreds of other success books and articles. A summary of *How to Win Friends and Influence People* is here offered as a microcosm of the personality ethic. Certain other typical, or important, success books of this school will be briefly discussed later. They are mostly refinements and variations, with certain additions, to the following basic principles for getting ahead by getting along with other people.[23]

Carnegie begins by teasing the fish into looking fondly at the hook. He sums it up as "Six Ways to Make People Like You." (Each of the following rules is a separate chapter. Each example is one of many interpretations of the rules.)

Rule 1: *"Become genuinely interested in other people."*
Example: C. M. Knaphle, Jr., hated chain stores. They refused to buy coal from him. In the public speaking course, Carnegie persuaded him to support chain stores in a debate. Mr. Knaphle called on an executive of the chain store organization he despised and asked a favor. He wanted information about the benefits of chain stores. Mr. Knaphle watched the interview grow from the promised one minute to close to two hours as the executive explained how chain stores rendered a service to humanity. As he was leaving, the executive put his arm around Knaphle's shoulder and said: "Please see me again later in the

spring. I should like to place an order with you for coal." Concluded a transformed Mr. Knaphle: "To me that was almost a miracle. Here he was offering to buy coal without my even suggesting it. I had made more headway in two hours by becoming genuinely interested in him and his problems than I could have made in ten years by trying to get him interested in me and my coal."

Rule 2: *"Smile."*

Rule 3: *"Remember that a man's name is to him the sweetest and most important sound in the English language."*

Rule 4: *"Be a good listener. Encourage others to talk about themselves."*

Rule 5: *"Talk in terms of the other man's interests."*

Example: Henry G. Duvernoy of New York sold bread. Every week for four years he had called on the manager of a certain New York hotel to sell him bread. He attended the same social affairs as the manager, even took rooms in the hotel in order to get the business. "After studying human relations," Mr. Duvernoy shifted his tactics. He learned that the manager was the enthusiastic president of the Hotel Greeters of America. Next day he began talking with the manager about the Greeters. "What a response I got. What a response!" Not a word was mentioned about bread while the manager signed up Mr. Duvernoy as a member of the Greeters. "A few days later, the steward of his hotel phoned me to come over with samples and prices. 'I don't know what you did to the old boy,' the steward greeted me. 'But he sure is sold on you!' Think of it! I had been drumming at that man for four years—trying to get his business—and I'd still be drumming at him if I hadn't finally taken the trouble to find out what *he* was interested in, and what *he* enjoyed talking about."

Rule 6: *"Make the other person feel important—and do it sincerely."*

Example: James Adamson, president of the Superior Seating Company, wanted to sell a large order of chairs to George Eastman "of Kodak fame." Though Eastman had "amassed a fortune of a hundred million dollars," he rose like a hungry trout for Adamson's bait. Adamson was warned to take no longer than five minutes to state his case. Many hours later, the president of the Superior Seating Company was enjoying an agreeable luncheon with Eastman at the latter's home. He got the order. How did he do it? Well, Adamson began the interview by praising Eastman's office, which was constructed of lovely woodwork. The conversation shifted to Eastman's many philanthropic activities, and then to an autobiographical account of his early struggles to get the business started. Adamson strategically posed questions at every opportunity to give Eastman a feeling of importance.

The friendly fish is now gazing fondly at the hook. How do you get him to swallow it? Carnegie offers "Twelve Ways to Win People to Your Way of Thinking."

Rule 1: *"The only way to get the best of an argument is to avoid it."*

Rule 2: *"Show respect for the other man's opinions. Never tell a man he is wrong."*

Rule 3: *"If you are wrong, admit it quickly and emphatically."* Example: Frederick S. Parsons, an income tax consultant, had been arguing for an hour with a government income tax inspector over whether a particular item should be taxed. The hotter the argument, the more stubbornly cool became the government tax inspector. Then Parsons began to play the game intelligently. "I suppose that this is a very petty matter in comparison with the really important and difficult decisions you are required to make," he soothed the inspector. "I've made a study of taxation myself. But I've had to get my knowledge from books. You are getting yours from the firing line of experience. I sometimes wish I had a job like yours. It would teach me a lot." Parsons adds that "I meant every word I said." The government inspector warmed to the appreciation and "talked for a long time about his work, telling me of the clever frauds he had uncovered. His tone gradually became friendly; and presently he was telling me about his children." Three days later the inspector called to report that he had decided the point in Parsons' favor.

Rule 4: *"Begin in a friendly way."*

Rule 5: *"Get the other person saying 'Yes, yes' immediately."* Example: Carnegie cites H. A. Overstreet as his authority. When a man says "No," "his entire organism—glandular, nervous, muscular—gathers itself together into a condition of rejection." When a person says "Yes," "the organism is in a forward-looking, accepting, open attitude." Carnegie suggests we follow the technique of "barefooted old Socrates . . . a brilliant old boy." Using the Socratic method, Socrates "kept on asking questions until finally, almost without realizing it, his opponent found himself embracing a conclusion that he would have bitterly denied a few minutes previously."

Rule 6: *"Let the other man do a great deal of the talking."*

Rule 7: *"Let the other fellow feel that the idea is his."*

Rule 8: *"Try honestly to see things from the other person's point of view."*

Rule 9: *"Be sympathetic with the other person's ideas and desires."*

Example: Joseph S. Webb of the Philadelphia Electric Company was disturbed because certain prosperous Pennsylvania Dutch farmers were not using electricity. They were said to be tightwads, and were irritated at the company to boot. He knocked at the door of a farmhouse and was met by the icy Mrs. Druckenbrod, a farmer's wife. Mr. Webb met her chilly reception with a ray of sunshine: "Mrs. Druckenbrod, I'm sorry we've troubled you. But I didn't come here to sell you electricity. I merely wanted to buy some eggs." Mr. Webb went on to praise brown eggs over white eggs for cake-making, remarked that he bet Mrs. D. made more money from her hens than her husband from the dairy. Well, one compliment led to another appreciative comment in the poultry house until Mrs. D. finally talked herself into the advantages of electricity. "Two weeks later, Mrs. Druckenbrod's Dominick hens were clucking and scratching contentedly in the encouraging glow of electric lights."

Rule 10: *"Appeal to the nobler motives."*

Rule 11: *"Dramatize your ideas."*

Rule 12: *"Throw down a challenge."*

Example: Landlord Hamilton J. Farrell persuaded a tenant not to break his lease by offering him the opportunity to do so.

Farrell avoided a messy scene and the expense of legal action by challenging the tenant's sense of honor. Said the landlord to the tenant, who was about to break the lease after enjoying the quarters for the most expensive part of the year: "But, I still believe you're a man of your word and will live up to your contract. For after all, we are either men or monkeys—and the choice usually lies with ourselves!" The tenant and his wife finally concluded that "the only honorable thing to do was to live up to their lease." When all else fails, Carnegie advises, try throwing down a challenge. "That is what every successful man loves: the game. The chance for self-expression. The chance to prove his worth, to excel, to win. That is what makes foot races and hog-calling and pie-eating contests. The desire to excel. The desire for a feeling of importance."

If the fish elusively refuses the hook, Carnegie offers "Nine Ways to Change People without Giving Offense or Arousing Resentment."

Rule 1: *"Begin with praise and honest appreciation."*
Example: "A barber lathers a man before he shaves him." (All good students of the personality ethic should soap up their man before applying the razor.) W. P. Gaw's company was constructing an office building in Philadelphia which was delayed by a Brooklyn firm making the ornamental bronze work to go on the exterior of the building. After burning the telephone wires between Philadelphia and Brooklyn, Mr. Gaw decided "to beard the bronze lion in his den." He returned to Philadelphia with "everything that he wanted without even asking for it." "Mr. Gaw," Carnegie assures us, "is an ordinary citizen like you and me." How did he do it?

As Mr. Gaw entered the president's office, he remarked: "Do you know you are the only man in Brooklyn with your name?" Mr. Gaw had picked up this bit of information from the telephone book while looking up the address. The president discoursed proudly on his unusual name and ancestry, then Mr. Gaw complimented him on the plant, they toured the plant, more compliments for president and plant, lunch, and finally home with the promise of delivery of the ornamental bronze work so that the office building could be completed on schedule.

Rule 2: *"Call attention to people's mistakes indirectly."*

Rule 3: *"Talk about your own mistakes before criticizing the other person."*

Rule 4: *"Ask questions instead of giving direct orders."*

Rule 5: *"Let the other man save his face."*

Example: Charles Schwab (a special hero of twentieth-century success writers) was a master of industrial diplomacy. One day, while walking through the steel mill, he came across some employees smoking, directly under a "No Smoking" sign. He walked over to the men, handed each one a cigar, and said: "I'll appreciate it, boys, if you will smoke these on the outside."

Rule 6: *"Praise the slightest improvement and praise every improvement. Be 'hearty in your approbation and lavish in your praise.'"*

Rule 7: *"Give a man a fine reputation to live up to."*

Rule 8: *"Use encouragement. Make the fault you want to correct seem easy to correct; make the thing you want the other person to do seem easy to do."*

Rule 9: *"Make the other person happy about doing the thing you suggest."*

Example: J. A. Want, head of the J. A. Want Organization, had a problem. The mechanic who fixed typewriters and other machines was always complaining about long hours and too much work. He wanted an assistant. Want did not give him any of these things, but he made the mechanic happy. How? He moved the mechanic into a private office. On the door of the office appeared his name and a new title: "Manager of the Service Department." The mechanic was "no longer a repair man to be ordered about by every Tom, Dick and Harry. He was now the manager of a department. He had dignity, recognition, a feeling of importance. He worked happily and without complaint."

The decades following the publication of *How to Win Friends and Influence People* in 1936 were rich in wealth for Carnegie. There was time now for meditative walks in a park near his modest stucco house in Forest Hills, New York, and time, too, for more leisurely vacations with the new Mrs. Carnegie. His first marriage ended with a divorce in 1931 after ten years of living hell. For a long time the popular mentor of human relations firmly denied that he had ever been married. If the news got out, what would people think about his section in *How to Win Friends and Influence People* entitled: "Seven Rules for Making Your Home Life Happier"? The year after his divorce, Carnegie published *Lincoln the Unknown,* which scalds the President's wife as a shrew who nagged at her husband for lacking the social graces. The friction generated in the Carnegies' home life, ironically enough, seems to have been caused by the complaint of his wife that her husband was similarly unfinished in the social graces. About the Lincoln volume, he once said: "The book is strictly autobiographical in every respect." [24]

After what he considered to be his own Lincolnesque experience, Dale Carnegie was cautious about a second try at marital felicity. Finally, in 1944, he succumbed to Mrs. Dorothy Price Vanderpool, a former secretary and divorcee from Tulsa, Oklahoma. The marriage could not have been safer. Dorothy was a graduate of the Dale Carnegie Course in Effective Speaking and Human Relations.

Out of their union came a daughter, whom Carnegie sired at the age of 62, and the Dale and Dorothy Carnegie Courses for Women. They were a productive husband and wife team in a tradition which recalls Charles and Mary Beard and Arthur and Kathryn Murray, Sidney and Beatrice Webb, and George Burns and Gracie Allen. In this case the driving force was the husband. But Dorothy was always there with the introspective advantage. The course for women was an adaptation of the older curriculum for mixed groups, directed specifically at the needs of career girls and housewives. After instructing in the course, Dorothy soon discovered that what most women really want more than anything else is a happy marriage to a successful husband. So she wrote a book in 1953 with the self-explanatory title, *How to Help Your Husband Get Ahead.* The one man who didn't need to read it, of course, was her husband.[25]

Dale Carnegie bore some resemblance to another famous man from Missouri of his generation, Harry Truman. Both men wore glittering eyeglasses, spoke with a nasal drawl, and were fond of cloaking their small, erect figures in dapper double-breasted suits. Carnegie was a bouncy kind of a man, effervescent with enthusiasm, and vigorous in his handshakes. A maker of many millions of dollars, he was a man as stingy with a dollar as he was free with an emotion. The curious fact about Carnegie is that he loved to argue, though he was always careful to strike the right note of humility. He was a "Why? I'll tell you why!" kind of a speaker and writer who frequently used the shock approach for dramatic effect. His favorite gambit for opening a conversation was: "Do you know what prevents you from becoming an idiot?" The answer was a paltry five cents' worth of iodine secreted by the thyroid gland, a hazard which Carnegie hastened to admit he shared with the human race. Now this may not have been the most intellectually stimulating conversation, but it did have a lapel-grabbing intensity which he felt produced results.[26]

Fame and funds had at last settled upon the self-styled "barefoot boy from Missouri" who once was so ashamed of his ill-fitting clothes. His thoughts on life were sent out over the airwaves and recorded in a syndicated newspaper column. More published collections of capsule biographies flowed from his pen, held together by the theme of a humble-origins-upward-to-fame-and-wealth narrative. In 1948 he was again on the nonfiction best-seller list in the number two spot behind Dwight Eisenhower's *Crusade in Europe*. Carnegie's own crusade was summed up in the title, *How to Stop Worrying and Start Living*. It is a competent book on the subject, but it can be boiled down into Carnegie's own 'team' of platitudes: 'Don't cry over spilt milk,' and 'Don't cross your bridges before you come to them.' In style and structure, it carries on in the effective manner of *How to Win Friends and Influence People;* in content, it is an unusual peace of mind book. *How to Stop Worrying and Start Living* is not a criticism of the success goal in favor of self-adjustment. If anything, the book worries about worry being a hindrance to achieving success.[27]

Though Americans in the post-World War II period seemed desperately in search of peace of mind, they were equally eager for material success. Dale Carnegie, his own cheerful, folksy self augmented by trained instructors, was right there on the job. On a scale of popularity and national recognition, the idea of success has never produced anything quite like the Dale Carnegie Course, though there have been, and are, many public speaking courses. Since that evening at the Y.M.C.A. back in 1912, more than a million people have been graduated. By the late 1960s, some 80,000 were enrolling each year in 1,210 communities in the United States and 92 communities abroad. With the exception of a few sourpusses who never could get into the spirit of the thing, the Dale Carnegie alumni body is as wildly and, occasionally, hysterically enthusiastic about their alma mater as the old grads at a football game cheering on twelve All American players to an undefeated season, coached by the mentor of the year.[28]

Any initial skepticism about the loyalty of this alumni body is washed away by the countless personal confessions of how the course has helped the timid to conquer fear, the friendless to gain popularity, and the ambitious to win a promotion with an increase in income. Though the list of things the course can do for you has increased over the years, they all, in one way or another, add up to achieving material success. The customers are satisfied. Some 75 per cent of new business is pulled in by the recommendations of former students. The *esprit de corps* generated is sometimes so feverish that graduating classes continue to meet after the Commencement Banquet. When last heard from, a group in Pennsylvania had been refueling at periodic meetings for over twenty years. There's even a Dale Carnegie Alumni Association, Inc.

What is it like to take the course? Some 40 men and women, already yoked together by an eagerness to improve themselves, meet at a hotel, club, or school. The course runs 14 weeks with each weekly meeting lasting about four hours. The tuition fee (about $210) includes all textbooks, class supplies, and a diploma. The world-wide Carnegie organization is very tightly controlled by the home office in Garden City, Long Island. The structure is a franchise set-up (which have become very valuable) on which royalties are paid to the parent organization on gross receipts. The instructors, who are carefully trained, are assisted by former students who have been elected to the honor by their classmates and serve joyfully free of charge for the fun and experience of it.

The textbooks pretty much define the subject matter of the course. There is Carnegie's manual on public speaking. Human relations is covered in *How to Win Friends and Influence People*, while more recently a bonus, mostly for home consumption, is offered in *How to Stop Worrying and Start Living*. Various gaps are filled in by such pamphlets as "How to Remember Names."

This is a form of adult education based on the "do-it-yourself" principle. Everyone gets the chance to speak at each session and to practice the techniques for an enthusiastic delivery and the development of a pleasing personality. It's every man his own valedictorian every week in the Dale Carnegie Course in Effective Speaking and Human Relations.

A stream of people continue to flow through the training. They represent a cross-section of national frustration. Here is the thick-tongued business executive who is increasingly called upon to make public speeches. He is graduated with a silver tongue. Here is the commercial artist, so choked with fear that he gets sick every time he thinks of exposing his work to the cynicism of advertising men. He will tell a demonstration meeting of candidates for the course how he licked the problem. (He confounded them by simply smiling.) Like the readers of much contemporary success literature, they come from all occupations, mostly from the middle class. There is the bright young man sent in at the corporation's expense (whole plants and offices can be serviced), and the old, bright young man who wonders what went wrong. Here is the doctor whose sharp manner somehow offends his patients, the technician who clams up at the weekly conference, the eager beaver busily determined to get ahead, the constricted clerk trying to loosen up, and salesmen by the droves. The point is to learn how to sell yourself and your ideas. "We are all *salesmen* every day of our lives," Charlie Schwab is cited as saying in one prospectus for the course. "We are selling our ideas, our plans, our enthusiasms to those with whom we come in contact." [29]

Authors in search of material about modern America would do well to visit a class. Every fourteen-week course is a setting for a play or novel, containing forty separate dramas of human life propelled from tragedy to comedy and back again. During his maiden speech a man from Brooklyn was so terrified that he found himself incapable of saying anything. He collapsed to the floor in a dead faint. Quick-witted Dale bounded to the platform, dramatically pointed to the fallen figure, and announced heroically: "One month from today, this man will make a speech from this platform." And he did.

One man was so timid he couldn't bring himself to lead his church group in silent prayer. A Wall Street man was so self-conscious that at board meetings he was too shy to second a motion. He started taking the course under an assumed name, but was seized with such terror when called on to speak that he ran out of the class. Desperately in need of help, he came to Carnegie and started once again. Soon he was thrilled with the sound of his own voice flowing over the audience. Early one Sunday morning he shook his wife awake and asked: "Is there any place in New York where I can make a speech today?" She drowsily informed him that if the Spirit moved him, anyone could speak at a Quaker meeting. At the other end of Brooklyn he located a Quaker meeting house and was so moved by the Spirit that he spoke for twenty minutes.[30]

Carnegie liked to take on one tough challenge to the personality ethic. How do you transform an engineer, absorbed in inanimate things, into a manipulator of people? "I suppose they were mostly engineers, or *like* engineers," he glowed brightly in 1943 about the Cornell Club in New York City, "and I would rather teach engineers than anything.... Have you ever seen an insincere engineer? Besides, they're so bad to start with that it's a great joy to see them learn how to open their mouths without chewing their tongues up." [31]

Carnegie's course has been responsible for helping thousands to gain promotions. What is more important, it has taught troubled men and women how to find happiness in the increasingly vital problem of getting along with other people. While President Roosevelt was assuring the nation that "the only thing we have to fear is fear itself," Dale Carnegie continued to challenge his students and readers to "do the thing you fear." In the jovial warmth of his classes, he and his instructors produced a form of group therapy for success and happiness not unlike the *esprit de corps* for sobriety and temperance of Alcoholics Anonymous.

Carnegie died in 1955 at the age of sixty-six and was taken home to be buried in the family plot in Belton, Missouri. There were no public proclamations such as celebrate the passing of a great statesman, but there were few students who would have felt it inappropriate to apply the cascading hallelujahs in Handel's *Messiah* to their earthly king. And king of the personality ethic he was. The impressive statistics racked up by *How to Win Friends and Influence People,* joined by the devotion of his students for the course, make him the most important and influential success writer in the decades following the 1930s. After that decade, neither the success idea, nor America, would ever be the same.

17

"I'M TALKING ABOUT A NEW WAY OF LIFE"

The personality ethic introduced a new way to success. The leverage factor was a knowledge of human relations. Dealing with customers and clients was one test of your ability to handle people. The other involved your shrewdness in getting along with people in your own firm or business—with your associates of equal power, with the employees who worked under you, and with your boss as the immediate representative in an ascending scale of superiors above you.

Using Dale Carnegie's twenty-seven rules as a point of departure, in what way did other self-help books of the personality ethic differ from the form, principles and presentation of *How to Win Friends and Influence People?*

Frequent use of a person's name was a standard principle of human relations in the personality ethic. While Carnegie claimed that "a man's name is to him the sweetest and most important sound in the English language," he neglected to offer instructions in how to remember the name you were supposed to repeat. Success writers sometimes borrowed from memory training the rules of accuracy, repetition, and association and devoted a chapter to this skill. (The Dale Carnegie Course in Effective Speaking, Leadership Training, and Human Relations fills this gap by distributing to its students a pamphlet on how to remember names.)[1]

There were certain skills within the personality ethic which

required specialized instruction. Advice on how to achieve
a radiant personal impression, which had been abundant before
the 1930s, became a "how to" mania after that decade. Through
charm schools and correspondence courses, newspaper features
and the radio, in books, articles, and 'hard sell' advertisements,
there was plenty of advice on how to make yourself more
personally and physically attractive to other people.[2]

In vocal and written communication, Sherwin Cody, his
pointed beard grayer now, was still fixing newspaper and magazine readers with his challenging gaze to correct those embarrassing blunders of pronunciation, grammar, spelling, and literary
expression. A phonograph record on proper pronunciation and
effective speaking brought the Cody correspondence course up-
to-date The Funk & Wagnalls course in voice training, using
seven double-faced records synchronized with the text of a two-
volume instruction manual, trilled the hope that "there is a
fortune in your voice, a real dollars-and-cents fortune. A good
speaking voice has a definite cash value. . . ." At the other extreme, the Beltone Hearing-Aid Company shouted from the front
flap of a packet of matches: "DOES *LOSS of HEARING*
ROB YOU of SUCCESS and HAPPINESS?" "The Magic of
Words" branch of Funk & Wagnalls expressed its alarm from
another match flap: "THOUSANDS ARE HANDICAPPED
BY POOR ENGLISH and don't know it! Unconscious of their
faulty grammar, mispronunciations and careless diction, they
never realize why they are barred from business advancement
and social acceptance. WHAT IS POOR ENGLISH COSTING
YOU? See test on back cover." [3]

Amidst this pragmatic exploitation of the social graces for
financial and social advancement, Ethel Cotton's course in how
to be a lively and entertaining conversationalist offers the unique
suggestion that at least one reason for trying to be an interesting
and stimulating conversationalist, besides a means to success,
is that it's lots of fun. Ethel Cotton refreshingly captures the
spirit, now and then, of Randolph Bourne's observation that
"good talk is like good scenery—continuous, yet constantly
varying, and full of the charm of novelty and surprise." [4]

There were also wide-ranging manuals in how to manipulate,

with conscious dexterity and studied skill, the responses of other people. How can you get people to like you? How can you win them to your way of thinking? How can you change their attitudes toward yourself, your product, your proposal, and your ideas? What is the secret of leadership?

The nuances success writers explored in answering these questions were multifarious; the substance was the same. The objective of controlling the responses of other people flowed from a theory of human relations based on a fixed concept of the nature of man. Man is a cluster of drives. In order to persuade him, you must appeal to these drives or wants. Man is egocentric, wrapped up in himself, yearns for a feeling of importance, and can be made to do only what he wants to do. If you wish to play upon the flute of man, you must first learn to touch the right stops. How yielding is this instrument to our mastery? Inquired one success writer: "Are people so difficult to fathom and control that the ability to handle them is almost as rare as the qualities of genius? Of course not! People are notoriously easy to mold to your way of thinking, if you want to mold them, and human nature is so simple a matter that it is tragic for anyone not to understand it thoroughly and use it consistently." [5]

A popular preacher with his own set of nuances for the personality ethic was a sales consultant known both to his intimates and audiences as "Mr. Sizzle." Elmer ("Don't Sell the Steak— Sell the Sizzle.") Wheeler of "Sizzle Ranch" in Texas, founder of "sizzlemanship," was a prolific lecturer and writer on how to be a "winner" instead of a "fizzler." In his 1947 book with the self-explanatory title, *How to Sell Yourself to Others*, Wheeler began with the inevitable claim that his teachings were practical and scientific, not theoretical. Rejecting a formal education and luck as necessary for success, he quickly asserted: "Regardless of who you are or what you want, your success will depend upon your ability to *sell yourself to others.* . . . The *ability to get along with people* is the principal ingredient of *success!!*" After establishing the dual principles that the only way to get a person to do something is to make him want to do it and that everyone has an egocentric interest primarily in himself, Wheeler advances techniques of manipulation which differ very little, and offer only a few minor additions, to the fundamentals of the game which we have already learned from *How to Win Friends and Influence People.*[6]

For example, Mr. Sizzle explains how to put some bite in the power of suggestion ("When we instructed the Walgreen Drug soda clerks to say, 'One or two eggs in your malt?' we sold many more than when they formerly said, 'Want an egg in the malt today?'"). He goes on to explore semantics and the power of words, advises on the proper use of the voice, cautions us to tell jokes *"Jack Benny style"* in order to make others feel superior, and fills humor with a cash value ("If you can tell jokes you can make fame and fortune. . . . You get less money when you make them cry."). Wheeler points out that in the "art of passing the buck . . . the trick is to make the other fellow feel that you personally agree with him—but some *third party* would object." He emphasizes the importance of getting children to like you ("A good way to make friends is to like the children. Every door-to-door salesman knows this."), outlines the standard procedure for remembering names, slides open a wardrobe full of sartorial suggestions (". . . Others should not 'see' your clothes—but rather 'feel' your taste."), and concludes with the *"secret ingredient"* that everything he advises must be executed with proper timing.[7]

Among major book publishers who could claim a list of respectable diversification, Prentice-Hall had shouldered aside Thomas Y. Crowell in this period and carved out the largest empire in the field of self-help success literature. The form in which the message was cast varied from full-length books to pamphlets, from wallet inserts to repetitious articles in magazines like *Your Life* and *Opportunity.* A simple expression was the "comic book" pamphlet designed for the factory worker. The story of *The Happiest Man in Town!* begins with a picture of the president of International Dynamics Industries. He has just arrived from the New York office and is congratulating the plant manager of the Midwestern division. The plant has achieved the highest output for all divisions. The felicitous scene is jarred by Ed Thompson, described by the plant manager as a "good mechanic," but "no diplomat." Ed strides into the office, begins griping about the supervisor, and boasts that he is a good worker. The plant manager suggests that he try to cooperate. The gray-thatched corporation president, looking sage throughout the discussion, hands Ed a leaflet with the comment: It "may help you to get ahead." Ed parts with the crack: "These two hands are all I need!"

After the plant lets out for the day, Ed boasts to his fellow workers how he told off the manager. When he suggests some bowling that evening, his fellow workers begin drifting away, trailing excuses. He calls his girl, Betty, for a date. She turns him down. Now disturbed and angry, Ed begins reading the leaflet the corporation president gave him. It contains an unsophisticated statement of the personality ethic's means to success. He reads that it pays to be courteous, friendly, and polite to everyone. Next day Ed is cooperative and "all smiles." One week later he is overwhelmed by invitations from his fellow workers for pinochle and "dinner with the wife and me." One month later he gets a raise. Two months later Ed's unit sets a new plant record. The corporation president returns for the denouement, while Ed confesses: "That leaflet you gave me changed my whole life." The corporation president admits: "Once I carried a chip on my shoulder, too. And I was getting nowhere fast. Then I took hold of myself and found real pleasure in being pleasant to everyone. Believe me, it made my rise up thru the ranks a lot easier!" The story ends with Ed's announcement that "best of all, Betty has agreed to be my wife!" [8]

In our analysis of the success idea, we ruled out at the start technical manuals in how to make money in specific occupations, e.g., how to grow rich in chemical engineering or how to raise a fortune by growing house plants. But what was once considered a separate occupation with its own skills reserved for that occupation was rapidly becoming in this period a way of life in which everyone, in one way or another, was compelled to participate. America was becoming a nation of salesmen. Publishers recognized the shift by directing their advertising of salesmanship books to the general market, as well as to the increasing number of men and women who were in merchandising. Many of the propagandists for the personality ethic had themselves been trained in marketing, sales consulting, or in the psychological clinics set up to pump life into the tired sales record of ailing businesses.

"How to" manuals on salesmanship were very similar to the general personality ethic success book with three exceptions. First, they were naturally partial to selling as an occupation. Second, they were more specific in outlining the step-by-step techniques in making a sale. Third, they carried over a kind of 1920s hustle and pep with the dictum that you have to get off the seat of your pants and make the call before you can close the sale.

The number four non-fiction best-seller in bookstores during 1950 was directed specifically at salesmen, particularly insurance salesmen. Frank Bettger's *How I Raised Myself from Failure to Success in Selling,* like most books of its type, is useful for anyone who must earn a living in modern America.[9]

Frank Bettger was one of five small children when his father died. At the age of eleven, he hit the sunrise trail at four-thirty in the morning, selling newspapers to help his widowed mother who took in washing and sewing. At fourteen, after six years of school, he signed on as a steamfitter's helper, at eighteen was playing professional baseball, and then moved up to the Big Leagues as an infielder for the St. Louis Cardinals. After an arm injury, he drifted back to his hometown of Philadelphia, and began selling life insurance. How Bettger developed the personality, character, and techniques to become one of the nation's leading salesmen of life insurance is told with frequent autobiographical asides in *How I Raised Myself from Failure to Success in Selling.* The danger of the autobiographical approach, of course, is the tendency to drift into boastful self-exaltation. Bettger avoids the perils of autobiographical arrogance with numerous 'before and after' descriptions. He too has suffered in the school of hard knocks in order to change toe-stepping blunders into back-scratching triumphs. During his career, Bettger made nearly 40,000 sales calls, which works out to about five calls every day for more than twenty-five years.

The first two chapters of Bettger's memoirs bubble with a go-getter's passion for enthusiasm and the importance of making sales calls. As in many recent success books, the writer was in some way touched by Dale Carnegie. In this case the influence was personal. One night at a Dale Carnegie public speaking course produced the decision to become an *enthusiastic* life insurance salesman which was "the turning point of my life." Filled with fear, Bettger had dragged through a training speech. Then the old master took over. Carnegie "gave our class a stirring talk on the power of enthusiasm. He got so excited during his talk, he threw a chair up against the wall and broke off one of its legs." After that trauma, never again could Frank Bettger be accused of conducting a droopy interview.[10]

The remainder of Bettger's book alternates between specific advice to salesmen (organize and plan your time, "the best way to outsmart secretaries and switchboard operators is never to try!") and case histories which illustrate how the standard rules of the personality ethic can be applied to concrete situations. The smart approach, of course, is to find out what the other fellow wants and talk to him in terms of his own interests. The brilliance of Bettger's book is its reduction of such rules for manipulation to a mechanical insertion of key phrases at crucial points in the interview. For example, you settle uneasily into the chair and the busy man behind the desk snarls: "What did you want to talk to me about?" *"You"* was a one-word reply Bettger found to be irresistible. Again, never argue, but there does come a time in the failing interview when salesman and client are locked into a 'no deal' situation. You have asked "Why?" to his objections and he has freely given them. After a small pause, say: "Mr. Jones, in addition to that, isn't there some other reason?" "In addition to that" probes for the "real reason, or the key issue" in his mind. (Though Bettger doesn't say so, it also implies that the client's previous objections are not compelling enough to merit a respectable rejection of your proposal.) Finally, after presenting the proposal and summarizing it, "look at the prospect and ask: 'How do you like it?' It is surprising how frequently he answers: 'I think I like it.' " [11]

The kind of people success writers of the personality ethic liked were woven into a congenial pattern. They applauded the shoeshine boy with the ingenious sign: " 'One Shoe Shined *Free*

—the other 10 cents!'" They praised the attention-getting cleverness of the red-haired boy who was applying for a job and found himself at the end of a long line. He slipped out and sent a telegram to the personnel interviewer: " 'DON'T HIRE ANYBODY UNTIL YOU SEE THE RED-HAIRED BOY AT END OF LINE.'" The kind of methods which saddened the personality ethic were exhibited by Woodrow Wilson's handling of the Republican Party and the Senate with respect to the League of Nations. It represented, at least for success writers, the best-known example in American history of the bungling of a momentous turning point in history by a failure in human relations. They much preferred the approach of Mark Twain, who described a fight in this way: " 'Placing my nose firmly between *his* teeth, I threw him heavily to the ground on top of *me!*' " All in all, there was something very wonderful for them in Will Rogers' famed observation: " 'I never met a man I didn't like.' " [12]

A standard technique of the personality ethic was the use of the success doctrine itself as a means to success. The objective was to entice the client into talking as if he just stepped out of the pages of a success book. If the client were a self-made man, the student was shrewdly instructed to guide the conversation back to those early struggles to get started. Frank Bettger was a master of this approach (recommended phrasing: "How did you ever happen to get started in this business?"). Since every American likes to think of himself as self-made, except when he and his wife are status-jumping into a higher social class, obstacles to be overcome can be constructed for even the president of an inherited business. [13]

A profitable approach is to coax the recalcitrant client into a discussion of his justification for success, which frequently amounts in American culture to a justification for existence. Get him to talk about the contribution of his job to the welfare of humanity. If he slowly leans back in his chair and starts sprinkling the conversation with the word "service," there is seemingly little to be done but nudge along the interview with questions and wait for what you want to be handed to you.

The purpose of all this was to melt the chill of a business

transaction into the warmth of a friendly relationship, to talk about anything but immediate business in order to get business. Dale Carnegie cites cases for both the self-made man and justification approaches, but is most enthusiastic about drawing the client into musings about his children. As the client raises before himself the image of his children, clad in nitey-nites romping around the living room, or going on to greater things in school or college, he is transported into a receptive mood.

Learning all these moves in the game of human chess are not qualities of character that you build into yourself. When James Farley suggested that the secret of his success was "hard work," Dale Carnegie could only snicker: "Don't be funny." The *character ethic* had sternly charged that the only path to wealth was a laborious inner development of moral virtues. The *personality ethic* dangled a cluster of psychological principles, easily learned, immediately productive, and with no necessity of a deep transformation in our hearts and minds. The focus had shifted from a development of character to a manipulation of people. As success writer Charles Roth put it, in the extreme: "Every day of your life you are in the presence of the only source of success, happiness, and achievement there is—some other person, or persons." [14]

Like a high school commencement speaker, it was unthinkable for any success writer to advocate dishonesty. Sneaking around a promise, misrepresenting a product, or engaging in financial chicanery was positively frowned on by some writers of the personality ethic. Many more, relative to the total volume of the literature, ignored or failed to emphasize the value and importance of honesty. What the personality ethic lacked was the nineteenth century's passionate defense of honesty as a moral absolute ingrained in our character.

The personality ethic, however, was plagued by a kind of honesty which never concerned the character ethic. What happens to honesty between human beings? A moral tug-of-war continually strains within the personality ethic over this question. On the one side stands honesty, sincerity, integrity, and candor. On the other, there lurks hypocrisy, deception, and insincerity mendacity, fraud, deceit, and duplicity. Most success writers of the personality ethic saw the dangers in the path down which they were guiding their readers. While the character ethic feared the quicksands of laziness and profligacy which sucked you down into failure, the personality ethic feared the cesspool of deceit. You could stay afloat and still be a success in such an environment, but soon you were unable to stand the smell of yourself.

Flattery and insincerity, they cried, would not work. You must express genuine appreciation. Operating on the faith there is some good in every man, your praise must unselfishly spring from the heart. "Sincerity is the magic touchstone," Elmer Wheeler exhorted, "that makes your personality sizzle instead of fizzle." Dale Carnegie is particularly representative: "No! No! No! I am not suggesting flattery! Far from it," he protested. "I'm talking about a new way of life. Let me repeat. *I am talking about a new way of life.*" [15]

Unquestionably the personality ethic was an expression of social and economic conditions which were forcing upon Americans a new way of life, though not in the sense that Carnegie meant it. It is also important to see the personality ethic as a new way of *looking* at life where people are used for the purpose of profit. Does Carnegie demand a deep change within ourselves, a revolution of ourselves? Or are his rules merely psychological principles to be superficially grafted on the self?

Let us take the universal rule of the personality ethic: *"Smile."* The final test of a smile, we find, is its cash-making potential. Carnegie warns us that a smile must not be insincere or mechanical; it must be honest and heart-warming, "the kind of a smile that will bring a good price in the market place." Though most of us, with Charlie Schwab as our ideal, cannot hope to flash a keyboard of teeth worth a million dollars, we can at least spread one with sufficient regularity to emulate William B. Steinhardt, a member of the New York Curb Exchange. After Mr. Steinhardt remodeled his sour puss, he joyfully reported: "I find that smiles are bringing me dollars, many dollars every day." [16]

Or let us take another universal rule entitled: *"The only way to get the best of an argument is to avoid it."* The following incident taught Carnegie "an invaluable lesson." He was at a dinner party in London. The man on his right told a humorous story which hinged on a quotation from Shakespeare—"There's a divinity that shapes our ends, rough-hew them how we will." The raconteur, however, erroneously said the quotation was from the Bible. Carnegie correctly protested it was from Shakespeare; the man on his right who told the story insisted it was from the Bible. They then put the question to the man on Carnegie's left who was a Shakespearean authority. All this had what would seem to be the makings of a lively intellectual argument. (After standing corrected, the man could argue, for example, that the Shakespearean quotation was at least an expression of Biblical theology.) The Shakespearean authority, however, had in view other ends than the pursuit of truth. He kicked Carnegie under the table and lied to them that the quotation was from the Bible. On the way home Carnegie put it to the Shakespearean authority. Wasn't the quotation from the bard? "Yes, of course," he replied, *"Hamlet,* Act V, Scene 2. But we were guests at a festive occasion, my dear Dale. Why prove to a man he is wrong? Is that going to make him like you?" [17]

The moral principles of the *character ethic* were absolute virtues. The psychological principles of the *personality ethic* were pragmatic, relative in their utility. How easy it is to drift into insincerity or condone the telling of a lie. Most success writers were aware of such duplicity, passionately protested against it, but continued to cite examples of hypocritical men who falsely massaged the affections of others for personal gain. In an earlier act, Hamlet bitterly cursed: "That one may smile, and smile, and be a villain; At least I am sure it may be so in Denmark." In America at mid-twentieth century, the villains and the virtuous read books to learn when to smile. It was a new way of life; it was, also, a new way of looking at life, at ourselves, and our relationship to our fellow man.

There were critics who sounded sour notes in the success-tuned orchestration for harmonious human relations. Many of them struck at the most famous merchant of the personality ethic. In 1937 Sinclair Lewis was outraged at *How to Win*

Friends and Influence People, with its lessons on "how to smile and bob and pretend to be interested in people's hobbies precisely so that you may screw things out of them. . . ." [18]

Irving Tressler's 1937 burlesque, *How to Lose Friends and Alienate People,* closely paralleled Carnegie's self-help tome. In his introductory remarks entitled "A Short Cut to Indistinction," "Thomas Lowell" tells all about Tressler's Institute of Human Relations Up To A Certain Point, which drew people who wanted "to learn how to make themselves talk, make themselves talk so that others would hate them. . . ." One of the Institutes' 'successful' graduates, whose income took a joyfully sharp plunge after the course, was Pat Burnblatt. Pat was so likable and so willing to listen to others talk that he had to give up "selling padded brassieres" when "his first customer, a 75 year old man, bought two dozen after two hours spent telling Pat about his visit to Yellowstone in 1911." For those who longed for privacy and seclusion, Tressler offered rules like *"Forget flattery. Be generous with your acid and lavish with your contempt. If you do, people will remember your words—remember them long after they have ceased speaking to you,"* and "If you really want people to dislike you upon first sight: *Snarl!"* [19]

Some twenty years later, a few articulate critics were still bucking the trend. In 1956 the *New York Times'* Harvey Breit, hearing that the "ingratiating way" had been formally exported to England, shouted across the Atlantic: "Carnegie Course, come home!" Breit's confession of national shame, however, must have been appeased by a realization that the English were quite capable of taking care of themselves. It was, after all, the Englishman Stephen Potter who devised a series of Lifemanship counter-ploys clever enough to ruffle the most polished pupil of the personality ethic. There were, of course, the irreverent stories. Humorists dreamed up fantastic conversations between Carnegie students. A favorite story was the executive who hurried to a business luncheon, eager to try out Carnegie's rules which he had been studying. Later he was overheard to observe ruefully: "I made a friend for life, but boy, what an enemy he made." No doubt there were some in business, choked up with being pleasant to a cantankerous boss, who longed to emulate the curate who had quarreled with his rector and was being shipped out. On the Sunday of his departure, the curate preached his farewell sermon. "I shall take as my text," he said, "those words from the moving story of Abraham: 'Tarry ye here with the ass, while I go yonder.'" In any case, the key principle in selling is honesty. Once you know how to fake that, you've got it made.[20]

Sincerity was virtually an insoluble problem for the personality ethic. But a few success writers, most of them psychologists, approached the sincerity problem with trained understanding. The trouble with most books on human relations, complained James Bender and Lee Graham in *Your Way to Popularity and Personal Power,* is their failure to recognize that "you are an individual. They try to impose a system of behavior that is supposed to fit you as well as a million other readers. But your differences in personality make this impossible. . . . There is only one *you* in this whole world. . . . If you were to follow the advice in these books, you'd become unnatural, irritating, and insincere. In your effort to conform to a pattern, your phoniness would break through. . . . If you don't think so, picture in your mind's eye the sort of person these books consider ideal. Do you see him clearly? He's constantly smiling. He praises everything. He lets the other fellow do all the talking. He never expresses a contrary opinion. He wouldn't dream of criticizing. He seldom gets angry and there's no one he dislikes. You can't say he isn't nice, but that's about all there is to it. And if you got to know him better, you'd have to admit that he was dull, mechanical, and not quite genuine." [21]

For Bender and Graham, "the core of the problem is this: *If you don't like yourself, you can't like other people; and if you don't like other people, they can't like you.* No magic formula will help you. This is a matter of keen self-analysis and deep self-understanding." Bolstered by self-analysis quizzes, in addition to advice paralleling much of the standard means to success, the authors emphasize the importance of liking yourself by probing into the *"inner you."* But for every searching effort to move back the process one step to change yourself, there were hundreds of books and articles which concentrated on changing the other fellow's opinion of yourself.[22]

The character ethic, the dominant means to wealth until the 1930s, was a creed. The creed consisted of (1) the means to success with various corollaries, e.g., statements about the equality and amount of opportunity in America, an exaltation of the self-made man, a tone of anti-intellectualism, etc. (2) an anti-materialistic warning about the dangers of a too greedy obsession with money-making (3) a definition of what was widely called 'true success,' and (4) a justification for material success. What was the creed of the personality ethic?

The personality ethic carried on the inspirational tradition of the success idea with respect to the following convictions: the amount and equality of opportunity in America was abundant (sometimes expressed more negatively in the personality ethic as a shortage of executive material); luck was not a factor in the making of a successful man; an individual's destiny depended on himself, not circumstances, and pressure was exerted on him to make something of himself; the self-made man was exalted; and the poor boy struggling up from a background of poverty had an advantage over the rich man's son. But on each point, the personality ethic was less demonstrative, less assertive in frequency and tone. This was as true for the decades following World War II as for the depression years of the 1930s.

Like the character ethic, the *intent* of success apostles of the personality ethic was not to write political propaganda but to teach people how to become a success. Why take a political position on, for example, severe income taxes on upper-income breadwinners? Engaging in a political wrangle on a controversial issue would only side-track the purpose of the book and offend prospective buyers. The *effect* of success literature, however, was politically conservative. By stating or implying that failure was the fault of the individual, not social and economic conditions, success writers blocked the reformer's justification for altering the *status quo* by means of government intervention.[23]

The personality ethic broke with one tradition in this part of the success formula. No more did self-help missionaries specify the advantages of the barefoot boy with rural origins. Into limbo, too, went the influence of a good mother. The character ethic believed that the young man from rural origins had always beaten out his counterpart in the city through force of character. He was eager to work hard and years of clean living had filled him with a moral strength to resist the temptations of urban life. Sweeping changes, many of them in transportation and population distribution, had erased forever that noble image of the country boy, his few small possessions folded into a red bandanna swinging from a fishing pole, striding down the road towards the fearful but exciting city, to begin his onward and upward rise to fame and fortune.

What about education? The character ethic, towards the close of the nineteenth century, had increasingly admitted the advantages, though not the necessity, of a formal technical or vocational education. A classical or liberal arts education was guaranteed to do more harm than good. The personality ethic did not choose sides or engage in the vocational vs. liberal arts battle. It agreed that a formal education was not necessary for success. On the one hand, Douglas Lurton hedged in *Make the Most of Your Life,* a college education unquestionably "can be of great help to the individual who uses his advantages well. . . ." On the other hand, "frequently a college education hinders rather than helps." In any case, "lack of it is no alibi for failure." Self-education is always available through correspondence courses and public libraries.[24]

The personality ethic was as sharply critical of the nation's schools and colleges as the character ethic had been towards the old classical curriculum. Formal education was ignoring the most important course in life's curriculum. That course, naturally, was in human relations. Dale Carnegie, for example, picks on Harvard University and the study of Latin as symbols on which to spill his contempt. He gleefully reports the speech of a wealthy owner of a carpet factory who was graduated from Harvard, came from an old New York family, and had his name in the Social Register. This aristocrat "declared that he had learned more in fourteen weeks through this system of training about the fine art of influencing people than he had learned about the same subject during his four years in college." Children should memorize, he went on, the advice of Charlie Schwab, who was paid a salary of a million dollars a year "largely because of his ability to deal with people." Instead of memorizing Schwab's words, our children are "wasting their time memorizing the conjugation of Latin verbs or the amount of the annual rainfall in Brazil. . . ." Our children, however, would do better to remember Schwab's words than emulate his destiny. Businessmen who are fond of citing Schwabian anecdotes should be aware that: (1) Charles M. Schwab died bankrupt in 1939, though he once made, in a time before high income taxes, $2,000,000 a year as United States Steel's first president. (2) He had often promised a $2,000,000 endowment to his alma mater, St. Francis College, in Loretto, Pennsylvania. (3) St. Francis, instead, was left holding the bag for a $25,000 loan that Schwab borrowed in 1932 and never repaid.[25]

The idea of success had always in it strains of anti-intellectualism. This characteristic was also true of the personality ethic. Though knowledge of your occupation or product was a basic requisite, an ability to get along with people and pull from them a desired response was more important than brains or a formal education. Just as the quality of the sales pitch seemed to be more important than the quality of the product, so was social intelligence more important than abstract intelligence. A love of learning, the arts, and things of the mind, by implication, were seductive thieves of ambition and time. What paid off was an understanding of human relations and its application to concrete profit-making situations.

A striking fact about the personality ethic is its comparative indifference to the philosophical implications of the success idea. Over the long road from Calvinism to Carnegieism, success apostles of the character ethic, of both a religious and secular persuasion, had usually paused for a moment to ponder such questions as: Will an obsessive greed for gold tarnish my soul, destroy my character, lead me into unhappiness? What is the ultimate goal in life, what is 'true success'? What is the justification for material success? Does making money possess any dignity? Is it ethically right to lay up treasures on earth?

The fear which continually nagged at the character ethic was the reality of success destroying those very qualities that produced success. Hard work and sobriety were the means to success, virtues in themselves. Money, with all its temptations of high living and soft pleasures, was always threatening the ascetic traits which produced it. The personality ethic was never moved to tremble before such a danger. Learning to talk in terms of the other man's interests, or memorizing his name, were hardly moral virtues in themselves. And a comfortable house in the country with servants, and a two-car garage filled with the most recent automotive look, did not threaten one's competence in handling people. Indeed, in the machinery of business and professional life, these advantages oiled the gears of human relations.

The traditional protests against total materialism were expressed almost entirely in the personality ethic by success writers who were trained psychologists. But they worried, not about the moral effects of wealth upon the qualities that made it, but about the psychological and physical effects resulting from the actual making of money. Bender and Graham, for example, offer the case of Willard Stone, who suffered from periodic attacks of a stomach ulcer. Stone "climbed from rags to riches in ten years, driven by an insatiable urge to be a 'success.' " Rejected in childhood by his parents and frustrated by a lack of affection, "he had decided early in life that he would win the approval he needed by fighting his way to the top. He acquired an outwardly pleasant manner to get people to like him." Churning with feelings of guilt, resentment, and a fear of failure, Stone regularly frets himself into ulcer attacks. The one sure cure for him is "to lose his resentment against his folks, which he has extended toward the rest of the world." Psychology-trained success writers, like Bender and Graham, worried about stomach ulcers and heart attacks resulting from a compulsive urge to succeed. They, and most of their colleagues of the personality ethic, were philosophically indifferent to the perils of materialism.[26]

What about 'true success'? The character ethic had defined this higher, or highest, goal in life as happiness, doing good to others, self-respect, a noble character, peace of mind, joy of living, the love of friends and family, doing your best, or developing the faculties that God has given you. Whatever the definition, it was asserted as a protest against money as the sole end in life. 'True success' was the *summum bonum* of life. It is what most people, if asked, would insist *should* be the definition of success.

On the surface, 'true success' for the personality ethic might seem to be popularity, lots of friends, or self-confidence in human relations. But this does violence to the traditional meaning of 'true success' as a revolt against a totally materialistic philosophy of life. Popularity was considered a worthy end in itself and was offered as a means to material success. But popularity was not an end in life which was asserted to be a more noble goal than the accumulation of wealth. The personality ethic, too, was less merciful because of its indifference to 'true success.' 'True success' had always been a refuge in which men who felt they had failed could comfort themselves with the self-respecting assurance that they had achieved something higher than wealth or fame. For all its terrible pressure to succeed, the character ethic had always been filled with a sense of Christian mercy.[27]

Proponents of the personality ethic were far more interested in the justification for material success than in the dangers of greed, or that wealth might be considered the final end in life. Like counselors of the character ethic, they presented both a secular and a religious interpretation. The *secular* justification for material success of the personality ethic was based on the concept of service. Wealth was a measure of service to other people, the community, and the nation. "About the most stupid thing that has ever been said is the old bromide, 'You have to be either crooked or lucky to make a million dollars,'" Elmer Wheeler protested. "All you need do is figure out something that you can *offer* other people. Some article that will make their life more interesting, happier, easier. The fortune you will make will depend upon the value of the thing you have to offer; and when you make yourself rich by service to others, you won't be a crook or lucky. You'll enrich millions of others *with* you. . . . 'Serving the needs of others,' is the great secret upon which all great fortunes have been built." [28]

To the standard justification of service, Wheeler added an insight less frequently expressed in the idea of success, though it does owe something to the old stewardship of wealth doctrine. Growth and progress, he maintained, is the result of the collective strength of individual men who have succeeded. "Advancement of the human race," claimed Wheeler, "has always depended upon *individual achievement*. . . . The best way a man can help other people is first to be successful himself. A poor man or a weak man can't do much good for others. It has always been the *successful* individual men who had lifted the race to higher levels of civilization. . . . If John D. Rockefeller had given all of his money to the poor when he was starting out, he couldn't have given them millions later on." [29]

Balancing the secular against the religious justification for material success, the religious justification was used much less frequently in the personality ethic than it had been in the character ethic. The *religious* interpretation, also based on service, is detailed in *Get Rich in Spite of Yourself* by Louis Grafe, who was an authority in the field of mail order advertising. Grafe begins by assuming that the amount of money a man makes is the measure of his service to his fellow man. He then strengthens his justification with a religious support by invoking the Bible and the sayings of Jesus: " 'Whosoever will be great among you, let him be your minister; and whosoever will be chief among you, let him be your servant.' " Paraphrased by Grafe, this means: " '*Whosoever will be great among you, let him minister unto the people's needs; and whosoever will be chief among you, let him give service in that field in which he is most skilled.'. . . To do your best, in giving service to your fellow men, is a duty you owe to your God.*" The 'chiefs' are those who have provided the most service. The Christian law, " 'Love thy neighbor as thyself,' " becomes " '*Serve thy neighbor as thyself,*' " for service is an expression of our love. Since service is an expression of our love for others, and money is the measure of that service to others, we love our neighbor as ourself when we make money by serving him.[30]

Why do the cars of Henry Ford command such a high trade-in value, Grafe asked? Because Henry Ford tried to serve the man who could only afford a used car. Ford's cars "have had, most of the time, the greatest value in the used car field. I imagine this was a totally unexpected reward for the service he gave, automatically increasing the demand for new cars. *Such unexpected rewards for service freely and eagerly given are what make men deservedly rich.*" Grafe calms the guilt feelings of those who might think that money-making lacks a Christian justification. He gives a lesson in Biblical history and then passes along the assurances of Jesus Christ wrapped up in the parable of the talents. "When the Bible speaks of the difficulty of rich men getting into Heaven, it is probably speaking of the rich of *that* day, most of whom gained their wealth through *other people's losses,* by conquest, chicanery, DISservice. There were few princes of service then, except for prophets and spiritual leaders. But in modern America we *do* have princes of service, people who have made their wealth *only* by *adding* to the security, comfort and happiness of their fellow men. Today these rich men are our best servants. And theirs is the reward promised in the parable of the talents: 'To him that hath shall be given.' " [31]

In summary, the personality ethic was indifferent to the dangers of materialism and the meaning of 'true success.' It was concerned about the justification for material success, but the religious interpretation was declining in importance. It is important to note that the personality ethic did not consciously enshrine the possession of wealth and material things as the *summum bonum* of life. In terms of the values of American culture, it is inconceivable that anyone would assert that the highest good in life, the end to which all our strivings on earth should point, and the goals which we should exalt above all others is the making of money for the power and things money can buy. The personality ethic never said that—but it never denied it either.

How can we explain these particular changes in the creed of

the success idea? In the first place, the success writer of the personality ethic came to his job with a different perspective. He was a technician, a dabbler or expert in psychology, a consultant who wrote his books out of personal experience or observation. He was no longer a bookish man, who liked to think of himself as a writer and a philosopher, musing about life and its meaning. He wrote only to teach the psychological principles of success which he had seen at work in the marketplace.

Second, the literature of the character ethic had been directed at young men. It throbbed with inspirational sermons for youth on the meaning of life. The literature of the personality ethic was written more for adults. It felt no duty to refine youthful minds with spiritual uplift.

Third, the decline in the religious justification for money-making contributed to the lack of interest in the dangers of materialism and the definition of 'true success.' Though the secular wing of the character ethic had been concerned about these problems, it was the religiously oriented success writer who expressed the gravest concern that Mammon might topple God's throne in the hearts of men. An ideological tension was always straining at the character ethic. The sin of greed might at any time overpower the goodness of a balanced ambition. This tension was missing in the personality ethic. The very words "avarice," "greed," and "covetousness," have a Biblical and old-fashioned mustiness about them, redolent of a spirit in success literature now quite out-of-date. As we shall see in a later chapter, the so-called 'return to religion' in the post-World War II period did little to revive this tension so important in the Puritan heritage of American religious thought.

18

SOURCES OF A
NEW WAY OF LIFE—
AND ITS PERILS

Developing a radiant personality and mastering techniques for handling people became a passion after the 1930s. From magazine articles to comic books, from courses in public speaking and charm development to full-length books charged with Carnegie-like rules for persuasion, an elephantine body of self-help literature was swinging the idea of success away from the character ethic. The way to get ahead was by a pleasing personality and the manipulation of other people.

Was there any evidence, as success writers claimed, that skillful human relations was an important factor in success? In business, "personality" and the ability to handle people were venerated. One placement man estimated that when hiring a new executive, "employers' judgments are based 20 per cent on the record and 80 per cent on personality." Perrin Stryker reported in 1955 that " 'getting along with people' " had been accepted by the modern corporation "as the first law in executive-development programs." [1]

When *Fortune*'s management poll asked executives in 1946, "Which one of the following qualities do you rate as having contributed most to your success?," a majority checked "ability to handle people" over the runner-up, "ability to make decisions." Some eight years later, a study of "a group of highly successful corporation officers" published in the *Harvard Business Review* corroborated *Fortune*'s findings. "A majority of the group members stated that skill in human relations was most important in their own advancement. Important qualities in this connection were the ability to get along with people, social poise, consideration of others, and tact in personal dealings. Next in importance . . . was the capacity to analyze facts and to understand and correctly solve problems." [2]

The importance of human relations reached down through the white collar ranks to the factory worker. While rating scales in earlier days emphasized descriptions of a worker's application, industriousness, and output, more and more in this period attention was being paid to the worker's relations with his fellow employees, subordinates, and superiors. Interpersonal relations were increasingly considered a vital factor in production and job stability.[3]

In the professions, as well as business, a different way of life demanded social intelligence in addition to technical competence. There were exceptions, for instance, the scholar absorbed in his lonely study or the natural scientist in another world of test tubes and mathematical figures. But outside of such 'loners,' the changing nature and importance of interpersonal relations in most occupations required qualities which heretofore had been polished to exacting brightness at the courts of European monarchies. This change in the American way of life was a matter of degree. In politics, of course, personal charm had always been an important factor. But the defeat of Robert A. Taft by Dwight Eisenhower at the Republican Convention in 1952 was a peculiar mid-twentieth century tragedy for the Senator from Ohio. Even fervent Taft supporters lamentably agreed that the chief quality Eisenhower enjoyed, and Taft lacked, was personality.

When a trim co-ed from Boston University, eager to learn the secret, asked the respected psychiatrist Dr. William C. Menninger, "what is the psychological key to success?" he replied flatly: "There's just one answer to that question: the difference between success and failure depends on knowing how to get along with other people. About 80 per cent of the people fired from their jobs are dismissed because they don't know how to get along with the people they work with or for." [4]

If we assume that there is some validity in the teachings of the personality ethic, the unavoidable question is—why? What caused this shift in the idea of success from the character ethic to the personality ethic? What forces were working in America to raise to such importance a pleasing personality and the ability to handle people?

The shock of the Great Depression hastened the shift. In 1933 the number of unemployed exceeded the number in the armed services during World War II a decade later. While the stock market plunged to new lows and the suicide rate climbed in the opposite direction, as self-reliant Americans swallowed their pride and fell in at the end of breadlines, the nation descended into the Great Depression and its most all-embracing crisis since the Civil War. The bitter decade of the 1930s seemed to mock the equation of hard work equals success. Now the urge was not so much to work hard, but to work.

The depression forced a reexamination of the old route to wealth. As usual, when things go wrong, you can blame it either on other people, 'the system,' or yourself. Americans bludgeoned the businessman, turned contemptuously on the symbol of Wall Street, lost faith in the system of freewheeling capitalism, but could not help but hold themselves partly responsible, as individuals, for whatever economic loss they had suffered.

> The fault, dear Brutus, is not in our stars,
> But in ourselves, that we are underlings.

Such a doctrine of personal responsibility for one's earthly destiny, though weakened, was too deeply engrained in American values to be cast aside. The success idea never permitted a whimpering resignation before uncontrollable economic and social forces. The cause of failure was located in one's own self; a crisis only prompted the search for new techniques of achievement.

The depression also posed the ludicrous paradox of poverty

in the midst of plenty, tragically symbolized by the slaughter of 'little pigs' while families were starving. With goods backing up on the shelves, the crisis would not be solved by working harder and producing more goods. It could only be solved by creating a desire and demand for the consumption of the goods. The depression intensified this paradox and pointed to a deeper cause for the final dominance of the personality ethic.

With or without the depression, the personality ethic was inevitable in a nation which over the years was undergoing a shift from a scarcity economy to an economy of abundance, from a production economy to an economy of consumption. The character ethic had been a realistic response to a set of social and economic exigencies—to feed, clothe, and house your family by the sweat of your brow and the strength in your back. The conflict was between man and the physical environment, between the individual and nature. Self-denying, ascetic qualities, such as thrift, stamina, and determination were a necessity. Goods were scarce because total demand was usually equal to or in excess of total supply. In such an economy, wealth accrued to the man who could organize and produce goods.

When mass production and the continuous flow assembly line broke through the scarcity barrier in the 1920s, potential supply began to outstrip demand. Growth was then no longer restrained by productive capacity, but by the capacity of the market to soak up goods in excess supply. (The wartime seller's market only interrupted a long-term trend.) Machines, with their inexhaustible energy, can keep products moving through the production process twenty-four hours a day every day. The problem is to keep the products moving after they roll off the end of the assembly line.

In a consumption economy of abundance, the nation can afford to, and must, pour more of its energies into the service occupations. There is a decline in the percentage of the working population engaged in the production of physical goods, i.e., agriculture, forestry and fishing, extraction of minerals, and manufacturing. There is an increase in the percentage of the working population engaged in service and distribution, i.e., trade, clerical pursuits, professional service, public service, communication, and transportation. With the increase of jobs revolving around people, rather than the production of things, a premium price is paid to those who are skillful in the manipulation of human beings, directly through personal contact, or indirectly through symbols.[5]

New jobs open up, and wealth begins flowing to those who can solve the problems of marketing, selling, advertising, promotion, and distribution—and the coordination of these fields with production, finance, and purchasing. The demand is for individuals who are interested in people rather than materials, who are product-wise rather than production-oriented. The trick in a consumption economy is not to build a better mousetrap, but to sell it. With an increasing proportion of everything offered for sale falling into the category of optional consumption, which the consumer can ignore without any serious personal inconvenience, the selling services must do more than simply move products. They must constantly create a desire for new products, or for old products packaged in a new dress.

The competition in business is as intense as it has ever been in the American experience. But the nature of competition is determined less by the character of the product's competitive price and the individual's perseverance to produce it, and more by the personality of the product and the individual who is engaged in the various phases of selling it. As price competition is relaxed through price leadership and the experiments in fair trade laws, as the performance and quality of products become more standardized by mass production, the major areas of competition lie in product initiation, product differentiation, and consumer attitudes. It is in the field of consumer attitudes, tastes, and preferences that the personality ethic becomes indispensable.

Where there is an oligopoly, such as the automobile industry, with prices controlled by a few giants, the nature of competition is considerably different than when Henry Ford, according to legend, offered a variety of colors for his Model T—so long as it was black. From 1914 to 1925, the Model T actually came only in black. Today Ford offers a dazzling choice of solid colors and two-tone combinations. While the local agencies of

Ford and Chevrolet bang bumpers in their annual battle for top sales, the echoes register with seismographic sensitivity not only in Detroit, but also in the advertising agencies along Madison Avenue. Because the price in relation to the quality and performance of competing automobiles, gasoline, toothpaste, cigarettes, soap, and so forth are relatively similar, the producer is at the mercy of the advertiser's effectiveness in controlling consumer choice. It is this fantastic range of consumer choice that intensifies competition, not only between producers of the same product, but between producers of different kinds of products. How *will* the Joneses spend their money? A bigger bed for Junior or an extra radio for the kitchen? Color television or a dishwasher? A new automobile or a better house? [6]

Advertising manipulates people indirectly through symbols. On the retail level, people are directly persuaded through personal contact and face-to-face relations. When price competition decreases, service competition increases. In the classical economy of Adam Smith, the market price is regulated by the invisible hand of supply and demand. The Keynesian economy of the personality ethic is pumped by the glad hand. The friendly gas station attendant, the courteous clerk, the smiling check-out girl help you to decide whether to buy Esso or Atlantic gasoline, shop at Woolworth's or Grant's, buy your food at the Acme or the A & P.[7]

On the executive level, with bigger stakes riding on each sale, the glad hand is less calloused, but the grip is just as tight. In the office and on the links, at the conventions or in the most expensive restaurants, the glad hand, firm and sincere, reaches out for the contract while Adam Smith's invisible hand withers away. All these factors reinforced the habit of combining business and pleasure—spheres of interest which Europeans like to keep separate, but which Americans always try to unite.

Golf, of course, has become the ideal recreation pursued for purposes other than purely relaxation, exercise, and fun. "Knowing how to play golf," said one Michigan industrialist, "is especially important for business people in sales and promotion. A lot of labor leaders are playing golf and bridge instead of poker and pinochle." A man of conviction, the industrialist turned philanthropist and handed over to Notre Dame University $5,000 to stimulate interest in golf and bridge. In Denver, Colorado, an investment banker, who plays a good game of golf, estimated that fully 50 per cent of his business comes from friends who enjoy taking the Eighteen with him. "Recently a friend called me to make up a foursome," he reported. "I told him I couldn't play because I had a quota of stock to sell. He said, 'Forget it; come on along. I'll take a third of it and we'll unload the rest on the other two.' " [8]

One's antennae must be sensitive enough to pick up the signals for conducting business at the country club. (At the better clubs, "contacts" are made, but specific business is seldom mentioned.) In *How to Win Friends and Influence People,* Carnegie approvingly reports the cagey technique of Constant, the head valet in Napoleon's household, who permitted Josephine to beat him at billiards. "Although I had some skill," he averred, "I always managed to let her beat me, which pleased her exceedingly." The personality ethic was not above forcing the true sportsman to suffer such agonies of self-sacrifice. But the whole approach could backfire. In 1953 Walter Winchell reported an awful disaster: "A leading ad agency just lost a $3-million account because an account exec's golf game was transparently phony. He let a sponsor 'beat him' which irked him to the point of dropping the agency!" It was, admittedly, an unforgivable blunder on the part of the account executive. He may, or may not, have misjudged the urge of his client to win, but it was inexcusable in terms of the personality ethic for him to get caught. Agency punishment in such cases is properly merciless.[9]

The federal government inadvertently blessed the glad hand approach by ruling that dollars spent in the pursuit of other dollars is a legitimate deduction from a company's taxable profits. The company expense account has forced American business to compete even more directly in terms of the personality ethic.

"Supposing you're selling carpet tacks," explained one salesman. "Three other fellows from three other companies are trying to sell carpet tacks to the same customer. The price is about the same and the quality is certainly the same. After all, how much difference can there be between carpet tacks? So which brand is the customer going to buy? The chances are that he'll buy from the salesman who puts him in the best frame of mind. If he likes you he'll buy from you—and one way to get him to like you is to spend some money on him. With carpet tacks it's as simple as A, B, C. And a lot of goods are in the carpet tacks category nowadays." [10]

It is debatable just how effective the hearty fellowship lubricated by an expense account is in massaging a client. Vincent Sullivan, in his hard-boiled *How to Sell Your Way into the Big Money,* thought it was important and frankly discussed some of its problems and uses. Remember to stay sober, Sullivan cautioned. As a defense against the heavy drinker, try the vermouth cocktail. "It consists of just vermouth and bitters. You can drink any martini luncher under the table in short order with these little darlings."

Confident that his readers will control themselves, Sullivan ventures to describe the call house of Miss Gloria, a twelve-room duplex apartment on Central Park West in New York City. Miss Gloria's luxurious barn is stabled with five extraordinarily beautiful girls—each one a bright carbon-copy of Hollywood's most sensual actresses of the moment. "This gilded palace of pleasure is maintained by the sales organization handling the advertising of a group of magazines that you probably read in your own living room weekly or monthly. As a salesman for this organization, the whorehouse is the final sales weapon. And it invariably produces the contract, too! This type of selling is known in the sales profession as whorehouse selling, and it is not at all uncommon."

Though Sullivan frowns on this style of business, as well as on lavish gifts, kickbacks, and fee-splitting, he respectfully describes the behavior of a married man who cleverly preserved his marital fidelity by this ruse: "He arranged those double dates for himself and his customer, but when it came time for him and his girl to disappear into the bedroom, they each mixed a couple of drinks, entered the bedroom and used the bed to play a couple of rounds of gin rummy. The girl, of course, was paid her full fee—after all her time is valuable—and [she] understood the arrangement. His wife didn't like the idea, naturally, but made the proviso that he stick strictly to vermouth cocktails for the evening." [11]

The *New Yorker's* John McCarten embellished for the chic readers of *Harper's Bazaar* the interesting historical comparison: "It's not so very long ago that enterprising youths of the stripe of Horatio Alger boys—Phil the Fiddler, Connie the Canoeist or Jed the Poor House Boy—were firm in the conviction that honesty, hard work and no liquor would inevitably lead to the presidency of a cordage works or the like. Nowadays, Phil, Connie and Jed probably couldn't progress beyond positions as name-plate polishers if they eschewed an occasional olive or cherry dip with the head man or his associates. As a matter of fact, it frequently appears that skill in handling a long-stemmed glass is virtually as important to the modern businessman as knowing how to work his way through a crowded ledger. This holds true of a lot of occupations. No author whom a publisher regards as being worth a place above the salt can issue a book without being dragooned into a cocktail party to celebrate the event. Neither can a soap manufacturer create a new detergent without baptizing the product in alcohol. Even a topflight poet, when he clambers down from his ivory tower to lay down his heavy ode, does so to the accompaniment of tinkling glasses and siphon swishes." [12]

What happened to frugality and thrift in the success idea? They were important for the character ethic. Now they are musty with disuse, quaint-sounding, and no longer ring with a moral tone. Why did the personality ethic ignore parsimony as a means to success?

Mass starvation would be the consequence if modern Americans were required to obey Poor Richard's stern command: "Rather go to bed supperless than rise in debt." Many families live within their means by borrowing to do it. Others live so far beyond their income that it might be said that they almost were living apart. Thrift as a value is wracked by ambivalent attitudes. In recent decades sometimes it was more patriotic to spend and keep the economy humming; at other times one was encouraged to save and check inflation. Is a mortgage on a house, amortized by monthly payments, an act of going into debt or a thrifty way of building equity through saving? Is father, who has hocked part of next year's salary on deferred payments for his car and appliances, a profligate, or is he thrifty because he will pay off the debt and increase his assets? What is the difference between the older habit of "putting something aside for a rainy day" and contemporary pensions, social security, and life insurance? [13]

Whether Americans are more or less thrifty is too complex for an off-hand generalization. We can say, however, that for the character ethic thrift and frugality were values which honored ascetic self-denial and deferred gratification. If we measure thrift in that sense, we can understand why the personality ethic ignored it as a means to success. The personality ethic was responding to a multitude of forces which were seducing that asceticism. Among those forces were: Installment buying, the charge account, and easy credit terms ('Nothing down and an eternity to pay.'); advertising's latest model appeals and a desertion by industry of the 'built to last' ideal; an increasingly higher standard of living and the fruitfulness of mass production in an abundance economy; inflation which nibbled at the value of the dollar; the warnings of the Keynesian economists that a sharp rise in savings could start the economy spinning into the downside of a business cycle; a government, itself deep in debt, spending astronomical sums in domestic and foreign affairs; a 'live it up' attitude sparked by high income and inheritance taxes ("The government will get it anyway."); and the decline of the Puritan tradition in American religion and values with its harsh demands, asceticism, and self-denial.

All these reasons are helpful in explaining why the personality ethic dropped thrift as a means to success. American life made the sugar bowl frugality of the past an anachronism. But a more direct explanation springs from a deep change in the structure of the American economy. It is this change in the structure of the economy which carries forward our explanation of why the personality ethic attained a position of dominance in the success idea.

As we noted in an earlier chapter, the character ethic served the needs of an economy of small proprietors. The nineteenth-century way to success was to start a firm, expand it in competition with others, and then drive on with it as high as one could go. An enterprising individual generally owned the property with which he worked, with his status and income determined by the qualities he himself put into the firm. The success of the firm was the measure of his own success. The traditional bourgeois values, such as thrift and frugality, were mandatory in the world of the small entrepreneur who was both owner and operator. With the rise of large corporations, however, these bourgeois values were transferred to the business concern, and it was possible for the entrepreneur himself to dispense with them.

The increasing consolidation and concentration of business into corporate structures during the twentieth century cut a new route to wealth. The character ethic's owner-operator is replaced by the manager who works his way up within an established bureaucratic hierarchy. He is a salaried employee on a bureaucratic scale. The ladder of success is already framed in place. The nineteenth-century owner-operator had to nail each succeeding rung on his own ladder of success. The modern corporation manager can see the established rungs above him which he must grasp.

The promotion of a corporation manager to a higher notch on the scale depends on the impression he makes on his superiors and associates. In the nineteenth century, the success of an expanding small proprietor depended more on the impersonal action of the market. His success was tied directly to the success of his own company. The avenue of ascent for the corporation executive, on the other hand, is closed or thrown open by the personal judgment of his superiors. Since promotion is controlled less by an invisible hand of supply and demand pointing an impersonal finger at the winner, the glad hand frequently exerts its own kind of pressure in shaping the decision.

In a corporate bureaucracy, a premium is put on the ability to work with and through people. An important part of the executive's job is to coordinate functions, to organize, lead and set an example for subordinates, and to advise and carry out the instructions of superiors. He works through and with other people. His decisions are not individual but corporate. Much of his time is spent in committees and conferences, writing or receiving reports and memoranda. That is one reason why success books of the personality ethic are essentially manuals on communication—how to handle people, how to control the responses of others, how to present ideas effectively and persuasively. In this type of business bureaucracy, as in a political or military bureaucracy, the concept of the smoothly organized and functioning "team" is lifted to an ideal. A business bureaucracy cannot tolerate, except in research, the offbeat, eccentric genius who disrupts the rhythm of human relations. In mid-twentieth-century America, the epithet "he's hard to get along with" can sting like the curse of dishonor in an earlier age.

Different qualities are necessary, of course, for the line executive, who is interested in the results of his specific orders on production and sales, and the staff executive, who suggests and advises by using persuasion. But from the line executive down to the section foreman, the authoritarian boss of seventy-five years ago who drove his shop of illiterates has become an anachronism. The workers are better educated, jobs are more highly skilled, the union is an attentive chaperon, and everyone is morale conscious. From the straw bosses to the big bosses in an ascending hierarchy, you not only have to get the job done, but you must also make certain that everyone is happy while they're doing it.[14]

Throughout the world of business, controlling the attitudes of other people lifted the word "relations" to new significance. Management must anticipate and direct relations with a variety of groups—customers, the local community, the public, labor, suppliers, financiers, and shareholders. Balancing the demands of these competing groups and keeping them happy has forced a relations-conscious management to seek assistance from new industrial types. Public relations, labor-management relations, and industrial relations became growth occupations.[15]

The interdependence of people was another cause contributing to the rise of the personality ethic. The life of the housewife, and men and women in business and the professions, was increasingly interwoven with the lives of other people in the shift from a rural-farm to an urban-suburban way of life. In the nineteenth century, the majority of Americans were farmers. The farming family lived an isolated existence. They worked with domesticated animals and the raw materials of the soil. Today, Americans are urbanites, suburbanites, exurbanites, or inhabitants of small towns. On the job, people are frequently the raw material out of which success is fashioned. During leisure hours, the group is the indispensable staple for a more gregarious definition of fun.

An extreme example of this way of life is the self-contained communities like Levittown and Park Forest, Illinois. *Fortune's* William H. Whyte, Jr., peeked into the picture windows and reported something about the life in look-alike housing developments. In these sprawling commuting dormitories of communal intimacy, life often seems dominated by the social demands of other people. Inflamed with a passion for group-organized activities, just about the nicest thing your neighbors can say about you and your wife is: "They are a wonderful outgoing couple." [16]

On the executive level, *Fortune* has explained how corporate bureaucracy has forced an interrelationship between business and the home. In company towns, and in the suburbs where managers of the same corporation live in close proximity, the long arm of the job has been poking into the sanctuary of the home and encircling the wife. Business is increasingly taking a long, hard look at the wife before hiring the husband, lending credence to the definition of marriage as a "mutual mobility bet." The ideal wife should be highly adaptable, highly gregarious, and realize that her husband belongs to the corporation. "The good corporation wife does not make her friends uncomfortable by clothes too blatantly chic, references to illustrious forebears, or excessive good breeding. And intellectual pretensions she avoids like the plague. It is interesting to watch one wife rearrange her magazine basket as she primps for callers; almost automatically, she shuffles her *Harper's* and *Atlantic Monthly* beneath the pile. The Girls might not understand." For the corporation wife who wants her husband to get ahead, "getting along with people . . . has become more than mere expediency; it has become a dedicated purpose." [17]

The anti-intellectual potential for 'groupthink' in the personality ethic is indicated in *Fortune's* survey: "Growth can mean many things; to the younger generation of executives it seems to mean an increasing ability to handle and mix with people. And the terms are the same for the wife. 'The wife who is not very sociable,' goes a highly typical male observation, 'might not affect the husband directly, but she can hurt him just the same. A lot of business is done week ends. If she doesn't go for this, her lack of growth can hold the man back.' Even the old idea of a wife as a sort of culture carrier is virtually dead; she is still expected to read and things like that, but for functional reasons. 'Sure I want her to read good books and magazines,' as one executive puts it, 'I don't want her to make a fool of herself in conversation.' " [18]

The ever-tightening linkage of human affairs helps to explain why the influence of a "good mother" drifted out of success books. In the more rural, small town training ground of the character ethic, a mother was constantly minting the quality of her son. In the more urban world of the personality ethic, youth organizations and universal, compulsory education diminished her influence.

The personality ethic transferred the leverage factor in success from mother to wife. (The character ethic, of course, had always praised the "good wife"—good defined as a strong moral character.) Tutors in the personality ethic dropped mother and increased the importance of the "good wife." A "good wife" bolstered her husband's self-confidence, was easy to get along with, and possessed a capacity for social and intellectual growth equal to her husband. Though not exactly a wife-made man, the careerist could quickly be unmade by the misery of an unhappy marriage.

The rush of American society into an interconnected way of life was speeded by mass transportation, mass communication, and various other "masses" from mass entertainment to mass education. How the automobile, the movies, radio, and television increased the interrelatedness of life and demanded a quick adaptation to changing situations and new people is obvious. Mass education, however, requires additional comment.

Universal, compulsory education lifted the child out of the focused contact of family life and enlarged his peer group contacts. Progressive education urged children towards a more social response to life. The theories of progressive education were translated into practice with varying degrees of acceptance in all but the most orthodox public schools, but to a far lesser extent in the private schools which fed into the better colleges and universities. The McGuffey Readers of the nineteenth century tried to build character into their children; progressive education was concerned also with personality development.

General education courses in "grooming" were frequently only the harassed expression of educators forced to keep disinterested students in school to a certain age. What is really important was the theory of progressive pedagogy which added up to a conception of education as much a social as an intellectual process. The emphasis was on 'teaching the child rather than the subject,' and training him to participate in group affairs. The process was 'learning by doing' through 'real life' problems and 'activity projects.' It was the whole child which must be taught, according to the progressive theories which caught on beginning in the 1920s. The child's social and emotional qualities were inseparable from and as important as a hard, intellectual, disciplined training of the mind. The stress was not, and the words are revealing, on the more solitary life of the mind, but on 'cooperation,' 'adjustment,' and 'integration.' Education as a *social* process should teach the mutual relations of mankind living in an organized society. It was unquestionably, as far as it goes, excellent training for what was called 'citizenship.' The end product was frequently *sociable*

—a boy or girl fond of company and society, companionable, genial, and affable, and good at mixing with others. In short, the kind of person who operated naturally and effectively in a society dominated by the personality ethic.

Here there is irony, however. The McGuffey Readers rein-forced every element in the formula of the character ethic Progressive education was good training in the personality ethic, but it could never be accused of supporting the competi-tive, ambitious spirit of the success idea, of urging a child to *exceed* his grasp. The child's level of aspiration must not be set too far above his level of potential. A wide gap might pro-duce several kinds of neuroses. A life adjustment curriculum educated for adjustment to 'life,' and for an adaptation of a child's life goals to his achievement potential.[19]

Modern parental upbringing reinforced progressive education. There was something vaguely undesirable about "introvert" children, but then Dr. Spock's famed paperback treasury on baby and child care was always on hand with helpful hints on how to encourage children to be more "outgoing." Cartoonists defined contemporary theories of child rearing by poking fun at them. In the *New Yorker,* Whitney Darrow, Jr., pictured a tweedy, pipe-smoking father seated on a sofa, leaning forward intently, while he discusses the matter of a report card in his hand with his small son standing before him on the carpet. His agitation has nothing to do with sinking academic grades in arithmetic. The report card has disappointed him with an apparently more grave discovery. "Young man, from now on," he says sternly, "I want you to get in there and integrate with the group." In another version, an equally disturbed mother, pointing out the window to a group of scrapping moppets, looks down at her sobbing son and issues the stern command: "Now get in there and integrate." Gardner Rea had an answer for that one in the *New Yorker.* While a group of boys tussle in the background, a perplexed child tries to explain to his camp counselor: "But I can't *fight* well enough to integrate with the group." [20]

All these causal forces, of varying degrees of power, conspired to swing the means to success away from the older bourgeois virtues to a pleasing personality and the ability to handle other people. In summary, the shock of the 1930s depression was less important than the long-term transition to an economy of abundance and consumption, the growth of service occupations, the importance of, and intense competition in, all those areas involving distribution and selling. While much of the American economy was shifting to a corporate bureaucracy, people were forced into closer contact through changes in population distribution, living habits, transportation, and communication. While modern education and child-rearing practices helped to break in coming generations of aspirants, new ways of conducting business reached out to encircle not only the husband, but his wife as well.

These changes, cutting deep into American life, made insufficient, though still indispensable, the older virtues of hard work, perseverance, and determination. The new route to riches and power was working through and with other people, controlling their responses and manipulating them to your way of thinking. Though success writers of the personality ethic unquestionably overemphasized human relations at the expense of other factors in money-making, here was indeed, as Dale Carnegie insisted, a new way of life for all Americans.

One consequence of these vast forces was the emergence of a new hero to stand with the Models of Devotion and Images of Aspiration noted in a previous chapter. Models of Devotion, like George Washington, symbolized abstract ideas, places, or things. Images of Aspiration were people whom one was eager to equal or excel occupationally. What we might call Idols of Entertainment were the playmates of leisure, marketable products for one's amusement.

It was the mass media, beginning in the 1920s with print joined to radio, the movies, and phonograph records, later expanded by television, which created our Idols of Entertainment. There is a heritage for this kind of fame which reaches back to the political orator of over a century ago. But it was a ladder to both wealth and fame for the performer as athlete, actor, comedian, musician, and singer in the middle decades of the twentieth century. In most businesses the rags-to-riches tale was steady and sure. In the communications industry the starvation-to-stardom saga was quick and unexpected. The thrilling sequence was from Starvation Flat, through the Big Break, the Smash Hit, and the Name Up There in Lights to the Plush Penthouse. As the *Fan Club Hollywood News* breathlessly announced: Elvis Presley "wasn't discovered, he just happened. Here is a life story which rivals any rags to riches fable ever written." In the mid-1960s Presley, an actor-singer with the most widely denounced pelvis in human history, was estimated in a good year to be earning as much as $5,000,000. Among Elvis' numerous automobiles was a gold-trimmed Cadillac spray-painted with 40 coats of crushed diamonds. In the elite arts it is the creator, the writer, the painter, the composer who is extolled. In the popular arts it is the entertainer, the actor, the singer, the comedian who is exalted. While many creative people able to appeal to the mass taste have made fortunes in the new opportunities of the lens and the microphone, it is the performers who have more often been rewarded with the dividend of popular fame.[21]

The entertainer exploits the mass media as much as it exploits him. Where else could one find an instant success of both wealth and fame which demands no risk of venture capital? Since the public appetite likes a varied menu, the advice of Jimmy Durante is sage: "Be awful nice to 'em goin' up, because you're gonna meet 'em all comin' down." The chance at instant fame exacts the risk of instant failure.[22]

In the world of the personality ethic, an executive gets ahead by selling himself as well as the product. The entertainer and professional athlete *are* the product. They are consumed as fantasy objects by the public.

In the nineteenth century fame was a reward for meeting certain basic needs of society—governing or protecting the nation. The new dimension that has been added is fame by entertaining the people. Just as the public has more discretionary income to spend on luxuries beyond necessities, so they also have more discretionary fame to lavish on performers who add to their lives the froth of glamour to lighten the dreariness of life. Making money has always been as simple in theory as it has been difficult in practice. You find, or create, a need and fill it at a profit. The new route to success in a consumption economy of mass communications is to become an entertainment product that the public voraciously consumes as a luxury of its leisure.

What psychological consequences did these changes, expressed in the personality ethic, have on the way Americans look at life, at themselves, and their fellow man? In the first place, the personality ethic reinforced an urge toward conformity and group-mindedness. The word conformity is used pejoratively to indicate a pressure to adjust to a particular pattern of living and thinking. It is important to remember, however, that there are shades of conformity and to ask: "conformity to what?" Pressure to learn considerate manners or to act like a gentleman is not undesirable; pressure to think in the same way or violate one's ethics is tyranny. The personality ethic, and the forces which it articulated, enforced a creeping conformity which was subtly tyrannous in its pressure to play the game according to the most effective rules, even though the rules might violate a person's ethical principles.

In a group-minded society orchestrated for conformity, adjustment of all instruments to a single timbre creates a sterile sound, a symphony of platitudes in which the way you play the notes is more important than the notes themselves, the slickness of the performance more interesting than the quality of the composition. "It is undeniably true that you don't have to be an s.o.b. to be creative," an editor of *Fortune* has observed. "It is equally true, however, that a real advance in any field frequently involves conflict. And unless people temper their worship of environment, they may well evolve a society so well adjusted that no one would be able—or willing—to give it the sort of hotfoot it regularly needs. We would all be too busy getting along with each other." In the personality ethic, intellectual timidity seems like sagacity; the sweet reasonableness of cliché-trading is safer than the sparkle of thoughtful, controversial conversation. Better to be cozy than controversial, wiser to use soft soap than the scrub brush, get in there and integrate, and always be easy to get along with.[23]

Second, the personality ethic stained those affections of people for each other which should flow from a *politesse de coeur*, from a love of men and women for what they are, and not what we can get out of them. In the nineteenth century of the character ethic, the way to success was through the exploitation of natural resources; in the personality ethic, the way to get ahead is through the exploitation of human beings. Instead of working with things, physical objects, you work with and through individuals or groups. People are the raw material out of which success is fashioned.

But people are not an unprocessed material of nature, like coal or iron ore. By humanistic standards, you are supposed to love people, not use them. Man is an end, not a means. By Christian principles, he is an end to a final salvation, not an object to be exploited for personal gain. To manipulate others for personal gain under the guise of liking and enjoying them for their own sake is a form of deceitfulness. It sets in motion a clash between values which are humanistic and religious and behavior which is repugnant to those values. It was this offense to his sense of values which prompted Sinclair Lewis to strike at Carnegie's book, with its lessons on "how to smile and bob and pretend to be interested in people's hobbies precisely so that you may screw things out of them. . . ." The personality ethic tarnishes all social relations. It is not easy to switch constantly from a feigned regard for a person towards whom you feel indifference to an honest expression of feeling towards those whom you cherish as friends or loved ones. To smile so frequently with mercenary intent is to rape the smile with self-seeking. Though success writers kept protesting against flattery, mostly for the dubious reason that it wasn't effective, sincerity was an insoluble problem for the personality ethic. Sincerity without selection is hypocrisy.[24]

There is much to be said in support of success writers of the personality ethic. They helped to resolve self-conscious agonies and inferiority feelings. They frequently untied knotted lives of daily panic and bound them to a warm self-confidence in human relations. In an increasingly interrelated society, they eased the strain of people forced to get along with one another. They taught those with a rubbery insensitivity to the feelings of others the effectiveness, and the gladness, of simple courtesy and tact. But there is a difference between persuading people with the understood intent of private gain, and manipulating them with psychological techniques which trespass upon integrity and honesty. In Carnegie's examples, cited so approvingly, what is the significance of Mr. Steinhardt who discovered that smiles brought dollars, of the Shakespearean authority who lied in order to be well-liked, of Constant who threw the billiard game to Josephine in order to please her, of the Philadelphia Electric Company's Mr. Webb who beamed to the icy Mrs. Druckenbrod: "I didn't come here to sell you electricity. I merely wanted to buy some eggs." Does Mrs. Druckenbrod know that Mr. Webb is buttering her up today in order to fry her with an electric bill next month? With the means to wealth so relative, with motivation so easily twisted from affection to expediency, what is spontaneous and what is contrived, who is sincere and who is a flatterer, what is genuine and what is false? What lurks behind the smiling mask? [25]

The answer can sometimes be alarming. In a life of mirthless smiles and superficial relationships, one can feel a terrible sense of isolation and aloneness. It's a kind of emptiness which a gluttonous craving for companionship cannot fill. A feeling of emotional phoniness seeping into much of life can result in self-accusations of hypocrisy and lost integrity. It leads to an estrangement from one's fellow men, followed by a contempt for oneself as well as other people, and finally an inability to love or feel loved. A. A. Roback read a representative book of the personality ethic, put the rules into practice, and then concluded his satire with the not so funny observation: "Perhaps you will understand . . . when I tell you I am losing my own friendship, I mean my faith in values and standards, faith in humanity; for something argued in me: 'What you are doing, others are doing too. You are kidding others, and others are kidding you. That's exactly how they are winning you!' Was there any way of recognizing what is chaff and what is wheat; what is soft soap . . . ?" [26]

Finally, the personality ethic not only created a stress situation by estranging men from one another, it also alienated men from themselves. In the character ethic, success was directly related to inner qualities. If you worked hard and saved money, you made money. In the personality ethic, success is related to the opinion of others about you. The means to success are not fixed, but relative to the response of others. Your attitude towards yourself, your sense of identity, is shaped by the attitude of other people toward you. So while you think you are controlling others, they are actually exercising final control over you, defining for you what you are. When a young man in W. H. Auden's *The Age of Anxiety* wonders:

> . . . It is getting late.
> Shall we ever be asked for? Are we simply
> Not wanted at all?

another character replies:

> Well, you will soon
> Not bother but acknowledge yourself
> As market-made, a commodity
> Whose value varies, a vendor who has
> To obey his buyer. . . .[27]

If other people are the raw material of success, you are a commodity, salable as a personality package in the marketplace. Your value is measured by the price others are willing to pay for you. Your sense of identity is defined by what others think of you. Not only what you are, but who you imagine yourself to be, is determined by their approval. You lose, therefore, identity with yourself. You become alienated from yourself. And the self-alienated man is an apprehensive and anxious man.

In *Gift from the Sea*, her beautiful book about the conflicts splintering the serenity of modern women, Anne Morrow Lindbergh observes: "How one hates to think of oneself as alone. How one avoids it. It seems to imply rejection or unpopularity. An early wallflower panic still clings to the word. One will be left, one fears, sitting in a straight-backed chair *alone,* while the popular girls are already chosen and spinning around the dance floor with their hot-palmed partners. We seem so frightened today of being alone that we never let it happen." Being alone, for both men and women, not only implies rejection and un-popularity, it robs you of the constant need to define your identity which others now command, to test your skill at charm-ing a favorable response from others. Who can afford solitude? People who work with things, and people whose primary purpose is the unfolding of truth, rather than the pursuit of commercial gain, those who write books, paint pictures, and labor in laboratories. Other folk, who must control the responses of people, indirectly through symbols, or directly through per-sonal contact, cannot afford solitude. Nor do they want it. Solitude means an absence of people, and it is only through people that the self-alienated product of the personality ethic can find his sense of identity.[28]

In the chapters that follow, we shall see how the apostles of mind power as a way to success fed upon these feelings of estrangement, self-alienation, anxiety, and helplessness. You can be, indeed you *are,* they affirmed, what you *think* you are. With the power of positive thinking, they lured post-World War II Americans to a philosophy which not only promised the material advantages of success but an escape from the torments of psychic distress

19

THE SEARCH FOR POWER

Power, in mathematics, can be obtained by multiplying a number by itself. It was in self-multiplying power that a popular group of success writers located the leverage for success. The route to riches was not strength of character. It was not a winning personality. The way to wealth lay in the self multiplied.

There were two sources of power. The religious interpretation located the source of power in God. He was called Infinite Intelligence, Universal Mind, or Divine Supply. Success writers who developed the religious interpretation expressed a theology called New Thought. In the post-World War II decades, it was most widely disseminated by the Reverend Norman Vincent Peale.

The secular interpretation located the power for success within man. Émile Coué's rhythmical jingle of autosuggestion, "Day by day, in every way, I am getting better and better," was its most dramatic expression before the 1930s. Secular mind power did not, like New Thought, imagine its devotees tapping the omniscience of All Supply. Many of its interpreters, though, admitted the existence of a supernatural being. They spoke of certain God-given powers within man and frequently quoted the Bible for support. The important distinction is that secular mind power did not require religious faith. The generating power for success was entirely within man or between men.

It was not a power supercharged by a contact between man and God.

Since the early 1930s one of the more popular works on secular mind power was Claude Bristol's *The Magic of Believing*. Published in 1948 by Prentice-Hall, it has sold over half a million copies with its promises still being advertised in the late 1960s. A piano player named Wladziu Valentino Liberace confessed in a lyrical introduction to the 1955 edition: "This book has been a constant and daily friend to me...." *The Magic of Believing* is lifted above such confessionals onto a more rewarding level of analysis by its wide-ranging summary of the secular mind power school of success literature. Bristol threshed through much of the literature, both secular and religious, and sifted what he thought to be, and what actually is, the essence of it.[1]

Claude M. Bristol was a newspaperman, an investment banker, student of the law, lecturer, and writer. While a newspaperman he was absorbed in the mystical world of the psychic and the occult. "For a two-year period I was church editor of a large metropolitan newspaper . . . ," he tells us. "I came in close contact with clergymen and leaders of all sects and denominations, mind-healers, divine-healers, Spiritualists, Christian Scientists, New Thought-ers, Unity leaders, sun and idol worshippers, and, yes, even a few infidels and pagans." Many years later "I was commissioned to write a series of articles on what is known in police parlance as the 'fortune-telling racket.' I visited everything from gypsy phrenologists to crystal-ball gazers, from astrologers to spiritualistic mediums." Fascinated by the psychic and the occult, he read "every book I could get my hands on dealing with religions, cults, and both physical and mental sciences. I have read literally thousands of books on modern psychology, metaphysics, ancient magic, Voodooism, Yogism, Theosophy, Christian Science, Unity, Truth, New Thought, Couéism, and many others dealing with what I call 'Mind Stuff,' as well as the philosophies and teachings of the great masters of the past." To this was added a boyhood background and interest in "wireless telegraphy, X-ray, high-frequency apparatus, and similar manifestations of electricity," and a familiarity with "such terms as radiations, frequencies, vibrations, oscillations, magnetic influences," and so forth.[2]

One night, during World War I when he was a soldier in France, came the moment. Without money for even a pack of gum or cigarettes, Bristol vowed that "when I returned to civilian life, 'I would have a lot of money.'" As an investment banker in the 1920s, he did not engage in useless doodling. "My 'doodling' was in the form of dollar signs like these '$$$$$—$$$$—$$$—$$' on every paper that came across my desk. The cardboard covers of all the files placed before me daily were scrawled with these markings, so were the covers of telephone directories, scratch-pads, and even the face of important correspondence." [3]

Out of this combined experience as a newspaperman and banker, concentrated reading and an urge to be rich, Bristol developed his technique for success which he claims saved his firm, and many others, from bankruptcy during the depression. "In laying before you this very workable science," Bristol explained his rejection of the religious approach, "I am aware that the subject has been handled before from many angles, largely from religious and metaphysical approaches, but I am also cognizant that many people shy away from anything that smacks of religion, the occult, or the metaphysical." [4]

Bristol was worried at first. "When I started out years ago to teach this science through the medium of lectures and my brochure, I wasn't certain that it could be or would be grasped by the ordinary individual; but . . . I have seen those who have used it double and triple their incomes." Unfortunately, "many apparently well-educated men and women in their respective fields, will, in their broad ignorance, condemn the idea of thought power and will make no endeavor to learn more about it; *and yet every one of them, if successful, has unconsciously made use of it.*" What is universal for everyone is that "you are the product of your own thought. What you believe yourself to be, you are. Thought is the original source of all wealth. . . . There will never be another business depression if people generally realize that it is with their own fear thoughts that they literally create hard times. . . . So it is with wars. When peoples of the world stop thinking depressions and wars, they will become non-existent. . . ." [5]

The source of power is in the subconscious mind. The subconscious mind is ageless, tireless, and sleepless, "rooted in instinct . . . a memory vault . . . a mighty storehouse of ever-ready material which can be placed at the disposal of the conscious mind, but also a powerhouse of energy with which the individual can be charged, thus enabling him to recover his strength and courage, and also his faith in himself." The subconscious mind is "beyond space and time. . . . It is fundamentally a powerful sending and receiving station with a universal hookup whereby it can communicate with the physical, mental, psychic, and, according to many investigators, spiritual worlds, past, present, and future. . . . The subconscious mind embodies the feeling and wisdom of the past, the awareness and knowledge of the present, and the thought and vision of the future." [6]

How do you tap this limitless power plant of a subconscious mind? Visualize mental pictures by using your imagination. Not only must you "*feel* and *think* yourself successful," you must "actually *see* yourself as already successful, either in the performance of some selected task or as actually occupying the position to which you are aspiring." Do you long for a new house? Cast an image of your dream house on the screen of your subconscious mind. "You want a better job? You'll get it when you give your subconscious mind a mental picture of yourself holding that job." Are you an executive in a sagging corporation? One oil refining company, smitten by serious financial difficulties, told its stockholders "to make a mental picture of the oil turning into money and coming from every still and every spigot—in short, to visualize the company as a money-maker." Apparently it worked. Are you a single woman longing for a husband? If "with your whole heart and soul you desire a certain type of man to walk into your life as a husband, merely picture him, not necessarily in physical form but in the abstract, setting forth in your thought projection the attributes that you would like to have in your man, and the day will surely come when you will meet him." [7]

There are helpful mechanics to assist in visualization. Write down on numerous cards what you want. Sprinkle these cards around your bedroom and bathroom. Visualize with your cards as often as you can, particularly just before going to sleep at night and upon waking in the morning. "See yourself actually doing the things you visualize and it will all work out, because every thought held constantly and persistently sooner or later materializes after its kind." [8]

The law of attraction works in harmony with the law of visualization. 'Like attracts like' means that "our fear thoughts are just as creative or just as magnetic in attracting troubles to us as are the constructive and positive thoughts in attracting positive results. So no matter what the character of the thought, it does create after its kind. When this sinks into a man's consciousness, he gets some inkling of the awe-inspiring power which is his to use." [9]

The laws of attraction and visualization, in both secular and religious mind power, had always offered a potential source for the manipulation of others. That potential was fulfilled more completely after the 1930s. For over a half a century standard advice had been that we are moulded by the thoughts of others and should therefore associate with monied people. The advice was now more specifically directed at influencing other people. Bristol felt that certain of his techniques were "a master method by which the mighty forces of the subconscious mind can be employed to influence those with whom you are dealing. Whether we know it or not, we're all engaged in selling something—if not our wares, then our personalities, our services, our ideas." Attention should be paid to "personal packaging." When properly attired, "you will feel within yourself that sense of power, which will cause people to give way before you and will even stir others to help you on your way." [10]

Like many merchants of mind power, Bristol was interested in thought transference. A belief in telepathy (communication from one mind to another independent of the recognized channels of sense) and psychokinesis (the direct action of mind on matter) had been encouraged by such scattered influences as the theory of electronics, ouija boards, mentalists like Joseph

Dunninger, and the extrasensory perception research of Dr. J. B. Rhine at Duke University. Bristol was uncertain what to call it, but he was convinced that everyone possessed latent powers to influence others at a distance and that many people consciously or unconsciously did just that. Have you ever wanted to get rid of people who were calling at your office or visiting your home? Well, try thought transference. One business executive banished "people who were taking up his time by simply repeating mentally to his visitor: 'It's time for you to go, leave now, leave now.' The visitor would shortly get fidgety, look at his watch or get up from his chair, reach for his hat, and soon be on his way out. You can get the same results when visitors overstay their time in your home. When you feel it is time for them to go, simply say to yourself, 'Go home now, go home now, go home now,' and you will find that they glance around the room looking for the clock and say, 'Guess it's about time we were leaving.' " [11]

The driving force for success is embodied in the law of affirmation. Whether the affirmation is an auto- (self) suggestion or a suggestion from an outside source (like a commercial on the radio), the constant repetition of a word or phrase drives and buries the thought into the subconscious mind. The subconscious mind, agitated by the suggestion, will then go to work for you (or the company sponsoring the commercial). Most useful is the self-stimulating urges of autosuggestion. One of its beauties is that you can recite your repetitive phrases anywhere. "One woman, a Unity student, told me that she and her sister never drove downtown without saying that they would find a parking space in or near a spot that they desired—and they always found it." Another woman "was arrested for violating the traffic signals, but according to the newspaper stories at the time, she convinced the judge that the green light was on when she crossed the intersection. She was a motherly woman and the judge freed her when she told him, 'Judge, the light just had to be green, and it always is for me because I keep repeating as I near an intersection "Green light be on, green light be on." ' " [12]

Like the card technique for visualization, Bristol forges a chain of mechanics to grapple with the law of affirmation. Stand in front of a mirror, come to attention, and "breathe deeply three or four times until you feel a sense of power, strength, and determination. Next, look into the very depths of your eyes, tell yourself that you are going to get what you want—name it aloud so you can see your lips move and you can hear the words uttered. Make a regular ritual of it, practice doing it at least twice a day, mornings and evenings. . . . As you stand before the mirror, keep telling yourself that you are going to be an outstanding success and that nothing in this world is going to stop you. . . . Once you start this mirror practice your eyes will take on a power that you never realized you could develop. . . . This power will give you that penetrating gaze that causes others to think you are looking into their very souls." [13]

While using the law of affirmation, supported by exercises in deep-breathing and the Magnetic Gaze, it is well to remember that "the simpler the words to express the ideas you wish conveyed to the subconscious, the better. For example, if you are unhappy, use the words, 'I am happy. . . .' Just repeat them to yourself twenty or thirty times. 'I am strong,' 'I am happy,' 'I am convincing,' 'I am friendly,' 'Everything is fine' are a few simple affirmations that you can use to change your mental point of view for the better. If the effects are to be permanent, the affirmations must be continued until the desired results are obtained." [14]

There are a few important qualifications. First, the yearning for your objective must consume your whole being. Second, confide in no one. If those who are envious of you were to find out what you were up to, they might set up thought vibrations to counteract your own. Also, when you talk about what you are going to do, you scatter your forces.

Finally, is it necessary to *do* anything besides sitting around tapping the subconscious by visualizing, attracting, and affirming? Mind power, particularly in its more bizarre extremes, was a rebuke to the character ethic as a way to get ahead. Though Bristol agreed that "something more than hard work is necessary," he attached more importance to action than is usually representative of the massive literature of mind power. "The toughest problem that confronts most people is the lack of money, and while I have read and heard of people finding bundles of $1000 bills by using this Mind Stuff, I think that money comes as a result of combining Mind Stuff and energized action. . . . It's doing the thing you have pictured to yourself that brings it into actual existence." A first-rate, experienced practitioner of mind power no doubt could sit in his office and visualize orders pouring over his desk, but the neophyte would find it hard going. On this point Bristol concluded that at least some elbow grease was necessary in rubbing the Aladdin's Lamp of mind power.[15]

While such power sources as "the will" and "habit" were not ignored, the subconscious, or unconscious, had overwhelmingly become the favorite power plant for the secular interpretation. There were variations, of course. Walter M. Germain in a book published in 1956 called it the "Supraconscious." The publisher, Hawthorn Books, then a division of Prentice-Hall, was apparently overwhelmed by the boldness of *The Magic Power of Your Mind:* "Dr. Walter M. Germain has set down on paper discoveries that were once thought too powerful to fall into the hands of common people!" [16]

In 1956 *Autoconditioning* at last appeared and excited a brief flurry on the best-seller lists. *Autoconditioning* had been ripening in the groves of academe where a Duke University Professor of Sociology named Hornell Hart had busied himself for some years trying to prove that "TODAY, SCIENCE CAN TEACH YOU TO BE HAPPY." "The discovery of Autoconditioning," the dust jacket's flyleaf announced boldly, "is a new breakthrough in the science of psychology, just as the discovery of atomic energy was a breakthrough in the science of physics and the discovery of antibiotics a breakthrough in the science of medicine." A trained scholar like Professor Hornell Hart, not to mention the editors of Prentice-Hall, should have known better. *Autoconditioning's* contribution is at best procedural, not substantive.[17]

Autoconditioning, like so much of mind power literature, promises the fulfillment of a number of goals in life. Success is but one goal. What can autoconditioning do for you? For success and advancement in your job, autoconditioning can release from 25 to 75 per cent more working energy, increase your efficiency, and ease frictions in getting along with other people. It can cure marital and family problems, bad habits, faulty human relations, and a wide range of mental depressions from worry and tension to fear and self-hate. For the happiness bound, there is a Mood-Meter which comes with each copy of the book. The Mood-Meter, a self-recording chart of thirty emotions from "Ecstatic" to "Miserable," assists you in checking your happiness rating from day to day.

Autoconditioning for success is basically the same as autoconditioning for most goals. But first there are some do's and don'ts by which to guide your life. Do not waste or destroy your vital powers by self-pity, quitting, running away, rushing impetuously into something, or vindictively attacking the challenges of life which most of us must face. Do put your energies to work by grappling intelligently and courageously with your problems, do "cooperate creatively" and try to work in harmony with other people, and do "adventure spiritually" by reaching out to admit the existence of something higher and beyond yourself. Very much in the spirit of the 1950s, Hart is careful to point out that autoconditioning can readily harmonize with religious faith if one has affirmative convictions about a "Superhuman Wisdom." [18]

How can you become a "skilled autoconditioner"? Where is the source of power? Hart's answer: It's in "the id." "This *id* is a kind of jungle chimpanzee who lives deep down in your own unconscious mind—your inner receptive mind. The id is what sends up the impulses, urges, hungers, and drives that move your conscious mind." When you are in a state of complete relaxation, let your real self, call it your "directing ego," speak silently to your unconscious or inner receptive mind. What happens? By "bringing your unconscious mind into line with the decisions and purposes reached by your directing ego at the moments of clearest vision and highest aspiration," you redirect your energies and change your attitudes. To put it another way, as your real self (your directing ego) speaks silently to your unconscious mind (your inner receptive mind), you bring "your id into line with your own best ideals and purposes. . . . Just silently tell your id, kindly but firmly, how you really want him to act."

That's the theoretical basis. Now, how do we get the id pulling for us rather than against us? Decide upon your problem. Choose a quiet room, sit down in a comfortable chair, dim the lights, close your eyes, and relax. Don't lie down. You might fall asleep. Your whole body is in a condition of complete relaxation. Now your directing ego starts talking silently to your inner receptive mind: " 'You are now going to relax deeply. . . . Let your hands become as limp as though they were two wet oak leaves lying on the trunks of fallen trees in a forest. . . . You are feeling a sense of peace.' " Linger over a variety of such phrases and thoughts, but don't let your mind wander and don't fall asleep. You should then reinforce your relaxed state by making the following suggestion: " 'You are now beginning to be deeply relaxed. This relaxation will go on getting deeper and deeper, until I count back to zero.' " At this point the neophyte should autocondition himself to be a more effective autoconditioner. Tell yourself that next time you will autocondition with increasing effectiveness by slipping more easily into a condition of complete relaxation.[19]

You have hypnotized yourself! Now comes the crucial point. Your directing ego should start feeding the suggestion into your inner receptive mind. Suppose you want to be a good listener. Say to yourself: " 'When next you meet that person you will feel active interest in his ideas and his purposes. You will encourage him to talk, and you will listen with active and genuine interest to what he has to say.' " Want to meet successfully a difficult situation in which you might panic? Try this: " 'When you get up before that audience (or go into that examination room, or are called in for that interview, or whatever) you will be at your best. You will feel self-possessed, at ease, and competent. All your mental resources will be easily and fully available.' " When you have finished feeding commands into your unconscious, you should come out of your self-hypnosis with a post-hypnotic suggestion. For a feeling of euphoria, ring down the curtain with: " 'After I have counted back to zero, you will come out of this deep relaxation, feeling cheerful, courageous, and enthusiastic. (Other adjectives may be substituted here, according to the wishes and tastes of the experimenter.) Five, four, three, two, one, zero.'" The whole process may take a half an hour for the beginner; old hands can run through it in two or three minutes.[20]

Autoconditioning is only part of it, albeit the larger part. The mind is also equipped with "a built-in receiving set. Some psychologists call this receiving set *intuition*." For help in making decisions and receiving those valuable flashes of insight or hunches, reverse the process of autoconditioning. "In autoconditioning, the line of action is from your directing ego to your inner mind; in hunches-to-order the line of transmission is through your inner mind to your directing ego."[21]

As a trained scholar, Hart felt called upon to offer a few caveats not usually included in mind power success literature. First, "induced intuition," or reversing the flow so that your inner mind guides your directing ego, should not be abused as "a substitute for logical thinking, nor for scientific research, nor for common sense—but rather as a supplement, to achieve those master insights that often decide the crises of our lives...." Second, Hart was careful to head off the natural criticism that autoconditioning might become a Pollyannian flight from reality, with practitioners darkly slipping off to quiet rooms to hypnotize themselves at the slightest provocation. One must "grapple courageously" with life, Hart insisted, while autoconditioning should not be flirted with indiscriminately but used only for important problems and for developing new basic attitudes.[22]

Finally, Hart admitted that there are other factors besides mind power which contribute to success. "What are the factors determining *your* present competitive advantage?" he asked. The sensible answer: "They might be broken down into four: (1) your innate ability—such as your IQ, your inborn aptitude for your special work, your physical stature and your innate bodily characteristics; (2) your past education, training, and development; (3) the amount of time, energy, enthusiasm, and concentrated attention you give your work; and (4) your value as a team member—your ease in getting along with co-workers, the extent to which they are able to do their best when working with you, the extent to which you are liked, admired, and wanted. Other elements may add to [your] competitive advantage, but if you score high on each of these four factors, your advance will be rapid and your success outstanding." On the first two quali- ties, innate ability and past training, which are rarely cited in success books, autoconditioning cannot help you. On the last two, releasing the efficient use of your energies and increasing your values as a team member, autoconditioning can mean the difference between success and failure.[23]

Most readers will recognize Hornell Hart's "new breakthrough in the science of psychology" as a more sophisticated procedure for applying Coué's autosuggestion or New Thought's law of affirmation. Of all the psychoanalytically inspired techniques for success, however, none was more appealing than the old Psycho-phone method. The correspondence course of the Cam- bridge Institute in Los Angeles, claiming "a completely *new method*," is appealing for two reasons. First, if you follow the simple instructions, you will not only become a success, but be unable to avoid it. Regardless of age, education, or "what you have been striving for, whether it be better health, financial success, vibrant personality improvement...YOU WILL BEGIN TO ACHIEVE IT...you will not be able to avoid it, for your sub-conscious mind will have been so conditioned and directed, that from now on, your every hope, your every wish, your every prayer, will be accomplished and fulfilled thru the tremendous powers of your very own sub-conscious mind."

Second, "There is required NO EFFORT ON YOUR PART! ...Without your doing a single thing (other than listening) or making any kind of effort, you will begin to notice gradual results and changes in your daily life. At first these will astonish you and cause you great wonder; then they will begin to delight you, for they are the beginning of a bright new life for you." You can listen your way to success! With fourteen courses on various subjects to choose from at $8.95 per course, ranging from financial success through sexual harmony to weight reduc- tion, you receive a record and a printed outline for each course. Set the record spinning on the phonograph, ease back into a comfortable chair, and "YOUR SUBCONSCIOUS MIND DOES IT FOR YOU . . . WHILE YOU RELAX!" [24]

But at the Armageddon of getting ahead, nobody's unconscious can equal the power of Infinite Intelligence. Faithless agnostics or orthodox Christians, disgruntled at New Thought's theology, might prefer the secular interpretation of mind power. But with just a little faith to get underway, New Thought's religious interpretation stood ready with an unbeatable source of power. New Thought did exploit the unconscious in conjunction with Infinite Intelligence, but standing alone, the unconscious was a toy steam engine compared to God's infinite power.

As we learned in earlier chapters, New Thought is an indigenous American religious movement. It is similar in many ways to Christian Science. Devoted primarily to healing the sick in mind and body, New Thought developed a success wing towards the close of the nineteenth century. In the post-World War II fanfare of religious mind power, what appears to be a freshly conceived doctrine actually enjoys a popular tradition of over a half a century.

There are no membership figures. Though New Thought does contain organized groups, it is not a formal Protestant denomination but a theological viewpoint, a mental attitude which has seeped into the American mind from church pulpits, lecture platforms, and published magazines and books. For many Protestants, and some Roman Catholics and Jews, it is an extracurricular activity outside of their own churches or synagogues. With no formal membership requirements for a believer, New Thought leapt ahead, buoyed along by a revival of interest in religion. How can its appeal to so many people be explained? What were the causes behind its popularity? [25]

New Thought is a religion for prosperous times. One observer perceived this some twenty years before the 1930s depression: "New Thoughtism does not flourish on an empty stomach or on a depleted pocketbook. . . . The propagandists of the new cults come from the middle class; they are no longer pursued by the wolf at the door. . . . The new ills of the upper and middle classes are caused by too little exercise, underwork, overeating, inordinate desire for money, political or social standing. . . . To the wage earner, to the man near the poverty line, to the overworked and under-nourished, new thoughtism offers little." The depression did not drive large numbers of people into the mind power way to success. To afford faith in thought, you have to be certain of the basic necessities in life.[26]

The decades fat with prosperity after World War II were the golden time for secular and religious mind power. What drove people into New Thought was not the memory of waiting rooms crowded with jobless people or the fear that an unstable economy might spiral into a depression. The New Thought disciple was not afraid of losing his job; he was desperate because he was not being promoted to a higher paying job with more prestige. Former neighbors sailed by in a newer car to a bigger home; he was treading water, which, in the rising tide of the American economy, means sinking into a lower economic and social class position.

Everywhere he turned, life jolted his ego. Home was no longer a castle of male supremacy but a discussion group run on democratic principles. His emancipated wife, supported by the law, had taken from him his authority as a husband; his children, who came first, had destroyed his priority as the father. He received, in return, a sensation of 'togetherness.'

Added to the older pressures to succeed and the constant stress situations of modern living were the newer problems of the personality ethic. By a curious irony, the effects of the personality ethic drove people into embracing mind power. When others are the raw material of success, we are estranged and alienated from them; when we ourselves are a commodity, we lose our identity and become alienated from ourselves. If we are incompetent in the expanding sphere of human relations so that no one bids up the price for our services as a commodity, we lose self-confidence and are plagued by feelings of helplessness and impotency.

Settled down now into a relentless undermining of man's faith in his own dignity were the shocks to old ways of thinking and living which created a market for religious mind power in its early years. After Darwin and kinship with lower animals came Freud and animalistic irrational impulses. If the realization that he was kin to the apes still troubled modern man in some deep way, the information that his unconscious was incestuous further eroded the confidence in a nobler self made in the image of God. That in childhood he longed to murder his father and sleep with his mother was not exactly designed to exalt a sense of self-dignity.

With the fall of France in 1940, America's national security was threatened by the loss of geographical isolation. That threat became reality with the development of, first, long-range aircraft, and later missiles, of atomic destruction. A psychologically unprepared America was now exposed to what Europe had long endured—sudden, unknowing attack by an aggressor. Now the threat of war became more anxiety-producing than being in a war. Matthew Arnold's conclusion in "Dover Beach" found ready quotation:

> And we are here as on a darkling plain
> Swept with confused alarms of struggle and flight,
> Where ignorant armies clash by night.

Others found an answer by interpreting that over-Donne observation in terms of One World internationalism: "No man is an *Iland,* intire of it selfe; every man is a peece of the *Continent,* a part of the *maine.* . . ." The increase in psychic distress between the 1930s and later decades was indicated by a middle-aged man in the James Thurber cartoon who remarked to his friend in 1948: "Do you remember, Crosby, when the only thing to fear was fear itself?" [27]

It was the person subject to these forces who was a candidate for the success message of New Thought. Though he shared many of the same problems as the seeker for health, happiness, and peace of mind, he was not the same person. A middle-class hustler with middle-brow sensibilities, he was buried under a daily avalanche of frustrations and anxieties. He felt himself overwhelmed by forces over which he could exert no control. Spiritually empty, he was not revolting from the severity of orthodox religion, like his counterpart at the turn of the century, but revolting from a belief in nothingness, a spiritual wasteland. Afraid, suffering from a damaged ego, lacking self-confidence with other people, alienated from himself and estranged from his fellow man, the buyer of New Thought was drifting unidentified in a lonely sea. He was ready to accept, with hope, the observation of Hamlet, another troubled man of long ago, that "there is nothing either good or bad, but thinking makes it so."

What a happy solution is New Thought. It not only teaches you how to change your thoughts; it endows thought with power. Everywhere New Thought pulses with the drive for power. Power is not a concept synonymous with the idea of success. The character ethic was not infatuated with the word, nor its equivalent. Though the personality ethic was intrigued by power over other people, the mind power ethic was obsessed with it. It filled a hunger for power within oneself, power over other people, and power over life itself. The New Thought believer wanted power because he felt insufficient to meet the demands of life. He was disinterested in the ancient theology of God's power over man, unresponsive to the contemporary emphasis on man's need of, and dependence on God. What he wanted was power of self. This he was assured of getting by becoming one with God.

Using scientific images, New Thought offered the timid, whose self-confidence had been destroyed by an inability to win friends and influence people, a source of personal magnetism as dazzling as bolts of electricity. The fearful and isolated, the alienated and helpless could connect with a celestial power plant mighty and magnificent enough to conquer all those forces which seemed so overwhelming in modern life.

Religious movements have struggled, often with bizarre consequences, to meet the peculiar needs of their followers. The Oneida Community practiced "complex marriage," while the Shakers shifted to the other extreme and practiced celibacy. One student of American religion noted that "Aimee Semple Mc-Pherson roared down the aisle of Angelus Temple one Sunday on a motorcycle. Daddy Grace ('Grace has given God a vacation.') baptized two hundred converts on the streets of Philadelphia with a fire hose. One sensation-seeking clergyman secreted himself on Easter morning in a coffin, had it brought into his church, and in the midst of the service leaped up crying, 'Resurrection day has come.' " A biographer of Father Divine reported that when a judge fined God (i.e. Father Divine) $500 and sentenced him to a year in jail, Father Divine's disciples declared: "The Jedge can't live long now. He's offended Almighty God." When the judge suddenly died three days later, Father Divine sighed from his cell: "I hated to do it." Here was power indeed, but it was all reserved for Father Divine. The need of the New Thought disciple was power for himself.[28]

Many followers of New Thought were drawn to formal groups so well organized that they amount to separate denominations. The Unity School of Christianity, for example, which is not affiliated with the International New Thought Alliance, has some 230 centers located throughout the United States and abroad, and 353 ordained ministers. Unity was founded in 1889 by Charles and Myrtle Fillmore. Charles was a cripple; Myrtle was tubercular. In collaboration with God, or rather by becoming one with God, they cured themselves.

What the Fillmores wrought is a tower of statistical strength. The Unity School of Christianity is a multi-million dollar organization humming with metaphysical manifestos and prayers from its plant near Lee's Summit, Missouri, eighteen miles from downtown Kansas City. A mass production religion with shipment provided by the U. S. Post Office Department, every month Unity sends out two million copies of its five magazines (e.g. *Wee Wisdom* for moppets under thirteen) and every year seven million additional books, pamphlets, letters, and related printed matter. Its radio broadcasts number about 1000 each week from more than 200 stations throughout the United States alone. One department, called Silent Unity, is on the job twenty-four hours a day in response to the 600,000 calls for prayer that arrive by letter, telegraph, and telephone during the course of each year. Silent Unity's 100 consecrated workers say a prayer for every request that arrives—from prayers for healing and protection to prayers for prosperity and a passing grade in an examination. Each request is then personally answered by mail. Such divine service helps to explain how the prosperous Unity School of Christianity can charge such small sums for its printed matter and rely for so much of its income on free-will 'love offerings.'

Like the New Thought movement as a whole, it is difficult to measure Unity's influence. Charles Braden estimated that during the 1950s and 1960s Unity was probably reaching five million people. Marcus Bach in 1957 guessed that more than one-third of the Christians in the United States with a denominational identification had read or were reading Unity material.[29]

Expressing a closer allegiance to orthodox Christianity than many New Thought groups, Unity is trinitarian based and biblically inspired, but God is not a separate personality. God is not powerful. He *is* power. God is the power *in* everybody and everything. Man becomes powerful by permitting that which God is to find expression in word and act. Unity differs from the main body of New Thought by asserting the doctrine of reincarnation. One Jewish businessman, overcome by the cheerfulness of a Unity funeral where the deceased did not die but underwent a "transition," requested that he too might be buried with a similar ceremony. "These Unity folks," he said, "make you glad you're dead." [30]

Unity's success message stresses the law of Divine Supply and the law of affirmation. Little attention is paid to the more bizarre possibilities inherent in the laws of attraction and visualization. "What we need to realize above all else," Charles Fillmore reassures us in *Prosperity*, "is that God has provided for the most minute needs of our daily life and that if we lack anything it is because we have not used our mind in making the right contact with the supermind and the cosmic ray that automatically flows from it. . . . It is a sin to be poor. . . . It is your birthright to be prosperous, regardless of who you are or where you may be." Of all Unity's prosperity prayers directed at God, who is variously addressed as Infinite Mind, Divine Mind, God-Mind, Principle, and Father-Mind, Fillmore touched immortality in his rendition of the 23rd Psalm:

> The Lord is my banker; my credit is good.
> He maketh me to lie down in the consciousness
>   of omnipresent abundance;
> He giveth me the key to His strongbox.
> He restoreth my faith in His riches;

He guideth me in the paths of prosperity for
　　His name's sake.
Yes, though I walk in the very shadow of debt,
I shall fear no evil, for Thou art with me;
Thy silver and Thy gold, they secure me.
Thou preparest a way for me in the presence of
　　the collector;
Thou fillest my wallet with plenty; my measure
　　runneth over.
Surely goodness and plenty will follow me all
　　the days of my life,
And I shall do business in the name of the Lord
　　forever.[31]

Perhaps the spirit of New Thought was expressed more conclusively by a workman whom a visitor overheard at Unity headquarters. As the visitor gathered with several Unity leaders on the terrace for luncheon, a workman strolled by singing the *Gloria Patri*. His rendition tried for the metrical rhythm, but soon wandered from the orthodox subject of adoration:

Praise God, from whom all blessings flow;
Praise Wealth, which helps us here below;
Praise Truth, the highest virtue known;
Praise Health, which everyone may own! [32]

THE POWER OF POSITIVE THINKING

New Thought was an expression of man's eternal quest for control of the uncontrollable. Its voice was heard across the land. Napoleon Hill's was the loudest from Chicago. "The world wants to know only one thing," Hill snapped in *Think and Grow Rich*. "HAVE YOU ACHIEVED SUCCESS?" From magazine articles, correspondence courses, and lecture platforms across the nation came the revelation of New Thought missionaries that a negative answer could only indicate some form of negative thinking.[1]

In the flourish of religious mind power after World War II, the most popular success merchant was no peddler of correspondence courses but an ordained minister of an upper-middle-class Protestant denomination. By the mid-1950s the buoyant pastor of Marble Collegiate Church on Fifth Avenue in New York City had authored a book which in the hard cover sweepstakes had smashed modern records for a long-time best seller. His words, in one form or another, were reaching out to encircle some 30,000,000 people a week. A select few, prepared to risk drowning under this wave of religious enthusiasm, publicly fretted that the portly pastor with the beaming face was tickling with a Satanic finger the soft underbelly of American Protestantism. But to the worry-torn and distressed, the cheerful minister was only placing a healing finger on wounds that had stubbornly resisted other forms of therapy. The go-getter of Marble Collegiate Church was, of course, New Thought's loudest voice in the 1950s, the "businessman's preacher," the Reverend Norman Vincent Peale.

"I certainly do not regard myself as a great voice among the world's spiritual leaders," Peale admitted, gazing out at the world through rimless spectacles, "but I like to believe humbly that I know how to sell my product effectively." The restlessly busy pastor joined advertising skills with mass communication for a persuasive holy hard sell of sloganized self-help. On and off during most of the 1950s his voice was heard daily on the radio from about 100 stations. Every week some 120 television stations sent out the image of his roundish figure and soft, mobile face. At $1,500 a lecture (donated to a Christian project) he was unable to exhaust the demand, though he rushed about the country speaking three or four times a week to all manner of gatherings, particularly businessmen, whom he delighted in addressing. Through the medium of print there was a weekly newspaper column, a fortnightly page in *Look,* weekly sermons which were printed and distributed to 250,000 persons, and the supervision of a monthly magazine of inspiration called *Guideposts* with a circulation of 750,000, heavily subscribed to by corporations which passed it along to their employees. For those who couldn't see, or who were too lazy to read, the friendly voice was ushered into living rooms through long-playing records. The response was awesome. Into Peale's office poured the staggering total of some 8,000 letters of personal mail a week.[2]

For visual and tactile inspiration there was the "Mustard Seed Remembrancer" for sale through retail stores and by mail from the Foundation for Christian Living in Pawling, New York. The "Mustard Seed Remembrancer," created by a fervent Pealite with the support of his wife, in "partnership with God," was inspired by Christ's words in Matthew: "'If ye have faith as a grain of mustard seed . . . nothing shall be impossible unto you.'" A mustard seed "of the type common in Biblical days" was set into a clear plastic sphere which was crowned by a three-tiered mounting representing faith, hope, and charity. This iconography was available in several forms of jewelry, from earrings and necklaces for the ladies to tie clasps and key rings for the gentlemen.

There is a story behind the Mustard Seed Remembrancer. Mr. Maurice Flint, who was negative-drowned in resentment and failure, was inspired by Christ's words through Peale, started carrying a mustard seed in his pocket, kept losing it, worked out a method of encasing the seed in a plastic ball, and began manufacturing the remembrancers from a factory in the Midwest. "The story of the lives that have been changed by this little device," Peale commented feelingly, "is one of the most romantic spiritual stories of this generation." Wagging a cautionary finger at consumers, Peale warned: "So popular and effective is it that others have copied it, but the Flint Mustard Seed Remembrancer is the original." [3]

In the book marts of the 1930s, Marble Collegiate's minister was just another clergyman who felt the call to put down the word of God between hard covers. Abingdon Press brought out two books in that decade which now and then faintly sketch the New Thought line but never draw it into a firm theological circle. In 1948 Prentice-Hall took over. They served up to a hungry public the New Thought recipe for best-sellerdom. *A Guide to Confident Living* held on to the lower rungs of the top ten non-fiction best sellers in bookstores during 1948 and 1949 in a kind of preliminary to the main event that was looming. [4]

In 1952 *The Power of Positive Thinking,* that titan of money-makers, settled into the best-seller lists and started growing roots. On Alice Payne Hackett's authoritative list, *The Power of Positive Thinking* was number five among the non-fiction best sellers in bookstores during 1952, number one in 1953 and 1954, and in 1955, in its fourth consecutive year, number two. (These ratings, of course, exclude the Bible, which was concurrently dressed up in a revised version, dictionaries, textbooks, and so forth.) By 1956 an unbudging fixture on the *New York Times* list for three and a half years, it had shouldered aside Lloyd Douglas' *The Robe* to become *the* long-time best seller in both the fiction and nonfiction (general) divisions. Statistics mounted to over 2,000,000 hardcover copies with serialization in more

than 85 newspapers and 13 national magazines, a revision into
the *Power of Positive Thinking for Young People,* and translation
into fourteen languages, including Afrikaans and Japanese. With
a healthy profit to the publisher and estimated royalties to the
author of over $1,000,000, Prentice-Hall pealed from a double-
page ad in 1956 that *The Power of Positive Thinking* had become "the best-loved inspirational book of our time." [5]

What did it offer? "There is no problem, difficulty, or defeat,"
Peale promised, "that you cannot solve or overcome by faith,
positive thinking, and prayer to God. The techniques are simple
and workable. . . . By using the techniques outlined here you can
modify or change the circumstances in which you now live,
assuming control over them rather than continuing to be directed
by them. Your relations with other people will improve. You
will become a more popular, esteemed, and well-liked individual.
By mastering these principles, you will enjoy a delightful new
sense of well-being. You may attain a degree of health not
hitherto known by you and experience a new and keen pleasure
in living. You will become a person of greater usefulness and
will wield an expanded influence." [6]

In the principles of positive thinking there is power to soothe
your mental agonies and to strengthen you for personal success.
Banish anxiety, tension, worry, sickness, and failure. Possess
peace of mind, happiness, health, and prosperity. All these gifts
are freely offered to you if you will only believe in God and
follow the route to his strength marked out by the Gospel according to Norman Vincent Peale. Sighed one citizen from
Enon, Ohio: "It's a book that makes you feel like a new person
inside." [7]

If the Lord helps those who help themselves, Somebody
Up There, to use a current idiom, likes Norman Vincent Peale.
The son of a Methodist minister, he was born in Bowersville,
Ohio, in 1898. His father, a practicing physician who had sev-
eral years earlier switched professions and assumed the cloth,
himself delivered the eldest of his three sons into the world.
Young Norman grew up with a monumental inferiority complex
as his poorly paid, but intellectually vigorous, father moved

from one small town Ohio pulpit to another. He recalled later the anguish of being teased as a minister's son and for being extremely thin. "Above everything else," he remembered, "I wanted to be fat and tough." In later years he achieved, primarily around the jowls, one of his longings.[8]

The shy, skinny minister's son used to choke with terror when called upon to recite in class. But he was already on fire with an ambition to be somebody important in the world—by doing the thing he feared the most. "As far back as I can remember," he said years later, "I wanted to grow up to be an orator. . . . I wanted to be a great political spellbinder and hold thousands of listeners magnetized. I even dreamed of becoming the governor of Ohio and of having my statue placed along with those of Garfield, McKinley, and Sherman on the capitol grounds at Columbus." While in high school he was elected head of a schoolboy Methodist group in Ohio. His brother Robert recalled the night of the great event. "We shared a room together, and he kept me up all night—declaiming in his sleep, over and over: 'President Peale, President Peale.' " This boyish pride in the symbols of success showed up later in his several offices in the form of plaques, awards, and inscribed photographs of prominent people, including an autographed picture of Dale Carnegie, while two flattering oil paintings complimented the walls of his Fifth Avenue apartment.[9]

When it was time for college, he entered Ohio Wesleyan. One collegiate experience made a profound impression. In class during his sophomore year he froze, as he often did, when called upon suddenly to recite. The professor held him after class and charged that it wasn't shyness or an inferiority complex, as Peale claimed, that threw him into tongue-tied confusion when reciting. It was a fear that he wasn't smarter than the other students. You're a minister's son, the professor added, you should know where to get help. Angry and humiliated, Norman wandered to the steps of the chapel and found help. He prayed. Soon he was talking his head off before assorted campus groups, doing the thing he feared the most. Even after years as a veteran speaker he was still hounded by a sense of inadequacy and fears that felt like butterfly wings. "Once he delivered a sermon," a friend recalled, "which I thought was good but he thought had gone badly. He went back to his study and I found him there—bawling like a baby." The subject of his sermon may offer a partial explanation. His friend remembered that "it had something to do with what we should offer God, not what we should expect from him." [10]

Peale was graduated from Ohio Wesleyan in 1920 and set out to be a newspaperman. He soon applied for a job to Grove Patterson, who was then managing editor of the *Detroit Journal,* and was taken on. He never forgot Patterson's advice: Keep it simple, interesting, and short. But the tug of the ministry was pulling him and after a year he stopped fighting it, obeyed the call and was enrolled at Boston University's school of theology. Ordained a minister in the Methodist Church, he served in Berkeley, Rhode Island, and then after a visit to New York, he decided he wanted to work there. The young pastor called on the Methodist bishop of New York City and asked for a church. The bishop was amused by the 120-pound young man's eagerness "to save New York," but he liked him. He was given a church in the flatlands section of Brooklyn with forty members and a shed-like wooden building. It was from that post in Brooklyn in 1924 that Peale's ecclesiatical star began its inexorable ascent.[11]

"Norman was never a particularly brilliant student," his brother Robert, a physician, recalled. (Leonard, the other brother, is a Methodist minister.) "When he started out in the ministry, no one would ever have said that Norman would set the world on fire. In a way, his inferiority complex was responsible for what happened to him. It made him work harder, and it provided him with his message." Observed a friend: "All his sermons are preached to himself." But the nature and appeal of his message, which had not yet developed in full, should not obscure Peale's first talent—a brilliance at organization.[12]

He got right down to business in Brooklyn. Sensing the opportunity in an expanding neighborhood, he persuaded an employee of the gas company to furnish him with the names of every new family for whom a gas meter was installed. On the day of the new family's arrival, the Methodist minister was right there with a cheery smile and a friendly invitation to come worship at his church. In three years membership skyrocketed from 40 to almost 900, a $100,000 church building was erected, the Sunday School mushroomed into the largest in Brooklyn, and urged on by advertising, over 3000 worshipers braved the rain one dreary Easter morning to hear him preach in a rented theater.

Rather plumpish now from a campaign of overeating, he moved on in 1927 to the University Methodist Church in Syracuse, New York, considered one of the most desirable pastorates in the state. The auditorium, with a seating capacity of 1500, largely drew faculty members from the nearby University of Syracuse campus. No man to be chained in by custom, the new pastor ran hortatory advertisements directed at the students in local newspapers. Soon the balconies were filled with interested young men and women. Ruth Stafford, the daughter of an Iowa Methodist minister, came to hear, but it was the minister who succumbed. He put the pretty senior on a banquet committee which seemed to require frequent conferences with the minister. After Ruth graduated, he kept her near by arranging a teaching post for her in Syracuse. They were married before a record-breaking crowd in the church with three clergymen officiating—the presiding Methodist Bishop, the Chancellor of Syracuse University, and Norman's father.[13]

The news of Peale's superb preaching was spreading. By 1932 the thirty-five-year-old minister had received calls from two of the most famous churches in the nation—New York's Marble Collegiate, and the First Methodist of Los Angeles, which boasted the biggest Methodist congregation in the world. Norman and Ruth prayed for guidance and received the same answer to their prayers. They packed up and headed for New York City.

Taking over Marble Collegiate, five blocks south of the Empire State Building at Fifth Avenue and 29th Street, meant switching from the Methodist to the Reformed ministry and being honored with possibly the oldest evangelical church in the country with a continuous ministry. Though Marble's soil was first tilled as long ago as 1628 and was richly endowed with real estate holdings, the fruits had withered on the vine. Almost three years without a regular pastor, Sunday attendance had slipped to 200. What Marble Collegiate needed, like any faltering company with strong assets, was dynamic management. It got just that—an efficient organizer, inventive promoter, and energetic salesman with a product tailored for the times. It was the bottom of the depression and the nation was soaked in negative thinking. The message of hope began to take shape.

Peale made no contribution to the basic design of New Thought theology, except to dress it up in a particularly attractive package. Of the writers who have had a decisive influence in his life, it is not surprising that he lists the seminal New Thought source of Emerson and the sympathetic work of William James. Unquestionably he plundered the abundant storehouse of New Thought literature that had been filling up over the years. However, unlike so many mind power success writers, both religious and secular, his message was empirically rooted in individual case studies. The parish minister, like a doctor, sees more of the basic tragedies and triumphs of life than most of us do. He is in on the rites of passage of birth, marriage, death, and he sees what happens to a man or woman when the certitudes of life are smashed by occupational failure, a marital crack-up, sickness, unbearable tension, or a child gone wrong. Marble Collegiate's minister did not always understand, and though an unsophisticated man theologically, he had enough intellectual humility and pioneering drive to do something about it.

He got together with Dr. Smiley Blanton, a pupil of Freud and an Episcopalian with an appropriate first name. Together they set up in 1937 a psychiatric outpatient clinic. The two worked in tandem with flexible methods. Their achievement was to help pioneer in the reciprocal benefits of religion and psychiatry. Blanton, for example, would bring the patient to a self-awareness of his guilt feelings established in childhood; Peale would take over and lead the patient to the religious therapy of faith, prayer, and love. After twenty years of successful practice the clinic had expanded to a staff of over twenty psychiatrists, psychologists, and clergymen. Many of them were full-time workers who attempted to nurse some 1500 troubled people a year back to health, while the more serious cases requiring years of analysis were referred to outside psychiatrists.

What happened in Brooklyn and Syracuse was repeated in New York. Sunday attendance jumped from 200 to a full house. Too inventive to be coerced by the tyranny of space, the ebullient minister increased the century-old building's capacity by installing television. On Sundays, 1600 worshipers squeezed into the church, while the overflow of 900 people spilled into other rooms in the building by means of a closed-circuit arrangement. So that everyone could be seated in the main church, Marble Collegiate finally decided to hold two identical services on Sunday mornings. Peale was not above using a daytime television technique on the heavy flow of transients, though it later was abandoned. At the get-together after the Sunday evening service, every guest who was observing a birthday was presented with a cake, while the queen for the day who had traveled the farthest received an orchid.

Peale's salary of close to $20,000 from Marble Collegiate during the 1950s was probably only a start on the payment of his Federal income tax. In New York City, Norman and Ruth Peale made their residence, as they do now, in a pleasantly furnished twelve-room apartment on upper Fifth Avenue. Home, too, for their two daughters and a son, was their 26-acre farm in Pawling, New York. The Peales often spent a Friday-Saturday weekend at Pawling in their eleven-room eighteenth-century farmhouse complete with a guest house, vegetable garden, orchard, and chicken coop. With no pretense at being a farmer, Peale tried to stop working long enough to see something of neighbors Lowell Thomas and Thomas E. Dewey, but with Sunday looming hours away, he meditated on his sermon, made notes, sank sometimes into irritable despondency that he would never again be able to deliver an inspiring address, and then when Sunday came and the hour tolled, he would stride to the pulpit without a note and lift up the hearts of his congregation.

"The secret of how he does so much," his wife explained, "is organization. Everything is carefully scheduled in advance. Some people rush when they have a deadline or two a month.

But he has several deadlines a week, so he can take them in his stride." Mrs. Peale fell into the rhythm of her husband's stride with a vivacity and energy which made her very much a part of the team. More often than in most occupations, a minister's wife shares the satisfactions and the labors of her husband's office life. Ruth Peale met the challenge with enthusiasm and intelligence. She was not only active in church organizations, but the partner, confidante, and business associate of her husband. The master of thought power was himself frequently nagged by a sense of powerlessness and faltering effectiveness. Ruth Peale was always there, ready to buck him up periodically, perhaps with a suggestion to try positive thinking. Of course they prayed together, and separately, for divine guidance before making important decisions.[14]

One of Mrs. Peale's more interesting activities was first reader of critical comments. In early 1955, when William Lee Miller launched a frontal assault in the *Reporter* on Pealism, Ruth Peale was so dismayed by the article that she advised her husband not to read it. It was well for his eternal optimism that he followed her advice. With increasing frequency, concerned psychiatrists, thoughtful clergymen, and disenchanted savants were aiming disparaging observations filled with negative thoughts in the direction of Norman Vincent Peale.

What was Peale's message? Collectors of later Pealiana soon recognize that, like most novels of Horatio Alger, Jr., if you've read one, you've read 'em all. What you read is the straight New Thought message. But New Thought is never mentioned, and seldom is there any indication that others have been dispensing the same doctrine for over a half a century. Indeed, critics of the Peale phenomenon seldom discuss the derivative nature of his theology in its historical perspective. Though Peale's bubbling casserole really simmers down to be nothing more than old New Thought stew, it is served up with the accomplishment of a master chef. The best statement of Peale's success message is his massive best seller, *The Power of Positive Thinking*. Of its kind, it is a first-rate book. It also happens to be, or rather inevitably is, a summary of his thought.

What are the qualities of a book like *The Power of Positive Thinking* that make for sales appeal? Every principle in the book is supported by Biblical quotations, frequent reassurances from doctors and counselors, before-and-after case histories of satisfied customers of the mind power approach, and incidents from the life of the author. Whenever inspiration burns low, Peale throws another human interest story on the fire. Whenever the tone gets preachy or the point fuzzy, he reminisces about his own personal problems. Unlike some mind power apostles, there is no wandering in a metaphysical fog, no sensation of sinking into an occult quagmire, no complicated explorations into philosophical idealism. The approach shoots straight from the shoulder like a luncheon address at the Rotary Club.

Much of Peale's appeal lies in his use of anecdotes. Like the parables of Christ, an abstract idea is more effective expressed in human interest terms through individuals and people. Ruth Peale discovered this early in their marriage. "When I baked my first pie," she recalled, "he expressed great praise for it but I noticed he actually was much more thrilled a few days later when I served him an inspirational anecdote, gleaned from my cleaning woman. He all but smacked his lips over the story and, after polishing it up a bit, used it in his sermon the next Sunday." With all its sudsy anecdotes and sloganizing, the book does have a measure of dignity about it, compared to the bulk of mind power success literature. You don't have to order *The Power of Positive Thinking* by mail in a plain wrapper.[15]

In the tradition of "how to" literature of any kind, there are always definite instructions on how to do the job. Like body-building techniques, you must perform certain exercises to reach your goal. "Many people who would like to find help in religion just don't know how to go about it," Peale and Smiley Blanton concluded. "When they are given a definite pattern of behavior to follow, it helps them to establish a relationship with the infinite." Peale's book offers a variety of goals, and many readers studied it for other ends than success. But the way to get ahead is the same way you cure alcoholism or relieve anxiety. You fix yourself by getting right with yourself and God. The exercises are the same whatever the goal.[16]

The Power of Positive Thinking is as pragmatic as the American spirit. "This is simply a practical, direct-action, personal-improvement manual," Peale explains. It "teaches applied Christianity; a simple yet scientific system of practical techniques of successful living that works." The laws of Christianity, contained in the Bible, are so precise that when properly demonstrated "religion may be said to form an exact science." [17]

The foundation for Peale's laws are a cause-effect relationship controlled by the power of thought. As one medical doctor explained: " 'Many of my patients have nothing wrong with them except their thoughts. . . . The prescription I write is a verse from the Bible, Romans 12:2. I do not write out that verse for my patients. I make them look it up and it reads: ". . . be ye transformed by the renewing of your mind. . . ." ' " Counsels Peale: "I recommend a mind-emptying at least twice a day, more often if necessary. Definitely practice emptying your mind of fears, hates, insecurities, regrets, and guilt feelings. . . . Immediately start filling your mind with creative and healthy thoughts. . . . Fill your personal and group conversations with positive, happy, optimistic, satisfying expressions. . . . You can think your way to failure and unhappiness, but you can also think your way to success and happiness. The world in which you live is not primarily determined by outward conditions and circumstances but by thoughts that habitually occupy your mind. . . . This great law briefly and simply states that if you think in negative terms you will get negative results. If you think in positive terms you will achieve positive results. That is the simple fact which is at the basis of an astonishing law of prosperity and success. In three words: Believe and succeed." [18]

To succeed you must believe in yourself and have faith in God, for faith releases power. "The ability to possess and utilize faith and gain the release of powers it provides are skills and, like any skills, must be studied and practiced to gain perfection." The way to achieve faith is by prayer. "Drive your prayers deep into your doubts, fears, inferiorities. Pray deep, big prayers that have plenty of suction and you will come up with powerful and vital faith." Is this not a promise of the Bible? " 'If ye have faith . . . nothing shall be impossible unto you. . . . If God be for us, who can be against us? . . . All things are possible to him that believeth. . . . I can do all things through Christ which strengtheneth me.' " Live with these thoughts and they will sink from your conscious into your subconscious mind. The process will change you into a believer. Naturally you must plan your work, avoid tension, and do your job in a mood of relaxed efficiency. Of course, just by believing, you are not going to get everything you want. However, don't worry about that, for "when you put your trust in God, He guides your mind so that you do not want things that are not good for you or that are inharmonious with God's will." [19]

Where is the source of power? Peale locates it in this way: "A friend in Connecticut, an energetic man, full of vitality and vigor, says that he goes to church regularly to 'get his batteries charged.' His concept is sound. God *is* the source of all energy—energy in the universe, atomic energy, electrical energy, and spiritual energy; indeed every form of energy derives from the Creator. . . . Contact with God establishes within us a flow of the same type of energy that recreates the world and that renews springtime every year. When in spiritual contact with God through our thought processes, the Divine energy flows through the personality, automatically renewing the original creative act. When contact with Divine energy is broken, the personality gradually becomes depleted in body, mind, and spirit. An electric clock connected with an outlet does not run down and will continue indefinitely to keep accurate time. Unplug it, and the clock stops. It has lost contact with the power flowing through the universe. In general this process is operative in human experience though in a less mechanical manner. . . . Every great personality I have ever known, and I have known many, who has demonstrated the capacity for prodigious work has been a person in tune with the Infinite. Every such person seems in harmony with nature and in contact with the Divine energy." Or in business terms, this is what is meant by effecting "a merger with God." [20]

While tapping the law of Divine Supply, it is necessary to understand the law of attraction. "When you expect the best, you release a magnetic force in your mind which by a law of attraction tends to bring the best to you. But if you expect the worst, you release from your mind the power of repulsion which tends to force the best from you." [21]

To exploit the law of attraction, practice the law of affirmation. While walking down the street, before going to bed at night or after rising in the morning, recite your positive phrases. Peale was particularly fond of two quotations from the Bible: " 'If God be *for* us, who can be *against* us?' " and " 'I can do all things through Christ which strengtheneth me.' " One woman was more specific. Selling vacuum cleaners from door to door, she learned to recite: " 'If God be for me, then I know that with God's help I can sell vacuum cleaners.' " Using the other laws at the same time, she was able to announce: " 'God helps me sell vacuum cleaners.' " Concludes Peale: "Who can dispute it?" [22]

The power of prayer is related to the law of affirmation. Prayer is not only "a sending out of vibrations from one person to another and to God," it is " 'something practical that fits a business problem.' " Prayer "driven deeply into your subconscious can remake you. It releases and keeps power flowing freely." To " 'prayerize' " means to discuss with God in a natural, normal manner any decisions that have to be made. One businessman "prayed as he walked or drove his car or performed other everyday activities. He filled his daily life full of prayer —that is, he lived by prayer. He did not kneel to offer his prayers but would, for example, say to God as to a close associate, 'What will I do about this, Lord?' or 'Give me a fresh insight on this, Lord.' He prayerized his mind and so prayerized his activities." [23]

Finally, "formulate and stamp indelibly on your mind a mental picture of yourself as succeeding. Hold this picture tenaciously. Never permit it to fade. Your mind will seek to develop this picture. Never think of yourself as failing; never doubt the reality of the mental image. That is most dangerous, for the mind always tries to complete what it pictures. So *always* picture 'success' no matter how badly things seem to be going at the moment. . . . Go about your business on the assumption that what you have affirmed and visualized is true. Affirm it, visualize it, believe it, and it will actualize itself. The release of power which this procedure stimulates will astonish you." [24]

This is the law of visualization. Peale reports that one minister suggested to a woman who was having marital difficulties that she "create an image or picture of herself as capable and attractive. He whimsically told her that 'God runs a beauty parlor' and that faith techniques could put beauty on a person's face and charm and ease in her manner." Exploiting the law of visualization for the goal of success, Peale advises: "Keep the idea of prosperity, of achievement, and of attainment firmly fixed in your mind. Never entertain a failure thought. Should a negative thought of defeat come into your mind, expel it by increasing the positive affirmation. Affirm aloud, 'God is now giving me success. He is now giving me attainment.' The mental vision which you create and firmly hold in consciousness will be actualized if you continually affirm it in your thoughts and if you work diligently and effectively. . . . Optimistic visualization combined with prayer and faith will inevitably actualize achievement." [25]

Peale expressed lucidly the substance of the religious mind power ethic in the decades since the 1930s. The creed did not differ markedly from what New Thought gospelers had been expounding since the end of the nineteenth and early years of the twentieth centuries. The laws of Divine Supply, affirmation, attraction, and visualization had been "discovered" and pronounced some three quarters of a century ago. The same holds true for the secular mind power ethic which we analyzed in the preceding chapter. The secular approach, however, did increasingly explain in a more detailed manner how to tap the subconscious as a source of power.[26]

How did the mind power ethic since the 1930s, both religious and secular, differ from the creed of the success idea expressed by the character ethic? Various elements in the formula held firm. The amount and equality of opportunity was inexhaustible; every individual was still the master of his own destiny; luck was an insignificant factor in achievement; the hero was still the self-made man; and the pressure on everyone to reach the top was intense. Though the intent of success books was to inflame the laggards with ambition and instruct the eager beavers in the techniques for getting ahead, the effect of the success idea was still politically conservative. If things were going badly, it was the self, not society and its institutions, that was "sick" and in need of repair.[27]

The mind power ethic continued to ignore education, even self-education, as a profitable pursuit for occupational mobility. The success idea expressed in the mind power ethic retained its ethical foundation, but it was weakened. Most writers stood for honesty and the golden rule, not because dishonesty violated an absolute code of ethics built into one's character, but because under the law of attraction and the inevitability of compensation, wrong action would attract disastrous results. Unethical behavior would boomerang and destroy you. Some writers ignored the relation of success to ethics altogether.

Indifference marked the general attitude of secular and religious mind power towards the dangers of greed and the lures to wickedness that wealth might dangle before the successful individual. 'True success' as an anti-materialistic goal higher than material success was seldom defined or discussed. The explanation for this may be that other goals besides success were frequently offered within the same book. Hence, there was no necessity to discuss 'true success' because mind power offered both prosperity and, for example, peace of mind. It could also be argued that the mind power ethic felt no moral responsibility for the evils traditionally associated with uncontrolled materialism. In any case, there was little concern for the moral dangers in success so fervently expressed by the character ethic.[28]

The justification for money-making had always forced its own kind of agonizing reappraisal by proponents of the character ethic, and to a lesser extent by those of the personality ethic. The mind power apostles were not exactly indifferent to the justification for success, but they never expressed very much interest in it either. When a justification was expressed, it was in terms of the doctrine of service. Perhaps an interest in justifying money-making was diminished by the variety of goals that

New Thought promised. Or it could be argued that New Thought enjoyed a built-in justification. If success comes only by tapping God's power, then success must be blessed, for it can only be achieved with God's assistance. God would not lend aid to anything that was not good. However, it might be suggested that New Thought's extreme egocentricism was a more important reason for its lack of interest in justifying success—both to man and to God.

When Norman Vincent Peale dropped into a bookstore in 1954 to see how his latest was doing compared to the Kinsey report, a salesgirl confided: "You know, religion is much more popular than sex this year." Checking the nation's pulse in the late 1940s and 1950s, other physicians of the public mood detected the loud thumpings of a religious revival. Examining the evidence, trend-sifters termed the impulse a 'return to religion.

In the first half of the 1940s, the Swedish scholar, Gunnar Myrdal, had observed: "America probably is still the most religious country in the Western world." The years that followed did not diminish the lead. During the 1950s, with church membership and attendance on the increase, pollsters discovered that over 95 per cent of United States citizens said they believed in God. While evangelists like Billy Graham, and television stars with the polished persuasion of Fulton J. Sheen, swayed masses of people, upper-brow theologians, led by Reinhold Niebuhr, were drawing intellectuals and college students into a serious study of Christianity and an awakening respect for its ancient faith. Religious books filled the best-seller lists. 1953 marked something of a climax. In that year six out of the top ten non-fiction best-sellers expressed a religious theme, or five out of the leading nine if the Revised Standard Version of the Bible is excluded in the listing.[30]

It had become fashionable in the 1950s to express an interest and even an enthusiasm for religion. President Eisenhower opened his Cabinet meetings with a silent prayer, while at the other end of Pennsylvania Avenue Congress passed a bill in 1956 making "In God We Trust" the official motto of the

United States. In suburbia, on most any winter Sabbath morning, indifferent or agnostic fathers could be seen depositing their children at Sunday school, an effort which expressed at least a respect for religion. Translating the American culinary contribution of the quick-lunch into spiritual refreshment, enterprising divines in the mid-1950s set up "Dial-a-Prayers" in many cities over the nation. Advertised Dr. John Sutherland Bonnell, minister of New York's Fifth Avenue Presbyterian Church: FOR A SPIRITUAL LIFE IN A BUSY DAY, DIAL-A-PRAYER, CIRCLE 6–4200: ONE MINUTE OF INSPIRATION AND PRAYER.[31]

Tin-pan Alley, registering like a super-seismograph to the 'Back to God' movement, exploited the 'Fellow Upstairs,' or better, the 'Big Fellow in the Sky.' From juke boxes across the nation lugubrious voices sobbed theological assurances, while bobbysoxers and boys in motorcycle modern shuffled around the dance floor in what could hardly be called a devotional mood. Tuning into the sounds of 'I've Got Religion,' the Ideal Toy Co. sold a doll that could be made to kneel in a praying position. "I love God," burbled film star Jane Russell. "And when you get to know Him, you find He's a Livin' Doll." The concluding lines to Number 13 in *Modern Screen*'s series on "How the Stars Found Faith" revealed the ample room Piper Laurie gave to 'Good Old God.' Returning twenty miles by jeep from the front lines in Korea, Piper was aware of the danger from night-time enemy patrols, but "I felt wonderful because I knew, somehow I just *knew* that there were not four of us, but five of us going back in that jeep. And the fifth passenger, I was certain, was *God*. He *was* with me." Choosing his side in the running warfare between science and religion, television celebrity Arthur Godfrey rolled up his metaphysical artillery and fired: "Don't tell me about science and its exact explanation of everything. Some things are bigger. God is the difference. He gets around." [32]

God was indeed getting around in the America of the 1950s. Believing in God was as fashionable then as questioning that belief became stylish a decade later. The Eisenhower years, in which the President was a shining symbol more important for what he was than what he did, was a decade of consolidation. It was a secure base which made it possible for America to tolerate in the 1960s the questioning of religious constructs by theologians and the challenge to bourgeois values by the rebellious young. The 1950s was dominated by World War II veterans. They made capitalism work after the doubts of the 1930s and, with their wives, reconfirmed the family unit (despite the high rate of divorce) after the turbulence of the war.

The 'return to religion' was a hunger for faith, of course, but it was a great deal more than that. It was: A suburban movement expressing family togetherness; a testament to religion as a vital ethical influence in raising "the kids"; a belongingness to a stable institution which had traditionally been in charge of values; a way to identify oneself in a pluralistic society as either a Protestant, Jew, or Roman Catholic; a misty feeling of security and goodness; and a bulwark against 'cold war,' atheistic communism. Belonging to the church of your choice, taking care of your family, cutting the grass, and voting was a way of defining yourself as a respectable, middle-class American.

What light does the 'return to religion' throw on developments in the success idea? The relationship of New Thought's success message to the religious revival was shot through with paradoxes. The widespread discovery of New Thought in itself did little to interrupt the declining influence of religion on American values. Nowhere is this paradox—increased church membership and institutional strength in the midst of a weakening religious influence over values—more apparent than in the fading away of the religious justification for money-making.

In the nineteenth century and before, the character ethic invoked religion to *justify* the accumulation of wealth. New Thought exploited religion as a *means* to money-making. The former was concerned with a philosophical problem involving the meaning of life—"why?" The latter was interested in "how to." It was the difference between getting ahead in order to get right with God and getting right with God in order to get ahead. The religious interpretation of the older character ethic expressed a need to assure the successful and the aspiring that their work glorified God through the stewardship principle, and later, through the concept of service. Religious and secular (i.e. secular means, not justification) mind power, combined with the personality ethic, reflect the contemporary philosophy of the success idea. They expressed no deep need for a religious justification. God was no longer a sanctioning authority favorably judging the value of success. In secular mind power and the personality ethic, he was mostly ignored. In the religious mind power of New Thought, he had become a Divine Dynamo for recharging tired batteries.

Another paradox is the use of New Thought's philosophical idealism for an end of worldly materialism. As pointed out in our discussion of the origins and development of New Thought, thought power is a philosophy of idealism. Power flows from mind, which is non-material, rather than from material things. The paradox lies in the exploitation of spiritual forces for material gain. In comparison to the character ethic, the paradox is deepened when New Thought relaxes the old moral tension between healthy ambition and destructive greed, between money as a means to an end and in itself an ultimate end in life. The character ethic was always hammering away at greed with anti-materialistic arguments and discrediting money as the *summum bonum* in life with definitions of 'true success.' New Thought relaxed this tension by its apathy towards the dangers of money-making and its indifference to what the final goals in life should be. Lost to the success idea, too, was the conviction that the means to wealth were a moral absolute. In the nineteenth century, a fine character was good in itself, even if it did not pay off. The laws of attraction or visualization, like the techniques of the personality ethic, were not moral absolutes in themselves, but relative to their results. They were good only if they worked.

A third paradox is New Thought's claim to be Christian while it is a perversion of traditional interpretations of Christianity. This self-contradiction is not applicable to those New Thought writers who are admittedly eclectic. But avowed trinitarians distort the sources, traditions, and symbols of Christianity in a spirit which church fathers have fought against for centuries. The distortion is the application of the pragmatic test to

Christianity. The pragmatic test makes the absolute nature of God something to be valued primarily for its consequences.

Norman Vincent Peale, musing on how a good idea can start out as a newspaper column, turn into a sermon, be expanded into a book chapter, and possibly wind up on a radio or television show, remarked: "A good idea is sort of like a roast beef. You can make a lot of things out of it before it ends up as hash." A lot of things can be made out of Christianity, but pragmatism grinds it up into hash. An indigenous American philosophy, pragmatism is a good idea when applied with all its native brilliance to the problems of technology. If a mechanical innovation works in a factory, it's good, even if it clashes with engineering theory. It is another thing to sell Christianity largely on the basis that it works, that it is useful in achieving success or becoming healthy. The point here is not whether positive thinking helps people, which in multitudes of cases it unquestionably does, but whether it is in the central Christian tradition. To judge religious mind power as an expression of Christianity because it helps people is to reduce Christianity to a pragmatic test. Whether or not Christianity helps anyone has nothing to do with its validity. It is not a dogma assessed by its consequences but an absolute.[33]

New Thought, also indigenous to America, was perfectly designed to break through the religious illiteracy of most modern Americans. Here was something meaningful outside the compartment reserved in one's mind for Sunday morning's sermon. Here was something that could be used during the week, spelled out with instructions as simple and detailed as a "how to" manual on building chairs or planting tulip bulbs. The further difference between traditional Christianity and New Thought is marked by polarities. It is the difference between religious growth in itself, and its use as a means to an end of wealth; between getting religion because you should, and because it is good for you; between satisfying a spiritual hunger by adoring God, and satisfying a hunger for material things by invoking spiritual concepts; between being an instrument of God for Christ's sake, rather than making an instrument of him for your own sake; between Thy will be done through me, rather than my will be done through Thee. As Eugene Carson Blake has commented, it is similar to changing the words of Jesus from " 'Seek ye first the kingdom of God, and His righteousness; and all these things shall be added unto you,' to the slightly different but idolatrous, 'Believe in "the Man upstairs" [or Infinite Intelligence] and he will make you prosperous and successful.' " [34]

Atop the spire of Marble Collegiate Church stands a golden cock. It is said to symbolize Peter's betrayal of Christ. By the middle of the 1950s, several church leaders began announcing in print that the cock had already crowed twice and that a limb of Protestantism was being delivered up for a sacrifice to Mammon. It was the dramatic popularity of Norman Vincent Peale that prompted theologians to express their alarm in sermons and newspaper articles. For several years many Protestant ministers had privately, rather than publicly, rebelled at the way Peale comforted the afflicted while they were doing their best to afflict the comfortable—a task always encumbered by Protestantism's lay control over the choice of local ministers. God, after all, was not a mental Band-aid or a spiritual tranquilizer, no matter how appealing to certain members of the congregation that interpretation might be.

In addition to the pragmatic nature of Peale's theology, what most critics objected to was considering Christianity a self-service supermarket where you could take what suits your fancy and leave the rest. Christianity may or may not be, as Peale stated, "a power mechanism" and religion "a scientific methodology for thinking your way through problems." What is subject to criticism is the content of Pealism. It ignores almost entirely the central meaning of the Christian faith. Where is there a recognition of the problem of evil, the nature of sin, the necessity of suffering, the reality of guilt? Peale, of course, did not ignore guilt. He talked about it all the time, but mostly with the amoral tone of a psychiatrist concerned with false guilt feelings. Seldom is there a discussion of the nature of sin, or that perhaps a person *did* sin and *should* feel guilty. The whole tone and approach is to think away the torturings of guilt and fear because they provoke "energy drainage." [35]

The central message of Christianity for the individual is the assurance of St. John that "God so loved the world that he gave his only Son, that whoever believes in him should not perish but have eternal life." Without an understanding of sin and suffering, God's act of redemption in Christ, and Christ's atonement for man's sins, become meaningless. The cross may be a plus sign, the emblem of the positive thinker; it is also the symbol of sacrifice and suffering, of thoughts of anguish as well as thoughts of assurance.

The contradictions within the religious revival are apparent when Peale's sunshine philosophy is contrasted with Reinhold Niebuhr's neo-orthodoxy or Billy Graham's evangelicalism. Perhaps theologians would have taken more kindly to New Thought if it had expressed the tradition of a militant religion going out to turn the world upside down to set it right side up. Also, New Thought's obsession with worry eliminated a concern for social problems. There are some problems, involving social action and responsibility, that people *should* worry about. Followers of Peale were not interested in changing the world. They were eager to adapt to it.

New Thought is always tiptoeing along the borders of blasphemy. The worst sin that man can commit is to assume that he is God. With none of the ancient Judaistic fear and awe of God, Pealites are always in danger of assuming that God's power flows into them as easily as current through a wall socket. The danger is magnified by the approach to God—not beseeching but affirming, not asking as a gift but commanding as one's birthright. The approach is quite different from that of an impoverished farmer asking God to make it rain in a drought, or a parent, half-crazy with anxiety, imploring God to make his sick child well. Both the farmer and the parent do God an injustice, it is true, but at least the approach is reverent. The law of affirmation has a "now look here, Divine Supply" tone that only a Godlet, a chip off the divine block, could carry off with any sense of assurance. It has all those egocentric dangers of regarding one's navel as the hub of the universe. Since the symbolic story of Adam and Eve, men and women have been trying to push God around and get him to do their will. For such a purpose, the law of affirmation is hard to beat.

Psychiatry offered serious criticisms. For the neurotic and mentally ill, there were admitted advantages to secular and religious mind power. It is cheaper than medical care. Unlike psychoanalysis, there is no painful confrontation with the unconscious and its great grief. While mind power offered the hope that an individual could do something about his problems, the initiative of "fix it yourself," a form of suburban therapy, could be dangerous when applied to "fix yourself." Self-administered brainwashing of personal problems by autosuggestion glosses over hidden causes of mental sickness, fails to expose the roots of a problem, and may place a temporary scab on a neurotic wound which would only make it more difficult to heal that wound in the future. A faith in any or all the laws of Divine Supply, affirmation (autosuggestion), attraction and visualization have undoubtedly helped a great many people with minor problems. But positive thinking may do positive harm to anyone balancing on the sharp edge between mental health and illness. Advising a person who is being sucked into the whirlpool of neuroses to try the techniques of mind power may be like throwing a drowning man both ends of a rope.

Though Peale himself was too modest a fellow to be harshly judged, the naivete of his inspirational balloons were fair game for pricking with a satirical stiletto. The likable dominie of Marble Collegiate Church made it a habit to pray for his critics, that is, when their negative thoughts could get to him through the protective screen that Mrs. Peale provided in her capacity as first reader of unfavorable criticism. Peale's satirical detractors were apparently unaware of the custom. "Uplift has been overdone. . . ." announced comedienne Anna Russell in 1955 in *The Power of Being a Positive Stinker.* "So I decided to explore 'Downlift.' . . ." Her autosuggestive slogan of disenchantment: "Twenty times a day repeat these words: 'I will not be a negative stinker; I will be a positive stinker!' " In *The Power of Negative Thinking,* Bernard W. Shir-Cliff came up with "the Negative Thinker's Basic Credo: 'I don't wanna.

Therefore I ain't gonna!' " When it came to evangelists, Adlai Stevenson was firm: "I find Paul appealing and Peale appalling." But it was a disillusioned Pealite from Texas who best spoofed the mechanical images of New Thought, perhaps unwittingly, when she wrote in to the pastor of Marble Collegiate: "I've done everything you suggested and tried to connect my life with God's circuit, but I'm beginning to think that I must be on A.C. and God on D.C." [36]

Peale was wired into the lively circuit generated by his critics, however. Though he may have been in tune with the Infinite, it was apparent that he was discordantly out of tune with a small orchestra of savants. Only a few scattered shots were fired at the minister of Marble Collegiate up to 1955. In that year the critics hit hard. In 1956 an injured Peale struck back in a magazine article with the defense that "I never preached that material success would come to anyone through the practice of the Gospel." In a special 1956 preface to the 2,000,000-copy anniversary edition of The Power of Positive Thinking, he inserted a rather astonishing denial. The book did not, he claimed, teach positive thinking "as a means to fame, riches, or power. . . ." In a 1957 response to his critics, Stay Alive All Your Life, he made an effort to protest against the material definition of success and the exploitation of God to achieve wealth. That protest did not interfere, somehow, with his instructions on how to get ahead. [37]

As America moved through the 1960s, the critics turned to bigger game—God himself, or rather man's conception of God —and social action problems involving the cities, the poor, and the Blacks. There were no dramatic best sellers for the mind power ethic, just steady, relentless sales and heavily attended New Thought services across the nation. Norman Vincent Peale continued to turn out his share of inspirational books and magazine articles. Marble Collegiate Church was jammed with two overflow services on Sunday mornings, and there were the usual free-lance lectures, radio programs, and a syndicated column going out to some 200 newspapers. [38]

Occasionally he would surface into the news. The decade

began with an egregious blunder which required massive doses of positive thinking. Peale had aligned himself with a group which publicly expressed doubt that a Roman Catholic President of the United States could resist pressures from the Vatican. With political passions running hot in the 1960 Kennedy-Nixon campaign, Peale was hit hard by accusations of bigotry from many quarters and soon recanted with a confession that his stand had been "unwise" and that he had "never been too bright anyhow." A year later he more safely aligned himself with Cardinal Spellman by defending the Cardinal's denunciation of a licentious motion picture called *Baby Doll*. No such assaults were hurled at *One's Man's Way*, a 1964 motion picture about Peale's life which Hollywood, quite accurately, turned into a moving inspirational success story.[39]

There were negative moments. After Peale had been nominated for the presidency of the Protestant Council of the City of New York in 1965, a dissident group declared that "if, as we believe, there has been a void in Protestant Council leadership, Dr. Peale will enlarge it." But the discords were faint and infrequent for a man so obviously in tune with Divine Supply. Above all there were the warm family moments—the marriage of a bright, attractive daughter to a Hotchkiss-Yale graduate (the other daughter married a Presbyterian minister), the ordination of an only son to the ministry, and the Pawling, New York, retreat, now expanded to a 225-acre estate with a sauna and indoor swimming pool where, at the insistence of Mrs. Peale, no liquor but grape juice is served at parties.[40]

As the 1960s drew to a close, relations with the President of the United States were decidedly more cordial than at the decade's beginning. Richard M. Nixon, defeated by John F. Kennedy, had returned in triumph in 1968 and a few months after the election, a Nixon daughter and an Eisenhower grandson were united in marriage at Marble Collegiate Church with Peale officiating. The nation had lived through the sophisticated style of the Kennedys and the cornballism of the agrarian Johnsons. In some symbolic way the hopeful dominie of New Thought was returning America to the decent, God-fearing, middle-class style of an Eisenhower-Nixon union. Maybe some of the disrupting problems of the 1960s could be affirmed away. As he told President-elect Nixon in a sermon: "God doesn't want anyone to be hungry and oppressed. He just puts His big arms around everybody and hugs them up against Himself." The most hopeful of all, perhaps, was the assurance that the message was still getting through. Champion Gary Player was carrying around a copy of *The Power of Positive Thinking* in his golf bag. By the end of the decade, sales of the book had mounted to the four-million mark while twenty million copies of Peale's other writings were annually being distributed. As the nation began a new decade and the 1970s, was it symbolic that the preacher at the first religious service in the White House after New Year's Day was the Reverend Norman Vincent Peale? President Nixon had positive thoughts. The President was moved to say later that "every American should have an interest in all Dr. Peale stands for. . . ." [41]

Unlike Norman Vincent Peale, the massive body of New Thought success literature was never sufficiently dramatic in its separate parts to draw to itself such specific attention. The mind power ethic, both religious and secular, was never so popular at any time to overthrow the character ethic, which was dominant through the 1920s, or the personality ethic which has reigned supreme since the 1930s. But the mind power route to riches continued to appeal to multitudes of practitioners as it expanded from its origins of some three-quarters of a century ago.

21

"I DON'T CARE
HOW WEAK OR SMALL
YOU ARE...."

The anthropologist Clyde Kluckhohn remarked not long after World War II that, with the possible exception of prewar Japan, "the worship of success [in the United States] has gone farther than in any known culture." Prodded by such worshipful urges, American ingenuity explored many byways to success. While these byways were not so heavily trod as the three main routes of character, personality, and mind power, travelers steadfastly moved along them with quickening hearts and high hopes that a pot of gold lay at the other end.[1]

The signposts set up along these various byways, with occasional variations, carried unchanging instructions for success. The period under discussion will not be limited to the decades since the 1930s but will embrace the entire twentieth century when all of these techniques were vigorously marketed and hungrily consumed. Each of these techniques was more popular in some decades than others. A few hit their peak in the nineteenth century and have been waning ever since. Taken together, they were always nibbling at the corners of the success market.

Fortunetelling is as old as the first witch doctor in a primitive tribe. In America it was a lively business with a low overhead. Advertising locally in newspapers, and nationally through magazines, a plethora of "Madames" and some "Professors" offered

341

not only wisdom in choosing a suitable occupation, but promised to predict the very all—in the shop or by mail. They peered into tea leaves for auspicious patterns; plotted the stars; traced lines on the palm of the hand; interpreted dreams (according to Madame Millie, dreams resulting from indigestion are without significance); dealt from a deck of cards; drew from a table spread with dominoes; and foresaw the future by the laws of molesophy. (There was no field of wartosophy. Warts, ephemeral and frequently transient, were without occult significance.)[2]

Palmistry and astrology were particularly elaborate systems for fortunetelling. Palmistry, as anyone who has walked a boardwalk or visited a county fair knows, is the practice of judging character and aptitude, and discerning someone's past and future, by examining the lines and marks in the palm of his hand. According to one lady engaged in the business, "all Destiny lines must rise and reach the Saturn mound to designate success in the material items of life." In her opinion, it was an inauspicious destiny line that faded away before reaching the Saturn mound. Most twentieth-century analysts did not limit themselves to the palm of the hand but examined the entire appendage for clues about the proper choice of an occupation. The inner man lay revealed through the size and shape of the hand, the texture of the skin, the structure of the fingers, the fingernails, and the thumb. Long, thick, knotty, straight fingers with square finger tips, according to one analyst, revealed personal qualities conducive to business success.[3]

Some tried reaching for the stars through the stars. "Prof." Jeremiah MacDonald of Binghamton, New York, was a representative astrologer on success who believed that the heavenly bodies influenced human affairs and that he could predict the future by their aspect and position. "Prof." MacDonald strangled his modesty in order to remind his readers that "all who read the papers know of my world famous predictions, for no uncommon event or phenomena has occurred that I have not predicted before it happened." He laid out a life plan for the twelve different groups of people divided by their birthday dates. "Leo People: Those born between July 23rd and August 23rd, any year, will do best on high ground. . . . Virgo People: Those born between August 23rd and September 23rd, any year, will do best in large cities, near rivers." Each group had its own "important day of the week." Anyone starting a business with the earth and moon outside of his zodiac sign has diminished his chances for success.[4]

Is this fatalism not repugnant to the success idea? If your destiny is controlled by the stars, what free will have you to control your fate? Star plotters had their answers ready. First, astrology is a tool that can help you to know yourself and settle you into the right job. Second, man has free will to utilize favorable planetary conditions for his own profit. He has the choice of following or disregarding his horoscope.[5]

The fortunetellers of this world may descend to a pitiful end in the next, far from the starry heavens. Diviners and soothsayers were consigned by Dante to one of the lower divisions of the Inferno. There, in the fourth chasm of Malebolge, the faces of fortunetellers were turned around until from the neck up they faced back.

> Mark how the shoulders now his bosom make.
> Because he wished too far before to see
> He looks behind and ever goeth back.

And as the fortunetellers, with their twisted necks, wept,

> I saw, that tears out of their eyelids prest
> Ran down their buttocks by the cleft behind.[6]

Three ancient techniques of self-analysis were enriched by scientific knowledge in the twentieth century. They were: phrenology (examining the skull as an indication of mental faculties and traits of character); physiognomy (discerning character and temperament from outward appearance, especially the face); and graphology (judging a person's character, disposition, and aptitudes from his handwriting). Self-help specialists in these fields agreed that just to look at a person's skull (phrenology), face (physiognomy), or handwriting (graphology) is to know his inner quality of will, habits, and unconscious, his character and his personality. A knowledge of these "sciences" could help an individual to know himself, teach him to improve deficient qualities, and locate him in a job most auspicious for his abilities. As one might expect, these schools for success responded to forces which produced the personality ethic. Though always clearly oriented in that direction, from the 1930s on, with increasing purpose, they were presented as techniques for analyz· ing other people.

For most phrenologists, there were from thirty-five to forty-five separate mental faculties located in specific regions on the surface of the brain. An increase in the acquisitive region, for example, would produce a corresponding anatomical change in the skull. If the skull bulged outside the acquisitive region, the skull's owner was probably a good bet for the money marts. The fascinating thing about the bumpological approach, however, were the number of possible combinations of these thirty-five to forty-five mental faculties. A person with strong "Acquisitiveness" and strong "Secretiveness," but with moderate "Conscience," is likely to be dishonest. On the other hand, if you detect from looking at your skull in the mirror, or feeling it, that you are strong on "Acquisitiveness" and strong on "Conscience," but weak on "Kindness," chances are you are honest all right, but stingy.[7]

Your Face Is Your Fortune offered a quick self-analysis by physiognomy. The instructions were to compare descriptions and pictures in the book with the shape of your head, face, profile, forehead, eyebrows, eyes, nose, lips, chin, jaw, ears, the color of your hair and eyes, and the texture of your skin and hair. Your character is as plain as the nose on your face. If your nose is large, "you are forceful"; if it is long, "you are reserved and inclined to be cautious and pessimistic." If it is small, "you are usually mild and gentle"; while if it is short, "you are lively, genial, and usually optimistic." Broad nostrils are a good sign that "you have energy, independence, courage and wit." Narrow nostrils might confirm what you already suspect, that "you are not very energetic and are somewhat inclined to be nervous."[8]

Though physiognomists found most of their clues in the face, they frequently explored everything visible from the neck up, and occasionally the structure and movement of the whole body. Personnel directors, not to mention everyone struggling to get ahead in the past few decades, ignored physiognomy at their peril. It was a canny device for sizing up the other fellow before he even opened his mouth.

Let's examine the lips. In *Face Value,* we learn that a person with an unusually prominent lower lip is "opinionated" and "inclined to be selfish and materialistic." A person with tight, thin lips has "will power," "self-control," and is "secretive and skeptical." Beware! "Don't flatter the long upper lip. He won't believe you. He is extremely independent and forms his own opinions." Concluded the author of *Face Value* with a metaphor we have no right to expect: "People's lips will tell you a whole mouthful if you will observe them." [9]

For graphological success writers, character is as plain as the handwriting on the wall. It is a picture which reveals the true nature of your subconscious. This picture consists of the size, slope and weight of the handwritten specimen; the spacings in margins; the spacings between words and letters; the way capitals, looped letters, and the letter "t" are formed; the manner in which words are ended; and the application of punctuation marks throughout a sentence. All these elements in handwriting hold up a mirror to our true selves and reflect the character of other people.

According to the author of *What Handwriting Reveals,* the basic principles are simple. Large letters indicate a love of big things; small letters show a preference for detail. Heavy pressure with the pen reveals determination; light pressure indicates unobtrusive delicacy of character. Lines which ascend reflect a cheerful ambition; lines which descend reveal a gloomy pessimism. You might tell all simply by the way you form the letter "t" —a very important letter for graphologists. If your handwriting expresses a "heavy and continued movement from left to right in each word, with the heavy pressure on the cross-stroke of the t, or t-bar, then you are naturally fitted for an executive position, where aggressiveness, timeliness and forcefulness are factors." [10]

For a smaller, but hardier band of missionaries, the body and its health became the propelling force for success. In the field of food and dietetics, body-care and body-building no figure glowed with quite the same joyous intensity as the fabulous fanatic of physical culture, Bernarr MacFadden. Described by his former wife as "one of the most mercurial and unpredictable personalities yet produced by the upper vertebrates," body-builder MacFadden made millions by publishing mazagines and a whacky reputation by preaching and living the doctrine of happiness and success through health. But he was only a 97-pound weakling compared to those statuesque strongmen who revealed the results of muscle building through bulging personal photographs in magazine advertisements.[11]

The strongmen pulled every ploy from the back of an advertiser's copy book in order to sell their self-help manuals. Siegmund Breitbart, muscles glistening in an impressive photograph, apologized for his selfishness: "I never realized how much you wanted the strength and power that I've gloried in. Even though for years I have been called the 'Super-man of the Ages,' I've never begun to know what I have been keeping from you. But now you can have it. Your response to my early announcements has given me a new realization of what this power of crushing strength means to *you*. Now *you* can know anything *I* know—just ask me. I want to tell you all. I DON'T CARE HOW WEAK OR SMALL YOU ARE I'LL give you a body to be proud of; health, vitality, pep and the Success that the new life will bring you." Just follow the photographs in the booklet. On page 21, "biting a steel chain in half with my teeth is illustrated. On page 39, there I am supporting a moving merry-go-round mounted with six men, on my chest. Again on page 44, I demonstrate that I actually hold 4,000 pounds of granite on my chest, while several husky men pound it with sledge hammers. Or on page 32 and 33, the motor cycle race, while I support the motor-drome on my chest. If you want a new start in life. . . ."[12]

Few physical culturalists were more familiar to Americans than "the World's Most Perfect Man." Muscles quivering, Charles Atlas threw out his challenge: "PULL AWAY FROM

THE CROWD OF WEAKLINGS! . . . FORGE RAPIDLY AHEAD! Business is slack—jobs are scarce—YOU can't afford to be laid off. HEALTH—Dominating, Wealth-Winning HEALTH is the DRIVING POWER behind Industrial Success! You need lots more of it. You need Strength—Stamina—Nervous Energy—Dauntless Courage and Daring. You need Pep and Personality and increased POWER to keep your job, win *quick* promotion, become a whirlwind SUCCESS! . . . Today's business, BIG business, demands BIG TWELVE-CYLINDER MEN, RED-BLOODED MEN, alert and alive, go-getters, top-notchers. . . . You'll never succeed, never progress while your body is sluggish, while your weak, unattractive figure repels instead of inspires. . . . GET OUT OF THE RUT!" [13]

In all the advertisements and books about success through health, none promised more of the good things of life with less effort than the apostles of dietics. Of all the foods, nuts seemed to hold a particular nutritional fascination for physical culturalists. "A FAILURE—HE DOESN'T KNOW IT—BUT FAULTY LUBRICATION IS TO BLAME," the copy writers of a pecan nut concern came right out and said it. Beside the headline stood the employer resting a kindly hand on the stooped, listless shoulders of Jones, seated in miserable dejection at his desk. "In firing Jones, the Boss doesn't know it but he's letting the firm lose a man who could be one of its very best. Jones doesn't know, either, why Something has always held him back —made him listless—dulled the keen edge of his brain and ability. For the insidious part about faulty lubrication is that only a few of its victims realize when it has a hold on them. . . ." Pecano, the Miracle Food, could give Jones just the kind of internal bath he so obviously needed. "It is powdered so finely that it needs no chewing, actually melts in your mouth—releases every single particle of the oil for instant lubrication of your entire system." [14]

Memory, an ancient division of the mind, was recalled as a technique for success. The use of memory, and mnemonics (devices for aiding the memory, e.g., 'Thirty days has September,

April, June, and November') were popularized by W. J. Ennever. Ennever founded the first Pelman Institute in London in 1898 and gave the English language a new word as he spread Pelmanism throughout the world. "Memory, as meaning the power of voluntary recall," one typical course in applied psychology instructed, "is wholly a question of trained habits of mental operation." The big idea in the memory message was recall by association. "The date or face or event that you wish to recall *is bound up with a multitude of other facts of observation and of your mind life* of the past. Success in recalling it depends simply upon your ability *to hit upon some idea so indissolubly associated with the object of search that the recall of one automatically recalls the other.*" [15]

For instance, how do you learn to remember names? You must be determined to remember the name and force yourself to concentrate. Get the name accurately and repeat it to yourself, while using the principle of association. You meet Mr. Whelan at some social or business affair. He's smiling. He's in the publishing business. According to one author, something like the following should be racing through your mind as the introduction takes place: "Here's Mr. WHELAN (pronounced Whalen), 'the smiling Irishman.' Mr. WHELAN, WHELAN, WHELAN has a whale of a smile, but his name is not spelled *Whalen* but WHELAN. Mr. WHELAN is a big *wheel* (Whalen) in publishing.

> You'll hear no wailin'
> From smiling Mr. WHELAN.

I'll remember the pleasant name of the pleasant Mr. WHELAN. See Mr. WHELAN *whalin'* in a *whale* boat with that *whale* of a smile." When learning a new name, if you bait the hooks of your memory with the principles of accuracy, repetition, and association, names will rise into your memory like hungry fish. The whackier the bait of association, the deeper the name will bite into your memory.[16]

A well-traveled byway was blazed by the midnight oil flickering over home-study courses in business affairs. Towards the close of the nineteenth century the success idea began to suggest that a formal education in a business college (as opposed to a classical or liberal arts education) could be a help. A substantial body of instructional literature in business affairs took shape. Throughout the twentieth century correspondence schools sold their courses (later called executive training programs) with the claim that cold, hard knowledge of business fundamentals is the foundation of success. The best known were the International Correspondence Schools, LaSalle Extension University, and the Alexander Hamilton Institute. "Once you feel that vital inspiration to get ahead . . . ," lectured one correspondence school in the 1920s, "you have made a splendid start in the race for Success. But how far you go and what laurels you win depend not alone on courage, or determination, or even upon natural ability, but on training!" This specialized training for the aspiring executive could range from business management through personnel organization to business law.[17]

Various magazines, newspapers, and book publishers, from time to time, exploited the tug of success and pitched their appeal in terms of knowledge, training, and executive skills. In the decades after World War II, one newspaper plastered selected railway stations in Commuterland with billboards announcing: EVERYWHERE THE MEN WHO KEEP GETTING AHEAD READ THE WALL STREET JOURNAL. The *Journal* was particularly fond of the testimonial confession in its advertising: "I was chatting with the postman who delivers my mail. He remarked that two families on his route who get the Wall Street Journal had recently moved into bigger houses. This started me thinking." After reading the *Journal* regularly, another eager beaver was convinced: "Now I know why men of wealth and prestige read the *Journal*. It is part of their secret. It is one of the things that helped them get where they are." The *Journal* was also certain of the answer to this question: Do they read the *Wall Street Journal* because they have more money, or do they have more money because they read the *Wall Street Journal*?[18]

"It Pays to Increase Your Word Power" has been a recent development in the history of the success idea. A product of the

1930s, the theoretical source can be traced directly to Johnson O'Connor of the Human Engineering Laboratory. O'Connor had been giving a battery of tests to occupational groups at his laboratory. He was struck by what appeared to be an orderly connection between high scoring on vocabulary tests and certain occupational groups. O'Connor announced the results in 1934 in the *Atlantic Monthly*. "Vocabulary and Success," the title of the essay, has been reprinted at least thirty times since that date.

The statistics cited in the essay intrigued O'Connor and alerted success writers to sharpen their pencils. He found that major executives scored higher in the English vocabulary test than any other selected group. Even college professors averaged 8 errors out of 150 words, while major executives averaged only 7 errors. O'Connor was convinced that he had tested his way into an important discovery. He announced that "an extensive knowledge of the exact meanings of English words accompanies outstanding success in this country more often than any other single characteristic which the Human Engineering Laboratories have been able to isolate and measure. . . . Although it is impossible to define success rigidly or scientifically, it seems to be true, nevertheless, that a large vocabulary is typical, not exclusively of executives, but of successful individuals. . . . Why do large vocabularies characterize executives and possibly outstanding men and women in other fields? The final answer seems to be that words are the instruments by means of which men and women grasp the thoughts of others and with which they do much of their own thinking. They are the tools of thought."

But, we ask, does he have a large vocabulary because he is a major executive, or is he a major executive because he has a large vocabulary? O'Connor hinted at, but did not state, the cause-effect relationship: "The large vocabularies of successful individuals come before success rather than after." The conclusion is obvious: "An exact and extensive vocabulary is an important concomitant of success. . . . Such a vocabulary can be acquired. . . . The balance of evidence at the moment suggests that . . . a consciously, even laboriously, achieved vocabulary is an active asset." [19]

A new field of success had been ploughed and planted; success writers began reaping the harvest. The fattest yield fell to Wilfred Funk. Lexicographer Funk, sometime president of Funk & Wagnalls publishing house, created and wrote for years the relentless vocabulary building feature in the *Reader's Digest,* "It Pays to Increase Your Word Power." He co-authored with Norman Lewis the most popular vocabulary-building success book in the history of American publishing. *30 Days to a More Powerful Vocabulary,* first issued in 1942, had sold by Funk's death in 1965 a staggering 4,700,000 copies of which 1,800,000 were hardbound.[20]

Grouping related words into chapters around various themes ("French Phrases You Can Use"), *30 Days to a More Powerful Vocabulary* gives the definition and pronunciation of hundreds of words and explains their meaning through illustrative sentences. In their inspirational introduction Funk and Lewis strengthened the cause-effect relationship between vocabulary building and success. Tests have revealed, they insisted, that "if your vocabulary is limited your chances of success are limited. . . . One of the easiest and quickest ways to get ahead is by consciously building up your knowledge of words." For three reasons. First, "the extent of your vocabulary indicates the degree of your intelligence. Your brain power will increase as you learn to know more words." Second, "words are your tools of thought. . . . The more words you have at your command the deeper, clearer and more accurate will be your thinking." Third, words are the tools of communication. You are judged by the words you use; you use words to convince and persuade other people. Since the vocabulary of the average person just about stops growing in his middle twenties, it is necessary to follow a plan. Fifteen minutes a day, for a month, will do the job. Conclude the authors of *30 Days to a More Powerful Vocabulary:* "A command of English will not only improve the processes of your mind. It will give you assurance; build your self-confidence; lend color to your personality; increase your popularity. Your words are your personality. Your vocabulary is you. . . . Words can make you great!" [21]

The final technique in this montage of miscellaneous means to success reaches back to the Greeks, but as a systematic procedure for getting ahead, it began in the 1930s. Professor Robert P. Crawford at the University of Nebraska had been holding classes in the subject since 1931, but its growth curve did not start soaring until World War II gave it a push. The man who more than anyone else promoted the technique was Alex F. Osborn. Bronx-born into a family of modest circumstances, haunted by financial insecurity, Osborn worked his way through Hamilton College, managed the football team, and edited the college newspaper. He quashed his fears of an impecunious life when he teamed up with that old success writer of the 1920s, Bruce Barton. Together they still represent 50 per cent of the nameplate on the plush Madison Avenue headquarters of Batten, Barton, Durstine, and Osborn.

This fast-growing technique has variously been called creative ideas, creative imagination, creative ideation, or free-wheeling. When individuals gather together into groups, it is called brainstorming, buzz sessions, group thinks, or idearamas. Behind all the hoopla generated by creative-thinking aficionados there lies a theory of problem solving.

"Our thinking mind," says Osborn, "is mainly two-fold: (1) *a judicial mind* which analyzes, compares, and chooses. (2) *a creative mind* which visualizes, foresees, and generates ideas." The end product of a judicial mind is a verdict; the end product of a creative mind is an idea. Though Osborn regards "imagination-without-judgment to be more deplorable than judgment-without-imagination," it is imagination which has been neglected. Our colleges concentrate almost entirely on training the mind to analyze, judge, and reason logically. (In order to induce a creative trend in education, Osborn established The Creative Education Foundation.) With most people "judgment grows automatically with years, while creativity dwindles unless consciously kept up. Circumstances force us to use our judicial mind every waking hour." Judgment, of course, is necessary, but an overgrown judgment can choke our inborn imaginative talent like weeds in a garden of flowers. While scientific testing has challenged personal judgment as a method of verification, there is no polling device or machine that can substitute for creative thinking.[22]

Imagination is "mankind's greatest gift." Indeed, "civilization, itself, is the product of creative thinking." All of us possess creative talent. "The difference is only in degree; and that degree is largely influenced by effort." It is "your *drive,* rather than your degree of *talent,* that determines your creative *ability"* (except women who are more creative than men but are held back by lack of self-confidence). The youthful are not more fruitful than the aged. Our native talent may stop growing, but our creative ability can keep growing year after year with effort. Though Osborn indicated his support of a liberal arts education, like all success writers he insisted that "the degree of one's creative power does not depend upon a degree. . . . There is no evidence that higher education induces creative power." This is so, not only because most colleges ignore the subject, but because people who go to work in their teens "tend to pack into their memories the *first-hand* experience which forms the richest fuel for creative lamps." When it comes "to creative efficacy, neither the extent of our knowledge nor the potency of our talent is as vital as our driving power." [23]

"Whether you are looking for a job, or trying to get ahead in a business, imagination is a key to achievement." Creative thinking can help you to enjoy a happier life, solve your personal problems, and improve your human relations.[24]

The aim of creative thinking is to pile up as many ideas or alternatives as possible for the solution of a particular problem. (An Osborn-chaired committee in Buffalo produced 3,800 alternative names for a multi-million-dollar bridge.) In creative thinking we must keep judgment and imagination separate. "In creative effort we have to be a Jekyll-and-Hyde. From time to time, we must turn off our judicial mind and light up our creative mind." We can produce new ideas by various processes—by combining two or more ideas, by associating ideas, by adapting, rearranging, reversing, and so forth. And we can do it individually or in groups in brainstorming sessions. Brainstorming is using "the *brain* to *storm* a creative problem—and to do so in *commando* fashion, with each stormer audaciously attacking the same objective." The average person can think up twice as many ideas when working in a group as when laboring alone because of the stimulative effect of rivalry and the cross-fire which sets off ideas like a string of firecrackers.[25]

The ideal number of people in an informal brainstorming session is between five and ten participants with substantially the same rank. The focus of 'storming' should be narrowed to a specific problem. There are four basic guides: "(1) *Criticism is ruled out.* Adverse judgment of ideas must be withheld until later. (2) *'Freewheeling' is welcomed.* The wilder the idea, the better; it is easier to tame down than to think up. (3) *Quantity is wanted.* The greater the number of ideas, the more the likelihood of winners. (4) *Combination and improvement are sought.* In addition to contributing ideas of their own, participants should suggest how ideas of others can be turned into *better* ideas; or how two or more ideas can be joined into still another idea." Chain-reactions have preference. If someone has an idea which was directly sparked by a previous idea and other hands are up, he snaps his fingers. He is hitch-hiking, i.e., making the most of the power of association and the leader will call on him immediately.[26]

There are lots of procedural guides which have been worked out, but the most important is still the major contribution of creative imagination to problem solving—keep imagination and judgment separate. As one brainstorming leader put it: "If you try to get hot and cold water out of the same faucet at the same time, you will get only tepid water. And if you try to criticize *and* create at the same time, you can't turn on either *cold* enough criticism or *hot* enough ideas. So let's stick solely to *ideas*— let's cut out *all* criticism *during* this session." Gently warn a transgressor. If he persists, squelch him. One fellow just couldn't turn off the cold water. The leader blasted him: "*Think* up or *shut* up!" he commanded.[27]

Any occupation or type of group can play, e.g., business, armed services, professions, clubs, community organizations, family unit, etc. Osborn describes how a group of Air Force officers brainstormed this problem: " 'If 700 miles of outside telephone wires were coated with three inches of frost so that long distance calls could not be made, how would you restore normal service as fast as possible?' " Cooking up ideas like popcorn, "the officers suggested 53 solutions in 25 minutes. As soon as an idea was uttered, it was chalked on a blackboard; and each idea was numbered consecutively." The 36th suggestion was the workable solution: Send helicopters flying over the wires. The downdraft from the giant blades will blow the frost off and restore long distance service. Osborn reports that about 10 per cent of the ideas produced in most brainstorming sessions are potentially usable.[28]

Hundreds of companies were brainstorming problems in the 1960s, while a number of colleges offered courses in creative thinking. Magazine articles promoted its possibilities. Brainstorming can be used to coin words (e.g., butts and ashes left in an ashtray: buttage, garbutts, cigamess), or to think up new inventions (e.g., an automatic bedmaker, a suitcase with rollers on the bottom, a watercooler that shines your shoes while you drink). Out of whacky ideas can come positive results like a portable electric dishwasher. The Aluminum Company of America calls it "imagineering," which means that "you let your imagination soar and then engineer it down to earth." It is the soaring that fires the ardor of brainstormers. That sage, sober executive with the musing mien, revered for his judgment, in their sessions must either think up or shut up.[29]

The idea of success, like its hero, the self-made man, is synonymous with individual achievement. But it is not creative thinking by the individual that has caught on, but brainstorming by the group. This is not unexpected in a world molded by forces which produced the personality ethic. What Ernest Benger of Du Pont observed is true: "No idea has ever been generated except in a single human mind. . . ." But not unlike the tendency of labor unions, brainstorming sacrifices individual recognition for the pooled satisfactions of group mobility. In buzz sessions, "no idea is identified by the name of its suggester. . . . The need for group congeniality far outweighs the good of granting individual credit." Brainstorming's delight in group achievement suggests only one direction in which the success idea might move in the next few decades.[30]

22

THE FAILURE OF
SUCCESS

How to live? What to live for? As the success idea offered its own set of answers, there evolved a series of problems which twisted themselves into dilemmas.

We move on from the historical development of the success idea expressed in self-help literature. Our concern now is for the relation of that idea to the American experience. The relationship is revealed through an examination of selected critics of the success idea and by an analysis of certain consequences of the success complex for American life.

The dilemmas which emerge in this and the following chapters were imposed on Americans by themselves. Between the ideals and the realities of American life, between the promise and the performance, there was always a void. In the quest for meaning and purpose, in the world of work and in leisure, what is was always less than what should have been.[1]

Chameleons, it is said, become nervous wrecks when moving across a plaid bedspread. As actors in the drama of life, we must play many roles. There is scarcely time to shift the scenery before we shift our identities. The tough-minded breadwinner by day, at night becomes the loving husband and father. When our actions conflict with our beliefs, when we don't practice what we preach in playing our conflicting roles, the consequences can be psychologically disturbing.

Christianity, the dominant ethical construct in America,

teaches that we should be filled with gentleness, forgiveness, sacrifice, and brotherly love. In real life we must be competitive and aggressive, impersonal and selfish. In the economic system of capitalism, the primary purpose of the job is to make money. Money is the trophy in the natural warfare between buyer and seller and between employees for the same promotion. If you run your own business or profession and forget that the *first* objective is to make money, you go under. If you work for somebody else and forget that it must be your employer's objective, you're stuck in the same job for life—or out of work. A "deal" is one in which everybody gains; sometimes the better deal is the one in which you gain at the other fellow's expense. The American system is constructed on competitive individualism for profits and promotion. It's a cold, ruthless, hard-boiled world of self-assertion.

Most people who vigorously engage American life are troubled by conflicts between creed and behavior. Some avoid the contradiction of the Get of capitalism and the Give of Christianity by removing themselves from the profit motive. They choose, perhaps, to become teachers. Others confidently construct their own scheme of humanistic values. Yet, for many men there are splinters of guilt on the ladder of business success. Just such a man was J. O. Bentall, a leading Baptist clergyman from Chicago. In a moving testament of his conversion, he explained in 1907 how he reconciled earning his living with living up to his ideals. He became a Socialist because he was a Christian.

Bentall explained: "There are certain cardinal principles in the Christian religion which I must adhere to in order to be a Christian. One of them is: 'Do unto others as you would that others should do unto you.' Another is: 'Love thy neighbor as thyself.' But it is impossible for me to obtain my living and at the same time adhere to these rules. In a society where competition obtains and is accepted as the system under which mankind must live, I cannot secure the means of life without taking something which my neighbor also tries to take and which I get only because I am ahead of him in time, superior to him in strength, above him in intelligence or possess a vantage point given me by some peculiar arrangement to which I was not entitled because of any of my own merits. If I thus take this article which my neighbor also tries to take, I must first prostitute the principle which is the corner stone in my religious structure and set it aside while I appropriate and use this article as my means of life. I could let my neighbor have this article in question, but that would only change the wrong from one person to another." [2]

But is there no choice within the system? "If I am in business, and my neighbor is also in business," Bentall continues, "I am compelled to look for the trade which my neighbor also looks for. If I do not succeed in getting that trade I do not love my neighbor. If I succeed in getting it my neighbor does not love me. Under competition my gain becomes my neighbor's loss and if I am to succeed and become prosperous he must of necessity go down and become bankrupt, providing competition has free play. It is only by checking competition that the two of us might possibly go up together and make equal gain."

Bentall goes on to explain by the Marxian theory of surplus value how his business success, measured in terms of profits, is actually achieved by depriving his employees of wealth that they have earned by their labor. Then he returns, in a lyrical passage filled with torment, to the personal agony of capitalistic competition. "Under the system of competition it is impossible to put into practice the principles which are indispensable to the Christian religion as it would be to further a man's happiness by transfixing him with a bayonet. I am therefore helpless as a Christian to carry out my desire, and Christianity, which came and gave me my ideals and opened my eyes and gave me a vision of holiness and love and justice and truth and righteousness, has become only a fiend that haunts me and prods me and tosses me from earth to heaven and from heaven to hell and gives me no rest and no peace and no comfort, only tears and suffering and woe and despair. . . . I am in a lamentable position. That which I would I do not, and that which I would not I do."

"Why am I a Socialist?" Bentall asks, and replies: "Because Socialism will make it possible for me to *attain* to my ideals."

Socialism is an economic system of cooperation which makes it possible to live by the Golden Rule. It is "the material side of that of which Christianity is the religious." When my neighbor works, he works for me. When I prosper, he prospers. He cannot take advantage of me and I cannot take advantage of him. We are bound together in love and affection working for a common goal.

As Bentall looked out on his America of the 1900s, he saw the rich fencing in for themselves the great storehouses of God's creation. Under Socialism, the storehouses would be opened to their rightful owners. Suffering and want would be eliminated. Socialism would abolish special privileges and the capitalistic source of legislative immorality. Legislatures would pass laws for all the people. Family life, with the poor now living in wretched conditions and the rich demoralized by idle luxury, would be restored to its true role as a Christian institution.

More than politics and family life, however, the church had suffered most of all. "In defending competition which is fundamentally immoral, the church which should be the exponent of the highest ethical principles has put the dagger into her own heart. The teachings of Jesus cannot be preached consistently together with upholding and defending the principles of competition. That the church has suffered because of her complicity in this immoral warfare, is not to be wondered at. She has been fighting with one hand to get people into the kingdom of God and with the other to get the kingdom of competition into the people. . . . The kidnapping of Jesus by capitalism is the greatest crime that has been committed since the Christian era began. A sorrowing world is running around wailing and lamenting and saying: 'They have taken away my Master and I know not where they have lain Him.' " [8]

Bentall's Christian Socialism questioned with the golden rule the success idea's justification for material success in an economic system of competitive capitalism. Bentall cried out his moral agony in the early years of the twentieth century. Though his anguish is timeless, for the apologists of capitalism, it was dangerous. They were certain that Christian Socialism, if it worked, would produce consequences which would be largely destructive of individual freedom.

It was the inner conflict of what we might call the Christian Capitalism of the success idea which produced the first dilemma. The clash was between capitalism as an economic system of organized selfishness and Christianity as a value system of unselfish love. On the one hand, if you struggle to be a success within the capitalistic system, you must always push for your own self-interest, throw yourself into competition with others, endure the strains of unethical behavior, squeeze the issue to a harder bargain, and *not* do unto your neighbor as you would have him do unto you. How, then, can you honor traditional Christian values? How can you express in your own life the beatitudes of the Sermon on the Mount and its Golden Rule? If you achieve even a small measure of success, how can you honestly witness that you are expressing in your life the ideals of a Christian society?

On the other hand, if you follow the dictates of Christianity, you must act toward your fellow man with gentleness, kindness, and compassion, you must be self-giving rather than self-seeking, you must give yourself to the interests of others rather than to your own self-interest. How, then, can you survive in business or the profit-oriented professions? At work, it's me rather than you, us rather than them. Does not successful economics make unsuccessful Christians?

Americans have always had a deep moral need to justify their actions—whether it was getting entangled in world wars or pushing toward success. We have seen how success writers of the character ethic tried to resolve the dilemma of self-seeking business success and self-giving Christian or humanitarian values. From the seventeenth through the nineteenth centuries, money-making was justified by the stewardship of wealth doctrine. Depending on the success philosopher, it followed a religious or a secular interpretation. The accumulation of wealth was both an evidence of God's favor and a way of glorifying God. Attention to business built within the individual a noble character strong with the ascetic virtues of industry and thrift. Not to work hard was to misuse talents which are a gift from

God. Since we are all stewards of the Lord, we must make good in order to do good. One ought honestly to make money, for the more we make the more we can give away for pious uses. The secular interpretation of the character ethic's justification for success by-passed God. Making money was a good thing to do for humanitarian reasons. It could be given away to help others after it was made. The supreme justification for success in the twentieth century has been the concept of service. The degree of success was the measure of one's service to the community. It was a yardstick measuring how much one had contributed to the welfare of others.

By an ingenious ideological assurance, the character ethic tried to resolve the dilemma of Christian values clashing with the spirit of capitalism. You love your neighbor by pursuing your own self-interest. Idealism justified materialism. It is one reason why Social Darwinism, with its doctrine of the fittest surviving in a struggle for existence, never captured the imagination of success writers and businessmen as a vindication for achievement. The success idea was Christian and humanitarian. In the stewardship of wealth doctrine, getting was justified because one had to get in order to give. In the concept of service, one gave to others in the process of getting for oneself.

While the character ethic tried to resolve what we might call the justification dilemma of self-seeking and self-giving, it made that dilemma insoluble by yoking it to a second dilemma. On the one hand, if the individual worked hard and accumulated wealth, would not this wealth destroy those qualities in him which helped him to make the money? If he gained the whole world, was he not in danger of losing his own soul? On the other hand, if the individual was a slacker without ambition, would he not be denying his God-given qualities? If he was a parasite easily satisfied with his lot in life, would he not be guilty of contributing less than he could to the welfare of the community?

The character ethic tried to resolve the first dilemma but then compounded it with this second dilemma. *If* your methods were honest; *if* you were generous according to the stewardship doctrine or contributed to the welfare of the community through the service concept; *if* material success was not the final goal in your life; *if* you understood the meaning of 'true success'; then you were fully justified in piling up treasures on earth. However, if you were unfaithful on any of these counts, your spirit was in danger. There was no easy way out. The character ethic sprinkled holy water on money-making or justified it on humanitarian grounds.But you were not permitted to enjoy the comforting resolution of the justification dilemma unless you endured the continual introspection of the personal dilemma.

A tension was created between material success and 'true success.' The task of the individual was to hold this tension in balance. It was a creative tension for work. Despite the guilt feelings engendered, it was psychologically healthy, if it is understood that the clash between man's self-love and love for others, between his base needs and higher inclinations, has always posed an insoluble dilemma. The nineteenth-century American may have ended the weak feeling guilty that he had not done better in the battle with Mammon. But at least he knew where he stood. If he was subjectively accountable, his achievement was objectively justifiable.

Since the 1930s, the personality ethic has been the dominant route to wealth in the success idea. The personality ethic was enthusiastic about service as a justification for material success, but the religious interpretation of the service concept declined in importance. In the Niagara of advice on how to manipulate other people in order to get ahead, the personality ethic was indifferent to the dangers of materialism and the meaning of 'true success.' It did not enshrine the possession of wealth as the *summum bonum* in life, but it did not deny it either. The personality ethic could tell you how to become a success and justify the process to give your achievement philosophical dignity, but it was uninterested in what kind of a person you would *be* after you had *become* something. Its attitude toward 'true success' was indifference.

The personality ethic tried to resolve the dilemma of Christianity and capitalism, but refused to compound it with the second dilemma. The tension had been relaxed. The success idea, now dominated by the personality ethic, had become impoverished as a philosophy of life. For most Americans, the amassing of possessions has never amounted to a satisfying ultimate goal in life. A philosophy without ultimates may be a notion to live on, but it has never been a doctrine to live by.

We have earlier suggested that this change in the success idea was caused by a number of factors. Success book writers themselves had become professional technicians of psychological persuasion. Adults, hungry for success advice, had supplanted young men in a reading market where too much literary boy-scoutism might seem unsophisticated. In the character ethic, it was the religious interpretation of the justification for success which had tightened the tension between material success and 'true success.' While the secular wing did hammer away at the spiritual threat of materialism, it was the religiously oriented success writer who feared most that Mammon might topple God's throne in the hearts of men.

In the personality ethic, the declining importance of the religious interpretation of the justification for success was an indication of the declining influence of religion on American values. The declining influence of religion was further evident in the indifference of the secular wing to the spiritual perils of materialism. Secular success writers were apparently not so conditioned by general religious values to consider such problems important.

How, then, can we explain this paradox: During the 1950s the nation was moving through a generally agreed "return to religion" while at the same time the idea of success (excluding New Thought for the moment) was experiencing a "departure from religion." Was the success idea moving against a national trend?

Statistics support a "return to religion." During the late 1940s and 1950s church membership increased dramatically. Funds flooded into every-member canvasses, parents strained the capacities of Sunday schools with their children, and in suburbia, where most of the bustle was evident, the churches increasingly became centers for social activity. But a community center is not the same thing as a Christian community. As a community center, the church had increasingly become a fraternal and recreational organization of congenial people knit together by compatible racial and social class identities. It was a sanctified outlet for American activism and busy organizational urges. While the heralded 'return to religion' may have been an earnest seeking for a metaphysical foundation upon which to construct one's life, there is little indication that it seriously interrupted the long-term decline of religious influences on the thinking of most Americans.

As the nation moved through the 1960s, the post-war 'religious revival' began tapering off. Did the success idea play a part? There is an absence of hard evidence, but it is suggested that a portion of the clergy ministering to middle-class, suburban congregations had lost touch with an older Protestant interpretation of material success.

The usual interpretation of the pastoral clergy is that they have been a conservative bulwark of the *status quo*. Their soothing sermons were supposed to have reinforced the capitalistic convictions of their bourgeois congregations. Yet it can also be argued that the Protestant clergy ministering to middle-class, upwardly mobile congregations were neutral about the Christian validity of capitalism and often even critical of getting ahead materialistically in American life.

One would hesitate to cite any sermon as a typical post-World War II statement about success to middle-class Protestant congregations living in increasingly affluent surroundings or attending fashionable big-city churches. A sermon representative of one position was delivered by Robert J. McCracken, pastor of New York City's famed Riverside Church. Americans have made a god of success defined as money, McCracken told his flock. Of course money in itself is neither good nor bad, he continued. It depends on how it is acquired and what is done with it after it is made. Yet material success "often brings with it fearful disillusionment." It cannot buy happiness. McCracken goes on to honor certain priceless qualities that we have come to know in this study as 'true success'—"friendship, love, nobleness of character, a tranquil conscience, and that greatest boon of all, the forgiveness and fellowship of God."

This is familiar ground. But McCracken proceeds to drive an insurmountable wedge between Christ and the weekday world of business. Christ's "scale of values is markedly different from ours." He blessed the poor, taught that life does not consist of possessions but that one must lose his life in Christ in order to find it, and warned that many who are first will be last and the last first. "The thing that really matters is what a person is, not what he has. . . . To find the real success we must be true to the highest we know; we must be true to God revealed in Christ." McCracken concludes that this interpretation of Christianity "with its reversal of materialistic standards has no prospect of becoming a popular creed." [4]

In his sermon, McCracken struck at materialism. But he neglected to justify material success. Because he did not resolve the first dilemma of justification, the second dilemma of ends and means becomes no dilemma at all. Instead of enduring the tension between self-getting and self-giving, the devout Christian would seem to have no choice. McCracken does not say that money-making is wrong, though one might easily infer that value judgment. There is no emphasis, however, that it is a moral objective in life. The businessman might well go forth to Monday's battle confused by Sunday's sermon. And if weekday breadwinning cannot be reconciled with Sunday's sermonizing, the consequence is a compartmentalized mind. As Lee Bristol, Jr., graphically put it: "A man's Sunday self and his weekday self are like two halves of a round-trip ticket—not good if detached." [5]

During the post-World War II years religion did serve to locate and identify the upwardly mobile suburbanite and his family as Protestant, Roman Catholic, or Jew. It did offer belongingness and established respectability in the community. But while religion was growing stronger as a church-going social ritual, it was growing weaker as an influence shaping values and behavior

The character ethic comforted the afflicted by giving meaning to economic life and mercy to failures through 'true success.' It afflicted the comfortable with stern warnings about the perils of materialism. It was the tradition of the mind power ethic, especially the doctrine of New Thought more recently expressed by Norman Vincent Peale, to comfort the comfortable by relaxing the tension of the personal dilemma. New Thought made religion pragmatic. God was no longer a sanctifying and restraining force but a power to be exploited for material purposes. The supernatural ceased to be a Divine Judge and became a Divine Dynamo uninterested in checking man's irresponsibility for self-seeking power.

The great task of the character ethic had been to spiritualize commerce without commercializing the spirit. The religious interpretation of the character ethic, when closest to its Puritan source, believed that wealth was a natural and proper incentive because man was ethically imperfect and driven by self-love. But at the same time wealth should not become an end in itself. Wealth should serve to glorify God by encouraging ascetic virtues in the individual and by building a community which could devote itself to a Christian life on earth.

In an affluent society the disenchanted are wont to cite Emerson:

> Things are in the saddle,
> And ride mankind.

But it was also Emerson who prophesied: "The pulpit and the press have many commonplaces denouncing the thirst for wealth; but if men should take these moralists at their word and leave off aiming to be rich, the moralists would rush to rekindle at all hazards this love of power in the people, lest civilization should be undone." [6]

The religion of ascetic Protestantism was a force for productivity. The clergy has often been criticized for encouraging materialism—and many of them did just that. In a scarcity economy productivity was vital to the survival of the community. The clergy's function was not to crush materialism but to promote and guide it at the same time. The task was somewhat like checking a runaway horse. If you break his spirit to run, you no longer have a useful horse. The character ethic put a bit in the mouth of the runaway horse of American materialism and tried to control its speed and direction.

In the seventeenth century the doctrine of the calling was just such a bit. Cotton Mather was no slavish apologist selling out to rich parishioners but a tough-minded disciplinarian of his society. You will recall that he put forth the doctrine that every Christian has two callings. In his general calling, a Christian should serve God. In his personal calling, a Christian should have an honest job which is useful to the community. A Christian should spend most of his time at his job so that "he may glorify God by doing of good for others and getting of good for himself." Mather quickened the incentive of his flock: "Come, come, for shame, away to your business. Lay out your strength in it, put forth your skill for it. . . . 'Solomon, seeing that the young man was industrious, he made him a ruler.' I tell you with diligence a man may do marvelous things." Having justified achievement, Mather cracked down. This was no easy voyage he proposed. The Christian in his two callings is like a man in a boat rowing for heaven. If he pulls only one oar (either the spiritual or the worldly one), he "will make but a poor dispatch to the Shoar of Eternal Blessedness." [7]

In the middle decades of the twentieth century the idea of success was like a rowboat spinning around in a whirlpool of philosophical confusion. The personality ethic and the mind power ethic were uninterested in checking materialism. A portion of the Protestant clergy were engaged in denouncing material success, demanding that counsels of impossible perfection become workable guidelines of behavior. The character ethic was moribund. But in its day the character ethic had tried to resolve the conflict between the idealism of Christianity and the materialism of capitalism. It justified the accumulation of wealth but charged that the task of the good man, working in an imperfect society with imperfect men, was to hold 'true success' and material success in some kind of tremulous balance.

While success writers were limited to philosophizing about the character ethic dilemma of material success and 'true success,' novelists and playwrights carry us deeper into the dilemma through the lives of their characters. What intrigues many thoughtful creative writers is what happens to the climber's soul as he scrambles up the success ladder. What kind of person has he become? How does it feel at the top? Imaginative writers illuminate how the becoming can change the being, how the outer success interacts with the inner self. They tell us that the success-driven man can be dying inside while he is making it outside. Sometimes the pilgrimage from rags to riches is a journey from rags to wretchedness.

In the German legend, the learned Dr. Faust sells his soul to the Devil for youth, knowledge, and magical power. In Clifford Odets' 1937 American drama, *Golden Boy,* twenty-one-year-old Joe Bonaparte is the allegorical representative of every artist who fled from his true self into commercialism, every 'serious' playwright who sold out Broadway for Hollywood, as Odets himself was accused of doing. Joe Bonaparte most of all loves music. He is on the threshold of a promising career as a violinist. But Joe hates obscurity and poverty and is consumed by an ambition to make money and be somebody. In American culture, Joe recognizes, hands that pummel other men bring quicker fame than hands that play the violin. The Fist will get you there quicker than the Fiddle.

Joe develops into a magnificent fighting machine as he moves closer to the title, but disintegrates within himself into hate and egotism. The girl he loves, Lorna, discerns that this unhappy Faust has sold his true self to the Devil of material success. "You're a miserable creature. You want your arm in *gelt* up to the elbow. You'll take fame so people won't laugh or scorn your face. You'd give your soul for those things. But every time you turn your back your little soul kicks you in the teeth. It don't give in so easy." Finally Joe kills a man in the ring and breaks his hand. There is no dilemma now. He believes he has murdered his finer self. His hands are useless for the violin. Joe has come to the realization that to conquer the world means

to be able to say: " 'I have myself; I am what I want to be!' "
Lorna hopes exultantly that they can start a new life together
in "some city where poverty's no shame—where music is no
crime!—where there's no war in the streets—where a man is
glad to be himself, to live and make his woman herself!" But
author Odets refuses the compromise and pays the Devil his
full price. Joe speeds off into the night with Lorna, unrepentant
and hostile. His finer self destroyed, there is only the shell of
Joe Bonaparte which is pronounced dead in the crash of his
Duesenberg—the cherished symbol of his material success.[8]

The failure of success was an irony that fascinated creative
writers. One novelist, who had written inspirationally about
success for Orison Swett Marden's magazine before fame
touched him as a creative writer, pondered on the nature of both
success and failure in American life. In *Sister Carrie*, Theodore
Dreiser juxtaposed a successful man's pitiful decline with a
woman's feeling of emptiness in achieving success. Carrie Mee-
ber leaves her rural home to work in Chicago. Unemployed and
penniless after losing her job, longing for fine clothes and the
manicured beauty that the city can offer, she becomes the mistress of a traveling salesman. Through him she meets and soon
takes up with handsome, affluent, though married, George
Hurstwood, manager of a plush Chicago bar. Hurstwood steals
from his employer's safe, tricks Carrie into fleeing to New York
with him by way of Montreal, and marries her.

In New York things go badly for Hurstwood. He begins a slow,
heart-rending descent down the occupational ladder. Carrie
leaves him. He sinks into menial jobs—a scab during a strike,
then begging. At last he is down to the soft cry of every man
whose problems have grown bigger than he is. He seals off his
shabby room, turns on the gas, and lies down to die with a
" 'What's the use?' " Carrie begins her rise as Hurstwood sinks
lower and lower. She goes on the stage as a chorus girl and
works her way up until she becomes a musical comedy star.
Carrie is now a success. She is well-known, owns a carriage,
dresses in beautiful clothes, and lives in a fine suite at the Waldorf. But she is lonely and unhappy. As Dreiser perceives, Carrie

can never find happiness in success because success for her, like so many others, is a journey, not a destination. There are always the unfulfilled dreams which lie above and beyond. For many people there is the hope that achieving the goal will bring final happiness. But it never does, because there is always another goal beyond the one reached, other worlds to conquer. There is no top of the mountain but only plateaus from which to begin another ascent.[9]

What the better novels and plays on the success theme teach us is that life is filled with dilemmas and ironies, conflicts and crises in which there is no easy solution. 'Slick' fiction describes the sun sinking into the west as the hero embraces his girl—*amor vincit omnia;* 'serious' fiction does not end its story with such a sunny contentment with life's problem.

In *Point of No Return,* John P. Marquand explored the principle which the major character in his *Sincerely, Willis Wayde* both stated and lived: "You had to sacrifice a lot of things if you made money." Charles Gray in *Point of No Return* is a likable, forty-three-year-old Dartmouth graduate and bank executive. For countless Charlie Grays, the job of life, or the life of the job, is a constant point of no return—the navigational point at which it is impossible to return to your place of departure. Now Charles is homing in on his destination. Whether he will safely land the job of vice president or miss the mark has whipped him and his wife into churning anxiety. He is in the grip of a system, and he is quite aware of it. There are forces within himself and forces of family responsibility which compel him to get on and move up. He is humbled by this system, reduced to anxieties about his promotion, robbed of his freedom by the single, supreme fact of increasing his salary at the bank. In his own thoughts of degradation, he is an ass trundling after a bundle of hay.

Charles gets the promotion and the Grays are still upward mobile. They will send their son to a New England boarding school, buy a bigger house in an even better neighborhood, turn in the tired old Buick, purchase a sailboat, and switch to a more fashionable country club. But Charles has lost more than his freedom to the system, for "in spite of all those years, in spite of all his striving, it was remarkable how little pleasure he took in final fulfillment." It was "a strangely hollow climax." Yet as Marquand sagely observes, if Charles had his life to live over, he would unhesitatingly step right onto the treadmill again. One suspects it is only a matter of time before the thoughts of Charles and Nancy anxiously begin drifting toward the nagging question—who is next in line for the presidency of the bank? [10]

Creative writers often yoked the success drive to the family unit and saw in the connection unhappy consequences. Wives nagged their faltering husbands to get ahead for prestige and status, or ambitious husbands neglected their wives and children and married their work, or parents pressured their children to reach impossible standards beyond their abilities. How imaginative insight can brilliantly probe the success complex is played out in what is quite possibly the greatest tragedy in the history of the American drama.

Arthur Miller's *Death of a Salesman* is a play about an unimportant man who aspired higher than he achieved. At sixty-three years of age, Willy has been covering the New England territory out of Brooklyn for some thirty-five years. He is exhausted, his commissions are dwindling, he is fired from his job, then pride is broken, and all confidence is lost. His favorite son, Biff, has been a bitter disappointment. Willy is on the brink of suicide. But the man has dignity. He has slaved for his family, about paid off the mortgage, and every year has squeezed through on the time payments for his appliances, though convinced that "they time those things. They time them so when you finally paid for them, they're used up." Now Willy's mind is slipping and his hallucinations and mutterings call back to him the crucial points in his life. While his wife tenderly knows that "he's only a little boat looking for a harbor," she fiercely defends him before his mocking son: "I don't say he's a great man. Willy Loman never made a lot of money. His name was never in the paper. He's not the finest character that ever lived. But he's a human being, and a terrible thing is happening to him. So attention must be paid. He's not to be allowed to fall into his grave like an old dog. Attention, attention must be finally paid to such a person." [11]

Yearning for success so passionately, the "terrible thing" for Willy is that he must endure the self-realization of failure. As he wonders what went wrong, what decisions he should have made to become rich and important, he increases the pressure on the thirty-four-year-old Biff to live out Willy's own dream of becoming an important businessman. Willy thinks he has the key, and in this 1949 play, it is the personality ethic. "It's not what you say," he advises his son, "it's how you say it—because personality always wins the day." Grades in school don't count so much as being a rugged, all-round boy who above all is well-liked and will be well-liked in the business world. But Biff loathes business and only wants to work in the outdoors under the sky on a western cattle ranch. A star athlete in school and a boy of promise, we come to learn that his faith in his father was shattered by finding, years before, a woman in Willy's hotel room in Boston. Now Biff returns once again to fulfill the impossible dream of his father to become a bigshot, though he knows that a business life in the city is a denial of his own true self and his hopes for the future. Biff knows he and his father are both second-rate, but Willy cannot bring himself to admit it. In a magnificent scene, father and son fiercely confront each other and Biff falls sobbing on Willy, begging to be released from his father's phony dreams about Biff's prospects for success. Willy interprets Biff's tears as an expression of love, refuses to give up his illusions, and with the conviction that Biff will fulfill the dream of success for both of them, drives off in his car to commit suicide so that Biff can get another start with the twenty-thousand-dollar life insurance money.[12]

At the funeral, Willy's best friend offers a peroration for all who struggle for the salesman's dream of success within the intangibles of the personality ethic: "Nobody dast blame this man. You don't understand: Willy was a salesman. And for a salesman, there is no rock bottom to the life. He don't put a bolt to a nut, he don't tell you the law or give you medicine.

He's a man way out there in the blue, riding on a smile and a shoeshine. And when they start not smiling back—that's an earthquake. And then you get yourself a couple of spots on your hat, and you're finished. Nobody dast blame this man. A salesman is got to dream, boy. It comes with the territory." [13]

Since its Broadway opening in 1949, *Death of a Salesman* has shaken audiences across the nation. The movie version, partly because this particular drama lends itself better to the stage, was a flop. In fact, it should have been the movie version which called forth the crack from a man leaving the theater: "I always said that New England territory was no damned good." The play made Americans, including tough-minded businessmen, cry unashamedly, and even the oversophisticated *New Yorker* magazine's John McCarten confessed that the play "had me gulping like a goldfish before it was fifteen minutes old." *Death of a Salesman* is a particularly, though not exclusively, American play. London playgoers were puzzled by the moving effect of the drama on Americans. They were inclined to despise Willy Loman's pathetic hunger for being well-liked, and they could not identify with the failure of a mere salesman—a response which suggests a marked difference, in degree rather than kind, however, between these two English-speaking peoples. [14]

Death of a Salesman is not a classical tragedy. No Greek hero or great king crashes from the heights. But every culture knows its own tragedies. A tragedy comes alive when it moves the living—and this one shook Americans. Willy is a common man, a part of the plain people, by his very name a low man, but he has stature. He is not pathetic, but tragic, for he has struggled and tried and cherished dreams like the rest of us. Arthur Miller intensifies the tragedy by expressing it through the family unit. Willy Loman is a free American, but he is a slave to a system of values. The last words of the play are delivered by Willy's wife. She weeps over his grave, tries to tell him that the last payment has just been made on the mortgage, and repeats again and again: "We're free . . . We're free . . ." But Willy was never free and did not want to be. He was never free of his phony dream that he could actually achieve his idea of success. It was not enough that Willy so committed himself to the idea of success that it destroyed him. He was determined to coerce Biff into the same system of values. He sold his life by suicide for the money in the insurance policy so that Biff could get a new start. He destroyed himself to perpetuate in his unwilling son the very thing that caused his own destruction. Willy Loman took his own sad life in order to justify the waste of it.[15]

What do 'serious' novelists and playwrights tell us about success? They articulate our own ambivalent feelings. In a later chapter we shall examine the response of several other significant imaginative writers to a different aspect of success. With respect to goals, the story is told in different ways, but the conclusion is consistent—success has its price. The struggle frequently destroys soul, honor, and integrity. It can make a person insensitive and callous toward human suffering. Success may disintegrate into the ashes of loneliness, family discord, emotional emptiness, or spiritual poverty. When the lives of the people we meet in many novels are peeled like an artichoke, we learn that there are limits to what money can buy. The good things of life do not equal the good life. Our better novelists and playwrights seem to be saying, in their gloomy, tragic-filled probings into the meaning of success, that there are only two tragedies: One is not getting what you want and the other is getting it. The one is the price of failure; the other is the price of success. The trouble with fame and status and money is that they seem to cost so much.

The character ethic in inspirational success literature was always warning about the dangers of greedy materialism and trying to define 'true success.' This much, at least, it had in common with 'serious' fiction. 'Serious' fiction began at the point where non-fiction success literature ended. While non-fiction success literature could only warn, the creative writer enjoyed the advantages of his own imagination and insights into the hearts and minds of people. He exposed the eternal tensions between material success and 'true success,' inordinate ambition and a balanced life, making money and finding happiness. The supreme irony was that outer success frequently destroyed inner contentment. Sometimes the price of success was absolute, paid in the wages of life itself.

Success was increasingly paid for in American society in the wages of counterfeit human relations. "The authentic Adversary today," declared Max Lerner, "is the manipulation of man, the tendency to see the human being as a target and use him as an object instead of respecting him as a subject. . . . The assault on the mind of manipulated man in our contemporary civilization is for me the darkest thing about it." From the world of the personality ethic, dominating the get-ahead gospel since the 1930s, emerged the third dilemma of the success idea.[16]

Salesmen were the individual expression of the personality ethic. The middle-class success striver in the middle decades of the twentieth century could hardly avoid being a salesman. If he were not hawking a product, he was peddling ideas or selling himself. In the corporate structure, there were the bosses above, subordinates below, and fellow associates, clients, and customers. The salesman's importance increased as product differentiation in price and quality decreased. The life insurance salesman might consider his calling a greater contribution to the general welfare than the drummer of deodorants. Both manipulated for gain. The one played upon the fear of body odor, the other upon the fear of death.

The 'new way of looking at life' of Dale Carnegieism, in its extreme form, was Eros masquerading as agape. People increasingly became the raw material for profit. Success writers, like mechanical engineers plundering nature, became human engineers constructing rules for manipulating man. The self was soiled by the necessity to sell the self or a product according to the rules of persuasion: Be interested in the other fellow, make him feel important, avoid an argument, smile, praise him. Behavior was not guided by principle. It responded to the dictates of a public relations mentality. The public relations mentality, entwined with the personality ethic, inexorably led to a public relations morality. The result was moral relativism. Unlike hard work or honesty, the techniques for messaging other people were not absolutes, good in themselves. They were good only if they achieved the desired results. Profit was exploited by controlling the responses of man; truth was something found in public opinion polls.

Advertising was the institutionalization of the personality ethic. Like selling oneself or a product, most middle-class success strivers were associated in one way or another with advertising. A manufacturer could deceive the consumer with a shabby product and a merchant could place a heavy thumb on the weighing scales. Advertisers, in the view of some critics, corrupted the nature of man. They preyed upon the weakness of people, hammered the mind into a pulpy worship of material things, and seduced society into following its own worst tendencies. In the opinion of some observers, advertisers were a virus which sickened society, infecting the mass media of television and radio, driving taste down to the lowest common denominator, and cheapening art with a corrupting market place mentality. A *New Yorker* cartoon sliced into the deceit. "Now let's decide which we like best—" puzzled one advertiser at a conference. " 'Remember, folks, Klenodent contains anethol!' or 'Klenodent contains *less* anethol than any other leading toothpaste.' " [17]

What we might call the personality ethic dilemma of hypocrisy vs. sincerity contained within itself an individual dilemma and an advertising dilemma. The torment of the individual dilemma emerges from the responsibility of earning a living in a consumption economy. On the one hand, if success depends more and more on getting along with people and manipulating their responses, how can we resist the temptations of hypocrisy and duplicity? How can we avoid a public relations mentality with its moral relativism? Are we exploiting people, not in the older sense of long hours, low wages, and miserable working conditions, but exploiting their emotional and spiritual lives as fellow human beings?

On the other hand, if we resist playing the game of the per-

sonality ethic, how can we get ahead in the scramble of business
and the professions—unless we retire to such 'loner' occupations as research and the creative arts? Yet, from the viewpoint
of society functioning efficiently, how can white-collar breadwinners work under pressure in close quarters without the
soothing empathy, at best, and at worst, the guile, of the
personality ethic?

The individual dilemma is institutionalized in the advertising
dilemma. On the one hand, if you are in advertising, or connected with a company that advertises its products, do you not
often reinforce the weaknesses of your fellow citizens by deceit-
fully exploiting human nature? Do you not translate yesterday's
luxuries into today's necessities, seduce people's minds away
from creative interests to the artificial and wasteful stimulation
of material wants, and drag down the mass media, especially
television and radio, to the lowest common denominator of a
tasteless market-place mentality?

On the other hand, without advertising, how can you guide
the consumer in the expenditure of his money? How do you
inform people about new and improved products? Won't you be
losing those many worthwhile added values that creative advertising superimposes upon a product? More important, without
the deplorable methods of advertising, is it still possible to stimulate wants, awaken the desire to spend, and thereby quicken
productivity upon which the prosperity of the nation depends?
While some observers were beginning to challenge the necessity
of an increasing Gross National Product, is a policy of checking
growth advisable? Without advertising, is it possible to introduce
new products, expand existing markets, generate new jobs, raise
the standard of living, and sustain a recession-defying growth
in the Gross National Product?

What gave these dilemmas a disturbing twist were the expanding opportunities for their expression and the increasing number
of people involved. Some critics were asking whether we had
reached the point at which we were beginning to make the
individual sick in order to make the economy healthy. The
daily clash was between the ideal of treating people honestly as

subjects and the reality of manipulating them hypocritically as objects. The dilemmas were intensified by the moral strain between values which honored man as a fellow human being and 'a new way of life' which exploited his responses for personal gain.

23

POLITICS

The political dilemma carries us deeper into the meaning of the success idea. All of us are alive to different loyalties in a pluralist society. We are Protestant, Catholic, or Jew; from the East, West, or South; big city or rural; immigrant or native; management or labor. Issues and circumstances from moment to moment shift the weight of our loyalties from one special-interest group to another. These endless divisions are vital for our democracy because they prevent any one special-interest group from ganging up on another and seizing all the power for itself. Multiple loyalties unite us as citizens by dividing us into groups.

One reason why a dilemma rather than a revolution emerged out of the political implications of the success idea was because success writers, especially apostles of the character ethic, and liberal reformers were really in agreement about the basic values of American society. Both agreed that it was good to get ahead, that honesty is the best policy, that the nation should provide equal opportunities, that 'true success' was a higher goal than material success. Indeed, it was the character ethic which articulated the means and goals of life which many liberal reformers adopted as standards to measure society's performance. Laying the canon of reality against the creed of success, these democratic reformers concluded that the American Dream was an illusion. But they came not as killers of the Dream's premises. They saw themselves as the saviors of its promises.

Gunnar Myrdal perceived in the 1940s that "the new immigrants, the Jews, and other disadvantaged and unpopular groups —could not possibly have invented a system of political ideals which better corresponded to their interests. So, by the logic of the unique American history, it was developed that the rich and secure, out of pride and conservatism, and the poor and insecure, out of dire need, have come to profess the identical social ideals. . . . This spiritual convergence . . . is what makes the nation great and what promises it a still greater future." The Socialist, Harold Laski, has pointed out, albeit somewhat ruefully, that "nowhere, in any society of major economic importance, have . . . the 'underprivileged' so fully accepted the assumptions upon which successful men have made their way to power." [1]

There were, of course, political critics outside the populist, progressive, and liberal mainstream for whom the success credo was rotten, neither capable of being saved, nor worth it. The revolutionary Marxist Socialists struck at the success idea from all angles. The great-man-in-the-process-of-becoming-great interpretation of history was translated into a class struggle between the owners of property and the property-less proletariat. The self-made man was no hero but a greedy exploiter of the poor with a fat cigar sticking out of his mouth and a gold watch chain encircling his bloated belly. 'Honesty is the best policy' was a sneering mockery in this decaying capitalistic system. For the Communists, there was only one way to move from an acquisitive to a classless society: Destroy the private ownership of the means of production. The immediate goal:The overthrow of the government by violence.

If the radical revolutionists, such as the Communists, advocated violence to secure change, the radical evolutionists stressed peaceful methods. Christian Socialists, like J. O. Bentall, hoped for a new economic system, achieved by the ballot box rather than by bullets. In their society, cooperation and love would replace competition and personal profit. A number of utopian communities actually abolished the capitalistic system by erasing private property and the profit motive. The nineteenth-century Aurora community in Oregon, for example, held property in common. The fruits of every man's labor flowed into a common treasury. What went into that treasury was according to every man's capacity; what flowed out of it was according to every man's needs. Like other attempts at idealistic, communal societies in America, secular or religious, scientific or romantic, it folded—though Aurora's light shone brightly for some twenty-five years.[2]

These movements have been insignificant in their consequences. It was the American consensus of shared values which was the glue that held together the puzzle of American civilization. Reformers in the populist, progressive, and liberal traditions did not want to rewrite America's favorite and conservative story; they only demanded that everyone have an opportunity to play hero. Compared to the European political experience within the past one hundred years, the battle was fought within a narrow ideological framework. Gradually, reformers settled upon the use of governmental powers, particularly the powers of the federal government, to equalize and enlarge the common man's opportunities to get ahead. Both reformers and conservatives in the twentieth century, sharing similar values, agreeing in their goals but differing in their policies for achieving the American Dream, were persuasive because each found its source of power in the ambivalent attitudes of the American people toward success.[3]

Reformers largely ignored individual success writers. They were dissenters with a political purpose and after bigger game —the ideas expressed by success writers which conservative groups were consistently exploiting to block reformist legislation.[4]

The reforming sociologist, Lester Frank Ward, set the stage in 1886 and joined the issue. Success in life, Ward asserted, is the product of two factors—qualities within the man and the social environment in which he lives. The real question is which of the two is more important. Unfortunately, "far greater praise is bestowed upon the internal than upon the external elements of success." The popular view is that success is limited by a scarcity of internal elements. This is a false view. "I venture to maintain that the rarity of success is chiefly due to the absence of its external elements . . . that the internal elements are not rare, but abundant, and that, if the external elements could be correspondingly supplied, what now pass for feats of genius would merely represent the normal activity of the race. . . . There is no need to search for talent. It exists already, and everywhere. The thing that is rare is opportunity, not ability." Furthermore, "there is no more vicious popular fallacy than that the powers of the mind are strengthened and improved by adversity. Everyone who has accomplished anything, against adverse circumstances, would have accomplished proportionately more had such circumstances been removed." The same holds true for competition. The struggle of mankind is like a lawn of grass which grows impoverished if it must compete with weeds, but flourishes when the competition with weeds is removed. Ward's plea was to expand opportunity, reduce obstacles, and diminish competition. How? By political legislation. "I regard the work of creating opportunities, by which gifted individuals can utilize their powers, as simply in the nature of police regulation, capable of being conducted by any body politic." [5]

For reformers, a self-made man was no more feasible than a self-fertilized egg. Men may indeed make circumstances, but the circumstances of life also make the man. It was the circumstances of crop failures, falling prices, and poor credit which produced the Populist movement of the 1890s. "You stand for the yearning, upward tendency of the middle and lower classes," the Populist leader, Tom Watson, told his followers. You are the "sworn foes of monopoly—not monopoly in the narrow sense of the word—but monopoly of power, of place, of privilege, of wealth, of progress." Watson recited the credo of the Populist agrarian reform movement when he charged: "Keep the avenues of honor free. Close no entrance to the poorest, the weakest, the humblest. Say to ambition everywhere, 'the field is clear, the contest fair; come, and win your share if you can!' " [6]

The great fear was that the gates of opportunity were snapping shut. The Populists, the Progressives in the 1900s, the supporters of Theodore Roosevelt's New Nationalism and Woodrow Wilson's New Freedom in the 1910s agreed with the success doctrine that men should get ahead by hard work and honesty in a climate of abundant opportunities. These reformist movements, much like the Jacksonian revolt before the Civil War, were not anti-capitalist but anti-privilege, not against wealth but against the corrupt acquisition of wealth. They did not call for the right to equal rewards and guaranteed results but the right to an equal access to the rewards. Let's play the careerist game, they agreed with the conservatives, but not with a crooked deal from a stacked deck of monopoly, legislative favors to special interests, bribery, and the arrogant exercise of economic power. All these outrages were a tissue of machinations against the promise of American life.

A worried Woodrow Wilson in the early 1910s voiced the nagging concern, always deep in the pride of his countrymen, that America might be losing its uniqueness and going the way of Europe: "This is the country which has lifted to the admiration of the world its ideals of absolutely free opportunity, where no man is supposed to be under any limitation except the limitations of his character and of his mind; where there is supposed to be no distinction of class, no distinction of blood, no distinction of social status, but where men win or lose on their merits. I lay it very close to my own conscience as a public man whether we can any longer stand at our doors and welcome all newcomers upon those terms." Wilson called for laws to bring American society into line with its credo, to heal the wound between the belief in equal opportunity and the reality of restrictions on ascent. The purpose of reform was to exercise political power to create for each individual, in the facts of existence, the success idea's visionary description of social and economic conditions.[7]

During the 1920s critical attention was drawn away from political action to the quality of American life, to the social and intellectual consequences of the success complex. By 1932, however, Franklin D. Roosevelt was telling a bewildered, fearful nation that "a glance at the situation today only too clearly indicates that equality of opportunity as we have known it no longer exists." From the depths of the depression the New Deal struggled to equalize and enlarge individual opportunity threatened by the concentration of economic power and to ensure ethical means to the accumulation of wealth. The New Deal, then the Fair Deal of the late 1940s and the New Frontier and Great Society of the 1960s vastly expanded the powers of the federal government to strike at the injustices of American life. The ideological clash between reformers and conservatives, with respect to the success idea, was joined over whether the New Deal and Fair Deal, in particular, were creating conditions to make the success idea a reality or were pushing through legislation to destroy its promise.[8]

Shock troops of opinion supported the long history of reformist legislation to make success literature an accurate description of American life. Journalists, essayists, and social scientists struck hard at the legend that 'honesty is the best policy' by exposing the methods which business tycoons used to heap up their riches. In the 1900s journalism's muckraking crusade drove deep into the American mind the image of the business titan. He was ruthless to his competitors, irresponsible to society, and choked with greed as he clawed his way up the ladder of success, praying one day a week and preying the other six, keeping the Sabbath and everything else he could lay his hands on, obeying only the law of the jungle while breaking all the rest.

To the inflammatory emotionalism of the muckrakers, professional historians and economists added the appearance of scientific objectivity. They descended from their ivory towers into an arena where ideas were beginning to crack conservative absolutes. Historians like Charles Beard invoked an economic interpretation of politics in the 1910s to question the motivations behind the shaping of the sacrosanct Constitution of the United States. During the 1920s a debunking group of historians and journalists mocked the revered heroes of the American past by pricking the bubble of their reputations with satirical stilettos. But it was not until the depression of the 1930s, when Main Street turned bitterly on Wall Street, that a larger number of the nation's productive historians began reexamining the role of the big businessman in exploiting the laborer, deepening depressions, and starting wars. Scholars, joined by free-lance journalists, took a hard look at the 'Robber Barons.' "Behind every great fortune there is a crime," the saying went, and an old English rhyme took on new meaning for both the past and the present:

> The law locks up both man and woman
> Who steals the goose from off the common,
> But lets the greater felon loose,
> Who steals the common from the goose.

During the 1930s and 1940s much of American history was rewritten with a decided sympathy for the evolutionary contribution of Populism, Progressivism, and the New Deal. Textbook history on the college level was largely interpreted throughout the twentieth century (with a pause in the 1920s) as the relationship between politics and economics. Since political history is at its dullest when conservatives are in power, and its liveliest when liberals are in command, American history in the twentieth century was told largely in terms of reformist administrations enacting social justice legislation for the general welfare by regulating corporate power and taxing the possessing classes. As it filtered down to a generation of college students, the 'goodies' were those who supported the Jeffersonian ends of human rights secured by the Hamiltonian means of a strong government. The moral implications were unavoidable. The reforming groups were for the defenseless underdogs, for social justice and human welfare. The 'baddies' were for the Hamiltonian ends of property rights.

If some historians and economists questioned the means by which the business elite amassed their 'riches,' other social scientists were taking a critical look at the 'rags' in which big business leaders began their ascent. Sociologists, joined by historians and economists, dug into the social origins of the business elite, surveyed the entire class structure in America, and questioned the reality of equal opportunity. This type of attack on the postulates of the success idea had always been a matter of undocumented opinion, easily beaten down by conservatives, especially during prosperous times. Measured judgment by trained social scientists exposing the discrepancy between credo and fact was something else, even though some of their findings were later challenged by other social scientists.

In 1925 Pitirim Sorokin examined the lives of over six hundred of America's wealthiest men. He concluded that "the wealthy class of the United States is becoming less and less open, more and more closed, and is tending to be transformed into a caste-like group." Several years later Taussig and Joslyn undermined the legend that business leaders hurdled the obstacle of poverty in their rise to wealth. They offered statistics to prove that "the present generation of American business leaders has been recruited in greater part from the sons of business men, and only to a minor extent from the sons of farmers and manual laborers." If Taussig and Joslyn's conclusions were boldly critical of the success idea, their explanation for the conclusions were not. They suggested that "lack of native ability rather than lack of opportunity is primarily responsible for the failure of the lower occupational classes to be as well represented as the higher classes." [9]

Throughout the 1930s, 1940s and early 1950s a number of respected social scientists were asserting that mobility was decreasing and class lines were hardening. The Lynds took another look at Middletown and decided that "the chance for the mass of the population to 'go up in the world' to affluence and independence appears to be shrinking noticeably." In the years after World War II Clyde Kluckhohn was certain that "the facts indicate that rapid rise through sheer ability and industry is much more difficult than it was a generation or two ago. Status is harder to achieve by one's own initiative and easier to acquire through family connections." Robert K. Merton continued the historical judgment: "The 'office-boy-to-president' imagery was once in approximate accord with the facts, in the loose sense that vertical mobility was probably more common then than now." William Miller returned to a statistical study of the business elite during the first decade of the twentieth century and proposed another explanation for Taussig and Joslyn's conclusion that lack of native ability rather than lack of opportunity

explained why the lower classes were not so well represented in
the business elite. The reason why "poor immigrant and poor
farm boys together are shown to have made up no more than
three per cent" of the business elite he studied, Miller asserted,
was not genetic but environmental. Gregory and Neu reached
back to the nineteenth century and threw down the challenge:

> Was the typical industrial leader of the 1870s,
> then, a "new man," an escape from the slums
> of Europe or from the paternal farm? Did he rise
> by his own efforts from a boyhood of poverty?
> Was he as innocent of education and of formal
> training as has often been alleged? He seems to
> have been none of these things. American by
> birth, of a New England father, English in na-
> tional origin, Congregational, Presbyterian, or
> Episcopal in religion, urban in early environ-
> ment, he was rather born and bred in an atmos-
> phere in which business and a relatively high
> social standing were intimately associated with
> his family life. Only at about eighteen did he take
> his first regular job, prepared to rise from it,
> moreover, not by a rigorous apprenticeship
> begun when he was virtually a child, but by an
> academic education well above average for the
> times.[10]

Shifting to his own times, C. Wright Mills was certain in the
early 1950s that America was developing an "increasingly
limited structure of opportunity," while W. Lloyd Warner reported that "there is strong proof now that the American worker,
as well as others, can no longer expect to advance and achieve
success with anything like the same probability as did his father
and grandfather." Other social scientists, such as J. O. Hertzler,
confirmed the gloomy view: "Upward mobility . . . is becoming
more difficult." [11]

The *coup de grâce* to one part of the American Dream was
executed by Lipset and Bendix in the late 1950s. From the
beginning, Americans had pridefully assumed that the New
World was unique in its bountiful offerings of opportunity for

the working man to rise in the world. Europe was encrusted with the weight of feudal traditions and discrimination in favor of the well-born; America was a special invitation to the common man to compete for rewards on the basis of merit. Lipset and Bendix sought to smash the uniqueness of the Dream by claiming that between America and industrialized Europe there were no significant differences in the rates of mobility as measured by individuals crossing the line between the manual working class and the non-manual middle class. The rate of mobility from working class to middle class was not determined by any special quality in the New World but by the occupational structure of industrialism which was common to all developed nations in Western Civilization.[12]

The shock troops of the social sciences, whatever their motivation, softened up the dogma of conservatism so that political liberals could more justifiably lay down a barrage of regulatory and welfare-state legislation. If huge fortunes were tainted at their source, then the rights of private property were less sacrosanct. If illegal methods of gain had been used to accumulate wealth, then the need to regulate big business was indisputable. If opportunity was not equal, if mobility was decreasing and class lines hardening, then legislative action was mandatory. Americans believed in achievement by merit for unequal rewards under conditions of equal opportunity. But if achievement was by a privileged class under conditions of marked unequal opportunity, then the only power available, government, must be used to tax great wealth and regulate monopolistic corporations so that life chances once again could become more equal.

The vast body of success literature, as we have seen in earlier chapters, was largely indifferent to the political implications of its ideology. The effect, however, was a support for the *status quo* after the middle decades of the nineteenth century. Dedicated conservatives vigorously exploited this effect in books and comic strips, stockholder statements and bank fliers, reinforcing and expanding the inspirational advice of success literature into a doctrine of political conservatism in defense of propertied interests.

The history of the American conservative in the twentieth century is a drama of the reluctant accepting the unthinkable. As the nation seemed to be staggering along toward socialism, the conservative could only pray that he would not get all the government he was paying for. The conservative stood for a limited government, sound dollar, and a free-market economy. He stressed frugality in government and the freedom of the individual from governmental restraints. Increasingly business conservatives were forced to come down from their ivory tower of action into the market place of ideas.

Both liberal reformers (as opposed to the radical Left) and conservatives (as opposed to the lunatic Right) were democratic to the core, but they stressed different elements in the American democratic faith. Liberals emphasized social justice and equality while conservatives stressed the freedom of the responsible individual to work with a minimum of regulation and a maximum return from his effort. As the liberal attacked from his democratic position, the conservative counterattacked from his, justifying with the construct of the success idea unequal rewards of money and property in a system of free enterprise.

Conservatives kept insisting that there was a direct connection between merit and achievement. But more important than merit, which could be interpreted as an advantage inherited at birth, were those personal qualities available to everyone whatever unequal gifts God had assigned them—hard work and persistence. Success was not bred in the bone; if anywhere, it was bred in the home.

"My father started me milking cows while I was still a small boy," Leonard E. Read, a theorist for conservatism, recalled in the early 1960s. "I learned the relationship between hard work and a quart of milk. All else in economics is but embellishment of this primary lesson." Reflected industrialist Henry J. Kaiser in the 1940s: "My mother used to say to me from the days of my earliest memories, 'Henry, nothing ever is accomplished without work. If I left you nothing else but a will to work, I would leave you the most priceless gift.'" The best helping hand is the one at the end of your shirtsleeve. As one pepigram in a bank flier to depositors asserted: "Success is a ladder which cannot be climbed with your hands in your pockets." [13]

Unlike liberalism's gloomy tale of injustices and inequalities, conservatism's cheerful story started with a poor boy in humble beginnings and ended with a triumph. The self-made man, whether nudged by vanity, an earnest public relations department, or simply by the wonder and gratitude for what his country had made possible for him, told how the American Dream had once again come true through him. Rich nen's sons did their best to qualify. When Raymond C. Firestone, son of founder Harvey S. Firestone, was elevated to board chairman of the Firestone Tire and Rubber Company in 1966, the *New York Times* carefully noted that Raymond "started work with the company in 1933 as a gas station attendant." [14]

Patricians who became reformers, like Franklin D. Roosevelt, were accused of selling out their class. Self-made men who started at the bottom were somehow classless. Who better expressed that view than the baldheaded billionaire in a dinner jacket, the rugged individualist of fluctuating fortune who always made it back to fabulous wealth—Daddy Warbucks. Since the 1920s, Daddy Warbucks has been the comic-strip foster father of Little Orphan Annie, and since the 1930s, with Annie and her dog Sandy ("arf! arf!"), he has been snapping at the New Deal and its liberal successors. Little Orphan Annie's creator, Harold Gray, so irritated the Communist *Daily Worker* that it retorted with its own comic strip, Little Lefty. While Annie, Daddy Warbucks, and Sandy were alerting the nation to the collectivist perils of the welfare state, Little Lefty and his dog, Spunky, who could talk, were getting in their licks against laissez-faire capitalism. But Little Lefty and Spunky could never properly accuse Daddy Warbucks of not being one of the people.

In a 1955 strip, Daddy Warbucks returns to his home town after a long absence. He visits his old Irish friend, Mike, who still lives in the poor shack where he was brought up. Mike tells Gray's Sunday morning readers in this strip what a democracy is all about as he lectures in an Irish brogue to his fabulously wealthy friend: "Ye've always *loved* th' teemin' millions who niver earn more 'n a meager livin'—but ye never yearned or struggled to *be wan* of 'em! Ye started yir life here, in poverty —and have been iver satisfied to earn and spind millions—not to strive indlessly to attain mediocrity! But at heart ye *are* one of us ordinary wans—y'can niver change!" And Daddy Warbucks says: "I never thought of it that way, Mike—but I hope you're right—." [15]

How is it possible, the conservative wondered, to have a class struggle when men like Daddy Warbucks and his colleagues love the teeming millions from whom they have risen by individual merit? Who knows, in a society of achieved rather than ascribed status, it may have been Mike who was wearing the dinner jacket while Warbucks was still living in the shack. The rich, the middle class, and the poor were bound together by an identity of democratic values which cared little for the distinctions of social class.

Capital and labor were bound together, or should be, by an identity of economic interests. Historian David Potter touched the feeling that conservatives liked to encourage when he observed: "Few Americans feel entirely at ease with the slogan 'Soak the rich,' but the phrase 'Deal me in' springs spontaneously and joyously to American lips." The big game in which everyone was dealt a fair hand was the free enterprise system. The self-made man was a hero, and it was the free enterprise system of capitalism which made his heroism possible. But this was no environmental interpretation of reformers stressing the importance of external factors over internal qualities. If it was the environment of a free economy which made possible the triumph of the self-made man, it was not the environment which deterministically decided who was to be great. Those who broke away from the pack did so because of qualities within themselves. [16]

What of luck? The conservative view denounced the belief that luck controls success because it challenged the cause-effect relationship between merit and achievement. If amoral luck handed out the rewards of success in society, then chance, not personal qualities, determined who was to be successful. The successful were then only lucky, not deserving. If they were not personally deserving, then perhaps they did not deserve the rewards they received from society. Success, after all, was the expression of a system of inequalities. Inequalities are more persuasively justifiable if they are earned inequalities.

When Sears, Roebuck and Company's Julius Rosenwald launched his widely quoted remark in 1929 that success was 95 per cent luck and 5 per cent ability, conservatives were distressed. Rosenwald had said that any number of men who worked for him could run his business just as well as he could. "They did not get the breaks—that's the only difference between them and me." The *Iron Age* struck back in an editorial. Rosenwald may be successful and he may be lovable, but his views were erroneous and mischievous. "If financial success were chiefly a matter of luck," *Iron Age* got right to the point, "there would be strong grounds for the surtaxes that governments so savagely levy on large incomes, for the voraciousness of unionized labor, and for the leveling processes of Socialistic doctrine. This is indeed the very negation of the theory that men get what they earn or earn what they get. . . . A man's earning capacity is a rough measure of his ability." [17]

The theme of opportunity was persistent. In 1903, the merchant, Louis Stern, promised that "chances are better now than they ever were." In 1961, just about the richest man in America, J. Paul Getty, assured the readers of *Playboy* that "there is a tremendous mass of evidence to prove that imaginative, resourceful and dynamic young men have more opportunities to achieve wealth and success in business today than ever before in our history." [18]

A number of scholars were challenging those shock troops of the social sciences whose findings could be interpreted as support for reformist objectives. Was mobility decreasing and were class lines really hardening in America? The President of the New York Stock Exchange obviously didn't think so, and he called on W. Lloyd Warner to prove it. "Many of our sociologist . . . ," Stock Exchange President G. Keith Funston said in 1955, "have been saying in recent years that opportunity is decreasing. One of them was Professor W. Lloyd Warner of the

University of Chicago who in 1952 wrote that 'there is strong proof now that the American worker ... can no longer expect to achieve success with anything like the same probability as did his father and grandfather.' But Professor Warner has just completed a survey which proves just the opposite, and he has been man enough to admit his former error. Last week he announced that his new research showed that 'the sons of men from the wrong side of the tracks are finding their way increasingly to the places of power and prestige in business.' " Indeed, Warner did reverse himself and concluded that his research indicated that "at the levels studied here American society is not becoming more castelike; the recruitment of business leaders from the bottom is taking place now and seems to be increasing. Mobility to the top is not decreasing; in fact, for the last quarter-century it has been slowly increasing." [19]

Other social scientists pointed out during the 1950s and 1960s that if the success idea's vision of opportunity and the class structure were fanciful, the critics had pushed the pendulum too far. If the class structure was not as open as the apologists claimed, it was less rigid than the critics affirmed. In historical perspective the distance between classes appeared to be shrinking, visible differences between classes were diminishing, and mobility was increasing.

Social scientists were drawing more meaningful distinctions between the intragenerational mobility of a man in his own lifetime and the intergenerational mobility of a son surpassing his father. Social mobility was also seen as not only promotion to a better job but the accumulation of property. In comparative perspective, Stephan Thernstrom labelled "bold and dubious" the implications of Lipset and Bendix's conclusion that there were no significant differences between America and industrialized Europe in the rates of mobility from manual working class to non-manual middle class. The conclusion considered only occupational mobility and ignored property mobility, i.e. the possession of property. It measured intergenerational mobility between father and son but disregarded intragenerational mobility as well as rates of mobility within the two very broad classes of manual and non-manual. "Certainly it is premature to dismiss entirely," Thernstrom protested, "the old belief that the opportunity level in the United States has been higher than in Europe." Other scholars were wondering how European visitors for over a hundred years, comparing their class system to the American, could all be wrong.[20]

Revisionist historians with professional credentials counterattacked in the 1940s, 1950s, and 1960s. They assaulted the 'Robber Baron' interpretation of big-business leadership. "In the past," Allan Nevins chided in the early 1950s, "our historians tended to a feminine idealism. They were apologetic about dollars, our race to wealth, our materialism. . . . They spoke scornfully of the robber barons, who were not robber barons at all. . . ." If the tycoons who emerged from the pages of revisionist history bore little resemblance to the "good guys" of success literature, they were considerably more admirable than the "bad guys" pictured by the critics of business leadership during the Gilded Age. "The architects of our material growth—," Nevins boldly proclaimed, "the men like Whitney, McCormick, Westinghouse, Rockefeller, Carnegie, Hill, and Ford—will yet stand forth in their true stature as builders, for all their faults, of a strength which civilization found indispensable." [21]

Amidst all the waste and brutality, the revisionist historians contended, the entrepreneur was a risk-taking innovator with limited capital responding in a free society to the cutthroat competition of the times. He harnessed vast natural resources, built factories, railroads, and financial institutions, and provided the organizing skill to increase the wealth of the nation. There were rogues among the business leaders, but the best were the great men of their time. With courage, ability, and a zest for achievement, they plunged into that arena of life which offered the most exciting opportunities for adventure and challenge. Their contribution to the growth of American civilization was at once indispensable and immeasurable.[22]

The decisive issue was how to justify differential success. How do you vindicate unequal rewards in a society? The modern conservative is not really very modern, John Kenneth Galbraith taunted in the 1960s. He is engaged in "one of man's oldest, best financed, most applauded and, on the whole, least successful exercises in moral philosophy. That is the search for a truly superior moral justification for selfishness." [23]

Was success just another name for selfishness? The idea of success in the nineteenth century had insisted that you must make good in order to do good. The stewardship of wealth doctrine called for the unselfish philanthropic dispensing of money to those who were less fortunate or deserved a chance. The stewardship doctrine was no elitist philosophy raising barriers to the admission of the worthy. Nor was it an aristocratic social class conservatism of a closed establishment. It represented a democratic economic class conservatism of achieved rather than ascribed status. The paradox, of course, is that as the stewardship principle declined as a justification for success, its actual usefulness to conservative interests increased. When inheritance taxes skyrocketed during the New Deal, tax-deductible donations to foundations and charities permitted propertied interests to maintain control over their money. The alternative was to have their funds taxed to fill governmental coffers for ends frequently at variance with their own political and economic convictions. Yet, the stewardship doctrine was really rather paternalistic and not a very effective defense for achievement amidst the egalitarian urges of the middle decades of the twentieth century.

The businessman, H. L. Mencken once observed, "is the only man above the hangman and the scavenger who is forever apologising for his occupation. He is the only one who always seeks to make it appear, when he attains the object of his labors, i.e., the making of a great deal of money, that it was not the object of his labors." Arnold Toynbee has observed that one of man's deepest religious needs is "a purpose transcending his petty personal aims." That need, in the words of Lucien Romier, explains why "the gospel of 'making money' has developed here the most preachy, the most 'moral' people in the world." Yet what moral purpose could there be in the self-seeking pursuit of profits? "He Profits Most Who Serves Best," answered Rotary for the business community. "Service Above Self." The service concept was a blending of Adam Smith's comforting assurance that the pursuit of self-interest adds up to the general good with the Christian command that one must give in order to receive and that he who is greatest is the servant of all.[24]

"Service," Henry Luce pointed out for the twentieth-anniversary issue of *Fortune* in 1950, "is not a kind of blackmail paid to representatives of social morality; it is the way money is made. Service is what the typical American businessman would do his best to render even if there weren't a cop or a preacher in sight. The businessman makes money in America, typically, by serving his fellow man in ways his fellow man wants to be served." [25]

In the success idea, the concept of service was a justification for achievement. In the ideology of conservatism, it was a justification for business profits as well. The service concept cleansed the profit motive of gross selfishness. Individual success and business profits were a consequence of service *pro bono publico*. The success of an individual and the profits of a business measured the contribution of each to the public good.

The success creed supported the conservative defense against the attacks of liberal reformers in the twentieth century. One postulate in the success creed was not exploited by conservatives, yet its importance in diminishing resentment against the *status quo* was immeasurable. If each individual was responsible for his own success, then there was no excuse for failure. But how could the masses of people who were downward mobile, or considered themselves less than a success, endure the shame and guilt? Would they not be driven to blame conditions rather than themselves for their low achievement? Would they not eagerly follow the call of reformers to use political power to regulate and equalize American society?

The success idea, particularly the character ethic, insisted that 'true success' was a higher goal than material success. Happiness, peace of mind, or self-respect were more noble ends than making money. From a humanitarian viewpoint, 'true success' was comforting and merciful. From a political viewpoint, it was an adaptive mechanism which drained away discontent by raising a goal which was above material success and which could be measured subjectively by the individual rather than objectively by the community. Further, the suspicion that the rich are miserable with their riches was an illusion which the poor used to reconcile themselves to their poverty. 'True success' was an opiate of the people.

There were two postulates in the conservative defense which were not contained in the success idea. One was the importance of incentive and the other the nature of freedom. Both, however, were implied assumptions of the success idea.

The bedrock assumption of the conservative defense was that individuals worked hardest and best when there was the incentive of a direct connection between achievement and reward. To diminish reward would reduce effort and ultimately weaken the strength of the nation. For the conservative, it was the free-enterprise system based on private property which had built the country. The free-enterprise system was no longer free to make the country greater if the government diminished ambition by destroying the incentive of its enterprisers—whether they be owner-managers or corporate managers.

"There is no doubt that this country is better off today than any other in the world," affirmed Lawrence Fertig in 1961. "But who and what is responsible for this? Government did not do it. Planning by federal agencies did not do it. It is due solely to the institutions of private capitalism, to *individual* work, to thrift, to enterprise, to production, to capital accumulation and investment." The managing director of the National Association of Manufacturers, Earl Bunting, knew what the spur to production was: "It is the profit incentive that energizes man's creative faculties and continually opens up new fields and new opportunities." [26]

Especially from the 1930s through the 1950s, conservative businessmen hammered away at the federal government as the Great Equalizer. Franklin D. Roosevelt's New Deal soon began to rub like sandpaper on their nerve ends. The push for equality often looked to them suspiciously like hatred of the rich masquerading as love for the poor. In the conservative mind you could not hurry history, and history was being driven to extremes. The enforced equality of the graduated income tax was striking at financial incentive. For the conservative, incentive was stimulated by reward scaled to individual effort and excellence. Money was the symbolic reward for the businessman as fame for the artist and critical approval for the scholar. Just as the prestige of a university was determined by the reputation of its faculty, so the profits of a business were determined by the competence of its management. The faculty, not the students, set the quality of a university; management, not the workers or 'forces,' was the key factor in a successful business. Dull the reward of management and you dull the drive to produce.

"It is distressing to see financial incentives weakened by ever more steeply progressive personal income taxes," lamented Du Pont's Crawford H. Greenewalt in 1951. The president of Du Pont rushed on to justify personal self-interest in terms of the national self-interest. "If financial incentive is the strongest of the incentives we have to offer, it must of necessity follow that the nation's vigor will be weakened by its removal. And it is for the nation, not the individual, that we should be primarily concerned." [27]

Welfare-state coddling was equally damaging. Charles E. Wilson, Eisenhower's Secretary of Defense and former boss of General Motors, blurted out what corporate public relations writers had so often softened into euphemisms. "I've got a lot of sympathy for people where a sudden change catches them," Wilson admitted. "But I've always liked bird dogs better than kennel-fed dogs myself—you know, one who'll get out and hunt for food rather than sit on his fanny and yell." Left-wing mischief-makers of the welfare state were encouraging the outstretched hand rather than the rolled-up sleeve. The decentralization litany was consistent and clear: The federal government should not do what the states can do, the states should not do what local governments can do, and no government should do for the individual what he can do for himself.[28]

A more serious charge than sapping individual initiative and a slavish dependency on the welfare state was the invasion of individual freedom by the tyranny of government. Reformers, particularly since the 1930s, had argued that government regulation and taxation were justified by the cause of human rights.

This was an appealing argument because everyone was for human rights. But conservatives pointed out that setting off human rights against property rights was a false dichotomy. "There are no rights but human rights," countered Paul L. Poirot, "and what are spoken of as property rights are only the human rights of individuals to property. . . . The issue is not one of property rights versus human rights, but of the human rights of one person in the community versus the human rights of another." [29]

The right to property is an absolute, essential to a free society. To take from an individual his rewards is to take from him what is rightfully his for the doubtful benefit of someone else. It is to deprive him of his freedom. The solution to economic inequality is to enlarge the pie, not to equalize the shares.[30]

The political dilemma of the success idea emerged out of a conflict between political equality and economic inequality. On the one hand, how to prevent majority rule, interested in social justice and the redistribution of wealth through welfare-state egalitarianism, from violating the minority rights of property? On the other hand, how to regulate the power of property used for the privilege of vested interests? How to preserve the right of equal opportunity without equalizing rewards? How to safeguard the right that he who plants the seed should reap the fruit while at the same time guaranteeing the equal right of everyone to plant a seed?

To put the political dilemma of freedom vs. equality another way: If the government limits itself to maintaining order and enforcing contracts in a market economy of the least restraints, then the individual will have the largest play of freedom to enjoy his rewards stimulated by maximum incentives. However, equal opportunity cannot be assured without regulation. The public sector cannot be financed without taxation of private property.

Yet, if the government increasingly involves itself in the lives of individual citizens, business, and the professions through regulation, taxation, and subsidies, then the freedom of the individual is restricted, incentive is diminished, and priorities are set by government edict rather than free-market choice resulting in the possibility of bureaucratic oppression. However, the consequences may be desirable. More equal conditions of opportunity are sustained, the services of the public sector, such as education, conservation, and urban assistance, are adequately financed, and social justice becomes a viable goal.

The central political issue in the twentieth century, waged decade after decade, has been to hold these contending affirmations of American values in some kind of democratic balance.

24

"BEWARE OF THE
MAN WHO RISES TO POWER
FROM ONE SUSPENDER"

For three-quarters of a century the critics within the political dilemma we have just examined focused on the *quantity* of American life. Their passion was for *opportunity*, and their concern was for *people* and the *good society*, though with the opposing conservatives they held *shared values*. Their discipline was the *social sciences*, especially politics. Within the get-ahead gospel their attention was directed at the *means to success* and its corollaries. Rather than grumble about the materialism of success, they argued that not enough Americans shared in that materialism.

For over a century another group of dissenters we are about to examine have deplored the impact of success on the *quality* of American life. Their passion was for *freedom*. Their concern was with the *individual* and the *good life* and they held *uncongenial values* with the mainstream of their society. Their discipline was the *humanities* and their focus was on *'true success.'*

We begin with the patricians, for whom certain consequences of the Industrial Revolution were scarcely bearable. If political reformers were concerned about the rejected underprivileged at the bottom of the heap, the patricians were distresesed at the possibility of accepting those who had found their way to the top. "A less interesting crowd I do not care to encounter," sniffed Boston Brahmin Charles Francis Adams in his *Autobiography* of 1916. "I have known, and known tolerably well, a good many 'successful' men—'big' financially—men famous during the last half-century. . . . Not one that I have ever known would I care to meet again, either in this world or the next; nor is one of them associated in my mind with the idea of humor, thought or refinement. A set of mere money-getters and traders . . . unattractive and uninteresting." Adams, a patrician with business experience as a railroad president, admitted that he was "a little puzzled to account for the instances I have seen of business success—money-getting. It comes from a rather low instinct." In any case, "certainly, so far as my observation goes, it is rarely met with in combination with the finer or more interesting traits of character." His brother, Henry Adams, executed the *coup de grâce:* "America," he loftily contended, "contained scores of men worth five millions or upwards whose lives were no more worth living than those of their cooks." [1]

The patrician attack echoed the traditional European growling about America. Europeans have long mocked with lofty scorn the money-grubbing nature of American life. The British observer Thomas Colley Grattan concluded, over one hundred years ago, in 1859, that the mental capabilities of young American businessmen had been "cribbed into narrow limits. There is constant activity going on in one small portion of the brain; all the rest is stagnant. The money-making faculty is alone cultivated. They are incapable of acquiring general knowledge on a broad or liberal scale. All is confined to trade, finance, law, and small, local provincial information. Art, Science, literature, are nearly dead letters to them." Seventy years ago a visiting minister, Ian Maclaren, reported that "nowhere is such importance attached to the amount of money which a man has acquired or possesses. . . . [The] dollar is a monotonous refrain in conversation." Quantity was not always quality, the biggest was not necessarily the best, the wealthiest could be the poorest in the things that really count. To vulgarize the world was the mission of America. [2]

The patrician in America, however, liked to think that he, at least, was not kneeling before what William James called in a letter to H. G. Wells in 1906 "the bitch-goddess SUCCESS" with her "squalid cash interpretation." The patrician was, after all, not only a gentleman of breeding, but of intellect. Snapped Theodore Roosevelt: "I am simply unable to make myself take the attitude of respect toward the very wealthy men which such an enormous multitude of people evidently really feel. I am delighted to show any courtesy to Pierpont Morgan or Andrew Carnegie or James J. Hill, but as for regarding any one of them, as for instance, I regard Professor Bury, or Peary, the Arctic explorer, or Rhodes, the historian—why, I could not force myself to do it, even if I wanted to, which I don't." [3]

In the Gilded Age and the Edwardian 1900s, unlettered men with their boring talk of prideful profits from factories were presuming upon the natural superiority of a family background supported by commerce and the land. The 'Outs' were threatening the power and esteem of the 'Ins,' and while that little game was nothing new in the nation's history, at no time previously had so many 'Outs' become so powerful so fast. The patrician was both to the manor and the manner born. He represented an elite polished by a classical education and wealth from childhood. Money had always somehow just been there, old money made by East Coast ancestors in commerce or by landed aristocrats on Southern plantations. In the South, for generations after the Civil War, the patrician response did effectively crush the spirit of business enterprise. In the North, as the Industrial Revolution rolled over America, the patrician resistance was like a matchstick trying to hold back a tidal wave.

Patricians may have shuddered at the acquisitive drive, but they never underestimated the fruits which multiplied from that gross motive. The base nature of money-getting was never confused with the privileges of money-having. Money was essential to purchase the education and leisure without which one could not act the patrician. Family background without money was like a handsome carriage dragged by tired horses. The American Victorian patrician, like his upper-class British counterpart, presumed that under the fire of economic reverses blood would tell. He could rise from 'reduced circumstances' to riches if he really had to. "Some kind of pace may be got out of the veriest jade by the near prospect of oats," James Russell Lowell proudly declared, "but the thorough-bred has the spur in his blood." [4]

The patricians who felt a sense of repugnance at the pushy new rich included the gentleman of taste and learning, the fallen aristocrat, the frightened community leader, and the sufferer from wounded *noblesse oblige*. John Hancock Otis, in Edgar Lee Masters' Midwestern town of Spoon River, raised a warning finger:

> As to democracy, fellow citizens,
> Are you not prepared to admit
> That I, who inherited riches and was to the manner
>   born,
> Was second to none in Spoon River
> In my devotion to the cause of Liberty?
> While my contemporary, Anthony Findlay,
> Born in a shanty and beginning life
> As a water carrier to the section hands,
> Then becoming a section hand when he was grown,
> Afterwards foreman of the gang, until he rose
> To the superintendency of the railroad,
> Living in Chicago,
> Was a veritable slave driver,
> Grinding the faces of labor,
> And a bitter enemy of democracy.
> And I say to you, Spoon River,
> And to you, O Republic,
> Beware of the man who rises to power
> From one suspender. [5]

And who can forget the plight of Edwin Arlington Robinson's Miniver Cheevy, whose visions of a romantic past paralyzed his will to action?

> Miniver scorned the gold he sought,
>   But sore annoyed was he without it;
> Miniver thought, and thought, and thought,
>   And thought about it.
>
> Miniver Cheevy, born too late,
>   Scratched his head and kept on thinking;
> Miniver coughed, and called it fate,
>   And kept on drinking. [6]

One of the smoothest expressions of the patrician haughtiness towards the self-made man came from the pen of that urbane Boston Brahmin, Oliver Wendell Holmes, Sr. Our own age cries "snob" to *The Autocrat of the Breakfast-Table,* but Holmes' reflections had a hard democratic core. Class lines in the nineteenth century were sharper than today. The upper class of family and wealth was not afraid to call itself the best people. It was an elite which cherished honor, now replaced by the more business-like word "integrity," and which tried to establish and measure up to, at least in public view, honored standards of conduct, learning, and taste.

"Of course everybody likes and respects self-made men," Holmes observed in the *Autocrat* in 1858. "It is a great deal better to be made in that way than not to be made at all." A self-made man "deserves more credit, if that is all, than the regular engine-turned article, shaped by the most approved pattern, and French-polished by society and travel. But as to saying that one is every way the equal of the other, that is another matter. The right of strict social discrimination of all things and persons, according to their merits, native or acquired, is one of the most precious republican privileges. I take the liberty to exercise it when I say that, *other things being equal,* in most relations of life I prefer a man of family."

What does Holmes mean by a "man of family"? He should have behind him four or five generations of gentlemen and gentlewomen, some family portraits, books, silver, and an appropriate study to house his inheritance. "No, my friends, I go (always, other things being equal) for the man who inherits family traditions and the cumulative humanities of at least four or five generations. Above all things, as a child, he should have tumbled about in a library. All men are afraid of books, who have not handled them from infancy." Holmes was no stuffed shirt puffed up with princely assumptions about the importance of place. His appeal was to free choice. "One may, it is true, have all the antecedents I have spoken of, and yet be a boor or a shabby fellow. One may have none of them, and yet be fit for councils and courts. Then let them change places. Our social arrangement has this great beauty, that its strata shift up and down as they change specific gravity, without being clogged by layers of prescription. But I still insist on my democratic liberty of choice, and I go for the man with the gallery of family portraits against the one with the twenty-five-cent daguerreotype, unless I find out that the last is the better of the two." [7]

For many patricians, the trouble with the self-made man was not so much that he was self-made, but that he so often did such a bad job of it.

In the view of success writers, the race for success was a thrilling opportunity to live up to the best within oneself. For some dissenters, the race was a rat race in which the rats were winning.

If we examined all the novels on the success theme published within the past one hundred years, we would see variations all the way from the shining hero overcoming obstacles to the ruthless monster gouging others to achieve his ends. The monster is caricatured mostly in 'slick' fiction. He is the ogre-ish business or professional man who has icepicked his way up the ladder of success over the fallen bodies of those he has used or betrayed. Some of this fiction occasionally rises to the level of satire; the worst of it is like a political cartoon. The caricature of intended distortions which makes a political cartoon good, makes literature bad. Many of the heels in these novels would not only sell their grandmother down the river, but, in the end, not deliver her.

In a sense it is true, as many students of the novel have concluded, that novelists writing about the businessman used carbolic acid rather than ink in their pens. Robert A. Kavesh has observed that in the twentieth-century novel, "business has loomed as a giant conspiracy and the businessman as a greedy opportunist or a vulgar and insensitive materialist." Charlotte Georgi has commented that since the 1920s, "the pattern for the businessman in fiction is set as either the grasping villain or the unimaginative dolt." [8]

Yet, the interpretation lacks refinement. "The question," Henry Higgins scolded Liza Doolittle in George Bernard Shaw's *Pygmalion*, "is not whether I treat you rudely, but whether you ever heard me treat anyone else better." America's better novelists have not been known consistently to bring out the violins for any occupational group, with the exception, perhaps, of prostitutes. Indeed, one can think of a number of sympathetic portrayals of the businessman, for example Henry James' *The American*, William Dean Howells' *The Rise of Silas Lapham*, Booth Tarkington's *The Plutocrat* and Sinclair Lewis' *Dodsworth*. Despite the businessman's whimpering about the shabby treatment he has received in American literature, a fair judgment would be that he has caught it no more nor less than other occupations.[9]

If the 'serious' novelist can be said to have a hero, it is the person who mirrors the novelist's own highest goals. It is the architect who designs for beauty, the doctor who heals for humanity, the research scientists, Sinclair Lewis' Martin Arrowsmith, perhaps, who goes off to do research for the sake of truth and knowledge. One day in 1912 Sherwood Anderson suddenly walked out of his office, dramatically leaving the world of business for the life of the mind. However apocryphal in detail, it is a famous story of choice in the biography of American writers —a choice which every 'serious' novelist and literary critic has symbolically shared.[10]

The 'serious' novelist, striving for artistic merit, is not interested in praising or condemning the businessman. He tries, in most cases, to understand him. Nor is he interested in how a business operates. That is not his task, which is no doubt fortunate, since most novelists have been writers all their lives and know no more about how a business operates than most businessmen know how to write a novel. The stuff of novels and plays is people who must choose. The story is how they respond to conflict and to stress situations within themselves and with the world around them. That is why most first-rate novelists are moral philosophers, for human conflict ultimately resolves itself into moral choice. The job of the man is less important than what the job does to the man. Success novels of quality are novels of characterization and manners in which the stage decorations of business are a backdrop for the drama of life.

In a previous chapter we examined one aspect of success which fascinated our better novelists and playwrights. Another

theme about success in 'serious' fiction and plays, this time
sharply at variance with inspirational success literature, revolved
around the nature of freedom. The idea of success revealed in
inspirational success literature expressed a philosophy of the
free individual. It boasted a faith that a man was free to rise
in the world by his own efforts. The critical fashion in fiction
and drama in the twentieth century has been the realist-naturalist
manner. The better novels and plays on the success theme for
three-quarters of a century have been constructed on that philosophy. The realist-naturalist philosophy was deterministic
and environmental. The people who live in such novels are free
moral agents, to be sure, but they are in the grip of forces which
exert control over them. In the following illustrations we can
watch 'serious' novelists and playwrights criticizing a fundamental postulate of the success idea.[11]

In *The Octopus* by Frank Norris, we are led to believe that
Shelgrim, the railroad magnate, is a villain in the cruel battle
between the railroad and the wheat farmers. Toward the close
of the novel, however, we find him to be rather pleasant and
sentimental toward his employees. Shelgrim explains the fierce
struggle between the railroad and the wheat farmers in an interview with a young man whose sympathies have previously been
entirely with the wheat farmers: "You are dealing with forces,
young man, when you speak of Wheat and the Railroads, not
with men. There is the Wheat, the supply. It must be carried to
feed the People. There is the demand. The Wheat is one force,
the Railroad, another, and there is the law that governs them—
supply and demand. Men have only little to do in the whole
business. Complications may arise, conditions that bear hard
on the individual—crush him maybe—*but the Wheat will be
carried to feed the people* as inevitably as it will grow. If you
want to fasten the blame of the affair at Los Muertos on any
one person, you will make a mistake. Blame conditions, not
men." [12]

In *The Grapes of Wrath* by John Steinbeck, the banking
system drives the Oklahoma farmers off the land. The owners
who reclaimed the land "were caught in something larger than
themselves." A bank or a company "don't breathe air, don't eat

side-meat. They breathe profits; they eat the interest on money. If they don't get it, they die the way you die without air, without side-meat. . . . The bank is something more than men, I tell you. It's the monster. Men made it, but they can't control it." [18]

For Frank Cowperwood in Theodore Dreiser's *The Financier,* the amoral and inexorable law of life is a kind of Social Darwinism. As a young man, at the beginning of the novel, Frank returns again and again to a marine tank at the fish market to watch in fascination the drama of living and dying which takes place there. A lobster gradually devours a squid over a period of several days. The squid was unarmed, Frank thought to himself, and had nothing to feed on. " 'That's the way it has to be, I guess. . . .' Things lived on each other—that was it. . . . For days and weeks Frank thought of this and of the life he was tossed into, for he was already pondering on what he should be in this world, and how he should get along." [14]

Budd Schulberg tried to answer the question of the title, *What Makes Sammy Run?,* in his novel about a ruthless opportunist who knifed his way to success in Hollywood. Sammy Glick was a Jewish boy from the Rivington Street slum on Manhattan's Lower East Side. The explanation for his cruel opportunism was not racial or ethnic. As Mama Glickstein lamented: "Sammy was not a real Jew any more. He was no different from the little wops and micks who cursed and fought and cheated. Sometimes she could not believe he grew out of her belly. He grew out of the belly of Rivington Street." Budd Schulberg offers an environmental interpretation. Sammy's friend, if it could be said he ever had a friend, puts the blame firmly on urban slums: "I thought of Sammy Glick rocking in his cradle of hate, malnutrition, prejudice, suspicions, amorality, the anarchy of the poor; I thought of him as a mangy little puppy in a dog-eat-dog world. I was modulating my hate for Sammy Glick from the personal to the societal. I no longer even hated Rivington Street but the idea of Rivington Street, all Rivington Streets of all nationalities allowed to pile up in cities like gigantic dung heaps smelling up the world, ambitions growing out of filth and crawling away like worms. I saw Sammy Glick on a battlefield . . . and I realized that I had singled him out not because he had been born into the world any more selfish, ruthless and cruel than anybody else, even though he had become all three, but because in the midst of a war that was selfish, ruthless and cruel Sammy was proving himself the fittest, the fiercest and the fastest." [15]

The realist-naturalist tradition in novels and plays has been the dominant creative movement because it was a reflection of the dominant intellectual thought of the century. The viewpoint of the 'serious' novelist and playwright, working within the realist-naturalist tradition, was critical of inspirational success literature. Their mood was pessimistic and their philosophy environmentalistic and deterministic. Many of the characters are pushed and shaped by inexorable forces, environmental conditioning, or in their lives testify to a Social Darwinist interpretation of survival. "This is the land of the great big dogs," young Chris screams, in Arthur Miller's *All My Sons,* "you don't love a man here, you eat him!" [16]

In the capitalistic system, all businessmen and profit-oriented professionals are driven by similar forces—the law of supply and demand, profit and loss statements, the necessity to compete. 'Serious' novelists seem to understand that in a capitalistic society freedom of choice does not include the choice to be free. However, there *is* freedom of choice *within* the system. The story then becomes the relation of the individual to success within the system. The system may deal the hand, but there is freedom in the way you play your cards.

There were other dissenters from the success gospel who were becoming entwined in a dilemma involving freedom. At no other time in the American experience was a disenchantment with particular aspects of success more stylistically expressed than in the decade of the 1920s.

The roaring part of the 1920s was a mutiny against Victorianism. The Jazz Age was the dividing line in personal codes and social conduct between the nineteenth century and our own times. It was a great watershed in values. The roaring part of the 1920s was an urban, middle-, and upper-class revolt against Victorianism's stuffy restrictions, codes of conventionality, and dull front of decency masking hypocritical proprieties. It was an exhilarating period in American history. Extremely rapid changes tumbled after one another. The urge to be free was expressed in the way people dressed, the manner in which men and women responded to each other, the forms of entertainment, and the subjects of conversation. The degree to which this new-found freedom was explored varied greatly. Children shocked their parents who shocked their own parents in turn, not to mention the rural areas and small towns. Bohemians shocked everybody. Short skirts, the emancipation of women, jazz, dancing, drinking, late parties, and bold subjects like sex—this much did young and middle-aged people in the urban upper-middle and upper classes have in common with varying and wide degrees of expression. However, for the overwhelming majority on this class level, as well as the rest of the nation, the dominant values of the age were symbolized, as we have seen, by the go-getter, the self-starter, the optimistic jingle of Coué, and Bruce Barton's comparison of Jesus Christ with the businessman.

Among the dissenters were intellectuals, largely creative writers and essayists, for whom a deeper meaning might have been expressed in Ernest Hemingway's 1926 novel, *The Sun Also Rises*. In that tragic story an American who was still capable of being aroused sexually, but whose instrument of fulfillment had been unmanned by a war injury, and a sexually adventuresome woman fall in love. Lacking a sense of fulfillment in their own way, this group of dissenters struck at the sources of their frustration.

In all American history, the 1920s was the time of widest cleavage between the intellectual and American culture. Harold Stearns reported in the early years of the decade that the younger generation of artists and writers "does dislike, almost to the point of hatred and certainly to the point of contempt, the type of people dominant in our present civilization, the people who actually 'run things.'" It was a time during which the intellectual, devoted to truth and beauty as he saw it, felt most alienated and most powerless. It was also a time of immense creative brilliance.[17]

C. P. Snow has emphasized the two cultures of the scientist and the humanist and the communications gap between them. A more meaningful two cultures for America has been the fissure between the intellectual and a business-dominated society. "We have in America two publics," explained Van Wyck Brooks in 1915, "the cultivated public and the business public, the public of theory and the public of activity, the public that reads Maeterlinck and the public that accumulates money: the one largely feminine, the other largely masculine." [18]

The two publics, the two cultures, were constantly circling each other distrustfully. For the intellectual in the 1920s there were two worlds which revealed his loneliness, prestige frustrations, and intellectual snobbery. There were the civilized few and the rest were barbarians. There were Bohemia and Philistia, Greenwich Village and Wall Street. Stretching back of the coastal cities was the hinterland—a wasteland with no one to talk to about books, art, and the things that really count. Even on the left bank of the Hudson there was a feeling of isolation that one never felt on the left bank of the Seine. Many fled to Europe. A few took the route of T. S. Eliot and retired to the more stratified society of Europe where a cultivated gentleman of sensitivity and learning could both appreciate and be appreciated.

The restrictions on freedom—the snooping, the book-censorship, groupthink, and Prohibition—disillusioned many intellectuals about their country. Equally distressing were the heroes of America and the values people lived by. While Bruce Barton was making his comparisons, debunkers were impudently comparing historical heroes to businessmen to the disadvantage of both. What the critics in the 1920s found distasteful was the businessman's obsession with material success, his anti-intellectualism, barren heartiness, and unrefined excesses of glad-handing boosterism. Many intellectuals were repelled by an acquisitive, pragmatic society in which Greetings ("How's business?") and total absorption ("The business of America is business.") excluded other interests ("Now you're getting philosophical!") and simplified the final judgment ("If you're so smart, why aren't you rich?"). It was all so damn vulgar and insensitive. And it all seemed to end in an idolatry of the ordinary and the average in an oppressive tyranny of conformity and standardization. The trouble with America was that it was too American.

Sinclair Lewis caught the mood. His 1922 novel, *Babbitt,* enriched the language with a new word. Most everyone will recall that George Follansbee Babbitt was a forty-six-year-old real estate broker who lived in a Middle Western city of several thousand inhabitants named Zenith. "He made nothing in particular, neither butter nor shoes nor poetry, but he was nimble in the calling of selling houses for more than people could afford to pay." A graduate of "that great department-store, the State University," Babbitt was contemptuous of "highbrows," spoke three languages (American, baseball, and poker), with commercial imagination referred to a second cocktail as "a little dividend," and occasionally bestowed the ultimate compliment on the ladies manufactured in the images of modern appliances and gadgets which he venerated: "You're looking like a new soda-fountain to-night, Louetta." [19]

Babbitt was a good husband to his plain wife and a responsible father to his three children. He did what was right because God would punish him if he did not, but he was not above stretching his ethics for a nice profit. A booster bubbling with enthusiasm, he was 200 per cent for an America defined by the Republican party, conservative editorials in the local paper, the Presbyterian Church, the Elks, and the Chamber of Commerce. When they spoke, he had an opinion.

But there was another Babbitt and Sinclair Lewis caught him at a time of crisis. Babbitt was fed up. Life had lost its sense of adventure. His family, business, religion, golf, friendships, and social life had become as mechanical as the ideas he lived by. He even questioned the joys of being a solid citizen. He wanted to be daringly free—to live and to think for himself. He tried nature and simplicity in the Maine woods (somewhat in the spirit of Thoreau), then an affair with a stylish woman, then dissipation with a group of self-styled Bohemians. Finally he fell under the influence of his old college classmate, the city's "radical" lawyer, Seneca Doane, and began to talk around the club during a strike about the rights of labor. Alarmed by his flirtation with liberal ideas, Babbitt's business friends crush him into conformity. They ostracize him, threaten the future prospects of his real estate firm, until at last he is coerced into declaring his loyalties by symbolically joining a right wing political organization. Babbitt slinks back to the old role gladly, after they permit him to save some face, but the spark of rebellion is struck again in the closing scene. Babbitt's son has eloped with the girl next door whom the son has loved for years. He wants to quit college, work in a factory, and become an inventor. "I've never done a single thing I've wanted to in my whole life!" Babbitt says and surprises his son. "But I do get a kind of sneaking pleasure out of the fact that you knew what you wanted to do and did it. . . . I'll back you. Take your factory job, if you want to. Don't be scared of the family. No, nor all of Zenith. Nor of yourself, the way I've been. Go ahead, old man! The world is yours!" [20]

Sinclair Lewis detests the values of Babbitt, but he has sympathy for Babbitt as a man. Like our better novelists, Lewis recognizes that Babbitt is a human being caught up in a system from which it is now too late for him to escape. He struggles as a freethinking individual but ultimately succumbs. The critics in the 1920s deplored what the "radical" lawyer Seneca Doane termed "standardization of thought." With commercial phrasing that Babbitt's friends could understand, what many critics of success in the 1920s stood for was free enterprise—of the mind.[21]

In different periods, for different reasons, critics challenged the success idea with their vision of a better America. In the 1920s intellectuals deplored the rigid bourgeois quality of American life. The muckrakers of the 1900s and the more militant liberals of the 1930s lashed out at the success idea because it did not live up to its boast of equal opportunity for all. The complaint was not against bourgeois values, but a protest that people were blocked from obtaining property which would make them bourgeois. Their stylistic mood favored the hatchet and the bludgeon.

History has made the differences an interesting counterpoint of contending criticisms. While many muckrakers of the 1900s and New Dealers in the 1930s would have settled for an America which translated into reality the opportunity which success books claimed, the critics in Coolidge America were horrified that success literature all too accurately reflected American life. It was not the ineffectiveness of American capitalism which alarmed them but its all too evident effectiveness. The lament of the 1920s was for social and intellectual freedom. Rather than the bludgeon of denunciation, the stylistic mood favored the stiletto of satire, the razor of mockery, the rapier of ridicule.

After the depression concern of the 1930s for opportunity, critics in the prosperous 1950s and 1960s focused once again on what they felt to be the consequences of the success complex —the need to conform, the erosion of individualism, the standardization of a mass culture. William H. Whyte, Jr., reflected the mood in his 1956 influential book, *The Organization Man*. Large-scale organizations were sapping initiative, huge corporations were even invading the sanctuary of the home to measure the wife's adaptability, sprawling suburban developments were a suffocating blanket of conformity, groupism was enveloping individualism, people were becoming as interchangeable as the parts in a machine. Babbitt, at least, was a self-employed businessman with some degree of independence. The organization man, though more sophisticated, was neither self-employed nor independent. In the early 1960s one joke making the rounds was about the man who became the surprised president of one of the nation's largest firms because someone with golf spikes stepped on his IBM card.[22]

In the political dilemma explored in the previous chapter, the critics of the success complex expressed a humanitarian concern for the common man. In the social democracy dilemma emerging here, the critics of the success complex were disillusioned that the common man was using his prosperous advantages for such common things. In the political dilemma the critics were concerned about the *quantity* of American life and called for majority rule to check the minority rights of property. In the social democracy dilemma the critics were unhappy about the *quality* of American life and a majority which appeared to be swamping the minority rights of freethinking, controversial opinions, and a sensitivity to the good, the true, and the beautiful.

The social democracy dilemma emerged out of egalitarian forces which were challenging the authority of taste leadership under peculiar American conditions. Gustave de Beaumont, Tocqueville's traveling companion in the 1830s, sniffed that "to have elegance in taste, one must first have elegant customs." He found little of either. "Do not look for poetry, literature, or fine arts in this country. The universal equality of conditions spreads a monotonous tint over all society." The British visitor, Thomas Colley Grattan, reported in the 1850s that there was no standard of manners because there was no "permanent class in society to be looked up to and imitated. . . . We find in the same circles most striking contrasts of style, 'every one' being, as might be said, 'his own gentleman.' " [23]

When everyone is his own gentleman, who possesses the authority to set standards of quality? If one man's opinion is as good as the next, why not the majority opinion? A small minority is usually superior in taste to the vast majority. When a powerful majority lacks deference to the taste of the minority, taste is debased to the level of the many rather than raised to the higher level of the few.

The power of the American people over national taste cannot be explained by their form of government. Other European nations shared a belief in *political* equalitarianism—that there should be equality *among* men with respect to the vote and before the law. The American stressed *social* equalitarianism —the equality *of* all men with respect to one another. American values respected success, but the successful man was not superior in the same sense that a prince was superior. American values respected a doctor or a self-made millionaire, but they were granted no cap-tipping deference from the populace. Success might be the measure of a man's worth, but to be a man—or rather to be an American—was to be as good as any other man. However torn by ambivalence this faith might have been by distinctions of family background, possessions, or occupation, an abiding belief in social equalitarianism nurtured a populace which instinctively recoiled from deferential attitudes and servile gestures. It was a brash response to authority not always easy for Europeans to understand.[24]

In their scheme of egalitarian values, Americans more willingly recognized economic class superiority than social class superiority. The people forbid their plutocracy to act like a cultivated aristocracy. The factory owner must chum with his workers on a first-name basis. The boss's son, fresh from one of those fancy private colleges, might try to play the cultivated aristocrat, but he was soon slapped down—or shipped out. There was to be no putting on of airs. An 1875 schoolbook was precise: *"We do not blame a man who is proud of his success, so much as one who is vain of his learning."* Since a certain amount of artificiality is necessary for polite learning, those who were touched with artificiality seemed to be tainted with effeminacy. Speech was better plain, direct, unlearned, without adornment or elegance. When specific writers or painters are said by other cultures to be most American—which generally means most unlike their own—they lack adornment. From the eighteenth-century painter John Singleton Copley to the twentieth-century poet Robert Frost, the American mode is the forthright, simple, honest manner, executed without embellishment.[25]

Social equalitarianism diminishes the authority of an elite. In a society in which status is ascribed rather than achieved, and when leadership is largely drawn from an elite establishment, leaders expect respect from the masses. In such a society, soaked in the deference of one class for the class above it, those qualities that distinguish the elite are played out in the public forum. When there is no authority to compel the expression of thought in the language of a cultivated gentleman, as in America, the expression of thought in the language of a gas station attendant may be considered more masculine, honest, and democratic.

In politics the debasing of style to the level of the masses was a 'give 'em hell' spectacle, particularly after the Jacksonian period. The politician was well advised to appear just as common as his unlettered constituents. The necessity to play 'just folks' to mass style in order to get votes fed upon itself. The cultivated gentleman of social position and property shrank from politics because to win required him to erase from his manner the very qualities that made him a gentleman. Polite learning sparkling with wit and sallies into abstract ideas simply couldn't compete with a candidate who was 'one of the boys.' This has been one reason why engaging in politics for an elected office since the Jacksonian period, with the exception of the higher offices of governor and senator, has never been an escalator into fashionable society.

A political democracy and a social democracy, America was also an economic democracy. The people exercised their free choice in the marketplace with a minimum of restraint. Under communism, economic democracy tends to slide into enforced equality. In America, economic democracy was constructed on the freedom of the individual. No civilization of comparable magnitude in the history of the world has extended to such a degree as in America the free choice of the marketplace. In no previous age have so many people enjoyed so many opportunities so often to exercise that choice. With little deference to an elite and a government checked in its authority, the marketplace was the court and the people sat enthroned as decision-makers. In the marketplace, every day was election day and the ballot was the dollar bill. The way to be a financial success was to get the people to vote for you with their money. In this sense the marketplace, like the political polling booth, was an expression of democracy. The democratic hero of that marketplace was the self-made man. A defector from Russian communism understood the point when he announced in 1965: "I am Nureyev, dancer, nothing more than that. I am on sale. It is free enterprise. If you like, you buy. If you don't like, you leave alone." [26]

The government, of course, was not powerless. It invoked massive regulatory powers. Its taxing power redistributed the wealth. The chief executive conferred honors by awards and recognition by invitations to White House affairs. The federal government itself spent billions upon billions in the economy. But the massive intrusions of the federal government were limited. The government restrained itself from controlling the tastes of its citizens. It withdrew from influencing people about who was or was not to be a success. There was little coercion to check free choice within the limits of reasonable laws. Compared to what it might have done with its awesome power to tell people what they should like, the United States Government was virtually *laissez-faire*.[27]

Although there was no central government, monarch, or elite to impose standards of taste, alternatives were available to escape the vulgarity of the public. Non-profit institutions were just such alternatives. In a mass-consumption economy, they provided a choice which was superior in taste and quality to the choice of the people. A distinction between business and non-business success is relevant. In a market situation, the question is simple: "Will it sell?" A non-profit institution asks: "Is it good?" Museums, foundations, and university presses asked that question because they could afford to ask it and they could afford to do so because their standards were not directly chained to the votes of the public in the marketplace.

The television industry is a clear illustration of the social democracy dilemma of freedom vs. authority. Throughout the 1950s and 1960s, sophisticated television critics were unanimous in deploring the quality of the top fifteen programs aired on prime evening time. Television had become an inane world of mindless distractions which impoverished rather than enriched life.

Those held responsible for low taste in programming were variously network executives, individual station managers, producers, corporate sponsors, and advertising agencies. But the villain was fingered by Bing Crosby in 1965 after several months with his own television show. "According to the rating, we haven't been doing so well," Bing sadly admitted. "I think I'd have to get on a glass-bottom boat to find the rating. It's a rat race. If you don't get a rating, they dump you." Two decades of audience measurement by ratings, though imprecise, have indisputably shown that the public has gotten what it has wanted in programming. The reason for the low taste of television has been the low taste of the American people.[28]

With a commendable zeal based more on hope than reality, Federal Communications Commissioner Newton Minow told broadcasters in 1961: "I am not convinced that the people's taste is as low as some of you assume." It was probably worse. Television programming would have descended to an even lower level of quality if it were not for the nagging of media critics, an occasional feeling of responsibility by some television executive for the positive contributions of the medium, and the Federal Communications Commission's power, seldom used, to refuse license renewals to stations not measuring up to standards. A mass medium like television does not lift the taste of the masses; the masses degrade it as an art form to their own level. Advertising, often chosen as the culprit, was only an intervening variable. Hollywood has been cranking out moving pictures since Follow-the-Bouncing-Ball without benefit of soap manufacturers and advertising. In total volume, the quality of both media has probably been about the same.[29]

One solution for avoiding the consequences of the social democracy dilemma would be to establish some form of taste authority. Control would be taken away from business, which paid the bills for television through advertising, and given to a government bureaucracy. Costs would be assumed by a license fee per television set and by a government subsidy. In either system, the people end up paying, through the cost of advertising added to the product they purchase or through taxes and fees imposed by the government. The important difference is that a taste authority decides what the public wants to see—or should see.

In both commercial and public television, the airways are the property of the public. In commercial television, broadcast channels are a public gift to businesses operated for profit. Ironically, public television, supported by a tin cup held before the government, foundations, and interested viewers, has not been television by public demand but freedom from mass public taste. Apparently European audiences who have lived with government television systems supported by license fees and subsidies have not differed much from American viewers. When given a choice between a gunslinger's blazing six-shooter and an information program, the majority dialed in the gunslinger. Thus, to chastise network executives for the quality of commercial television is to spank the monkey and ignore the organ grinder. The attack should be launched at a television system operated for profit. The solution would be to establish a bureaucratic authority to shield the people from their own deplorable taste.

If television executives and performers are puppets at the end of a string jerked by the public's twirling television dial, politicians must periodically face the public's demands at the ballot box, and those desirous of business success on the private pay scale must chase the public's dollar bill in the marketplace. The consequences of this system represent the price that America has had to pay for being an economic, political, and social democracy, for awarding power to the people.[30]

Winston Churchill once recalled for the House of Commons the observation that "democracy is the worst form of Government except all those other forms that have been tried from time to time." America, as an economic, political, and social democracy, has been a counterpoint of contending promises as well as criticisms. It is in the counterpoint of freedom and authority, expressed in the dilemma of a social democracy, that success values and the quality of American life must be judged.[31]

On the one hand, if the idea of success in America takes its cues from a free-enterprise economy and a fluid class system where the court is the marketplace and the consumer is sovereign, if America is a social democracy with little taste leadership from an authority resting in the government or an elite to which deference is expressed, then the free choice of the individual citizen is enlarged. But the price for this social democracy must be paid. In the absence of fixed criteria for establishing position, the marketplace fashions a materialistic yardstick for measuring a man's worth, money largely establishes status, and making it becomes crucial. What is salable becomes valuable, gold not goodness is the criterion, quantity not quality, income not intellect, and culture is democratized to the low taste of the people.

On the other hand, if values are imposed upon the individual by an authoritarian system, by a social class elite in a stratified society or by governmental coercion, if success is not defined and decided upon by the sovereign consumer in the market-place but determined by prestige and a status which is fixed by family background in a society trained to deference or estab-lished by governmental edict, then the price must be paid for this elitist system in the diminished freedom of the individual. However, status is then measured by other criteria than money-making and the low taste of the people no longer enjoys its sovereignty. The government, or a cultivated elite, financially secure and enjoying deference, imposes its own values on so-ciety. The life of the mind is revered for its own sake, facility in the arts carries its own prestige, while quality, not quantity, intellect not income are honored. The people are saved from the impoverishment of their own vulgarity at the expense of their freedom.

One solution: Substitute medals for money as the general badge of success. But who would decide who gets the medals?

25

"A DIFFERENT DRUMMER"

A civilization is a tapestry. The success complex was woven into the tapestry of the American experience in a design of relationships. The design in the final dilemma is woven largely out of the relationship of success to happiness and leisure.

Living in the middle decades of the twentieth century, Erich Fromm saw signs that "people are increasingly dissatisfied and disappointed with their way of life. . . . Man's happiness today consists in 'having fun.' Having fun lies in the satisfaction of consuming and 'taking in' commodities. . . . The world is one great object for our appetite, a big apple, a big bottle, a big breast; we are the sucklers, the eternally expectant ones, the hopeful ones—and the eternally disappointed ones. . . . Modern man is alienated from himself, from his fellow man, and from nature." [1]

Life indeed may have been just awful in recent decades, but an historical judgment compels us to ask, in terms of happiness, whether it was ever any better. Over one hundred years ago Alexis de Tocqueville observed that "in America I saw the freest and most enlightened men placed in the happiest circumstances that the world affords; it seemed to me as if a cloud habitually hung upon their brow, and I thought them serious and almost sad, even in their pleasures." Tocqueville remarked, in this the 1830s, upon "that strange melancholy which often haunts the inhabitants of democratic countries in the midst of their abundance, and that disgust at life which sometimes seizes upon them in the midst of calm and easy circumstances." [2]

One hundred years ago Thomas Nichols spoke intelligently to the point: "We talk in America of our great, our enlightened, our free, and, above all, our happy country! I never thought America *was* a happy country—only that it ought to be. In all the years of peace and plenty we were not happy. In no country are the faces of the people furrowed with harder lines of care." Nichols takes us beyond description into the causes of unhappiness: "It is seldom that an American retires from business to enjoy his fortune in comfort. Money-making becomes a habit. He works because he always has worked, and knows no other way."

Nichols thought he knew what the first element of happiness was. It was enjoyment of life, contentment. But "there is no such thing in America as being contented with one's position or condition. The poor struggle to be rich, the rich to be richer. Everyone is tugging, trying, scheming to advance—to get ahead. It is a great scramble, in which all are troubled and none are satisfied. In Europe, the poor man, as a rule, knows that he must remain poor, and he submits to his lot, and tries to make the best of it. . . . Not so in America. Every little ragged boy dreams of being President or a John Jacob Astor. The dream may be a pleasant one while it lasts, but what of the disappointing reality? What of the excited, restless, feverish life spent in the pursuit of phantoms? . . . America is a great country; it has been and may still be a prosperous country; it cannot yet be truly called a happy one." [3]

Observers in recent decades may well be right that Americans were not happy in the 1950s and 1960s. Who can say whether they were less happy, or more happy, than in the past? What we can say with certainty, however, is that there were psychological consequences of the success complex which contributed to feelings of both happiness and unhappiness.

Freud suggested in his last major work on society in 1930 that "men are beginning to perceive that all this newly won power over space and time, this conquest of the forces of nature, this fulfillment of age-old longings, has not increased the amount of pleasure they can obtain in life, has not made them feel any happier." He goes on to explain why: ". . . The price of progress in civilization is paid in forfeiting happiness through the heightening of the sense of guilt." We all have known at least one person who could not enjoy his success. His conscience was soaked in guilt. He worked and sacrificed to reach a goal, yet once achieved, could not delight in it. His conscience whispered: "You do not deserve it." Or his conscience accused: "You have displaced someone else to get what you want." [4]

There were other types who were denied the psychic rewards of success. There was the person for whom a challenge conquered could only be the signal for a new challenge. Achievement was a mountain top which soon became only a resting place to begin a fresh assault. He must conquer lest the self-accusation of incompetence, or impotence, be proven. We have known, too, the individual for whom the battle crushed the capacity to enjoy anything but victory. There just wasn't any sensitivity left for anything else. Familiar, too, was one tragedy of success: Promotion out of the kind of work in which an individual had found a deep personal satisfaction. The teacher was promoted to administrator, the salesman to sales manager, the foreman moved up from the factory floor to the front office where shuffling papers replaced the machines he once enjoyed working with so much. Success sometimes meant managing people to do the kind of work you once found deep fulfillment in doing yourself. [5]

The agony of failure can be sudden; it may be the sad, quiet slide from promising beginnings. The psychological consequences of a frayed white collar can be ugly. If his social-class position is slipping while others are on the rise, he becomes a special prey to authoritarianism and prejudice. Banked with frustration and fear, he burns with a hatred of Jews, Communists, Negroes, the new rich, or any group that can relieve him of his self-contempt and soak up the blame for his slipping status.

Change of status in either direction—success or failure—may

cause psychic distress. The man on the way up is exposed to his own share of problems. He and his wife are moving through layers of society which strain their ability at social adaptation. The history of America has been the horizontal movement of people from one place to another and a vertical movement from one social status to another. Social class mobility to a higher status is an expression of democracy. Norman Podhoretz had a different feeling about it. A lower-class boy from Brooklyn, Podhoretz, by a combination of hard work, brilliance, and *chutzpah*, in one generation leaped into the upper middle class. "There was," Podhoretz confessed, "a kind of treason in it: treason toward my family, treason toward my friends." Even if people remain in their class level, they may experience a psychological change of class level through a rising national standard of living. Into a low-cost suburban housing development may flow people from the same social-class level, but they are all moving up together and experiencing the strains of social change to a new way of life.[6]

Moving from the rural areas to the city, or from the city to the suburbs, increases the stresses that people must bear. The husband, joined to his wife in that "mutual mobility bet," may find it a bad wager if she is unequal to his capacity for social growth. She must also be socially tougher in a world of strangers than in a stable community of old friends and family connections. The husband as breadwinner, straining to meet his awesome monthly responsibilities, goes forth to the daily struggle and the necessity of pretending that he is somebody and something more than he is. Success is a change of status and a source of stress. Inability to cope with stress may result in serious emotional symptoms.[7]

The drive to get ahead can be damaging to physical as well as mental health. The competitive go-getter feels guilty about not working during leisure hours, burns to be recognized, strains with impatience when he misses a slot in a revolving door, and attacks his exercise, if any, as if he were excelling at work. Another type of success striver plays it cool on the outside but is sweating inside. There are success strivers who live in terror of being occupational sliders. There are strainers for status who are anxious about skidding into a lower social class position. Whether an individual functions productively in relation to his aspirations, expectations, and achievement, or is physically impaired by them, depends on a host of variables. It depends on his ego structure and his entire makeup as a person, on his education, early conditioning, diet patterns, and family medical history. The drive to succeed can result in organic diseases of a coronary or gastrointestinal nature. But heart attacks are not caused by success. They may be caused, with other factors, by the inability of the individual to adapt to the stress of success or failure. It is the inability of an individual to handle the stress situations of mobility in either direction which contributes to a physical breakdown of an organic nature.

At one time an ulcer was a badge of distinction for the dynamically successful. With better medical understanding it is now a scarlet letter of inner stress reflecting an ambitiously aggressive man of ability who may, among things, be afraid he's not good enough. It isn't overexercised brilliance of mind but overworked emotions which agitate the vagus nerve to secrete an excessive amount of hydrochloric acid. In one *New Yorker* cartoon there is wry humor in the complaint of a wife to her girl friend as they sip a cocktail: "What gets me is his having ulcers and being a *failure.*" The lamentation of the self-made man indicates the price-of-success irony: "When I was poor, I didn't have enough to eat. Now that I have enough to eat, I have an ulcer." [8]

The scramble for success often collided with the pursuit of happiness. Overtaking the next goal is self-winning, but it is self-defeating because there can never be an ultimate victory. Goals which would seem to be restful destinations become signposts. The asceticism and self-denial, the long hours and the hard work, the compromises and the opportunism may turn the sweet smell of success rancid, the taste of it sour. The fire of ambition burns itself out in the ashes of an achievement incapable of stimulating sensations of either joy or lasting pleasure. In the insight of Horace Gregory,

> It is not money, but power that lives in money
> That heats the blood and turns the soul to ashes,
> Freezes the heart, and changes life to clay,
> Invisible spirit against the human spirit.

What it takes to get always affects what is gotten. The spirit of success never failed to affect the human spirit that pursued it.[9]

What has been the relationship of the success complex to happiness in an increasingly industrial and affluent American society in recent decades? In many developing nations people living in poverty believe that having more of the good things of life should lead to greater happiness. A lure of industrialism is that the better off people are, the happier they should be. What makes the equation suspect is that the values which produce the good things of life are not always the values that make for the good life.[10]

Immanuel Kant once defined happiness as "the satisfaction of all our desires. . . ." If desires remain constant and satisfactions increase in intensity, duration, and kind, then the chances of happiness should be greater. On the other hand, if desires increase but satisfactions remain constant or decrease, then the chances for happiness are diminished. A third alternative is revealed in the American experience. Satisfactions increased but so did desires. Aspirations were always running in advance of achievement. The idea of success was a self-defeating mechanism for happiness, an engine of discontent incessantly pushing expectations ahead of satisfactions.[11]

A key to understanding happiness in America, therefore, is not the degree of affluence in any period but the values of a striving society which produced the affluence. If Americans were getting more of what they wanted, it was apparent that the values of the culture did not permit them to be satisfied with what they got. Advertising's transformation of this year's luxuries into next year's necessities was only an economic expression of a value construct which demanded that this year's success become next year's point of departure for further achievement.

The rest of the world has always admired the abundance of

opportunity in America to better oneself. But that opportunity was not necessarily an invitation to bliss. In more stratified societies of ascribed status in which there are recognized ceilings on the height to which one is expected to rise, the pressure on the individual is eased. In American society, most everyone was expected to rise above the station in which he was born. Position in life, ever uncertain, was both a support and a threat to self-esteem.

In an affluent society people are constantly reminded that everyone is supposed to be doing better. For those who feel they are being left behind, there is status anxiety. For those who are actually doing better, there is the anxiety generated by unfamiliar life styles with all the demands and pretensions of being something you are not.

As people became better educated and worked in higher status jobs, they gained more satisfaction from their work but also more frustration. The solicitude expressed by many social scientists for the boring routine of certain blue collar workers may sometimes be a reflection of the intellectuals' own repugnance for this kind of work. Some people are more contented in a set routine which does not demand of them constant decisions. Higher status jobs demand greater ego involvements from which flow greater ego gratifications but also greater worries and distress. The better educated one was and the more sophisticated the job, the more opportunity there was for self-fulfillment, but also the greater possibilities for frustration and dissatisfaction.[12]

The Declaration of Independence guarantees that the pursuit of happiness is an inalienable right. It might better have guaranteed the pursuit of success as such a right. Happiness is not something you can pursue. It overtakes you. It is a by-product. If happiness is a by-product, then a concluding point about the relation of success to happiness might emphasize certain forces which influenced feelings of happiness and unhappiness. Over the course of the past century the characteristic which George Jean Nathan and H. L. Mencken thought most distinctly American was perhaps also the single most important characteristic which weighed against happiness: "The thing which sets off the

American from all other men . . . is . . social aspiration. . . . His dominant passion is a passion to lift himself by at least a step or two in the society that he is a part of. . . . *The American is a pusher.* His eyes are ever fixed upon some round of the ladder that is just beyond his reach, and all his secret ambitions, all his extraordinary energies, group themselves about the yearning to grasp it. . . . By the same token he is sickeningly fearful of slipping back. . . . Such a thing as a secure position is practically unknown among us." [13]

But what about change? Was living in the world of the nineteenth century character ethic different from living in a society driven by the personality ethic? We venture to suggest several changes, largely in degree rather than kind, which took place in the psychological effects of living in these two worlds.

The first change is a difference in the nature of individual dependency and helplessness. The nineteenth-century American felt helpless before impersonal forces which he tried to control by foresight and placate by faithful prayers. The modern American feels helpless before human forces. In a large corporation, promotion depends on the opinion of superiors. People determine an individual's success more than they used to. It's the difference between the impersonal forces of the weather and the capricious attitudes, opinions, and tastes of people. While today's organization man might feel uneasy about this kind of insecurity, he could recall that the creative intellectual has long endured the critic. And the destiny of the academic man has long been controlled by the critical judgment of his departmental and administrative superiors. If the scholar-teacher is in an occupation marked by its independence, he is also dependent for success on the opinions of a small group.

Have feelings of helplessness and powerlessness increased in the past two or three generations? One suspects so, if we mean that the individual's center of reality has mushroomed into a multitude of contacts which can affect him and which he constantly struggles to control. The paradox, which is so often misunderstood, is that the freedom of the individual has been expanding while at the same time he has become more dependent on institutions and other people. It is tempting to draw an analogy to the nation itself and its accelerated participation in foreign affairs. Increased national participation in foreign affairs can augment power without necessarily increasing a feeling of power. It increases the number of things over which the nation has power, but it may also increase numerically the things before which it feels powerless.

A second change is a different feeling about personal failure. When the nineteenth-century American of the character ethic failed to meet his goals, he felt guilt and self-contempt for himself and shame and humiliation before his family, friends, and associates. The modern American is heir to these psychological effects. He also places his ego eggs in one basket, but they are more exposed to breakage. With the exception of the "loner" occupations, the modern American must be a salesman versed in communication. He must be able to handle people, get along with them, control their responses by presenting ideas effectively and persuasively. In intensely competitive situations with diminishing product differentiation, he helps to sell the product by selling himself. Then he may feel *he* is the product. His self is on the marketplace. When they don't buy the product or the idea, they don't buy *him*. He is vulnerable to gnawing anxiety about his own powers. His anxiety is fed by apprehensions about whether or not he is popular and well-liked. His identity, the "who and what am I?," is in search of an answer which is only as stable as the changeable opinion of other people. "I like to work with people" may really mean "I need to work with people," because only if I am constantly accepted by people can I accept myself. To buy from me is to accept me, or to put it another way, to buy from me is not to reject me.

A third change, again in degree, is an increased feeling of emotional isolation in the company of other people. It is incorrect to assume that the nineteenth-century American cared less than the modern American about what people thought of him. The Victorian Age was very self-conscious about the opinion of other people and kept up appearances with elaborate hypocrisies. Its architecture is a fantastic exercise in front. Both the Victorian and the modern American wanted to be thought of as successful. The difference is that the Victorian needed to feel that he was respected by other people while the modern American needs to feel he is popular with them. While both cared deeply what other people thought of them, the modern American must be more attuned to other people in order to get ahead. People are the raw material out of which success is exploited. But business success is sometimes an act of aggression veiled in good fellowship. 'Public Relations' has a way of corrupting human relations. The smiling mask must disguise true feelings. The personality ethic increases the temptation to erase the self to make the sale. Done often enough, the self loses its content to become a forgery in conformity to what is salable.

The irony is that increased face-to-face contacts may intensify feelings of loneliness. It is not the number of people one sees but one's relationship with them that banishes loneliness. While friends in the office joke with one another, the unguarded spontaneity of fellowship with trusted friends is not possible if the competitive edge is so often determined by the opinion of higher-ups. The executive must be the computer with the smiling face, outwardly friendly but inwardly ticking with mechanical precision. He is in control only when he is in control of himself.

Success is the translation of money into recognized status. In a highly mobile society where people must tear up roots and move on to new surroundings, there are others just like you. And it is the others, just like you, who judge your taste in choosing status symbols. They are under the same strain, just as afraid, and just as anxious to be wanted and asked to social affairs, to be accepted and liked. "I think socially we're flying apart," perceived one minister in a Boston suburb. "We don't meet heart to heart any more, we meet at cocktail parties in a superficial way. We value smartness rather than depth, shine rather than spirit. But I think people are sick of it; they want to get out of it." [14]

Finally, forces surrounding the personality ethic contributed to feelings of emotional isolation while they increased the need for affection. Many turned to the family unit to fill this need. The family became a refuge to which the shattered American breadwinner retired each evening. In an agricultural community the family is an economic unit and children are a working asset.

In older urban settings children frequently cared for the parents in their old age. In modern America children have become less an economic asset and more of an emotional asset, less income earning and more income spending. So during the day the breadwinner competes and struggles, smiles and manipulates, masking competitive anxieties with trained insincerity. At the end of the day he retires to his family, his fortress and his refuge, where he hopes to recapture the sincerity of a loving relationship with his wife, and especially his children, and where he yearns to find the supporting trust of friends.

Oliver Wendell Holmes, Jr., once remarked that "life is painting a picture, not doing a sum." Every major country has painted its own picture of happiness in the design of its values. For every major country is not only a piece of real estate, it is an idea. The difficulty in America has always been that the idea of success and the idea of happiness were not the same.[15]

Early in the 1950s Justice of the Peace Horace Cooper of Langhorne, Pennsylvania, was sentenced to a prison term of from one to three years. A prominent member of the community, he was forced to sign a judgment note against his house and dispose of his boat, horse, and two automobiles. The offense: embezzling police fines in excess of $8,000. The district attorney asked Justice of the Peace Cooper why he had done it. "It was partly carelessness in keeping records and handling the money," he confessed. "My wife was sick and living conditions were too high and it was partly trying to keep up with the Joneses."[16]

For the past one hundred years spectacles of economic and political scandal have oozed across the stage of American life. The more notorious stories were often written in the lexicon of success—money, prestige, and power. One can recall the methods of the Robber Barons in the last quarter of the nineteenth century, the political and economic exposures of the muckrakers in the 1900s, the prohibition era of the 1920s, and the banking scandals of the 1930s—to single out only the better known instances of crime and unethical conduct.

Since World War II, in the nation's capital, there were mink coats and deep freezes, vicuña coats and oriental rugs, avaricious

Supreme Court Justices, influence peddling, and the fix. Sometimes the most respected members of society were caught and exposed to dishonor. West Point cadets were expelled for cheating, college basketball players threw games, rigged television shows were exposed as deceitful frauds, and a new word, payola, was introduced to describe how disc jockeys were bribed to plug records.

Wave after wave of exposures broke over the decades of the 1950s and 1960s—bid rigging by mighty electrical equipment companies, labor union corruption, collusion between the big city police and the rackets of organized crime, home repair frauds, bank embezzlements, faked insurance claims, faked academic dissertations, shoplifting in supermarkets, and the steady, relentless evasions of the federal income tax. In one way or another most of them added up to crimes of making or stretching a buck.

Frustrated ambition is the wet nurse of crime. As an undesirable consequence of the success drive, crime can be explained as a way of closing the gap between wanting and getting. It is the use of illegal or unethical means to achieve a desired end. Crime for success is a deviant shortcut. It's the young man, busting to be a bigshot. He robs a store, buys a flashy car, goes joyriding with his friends. Then there's crime as a traditional form of mobility for ethnic groups. As a first- or second-generation American, he's in a hurry in the land of opportunity. He organizes an illegal racket for prostitution, bootlegging, or gambling and runs it as a business for profit. The problem is how to translate dirty money into respectability. The great equalizer varies with the criminal. For the punk and the gangster, it's a gun; it's a pen for the embezzling clerk seething with resentment against those who have more, the frustrated white-collar worker who believes his merit deserves a greater reward, the overextended executive plotting devices to live on his expense account, and the Jones-chasing American citizen wrestling with his conscience as he fills out his income tax form.[17]

The insistent spur of American culture is the promise of success for all. Societies with a more rigid class stratification and respect for authority can more readily check the aberrant ambitions of their subjects. They may, like England, breed an inner discipline in their people or stifle ambition. Not so long ago America was an expanding frontier where independent folk were impatient with restraints and controls and, if necessary, would take the law into their own hands. For the past one hundred years the capitalistic system has rewarded the pioneering virtue of risk-taking. In business, risk-taking for gain demands innovation—the launching of new ideas, products, and methods. With such a premium on risk-taking, the law is an objectionable form of restraint. In a competitive system, you are seduced into cutting corners just as closely as your nearest competitor. The business philosophy of pragmatism—whatever works is good—has always endangered ethics by defining good in terms of the long-term profit and loss statement. America has been for over half a century a law-making but not a law-abiding society. There is reverence for law as the great protector of self, but an irreverence for law as a restraining check on personal and business ascent.

There have always been the crooks for whom ethical means break down under the thrust for money and power. For most middle-class Americans, however, the problems involving means and ends are daily and endless. The pressures to get ahead are in incessant conflict with countervailing pressures of conscience, reputation, and integrity.

In poorer societies, leisure often corrupts work and success is a "problem." In American society, work has corrupted leisure and leisure is said to be the "problem." [18]

What is leisure? A charming definition is in Mark Twain's *The Adventures of Tom Sawyer*. You will recall that Aunt Polly had given Tom the disagreeable chore of whitewashing a huge fence. Slyly he persuaded his chums to complete the entire job for him by making the task seem like a special treat which required particular skill. Tom had translated whitewashing the fence into a form of leisure for his 'friends' by making them pay for the privilege of doing it. ("If he hadn't run out of whitewash, he would have bankrupted every boy in the village.") For Mark Twain, the lesson was revealing: "Work consists of whatever a body is *obliged* to do, and . . . play consists of whatever a body is not obliged to do." [19]

Just as discretionary income is money left over to spend as you freely choose, leisure is discretionary time involving a free choice as to how you wish to spend it. Leisure involves not what you do, but your relationship and attitude toward it. It is the difference between *having* to do something as a duty, for a profit, or for personal gain, and doing something by choice for its own sake and for the pleasure of it.[20]

The success drive was leisure's thief. During the 1950s and 1960s popular magazine articles were describing a "leisure problem" resulting from a reduced standard work week and an abundance of free but unrewarding time. The way free time was spent may have been unrewarding, but part of the so-called "leisure problem," the abundance of free time, was not the problem. The real leisure problem for many people was not enough free time. The problem played itself out in several ironies.

One irony is that as the middle-class American's standard of living rose in the post-World War II decades, free time for many decreased. A move to the suburbs multiplied time-consuming responsibilities. Life was more complex, from commuting and paper work to grass cutting and community affairs. One reason for the guilt feelings of some commuting fathers about not spending enough time with their children was that children were not a part of either work or leisure, but competed with both for the fathers' time.

Another irony is that the more money one earned per hour, the more costly became the choice of leisure over work. Leisure then began to steal time from work which produced money to buy things that people thought they needed for a leisure that they didn't have time to enjoy. The more money a rising breadwinner made each year, the more remunerative became each hour of work, and therefore the more valuable each hour of leisure. The choice of whether to slow down, sustain, or accelerate the number of hours of work became more troublesome when expenses were running ahead of an income which was the foundation for the rising status of the entire family.

When the Industrial Revolution raised its 'dark, satanic mills' in the nineteenth century, everyone worked long hours regulated by the factory whistle. In the twentieth century what has happened is that the work hours of the blue-collar worker in his primary job, and the hours of wage-earners in low status jobs, have been drastically reduced with a commensurate increase in leisure. But the boss and the salaried success strivers in the front office were no better off than their nineteenth-century counterparts. They shared this opportunity to work long hours with professional folk, such as lawyers, doctors, and professors, with officials of various kinds, with owner-managers and corporation executives, with merchants and proprietors, with manufacturers, and with salesmen who worked on commissions, draws, and bonuses.[21]

For those who had the freedom to set their own work schedules, there was no time clock to punch, no closing bell to signal the end of the day. Decision-making was endless. The decision-making process is not a job you go to; it is a responsibility you live with. One study of business executives in the 1950s indicated that the average executive's time spent at the office was 43 hours per week. Paper work and business reading at home consumed another seven hours or so, with studying to further his career three and a half hours. Business entertaining gobbled up about two and a half hours at home and close to three hours outside the home. The sum of this working time came to 59 hours a week. To this figure could be added over five hours traveling between home and office. For some jobs, pile on a variable number of hours for business travel and out-of-town trips. The load begins to swell.[22]

Much has been made in an expense account society of the blending of work and play. The play-work blend has been overdrawn by those who assume that the pleasure is in the cake rather than in the circumstances which surround the eating of it.

It is also an irony that those who were winning a shorter work week with higher pay in twentieth-century America had the least capacity for leisure's creative use. Wage-earners on fixed hours were least able to exploit the self-fulfilling opportunities of free time. But like the business and professional men in the previous irony, when the wage-earner had the choice between translating free time into leisure, or into money-making, he chose money-making.[23]

George Brooks of the paper workers' union clarified in 1959 the issue of work vs. leisure in organized labor. With respect to hours, he explained, "the most numerous and persistent grievances are disputes over the sharing of overtime work. The issue usually is not that someone has been made to work, but that he has been deprived of a chance to make overtime pay." Workers "are eager to increase their income, not work shorter hours." Arnold Green reported in 1964 that "polls disclose that most workers do not want a shorter work week; they do want a shorter defined work week that will grant an increase in time-and-a-half pay." The urge in the labor union movement toward earlier retirement and longer vacations was not to provide workers with more hours of leisure but to soften the blow of automation by spreading the work thinner.[24]

The business and professional man was free to work around the clock in the hopes of a higher income or promotion. The wage-earner was forbidden to work more than a fixed number of hours. So he got a second job. The moonlighter was a multiple jobholder who could take a second job for a variety of reasons, e.g. the diversity of another kind of occupation. Mostly he was a breadwinner caught in a squeeze between the aspirations of his family and the limits of his income. And his need for income was greater than his desire for leisure. So he relaxed the squeeze by a second job. The president of the New York City's Patrolmen's Benevolent Association estimated in 1960 that from 60 to 70 per cent of the city's police force were holding outside jobs. "I was amazed myself," declared Mr. Cassese after an informal poll, "but it is like everything else, you can't make ends meet...."[25]

A sharpened perspective on the amount of leisure in America also demands an accounting of the number of wives who held jobs. The "kitchen revolution" of electrical appliances and prepared foods softened household drudgery. But the housewife often left the kitchen during the day only to labor in it at night. To help pay for the revolution, a whopping 41 per cent of married women from age twenty to sixty-four had paying jobs in 1968. If a moonlighter was a two-job husband, his working spouse was a two-job wife.[26]

If the success complex was leisure's thief, it was also leisure's tyrant. It imposed itself on free time. Success, achieved through work, was made visible through activities in free time. The reward of work, money, had to be translated into recognized status. Indeed, success was the result of work transformed into the symbols of leisure. Leisure became, therefore, not something standing outside of work, not a bloc of time sacred to itself, but an instrument for success. It became a function of work. In some societies, work is viewed as an interruption of free time in order to make the pleasures of leisure possible. In America, work was the continuum interrupted by leisure. Thus, the consecration of work exalted success, success intensified the importance of work, and in varying degrees, depending on the individual, leisure became a slave of status rather than a liberator for self-fulfillment.

Success has been the thief and tyrant of leisure because the rewards of work meant more to Americans than the rewards of leisure. Werner Sombart observed some sixty-five years ago that "the life ideal of the Americans is not found in the pleasurable development of self, nor in the beautiful harmony of a well-rounded life, but only in 'getting ahead.' . . . The term 'restless' is often applied to this struggle, but it is still more evidently *endless;* for any endeavor must be endless that seeks only quantity, since this is always boundless." [27]

Fifty-five years ago Van Wyck Brooks probed deeper. The typical American, he said, "has not been taught that life is a legitimate progress toward spiritual or intellectual ends. . . . He has had it embedded in his mind that the getting of a living is not a necessity incidental to some higher and more disinterested end, but that it is the prime and central end." Brooks wisely perceived that "economic self-assertion still remains to most Americans a sort of moral obligation, while self-fulfillment still looks like a pretty word for selfishness." [28]

There were those throughout the course of the American experience who denied that "economic self-assertion" was a "moral obligation" and "self-fulfillment" an act of "selfishness." They were rebels against the respectability of conventional success. For them, enlarging the house was not permitted to interfere with enlarging the self.

Over one hundred years ago an offbeat Harvard graduate, nature-loving poet, and freethinking transcendentalist from Concord, Massachusetts, escaped from the rat race of his own day. He penned a magnificent expression of the yearning to be free, still fresh, still relevant. Henry David Thoreau rebelled against the established conventions of his time. Cherishing privacy and the sweet solitude of nature, he turned his back on money-grubbing and retired in 1845 for two years, two months, and two days to the sylvan isolation of Walden Pond. Thoreau was a brusque man with a kind of frankness which put many people off. He never made a respectable living, was a bachelor with no family responsibilities, and his private education had already been paid for by someone else. Thoreau's courage is no greater than that of the fellow who can tell off his boss because he is an unambitious bachelor supported by a large independent income. His greatness was his philosophy of individualism. Unlike some philosophers, he not only philosophized about it but lived it.

Thoreau wanted to be his own kind of self-made man at Walden Pond. He tried to live as self-sufficiently as possible, building his own shelter, growing his own food, and providing his own fuel. By simplifying the necessities of life and avoiding its superficialities, he gained precious leisure. He found freedom to enjoy nature, to read, meditate, and write. "I wanted," he said, "to live deep and suck out all the marrow of life. . . ." [29]

"The mass of men," Thoreau observed, "lead lives of quiet desperation." They lay up "treasures which moth and rust will corrupt and thieves break through and steal. It is a fool's life, as they will find when they get to the end of it, if not before." Most people are in debt and are constantly debasing themselves to sell things. Who can speak of any divinity in man? "We live meanly, like ants. . . . Our life is frittered away by detail." Most luxuries and many "so-called comforts" of life are "positive hindrances to the elevation of mankind." The purpose of clothing is to retain vital heat and cover nakedness. Yet, "the head monkey at Paris puts on a traveller's cap, and all the monkeys in America do the same." There were "three pieces of limestone on my desk, but I was terrified to find that they required to be dusted daily, when the furniture of my mind was all undusted still, and I threw them out the window in disgust." If we read in the newspapers of one man robbed, a house burned, or a mad dog killed, "we never need read of another. One is enough. If you are acquainted with the principle, what do you care for a myriad instances and applications? To a philosopher all *news,* as it is called, is gossip, and they who edit and read it are old women over their tea. . . . What news! how much more important to know what that is which was never old!" [30]

Thoreau's economic philosophy was based, not on a labor theory of value, but on a life theory of value. "The cost of a thing," he said, "is the amount of what I will call life which is required to be exchanged for it, immediately or in the long run." How we have mortgaged life's precious time for our possessions! "Our houses are such unwieldy property that we are often imprisoned rather than housed in them. . . . We do not ride on the railroad; it rides upon us. . . . Men have become the tools of their tools." Thoreau found more independence as a day-laborer. He was finished at the end of the day, while the employer was at it all the time. [31]

Thoreau wanted people to be themselves, if necessary to be different and follow their own way, not their parents' or their neighbors'. Every man must live his own parable of self-discovery. At Walden Pond Thoreau lived his. "Every morning was a cheerful invitation to make my life of equal simplicity, and I may say innocence, with Nature herself." He wondered: "Why should we live with such hurry and waste of life? . . . Superfluous wealth can buy superfluities only. Money is not required to buy one necessary of the soul." The answer was clear for Thoreau: "Simplify, simplify." If there is to be conformity, lead a "life in conformity to higher principles. If the day and the night are such that you greet them with joy, and life emits a fragrance like flowers and sweet-scented herbs, is more elastic, more starry, more immortal,—that is your success. All nature is your con-

gratulation, and you have cause momentarily to bless yourself."
For anyone in the 1970s who is moving towards his own goal
while family and friends mutter the conformists' criticism that
everyone is out of step but he, Thoreau produced over one
hundred years ago a squelching twist on the conformists' march-
ing analogy: "Why should we be in such desperate haste to succeed and in such desperate enterprises? If a man does not keep
pace with his companions, perhaps it is because he hears a
different drummer. Let him step to the music that he hears,
however measured or far away." [32]

Thoreau was joined by those dissenters from the success
creed, discussed in the previous chapter, who were concerned
about the quality of American life. One critical response in the
1960s and early 1970s carried forward in its own way this
heritage of disaffection. It is too early to judge its historical
significance, which could be immensely influential on the future
of American values, but it is possible to describe its mood.

The New Romantics of the 1960s were the symbolic children
of that Babbitt who at a crisis point in his life struggled to be
daringly free. They could afford to carry the restless bourgeois'
occasional and ineffectual revolt against conformity to the extremes of 'doing their own thing.' Unlike the 'Up-against-the-
Wall' radical revolutionaries, the New Romantics (with a strong
Hippie element) were social evolutionists engaged in a peaceful,
non-political protest against the competitive ethic of success.
Dropouts from the traditional values of steady work, competition, and status-seeking (with its anxieties), they proclaimed a
life of meditation, cooperation, sensory gratification, and pleasure now.[33]

The New Romantics thumbed their nose at the likes of Henry
Ward Beecher who in the 1840s was wagging a stern index
finger at the youth of America and intoning: "Mere pleasure,—
sought outside of usefulness,—existing by itself,—is fraught with
poison." They put down John Cotton, the grandfather of Cotton
Mather, who decreed that a Christian may "bestir himself for
profit, this will he doe most diligently in his calling: And yet bee
a man dead-hearted to the world. . . ." To the Old Puritanism of

being "dead-hearted to the world," the New Romanticism decreed: "I feel, therefore I am." Wordsworth reflected their suspicion of reason:

> Our meddling intellect
> Mis-shapes the beauteous forms of things:—
> We murder to dissect.

And it was Jean Jacques Rousseau, not the success idea's John Calvin, who felt the same way they did about the nature of man. For the old Puritan, it was the evil in man which corrupted society. For the New Romantic, it was society which corrupted the goodness in man.[34]

The uptight organization man was an emotional ball-bearing bucking to be a big wheel. The New Romantics were all sensitive antennae tuned in on beauty, love, honesty, and fun. They were diverse as a movement and ephemeral in membership, but in one body they turned their backs on the American goals of mobility and crass achievement. Blowing marijuana smoke in the face of the middle-class dream, a dream which had sustained their parents through the struggles of the 1940s and 1950s, the New Romantics were not only asking, but actively seeking answers to an old question of increasing contemporary relevance: If I am not who I am, who will I be? Some sixty years ago James Terry White offered counsel sympathetic to their tradition:

> If thou of fortune be bereft,
>   And in thy store there be but left
> Two loaves—sell one, and with the dole
> Buy hyacinths to feed thy soul.[35]

The challenge of the New Romanticism to traditional life styles and life goals leads directly to our final dilemma. The alternatives bear upon happiness, leisure, and those consequences of psychic distress and ethical strain which we have examined in this chapter. The dilemma touches the ultimate concern of any society—survival.

The idea of success was nurtured in peace, but it was the threat of war that exploited it as a weapon of American foreign policy. The success idea became a weapon of American foreign policy because it was the keystone value contributing to an industrial strength upon which the national security of the United States was constructed. Just as each individual must pay a price for his own success, so the United States had to pay a price for assuming the leadership of the free world. That price was paid for in the tyranny of a national defense goal over domestic and personal goals in American life.

Work vs. leisure has always represented a dilemma for Americans, but in times of national peril the call to work was clamorous. In 1964 Alden B. Hoag, a newspaper editorial writer in Boston, asserted: "The Bomb is the stunning challenge of our times that extorts from us such an attention to world affairs as will not let us lapse into a preoccupation with leisure and satisfied stomachs. . . . We have to do better, for our national destiny depends upon it." In 1965 Boston University's dean of the chapel, Robert Hamill, could only point hopefully to a cybernetic revolution when automated machinery, coupled to the computer, would offer a guaranteed annual wage to all. In that bliss-filled future, Hamill promised, it will be an "absolute moral necessity that love and laughter replace the gross national product as the supreme value in the land." [36]

History, with a shrug of her shoulders, is weary of warning that civilizations decline and fall from within rather than from without. One hundred and fifty years ago Ezra Sampson quoted approvingly an interpretation of the fall of the Roman republic which he thought worth America's attention: "The course that a free nation runs, is from virtuous industry to wealth; from wealth to luxury; from luxury to an impatience of discipline and corruption of morals; till by a total degeneracy and loss of virtue, being grown ripe for destruction, it falls at last a prey to some hardy oppressor, and with the loss of liberty, loses every thing else that is valuable." [37]

The national security dilemma of individual self-fulfillment vs. national power has long tormented the United States but in particular since the 1940s. On the one hand, if the idea of success placed so much pressure on the individual to get ahead, then was it not doing so by misrepresenting the nature of opportunity in America and helping to create a world in which failure was shameful and happiness improbable? Success values encouraged neurotic or criminal behavior in some people whose level of aspiration was set above their level of potential. It was a source of anxiety, humiliation, and guilt. The success complex was a force for anti-intellectualism and a thief and tyrant of leisure.

At the same time, the success idea was the fuel which fed the engine of American growth. It was the keystone value which supported the material strength of a nation which was charged for several decades with the defense of the free world against totalitarianism.

On the other hand, if pressures on the individual to succeed were relaxed, if he were persuaded that his reach should not exceed his grasp, if Americans were no longer dissatisfied with their station in life, ceasing to hunger for material things to express their status, if incentive dissolved into a sweet contentment with one's lot, while 'true success' became the goal and not material success, then many of the frustrations and anxieties, the nagging guilt and the shame would more easily dissolve into a glow of inner peace and happiness. The Old Puritanism, which helped to build America by channeling human energy into productivity, would be transformed into the New Romanticism's willingness to risk feelings. For others, a decreasing attention to getting ahead in the job would permit an increasing absorption in the life of the mind for its own sake. Leisure would become a rewarding exercise in pleasurable self-development, while the arts, learning, and the intellect might still not get you anywhere, but getting somewhere in competition with others would become less important.

At the same time, wouldn't this shift in values check the nation's material growth? What would happen to the percentage increase in the Gross National Product if Americans stepped to a "different drummer" rather than to the Pied Piper of Success? Without the absorption in work and the drive for innovation, America would begin to slip from its position as the mightiest industrial nation in the world. The United States, for so long the bulwark against those powers which would destroy the free individual in a free society, would begin to crumble, and at last fall "prey to some hardy oppressor, and with the loss of liberty, lose every thing else that is valuable." [38]

During the middle decades of the twentieth century, first a Hot War with nazism and fascism, then a Cold War with communism, threatened what most Americans were convinced was the national security of the United States. During the 1950s and 1960s, they saw the nation in a race with Soviet Russia, which if lost, would deprive them of the right to live as free men. It was a competitive race geared to the driving force in the American ethos. At the founding of American Civilization, the Puritans were urged to choose work rather than leisure for the greater glory of God. By the middle decades of the twentieth century, Americans were encouraged to choose work over leisure for a secular God which was the national security of the nation.

26

BITCH GODDESS OR
COY MISTRESS?

A monumental paradox in American values is that nobody really approves of the definition of material success, but almost everybody wants to become the definition they deplore. In the first chapter we maintained that the cultural definition of business success was making money and translating it into status, or becoming famous. But we suggested that the cultural definition of success does not really tell us very much about what it was like to be an American. Indeed, one of the things we have discovered is that Americans have felt that success *ought* to be something else. It should have nothing to do with money. Thus we have the paradox: The individual American thought success should be defined in *non*-materialistic terms, but collectively, as a society, Americans measured success by a materialistic criterion. It is a paradox which may be confusing unless it is understood what Americans were trying to say about those values which gave meaning to their life.

When a middle-class American asserted that success ought *not* to be defined in materialistic terms, he was expressing a hierarchy of values. He was really saying that there are two kinds of success. And he was saying that the cultural definition of success which ranks people by material criteria is all right, except that it is wrong to assume that this kind of success is the *summum bonum* in life. The highest good in life cannot be measured by money. This personal definition of success was often referred to as 'true success.'

448

Robert Graves was reaching for a definition of true success when he quipped: "If there's no money in poetry, neither is there poetry in money." The poetry of a man's life is not in the things of "so-called success." True success is within ourselves—in peace of mind or happiness. When it is outside of ourselves, it flows from self-giving rather than self-seeking. It is measured by a happy family life or service to others. It flows out of what we are taught is our better selves. It is marked not by what assets we have accumulated in our estate but what good deeds we have sent before.[1]

The cultural and personal definitions of success were an expression of the ambivalence Americans felt about life goals. It is questionable whether the United States could function as a society if its people were no longer encouraged to hold conflicting feelings about success. Could one psychologically survive in a society driven forward by such anxiety-producing values without the comforting security of ambivalent attitudes? A life with illusions may be intolerable, but a life without illusions is unbearable.

We say to ourselves: "If *I* could be rich and famous, I would be happy." On the other hand, we think to ourselves: "Well, *he* may be rich and famous, but it's no guarantee he's happy, and in fact he probably isn't." Money cannot buy anything that really matters—the love of my family or good friends—but if I maybe had just a bit more of it, I would be a lot happier. At the same time, being a successful human being, having peace of mind, is a lot more important than being a success which is after all only what society thinks of me in terms of pretty crude standards.

That "money won't buy you happiness" is a folklore cliché which may or may not be true. That the rich don't enjoy their wealth as much as the common folk enjoy the little they have was a favorite theme in popular literature and films. We all have an image of the "poor, little rich girl," the withered crone alone with her wealth, the friendless crank in the "house on the hill." The rich are lonely. Husband and wife sit separated from each other at a long, elegantly appointed dining room table or glide by silently in a big yacht. Middle-class folk exude an air of merriment around their dinner tables and their perky little boats are alive with children's laughter and the coziness of family contentment.

The sufferings of the rich are among the sweetest pleasures of the poor. A whole generation of Americans grew up believing that John D. Rockefeller, Sr., could not enjoy a simple meal. Because of a bad stomach, he was reduced to nibbling crackers and sipping milk. The story is probably apocryphal, but the satisfaction it gave to millions of people is not. When Edwin Arlington Robinson strips away the appearance of contentment in "Richard Cory," are we really surprised?

> Whenever Richard Cory went down town,
> We people on the pavement looked at him:
> He was a gentleman from sole to crown,
> Clean favored, and imperially slim.
>
> And he was always quietly arrayed,
> And he was always human when he talked;
> But still he fluttered pulses when he said,
> "Good-morning," and he glittered when he walked.
>
> And he was rich—yes, richer than a king—
> And admirably schooled in every grace:
> In fine, we thought that he was everything
> To make us wish that we were in his place.
>
> So on we worked, and waited for the light,
> And went without the meat, and cursed the bread;
> And Richard Cory, one calm summer night,
> Went home and put a bullet through his head.[2]

Franklin P. Adams couldn't resist mocking the ambivalence:

> The rich man has his motor-car,
>   His country and his town estate.
> He smokes a fifty-cent cigar
>   And jeers at Fate.
>
> He frivols through the livelong day,
>   He knows not Poverty her pinch.
> His lot seems light, his heart seems gay,
>   He has a cinch.

> Yet though my lamp burns low and dim,
>   Though I must slave for livelihood—
> Think you that I would change with him?
>   You bet I would! [3]

Separately, and together, the cultural definition of material success and the personal definition of true success are shot through with paradoxes and ironies, ambivalences and ambiguities. If there is a crude success which society can measure, there is a finer success which we hold in our hearts' core. Getting to the top may be a whole lot more fun than being there. If we disdain what we desire, the only thing as sad as not realizing our dreams is to have them come true.

The holding of conflicting opinions toward success helps to explain the nature of American materialism—about which more heat than light is often generated. (For example, the surmise that the unfavorable consequences of industrialism were due to Americanism.) Americans were more materialistic than Europeans, not because they were greedier or liked money more, but because they used money more readily as a form of measurement. In the American open class system there were fewer criteria by which to measure another individual. Thus, materialism was a consequence of egalitarianism. Because of the greater symbolic significance of money, the profit motive was stimulated because money became an index measuring individual worth.

The American doctrine of materialism was a force for individual and national strength. Other doctrines of materialism, for example, certain forms of hedonistic pleasuring or a submergence in possessions purely for their own sake, could start a nation skidding into decline. American wealth began with personal austerity and self-denial. The enticements of increasing opulence eroding pioneering fiber might pose a threat to societies with a different set of values. In America, as long as competition for material rewards was keen and ambition to achieve these rewards was strong, what resulted was not weakness through self-indulgence but power through productivity.

If Americans were materialistic, they were also idealistic. The two most powerful nations on the globe are materialistic.

But the philosophical materialism of Marx is not at all the same as American materialism. For Marx all life could be reduced to matter and to a dialectical materialism which is shaped and controlled by economic determinism. American values express a belief in a dual reality of matter *and* the human spirit which transcends matter. This dualism between the materialism of success and the idealism of 'true success' helps to explain how American culture can be both materialistic and at the same time deeply spiritual. It is a philosophical position, for all its hypocrisy, which has probably done less mischief in the history of mankind than ideologies which have been reduced to a purer form of materialism or, at the other extreme, raised to a single-minded obsession with idealism.[4]

The ambivalence about success was revealed, as well, in certain beliefs and concepts. "Honesty is the best policy," yet it is true that more than one lavish house has been mortared with the slime of bribery and theft. Success is achieved by merit and 'know-how,' but somehow 'contacts' and 'know-who' is involved in getting ahead. An able man makes his own opportunities and luck is not very important, yet available opportunities and luck are important. We take pride in the self-made man's achievement as an expression of our social democracy, yet he is a bit crude, unlettered, and lacking in refinement.[5]

The self-made man expressed something of this ambivalence himself. At a speech-making luncheon at Rotary or Kiwanis, he thundered from the podium how he had come up the "hard way" in the University of Hard Knocks where the colors were black and blue and the college yell was "Ouch!" The Latin motto was no doubt *Per Aspera ad Astra.* Still, it was Brutus who reminds us in Shakespeare's *Julius Caesar:*

> But 'tis a common proof
> That lowliness is young ambition's ladder,
> Whereto the climber-upward turns his face;
> But when he once attains the upmost round,
> He then unto the ladder turns his back,
> Looks in the clouds, scorning the base degrees
> By which he did ascend.

If at the service club or luncheon he was to struggle born, at
the country club that evening he was to the manor born, though
his manner may deny it.[6]

Bitch Goddess or Coy Mistress? Perhaps the shape of both
were woven into the tapestry of the American experience. It
was a design of relationships in which the form and substance
of the one was dependent upon the other. How does one unravel
the less pleasing threads without changing the special quality
of the design? The special quality of that design was partially
woven out of the dilemmas of the success complex. The six
dilemmas are here summarized in the order in which they
emerged in this study.

The justification dilemma of self-giving vs. self-seeking is a
moral issue which the success idea tried to resolve. Is it possible
to be a Christian and a Capitalist, too? We should be loving,
kind, and self-giving. Yet we find ourselves in a world in which
we must be self-seeking, grasping, and self-interested. The character ethic, which dominated success literature until the 1930s,
sought to resolve this dilemma by the stewardship of wealth
doctrine. The religious interpretation of the stewardship doctrine justified money-making because it was an evidence of
God's favor and was also a way of glorifying Him. It was man's
duty to develop the best within himself through the character-
building ascetic virtues of hard work and thrift. As a steward
of the Lord, one ought honestly to make money so that one
could do good with it by giving it away for pious uses. The
secular interpretation of the stewardship doctrine stressed a
humanitarian justification. You have to get in order to do good
through giving. By the 1920s the supreme justification for success was the concept of service. In both its religious and secular
interpretations, the degree of one's success was the measure of
service to the community. To pursue your own self-interest is
to love your neighbor. In the concept of service, to get for
oneself is a process which gives to others.

The character ethic bound this dilemma to another dilemma.
The justification for success was not automatic; it depended

on certain conditions. The issue was joined in the character ethic dilemma of material success vs. 'true success.' It was the duty of every individual to work hard and try to become a success in his occupation. But the rewards of success might destroy the very virtues of character that made that success possible. There was always the danger, too, that material success would become an end in itself, that an individual would be tempted to believe that money-making and its rewards were the *summum bonum* in life. With varying degrees of emphasis, the character ethic incessantly warned that making success the final goal in life was a one-way ticket to damnation and personal disaster. The final goal in life should be 'true success,' that is, happiness or a noble character or peace of mind. Therefore, money-making was justified only if you were honest, contributed to the community through the stewardship doctrine or the concept of service, and recognized that 'true success' was the final goal in life. A tension was created between material success and 'true success.' The task of the individual was to hold this tension in balance. You were not permitted the comforting resolution of the justification dilemma unless you endured the continual introspection of the character ethic dilemma. Achievement was objectively justifiable only because each individual was subjectively accountable for his values and the manner in which he expressed them throughout his life in his thinking and in his behavior.

The personality ethic of manipulating other people has been the dominant means to success in self-help literature since the 1930s. It is not a philosophy to live by but a technique to earn a living with. Almost everyone in a responsible position has become a salesman, selling either himself, an idea, or a product. A breadwinner massaging other people to his way of thinking is the individual expression of the personality ethic. Advertising is its institutionalized expression. The difference between them is only a matter of degree. The personality ethic dilemma of hypocrisy vs. sincerity was shaped by the necessity in a consumption economy to manipulate people for personal or corporate gain. What happens to moral honesty when people become objects, when relationships are stained by the need to sell, when the self is soiled by the demand to sell the self? In personal affairs the insincerity and deceit of Dale Carnegieism becomes a smiling corruption of human relations. In administrative affairs hypocrisy and deception sink into the moral relativism of a public relations mentality in which truth is no longer in principles but in public opinion polls. Advertising as a formal occupation may resolve this dilemma by justifying the exploitation of human weaknesses in order to persuade people to spend their money. If luxuries do not progressively become necessities, the nation will slide into a recession. For some, the end justifies the means. For others, working in the enveloping world of the personality ethic, every day is a confrontation of their ideals with the realities of earning a living. ·

The political dilemma of freedom vs. equality evolves out of the clash between the critics of the success idea and its conservative defenders. To what extent must free individuals and corporations be regulated and taxed in the interests of the general welfare? The demands of the public sector must be measured against the freedom in the private sector to act and to own. Political equality and economic inequality must be held in some kind of democratic balance. Majority rule can break in upon the rights of property by redistributing wealth through a graduated tax in the interests of social justice. The concentration of economic power can disregard the public good by controlling political power for the privilege of vested interests. The task of government has been to sustain the right of equal opportunity while at the same time safeguard the right to unequal rewards.

The intertwining of desirable and undesirable cause and effect relationships is particularly revealed in the social democracy dilemma of freedom vs. authority. The individual American expresses his freedom in political democracy through the exercise of his franchise, in economic democracy through his sovereignty as a consumer in the marketplace, and in social democracy through a lack of deference for his 'betters.' From this kind of society, with its free choice and fluid class system, flows much of the criticism for which Europeans and intellectuals have lashed America—the absorption in money-making, a materialistic yardstick for the measurement of things that should be judged by other criteria, the vulgarity and low taste, and the sterility of anti-intellectualism. Much could be changed for the better by the existence of an elite of breeding and wealth toward which people felt a sense of deference in obedience to its taste leadership. An authoritarian style of government could exert its own taste leadership by exalting, for example, the arts, and most certainly by reordering the rewards of success. The dilemma involves the degree to which the reduction of individual freedom is worth the advantages of a more authoritarian economic and social system. The American form of materialism and anti-intellectualism is the price that has been paid for a social democracy.

The final dilemma expresses the conflict between the growth of the individual and the growth of the nation. The national security dilemma of individual self-fulfillment vs. national power expanded to survival dimensions during the 1940s and beyond. The success idea was one of the keystone values in the achievement of American economic growth. The massive Gross National Product of the United States was the foundation upon which the free world constructed its defense against the threat of aggressive totalitarianism. The price that American citizens have had to pay was a supreme national goal that cherished, not their spiritual and aesthetic growth as human beings, but the material growth of the United States. The two are not always synonymous either as goals or in terms of the methods necessary to achieve these goals. The success idea as a cluster of values fueled the engine of American material strength. But the price of manufacturing that fuel was costly. It was paid for by misrepresenting individual potential in relation to opportunity, sustaining anxiety-ridden pressures for success, provoking crime against person and property, increasing feelings of guilt and humiliation in failure, intensifying forces for unhappiness, and encouraging a vulgar grasping for success and status as a testimony to one's worth. The success idea and its expression in American life was the thief and tyrant of leisure. It plundered leisure of its delights as a civilizing refinement of the spirit and a pleasurable exercise of the mind. In America, where getting somewhere was crucial to self-esteem, the trouble with leisure was that it didn't get you anywhere.

It was Ralph Waldo Emerson, America's most respected nineteenth-century philosopher, who said about his country: "Our whole history appears like a last effort of the Divine Providence in behalf of the human race." For Lincoln, the United States was "the last best hope of earth." Such expressions of faith in that vast and visionary dream which is the promise of American life scarcely seem believable to those in despair about the gap between promise and national performance, between the rhetoric of preachment and the brute practice. Perhaps America has always been a dream incapable of realization, a promise too demanding to keep. Yet the incessant self-scrutiny which has always revealed a failure to honor the dream and live up to the promise has been another way of reaffirming the hope of both.[7]

Dilemmas, alas, cannot be resolved in the manner of King Solomon's legendary decision to divide the baby between the contending women. Absolutists with authoritarian mindsets have always found dilemmas unbearable. But it is the very existence of choice within a free society to which the dilemmas owe their existence. We do good only when we are free to do wrong.

Success is not a harbor but a voyage with its own perils to the spirit. The game of life is to come up a winner, to be a success, or to achieve what we set out to do. Yet there is always the danger of failing as a human being. The lesson that most of us on this voyage never learn, but can never quite forget, is that to win is sometimes to lose.

ACKNOWLEDGMENTS

A scholar's duty, ambition, and satisfaction is to serve the truth. It is a pleasure to single out some very special people who have helped me draw closer to it.

Ralph H. Gabriel, now professor emeritus at Yale University, was always encouraging me to strike out into new fields. Another counselor was John Sirjamaki who opened for me vistas in the social sciences. To Eric F. Goldman I owe a writer's debt—a concern for form as well as content, a respect for style as well as substance.

Scholars who have read selected chapters, or in a few cases the entire manuscript, and have offered valuable suggestions are Nathaniel Burt, Charles Braden, Freeman Champney, Ralph Gardner, David Hirst, Suzanne Keller, Leonard Labaree, Dieter Seibel, and Willard Thorp. I have plundered their most cherished possession—time—and am grateful to them for their gift of it to me.

I owe a special debt of gratitude to the staff of the Princeton University Library. William Dix, James Keels, Robert Winters, and Frederick Arnold, in particular, carried their thoughtfulness beyond the normal course of their duties. The reference staffs of the Yale University Library and the New York Public Library were particularly helpful. I appreciate the space made available to me to do research at the Library of Congress.

Of course, I alone am responsible for any imperfections of this book.

REFERENCES AND BIBLIOGRAPHY

I hope the references do not, in Samuel McChord Crothers' image, "run along, like little angry dogs, barking at the text." They are meant to be skimmed before or after reading a chapter.[1]

The purpose of the references and bibliographical notes is to identify quotations and supporting evidence, provide selected bibliographical information, and acknowledge secondary authorities upon whom I have drawn heavily or who have influenced my own thinking.

FOREWORD

[1] James Michener, "The Revolution in Middle-Class Values," *New York Times Magazine*, August 18, 1968, p. 87.

[2] Peter De Vries, *The Tunnel of Love* (Boston, 1954), p. 136.

CHAPTER 1

[1] Ralph Barton Perry, *Characteristically American* (New York, 1949), p. 10; and Harold J. Laski, *The American Democracy* (New York, 1948), p. 41.

[2] Quoted in *Time*, 73 (March 23, 1959), 63.

For the professions, see Howard M. Vollmer and Donald L. Mills eds., *Professionalization* (Englewood Cliffs, N. J., 1966); Kenneth S. Lynn and the editors of *Daedalus* eds., *The Professions In America* (Boston, 1965); Sigmund Nosow and William H. Form eds., *Man, Work, and Society* (New York, 1962).

[3] The quotation is from Ralph Ross and Ernest Van Den Haag, *The Fabric of Society* (New York, 1957), p. 750. I have tried to avoid the technique of quoting secondary authorities only as a foil. My objective, rather, is to open to thoughtful examination the cultural definition of success in America. Surprisingly, there exists no systematic analysis of that subject. Ross and Van Den Haag are perceptive observers of the American scene, and I quote them only to reflect a widely held viewpoint.

Naturally, considering the imprecision of the materials, the definition emerging from this analysis is imprecise. A minister could make a profit through royalties if his book of sermons became a bestseller. What is meant by non-profit is that the purpose of the occupation is not-for-profit. The complexity of the American economy in terms of the profit-seeking and not-for-profit sectors is discussed in Eli Ginzberg, Dale L. Hiestand, and Beatrice G. Reubens, *The Pluralistic Economy* (New York, 1965).

In this study, "success" and "achievement" are used synonomously.

[4] "The Standards Controlling Listing in Who's Who in America," *Who's Who in America* (Chicago, 1966), 34, 2; Cedric A. Larson, *Who: Sixty Years of American Eminence, The Story of Who's Who in America* (New York, 1958); R. W. Apple, Jr., "Who's Who Updated," *New York Times Magazine*, May 3, 1964, pp. 94ff.

[5] John C. Van Dyke, *The Money God* (New York, 1908), p. 52; A. B. Hollingshead, *Elmtown's Youth* (New York, 1949), p. 450.

[6] By status I mean a recognized position in society. Economic and social class ranking is a part of status. For social class and status see the relevant bibliographical references in Chapters 8, 23, and 24, and the following: Reinhard Bendix and Seymour Martin Lipset, eds., *Class, Status, and Power* (New York, 1966), second edition; Leonard Reissman, *Class in American Society* (Glencoe, Ill., 1959); John F. Cuber and William F. Kenkel, *Social Stratification in the United States* (New York, 1954); Seymour Martin Lipset and Reinhard Bendix, *Social Mobility in Industrial Society* (Berkeley and Los Angeles, Calif., 1959); Gerhard E. Lenski, *Power and Privilege* (New York, 1966); C. Wright Mills, *White Collar* (New York, 1951), and *The Power Elite* (New York, 1956); Suzanne Keller, *Beyond the Ruling Class: Strategic Elites in Modern Society* (New York, 1963), and "Social Class in Physical Planning," *International Social Science Journal*, 18 (December 1966), 494–512.

Social class and status is viewed from an historical perspective in Max Lerner, *America as Civilization* (New York, 1957); Seymour Martin Lipset, *The First New Nation* (New York, 1963); Oscar Handlin, *The Americans* (Boston, 1963); Jackson Turner Main, *The Social Structure of Revolutionary America* (Princeton, N. J., 1965); Douglas T. Miller, *Jacksonian Aristocracy: Class and Democracy in New York, 1830–1860* (New York, 1967); and Stephan Thernstrom, *Poverty and Progress: Social Mobility in a Nineteenth Century City* (Cambridge, Mass., 1964).

Stratification changes during the colonial period are explained in Gary B. Nash, *Class and Society in Early America* (Englewood Cliffs,

N. J., 1970); and John Demos, *A Little Commonwealth: Family Life in Plymouth Colony* (New York, 1970).

[7] Ben Hecht, *A Child of the Century* (New York, Signet Book Edition, 1955), p. 314.

[8] Walter Bagehot, "Introduction to the Second Edition, 1872," *The English Constitution* (London, 1964), p. 282.

[9] Quoted in Richard J. Whalen, "Joseph P. Kennedy: A Portrait of the Founder," *Fortune,* 67 (January 1963), 111. The full biography is Richard J. Whalen, *The Founding Father: The Story of Joseph P. Kennedy* (New York, 1964).

[10] Arthur Miller is quoted in *The New York Times,* December 6, 1967, p. 40; Fyodor Dostoyevsky, *The Brothers Karamazov* (New York: The Modern Library, [1950]), p. 302; Friedrich Nietzsche, *The Will to Power* (New York, 1967), p. 417. In the Nietzsche quotation I have added punctuation to the word "how" to make it read more clearly.

[11] [Anonymous], *The Pleasant Art of Money-Catching . . . To Which is Added, The Way How to Turn a Penny: Or The Art of Thriving* (London, 1714), Third edition, Preface (page numbers vary).

CHAPTER 2

[1] For propaganda about America as the land of opportunity, see John Smith, *A Description of New England* (1616) in *The American Mind: Selections from the Literature of the United States,* eds. Harry R. Warfel *et al.* (New York, 1947), pp. 6–8, and Josephine K. Piercy, *Studies in Literary Types in Seventeenth Century America, 1607–1710* (New Haven, 1939), p. 17. For those who turned around and went back, see Wilbur S. Shepperson, *Emigration and Disenchantment* (Norman, Oklahoma, 1965).

[2] The statistic on the proportion of farmers is from Arthur M. Schlesinger, "What Then Is the American, This New Man?," *American Historical Review,* 48 (January 1943), 229. See also Louis B. Wright, *The Cultural Life of the American Colonies, 1607–1763* (New York, 1957).

[3] Cotton Mather, *A Christian at his Calling* (Boston, 1701), pp. 37, 38, 41, 42. In quoting from works published prior to 1800, capitalization and punctuation have generally been translated into modern usage, but in no case has the spelling, language, or meaning been changed.

[4] *Ibid.,* pp. 47–49.

[5] *Ibid.,* pp. 65, 38, 62, 22. (Page numbers for citations are not necessarily in numerical order but are in sequence of quotation.)

[6] Cotton Mather, "The True Cause of Loosing," [sic] in *Durable Riches* (Boston, 1695), p. 5; *Sober Sentiments* (Boston, 1722), p. 26. See also "The True Way of Thriving," in *Durable Riches* (Boston, 1695), and *Essays to do Good* (New York, 1815).

E. A. J. Johnson, *American Economic Thought in the Seventeenth Century* (London, 1932), pp. 9, 86–100, 266–267, discusses the Puritan attitude toward wealth, while Robert S. Michaelsen, "Changes in the Puritan Concept of Calling or Vocation," *New England Quarterly*, 26 (September 1953), 315–336, points up changes in the Puritan concept of the calling during the course of the seventeenth century.

Useful general discussions of Puritanism are George M. Waller, ed., *Puritanism in Early America* (Boston, 1950); Perry Miller, *The New England Mind from Colony to Province* (Cambridge, Mass., 1953); Winthrop S. Hudson, *Religion in America* (New York, 1965); Stow Persons, *American Minds: A History of Ideas* (New York, 1958); Howard Mumford Jones, *O Strange New World. American Culture: The Formative Years* (New York, 1964).

A bibliography of attitudes toward Puritanism, favorable and unfavorable, is offered in Nelson R. Burr, *A Critical Bibliography of Religion in America* (Princeton, N. J., 1961), IV, Part 2, 105–109.

[7] William Penn, *The Advice of William Penn to his Children.* Quoted in Frederick B. Tolles, *Meeting House and Counting House: The Colonial Merchants of Colonial Philadelphia, 1682–1763* (Chapel Hill, 1948), p. 45.

[8] *Ibid.*, pp. 45–84; Joseph Dorfman, *The Economic Mind in American Civilization, 1606–1885* (New York, 1946), I, 78–92; Frederick B. Tolles, *Quakers and the Atlantic Community* (New York, 1960), pp. 55–65.

[9] For an analysis of bourgeois morality reflected in success handbooks of sixteenth- and seventeenth-century England, see Louis B. Wright, *Middle-Class Culture in Elizabethan England* (Chapel Hill, N. C., 1935), pp. 165–200.

The character ethic was no monopoly of Protestantism. Since the sixteenth century secular writers had been pointing out the obvious connection between working hard and making money.

[10] For examples of British eighteenth-century success literature, see [Anonymous] *The Way to be Wise and Wealthy, or The Excellency of Industry and Frugality: In Sundry Maxims Suitable to the Present Times* (Dublin, 1769); [Anonymous] *The New Art of Thriving; or, The Way to Get and Keep Money* (Glasgow, 1797); A Merchant, *The Way to be Wise and Wealthy; Recommended to All*, 2nd edition (London, 1755).

[11] Werner Sombart, *The Quintessence of Capitalism* (New York, 1915), pp. 103–124, states that the bourgeois type began to appear towards the close of the fourteenth century.

[12] Harold J. Laski, *The American Democracy* (New York, 1948), p. 39. Benjamin Franklin, "Letter to Jean-Baptiste Le Roy," in *The Writings of Benjamin Franklin*, ed. Albert H. Smyth (New York, 1906), IV, 572–573. The Smyth edition, published in ten volumes from 1905 to 1907, has been for a half century the standard edition but is being superseded by the successive volumes of *The Papers of Benjamin Franklin*, published by the Yale University Press.

The number of Franklin's children is confirmed in a letter to the author from Leonard W. Labaree dated July 9, 1969.

[13] Benjamin Franklin, *Autobiography* in *Writings,* I, 253–255. A useful narrative bibliography about Franklin is Charles L. Sanford, ed., *Benjamin Franklin and the American Character* (Boston, 1955), pp. 99–102. The selections in this volume are well-chosen and revealing. See also Robert E. Spiller et al. eds., *Literary History of the United States* (New York, 1948), III (bibliography), 507–515, and the footnotes in Richard D. Miles, "The American Image of Benjamin Franklin," *American Quarterly, 9* (Summer 1957), 117–143.

[14] Benjamin Franklin, *Writings,* I, 226. *The Way to Wealth* was first printed in the almanac of 1758 as *Father Abraham's Speech,* but the title used here was more frequently employed in reprinting the essay. For the sources of the maxims, the originals and the changes made by Franklin, see Bernard Fay, *Franklin, The Apostle of Modern Times* (Boston, 1949), pp. 30–33, 158–169, and Carl Van Doren, *Benjamin Franklin* (New York, 1938), pp. 109–113, 266–268. For a comparison of Franklin to early Scandinavian success literature, see Rosalie and Murray Wax, "The Vikings and the Rise of Capitalism," *American Journal of Sociology,* 61 (July 1955), 1–10.
Leonard W. Labaree, Ralph L. Ketcham, Helen C. Boatfield, and Helene H. Fineman, "Introduction," in *The Autobiography of Benjamin Franklin* (New Haven, 1964), pp. 1–40, is the point of departure for that work.

[15] Benjamin Franklin, *The Way to Wealth* in *Writings,* III, 407–418, and *Writings,* II, 372.

[16] Benjamin Franklin, *Writings,* I, 326–339.

[17] Franklin, of course, did not *deny* the importance of intelligence and learning as a means to success, but the shadings of emphasis are indicative.

[18] Louis B. Wright, "Franklin's Legacy to the Gilded Age," *Virginia Quarterly Review,* 22 (1946), 268–279; A. Whitney Griswold, "Three Puritans on Prosperity," *New England Quarterly,* 7 (September 1934), 483–488; Irvin G. Wyllie, *The Self-Made Man in America* (New Brunswick, N. J., 1954), pp. 12–13; I. Bernard Cohen (ed. with extensive commentary), *Benjamin Franklin: His Contribution to the American Tradition* (Indianapolis and New York, 1953), pp. 112–163, emphasize the Puritan strain in Franklin, but in fairness they did so to correct a position that had underestimated the Puritan influence on Franklin. Alfred Owen Aldridge, *Benjamin Franklin and Nature's God* (Durham, North Carolina, 1967), is a full-length study of Franklin's religious attitudes.

[19] The quotation is from Benjamin Franklin, *Writings,* III, 416. In the *Autobiography,* "sack" replaces "bag." (I, 343.) Mather's charge on tithing is in *Essays to do Good* (1710) (New York, 1815), pp. 157–168. This is the title under which it was often republished. Franklin read Mather's book as a youth in Boston.
Cf. Herbert W. Schneider, *The Puritan Mind* (New York, 1930), pp. 241, 246, 248–256, and *A History of American Philosophy* (New

York, 1946), pp. 39–42; Max Weber, *The Protestant Ethic and the Spirit of Capitalism* (New York, 1930), pp. 160–162, 180; R. H. Tawney, *Religion and the Rise of Capitalism* (New York, 1936), p. 238.

[20] *The Autobiography of Benjamin Franklin,* eds. Leonard W. Labaree et al. (New Haven, Conn., 1964), p. 45, and Benjamin Franklin, *Writings,* III, 409, 417. See also *Advice to a Young Tradesman, Writings,* II, 372.

[21] Benjamin Franklin, *Writings,* I, 357. In at least five separate places, Franklin made the point that the most acceptable service we can render to God is doing good to his children. Though this could be construed as a religious justification for success, the whole spirit of Franklin's philosophy is firmly constructed on a humanistic rather than a supernatural justification. Franklin's point in the following references is that our most acceptable service to God is not praying and performing church ceremonies but doing good to mankind. The five separate places are *Autobiography* in *Writings,* I, 325, 332, 341; "Letter to Joseph Huey" (1753), III, 143–146; "Letter to Ezra Stiles" (1790), X, 83–85.

[22] *Aristotle's Ethics for English Readers,* trans. H. Rackham (Oxford, 1943), p. 28.

[23] For Franklin's statements about anti-materialism, long buried in almanacs seldom disturbed, see Carl Van Doren, "Concluding Paper," in *Meet Dr. Franklin* (Philadelphia, 1943), p. 232, and Whitfield J. Bell, Jr., "Benjamin Franklin as an American Hero," *Association of American Colleges Bulletin,* 43 (March 1957), 128. See, also, Harold A. Larrabee, "Poor Richard in an Age of Plenty," *Harper's,* 212 (January 1956), 64–68.

[24] Benjamin Franklin, *Writings,* I, 323. Ben's father, influenced no doubt by Puritanism, used the word "calling" rather than "business." The biblical reference is Proverbs xxii:29.

[25] The quotation is from Nathaniel Hawthorne, *Tales, Sketches, and Other Papers, The Works of Nathaniel Hawthorne* (Boston and New York, 1883), XII, 202. Hawthorne also made it clear that he thought Franklin's Poor Richard expressed a limited philosophy. The statistic is the opinion of Paul L. Ford, *A List of the Books Written by or Relating to Benjamin Franklin* (Brooklyn, N. Y., 1889), p. 55.

[26] Max Weber, *The Protestant Ethic and the Spirit of Capitalism* (New York, 1930), p. 180.

CHAPTER 3

[1] Mary S. Holmes, "Happy Memories," letter to the editor of the *New York Times Magazine,* June 3, 1951, p. 4.

[2] For sales, see Richard D. Mosier, *Making the American Mind: Social and Moral Ideas in the McGuffey Readers* (New York, 1947), p. 168. After judging the conflicting statistics on sales, Mosier sides with the figures of Mr. Louis Dilman, president of the American Book Com-

pany. Mr. Dilman's statistics are cited in John L. Clifton, *Ten Famous American Educators* (Columbus, 1933), p. 75. For influence, see Mark Sullivan, *Our Times* (New York, 1927), II, 22. In a "rather painstaking survey," Sullivan found that McGuffey's influence "never reached any of New England except the one small southwestern corner close to New York City. Elsewhere, McGuffey's [influence] was almost universal." (Page 18, n. 1.) For the nineteenth-century textbook warfare between the McGuffey Readers and Appleton Readers, see p. 20, n. 1.

Harry R. Warfel, *Noah Webster: Schoolmaster to America* (New York, 1936), and Merle Curti, *The Social Ideas of American Educators* (New York, 1935), pp. 31–34, tell the story of Noah Webster. For an analysis of adolescent values reflected in children's literature of the nineteenth century, see Henry S. Commager, *The American Mind* (New Haven, 1950), pp. 35–40.

[3] See Richard M. Mosier, *Making the American Mind: Social and Moral Ideas in the McGuffey Readers,* pp. 154, 164–165. This is the best study of the ideology of the McGuffey Readers. The life of McGuffey is told in Harvey C. Minnich, *William Holmes McGuffey and His Readers* (Cincinnati, 1936). We have concentrated on the success theme in McGuffey, but as Henry Steele Commager, "McGuffey and His Readers," *Saturday Review,* 45 (June 16, 1962), 50ff., points out, the Readers, the Fifth and Sixth especially, were cosmopolitan rather than parochial in their selection of English and American literature. Henry F. Graff, "McGuffey's Lessons—and Non-Lessons," *New York Times Magazine,* December 3, 1961, pp. 50ff., comments on the relevance of the Readers to the upbringing of today's youth.

[4] "Waste Not, Want Not" is from *McGuffey's New Fourth Eclectic Reader* (Cincinnati and New York, 1866), pp. 63–65. L. S. Dutton in a letter to the author, December 3, 1957, concludes that the story probably first appeared in the extensively revised 1857 edition. The second quotation is from *McGuffey's Newly Revised Eclectic Third Reader* (Cincinnati, 1853), p. 184. Quoted in R. D. Mosier, *Making the American Mind,* p. 22.

There was a great deal of borrowing back and forth in these children's stories. For example, in *The Parents Assistant* (Philadelphia, 1853), pp. 394–424, the popular Irish author, Maria Edgeworth, spins a similar yarn over a great many more pages. Miss Edgeworth's stories for children were first published in the early years of the nineteenth century.

[5] *McGuffey's Newly Revised Eclectic Second Reader* (Cincinnati, 1844), p. 47. Quoted in R. D. Mosier, *Making the American Mind,* p. 106.

[6] See Phyllis McGinley, "Lessons for Today: From McGuffey," *New York Times Magazine,* May 20, 1951, pp. 9ff.

[7] Sinclair Lewis, "Foreword," in *Henry Ward Beecher: An American Portrait* by Paxton Hibben (1927) (New York, 1942), p. vii. The Hibben book is a sharp, often vicious, attack in the debunking tradition. Lyman Abbott, *Henry Ward Beecher* (Boston and New York, 1903), is

sympathetic but discriminating. Friendly but judicious is Harris E. Starr in *Dictionary of American Biography* s.v. "Beecher, Henry Ward." Robert Shaplen, *Free Love and Heavenly Sinners* (New York, 1954), is a detailed account of the trial.

⁸ Henry Ward Beecher, *Lectures to Young Men* (1844) (Boston and New York, 1846), pp. 28, 48. The quotation is from Proverbs xxii: 29. The title varies for this collection of lectures.

⁹ *Ibid.*, pp. 80–81.

¹⁰ *Ibid.*, pp. 86, 88, 90.

¹¹ *Ibid.*, pp. 93, 95.

¹² James D. Hart, *The Popular Book: A History of America's Literary Taste* (New York, 1950), p. 109; Allan Nevins in *Dictionary of American Biography* s.v. "Arthur, Timothy Shay"; Hervey Allen, *Israfel: The Life of Edgar Allan Poe* (New York, 1926, 1934), p. 335.

¹³ The quotation is from Timothy Shay Arthur, *Advice to Young Men* (1847) (Boston, 1853), p. 158. *Ten Nights in a Bar-Room, and What I Saw There* (1854) (Philadelphia, 1858); *Where There's a Will There's a Way* in *The Way to Prosper . . . And Other Tales* (1851) (Boston and Philadelphia, 1854); *True Riches or Wealth without Wings* (1853) (Philadelphia, 1859); *A Way to be Happy* and *How to Attain True Greatness* in *The Last Penny and Other Stories* (1852) (Philadelphia, 1859); *Retiring from Business* (New York, 1847). Warren G. French, "Timothy Shay Arthur: Pioneer Business Novelist," *American Quarterly*, 10 (Spring 1958), 55–65, points up the strong strain of anti-materialism in Arthur's fiction. For the moral flavor of ante-bellum America, see Carl Bode, *The Anatomy of American Popular Culture*, 1840–1861 (Berkeley and Los Angeles, 1959).

¹⁴ Andrew Carnegie, *Triumphant Democracy* (New York, 1885), p. 1; Charles and Mary Beard, *The Rise of American Civilization*, revised edition (New York, 1933), II, 176, 205.

¹⁵ C. and M. Beard, *op. cit.*, 52–121. At the same time, as Thomas C. Cochran, "Did the Civil War Retard Industrialization?" *Mississippi Valley Historical Review*, 48 (September 1961), 197–210, points out, the Civil War probably retarded rather than accelerated rates of economic growth.

¹⁶ The quotation is from *Washington Star*, October 26, 1905, and is cited in Henry F. Pringle, *Theodore Roosevelt* (New York, 1931), p. 371. For southern authors, see, for example, the works of Margaret Mitchell, William Faulkner, Erskine Caldwell, Lillian Smith, Tennessee Williams, and the Negro writers, Frank Yerby and Richard Wright. For a discussion of aspirations, see Wilbert E. Moore and Robin M. Williams, "Stratification in the Ante-Bellum South," *American Sociological Review*, 7 (June 1942), 343–351.

¹⁷ For interpretations which accentuate the differences between the South and the nation, see C. Vann Woodward, *The Burden of Southern History* (Baton Rouge, Louisiana, 1960), and "The Southern Ethic in a Puritan World," *William and Mary Quarterly*, 25 (July 1968), 343–

370, especially pp. 365–370 which is a moving, sorrowful statement about the tragedy of the southern experience since the Civil War; Seymour Martin Lipset, *The First New Nation* (New York, 1963), pp. 319–320; and David Bertelson, *The Lazy South* (New York, 1967). For interpretations which diminish the 'differentness' between the South and the North, or between the South and the rest of the nation, see Charles Grier Sellers, Jr., *The Southerner as American* (Chapel Hill, North Carolina, 1960); Howard Zinn, *The Southern Mystique* (New York, 1964); and David M. Potter, "The Historian's Use of Nationalism and Vice Versa," *American Historical Review,* 67 (July 1962), 924–950.

[18] The first quotation is from C. Vann Woodward, *Tom Watson: Agrarian Rebel* (New York, 1938), p. 89. The Grady quotation is from *Atlanta Constitution,* August 15, 1880, and is cited in Woodward, *Tom Watson,* p. 90. See also, C. Vann Woodward, *Origins of the New South: 1877–1913* (Louisiana State University Press, 1951), pp. 142–174.

[19] Bliss Perry, *The American Mind* (Boston and New York, 1912), p. 84; Clyde and Florence R. Kluckhohn, "American Culture: Generalized Orientations and Class Patterns," in *Conflicts of Power in Modern Culture,* ed. Lyman Bryson et al. (New York, 1947), p. 115. This was an ambivalent attitude. As the Kluckhohns point out, there was also a tendency "to snipe at superior individuals. . . ." (p. 115) Thorstein Veblen's phrase was that America was the self-made man's "native habitat." *The Theory of Business Enterprise* (1904) (New York, 1932), p. 273.

[20] Cf. Lester Frank Ward, "Broadening the Way to Success," *Forum,* 2 (December 1886), 343–344.

[21] Ralph Barton Perry, *Puritanism and Democracy* (New York, 1944), p. 308.

[22] For the self-made man designation as a political advantage, see William Burlie Brown, *The People's Choice: The Presidential Image in the Campaign Biography* (Baton Rouge, La., 1960), pp. 48–61, and John William Ward, *Andrew Jackson: Symbol for an Age* (New York, 1955), pp. 166–180. For suggested changes, see Henry F. Graff, "Decease of the 'Log Cabin' Legend," *New York Times Magazine,* June 30, 1963, pp. 8ff. Sidney H. Aronson, *Status and Kinship in the Higher Civil Service: Standards of Selection in the Administrations of John Adams, Thomas Jefferson, and Andrew Jackson* (Cambridge, Mass., 1964), measures the distance between the image and the reality in the democratization of the governing elite in Jackson's administration.

[23] Henry Clews, *Fifty Years in Wall Street* (New York, 1908). Quoted in Matthew Josephson, *The Robber Barons* (New York, 1934), p. 315; Henry Seidel Canby, *The Age of Confidence: Life in the Nineties* (New York, 1934), p. 241.

[24] Harold Laski, *The American Democracy* (New York, 1948), pp. 165, 172; *Speeches of William Jennings Bryan* (New York, 1909), I, 241. See also, for example, Solon J. Buck, *The Agrarian Crusade* (New

Haven, 1920), p. 128, which notes that the Southern Alliance in 1887 declared itself "a business organization for business purposes. . . ."

[25] A third classification of heroes, Idols of Entertainment, is suggested in a later chapter.

Measuring historical changes in exemplars of children is loaded with methodological pitfalls. My own feeling is that the changes in substance are much less than one might suspect. Beginning with the 1898 Estelle M. Darrah survey, Fred I. Greenstein, "New Light on Changing American Values: A Forgotten Body of Survey Data," *Social Forces,* 42 (May 1964), 441–450, takes a plunge into the problem. For heroes, see Dixon Wecter, *The Hero in America* (New York, 1941), p. 317; Morton Yarmon, "Changing Fashions in Our Heroes," *New York Times Magazine,* May 15, 1955, pp. 28ff.; Marshall W. Fishwick, *The Hero, American Style* (New York, 1969); and Theodore P. Greene, *America's Heroes: The Changing Models of Success in American Magazines* (New York, 1970), which is not so much about success as the admired qualities of heroes depicted in biographical articles in selected. popular magazines from the 1890s to the 1910s.

[26] Edwin T. Freedley, *A Practical Treatise on Business* (1852) (Philadelphia, 1856), p. 5; *Appleton's Cyclopedia of American Biography* s.v. "Freedey, Edwin Troxell."

[27] The quotation is from Freeman Hunt, *Lives of American Merchants* (1857) (New York, 1858), I, vi. See also A. Everett Peterson in *Dictionary of American Biography* s.v. "Hunt, Freeman," and Jerome Thomases, "Freeman Hunt's America," *Mississippi Valley Historical Review,* 30 (December 1943), 395–407.

[28] E. T. Freedley, *A Practical Treatise on Business,* p. 7; Freeman Hunt, *Worth and Wealth* (New York, 1856), p. 403.

[29] Edwin T. Freedley, *A Practical Treatise on Business,* pp. 58–60, 37–38, 46–57. The quotations are from pp. 58–59.

[30] Freeman Hunt, *Worth and Wealth,* pp. 60–63, 45, 248, 352. The quotations are from pp. 182, 31, and 293. For the dangers inherent in money, see p. 404. For an ideal successful man, see pp. 62–64.

[31] Matthew Hale Smith, *Bulls and Bears of New York* (1873) (Hartford and Chicago, 1875), p. 541; *Successful Folks* (Hartford, 1878), p. 496.

[32] James A. Garfield, *Elements of Success* (Philadelphia, n.d.), pp. 8–9, 13, 14.

[33] Horace Greeley, *An Address on Success in Business* (New York, 1867), p. 3. The description is from a letter by S. S. Packard preceding the published address.

[34] *Ibid.,* pp. 38, 35. For Greeley's faith in opportunity in the West, see James Parton, *The Life of Horace Greeley* (Boston, 1889), p. 534. L. U. Reavis, *A Representative Life of Horace Greeley* (New York, 1872), pp. 501–503, celebrates Greeley as equal, if not superior, to Benjamin Franklin as "the greatest of all self-made men this country has produced." (p. 502)

CHAPTER 4

[1] For a discussion of agrarian opportunity, see Henry Nash Smith, *Virgin Land: The American West as Symbol and Myth* (Cambridge, Mass., 1950).

[2] The first two quotations are from the introductory statement of Horatio Alger Awards Committee of the American Schools and Colleges Association, Inc., *Opportunity Still Knocks* (New York, 1958). The Sarnoff quotation is from the *New York Times,* May 10, 1957, p. 20. See also "Horatio Alger, Inc.," *Time,* 50 (July 21, 1947), 80.

[3] The novel count was arrived at by subtracting Alger's other works from the total given in Ralph D. Gardner, *Horatio Alger, or The American Hero Era* (Mendota, Ill., 1964), pp. 355–390. The estimate of sales varies widely. Quentin Reynolds, *The Fiction Factory* (New York, 1955), p. 83, cites an estimate of 250,000,000. Ralph Gardner, *op. cit.,* p. 356, seems to favor a total of 400,000,000. Frank Luther Mott, *Golden Multitudes: The Story of Best Sellers in the United States* (New York, 1947), pp. 158–159, says that "a sale of a hundred million in these years is preposterous." Mott stands on an aggregate sale of 16,000,000 to 17,000,000.

Ragged Dick was chosen by the Grolier Club as one of the 100 influential American books printed before 1900. See the Grolier Club, *One Hundred Influential American Books Printed Before 1900* (New York, 1947), p. 107.

[4] Herbert R. Mayes, *Alger: A Biography Without a Hero* (New York, 1928).

Attempts to find the diary are detailed in correspondence between Mayes, the author, and Malcolm Cowley in 1957 and 1958, on deposit in the Princeton University Library. Cowley raised suspicions about the diary's authenticity in "The Alger Story," *New Republic,* 113 (September 10, 1945), 319. John Seelye, "Who Was Horatio? The Alger Myth and American Scholarship," *American Quarterly,* 17 (Winter 1965), 749–756, adds further documentation to the story.

A biography of Horatio Alger, Jr., is needed. Frank Gruber, *Horatio Alger, Jr.: A Biography and Bibliography* (West Los Angeles, 1961), is solid but not sufficiently comprehensive, while Ralph Gardner, *Horatio Alger, or The American Hero Era* (Mendota, Ill., 1964), is flawed by imaginary conversations, though the scholarship is careful and the bibliographical sections superior. The pre-Mayes, published, biographical information in Grace Williamson Edes, *Annals of the Harvard Class of 1852* (Cambridge, Mass., 1922), *passim,* is to be preferred to John Tebbel, *From Rags to Riches: Horatio Alger, Jr., and the American Dream* (New York, 1963), who concluded that Mayes's biography "can hardly be improved upon four decades later . . . . Mr. Mayes's research was definitive . . . ." (p. v). It will take some time to correct the errors of what was no doubt a 1920s debunking caper.

[5] For this new light on Alger I am grateful to Mrs. Curtis Eldridge, clerk of the First Parish in Brewster, for church documents requested.

The reasons given by Gruber and Gardner for Alger's departure are also no doubt true—as far as they go. Frank Gruber, *op. cit.,* pp. 22, 25–26; Ralph Gardner, *op. cit.,* p. 183.

[6] We are searching for a very broad overview of Alger's novels and not marking exceptions to these generalizations. Alger, for example, wrote a novel, *Tattered Tom* (1871), about a girl. She was, however, a tomboy.

The bibliography of Alger's works in Ralph Gardner, *op. cit.,* pp. 394–497, is a monumental piece of work and supersedes all others. For discussions of Alger's novels, see Gardner and Frank Gruber, *op. cit., passim,* other works cited in this section, and the following: S. N. Behrman, "Two Algers," in *Strive and Succeed* (New York, 1967), pp. v–xii; Robert Falk, "Notes on the 'Higher Criticism' of Horatio Alger, Jr.," *Arizona Quarterly,* 19 (Summer 1963), 151–167; Norman N. Holland, "Hobbling with Horatio, or the Uses of Literature," *Hudson Review,* 12 (Winter 1959–60), 549–557; John G. Cawelti, *Apostles of the Self-Made Man* (Chicago, 1965), pp. 101–123; Clifton Fadiman, "Party of One," *Holiday,* 21 (February 1957), 6ff., and *Any Number Can Play* (Cleveland and New York, 1957), p. 39; R. Richard Wohl, "The 'Rags to Riches Story': An Episode of Secular Idealism," in Reinhard Bendix and Seymour Martin Lipset, eds., *Class, Status and Power* (New York, 1966), pp. 501–506, and (edited by Moses Rischin), "The 'Country Boy' Myth and Its Place in American Urban Culture: The Nineteenth-Century Contribution," *Perspectives in American History,* 3 (1969), 77–156; "Holy Horatio," *Time,* 46 (August 13, 1945), 98ff.; Russel B. Nye, *The Unembarrassed Muse: The Popular Arts in America* (New York, 1970), pp. 62–72.

[7] Horatio Alger, Jr., *Ragged Dick* and *Phil, the Fiddler* in *Struggling Upward and Other Works* (New York, 1945); *Luck and Pluck* (1869) (Philadelphia, n.d.). *Phil, the Fiddler* is particularly significant because it helped to destroy the padrone system by which little street musicians were brought over from Italy and kept in virtual slavery.

[8] Henry F. and Katherine Pringle, "The Rebellious Parson," *Saturday Evening Post,* 223 (February 10, 1951), 30.

[9] Horatio Alger, Jr., *Bound to Rise or Up the Ladder* (New York, 1908), p. 1.

[10] Russel Crouse, "Introduction," in Horatio Alger, Jr., *Struggling Upward and Other Works* (New York, 1945), p. viii.

[11] Benjamin Shurtleff, *The History of the Town of Revere* (n.p., 1938), pp. 277 and 291, gives the date of assignment as April 13, 1844.

[12] Horatio Alger, Jr., *From Canal Boy to President or The Boyhood and Manhood of James A. Garfield* (New York, 1881), p. 9; *The Backwoods Boy or The Boyhood and Manhood of Abraham Lincoln* (Philadelphia, 1883), p. 9. For a discussion of the Lincoln book, see Jordan D. Fiore, "Horatio Alger, Jr., as a Lincoln Biographer," *Journal of the Illinois State Historical Society,* 46 (Autumn, 1953), 247–253. For comments on the log cabin in American folklore, see Harold R. Shurtleff,

The Log Cabin Myth, ed. Samuel Eliot Morison (Cambridge, Mass., 1939), pp. 5–6.

[13] The quotations are from Horatio Alger, Jr., *From Farm Boy to Senator or The Boyhood and Manhood of Daniel Webster* (Philadelphia, 1882), p. 300, and *The Backwoods Boy,* p. 10.

[14] *Lamb's Biographical Dictionary of the United States* s.v. "Thayer, William Makepeace"; Verne L. Samson in *Dictionary of American Biography* s. v. "Thayer, William Makepeace."

[15] William M. Thayer, "Introduction," *The Farmer Boy and How He Became Commander-in-Chief* by Uncle Juvinell [Morrison Heady] (New York, 1863), p. 4.

[16] William M. Thayer, *Turning Points in Successful Careers* (New York, 1895), p. iii. The passage is from *Julius Caesar,* IV, iii.

[17] *Ibid.,* pp. 74, 308, 350, v.

[18] Albert G. Boyden, "Introduction," *Ethics of Success* by William M. Thayer (Boston, 1893), p. 6.

[19] W. M. Thayer, *Ethics of Success,* pp. 17, 18, 247. In *Tact, Push, and Principle* (1880) (Boston, 1881), p. 37, tact is defined as "the ability to use natural powers, acquisitions, and opportunities to the best advantage."

[20] *Ibid.,* p. 432. For the Bible considered as a "business manual" with a number of supporting quotations from it, see pp. 439–444. See also W. M. Thayer, *Onward to Fame and Fortune or Climbing Life's Ladder* (New York, 1893, 1897).

[21] Agnes Rush Burr, *Russell H. Conwell and His Work* (Philadelphia, 1926), p. 19. This is the 'official' biography.

[22] The quotations are from W. C. Crosby, "Acres of Diamonds," *American Mercury,* 14 (May 1928), 111.

[23] Maurice F. Tauber, *Russell Herman Conwell, 1843–1925: A Bibliography* (Philadelphia, 1935), item number 22, gives the figure as 6,125. Robert Shackleton, *Russell H. Conwell: His Life and Achievements* in *Acres of Diamonds* by R. H. Conwell (New York, 1915), p. 168, states that "several millions of dollars, in all, have been received by Russell Conwell as the proceeds from this single lecture."

In a letter to the author, dated December 16, 1957, Richard H. Wissler, Curator of the Conwellana-Temple Room at Temple University, states that *Acres of Diamonds* "netted close to seven million dollars." Wissler reports that Conwell's son recalled that his father told him that the lecture was first given in 1870 under the title, "Lessons of Travel." For background material, see Russell H. Conwell, "Fifty Years on the Lecture Platform," in *Acres of Diamonds* by R. H. Conwell (New York, 1915), pp. 173–181.

For Conwell's college days and their influence, see Agnes Rush Burr, *Russell H. Conwell and His Work,* pp. 101–105, 310–311.

[24] The quotation is from Victoria Case and Robert Ormond Case, *We Called It Culture* (Garden City, N. Y., 1948), pp. 65–66. See also

Mary Louise Gehring, "Russell H. Conwell: American Orator," *Southern Journal of Speech,* 20 (Winter 1954), 117–124.

[25] Russell H. Conwell, *Acres of Diamonds* (New York, 1915), pp. 6, 8. Maurice F. Tauber, *Russell Herman Conwell, 1843–1925: A Bibliography,* item number 25, notes this edition as "probably the best and most used." The speech was first published in 1887 by the Businessmen's Association of Grace Baptist Church in a collection of Conwell's sermons. In 1890, the first of many editions in book form was published by the Philadelphia industrialist, J. Y. Huber. For other works by Conwell on success, see Maurice F. Tauber, item numbers 44, 45, 57, and 60.

[26] *Ibid.,* pp. 17–18.

[27] *Ibid.,* pp. 18, 20, 21.

[28] *Ibid.,* pp. 21–22, 24, 26.

[29] *Ibid.,* pp. 30, 50, 58–59.

CHAPTER 5

[1] Wilbur F. Crafts, *Successful Men of To-Day and What They Say of Success* (1883) (New York, 1894), pp. 15, 17, 20. This poll should be considered more a reflection of thought than accurate empirical evidence. An important criticism, and by no means the only one, is that he used the population statistics of his own day in treating returns. He should have used statistics taken forty or fifty years earlier to correspond to the childhood years of his respondents. For a biographical sketch, see *National Cyclopedia of American Biography* s.v. "Crafts, Wilbur Fisk."

[2] *Ibid.,* pp. 24, 31.

[3] *Ibid.,* pp. 92, 98, 111, 112, 113, 81.

[4] *Ibid.,* pp. 138, 149, 129.

[5] R. Hofstadter, *Social Darwinism in American Thought* (Boston, 1955), p. 44 (rev. ed.); J. J. Spengler, "Evolutionism in American Economics, 1800–1946," in *Evolutionary Thought in America,* ed. Stow Persons (New Haven, 1950), p. 212; T. C. Cochran and W. Miller, *The Age of Enterprise* (New York, 1942), p. 120. For additional supporting evidence, see Irvin G. Wyllie, "Social Darwinism and the Businessman," *Proceedings of the American Philosophical Society,* 103 (October 15, 1959), 609–615.

[6] The J. D. Rockefeller, Jr., quotation differs with the reporter. The source used here is W. J. Ghent, *Our Benevolent Feudalism* (New York, 1902), p. 29. Because Ghent does not make the source of the quotation clear, when cited by secondary authorities, the quotation is usually, and incorrectly, attributed to J. D. Rockefeller, Sr. For Social Darwinism used by a businessman to defend consolidation, see James J. Hill, *Highways of Progress* (New York, 1910), pp. 126, 137. Chester M. Destler, "The Opposition of American Businessmen to Social Control during the 'Gilded Age,' " *Mississippi Valley Historical Review,* 39 (March 1953), 641–672, does not make clear the differences between Social Darwinism

used as an argument against government intervention and as a justification for personal success. He confuses the distinction between the paid or unpaid spokesmen for business interests and the businessmen themselves. The article, however, does offer evidence that the paid spokesmen for business interests invoked Social Darwinism to fight government intervention. For an indication of how Social Darwinism could be used to support contradictory economic and political arguments, see James H. Bridge, ed., *The Trust: Its Book* (New York, 1902), especially the appendix.

[7] It is significant that Carnegie's sometime literary assistant, James H. Bridge, was a worshipful disciple of Herbert Spencer. For an example of Social Darwinism used as a justification for the success of specific businessmen by the man who was at one time Carnegie's ghost writer, see James H. Bridge, *The Inside History of the Carnegie Steel Company* (New York, 1903), p. viii. For background on this ghost writer who was a bridge between Carnegie and Spencer, see James H. Bridge, *Millionaires and Grub Street* (New York, 1931), pp. 1–65. How thrilling the discovery of Darwin and Spencer was to Carnegie as a younger man is revealed in his *Autobiography* (Boston and New York, 1920), pp. 338–339.

Two businessmen who are exceptions and did use Social Darwinism as a justification for personal success are Henry Clews, *Fifty Years in Wall Street* (New York, 1908), p. 6, and Chauncey M. Depew, *My Memories of Eighty Years* (New York, 1922), pp. 383–384. It is worth noting that these men do not press the Social Darwinist justification, nor do they apply it directly to their own success. The important point is that for every stray quotation using Social Darwinism as a justification for personal success (except by business spokesmen, intellectuals, theorizing philosophers, etc.), scores of quotations from businessmen and success writers can be cited which prefer the stewardship principle or the concept of service.

[8] Quoted in B. J. Hendrick, *The Life of Andrew Carnegie* (New York, 1932), I, 146–147. For family background, see Robert Green McCloskey, *American Conservatism in the Age of Enterprise: A Study of William Graham Sumner, Stephen J. Field, and Andrew Carnegie* (Cambridge, Mass., 1951), pp. 127–167.

For an interesting diary confession of the pre-Civil War merchant prince from Boston, William Appleton, on the tormenting clash between an uncontrollable ambition and Christian humility, see the discussion in Cleveland Amory, *The Proper Bostonians* (New York, 1947), pp. 78–87.

[9] Andrew Carnegie, "Wealth," *North American Review,* 148 (June 1889), 655.

[10] *Ibid.*, pp. 661–662, 664. "In bestowing charity," Carnegie advised, "the main consideration should be to help those who will help themselves" (p. 663). In "The Best Fields for Philanthropy," *North American Review,* 149 (December 1889), 682–698, he suggested such fields as education, libraries, and public parks.

The point at which Social Darwinism was influential on businessmen was the reassertion of many philanthropists in this period that the Lord (or evolution) will help those, who are given the opportunity and take it, to help themselves in their struggle for a more desirable existence.

[11] Andrew Carnegie, *The Empire of Business,* p. 141; Andrew Carnegie, *The Gospel of Wealth and Other Timely Essays,* p. 68. Carnegie cited John Wesley's sermon which charged Methodists 'to gain all you can, save all you can, give all you can.' "Upon this sermon the gospel of wealth seems founded," he asserted. "Indeed, had I known of its existence before writing upon the subject, I should certainly have quoted it" (p. 69). Though Carnegie's stewardship was not tied to religion, he did not hesitate to corroborate it by Christianity. See Andrew Carnegie, "The Best Fields for Philanthropy," *North American Review,* 149 (December 1889), 698.

[12] Andrew Carnegie, "Wealth," *North American Review,* pp. 659, 660. For an equally shocking viewpoint that wealth is not the product of individual effort but largely the joint product of the community, see Andrew Carnegie, "How Men Get Rich, and the Right View of Wealth," *World's Work,* 17 (December 1908), 11047–11053.

[13] Charles S. Peirce, "Evolutionary Love," *Monist,* 3 (January 1893), 182.

[14] On the point of Social Darwinism implying that the fittest survive while others perish, note the battlefield metaphors employed by Professor C. R. Henderson of the University of Chicago in his essay, "Business Men and Social Theorists," *American Journal of Sociology,* 1 (January 1896), 385–386.

[15] *Struggles and Triumphs: Or, Forty Years' Recollections of P. T. Barnum Written by Himself* (New York, 1871), p. 499. The quotation is from the chapter "The Art of Money Getting" which contains part of the lecture which a debt-ridden Barnum delivered close to one hundred times in England during 1859. The lecture is representative of the character ethic, though there is an unusual attention to the importance of advertising.

[16] The first quotation is by Rev. Dr. Newell Dwight Hillis in the *Commoner,* 5 (April 21, 1905), 1. His recording of Rockefeller's statement differs in wording from Ghent's. The second quotation is by Bishop Charles D. Williams and is quoted in Allan Nevins, *John D. Rockefeller* (New York, 1940), II, 545.

[17] The word quoted is from John D. Rockefeller, *Random Reminiscences of Men and Events* (1909) (New York, 1916), p. 146.

[18] [John D. Rockefeller], "John D. Rockefeller on Opportunity in America," *Cosmopolitan,* 43 (August 1907), 368–372. The editor noted that "during a visit to Compiegne, France, last summer Mr. Rockefeller expressed himself freely in answer to a series of questions by a correspondent who was a companion of his leisure hours. From careful and accurate notes of these talks the following article has been transcribed." (Editor's note, p. 368.) The questions were not included in the article.

Ghostly fingers were no doubt at play in most of Rockefeller's writings. By the canons of scholarship we can take the position that his writings reflect what he wanted people to think was true. It is the same principle which permits us to assume that speeches by the President of the United States, which are ghost-written, represent the President's thinking, unless there is evidence to the contrary.

[19] The first quotation is from Allan Nevins, *John D. Rockefeller*, p. 258; the second is from Matthew Josephson, *The Robber Barons* (New York, 1934), p. 325; the third is from Orison Swett Marden, *How They Succeeded: Life Stories of Successful Men Told by Themselves* (Boston, 1901), p. 194. On p. 713 Nevins gives another version of the first quotation as "God gave me the money." John Wesley's influential sermon is "Causes of the Inefficacy of Christianity" (Sermon CXX), *Sermons on Several Occasions* (New York, 1851), II, 441.

[20] John D. Rockefeller, *Random Reminiscences of Men and Events* (1909) (New York, 1916), p. 143. The exact figure is somewhere between $500,000,000 and $600,000,000.

CHAPTER 6

[1] The quotation is from David A. Balch, *Elbert Hubbard: Genius of Roycroft* (New York, 1940), p. 101.

[2] Harry T. Levin, "The Discovery of Bohemia," in *Literary History of the United States,* ed. Robert E. Spiller et al. (New York, 1948), p. 1067. The biographical facts of Hubbard's life are taken from David A. Balch, *Elbert Hubbard: Genius of Roycroft* (New York, 1940), and Felix Shay, *Elbert Hubbard of East Aurora* (New York, 1926). The most recent biography is Freeman Champney, *Art & Glory: The Story of Elbert Hubbard* (New York, 1968).

[3] The first quotation is from D. A. Balch, *Elbert Hubbard*, p. 103; the second is from [Elbert Hubbard et al.], *The Roycroft Dictionary Concocted by Ali Baba and the Bunch on Rainy Days* (East Aurora, N. Y., 1914), p. 144. See also Elbert Hubbard, *The Man of Sorrows* (East Aurora, N. Y., 1905); *John B. Stetson* (East Aurora, N. Y., 1911).

[4] The first quotation is from Felix Shay, *Elbert Hubbard*, p. 159. For "Bert's" version, see Freeman Champney, *Art & Glory: The Story of Elbert Hubbard* (New York, 1968), p. 90. Stewart H. Holbrook, *Lost Men of American History* (New York, 1946), pp. 296–301, tells the story of Rowan and concludes that "Hubbard got nearly all of the facts wrong" (p. 297).

The second quotation is from George Daniels' note on title page of *A Message to Garcia,* No. 25 of the *Four-Track Series* of the New York Central and Hudson River R. R. (New York, 1900). For background, see Felix Shay, *Elbert Hubbard*, pp. 159–167, and D. A. Balch, *Elbert Hubbard*, pp. 208–245.

[5] Elbert Hubbard, *A Message to Garcia and Thirteen Other Things* (East Aurora, N. Y., 1901), pp. 9–16. Hubbard does invoke the concept

of the "survival of the fittest," but he uses it to justify weeding out incompetent employees rather than a justification for success.

[6] Charles Howard Hopkins, *The Rise of the Social Gospel in American Protestantism, 1865–1915* (New Haven, 1940); James Dombrowski, *The Early Days of Christian Socialism in America* (New York, 1936).

[7] The quotation is from Lyman Abbott, *Reminiscences* (Boston and New York, 1915), p. ix.

[8] Lyman Abbott, "The New Puritanism," in *The New Puritanism* (New York, 1897), pp. 25–73; *Henry Ward Beecher* (Boston and New York, 1903), pp. vii–ix; *Reminiscences*, pp. vii–viii; *The Theology of an Evolutionist* (Boston and New York, 1897), pp. 176–191. Ira V. Brown, *Lyman Abbott* (Cambridge, Mass., 1953) is the only biography.

[9] The quotation is from Lyman Abbott, *Reminiscences*, p. 395. A comma has been inserted after "wealth." Lyman Abbott, *The Industrial Problem* (Philadelphia, 1905).

[10] Lyman Abbott, ed., *How To Succeed* (New York, 1882), pp. v, vi, vii, 123, 125, 126.

[11] Lyman Abbott, "The Ethical Teachings of Jesus: II.—Righteousness," *Outlook,* 94 (March 12, 1910), 576–578. This is the second of four essays on the ethical teachings of Jesus. Originally delivered as a lecture, they were later published in book form under the major title.

The exact quotation closest to Abbott's, which he purposely altered, is in Mark viii:36: "For what shall it profit a man, if he shall gain the whole world, and lose his own soul?" See also Lyman Abbott, *The Industrial Problem*, pp. 161–196.

[12] Lyman Abbott, "The Ethical Teachings of Jesus: I.—Sobriety," *Outlook,* 94 (March 5, 1910), 534; "The Ethical Teachings of Jesus: II. —Righteousness," *Outlook,* 94 (March 12, 1910), 580. For the stewardship principle with rich men obligated to act as trustees, see Lyman Abbott, *Christianity and Social Problems* (Boston and New York, 1896), pp. 66–99 and *passim*.

[13] The quotation is from William Lawrence, "The Relation of Wealth to Morals," *World's Work,* 1 (January 1901), 286–292.

CHAPTER 7

[1] Rollo May, "Introduction: The Significance of Symbols," in *Symbolism in Religion and Literature,* ed. Rollo May (New York, 1960), p. 34.

[2] Ruth Miller Elson, *Guardians of Tradition: American Schoolbooks of the Nineteenth Century* (Lincoln, Neb., 1964), p. 338, comes to the same conclusion about nineteenth-century schoolbooks, i.e., the pedagogical arrangements changed but the basic values remained consistent and unresponsive to conditions throughout the century.

[3] The translation by U Nu is referred to in Richard H. Rovere,

The American Establishment and Other Reports, Opinions, and Speculations (New York, 1962), p. 133.

[4] The first quotation is from Matthew Hale Smith, *Bulls and Bears of New York* (Hartford and Chicago, 1875), p. 541. The second is from "The Ladder of Saint Augustine," *The Complete Poetical Works of Henry Wadsworth Longfellow* (Boston and New York, 1902), p. 230. The frequent use of this quotation was perhaps at variance with Longfellow's intent in this poem.

In this study success writers are those who inspire and instruct others in how to make money. What they wrote is success literature. The analysis is based on non-fiction success literature.

[5] Matthew Hale Smith, *Successful Folks* (Hartford, 1878), p. 505; *National Cyclopedia of American Biography* s.v. "Smith, Matthew H."; *Lamb's Biographical Dictionary of the United States* s.v. "Smith, Matthew Hale."

[6] Cotton Mather, *Essays to do Good* (New York, 1815), pp. 158–159, 163.

[7] For the nineteenth-century route to success, see Werner Sombart in *Encyclopaedia of the Social Sciences* s.v. "Capitalism."

[8] For comments on the historians' role in this story, see William Miller, "American Historians and the Business Elite," *Journal of Economic History,* 9 (November 1949), 184–208.

[9] *Register of Debates in Congress . . . of the First Session of the Twenty-Second Congress* (Washington, 1833), Part 1,VIII, 277. By the 1840s the phrase was being used in the title of a novel—Emily Chubbuck [Judson], *Allen Lucas: The Self-Made Man* (1847) (New York, 1871). See also Irvin G. Wyllie, *The Self-Made Man in America* (New Brunswick, N. J., 1954), pp. 151–167; Ralph H. Gabriel, *The Course of American Democratic Thought* (New York, 1940), pp. 143–160; Merle Curti, *The Growth of American Thought* (New York, 1943), pp. 633–656.

[10] This, of course, was true for the less wealthy as well, and was part of the American tradition of generosity. See, for example, Geoffrey Gorer, *The American People* (New York, 1948), pp. 178–179. Raymond B. Fosdick, *The Story of the Rockefeller Foundation* (New York, 1952), p. x. See Wilmer Shields Rich and Neva R. Deardorff, eds., *American Foundations and Their Fields* (New York, 1948); Robert S. Bremner, *American Philanthropy* (Chicago, Ill., 1960); Arnaud C. Marts, *The Generosity of Americans* (Englewood Cliffs, N. J., 1966).

CHAPTER 8

[1] Max Lerner, *America As a Civilization* (New York, 1957), p. 59; *Reports of the Mosely Educational Commission to the United States of America,* October–December 1903 (London, 1904), p. 183.

[2] The first quotation is from Sylvia L. Thrupp, *The Merchant Class*

of Medieval London, 1300–1500 (Chicago, 1948), p. 300; the second is from Gunnar Myrdal, *An American Dilemma* (New York, 1944), p. 710.

In the seventeenth century the Puritans set up rigid, intolerant communities. For example, John Cotton tried to enforce the medieval concept of "just price" and "fair wages," but new world conditions began to dissolve the controls and restrictions on mobility.

[3] The historiography of religion as a causal force is itself an interesting exercise in intellectual history. The hypothesis of Max Weber in *The Protestant Ethic and the Spirit of Capitalism,* trans. Talcott Parsons (London, 1930) (first published as an essay in German in 1905), connecting Protestantism and the emerging spirit of capitalism in Europe has been alternately attacked and defended for decades. Our concern is not with the causal relationship between Puritanism and capitalism but the fact that there was an affinity between them. Our interest is in the consequences of the religious factor, specifically Puritan Protestantism.

The best introduction to the Weber controversy is a selection of readings: Robert W. Green, ed., *Protestantism and Capitalism: The Weber Thesis and Its Critics* (Boston, 1959). The latest and most workable bibliography, divided into subject headings, is S. N. Eisenstadt, ed., *The Protestant Ethic and Modernization: A Comparative View* (New York, 1968). Weber's harshest critic to date is Kurt Samuelsson, trans., E. Geoffrey French, *Religion and Economic Action* (1957) (London, 1961).

With respect to the American experience, discussions of the past and empirical studies of the present are controversial and inconclusive about the significance of the religious factor. There is, alas, no predictor variable. One must be careful not to attribute to religion what belongs to ethnicity—and vice versa. For a sampling of some of the literature, with references, see Seymour Martin Lipset and Reinhard Bendix, *Social Mobility in Industrial Society* (Berkeley and Los Angeles: Paperbound edition, 1959), pp. 48–56. More recent discussions include Bernard C. Rosen, "Race, Ethnicity, and the Achievement Syndrome," *American Sociological Review,* 24 (February 1959), 47–60, and the following from *American Sociological Review,* 27 (April 1962): Harry J. Crockett, Jr., "The Achievement Motive and Differential Occupational Mobility in the United States," 191–204; Joseph Veroff, Sheila Feld, and Gerald Gurin, "Achievement Motivation and Religious Background," 205–217; Albert J. Mayer and Harry Sharp, "Religious Preference and Worldly Success," 218–227.

See also Gabriel Kolko, "Max Weber on America: Theory and Evidence," *History and Theory,* 1 (1961), 243–260; Richard L. Means, "Weber's Thesis of the Protestant Ethic: The Ambiguities of Received Doctrine," *Journal of Religion,* 45 (January 1965), 1–11, and "American Protestantism and Max Weber's Protestant Ethic," *Religious Education,* 60 (March–April 1965), 90–98; Andrew M. Greeley, "Influence of the 'Religious Factor' on Career Plans and Occupational Values of College Graduates," *American Journal of Sociology,* 68 (May 1963), 658–671, and "The Protestant Ethic: Time for a Moratorium," *Sociological*

Analysis, 25 (Spring 1964), 20–33; David C. McClelland, *The Achieving Society* (New York, 1961); Gerhard Lenski, *The Religious Factor* (New York, 1961).

⁴ Erich Fromm, *Man for Himself* (New York, 1947), p. 81.

⁵ Adam Smith, *An Inquiry into the Nature and Causes of the Wealth of Nations* (1776) (New York: Modern Library Edition, 1937), p. 423.

⁶ Ralph Waldo Emerson, "American Civilization," *Miscellanies* in *Emerson's Complete Works* (Boston, 1883), XI, 279.

These are the closing lines of the Emma Lazarus sonnet. They are reproduced from the actual bronze plaque which in 1903 was placed within the sally port entrance to Fort Wood. In many standard reference works, the poem is quoted inaccurately and the location is given incorrectly. At this writing, the plaque is being moved to a new location. The part of the sonnet reproduced here indicates a quotation because the Statue, "with silent lips," is speaking.

⁷ Woodrow Wilson, *The New Freedom* (New York, 1913), p. 17, and H. L. Mencken, *Prejudices, Third Series* (New York, 1932), p. 56.

For the defenders and the critics of opportunity and mobility in America, see Chapter 23. Attitudes toward opportunity are examined in Boyd C. Shafer, "The American Heritage of Hope, 1865–1940," *Mississippi Valley Historical Review,* 37 (December 1950), 427–450; Clarke A. Chambers, "The Belief in Progress in Twentieth-Century America," *Journal of the History of Ideas,* 19 (April 1958), 197–224; Stephan Thernstrom, *Poverty and Progress: Social Mobility in a Nineteenth Century City* (Cambridge, Mass., 1964), pp. 163–165; and Ephraim Harold Mizruchi, *Success and Opportunity: A Study of Anomie* (New York, 1964), pp. 83, 89.

On the migration factor, see Everett S. Lee, "The Turner Thesis Reexamined," *American Quarterly,* 13 (Spring 1961), 77–83; George W. Pierson, "The M-Factor in American History," *American Quarterly,* 14 (Summer Supplement 1962), 275–289, and " 'A Restless Temper . . .,' " *American Historical Review,* 69 (July 1964), 969–989.

⁸ George Bernard Shaw, "Preface," *Pygmalion* (New York, 1939), p. 1.

⁹ D. W. Brogan, *The American Character* (New York, 1944), pp. 6–7; Karen Horney, *Neurosis and Human Growth* (New York, 1950), p. 26.

¹⁰ The nature of money is examined in Talcott Parsons, *The Social System* (Glencoe, Illinois, 1951), p. 424; Nicholas M. Spykman, *The Social Theory of Georg Simmel* (Chicago, 1925), pp. 232–251; and Robert K. Merton, *Social Theory and Social Structure* (Glencoe, Illinois, 1949), pp. 129–130, 137.

¹¹ William Kaufman, "Some Emotional Uses of Money," *Acta Psychotherapeutica Psychosomatica et Orthopaedogogica,* 4 (1956), 28.

¹² Otto Fenichel, "The Drive to Amass Wealth," *The Collected*

Papers of Otto Fenichel (New York, 1954), Second Series, p. 98, and James A. Knight, *For the Love of Money* (Philadelphia, 1968), p. 41. The seminal essay is Sigmund Freud, "Character and Anal Erotism," *Collected Papers,* II, 45–50. See also Ernest Jones, "Anal-Erotic Character Traits," *Papers on Psycho-Analysis* (Boston, 1961), pp. 413–437.

[13] S. Ferenczi, "The Ontogenesis of the Interest in Money," *Sex in Psychoanalysis* (New York, 1950), pp. 327, 328. For a comment on Ferenczi, see Norman O. Brown, *Life Against Death: The Psychoanalytical Meaning of History* (Middletown, Conn., 1959), pp. 287ff.

The relation between physiology and success cannot be ignored. The number of famous people in history who have suffered from gout is well-known. Too much port wine was thought to be the cause. Did wealthy or famous men have gout because they could afford port wine, or could they afford port wine because they had gout? Imaginative researchers discovered that gout, a painful inflammation of the joints, is not caused by an excessive swilling of port wine, though imbibing may precipitate it. Gout is caused by an excess of uric acid in the blood. Uric acid acts in some way as a brain stimulant. The researchers then discovered that men with a dynamic drive to get ahead contained an excess of uric acid in their blood.

George W. Brooks and Ernst Mueller, "Serum Urate Concentrations among University Professors," *Journal of the American Medical Association,* 195 (February 7, 1966), 415–418, is a recent study with references to previous research. See also an editorial "Which Comes First —the Success or the Gout?" *Journal of the American Medical Association,* 185 (August 10, 1963), 534–535, and Robert G. Whalen, "Gout Is 'In,' " *New York Times Magazine,* May 1, 1966, pp. 66ff. Correlations in these studies are also made to other human characteristics beside achievement motivation. It should be noted that too much uric acid can lead to mental retardation.

[14] Dr. Thomas L. Nichols, *Forty Years of American Life* (London, 1864), I, 402–404.

[15] Geoffrey Gorer, *The American People* (New York, 1948), p. 178; Lincoln Steffens, *The Autobiography of Lincoln Steffens* (New York, 1931), p. 709. Gorer's measure of America has been sharply criticized, but his emphasis on the relative nature of success is perceptive. See pp. 172–187.

[16] Charles Horton Cooley, "Personal Competition," *Sociological Theory and Social Research* (New York, 1930), p. 226. The essay was first published in 1899. See also Lester Frank Ward, "Plutocracy and Paternalism," *The Forum,* 20 (November 1895), 301; Thorstein Veblen, *The Theory of the Leisure Class* (1899) (New York: Modern Library Edition, 1934), pp. 22ff.; and Abram Kardiner, *The Psychological Frontiers of Society* (New York, 1945), pp. 444–445.

[17] Margaret Mead, *And Keep Your Powder Dry* (New York, 1942), pp. 40–53, 88–113, 155. The quotation is from p. 113.

The Mead reference, and several others in this section on childrearing, extend beyond our time limit, but are relevant to the period from the middle decades of the nineteenth century to the early decades of the twentieth.

[18] David C. McClelland, *The Achieving Society* (1961) (New York: Free Press Edition, 1967), pp. 336–390, and *The Roots of Consciousness* (Princeton, N. J., 1964), pp. 39–40.

This discussion is limited to male children.

The psychology of motivation is, of course, terribly complex. Robert R. Blake and Jane S. Mouton, "Personality," *Annual Review of Psychology,* 10 (1959), 218, assessed studies relating to the need for achievement and concluded: "It is almost as though for every study which reports findings in one direction, there is another with opposite results." Thoughtful discussions, in addition to McClelland's work, are Ralph Norman Haber, ed., *Current Research in Motivation* (New York, 1966); John W. Atkinson, *An Introduction to Motivation* (Princeton, N. J., 1964); John W. Atkinson and Norman T. Feather, eds., *A Theory of Achievement Motivation* (New York, 1966); John W. Atkinson, ed., *Motives in Fantasy, Action, and Society* (Princeton, N. J., 1958); Bernard C. Rosen, Harry J. Crockett, Jr., and Clyde Z. Nunn, eds., *Achievement in American Society* (Cambridge, Mass., 1969); and Rose Laub Coser, ed., *Life Cycle and Achievement in America* (New York, 1969).

An interpretation which stresses the intensity of motivation in relation to minority group status is Everett S. Hagen, *On the Theory of Social Change* (Homewood, Ill., 1962).

The relative nature of ambition is examined in Robert K. Merton, *Social Theory and Social Structure* (Glencoe, Ill., 1957), pp. 170–176; Suzanne Keller and Marisa Zavalloni, "Ambition and Social Class: A Respecification," *Social Forces,* 43 (October 1964), 58–70; and Ephraim Harold Mizruchi, *Success and Opportunity: A Study of Anomie* (New York, 1964).

The theory of causation upon which this study is constructed is explained in Charles A. Beard and Sydney Hook (written by Hook), "Problems of Terminology in Historical Writing," in Social Science Research Council, *Theory and Practice in Historical Study* (New York, n.d.), pp. 110–115. See also Social Science Research Council, *The Social Sciences in Historical Study* (New York, 1954), *passim.*

[19] The quotation is from Bernard C. Rosen and Roy D'Andrade, "The Psychosocial Origins of Achievement Motivation," *Sociometry,* 22 (September 1959), 216. See also Bernard C. Rosen, "Race, Ethnicity, and the Achievement Syndrome," *American Sociological Review,* 24 (February 1959), 47–60.

[20] John W. M. Whiting et al., "The Learning of Values," *People of Rimrock,* eds., Evon Z. Vogt and Ethel M. Albert (Cambridge, Mass., 1966), pp. 83–125; Bernard Bailyn, *Education in the Forming of American Society* (Chapel Hill, N. C., 1960), pp. 15–17, 22–29, 61–62, 75–78; Richard L. Rapson, "The American Child As Seen by British Travelers, 1845–1935," *American Quarterly,* 17 (Fall 1965), 520–534.

Under the impact of industrialism, of course, the British family was also undergoing modifications. For a cross-cultural comparison, see Maurice L. Farber, "English and Americans: Values in the Socialization Process," *Journal of Psychology,* 36 (October 1953), 243–250. For ethnic groups, see Fred L. Strodtbeck, "Family Interaction, Values, and Achievement," in *The Jews,* ed., Marshall Sklare (Glencoe, Ill., 1958), pp. 147–165. A critical essay is Edward N. Saveth, "The Problem of American Family History," *American Quarterly,* 21 (Supplement) (Summer 1969), 311–329.

[21] Bernard Berelson and Gary A. Steiner, *Human Behavior: An Inventory of Scientific Findings* (New York, 1964), pp. 468–469; Seymour Martin Lipset and Reinhard Bendix, *Social Mobility in Industrial Society* (1959) (Berkeley and Los Angeles, 1966), 254–255.

[22] Alfred A. Messer, "The Self-Made Man As Father," *New York Times Magazine,* March 19, 1967, pp. 123–125.

[23] The quotation is from Samuel J. Warner, *Self-Realization and Self-Defeat* (New York, 1966), p. 172.

The classic psychoanalytic book on the subject with an American setting is Karen Horney, *The Neurotic Personality of Our Time* (New York, 1937). Evelyn Ellis, "Social Psychological Correlates of Upward Social Mobility Among Unmarried Career Women," *American Sociological Review,* 17 (October 1952), 558–563, focuses on the unsatisfactory early primary group relations of mobile women. Relevant discussions may be found in W. Lloyd Warner and James C. Abegglen, *Big Business Leaders in America* (New York, 1955), and Robert Presthus, *The Organizational Society* (New York, 1962). For a recent addition to the reference group theory of achievement motivation, see Theodore D. Kemper, "Reference Groups, Socialization and Achievement," *American Sociological Review,* 33 (February 1968), 31–45. Also useful are Franz Alexander, *Our Age of Unreason* (Philadelphia, 1942); Albert Lauterbach, *Man, Motives, and Money: Psychological Frontiers of Economics* (Ithaca, N. Y., 1954); Harry Walker Hepner, *How To Live and Work Successfully with People in Business* (New York, 1952); and references in Chapter 25.

Surveys, as well as psychoanalysts, have also stressed an unhappy family background in shaping aspiration or achievement. Russell R. Dynes, Alfred C. Clarke and Simon Dinitz, "Levels of Occupational Aspiration: Some Aspects of Family Experience As a Variable," *American Sociological Review,* 21 (April 1956), 212–215, surveyed predominantly urban, middle-class, middle Western, Protestant university students. It was discovered that those with high aspirations (compared with those of lower aspirations) had experienced feelings of rejection and of not being wanted by their fathers or their mothers. They indicated less attachment to their parents, confided less frequently in their fathers, were more fearful of punishment, and felt that their parents showed favoritism towards a brother or sister.

[24] The Heraclitus quotation is from Fr. 45, *Diogenes Laertius,* IX, 7, and is quoted in G. S. Kirk and J. E. Raven, *The Pre-Socratic Philosophers* (Cambridge, England, 1957), p. 205

CHAPTER 9

[1] Quoted in Ernest Holmes and Maude Allison Lathem, eds., *Mind Remakes Your World* (1941) (New York, 1949), p. xiii. For an introduction to New Thought, see Horatio W. Dresser, *A History of New Thought* (New York, 1919) and Charles S. Braden, *Spirits in Rebellion: The Rise and Development of New Thought* (Dallas, Texas, 1963). William Walker Atkinson, *New Thought: Its History and Principles* (Holyoke, Mass., 1915), is sloppy history, but an excellent and clear statement of principles. Leighton Allen in *Encyclopedia of Religion and Ethics* (New York, 1917) s.v. "New Thought," is thoughtful and brief. A good general analysis of the movement is Charles S. Braden, *These Also Believe: A Study of Modern American Cults and Minority Religious Movements* (New York, 1949). Secondary authorities which have not been cited in the following references under specific subjects, but which contain useful general accounts, are Charles W. Ferguson, *The Confusion of Tongues: A Review of Modern Isms* (1928) (New York, 1929); Charles Baudouin and A. Lestchinsky, *The Inner Discipline* (London, 1924); Gilbert Seldes, *The Stammering Century* (New York, 1928), pp. 348–365; and F. E. Mayer, *The Religious Bodies of America* (St. Louis, Mo., 1954), pp. 540–545.

The secondary authorities cited in this bibliographical note, and in the following references, concentrate almost entirely on the mental healing and spiritual fulfillment aspects of New Thought. Scholars within the movement consider New Thought a mental healing faith and pay scant attention to the dollar-chasing wing of writers who teach the use of mind power for the accumulation of wealth. For lack of any solid work on the subject, scholars outside of the movement have generally followed along, stressing the mental healing side of the movement and often ignoring the success wing entirely. An exception to this is A. Whitney Griswold, "New Thought: A Cult of Success," *American Journal of Sociology,* 40 (November 1934), 309–318, which is pioneering and useful, but overemphasizes the significance of the success wing in New Thought as most secondary authorities underemphasize it. Edmund H. Schoeffler, "A History of the New Thought Movement," (Undergraduate Thesis, Princeton University, 1952), is better balanced and particularly valuable for a history of New Thought in the first three decades of the twentieth century. Hugo Hume, *The Superior American Religions* (Los Angeles, 1928), pp. 69–73, is a brief discussion of success by New Thought. See also Louis Schneider and Sanford M. Dornbusch, *Popular Religion* (Chicago, 1958) and Donald Meyer, *The Positive Thinkers* (Garden City, N. Y., 1965).

[2] Norman Vincent Peale, *A Guide to Confident Living* (New York, 1948), and *The Power of Positive Thinking* (New York, 1952). *The Power of Positive Thinking* was number six in 1952. Alice Payne Hackett, *Seven Years of Best Sellers: 1945–1951* (New York, 1952); "Best Sellers of 1952 According to Bookstore Sales," *Publisher's Weekly,* 163 (January 24, 1953), 278; "The Best Sellers of 1953 in the Bookstores," *Publishers' Weekly,* 165 (January 23 1954), 300.

³ Charles S. Braden, *These Also Believe* (New York, 1949), pp. 128–129. Ernest Holmes and M. A. Lathem, eds., *Mind Remakes Your World,* p. xi, define metaphysics, in terms of New Thought, as "a practical idealism, which emphasizes spiritual causation and the accessibility of spiritual mind power, acting in accord with law and available to all people."

⁴ The quotations are from William James, *The Varieties of Religious Experience* (New York, 1902), p. 92 (Modern Library Edition), and John Herman Randall, "Foreword," in *A New Philosophy of Life* (New York, 1909–1911), pp. 10–11.

The World War I estimates are from *New International Encyclopedia* (New York, 1916) s.v. "New Thought," and Alfred W. Martin, *Psychic Tendencies of Today* (New York, 1918), p. 36. The World War II statistics are from Ernest Holmes and Maude A. Lathem, *Mind Remakes Your World,* p. xii. The estimates do not include the influence of Christian Science.

Because New Thought groups are not listed in the government census reports, and other statistics are unreliable, it is impossible to compile accurate membership figures.

⁵ Ralph Waldo Trine, *In Tune with the Infinite* (Indianapolis, 1897): Charles S. Braden, *These Also Believe,* p. 142; James D. Hart, *The Popular Book* (New York, 1950), p. 168; Alice Payne Hackett, *70 Years of Best Sellers, 1895–1965* (New York, 1967), p. 33; "Ralph Waldo Trine's Third of a Century Best Seller," *Publisher's Weekly,* 119 (March 14, 1931), 1387–1388. The quotation is from p. 1388.

⁶ Cf. Federal Council of the Churches of Christ in America, "Social-Economic Status and Outlook of Religious Groups in America," *Information Service,* 27 (May 15, 1948), 1–8; Willard L. Sperry, *Religion in America* (1946) (New York, 1948), p. 77.

⁷ Charles S. Braden, *These Also Believe,* p. 143.

⁸ Horatio W. Dresser, *A History of the New Thought Movement* (New York, 1919), p. 35; George A. Quimby, "Phineas Parkhurst Quimby," *New England Magazine,* 6 (March 1888), 267–276; Horatio W. Dresser, *The Quimby Manuscripts* (New York, 1921), *passim;* Ernest Sutherland Bates in *Dictionary of American Biography* s.v. "Quimby, Phineas Parkhurst."

⁹ The standard work, Horatio W. Dresser, *A History of the New Thought Movement* (New York, 1919), is prejudiced against Christian Science and its influence. A careful corrective of Dresser's position, which is too often accepted by scholars, is Israel Regardie, *The Romance of Metaphysics* (Chicago, 1946), especially pp. 115–120.

¹⁰ Alfred W. Martin, *Psychic Tendencies of Today* (New York, 1919), pp. 58–59; Charles Brodie Patterson, "What the New Thought Stands For," *Arena,* 25 (January 1901), 9–16.

¹¹ Horatio W. Dresser, *A History of the New Thought Movement* (New York, 1919), pp. 135–136, 145–146, 179; William Walker Atkinson, *New Thought: Its History and Principles* (Holyoke, Mass., 1915),

pp. 6–15; William James, *The Varieties of Religious Experience*, pp. 93, 99; Horatio W. Dresser, "What Is New Thought?," *Arena*, 21 (January 1899), 30–32; C. H. A. Bjerregaard in *Encyclopedia Americana* (New York, 1952) s.v. "New Thought."

[12] H. W. Dresser, *A History of the New Thought Movement*, p. 158; W. W. Atkinson, *New Thought: Its History and Principles*, pp. 13–15. New Thought makes no distinction between organic and functional diseases and does not employ medical diagnosis. In the "age of anxiety" during recent years, however, the more popular writers and lecturers have united psychology and religion to focus more specifically on cures for mental and nervous disorders. An early attempt to use religion and psychology was the Emmanuel Movement started in Boston in 1906. The Emmanuel Movement permits treatment only of nervous and functional disorders. No case is accepted by a minister for psychotherapeutic treatment without the diagnosis and cooperation of a physician. See Elwood Worcester, Samuel McComb, and Isador H. Coriat, *Religion and Medicine: The Moral Control of Nervous Disorders* (New York, 1908); Elwood Worcester and Samuel McComb, *The Christian Religion as a Healing Power* (New York, 1909); Edward E. Weaver, *Mind and Health: With an Examination of Some Systems of Divine Healing* (New York, 1913), pp. 284–310; Raymond J. Cunningham, "The Emmanuel Movement: A Variety of American Religious Experience," *American Quarterly*, 14 (Spring 1962), 48–63.

[13] For a brief history of mental healing, see A. M. Bellwald, *Christian Science and the Catholic Faith* (New York, 1922), p. 1–9. Walter Bromberg, *The Mind of Man* (New York, 1937), and Pierre Janet, *Psychological Healing* (London, 1925), 2 vols., are extended discussions of the subject.

[14] Quoted in an advertisement for the *Nautilus* magazine in William Walker Atkinson, *New Thought: Its History and Principles*, p. 37. Mrs. Kaemmerling wrote under the pseudonym of Aldis Dunbar. Horatio W. Dresser, *A History of the New Thought Movement*, pp. iv, 153–156, 309. A. Whitney Griswold, "New Thought: A Cult of Success," *American Journal of Sociology*, 40 (November 1934), 309–318, establishes it as a metropolitan religion.

[15] Quoted in H. W. Dresser, *A History of the New Thought Movement*, pp. 250–251.

[16] *Ibid.*, p. 216.

[17] *Ibid.*, pp. 267, 279–280. "Make," an obvious misprint, has been changed to "makes."

[18] The first two quotations are from P. A. Jensen, "The No-Thought Absent Treatment," *Overland Monthly*, 57 (January 1911), 67. The next three are from a review of George M. Gould, *Borderland Studies* (Philadelphia, 1896–1908), *Current Literature*, 46 (January 1909), 97. The next two quotations are *ibid.*, p. 98. In the review of the Gould book, the references are to quotations from *Borderland Studies*. The observer is Alfred W. Martin, *Psychic Tendencies of Today* (New York, 1918), p. 63.

[19] Helen Wilmans, *The Conquest of Poverty* (1899) (Seabreeze, Florida, 1901). The 1899 edition is entitled *A Conquest of Poverty.* Seabreeze was spelled both as one word and two words.

[20] Advertisement in the back pages of Helen Wilmans, *A Conquest of Poverty* (Seabreeze, Florida, 1899). Helen Wilmans, *New Psychology and Brain Building* (New York, 1921) is her home study course which sold in the 1890s for $5 reduced from $25. In the 1921 edition, the Efficiency Study guides for "the mastery of the course" were prepared under the supervision of efficiency expert Edward Earle Purinton. Indispensable for a study of Helen Wilmans, whose married name was Helen Wilmans Post, is the scrapbook at the New York Public Library of over 100 pages entitled "The Life Work (A Testimonial) of Helen Wilmans (Post) 1831–1907 presented by Eugene Del Mar." Useful is Horatio W. Dresser, *A History of the New Thought Movement*, pp. 331–334.

For financial gain by absent treatment, for the price of "one dollar per month, invariably in advance," see Charles W. Close, *Business Success through Mental Attraction* (Bangor, Maine, 1896).

[21] W. W. Atkinson, *New Thought: Its History and Principles*, pp. 3–37; Abel Leighton Allen in *Encyclopedia of Religion and Ethics* (New York, 1917) s.v. "New Thought."

[22] Abel Leighton Allen in *Encyclopedia of Religion and Ethics* (New York, 1917) s.v. "New Thought."

[23] Prentice Mulford, "The Necessity of Riches," in *Your Forces and How to Use Them* (1888) (New York, 1890), II, 7; "The Religion of Dress," *ibid.*, II, 15. The quotations in capital letters are a few of the slogans spread throughout various chapters in the six volumes of *Your Forces and How to Use Them.* Mulford was not the first to make the connection between mind power and success, but he was the first writer of any influence and popularity, that I have been able to find, who devoted a large part of his works to that theme. For comments on the circulation and influence of his pamphlets, see Horatio Dresser, *A History of the New Thought Movement* (New York, 1919), p. 149, and William W. Atkinson, *New Thought: Its History and Principles* (Holyoke, Mass., 1915), p. 19.

Dresser gives no indication of the beginnings of the success wing, and it is clear that he sniffs at such corrupting sidelines. Henry Wood, *The New Thought Simplified: How to Gain Harmony and Health* (Boston, 1903), p. 95, scornfully remarked that "it is a degradation to make the new philosophy a money-making scheme."

[24] Prentice Mulford, "A Plea for Laziness," in *Prentice Mulford's California Sketches,* ed. Franklin Walker (San Francisco, 1935), pp. 92, 93, 95.

[25] The quotation is from Prentice Mulford, "About Prentice Mulford," in *Your Forces and How to Use Them* (New York, 1892), VI, p. 4. Prentice Mulford, *Prentice Mulford's Story: Life by Land and Sea* (New York, 1889) is an autobiography which ends with his departure from California. Prentice Mulford, *The Swamp Angel* (Boston, 1888)

tells about his life in the New Jersey woods. Prentice Mulford, "About Prentice Mulford," in *Your Forces and How to Use Them* (New York, 1892), VI, 1–16, is a brief autobiographical sketch which includes three short biographical accounts. There is no biography of Mulford. Useful studies are Franklin Walker, "Introduction," in *Prentice Mulford's California Sketches* (California, 1935); "One of His Old Friends," "Some Personal Reminiscences of Prentice Mulford," *Occult Review,* 22 (December 1915), 323–334; Irene Van Fossen in *Dictionary of American Biography* s.v. "Mulford, Prentice"; Arthur Edward Waite, "Introduction," in *The Gift of the Spirit: A Selection from the Essays of Prentice Mulford* (London, n.d.); *National Cyclopedia of American Biography* s.v. "Mulford, Prentice"; Charles Warren Stoddard, "Prentice Mulford, the New Gospeler," *National Magazine,* 22 (April 1905), 94–101; C. W. Stoddard, "Passing of Prentice Mulford," *National Magazine,* 24 (September 1906), 563–569; Eva Martin, *Prentice Mulford* (London, 1921). Several of these accounts state that John Greenleaf Whittier wrote a poem about Mulford when he died. The poem was actually about Elisha Mulford, a clergyman, who died in 1885. James D. Hart, *The Popular Book* (New York, 1950), p. 143, and Robert E. Spiller, et al., *Literary History of the United States* (New York, 1948), II, 661, 866, locate Mulford in the stream of American literature.

26 Prentice Mulford, "The Law of Success," in *Your Forces and How to Use Them* (1887) (New York, 1890), I, 3. In the following citations, the chapter titles are given because in each volume the pagination begins and ends with each chapter. The full reference for the six-volume series used in this study is Prentice Mulford, *Your Forces and How to Use Them* (1887–1892) (New York, 1890–1892), 6 volumes. It will hereafter be referred to as *Your Forces.* The dates 1887–1892 represent the copyright dates, and the dates 1890–1892 are from the title pages. The following analysis does not consider Mulford's philosophy of mental healing, but the principles upon which he based his philosophy of success and mental healing are, of course, similar.

27 Prentice Mulford, "The Law of Success," *Your Forces,* I, 3–4.

28 *Ibid.,* p. 5.

29 *Ibid.,* pp. 8, 13.

30 Prentice Mulford, "The Drawing Power of Mind," *Your Forces,* IV, 1, 15.

31 Prentice Mulford, "How to Push Your Business," *Your Forces,* III, 16.

32 Prentice Mulford, "The Necessity of Riches," *Your Forces,* II, 10.

33 Prentice Mulford, "The Church of Silent Demand," *Your Forces,* III, 2–3.

34 Prentice Mulford, "The Necessity of Riches," *Your Forces,* II, 3,1.

35 Prentice Mulford, "How to Push Your Business," *Your Forces,* III, 10.

36 Prentice Mulford, "Buried Talents," *Your Forces,* VI, 5. Mulford quoted Christ as saying: " 'It is better to give than to receive.' " In his plea

for funds to build The Church of Silent Demand, he agreed with this doctrine of Christ, but in a spirit completely opposite to Christ's interpretation. It is clear that Mulford's *justification* for success was based on the virtue of taking, not giving. See Prentice Mulford, "The Church of Silent Demand," *Your Forces,* III, 9–11.

[37] Prentice Mulford, "The Church of Silent Demand," *Your Forces,* III, 2, 8.

[38] Prentice Mulford, "Love Thyself," *Your Forces,* VI, 14.

[39] The quotations are from Prentice Mulford, "The Church of Silent Demand," *Your Forces,* III, 14, 8–9. See Prentice Mulford, "God's Commands Are Man's Demands," *Your Forces,* V, 2; Eva Martin, *Prentice Mulford* (London, 1921), pp. 69–70.

[40] *New York Times,* June 1, 1891, p. 1.

CHAPTER 10

[1] For early success writers of the late 1890s and early 1900s, see the works, specifically on success by religious mind power for these years, of Elizabeth Towne, Helen Wilmans, William Walker Atkinson, Henry Harrison Brown, and Charles W. Close. There was some work being done on the subject between Prentice Mulford, at the end of the 1880s, and the turn of the century, but success by New Thought did not really gather momentum until ten years after Mulford's influential work. For a list of the numerous New Thought magazines which began publication in the late 1890s and early 1900s, but without distinction between health and success as goals, see Frank Luther Mott, *A History of American Magazines* (Cambridge, Mass., 1957), IV, 283–285.

[2] Margaret Connolly, *The Life Story of Orison Swett Marden* (New York, 1925), p. 296. The facts of Marden's life are taken largely from this lyrical biography. It is a good detailed biographical description to 1894, but sketchy thereafter. The analysis of Marden's thought is brief, oversimplified, and unreliable. A summary, taken mostly from Connolly, is by Edward M. Hinton in *Dictionary of American Biography* s.v. "Marden, Orison Swett."

[3] M. Connolly, *The Life Story of Orison Swett Marden,* p. 101. Asa Briggs, *Victorian People* (London, 1954), pp. 124–149, is an essay on Samuel Smiles. I have not ventured in this book a cross-cultural comparison of the idea of success with Britain except to point out the heritage of the American success idea. To do so, without a thorough and detailed study of British success literature, would be to risk unsupported generalizations. I have also not explored the translation of American success literature into foreign languages nor measured the degree of its reception in other nations. To what extent, for example, did achievement-oriented cultures like Japan respond with greater enthusiasm to American success literature in translation than other cultures, e.g., Italy or Spain—and, of course, why?

[4] *Ibid.,* pp. 102, 104.

⁵ *Ibid.*, p. 125.

⁶ *Ibid.*, p. vii.

⁷ *Ibid.*, p. 206.

⁸ The statistics are from M. Connolly, *The Life Story of Orison Swett Marden*, pp. 197–207, and James D. Hart, *The Popular Book* (New York, 1950), pp. 160–161. The McKinley quotation is from an advertisement in the back of O. S. Marden, *The Exceptional Employee* (New York, 1913); Judge Lindsey's is from M. Connolly, *op. cit.*, pp. 283–284.

⁹ O. S. Marden, *Hints for Young Writers* (New York, 1914), pp. 12–13.

¹⁰ O. S. Marden, *Pushing to the Front* (Boston and New York, 1894), *passim.*

¹¹ *Ibid.*, p. 217. Cf. the following: "Yet one of the great lessons to teach in this century of sharp competition and the survival of the fittest is how to be rich without money, and to learn how to do without what is popularly and falsely called success." O. S. Marden, *Character: The Grandest Thing in the World* (New York, 1899), p. 41. "In the days of trusts and monopolies, when everything tends to great centres and enormous establishments, when the great fish eat up the little ones, when wealthy men are becoming wealthier, and poor men poorer, one should be extremely cautious about advising young men and young women to go into business with their little, hard-earned savings." O. S. Marden, *The Young Man Entering Business* (New York, 1903), p. 110. Marden also warned occasionally about the frustrating dangers of setting one's level of aspiration too high. See, for example, O. S. Marden, *Pushing to the Front*, pp. 383–384; *The Making of a Man* (Boston, 1905), p. 19; (with the assistance of Abner Bayley), *Stepping Stones: Essays for Everyday Living* (Boston, 1902), p. 320.

¹² O. S. Marden, *Pushing to the Front*, p. iv.

¹³ *Ibid.*, pp. 210–231. The quotation is from p. 384.

¹⁴ See, for example, O. S. Marden, *Architects of Fate* (Boston and New York, 1895); *How to Succeed* (New York, 1896); *Success* (Boston, 1897); *The Secret of Achievement* (New York, 1898); *Character* (New York, 1899); *Cheerfulness* (New York, 1899); *The Hour of Opportunity* (New York, 1900); *Good Manners* (New York, 1900); (with the assistance of Abner Bayley), *An Iron Will* (New York, 1901); (ed. by O. S. Marden), *Talks with Great Workers* (New York, 1901); (with the assistance of Abner Bayley), *Stepping Stones* (Boston, 1902); *The Young Man Entering Business* (New York, 1903); (ed. by O. S. Marden), *Little Visits with Great Americans* (1903, 1904) (New York, 1905); *Stories from Life* (New York, 1904); *The Making of a Man* (Boston, 1905). In addition, see the editorials in *Success* magazine.

¹⁵ An exception is O. S. Marden (with the assistance of Arthur W. Brown), *Economy* (New York, 1901). The subject of *Economy* is the proper administration of one's financial affairs with particular attention to frugality; the goal is the accumulation of wealth; the justification is

the doctrine of stewardship, and wealth as the measure of service to the community. *Economy,* a relatively short book, mostly quotations, on a subject which logically leads to the accumulation of wealth, may have been largely the work of Arthur W. Brown.

O. S. Marden, *How They Succeeded: Life Stories of Successful Men Told by Themselves* (Boston, 1901), is unusually materialistic with an emphasis on philanthropy as the justification for the great wealth of such men as Rockefeller and Carnegie.

[16] O. S. Marden, ed., *Little Visits with Great Americans* (1903, 1904) (New York, 1905), p. 11.

[17] O. S. Marden, *The Making of a Man* (Boston, 1905), p. 65.

[18] Margaret Connolly, *The Life Story of Orison Swett Marden,* p. 212.

[19] See John F. Huth, Jr., "Theodore Dreiser, Success Monger," *Colophon,* New Series, 3 (Winter 1938), 120–133, and "Dreiser and Success: An Additional Note," *ibid.,* 3 (Summer 1938), 406–410; Myrta Lockett Avary, "Success—and Dreiser," *ibid.,* 3 (Autumn 1938), 598–604; Walter Blackstock, "Dreiser's Dramatizations of American Success," *Florida State University Studies,* No. 14 (1954), 107–130. *Sister Carrie* was virtually suppressed as immoral by its publishers for twelve years after publication. The publishers of *Little Visits with Great Americans* felt differently about their volume, which contained many unsigned articles by Dreiser: "We regard them as a trust. We do not feel that we have a right to withhold them from the public." The Publishers, "Preface," in *Little Visits with Great Americans,* ed. O. S. Marden (1903, 1904) (New York, 1905), p. 2.

[20] O. S. Marden, *Pushing to the Front,* p. 10; Margaret Connolly, *The Life Story of Orison Swett Marden,* p. 234. Key circulation figures for *Success* were: 1904, 300,000; 1905, 308,946; 1906, 303,261.

[21] The quotation is from Margaret Connolly, *The Life Story of Orison Swett Marden,* p. 235; *ibid.,* pp. 226–229 sketches the broad outlines, while Louis Filler, *Crusaders for American Liberalism* (New York, 1939), pp. 161, 346–347, 363–365, fills in the details. *Success* folded after the December 1911 issue. Frank Luther Mott, *A History of American Magazines* (Cambridge, Mass., 1968), V, 286–292, suggests that the failure of *Success* was due to bad timing, the loss of its specialized audience, and the pursuit of contradictory editorial goals.

[22] O. S. Marden (with the assistance of Abner Bayley), *An Iron Will* (New York, 1901), quotes Prentice Mulford (p. 15) and hints at New Thought (pp. 26, 48). Connolly ignores the impact of New Thought on Marden's life and thought. Horatio W. Dresser, *A History of the New Thought Movement* (New York, 1919), p. 243, notes that Marden was President of The League for the Larger Life, a clearing house for New Thought groups in New York.

[23] O. S. Marden, *Prosperity: How to Attract It* (New York, 1922), pp. 4–5.

[24] *Ibid.,* p. 1.

[25] *Ibid.,* p. 59; O. S. Marden, *How to Get What You Want* (New York, 1917), p. 235.

[26] O. S. Marden, *Prosperity,* pp. 12, 15–16.

[27] *Ibid.,* pp. 22, 109, 106; O. S. Marden, *He Can Who Thinks He Can* (New York, 1908), p. 15. Everything, from inventions and discoveries, to hospitals and homes, Marden claimed, we owe to the law of attraction. O. S. Marden, *Prosperity,* p. 11.

[28] O. S. Marden, *How to Get What You Want,* pp. 148–149. The reference to Walt Whitman is in O. S. Marden, *Prosperity,* p. 29.

[29] *Ibid.,* p. 237.

[30] O. S. Marden, *Prosperity,* pp. 130–131, 134, 136–137.

[31] O. S. Marden, *Training for Efficiency* (New York, 1913), pp. 201–202, 207–208.

[32] The following works by Marden reflect a pure character ethic: *Success Nuggets* (New York, 1906); *Not the Salary but the Opportunity* (New York, 1909); *Getting On* (New York, 1910); *The Exceptional Employee* (New York, 1913); *I Had a Friend* (New York, 1914); (with the assistance of Joseph F. MacGrail), *Selling Things* (New York, 1916); *Thrift* (New York, 1918).

The following works are a mixture of the character ethic and New Thought: *Choosing a Career* (Indianapolis, 1905); (with the assistance of Ernest R. Holmes), *Every Man a King* (New York, 1906); *The Optimistic Life* (New York, 1907); *He Can Who Thinks He Can* (New York, 1908); *Be Good to Yourself* (New York, 1910); *Self-Investment* (New York, 1911); *Training for Efficiency* (New York, 1913); *The Progressive Businessman* (New York, 1913); *Everybody Ahead* (New York, 1916)—also published under the title, *Heading for Victory* (1916, 1920) (New York, 1920); *Making Life a Masterpiece* (New York, 1916); *Ambition and Success* (New York, 1919); *Success Fundamentals* (New York, 1920); *Making Yourself* (New York, 1923).

The following works are overwhelmingly New Thought: *Peace, Power and Plenty* (New York, 1909); *The Miracle of Right Thought* (New York, 1910); *The Victorious Attitude* (New York, 1916); *How to Get What You Want* (New York, 1917); *The Law of Financial Independence* (New York, 1919); *Prosperity* (New York, 1922); *Self-Discovery* (New York, 1922).

[33] O. S. Marden, *Prosperity,* p. 10. For the self-made immigrant boy theme, see O. S. Marden, *Success Fundamentals,* 224–225.

[34] O. S. Marden, *Prosperity,* pp. 325, 86.

[35] O. S. Marden, *Success Fundamentals,* p. 214.

[36] O. S. Marden, *Prosperity,* pp. 180, 161. For luck in relation to the character ethic, see O. S. Marden, *He Can Who Thinks He Can,* p. 218.

[37] O. S. Marden, *Prosperity,* p. 25.

[88] O. S. Marden, *The Exceptional Employee*, p. ix. See also, O. S. Marden, *He Can Who Thinks He Can*, pp. 242–243.

[39] O. S. Marden, *Peace, Power, and Plenty*, p. 19; *Prosperity*, pp. 30–31. See also in *Prosperity*, pp. 307–308.

[40] O. S. Marden, *Prosperity*, p. 17.

[41] It is interesting that when Marden praises the value of education, he surrounds it with the spirit of the character ethic. O. S. Marden, *Training for Efficiency* (New York, 1913), is a mixture of the character ethic and New Thought. It is distinctly the former mood which leads him to assert: "I believe that the business colleges are among the greatest blessings in American civilization to-day. . . ." (p. 233). O. S. Marden, *Prosperity* (New York, 1922), is an overwhelmingly New Thought book. When Marden interrupts the discussion of religious mind power to praise self-education, he immediately begins to use a vocabulary of struggle and sweat. See pp. 165, 252–257.

[42] O. S. Marden, *Choosing a Career* (Indianapolis, 1905), was the first book in which Marden expressed a particular interest in New Thought. On page 98, for example, there is a strong protest against materialism. Under the increasing influence of New Thought as the years passed, such protests gradually softened and appeared less frequently.

[43] O. S. Marden, *The Victorious Attitude* (New York, 1916), p. 89; *Prosperity*, pp. 61–62.

[44] O. S. Marden, *Success Fundamentals*, p. 262; *Prosperity*, pp. 205–206. To correct an obvious misprint, a comma has been removed between "courage" and "thought" and a hyphen added.

[45] Joshua Loth Liebman, *Peace of Mind* (New York, 1946); Alice Payne Hackett, *70 Years of Best Sellers, 1895–1965* (New York, 1967), pp. 174–180.

[46] O. S. Marden, *Prosperity*, pp. 217, 225.

[47] O. S. Marden, *How to Get What You Want*, p. 243.

[48] O. S. Marden, *Masterful Personality* (New York, 1921), pp. 61, 51. O. S. Marden, *The Power of Personality* (New York, 1906), emerging out of the character ethic tradition, stresses good manners, a good appearance, and the courage to overcome shyness in order to develop a "magnetic personality."

[49] Margaret Connolly, *The Life Story of Orison Swett Marden*, pp. 10, 284, 286. The quoted phrase "scores of people" is from p. 10. H. L. Mencken, review of Margaret Connolly, *The Life Story of Orison Swett Marden*, in *American Mercury*, 7 (February 1926), 253.

[50] Marden died in California where he had gone to recover from a lingering illness. The funeral services were held in Los Angeles; his friends in the East met at New York's Unity Church on the same day at the same hour. Margaret Connolly, *The Life Story of Orison Swett Marden*, p. 266. "Prosperity Treatment Stations" are described in O. S. Marden, *Masterful Personality*, pp. 277–278.

CHAPTER 11

[1] The literature of the impact of pure and applied science on religion is voluminous. An extensive bibliography is Nelson R. Burr, *A Critical Bibliography of Religion in America*, Parts 1 through 5 of *Religion in American Life*, James Ward Smith and A. Leland Jamison, eds. (Princeton, N. J., 1961). Gaius Glenn Atkins, *Modern Religious Cults and Movements* (New York, 1923), pp. 46–81, and Alfred W. Martin, *Psychic Tendencies of Today* (New York, 1918), pp. 1–33, deal specifically with the relation of science to religious idealism.

[2] Henry S. Commager, *The American Mind* (New Haven, 1950), pp. 41–54, argues persuasively that modern America began in the years between the mid-1880s and the Spanish American War of 1898.

[3] The quotation is from R. W. Trine, *In Tune with the Infinite* (New York, 1899), and is cited in William James, *The Varieties of Religious Experience* (New York, 1902), pp. 99–100 (The Modern Library Edition). James strung together scattered passages from the 1899 edition.

[4] William James, *The Varieties of Religious Experience* (New York, 1902), pp. 92, 95, 120 (The Modern Library Edition). For additional favorable references to New Thought, see William James, "The Energies of Men," in *On Vital Reserves* (New York, 1922), pp. 10–11, a lecture first published in 1907; "The Gospel of Relaxation," in *On Vital Reserves*, p. 73. James' essay on habit influenced both religious and secular mind power success writers. See William James, *The Principles of Psychology* (New York, 1890), I, 104–127. For an example of this influence, see the chapter on "Habit and Personal Supremacy," in Orison Swett Marden, *Masterful Personality* (New York, 1920), pp. 123–132.

[5] Charles Thomas Hallinan, "My 'New-Thought' Boyhood: An American Adventure," *Living Age*, 308 (March 5, 1921), 606–611. The essay was originally published in *Hibbert Journal*, 19 (1920), 240–248, and is also reprinted in Robert M. Gay, ed., *Fact, Fancy and Opinion* (Boston, 1923), pp. 268–277. Hallinan's experience probably took place between 1897 and 1899. See the references to Ralph Waldo Trine and Helen Wilmans on p. 611.

[6] *Ibid.*, pp. 610, 611. Evelyn Underhill, *Mysticism* (1911) (London, 1949), pp. 152ff., points out the distinctions between mysticism and New Thought.

[7] J. B. Priestley, "Noo Thought," *Saturday Review*, 147 (April 13, 1929), 500–501; Filson Young, "Quack Religions," *Living Age*, 269 (May 27, 1911), 571–574; Willard L. Sperry, *Religion in America* (1946) (New York, 1948), pp. 105–106; Frances Maule Björkman, "The Literature of 'New Thoughters,'" *World's Work*, 19 (January 1910), 12471–12475.

[8] Henry Harrison Brown, *Dollars Want Me* (San Francisco, 1903), p. 11. Henry Harrison Brown, *New Thought Primer* (San Francisco, 1903), pp. 51–55, lists some twenty New Thought magazines. Frances Maule Björkman, "The Literature of 'New Thoughters,'" *World's Work*,

19 (January 1910), 12471–12475; Woodbridge Riley, "The New Thought," *American Mercury,* 1 (January 1924), 104–108. For New Thought in fiction and the drama, see Horatio W. Dresser, *A History of the New Thought Movement* (New York, 1919), pp. 168, 324–325. Sinclair Lewis, *Babbitt* (New York, 1922), pp. 356–360, is an irreverent description of a New Thought meeting.

⁹ [Elizabeth Towne] *Elizabeth Towne's Experiences in Self-Healing* (Holyoke, Mass., 1905), p. 66.

¹⁰ [Elizabeth Towne] *Elizabeth Towne's Experiences in Self-Healing* is her autobiography. Brief, but useful, are Thomas Dreier and others, *The Story of Elizabeth Towne and the* Nautilus (Holyoke, Mass., n.d. [circa 1911]); *National Cyclopedia of American Biography,* current volume A, s.v. "Towne, Elizabeth Lois"; and M. N. Bunker, "A Woman the West Has Given," *Overland Monthly,* 67 (April 1916), 338–340.

¹¹ The first quotation is from pp. 5–6 of Elizabeth Towne, *Making Money: How to Grow Success* (Holyoke, Mass., 1904, 1929), pp. 5–6, 26, 69, 78. Elizabeth Towne, *15 Lessons in New Thought* (1910) (Holyoke, Mass., 1921), p. 44; Elizabeth Towne, *Making Money,* p. 56.

¹² Elizabeth Towne, *Just How to Concentrate* (Holyoke, Mass., 1904), p. 22; Elizabeth Towne, *Practical Methods for Self-Development* (Holyoke, Mass., 1904), p. 30.

¹³ Elizabeth Towne, *Just How to Concentrate,* p. 25; Elizabeth Towne, *Making Money,* pp. 32–33, 23. See also, Elizabeth Towne, *Thought Force for Success* (1910) (Holyoke, Mass., 1918). For happiness by affirmation, see Elizabeth Towne, *Joy Philosophy* (New York, 1903), 33–34.

¹⁴ Elizabeth Towne, *Just How to Wake the Solar Plexus* (1907) (Holyoke, Mass., 1926), pp. 4, 15, 28.

¹⁵ Elizabeth Towne, *Elizabeth Towne's Experiences in Self-Healing,* p. 68. *New York Times,* June 2, 1960, p. 33, is the obituary.

¹⁶ What we are looking for in these schools of success is a mindset. I have identified four laws which I believe are the essence of the New Thought success doctrine. They are terms which flow out of the literature. Variations and additional techniques, like Elizabeth Towne's deep-breathing explorations into the solar plexus, were of course inevitable given New Thought's lack of authoritative dogma. However, the substance of religious mind power is in these four laws, though different names are possible. For example, when Wallace D. Wattles impressed thought upon formless substance and thereby caused the thing thought about to be created, he called the concept "creative thought." Most of his colleagues would have been more likely to use the verb "to visualize" somewhere in their discussion. Wallace D. Wattles, *Financial Success through Creative Thought or The Science of Getting Rich* (Holyoke, Mass., 1915).

¹⁷ For other popular New Thought self-help writers who published in the decades before 1930, see, for example, the works, specifically about success by religious mind power, of Frank Haddock, Julia Seton, Ethel Whitney, Paul Ellsworth, Benjamin Johnson, Christian D. Larson,

William Walker Atkinson, Fenwicke L. Holmes, Brown Landone, William Ellis Bellis Meyrick Williams, Genevieve Behrend, and Bruce MacLelland, pseud. [Joseph Erwin Tuttle].

It is correct to place Frank Haddock among New Thought success writers, but not on the basis of his frequently cited, best-selling *Power of Will* (Auburndale, Mass., 1907). The source of power in this book is secular, an applied psychology of the will, and not a supernatural faith in some source outside of man. For a New Thought example of Haddock's success magnetism by vibration with the All, see *Power for Success* (1903, 1910) (Meriden, Conn., 1914).

CHAPTER 12

[1] The Henry Ford quotation is from the end cover of Émile Coué, *Self-Mastery through Conscious Autosuggestion* (New York, 1922); Genevieve V. Aram, "Émile Coué and His Method of Healing by Conscious Auto-Suggestion: An Interview with M. Coué," in G. V. Aram, Elizabeth Towne, and William Towne, *The Gist of Coué* (Holyoke, Mass., 1923), p. 8.

[2] [Allan P. Poole] *The Success Course of Will-Culture and Concentration for Power and Success: I Will Be What I Will to Be* (New York, 1918), pp. 8, 14–15. In the original text, the word "alternate" reads "alternating."

[3] Foster Correspondence Schools, *Will and Brain Power* (Scranton, Pa., 1918), I, 31, 24; II, 9. The will was frequently used in New Thought metaphysics as a leverage for success. (An early example is Charles W. Close, *The Secret of Opulence* [Bangor, Maine, 1902].) For the justification for success as the good things in life for your family, the respect of others, and the increased possibilities for service, see II, 16–22. For exercises to train the will and habit, see Frank Haddock, *Power of Will* (Auburndale, Mass., 1907).

[4] Eugene R. Dukette, *Psychoanalysis: The Key to Your Success* (Oakland, California, 1927), pp. 92–125. The quotations are from pp. 112 and 113. William Warner, "New Nerves for Old in One Evening," a full-page advertisement of Lagaren's book in *Psychology*, 3 (September 1924), 81.

[5] Psycho-Phone Company advertisement, "Get the Things You Want —While You Sleep," *Psychology*, 13 (September 1929), 72; J. V. D. Latimer, "Putting the Psyche to Work," *American Mercury*, 14 (June 1928), 150.

[6] Herbert A. Parkyn, *Auto-Suggestion: What It Is and How to Use It for Health, Happiness, and Success* (Chicago, 1909), pp. 127, 124, 132. Parkyn was editor of *Suggestion*, a magazine devoted to suggestive therapeutics, hypnotism, rational hygiene, and psychic research. Though there was some consideration of success in *Suggestion's* articles and advertisements, it was primarily interested in the psychic phases of medicine. The work cited above is from a series of articles first published

in *Suggestion* in 1903 and 1904, and then revised and expanded into book form in 1909.

[7] The quotations are from "Growing Better with Monsieur Coué," *Current Opinion*, 73 (November 1922), 587; Orlo Williams, "Healing by Autosuggestion," *Living Age*, 313 (May 20, 1922), 467; Robert Littell, "Émile Coué," *New Republic*, 33 (January 24, 1923), 224, 225.

[8] Émile Coué, *Self Mastery through Conscious Autosuggestion*, pp. 9, 12.

[9] *Ibid.*, pp. 60, 15. The exact wording of the phrase differed from "Every day, in every respect," to "Every day, in every way," to "Day by day, in every way." The latter was the most popular translation from the original French.

Coué's particular system of mental healing contained the following additional important distinctions: (1) He claimed no powers as a healer but insisted that the patient cured himself by transferring external suggestions into internal autosuggestions. (2) It is not necessary to know which organ is affected in order to be cured because the unconscious will detect it for you. (3) Whatever you want to do must be within your power to do it. (4) It is within your power to cure organic, as well as functional and nervous disorders, e.g., tumors, tubercular lesions, varicose ulcers, etc. How can a fibrous tumor be made to disappear? "The *unconscious* having accepted the idea 'It is to go' the brain orders the arteries which nourish it, to contract. They do so, refusing their services, and ceasing to nourish the tumor which, deprived of nourishment, dies, dries up, is reabsorbed and disappears." Émile Coué, *Self Mastery through Conscious Autosuggestion*, p. 27.

Coué touched off a sensation of controversy, particularly among doctors and clergymen. Opinion was by no means entirely critical. Most doctors agreed that autosuggestion could be used to some extent for nervous and functional disorders, but not for organic diseases. Two of the more thoughtful ecclesiastical criticisms, which also offer medical opinions, are William Ralph Inge, *Lay Thoughts of a Dean* (New York, 1926), pp. 230–242, and the Editor, "Couéism and Catholicism," *Catholic World*, 116 (March 1923), 790–803. The editor of the *Catholic World* argued that the will is indispensable for any moral struggle against evil.

There are a number of personal reminiscences and studies of Couéism. The best is Charles Baudouin, *Suggestion and Autosuggestion* (London, 1924), first published in 1920, which contains an additional preface in answer to criticism.

[10] Émile Coué, *My Method, Including American Impressions* (New York, 1923), p. 142. Further evidence of Cleveland's response to Coué is the *New York Times*, January 22, 1923, p. 14.

[11] Émile Coué, *Self Mastery through Conscious Autosuggestion*, pp. 38, 40, 52–53. The quotations are from pp. 40, 52–53. Coué felt that an idle man was a useless man, and that work was essential for a life of satisfaction.

[12] Émile Coué, *My Method, Including American Impressions*, pp. 104, 187.

[13] Alice Payne Hackett, *Fifty Years of Best Sellers: 1895–1945* (New York, 1945), p. 47, lists the best sellers for 1923.

[14] Elizabeth Towne, "The Fundamentals of New Thought Healing," in G. V. Aram, Elizabeth Towne, and William E. Towne, *The Gist of Coué* (Holyoke, Mass., 1923), p. 20.

CHAPTER 13

[1] Stuart Chase, *Prosperity: Fact or Myth* (New York, 1929), p. 40; Harold Laski, *The American Democracy* (New York, 1948), p. 165; Frederick Lewis Allen, *Only Yesterday* (1931) (New York, 1946), p. 201. (Bantam Book edition.)

[2] The quotations are from Henry Morton Robinson, *Fantastic Interim* (New York, 1943), p. 97, and Harold U. Faulkner, *From Versailles to the New Deal* (New Haven, 1950), p. 124. For an on-the-scene gasp of astonishment at the new phenomenon of hero-making, see Charles Merz, *The Great American Bandwagon* (New York, 1928), pp. 215–229.

[3] Irving Bacheller, *Keeping up with Lizzie* (New York, 1911), pp. 5, 28–29, 31, 53.

[4] I am indebted to Malcolm O. Young for suggesting that I begin the research on "keeping up with the Joneses" with Irving Bacheller. A. J. Hanna, "A Bibliography of the Writings of Irving Bacheller," *Rollins College Bulletin*, 35 (September 1939), 24–27; Charles E. Funk, *Heavens to Betsy! and Other Curious Sayings* (New York, 1955), pp. 141–142.

[5] Lucien Romier, *Who Will Be Master: Europe or America?* (New York, 1928), pp. 187, 193.

[6] The quotation is from J. A. Spender, *Through English Eyes* (New York, 1928), p. 85. For background, see Thomas C. Cochran and William Miller, *The Age of Enterprise* (New York, 1942), pp. 309–312; Frederick Lewis Allen, *Only Yesterday,* pp. 192–199.

The actual economic foundation upon which prosperity was constructed, and the degree of poverty in America at this time, is discussed in a later chapter.

[7] Julian Sherrod, *Scapegoats* (New York, 1931), pp. 18, 23.

[8] Peter B. Kyne, *The Go-Getter: A Story that Tells You How to Be One* (New York, 1921), pp. 58, 62.

[9] William W. Woodbridge, *"Bradford, You're Fired!": A Story of the Super-Self* (n.p., 1917), pp. 12, 9, 21, 24. The spelling of "figure's" has been changed from "figuure's."

[10] *Ibid.,* pp. 24–25.

[11] *Ibid.,* pp. 47–48. The recurring title in Woodward's story is similar to Elbert Hubbard's technique in *A Message to Garcia.*

[12] S. A. Harrington, *Success Nuggets: "Pep" in Capsule Form* (Akron, Ohio, 1922), pp. 7, 73, 44, 79, 89, 93, 9, 176.

[13] *Ibid.,* pp. 112, 163.

CHAPTER 14

[1] George Seldes, "Barton, Barton, Barton, and Barton," *New Republic*, 96 (October 26, 1938), 327.

[2] [William E. Barton] *The Autobiography of William E. Barton* (Indianapolis, 1932); William E. Barton, *Lieutenant William Barton of Morris County, New Jersey, and His Descendants* (Oak Park, Illinois, 1900); Frederick T. Persons in *Dictionary of American Biography* s.v. "Barton, William Eleazar."

[3] The first quotation is from Bruce Barton, "The Most Unforgettable Character I've Met," *Reader's Digest*, 69 (July 1956), 33; the second is from Bruce Barton, "My Thirty-Two Years at School," *American Magazine*, 87 (April 1919), 34. See also Bruce Barton, "Introduction," *The Autobiography of William E. Barton*, pp. vii–xx.

[4] Bruce Barton, *More Power to You: Fifty Editorials from Every Week* (New York, 1917), pp. 117, 100. An apparent contradiction of the success philosophy, Bruce Barton, "Do You Believe in Luck? I Do," *American Magazine*, 105 (April 1928), 16ff., concludes that luck comes to those who deserve it by being ready for it.

[5] *Ibid.*, p. 25; Bruce Barton, "My Thirty-Two Years at School," *American Magazine*, p. 73.

[6] Bruce Barton, *On the Up and Up* (Indianapolis, 1929), p. 95; Bruce Barton, "My Thirty-Two Years at School," *American Magazine*, p. 73; Bruce Barton, *More Power to You*, pp. 25, 28; Bruce Barton, *It's a Good Old World: Being a Collection of Essays on Various Subjects of Human Interest* (New York, 1920), pp. 188, 152.

[7] Bruce Barton, "My Thirty-Two Years at School," *American Magazine*, p. 68; Bruce Barton, "All Dressed Up and No Place to Go," *Reader's Digest*, 68 (February 1956), 138–140.

[8] *New York Times*, September 23, 1926, p. 4. Senator Bayard's statement is from the *New York Times*, September 28, 1926, p. 27.

[9] The quotation is from Bruce Barton, "My Thirty-Two Years at School," *American Magazine*, p. 34. On the work attitude, see Ben Duffy, "What Is He Like at Work?—5: Bruce Barton," *Youth's Companion*, 100 (February 4, 1926), 89, and Bruce Barton, *The Man Nobody Knows* (Indianapolis, 1925), pp. 179–180.

[10] Personal interview with a former employee.

[11] The first quotation is from "With Hustle & Hope," *Time*, 54 (October 24, 1949), 82; the second is from a letter from Barton to Bedner, November 30, 1948, in Robert R. Bedner, " 'And There Arose a New King Which Knew Not Joseph': A Biography of Bruce Barton" (Undergraduate thesis in Princeton University Library, 1949), p. 69.

For background, see Robert E. Sherwood, *Roosevelt and Hopkins* (New York, 1950), I, 232–233, and "Bruce Barton of New York is Salesman of a Liberal G. O. P.," *Life*, 4 (October 21, 1940), 100. A sketch of Barton's political career is Robert L. Bishop, "Bruce Barton

—Presidential Stage Manager," *Journalism Quarterly,* 43 (Spring 1966). For a front-page obituary and details of the estate, see *New York Times,* July 6, 1967, pp. 1ff., and July 25, 1967, p. 18.

[12] Bruce Barton, *On the Up and Up,* p. 110; Bruce Barton, *More Power to You,* pp. 103, 104.

That a gradual rise to success based on service is better than getting rich quickly by speculation is the lesson of Barton's novel, *The Making of George Gorton* (New York, 1918).

[13] Bruce Barton, *More Power to You,* pp. 199, 202.

[14] Charles Fiske, "The Confessions of a Penitent and Puzzled Parson," *Scribner's Magazine,* 82 (December 1927), 660; Jesse Rainsford Sprague, "Religion in Business," *Harper's,* 155 (September 1927), 431–439; William T. Doherty, "The Impact of Business on Protestantism, 1900–1929," *Business History Review,* 28 (June 1954), 141–153.

[15] Bruce Barton, *The Man Nobody Knows* (Indianapolis, 1925). The hope was expressed in the prefatory "How It Came to Be Written," which is without page numbers. The heart of Barton's religious faith may be found in *What Can a Man Believe?* (Indianapolis, 1927), p. 157: "Because I have intelligence there must be Intelligence behind the universe. Why? Because otherwise the universe has created something greater than itself, for it has created me; and the assumption that the lesser can produce the greater, that something can come out of nothing, does violence to my common sense. I can not conceive or accept it. In other words, because I am, I believe God is."

Alice Payne Hackett, *Fifty Years of Best Sellers: 1895–1945* (New York, 1945), pp. 51, 53; Charles M. Sheldon, *In His Steps* (1897) (Chicago, 1899). 1897 is the year in which it was published in book form. For an entirely different interpretation of Jesus as a poor workingman and a leader of the proletariat who would be head of the revolutionary labor movement, see Bouck White, *The Call of the Carpenter* (New York, 1911).

[16] Bruce Barton, *The Man Nobody Knows.* The quotation is from the prefatory note which is without page numbers.

[17] *Ibid.,* pp. 18–19, 43, 86, 62, 64.

[18] *Ibid.,* pp. 104, 106.

[19] *Ibid.,* pp. 126, 129, 143.

[20] *Ibid.,* pp. 162–164, 177, 166.

[21] *Ibid.,* pp. 166–167, 177, 168, 170, 173.

[22] *Ibid.,* pp. 179–180.

[23] *Ibid.,* pp. 189, 191. Barton used the word "success" in a very loose and convenient manner to mean both material success and "true success."

[24] Alice Payne Hackett, *Fifty Years of Best Sellers, 1895–1945,* p. 53. In this same year, *The Book Nobody Knows* was number seven on Hackett's list. The "book," of course, was the Bible.

CHAPTER 15

[1] Herbert Hoover, "Accepting the Republican Nomination for the Presidency," the *New York Times,* August 12, 1928, p. 3; George Sutherland, "Principle or Expedient?," *Proceedings of the New York State Bar Association,* 44 (1921), 279; Grace A. Turkington, *My Country: A Textbook in Civics and Patriotism for Young Americans* (Boston, 1918), pp. 15–16. Quoted in Bessie Louise Pierce, *Civic Attitudes in American School Textbooks* (Chicago, 1930), p. 167. See also, Herbert Hoover, *American Individualism* (1922) (New York, 1934), *passim.*

[2] Harold U. Faulkner, *From Versailles to the New Deal* (New Haven, 1950), pp. 90, 120; George Soule, *Prosperity Decade* (London, 1947), pp. 283–285; Eric F. Goldman, *Rendezvous with Destiny* (New York, 1952), pp. 293–298, 308–309; Thomas C. Cochran and William Miller, *The Age of Enterprise* (New York, 1942), p. 323.

[3] Gertrude Werner, "Foreword," in *101 Unusual Experiences Gleaned from the Careers of Business Leaders, and Others* by B. C. Forbes (New York, 1952), p. 7; *Current Biography* (1950) (New York, 1951) s.v. "Forbes, B(ertie) C(harles)."

[4] "B. C. Forbes Interviewed," *Forbes,* 60 (November 15, 1947), 180; B. C. Forbes, *Finance, Business and the Business of Life* (n.p., 1915), pp. 147, 300, 331, 311–313, 326–327.

[5] B. C. Forbes, *How to Get the Most out of Business* (New York, 1927), pp. 68–70. See Eric F. Goldman, *Two-Way Street: The Emergence of the Public Relations Counsel* (Boston, 1948).

[6] B. C. Forbes, "My Adventures in Self-Reliance," *American Magazine,* 90 (November 1920), 64.

[7] *Ibid.,* p. 174.

[8] *Ibid.,* pp. 178, 179–181. For the credo of *Forbes* "to humanize business," see B. C. Forbes, "Fact and Comment," *Forbes,* 60 (October 1, 1947), 10. For biographical information, see "B. C. Forbes Interviewed," *Forbes,* 60 (November 15, 1947), 180–181; *Current Biography* (1950) (New York, 1951) s.v. "Forbes, B(ertie) C(harles)"; *Who's Who in America, 1952–1953* s.v. "Forbes, B(ertie) C(harles)"; "Tycoon's Pal," *Time,* 36 (December 2, 1940), 74–76; "Forbes's 50." *Time,* 50 (November 17, 1947), 91–92; *New York Times,* May 7, 1954, p. 24.

[9] B. C. Forbes, *101 Unusual Experiences Gleaned from the Careers of Business Leaders, and Others,* p. 218, describes reporting experiences.

[10] The quotations are from B. C. Forbes, *Finance, Business and the Business of Life,* pp. 65, 90; 33, and *Keys to Success: Personal Efficiency* (New York, 1917, 1918, 1926), p. 69.

[11] B. C. Forbes, *Forbes Epigrams: 1000 Thoughts on Life and Business* (New York, 1922), pp. 17, 18, 25, 24, 36, 38, 43, 63, 66, 51, 78, 116, 160.

[12] B. C. Forbes, *Finance, Business and the Business of Life,* pp. 20, 30, 224, 46, 68–70.

[13] B. C. Forbes, *How to Get the Most out of Business,* p. 7; *Finance, Business and the Business of Life,* pp. 172, 270, 319.

[14] B. C. Forbes, *How to Get the Most out of Business,* preface without pagination, pp. 1–3. The quotation is from page 1. B. C. Forbes, *Finance, Business and the Business of Life,* pp. 29–30, 218. For a discussion of inner and outer "true success," see also pp. 148–150, 172–174, 218–220, 275–277, 290–292, 309–310, 322–324.

[15] For example, see the twenty biographies in B. C. Forbes and O. D. Foster, *Automotive Giants of America: Men Who Are Making Our Motor Industry* (New York, 1926). B. C. Forbes, *Finance, Business and the Business of Life,* p. 114; *Keys to Success,* pp. 199, 201. Forbes occasionally suggested the concept of stewardship as a justification for success, but his emphasis was overwhelmingly on the principle of service. See, for example, *Finance, Business and the Business of Life,* pp. 277, 317. An excellent, brief statement of the component parts of the idea of success is outlined in B. C. Forbes, *Men Who Are Making America* (New York, 1917, 1918), pp. v–xi. The statement reinforces Forbes' tendency to emphasize the non-character qualities of innate intelligence and brains necessary for *exceptional* rather than just moderate success. Thirty years later, in 1947, Forbes evidently had not changed his mind one bit. For a summary of the component parts of the idea of success similar to the one cited above, see B. C. Forbes, "Today's 50 Foremost Business Leaders," *Forbes,* 60 (November 15, 1947), 37ff.

[16] For scientific management, see Horace B. Drury, *Scientific Management: A History and Criticism,* Studies in History, Economics and Public Law, LXV (New York, 1915); C. Bertrand Thompson, *The Theory and Practice of Scientific Management* (Boston, New York, and Chicago, 1917); Edward E. Hunt, ed., *Scientific Management Since Taylor* (New York, 1924).

[17] Herbert Kaufman, *Do Something! Be Something!: A New Philosophy of Human Efficiency* (London, 1912); *The Efficient Age* (New York, 1913). Sumner H. Slichter in *Encyclopaedia of the Social Sciences,* s.v. "Efficiency," gives the etymology of efficiency.

[18] The "Efficiency Question Box" begins in the *Independent,* 80 (December 28, 1914), 480. The Canadian, Herbert N. Casson, was influential in developing personal efficiency, but spent more of his time in England.

[19] E. E. Purinton, *Purinton Practical Course in Personal Efficiency* (New York, 1919), Manual One, Preface; Manual Five, pp. 27–30; Manual Seven, pp. 33–34; *Personal Efficiency in Business* (New York, 1919), pp. 94–111 (the quotation is from p. 94).

[20] E. E. Purinton, "The Efficient Man's Money," *Independent,* 83 (July 26, 1915), 116.

The component parts of the success idea are stated in *ibid.,* pp. 116–118; *Purinton Practical Course in Personal Efficiency,* Manual Seven, p. 33; E. E. Purinton, *The Triumph of the Man Who Acts and Other Papers* (New York, 1916), pp. 12, 13. Service was also a means to success. See E. E. Purinton, *Personal Efficiency in Business,* p. 18—"You reap a royal salary by sowing a royal service." Without any influence of efficiency, the component parts of the idea of success with a secular justification are sketched out in E. E. Purinton, *Petain, The Prepared* (New York, 1917).

[21] Frank B. Copley, *Frederick W. Taylor: Father of Scientific Management* (New York, 1923), I, 83. The principles of efficiency expressed as a formal system are contained in Everett W. Lord, *A Plan for Self-Management* (New York, 1925). For comments on the efficiency movement in general, see Edwin D. Schoonmaker, "The Moral Failure of 'Efficiency,' " *Century*, 90 (June 1915), 187–192; [Anonymous] "The Moral Failure of the Modern Cult of 'Efficiency,' " *Current Opinion*, 59 (July 1915), 39–40. Samuel Haber, *Efficiency and Uplift: Scientific Management in the Progressive Era, 1890–1920* (Chicago, 1964), is an historical treatment.

[22] Charles F. Marden, *Rotary and Its Brothers* (Princeton, 1935). pp. 136–141. The exact wording and capitalization of the motto varies. Marden gives the following version: "He profits most who serves the best" (p. 137).

[23] Charles C. Chapman, *The Development of American Business and Banking Thought, 1913–1936* (New York, 1936), pp. 98–105; Herman E. Krooss, "Business Opinion between Two Wars: A Survey of Statements of Business Leaders on Economic Issues" (Manuscript at the New York University Library, School of Commerce, Accounts, and Finance, 1947), pp. 24–40.

[24] J. A. Spender, *Through English Eyes* (New York, 1928), pp. 311–312. For a similar statement, see pp. 96–97.

[25] André Siegfried, *America Comes of Age* (New York, 1927), pp. 37, 179.

CHAPTER 16

[1] At the beginning of the analysis of the third major school of success literature, I might explain why the designating terms were chosen. Character, mind power, and personality were words used by success writers themselves. Possible substitutes for the character ethic would have been "Protestant ethic" or "Puritan ethic." Both are too narrow because they exclude a secular interpretation. At the same time Protestant ethic for a specific religious interpretation is too broad because the religious impulse was specifically ascetic Puritan Protestantism. "Bourgeois morality" is loaded with political implications while "middle class values" is too loose. Character ethic, with either a religious or secular interpretation, seemed to me to be more precise. One disadvantage is that "character" and "personality" can have specialized meanings in the behavioral sciences. The terms are used here in their popular meaning, i.e., he has a good character or a pleasing personality.

[2] A character ethic success book which reflects a typical imbalance between character and personality is William M. Thayer, *Ethics of Success* (Boston, 1893). George H. Knox, *Ready Money* (Des Moines,

Iowa, 1905), particularly emphasizes the equivalent of personality. A grab bag work which advocates the major means to success of character, mind power, and personality is Welburn M. Guernsey, *107 Positive Ways to Easily Gain Health, Happiness, and Success* (Indianapolis, 1927). For an example of a 1920s transition success book defining personality as "character—plus," see B. C. Forbes, *Keys to Success: Personal Efficiency* (New York, 1917, 1918, 1926), pp. 231–237.

³ Earl of Chesterfield, *Letters to His Son* (New York, 1901), I, 41; Arthur M. Schlesinger, *Learning How to Behave* (New York, 1946), pp. 11–12; Frank Luther Mott, *Golden Multitudes* (New York, 1947), p. 304; Gerald Carson, *The Polite Americans* (New York, 1966), pp. 29–32.

⁴ Benjamin Franklin, *Autobiography* in *The Writings of Benjamin Franklin,* ed. Albert H. Smyth (New York, 1905), I, 350–351, 244–245, 337–339, 307–308. For success books of the personality ethic that cite Franklin, see Ewing T. Webb and John J. B. Morgan, *Strategy in Handling People* (Chicago, 1930), Frank Bettger, *How I Raised Myself from Failure to Success in Selling* (New York, 1949), and Dale Carnegie, *How to Win Friends and Influence People* (New York, 1936).

⁵ The New Thought works of William Walker Atkinson particularly emphasized control over others. In *Thought-Force in Business and Everyday Life* (Chicago, 1901), p. 19, Atkinson remarked that "success in life depends largely upon our ability to interest, attract, influence and control our fellow men." The way to do it was by "Personal Magnetism" based on "the law of Mental Control."

⁶ "His Simple Invention . . ." advertisement of Sherwin Cody School of English in *Psychology,* 3 (September 1924), 7. Sherwin Cody, *the Sherwin Cody 100% Self-Correcting Course in [the] English Language* (Rochester, N. Y., 1921), and *How to Deal with Human Nature in Business* (New York, 1915). Cody, a graduate of Amherst, died in 1959 at the age of ninety. Another language school stressing correct and persuasive written and spoken English is the Career Institute of Chicago, Illinois.

⁷ "Of Course I Want to See You!" advertisement of P. F. Collier & Son Co. in *Physical Culture,* 55 (January 1926), 107; "Your Reading Problem . . . ," advertisement of P. F. Collier & Son Co. in *American Magazine,* 97 (May 1924), 173; "They Laughed . . ." advertisement of the U. S. School of Music in *Popular Science Monthly,* 110 (February 1927), 135.

⁸ The quotation is from a reproduction of an advertisement in "Mr. Countway Takes the Job," *Fortune,* 22 (November 1940), 99. The article is on Lever Brothers' President Countway. For toothpaste, see "Those Winning Smiles Which Mean So Much . . . Commercially, Socially . . . ," advertisement of The Pepsodent Co. in *Physical Culture,* 55 (January 1926), 76. For comedones, i.e., blackheads on the face or nose, see "Next in Line–Yet Never Chosen–Perhaps It's Comedones," advertisement of The Pompeian Laboratories in *Popular Science Monthly,* 110 (February 1927), 101. Warned the makers of Pompeian Massage

Cream: "Comedones often interfere with business success, for you can't be clean cut and attractive when they are present. Do *you* wonder why you don't get ahead? Perhaps it's *comedones.*"

[9] A better-than-average volume on the subject of salesmanship is in the Alexander Hamilton Institute series, John G. Jones, *Salesmanship and Sales Management* (New York, 1917).

[10] F. Alexander Magoun, *Problems in Human Engineering* (New York, 1932), p. vii. See also, Dr. Harry Myers, *Human Engineering* (New York, 1932); Charles R. Gow, *Foundations for Human Engineering* (New York, 1931), and *Elements of Human Engineering* (New York, 1932). The term "human engineering" is used in physiology in a much different sense than human relations. See Reference Section, ASTIA Reference Center, Library of Congress, *Human Engineering: A Selected Bibliography of Technical Reports & a Guide to the Literature* (Washington, 1953).

[11] The statistics are in a letter dated July 2, 1969, from Simon & Schuster, Inc., to the author.

Frank Luther Mott, *Golden Multitudes* (New York, 1947), pp. 259–261, provides facts while George Stevens, *Lincoln's Doctor's Dog* (Philadelphia, 1938, 1939), pp. 46–48, discusses the early months of publication.

[12] Carnegie's books, cited elsewhere, are studded with autobiographical incidents. The following biographical sources are useful: Margaret Case Harriman: "He Sells Hope," *Saturday Evening Post,* 210 (August 14, 1937), 12ff.; Lowell Thomas, "A Short-Cut to Distinction," in *How to Win Friends and Influence People,* pp. 1–11; *Current Biography* (1941) s.v. "Carnegie, Dale"; Collie Small, "Dale Carnegie: A Man with a Message," *Collier's,* 123 (January 15, 1949), 26ff.; Harold B. Clemenko, "He Sells Success," *Look,* 12 (May 25, 1948), 60–69; Adolph E. Meyer, "How Dale Carnegie Made Friends, Etc.," *American Mercury,* 57 (July 1943), 40–48; "World of Carnegie," and "Friend with Influence," *Newsweek,* 46 (August 8, 1955), 70 and 71; *Who's Who in America* s.v. "Carnegie, Dale"; *New York Times,* November 2, 1955, p. 35.

[13] Most of the information about Carnegie's career, at what is now called Central Missouri State College, was lost in a 1915 fire which destroyed student records. Many of the details about his student life, including both quotations, are taken from letters to the author from Mrs. Monia C. Morris, dated December 7, 1955, December 21, 1955, and May 10, 1956.

[14] Letters from Howard Lindsay to the author, dated November 21, 1955, and December 6, 1955.

[15] Ewing T. Webb and John J. B. Morgan, *Strategy in Handling People* (Chicago, 1930).

[16] The quotation is from Dale Carnegie, *How to Win Friends and Influence People,* p. 14. Dale Carnegie, *Public Speaking* (New York,

1926), 2 vols. The title in later editions was changed to *Public Speaking and Influencing Men in Business.* Eleven years earlier, before changing the spelling of his name, Carnegie had co-authored a book on the subject, J. Berg Esenwein and Dale Carnagey, *The Art of Public Speaking* (Springfield, Mass., 1915). *Lincoln the Unknown* (New York, 1932); *Little Known Facts about Well Known People* (New York, 1925). H. A. Overstreet, *Influencing Human Behavior* (New York, 1925).

[17] Dale Carnegie, *How to Win Friends and Influence People,* pp. 71, 67.

[18] *Ibid.,* pp. 16, 73. The personality ethic was particularly keen on a quality of character shared by the 1920s. See Dale Carnegie, "What's the Secret of Successful Leadership and Living? Why, It's Enthusiasm!," *Rotarian,* 82 (February 1953), 8–9.

[19] Dale Carnegie, *How to Win Friends and Influence People,* pp. 12–13.

[20] *Ibid.,* p. 17. On page 189, Carnegie again quotes James, but changes "compared to" to "compared with."

Another favorite quotation of the personality ethic was attributed to John D. Rockefeller: "The ability to deal with people is as purchasable a commodity as sugar or coffee. . . . I will pay more for that ability than for any other under the sun." (p. 13)

[21] *Ibid.,* pp. 27, 30.

[22] *Ibid.,* pp. 29, 39. An obvious misprint, "grssshopper," has been changed to the correct spelling.

[23] *Ibid.,* p. 116. No page numbers are cited in the following analysis. The examples can usually be found in the appropriate chapter following the rules they interpret.

Part Six poses rules for a happier home life. They are not offered as specific means to material success. The seven sensible rules for marriage are: Don't nag; Don't try to make your partner over; Don't criticize; Give honest appreciation; Pay little attentions; Be courteous; Read a good book on the sexual side of marriage.

[24] Margaret Case Harriman, "He Sells Hope," *Saturday Evening Post,* 210 (August 14, 1937), 34.

[25] Mrs. Dale Carnegie, *How to Help Your Husband Get Ahead* (New York, 1953). How much assistance Dorothy Carnegie received in writing the book is not known. There is some discrepancy in who should get credit for setting up the course for women. In a letter to the author, dated November 22, 1955, Marylin C. Burke, assistant to Dorothy Carnegie, was authorized to say that the course "was planned, outlined and written solely by Mrs. Carnegie. In the operation of the course Mrs. [Florence] Schoonmaker has made some valuable suggestions—but the actual course itself can be attributed to Mrs. Carnegie alone." The literature advertising the course presents a different interpretation. It states that Dale Carnegie "has adapted his specialized tech-

niques to the particular needs of women, with the able assistance of his wife, Dorothy Carnegie."

[26] Margaret Case Harriman, "He Sells Hope," *Saturday Evening Post,* 210 (August 14, 1937), 33. The iodine story is also repeated in *How to Win Friends and Influence People,* p. 144.

[27] Dale Carnegie, *Five Minute Biographies* (New York, 1937); *Dale Carnegie's Biographical Roundup* (Forest Hills, N. Y., 1944); "We Have with Us Tonight," *Rotarian,* 49 (November 1936), 35–37. Collie Small, "Dale Carnegie: A Man with a Message," *Collier's,* 123 (January 15, 1949), 70, is the source for Carnegie's summary of *How to Stop Worrying and Start Living.* Alice Payne Hackett, *Seven Years of Best Sellers, 1945–1951* (New York, 1952), p. 12.

Dale Carnegie, *How to Stop Worrying and Start Living* (New York, 1944–1948). To support the above interpretation, contrast p. 20 with the whole tone of the book, e.g., pp. 42, 56, 134, and 205. Pages 89–100 teaches a form of secular mind power to overcome worry. For an earlier buck-up article directed at economic insecurity in the midst of the 1937–1938 recession, see Dale Carnegie, "Grab Your Bootstraps," *Collier's,* 101 (March 4, 1938), 14ff.

[28] For information about the Dale Carnegie Course, see the biographical references cited above and J. P. McEvoy, " 'Do the Thing You Fear,' " *Reader's Digest,* 53 (November 1948), 22–24, and William Longgood, *Talking Your Way to Success: The Story of the Dale Carnegie Course* (New York, 1962), which is the 'official' fiftieth anniversary account.

The description of the course is also based on advertising literature from the Carnegie organization and personal observations of a demonstration meeting and a class meeting. When various sources have disagreed on details about the course, as well as Carnegie's life, I have relied on letters from Harrison B. Taylor, vice-president of Dale Carnegie Publishers, Inc., dated November 18, 1955, and from L. Gray Burdin, vice-president of Dale Carnegie & Associates, Inc., dated May 14, 1969.

Henry Lee, "Talk Your Way to Success," *Coronet,* 30 (September 1951), 148ff., indicates the spread of public speaking courses, while E. M. D. Watson, "What 'Success' Schools Really Can Do," *Reader's Digest,* 74 (June 1959), 110–113, discusses their effectiveness.

[29] The quotation is from *What the Dale Carnegie Course Can Do for You* (New York, 1955), p. 14.

[30] After frequent retelling, these stories have begun to vary in detail and quotation. They still retain the same substance, however. See Harold B. Clemenko, "He Sells Success," *Look,* 12 (May 25, 1948), 62, 65; Collie Small, "Dale Carnegie: A Man with a Message," *Collier's,* 123 (January 15, 1949), 69; J. P. McEvoy, " 'Do the Thing You Fear,' " *Reader's Digest,* 53 (November 1948), 22; William Longgood, *Talking Your Way to Success,* p. 61.

[31] "Friends and Influence," *New Yorker,* 19 (March 20, 1943), 14.

CHAPTER 17

[1] Dale Carnegie, *How to Win Friends and Influence People* (New York, 1936), p. 103. For instruction on mnemonics, see Frank Bettger, *How I Raised Myself from Failure to Success in Selling* (New York, 1949), pp. 152–162.

[2] Advice on clothes, for example, is offered in Bert Bacharach, *Right Dress: Success through Better Grooming* (New York, 1955). The importance of a specific item of apparel, namely one's hat, is reiterated in a series of advertisements by Disney: The Hat of Presidents, i.e., corporation presidents. A representative advertisement is in *Time*, 68 (May 10, 1954), 5.

[3] "Do You Make These Mistakes in English?" advertisement of the Sherwin Cody Course in English in *New York Times Book Review*, September 6, 1953, p. 16, and literature mailed on request from the Cody organization. Since the 1920s, the name has been changed from the Sherwin Cody School of English to the above. The first quotation is from *Dramatizing Your Voice*, p. 2, one of many items sent through the mails by request from the Funk & Wagnalls Company. A representative advertisement is "New Idea. . . ." advertisement of the Funk & Wagnalls Company in the *New York Times Book Review*, February 4, 1951, p. 19. The second quotation is from the front flap of a packet of matches which urges the reader to write in for further information to the Beltone Hearing-Aid Company. The third quotation is from the front flap of a packet of matches which advertises the work of Clarence Stratton, a well-known writer in this field. Stratton is published by Funk & Wagnalls.

[4] The Bourne quotation is from literature mailed on request from Conversation Studies, a Chicago company, which distributes the Ethel Cotton course. See *The Ethel Cotton Course in Conversation* (Chicago, 1935–1937), a series of twelve separate lessons. A representative advertisement is "Make Your Conversation Pay Dividends," advertisement of Conversation Studies in *Glamour*, 26 (January 1952), 115.

[5] Charles B. Roth, *Winning Personal Recognition* (Englewood Cliffs, N. J., 1954), p. 29. For the nature of man, see also Ernest Dichter, *The Strategy of Desire* (New York, 1960).

[6] Elmer Wheeler, *How to Sell Yourself to Others* (New York, 1947), pp. xi, 199, 129, 1, xiv. For a variation on the nature of man interpreted through the "pleasure-pain" principle of human behavior, see pp. 215–222.

[7] Elmer Wheeler, *How to Sell Yourself to Others* (New York, 1947), pp. 59–60, 171, 176, 227, 267, 285, 300. During and after World War II, success writers began to incorporate into their work studies in public opinion persuasion and propaganda analysis. Particularly influential on Wheeler was Clyde R. Miller, *The Process of Persuasion* (New York, 1946). Elmer Wheeler, *Magic Words That Make People Buy* (New York, 1939), is a very humorous speech and a classic on retail selling. The means to success in Elmer Wheeler, *How to Make Your Daydreams Come True* (New York, 1952), are character, mind power,

personality, and creative ideas or imagination. No classic, but one that should be, is the affectionately hilarious satire on sales meetings, Peter De Vries, "A Live Wire," *New Yorker*, 27 (February 14, 1953), 86ff.

[8] *The Happiest Man in Town!* (Feature Publications, Inc., New York, 1955). *Secrets of Successful People* (Aristocrat Leather Products, Inc., n.p.) is an example of a small pamphlet inserted in the Inner Sanctum Wallet sold by this company.

[9] Alice Payne Hackett, *Seven Years of Best Sellers, 1945–1951* (New York, 1952), p. 18.

[10] Frank Bettger, *How I Raised Myself from Failure to Success in Selling* (New York, 1949), p. 7. Bettger's career with the St. Louis Cardinals was not quite so august as he indicates. One record book credits him with having played in only 27 games in the year 1910, batting .202. Bettger says he played third base; the record book lists him as a shortstop. See H. Y. Turkin and S. C. Thompson, *The Official Encyclopedia of Baseball* (New York, 1956), p. 77.

[11] *Ibid.*, pp. 203, 224, 237, 94, 231. Frank Bettger, *How I Multiplied My Income and Happiness in Selling* (New York, 1954), is a sequel with many case studies of actual selling experiences. The special techniques of another insurance salesman are described in Elmer G. Leterman, *The Sale Begins When the Customer Says No!* (New York, 1953), and *Personal Power through Creative Selling* (New York, 1955). The company approach is expressed in The Cleveland Heater Company, *Enthusiasm, Personality and Friendships* (Cleveland, Ohio, 1945). Daniel Seligman, "The Latest 'Secrets' of Selling," *Fortune*, 53 (June 1956), 123ff., analyzes books on selling. Ira Wallach, *Hopalong-Freud Rides Again* (New York, 1952), pp. 11–22, is a satire of Bettger.

The following are examples of other types of literature within the personality ethic. Everett B. Wilson and Sylvia B. Wright, *Getting Along with People in Business* (New York, 1950), concentrates on manipulating the boss. Louis A. Rice et al., *Personality and Human Relations in Business* (New York, 1953), is a brightly presented textbook for adults, with references for further reading at the end of each chapter which list the better books on personality development and human relations. A textbook for children, in four parts, is Ray C. Beery, *How to Make Your Dreams Come True* (Pleasant Hill, Ohio, 1950). James S. Knox et al., *Personality in Action* (Oak Park, Illinois, 1953), is an example of an author who also publishes his own books through the Knox Business Book Co. One of the longest excursions into the personality ethic is Richard W. Wetherill, *The Dynamics of Human Relations* (New York, 1949), 3 vols.

[12] The stories and anecdotes varied in form and wording with the particular success writer, but the substance was the same. The quotations are from Elmer Wheeler, *How to Sell Yourself to Others*, pp. 41, 85, and K. C. Ingram, *Winning Your Way with People* (New York, 1949), p. 40. For a representative attitude toward Wilson and the League, see Dale Carnegie, *How to Win Friends and Influence People*, p. 197.

¹³ Frank Bettger, *How I Raised Myself from Failure to Success in Selling,* p. 144. A discussion of the client's hobbies was also frequently recommended in the personality ethic.

¹⁴ Dale Carnegie, *How to Win Friends and Influence People,* p. 73; Charles B. Roth, *Winning Personal Recognition,* p. vii. Social scientific concepts which are related to the personality ethic are Erich Fromm's concept of the "marketing orientation," C. Wright Mills' "competitive personality," Leo Lowenthal's "idols of consumption," David Riesman's "other-direction," and Arnold Green's "status-adulterated friendship." Riesman developed his concept more extensively than the others and has been on the receiving end of judicious criticism from a variety of disciplines. The criticism in no way detracts from the fact that he is a seminal thinker in the social sciences. For references to these concepts, see Erich Fromm, *Man for Himself* (New York, 1947); C. Wright Mills, "The Competitive Personality," *Partisan Review,* 13 (September–October 1946), 433–441, and *White Collar* (New York, 1951), pp. 161–188; Leo Lowenthal, "Biographies in Popular Magazines," in *Radio Research,* 1942–1943, ed. Paul F. Lazarsfeld and Frank N. Stanton (New York, 1944), pp. 507–546; David Riesman, in collaboration with Reuel Denney and Nathan Glazer, *The Lonely Crowd* (New Haven, 1950); and Arnold W. Green, "Duplicity," *Psychiatry,* 6 (November 1943), 411–424.

The point of departure for a criticism of *The Lonely Crowd* is Seymour Martin Lipset and Leo Lowenthal, eds., *Culture and Social Character: The Work of David Riesman Reviewed* (New York, 1961).

¹⁵ Elmer Wheeler, *How to Sell Yourself to Others,* p. 14; Dale Carnegie, *How to Win Friends and Influence People,* p. 37. The phrase, "a new way of life," is repeated three times, with and without italics, on pp. 37, 54, and 208.

¹⁶ Dale Carnegie, *How to Win Friends and Influence People,* pp. 72, 68, 69.

¹⁷ *Ibid.,* pp. 109, 104, 105. Italics have been added to "Hamlet."

¹⁸ Sinclair Lewis, "Car-Yes-Man," *Newsweek,* 10 (November 15, 1937), 31.

¹⁹ Irving D. Tressler, *How to Lose Friends and Alienate People* (New York, 1937), pp. 14, 16–17, 45, 65.

²⁰ Harvey Breit, "In and Out of Books," *New York Times Book Review,* June 10, 1956, p. 8; Stephen Potter, *Lifemanship* (New York, 1951). Other satires are Alan Harrington, *The Revelations of Dr. Modesto* (New York, 1955), James Thurber, *Let Your Mind Alone!* (New York, 1937), pp. 77–79, and Shepherd Mead, *How to Succeed in Business without Really Trying* (New York, 1952). Laurence J. Peter and Raymond Hull, *The Peter Principle* (New York, 1969), is more a satire on success in general than specifically the personality ethic.

²¹ James Bender and Lee Graham, *Your Way to Popularity and Personal Power* (New York, 1950), pp. 11–12. This is the New American Library Edition. Bender is a psychologist; Graham is a free-lance writer.

[22] *Ibid.,* p. 12. An author who discusses human relations with a respect and warm feeling for mankind is K. C. Ingram in *Winning Your Way with People* (New York, 1949).

[23] There were exceptions, of course. Elmer Wheeler, *The Wealth Within You* (New York, 1955), pp. 32–34n, does engage in a political discussion of the benefits of capitalism over socialism, but it is significant that it takes place in a long footnote of three half-pages and not in the text.

[24] Douglas Lurton, *Make the Most of Your Life* (London, 1946), pp. 66, 67. The American edition was published in 1945. Lurton has been an important editor and publisher of various success magazines since the 1930s. *Make the Most of Your Life* incorporates the means to success of character, personality, and "creative imagination," with a strong emphasis on overcoming fear and self-consciousness. Douglas Lurton, *The Power of Positive Living* (New York, 1950), asserts that success is achieved by positive thoughts and a positive outlook on life, while *The Complete Home Book of Money-Making Ideas* (New York, 1954), does suggest something of the creative ideas approach.

[25] The quotations are from Dale Carnegie, *How to Win Friends and Influence People,* pp. 17 and 34. See also pp. 81, 48, 85, and 94. For Schwab, see "Bankrupt Millionaire," *Time,* 37 (May 26, 1941), 87, and "Castle and College," *Time,* 40 (November 2, 1942), 70.

[26] James Bender and Lee Graham, *Your Way to Popularity and Personal Power,* pp. 83–84.

[27] Though Dale Carnegie is typically uninterested in this philosophical implication of the success idea, he does permit Mr. William B. Steinhardt to philosophize about 'true success.' After applying certain principles of human relations, Mr. Steinhardt confesses: "And these things have literally revolutionized my life. I am a totally different man, a happier man, a richer man, richer in friendships and happiness —the only things that matter much after all."—*How to Win Friends and Influence People,* p. 69. Carnegie offers no arguments against materialism and does not articulate a justification for material success.

P. J. Redford, *Help Yourself to Advancement* (New York, 1953), is an exception. Redford concludes his book with an anti-materialistic argument and a plea for the importance of 'true success,' defined as an inner growth of the individual self, "a projection of that self into harmonious and mutually satisfying relations with other individuals and humanity in general," a well-balanced, well-rounded life for a "sense of peace, contentment and achievement without which real and lasting happiness is not possible. . . ." (pp. 103–105).

[28] Elmer Wheeler, *How to Sell Yourself to Others,* pp. 141–142, 240, 179, 238. The quotations are from pp. 141–142 and 240. Like the character ethic, the personality ethic frequently considered service a means to success.

[29] *Ibid.,* p. 7.

[30] Louis M. Grafe, *Get Rich in Spite of Yourself* (New York, 1945, 1954), pp. 11, 63, 14, 15.

[31] *Ibid.,* pp. 16, 72.

CHAPTER 18

[1] Cited in Perrin Stryker, "How Executives Get Jobs," *Fortune,* 48 (August 1953), 182; "Which Route Is Up?" *Fortune,* 51 (June 1955), 158. Stryker felt in the 1955 article that it was time to take a critical look at "the whole human-relations business that has so pervaded the thinking of the business schools and their young hopefuls" (p. 158).

[2] "The Management Poll," *Fortune,* 34 (October 1946), 16; Robert M. Wald and Roy A. Doty, "The Top Executive—A Firsthand Profile," *Harvard Business Review,* 32 (July–August 1954), 45, 50. For further evidence, see Richard Butter, "Along the Highways and Byways of Finance," *New York Times,* Section 3, April 17, 1955, p. 3; "Personality Rates High in University Job Study," *New York Times,* Section 4, February 18, 1951, p. 9; Loire Brophy, *There's Plenty of Room at the Top* (New York, 1946), pp. 47, 92; "The Crown Princes of Business," *Fortune,* 48 (October 1953), 268; J. Elliott Janney, "Company Presidents Look At Themselves," *Harvard Business Review,* 30 (May–June 1952), 59–70.

[3] Donald E. Super, "The Criteria of Vocational Success," *Occupations, the Vocational Guidance Journal,* 30 (October 1951), 7; F. J. Roethlisberger et al., *Management and the Worker* (1939) (Cambridge, 1947).

[4] Dr. William C. Menninger, "Why Men Fail," *This Week Magazine,* March 27, 1955, p. 7.

[5] Alba M. Edwards, *Sixteenth Census of the United States: 1940—Population: Comparative Occupation Statistics for the United States, 1870 to 1940* (Washington, D. C., 1943), pp. 100–103. C. Wright Mills, *White Collar* (New York, 1951), pp. 63–76, is a thoughtful interpretation of these occupational trends. David M. Potter, *People of Plenty* (Chicago, 1954), is a stimulating discussion of the impact of economic abundance on American life.

[6] For an example of an expensive insensitivity to consumer attitudes by a management top-heavy with engineers, see the explanation of Chrysler's descent into a definite third place position behind Ford and General Motors in 1953—William B. Harris, "Chrysler Takes the Bumps," *Fortune,* 49 (April 1954), 127ff.

[7] Advertising Federation of America, *Books for the Advertising and Marketing Man* (New York, 1951), gives the range of literature on advertising, marketing, selling, and related subjects. Perrin Stryker, "Motivation Research," *Fortune,* 53 (June 1956), 144ff., is an interesting discussion of how the social sciences are moving into the field of advertising. The metaphor of the "glad hand" is used by David Riesman, *The*

Lonely Crowd (New Haven, 1950), p. 142. Useful discussions of the nature of competition in the American economy are Lewis Galantiere, *An Examination of the American Economic System* (New York, 1952), second part (a digest report of the American Round Table's fourth session), and "The New Competition," *Fortune,* 45 (June 1952), 98ff., which also comments on Galbraith's concept of countervailing power.

[8] Quoted in "Scoreboard," *Time,* 66 (October 10, 1955), 82; "Country Clubs," *Time,* 66 (August 8, 1955), 74.

[9] Dale Carnegie, *How to Win Friends and Influence People,* p. 108; quoted in column of Walter Winchell, *Philadelphia Inquirer,* December 21, 1953, p. 27.

[10] Quoted in Ernest Havemann, "The Expense Account Aristocracy," *Life,* 34 (March 9, 1953), 148 and 151.

[11] Vincent F. Sullivan, *How to Sell Your Way into the Big Money* (New York, 1954), pp. 151, 161, 168. It is not suggested that Sullivan's book is a representative work of the personality ethic. We are discussing here, not the ideology of the personality ethic, but the causal relationships between that ideology and social and economic conditions in American life.

[12] John McCarten, "Easy on the Vermouth," *Harper's Bazaar,* No. 2864 (July 1950), p. 94. See also, John Brooks, "Business Parties . . . and the Free-Loader," *Harper's,* 208 (April 1954), 85ff., and Mary Van Rensselaer Thayer, "Washington Society is Serious Business," *New York Times Magazine,* February 25, 1951, pp. 13ff.

[13] The Poor Richard quotation is from Benjamin Franklin, *The Writings of Benjamin Franklin,* ed. Albert H. Smyth (New York, 1905), III, 417.

[14] This discussion has drawn heavily upon Peter F. Drucker, "How to Be an Employee," *Fortune,* 45 (May 1952), 126ff.; Perrin Stryker, "Who Is an Executive," *Fortune,* 52 (December 1955), 107ff., and "Which Route Is Up?" *Fortune,* 51 (June 1955), 104ff.; William Miller, "The Business Elite in Business Bureaucracies," in *Men in Business,* ed. William Miller (Cambridge, Mass., 1952), pp. 286–305; Crawford H. Greenewalt, *Key to Progress—the Uncommon Man* (n.p., April 26, 1956), a pamphlet recording a speech, also printed in the *New York Times,* April 27, 1956, p. 18; C. Wright Mills, *White Collar, passim;* and Robin M. Williams, Jr., *American Society* (New York, 1951), pp. 182–183.

[15] Public relations is examined in "Management's Self-Conscious Spokesmen," *Fortune,* 52 (November 1955), 108ff., and Eric F. Goldman, *Two-Way Street: The Emergence of the Public Relations Counsel* (Boston, 1948).

[16] William H. Whyte, Jr., "The Outgoing Life," *Fortune,* 48 (July 1953), 84. The series begins with "The Transients," *Fortune,* 47 (May 1953), 112ff. The example is "extreme" because the series sometimes overplays its point.

[17] William H. Whyte, Jr., and the editors of *Fortune, Is Anybody*

Listening? (New York, 1952), p. 158; "In Praise of the Ornery Wife," *Fortune*, 44 (November 1951), 75. The definition of marriage as a "mutual mobility bet" is by Everett Hughes and is quoted in *Is Anybody Listening?*, p. 172, without attribution. I am indebted to Marvin Bressler for recalling that it was Hughes who coined the phrase. For comments on the role of the government wife in foreign countries, see Helen Hill Miller, "Ambassadresses of Good Will—or Ill," *New York Times Magazine*, February 19, 1956, p. 26.

[18] W. H. Whyte, Jr., and the editors of *Fortune, Is Anybody Listening?*, pp. 172–173.

[19] The definitions of "social" and "sociable" are taken from Clarence L. Barnhart, ed., *The American College Dictionary* (New York, 1948), s.v. "social." The definitions have been adapted to education.

For this study, very useful material about the aims of American elementary and secondary school education, sharply defined by the running controversy between progressive and orthodox principles, has been newspaper and magazine articles collected over the past few decades. Interviews with a number of school principals and teachers have been helpful. An illuminating interpretation relevant to this study is David Riesman, *The Lonely Crowd* (New Haven, 1950), pp. 59–64. A criticism of progressive education, springing from a concern about the con.emporary aims of education and not from a desire to wreck the school system, is Arthur E. Bestor, *Educational Wastelands* (Urbana, Illinois, 1953), and *The Restoration of Learning* (New York, 1955). The later title is an expanded version of the earlier book.

[20] Benjamin Spock, M.D., *The Pocket Book of Baby and Child Care* (New York, 1946), *passim*, esp. pp. 244–245, 303–304. The Darrow cartoon appeared in the *New Yorker*, 24 (April 10, 1948), 32; the Rea cartoon in the *New Yorker*, 27 (July 21, 1951), 23.

[21] *Fan Club Hollywood News*, vol. 6, no. 6 (no date). The information on Presley is from the *New York Times*, November 22, 1964, Section 2, p. 9, and *Time*, 85 (May 7, 1965), 61. For the mechanics of fabricated fame, see Edith Efron, "How to Manufacture a Celebrity," *TV Guide*, 15 (August 5, 1967), 15ff.

[22] The quotation is from Franklin Pierce Adams, *FPA Book of Quotations* (New York, 1952), p. 761.

[23] William H. Whyte, Jr., and the editors of *Fortune, Is Anybody Listening?* (New York, 1952), pp. 204–205.

[24] The quotation is from Sinclair Lewis, "Car-Yes-Man," *Newsweek*, 10 (November 15, 1937), 31.

[25] Dale Carnegie, *How to Win Friends and Influence People*, p. 141.

[26] The quotation is from A. A. Roback, *I Am Winning Friends* (Cambridge, Mass., 1938), p. 21. See also Ethel Ward McLemore, "Manifesto from a Corporation Wife," *Fortune*, 65 (March 1952), 83ff.

[27] W. H. Auden, *The Age of Anxiety* (New York, 1947), pp. 42–43. This entire section on the psychological effects of the personality ethic has drawn heavily on the insights of the following: Erich Fromm, *Escape*

from Freedom (New York, 1941), pp. 119–120, *Man for Himself* (New York, 1947), pp. 67–82, *The Sane Society* (New York, 1955), pp. 120–151; Arnold W. Green, "Duplicity," *Psychiatry,* 6 (November 1943), 411–424; Rollo May, *The Meaning of Anxiety* (New York, 1950), *passim, Man's Search for Himself* (New York, 1953), *passim.*

[28] Anne Morrow Lindbergh, *Gift from the Sea* (New York, 1955), p. 41.

CHAPTER 19

[1] Liberace, "Introduction," in Claude M. Bristol, *The Magic of Believing* (New York, 1955), p. ix. This is the "Special Liberace Edition," illustrated with pictures. John Haverstick, "Lick Those Defects," *Saturday Review,* 37 (October 16, 1954), 35, tells how 8,000 copies were sold in one year from one bookstore in Portland, Oregon. A simplified version is Claude M. Bristol (adapted by Helen and Horace Johnson), *The Magic of Believing for Young People* (Englewood Cliffs, N. J., 1957). For an advertisement, see *New York Times Book Review,* February 25, 1968, p. 39.

In letters to the author (May 19, 1969, and May 27, 1969), Prentice-Hall reported that more than 375,000 hardbound copies of *The Magic of Believing* had been sold while Cornerstone Library stated that approximately 150,000 paperback copies had been sold.

[2] Claude M. Bristol, *The Magic of Believing* (New York, 1948), pp. 3, 5, 6, 8.

[3] *Ibid.,* pp. 8, 11.

[4] *Ibid.,* p. 14.

[5] *Ibid.,* pp. 2, 18, 29, 75–76.

[6] *Ibid.,* pp. 60–61.

[7] *Ibid.,* pp. 63, 83, 103, 223–224.

[8] *Ibid.,* p. 140.

[9] *Ibid.,* p. 40.

[10] *Ibid.,* pp. 144, 166, 168.

[11] *Ibid.,* p. 185.

[12] *Ibid.,* pp. 101–102.

[13] *Ibid.,* pp. 146, 147.

[14] *Ibid.,* p. 122.

[15] *Ibid.,* pp. 34, 132, 112. Bristol was not typical, also, in his emphasis on initiative, preparation for the job, and saving. His mind power confreres usually ignored such advice, particularly saving, which might nourish the negative thought of stinginess.

Claude M. Bristol and Harold Sherman, *TNT: The Power Within You* (New York, 1954), which made the best-seller lists in its year of publication, was also used as the basis for a movie. See "Shop Talk," *Publishers' Weekly,* 166 (December 18, 1954), 2335–2336. *TNT,* probably influenced by Harold Sherman, who put the book together after Bristol's death, occasionally goes beyond the God-given powers interpretation to flirt with the idea of a supernatural source of power. Claude M. Bristol, *T.N.T.: It Rocks the Earth* (Portland, Oregon, 1932, rev. ed. 1933) is an early exploration into the subject of secular mind power.

[16] Advertisement for Walter M. Germain, *The Magic Power of Your Mind* (New York, 1956) in *New York Times Book Review*, October 28, 1956, p. 33.

For other examples of the power source located in the subconscious mind, see Joseph Murphy, *The Miracles of Your Mind* (San Gabriel, Calif., 1953), and Melvin Powers, *Positive Thinking* (Los Angeles, 1955).

[17] The first quotation is Hornell Hart, *Autoconditioning: The New Way to a Successful Life in Business* (Englewood Cliffs, N. J., 1956), p. 1. Prentice-Hall published three separate books which were the same, except for the subtitle and a different introductory insert on colored paper bound into each volume. The three subtitles are: *The New Way to a Successful Life, The New Way to a Successful Life in Business,* and *The New Way to a Successful Life in Selling.* For earlier explorations, primarily into the subject of happiness, see Hornell Hart, *Chart for Happiness* (New York, 1940), and *New Gateways to Creative Living* (New York, 1941). Hart died in 1967 at the age of seventy-eight.

[18] *Ibid.,* pp. 44, 45, 213.

[19] *Ibid.,* pp. 59, 60.

[20] *Ibid.,* pp. 123, 63.

[21] *Ibid.,* pp. 78, 85.

[22] *Ibid.,* pp. 90, 111. See p. 207 for a list of safeguards.

[23] *Ibid.,* p. 143.

[24] Advertising literature sent by mail from the Cambridge Institute, 1157 South Robertson Blvd., Los Angeles 35, California. The literature is not dated, but it probably was composed and printed in 1953 or 1954. One mailing piece has reproduced post marks from envelopes sent in by applauding students. Most of the dates are stamped November and December of 1953. For "sleep learning" for success, see the current literature of the Stanford Institute, 26101 Euclid Avenue, Cleveland, Ohio.

[25] Edgar C. Hanford, "Growth of 'New Thought' Noted," *Christian Century,* 72 (September 7, 1955), 1036, reports that in 1955 the International New Thought Alliance claimed that "membership in New Thought churches in the United States has quadrupled in the past two years." For comments on the growth of health through mind power, see Thomas Sugrue, "Strictly Personal," *Saturday Review,* 27 (November 4, 1944), 13–14.

[26] Frank T. Carlton, "The Correlation of Unrest," 22 (July 3, 1909), 474–475.

[27] Matthew Arnold, "Dover Beach," *The Works of Matthew*

Arnold: Poems (London, 1903), II, 56–57; John Donne, "Devotions, XVII," *Complete Poetry and Selected Prose,* ed. John Hayward (Blooms-bury, England), p. 538; Cartoon by James Thurber, *New Yorker,* 24 (October 2, 1948), 27. See also Robert A. Nisbet, *The Quest for Community* (New York, 1953), *passim,* and Albert Lauterbach, *Man, Motives, and Money* (Ithaca, N. Y., 1954), pp. 100–109.

[28] J. Paul Williams, *What Americans Believe and How They Worship* (New York, 1952), p. 327; John Hoshor, *God in a Rolls Royce* (New York, 1936), pp. 84–85.

[29] Charles S. Braden, *These Also Believe* (New York, 1949), p. 175, and letter to the author dated April 30, 1969; Marcus Bach, "Pioneer in 'Positive Thinking,'" *Christian Century,* 74 (March 20, 1957), 358. In a letter to the author, dated May 17, 1957, Marcus Bach stated: "I would judge that Unity has directly touched the lives of 40,000,000 Americans." All statistics of New Thought's influence are guesses.

[30] Quoted in Clarence Woodbury, "Merchandisers of Faith," *American Magazine,* 143 (March 1947), 84. Most of the statistics and much of the information on Unity have been taken from letters from the Unity School of Christianity to the author, dated February 25, 1957, May 22, 1957, and April 29, 1969, and assorted pamphlets received by mail.

An authorized history is James Dillet Freeman, *The Story of Unity* (Lee's Summit, Mo., 1954). Useful secondary authorities are Charles S. Braden, *Spirits in Rebellion: The Rise and Development of New Thought* (Dallas, Texas, 1963), pp. 233–263; Israel Regardie, *The Romance of Metaphysics* (Chicago, 1946), pp. 183–239; Charles W. Ferguson, *The Confusion of Tongues* (New York, 1928), pp. 214–230; Charles S. Braden, *These Also Believe,* pp. 144–179; Marcus Bach, *They Have Found a Faith* (Indianapolis, 1946), pp. 222–253; Jan Karel Van Baalen, *The Chaos of Cults* (Grand Rapids, Mich., 1956), pp. 116–133; and James W. Teener, *Unity School of Christianity* (Chicago, 1942). An official statement of principles is Lowell Fillmore (compiled from the writings of Charles Fillmore), "Unity School of Christianity," in *Religions and Philosophies in the United States of America,* ed. Julius A. Weber (Los Angeles, 1931), pp. 211–216.

[31] Charles Fillmore, *Prosperity* (Lee's Summit, Mo., 1936, 1955), Foreword, pp. 60, 87, 69. In the first quotation, "supermind" is not capitalized and is perhaps a misprint. The strong strain of anti-materialism in Unity is commented on in the following chapter. Lowell Fillmore, ed., *The Unity Treasure Chest* (New York, 1956), is "a selection of the best of Unity writing." For success books, all or a part of which have appeared in Unity publications, see *Prayer in the Market Place* (Lee's Summit, Mo., 1950); Georgiana Tree West, *Prosperity's Ten Commandments* (New York, 1944); and William I. Hoschouer, *You Can Be Prosperous* (New York, 1947).

[32] Quoted in Marcus Bach, *They Have Found a Faith,* p. 251.

CHAPTER 20

[1] Napoleon Hill, *Think and Grow Rich* (1937) (Cleveland, Ohio, 1956), p. 370. Advertised sales figures seem a bit high. The statistics of Alice Payne Hackett, *70 Years of Best Sellers, 1895–1965* (New York, 1967), pp. 25, 54, are substantial enough: Over 1,200,000 combined paperback and hardbound sales.

Think and Grow Rich is a particularly fuzzy statement, with two variations, of the laws of Divine Supply, affirmation, attraction, and visualization. The first variation is the secret of the "Master Mind" which Hill claims Andrew Carnegie personally revealed to him. Though the point is not exactly clear, it appears that the Master Mind is none other than Infinite Intelligence come to the aid of an harmoniously functioning group. The second variation revolves around the conviction that "the men of greatest achievement" had "highly developed sex natures" and "were motivated by the influence of a woman." They did great things because they "transmuted" their sex drive into their work. In an ingenious rationalization for hiring a sensually exciting secretary, Hill explained: "One of America's most able business men frankly admitted that his attractive secretary was responsible for most of the plans he created. He admitted that her presence lifted him to heights of creative imagination such as he could experience under no other stimulus." (pp. 251, 261, 262, 274–275)

Hill, who was born in a log cabin in the Virginia mountains and died in 1970 at the age of 87, wrote a number of books, which it seems unnecessary to list here, except to point out that the contents of *Think Your Way to Wealth* (Los Angeles, 1948) and *How to Raise Your Own Salary!* (Chicago, 1953) are practically the same.

The Napoleon Hill Institute in Chicago mailed an individual study course in the 1950s entitled the "Science of Success' which cost about $100. Hill was part of the W. Clement Stone organization which publishes the magazine, *Success Unlimited,* and other personal development literature.

[2] Norman Vincent Peale, "Have Faith in People—They Are Basically Good," in *America's Twelve Master Salesmen* (New York, 1952), p. 156. The statistics are taken from the following sources: A letter from a spokesman for Dr. Peale (Howard M. LeSourd) to the author dated March 21, 1957; Irwin Ross, "Norman Vincent Peale," *New York Post,* October 3, 1955, p. 4; "Dynamo in the Vineyard," *Time,* 64 (November 1, 1954), 68; "Questions & Answers," *Time,* 65 (April 18, 1955), 80; advertisement of Prentice-Hall in *Publisher's Weekly,* 171 (January 21, 1957), unpaginated front section.

[3] The quotations are from Norman Vincent Peale, "Have Faith in People—They Are Basically Good," in *America's Twelve Master Salesmen,* p. 147; Norman Vincent Peale, *The Power of Positive Thinking* (New York, 1952), p. 168; Foundation for Christian Living, *Practical Helps for Effective Living* (Pawling, New York, n.d.), no pagination.

[4] Alice Payne Hackett, *60 Years of Best Sellers, 1895–1955* (New

York, 1956), pp. 190, 193. Other books by Peale from the 1930s through the 1950s include: *The Art of Living* (New York, 1937); *You Can Win* (New York, 1938); (with Smiley Blanton), *Faith is the Answer* (New York, 1940); *A Guide to Confident Living* (New York, 1948); (with Smiley Blanton), *The Art of Real Happiness* (New York, 1950); *Stay Alive All Your Life* (Englewood Cliffs, N. J., 1957). A compilation of various pamphlets by Peal is *Inspiring Messages for Daily Living* (Englewood Cliffs, N. J., 1955). *The Coming of the King: The Story of the Nativity* (Englewood Cliffs, N. J., 1956) is a children's book. *Not Death at All* (New York, 1949) is a chapter from *A Guide to Confident Living.*

Peale edited during the 1940s and 1950s a number of volumes compiled from the magazine *Guideposts: Guideposts* (New York, 1948); *New Guideposts* (New York, 1951); *The Guideposts Anthology* (Pawling, N. Y., 1953); *Faith Made Them Champions* (New York, 1954); *Unlock Your Faith-Power* (Englewood Cliffs, N. J., 1957).

[5] The quotation and statistics are from an advertisement by Prentice-Hall in the *New York Times Book Review,* April 8, 1956, p. 16. Alice Payne Hackett, *60 Years of Best Sellers, 1895–1955* (New York, 1956), pp. 202, 205, 208, 211. Since the seventeenth century, in keeping with standard procedure, this study has omitted the Bible from best-seller listings. *The Holy Bible: Revised Standard Version* (New York, 1946, 1952) has been omitted and Peale's book moved up one place, except for the year 1955 when Miss Hackett disqualified the revised version and ceased to list it. The *New York Times* statistic is in Harvey Breit, "In And Out Of Books," *New York Times Book Review,* April 8, 1956, p. 8, and Lewis Nichols, "In And Out Of Books," *New York Times Book Review,* October 11, 1959, p. 8. Norman Vincent Peale, *The Power of Positive Thinking for Young People* (New York, 1952, 1954) is a revised and shortened version of the longer book. The estimated royalties to the author from all sources is very rough and was not supplied by either author or publisher.

[6] Norman Vincent Peale, *The Power of Positive Thinking,* pp. 275, viii–ix.

[7] Quoted in an advertisement by Prentice-Hall in the *New York Times Book Review,* April 4, 1954, p. 15.

[8] Clarence Woodbury, "God's Salesman," *American Magazine,* 147 (June 1949), 140.

The following biographical sketch is based on a number of sources. The sources cited for quotations in the biographical sketch are not repeated in this footnote. Additional useful biographical or autobiographical descriptions are: "Dr. Peale: An Articulate Leader of Christianity," *Newsweek,* 42 (December 28, 1953), 43ff.; *Current Biography* s.v. "Peale, Norman Vincent"; Frank S. Mead, "Grassroots in Manhattan," *Christian Herald,* 66 (November 1943), 13ff.; "Norman Vincent Peale: Minister to Millions," *Look,* 17 (September 22, 1953), 86ff.; Arthur Gordon, "The Power of Norman Vincent Peale," *McCalls,* 81 (January 1954), 26ff.; Lewis Nichols, "Talk with Dr. Peale," *New York Times*

Book Review, October 31, 1954, p. 18; Comment of Peale in "These Hit Me Hard," *New York Times Book Review,* December 4, 1955, p. 60; Norman Vincent Peale, "Have Faith in People—They Are Basically Good," in *America's Twelve Master Salesmen* (New York, 1952), pp. 141–156; Norman Vincent Peale, "Why I Preach As I Do," *Christian Herald,* 79 (January 1956), 24ff., and "Why I Preach As I Do, Part II: God's Help Is Available to You," *Christian Herald,* 79 (February 1956), 32ff.; *Stay Alive All Your Life,* pp. 113–115, 254–256.

The Irwin Ross series ran in six issues of the *New York Post* from October 3 through October 9, 1955, under various titles. The authority for certain statistics about which the sources disagree are letters from Howard M. LeSourd to the author dated March 21, 1957, and May 31, 1957, and a telephone conversation of June 23, 1969. The 'official' biography is Arthur Gordon, *Norman Vincent Peale: Minister to Millions* (Englewood Cliffs, N. J., 1958).

[9] Eugene E. White and Clair R. Henderlider, "What Norman Vincent Peale Told Us About His Speaking," *Quarterly Journal of Speech,* 40 (December 1954), 408; Irwin Ross, "Norman Vincent Peale," *New York Post,* October 4, 1955, p. 4.

[10] The quotation is from Irwin Ross, "Norman Vincent Peale," *New York Post,* October 3, 1955, p. 35. The collegiate experience with the professor differs in detail depending on the source. I have taken this account from Arthur Gordon, *Norman Vincent Peale* (Englewood Cliffs, N. J., 1958), pp. 53–55.

[11] Clarence Woodbury, "God's Salesman," *American Magazine,* 147 (June 1949), 141.

[12] Irwin Ross, "Norman Vincent Peale," *New York Post,* October 3, 1955, p. 35.

[13] In some biographical accounts, Ruth Stafford's father is identified as a Detroit Congregational minister, which is also correct. Mrs. Peale's father retired and then accepted a parish in a Congregational church in Detroit. I have identified him here as an Iowa Methodist minister because Mrs. Peale was raised in Iowa as a Methodist, not in Detroit as a Congregationalist.

[14] Irwin Ross, "Norman Vincent Peale," *New York Post,* October 5, 1955, p. 26.

[15] Mrs. Norman Vincent Peale, "What I've Learned from My Husband," *Woman's Home Companion,* September 1954, p. 88. How biographical anecdotes are collected is indicated in Norman Vincent Peale, "Meet Some of My Favorite People," *American Magazine,* 159 (February 1955), 37ff.

[16] Norman Vincent Peale, D.D., and Smiley Blanton, M.D., "Are You Looking for God?," *American Magazine,* 144 (October 1947), 142. On the point of Peale's relationship to New Thought and its influence on him, he commented: "I had long observed the practice of such religious groups as Christian Science, Unity and metaphysical organizations. I observed that they all outlined in a simple one-two-three form,

the 'how' of the spiritual life." Norman Vincent Peale, "Why I Preach As I Do, Part II: God's Help Is Available to You," *Christian Herald,* 79 (February 1956), 66. Also on this point of the relationship of Peale to New Thought, he entitles a chapter in *The Power of Positive Thinking,* "Inflow of New Thoughts Can Remake You" (p. 201).

[17] Norman Vincent Peale, *The Power of Positive Thinking,* pp. viii, ix, 220.

[18] *Ibid.,* pp. 21–23, 28, 203–205.

[19] *Ibid.,* pp. 7, 9, 109, 128, 106. Something of the personality ethic is expressed in pp. 232–245. In at least one instance, Peale turned away completely from mind power. In "Norman Vincent Peale Answers Your Questions," *Reader's Digest,* 66 (April 1955), 89, he stated that the chief elements for making a success in life were "1) Work. 2) Work. 3) Work. 4) Forget yourself. 5) Have a Goal. 6) Get along with People." This is an excerpt from his regular department in *Look.*

[20] *Ibid.,* pp. 36, 39, 160. The last quotation is Peale's, but it is quoted back to him by a businessman.

[21] *Ibid.,* p. 107.

[22] *Ibid.,* pp. 16, 3, 119, 120.

[23] *Ibid.,* pp. 61, 50, 52, 55–56.

[24] *Ibid.,* pp. 16, 15.

[25] *Ibid.,* pp. 57, 210, 211. For another rendition of God running a beauty parlor, see p. 114.

[26] For other New Thought self-help writers who published in the decades since 1930, see, for example, the works, specifically about success by religious mind power, of Mary Elizabeth Simpson, Frederick Clifton Bond, Ernest Holmes Raymond Charles Barker, Lucius Humphrey, Paul Martin Brunet, Frank M. Welsh, Frances L. Gordon, Charles Edward Popplestone, Brown Landone, and John K. Williams. For New Thought in Los Angeles, a natural center for such activities, see Carey McWilliams, *Southern California Country* (New York, 1946), pp. 256–258.

For a more occult route to riches via the supernatural, see the literature sent on request by AMORC, The Rosicrucian Order, Rosicrucian Park, San Jose, Calif.; H. Spencer Lewis, *Rosicrucian Principles for the Home and Business* (San Jose, Calif., 1929, 1953); R. Swinburne Clymer, "The Hermetic Concept of Success," *A Compendium of Occult Laws* (Quakertown, Pa., 1938), pp. 11–50; and Edwin John Dingle, *Breathing Your Way to Youth* (New York and Santa Monica, Calif., 1931), which is a statement of "The Mentalphysics School of Wisdom."

[27] The discussion of the success formula is an attempt to generalize about mind power success literature as a whole. However, a few exceptions must be noted. It should be pointed out that Napoleon Hill, who was cited earlier in the chapter, is untypical of the literature in several ways, especially in his intent to propagandize politically. See, for example, the last chapter of *How to Raise Your Own Salary!* (Chicago,

1953), in which he defends "The American System of Free Enterprise." Norman Vincent Peale, for example, is more representative on this point. He does not insert his specific political opinions into his success books, but reserves them for articles such as "Let the Church Speak Up for Capitalism," *Reader's Digest,* 57 (September 1950), 126–130.

[28] An exception is Charles Fillmore and much of the literature of the Unity School of Christianity which vigorously assert that the love of money is a root of evil. Hornell Hart, *Autoconditioning,* p. 189, offers the warning that an overly ambitious desire to acquire wealth may destroy the capacity to enjoy it. Norman Vincent Peale's pre-New Thought books, published in the 1930s, worry about the selfish use of religion to get ahead and the relationship of the accumulation of wealth to happiness. Peale's major New Thought books, of wide popularity prior to 1956, *A Guide to Confident Living* and *The Power of Positive Thinking,* are not only indifferent to the problem, but argue that one should slow down in order to achieve the pace that wins. For a modification of Peale's indifference in response to his critics, see below.

[29] "Dynamo in the Vineyard," *Time,* 64 (November 1, 1954), 70.

[30] Gunnar Myrdal, *An American Dilemma* (New York, 1944), p. 11. For the polls on the belief in God, see "Do Americans Believe in God?," *Catholic Digest,* 17 (November 1952), 1–5, and George Gallup, "Americans Express Almost Universal Belief in God," *Public Opinion News Service,* December 18, 1954. For best sellers in 1953, see Alice Payne Hackett, *60 Years of Best Sellers, 1895–1955,* pp. 84, 205.

From an historical viewpoint, the phrase 'return to religion' makes one uncomfortable. The 'return' is to which period in the past after passing through what intervening period? What is the 'return' in terms of—church membership, church-going, devotional faith? I use the phrase to indicate a mood and interest. Seymour Martin Lipset, *The First New Nation* (New York, 1963), pp. 140–169, is thoughtful on the issue.

[31] Advertisement of Dr. John Sutherland Bonnell, Fifth Avenue Presbyterian Church, in the *New York Times,* October 27, 1956, p. 15.

[32] For the toy doll, see *Time,* 64 (September 20, 1954), 65. For Jane Russell's "Livin' Doll," see *Time,* 63 (June 28, 1954), 46. Piper Laurie, "The Fifth Passenger," *Modern Screen,* 45 (August 1952), 68; Arthur Godfrey, "So Long Son," *Guideposts,* 5 (March 1950), 2.

[33] Peale's 'roast beef' quotation is from Arthur Gordon, "The Power of Norman Vincent Peale," *McCalls,* 81 (January 1954), 68.

[34] Dr. Eugene Carson Blake, "Is the Religious Boom a Spiritual Bust?" *Look,* 19 (September 20, 1955), 30.

[35] The quotations are from N. V. Peale, *A Guide to Confident Living,* p. 151; *Stay Alive All Your Life,* p. 147; *The Power of Positive Thinking,* p. 45. The golden cock as a symbol from the New Testament is from Frank S. Mead, "Grassroots in Manhattan," *Christian Herald,* 66 (November 1943), 13ff.

The following critics, listed in chronological order, attack either Peale directly or positive thinking in general, from a theological or a psychiatric viewpoint, or both. The majority of them are ecclesiastics or Christian laymen. Albert N. Williams, "Our Prettified Prophets," *Saturday Review*, 37 (April 10, 1954), 26–28; Wayne E. Oates, "The Cult of Reassurance," *Review and Expositor*, 51 (July 1954), 335–347, which is reprinted in *Religion in Life*, 24 (Winter 1954–55), 72–82; A. Roy Eckardt, "The New Look in American Piety," *Christian Century*, 71 (November 17, 1954), 1395–1397, which is mostly about the peace of mind movement; William Lee Miller, "Some Negative Thinking about Norman Vincent Peale," *Reporter*, 12 (January 13, 1955), 19–24; Paul Hutchinson, "Have We a 'New' Religion?" *Life*, 38 (April 11, 1955), 138ff.; R. C. Murphy, Jr., "Think Right! Reverend Peale's Panacea," *Nation*, 180 (May 7, 1955), 398–400; Donald Meyer, "The Confidence Man," *New Republic*, 133 (July 11, 1955), 8–10; Dr. Eugene Carson Blake, "Is the Religious Boom a Spiritual Bust?" *Look*, 19 (September 20, 1955), 27ff.; Gustave Weigel, S.J., "Protestantism As a Catholic Concern," *Theological Studies*, 16 (1955), 214–232; Edmund Fuller, "Pitchmen in the Pulpit," *Saturday Review*, 40 (March 9, 1957), 28–30; Curtis Cate, "God and Success," *Atlantic Monthly*, 199 (April 1957), 74–76; A. Roy Eckardt, *The Surge of Piety in America* (New York, 1958), pp. 73–92.

The following references report critical viewpoints. "Educator Decries Dr. Peale's Views," *New York Times*, February 8, 1955, p. 25, which records the remarks of the Reverend Dr. Paul Calvin Payne; William Peters, "The Case Against 'Easy' Religion," *Redbook*, 105 (September 1955), 22ff.; Irwin Ross, "Dr. Peale and His Critics," *New York Post*, October 9, 1955, p. 5 (magazine section).

Peale, of course, had his defenders. See Arthur Gordon, "The Case for 'Positive' Faith," *Redbook*, 105 (September 1955), 24ff. Harvey Breit, "In And Out Of Books," *New York Times Book Review*, May 12, 1957, p. 8, examined 75 reviews of *Stay Alive All Your Life* and discovered that 30 were favorable, 15 were unfavorable, and 30 took no position.

[36] Anna Russell, *The Power of Being a Positive Stinker* (New York, 1955), no pagination; Bernard W. Shir-Cliff in *The Power of Negative Thinking* (New York, 1955), p. 35; Stevenson is quoted in *Time*, 92 (December 20, 1968), 18; the letter writer is quoted in Arthur Gordon, "The Power of Norman Vincent Peale," *McCalls*, 81 (January 1954), 67. For other satires on mind power, see Ira Wallach, *How to Be Deliriously Happy* (New York, 1950), *passim*, and *Gutenberg's Folly* (New York, 1954), pp. 106–113.

[37] Norman Vincent Peale, "Why I Preach As I Do, Part II: God's Help Is Available to You," *Christian Herald*, 79 (February 1956), 65; *The Power of Positive Thinking* (Englewood Cliffs, N. J., 1952, 1956), p. vi. *Stay Alive All Your Life* (Englewood Cliffs, N. J., 1957) differs from Peale's previous New Thought books in three ways. First, it condemns the use of spiritual causation for material gain, protests against a material definition of success, and defines 'true success' as self-development, a goal we are obliged by God to pursue. Second, it offers the concept of service as a motivation for material success. Third, it places

greater emphasis on enthusiasm, along with mind power, as the means to material success. Peale was apparently not very happy about *Stay Alive All Your Life,* and it was a great effort to write. "Next time I write a book," his 'official' biographer reports him as saying to his wife, "I'll pay no heed to the critics. I'll say what I want to say—and let them rave!" Quoted in Arthur Gordon, *Norman Vincent Peale: Minister to Millions* (Englewood Cliffs, N. J., 1958), p. 259. See also pp. 258 and 280. Chapter XI, one of two new chapters in the 1956 revised edition of Norman Vincent Peale, D.D., and Smiley Blanton, M.D., *The Art of Real Happiness* (Englewood Cliffs, N. J., 1950, 1956), quickly points out that a Negro porter, who went at prayer with the specific intent of success, was turned down by God.

[38] For a book tailored specifically for executive success, see Norman Vincent Peale, *The New Executive Edition of Enthusiasm Makes the Difference* (Englewood Cliffs, N. J., 1968). The book was published by Executive Reports Corporation, a subsidiary of Prentice-Hall. Prentice-Hall, with its subsidiary, Parker Publishing Company, was by far the leading major publisher of success literature in the 1960s.

[39] Quoted in the *New York Times,* September 19, 1960, p. 39. For Cardinal Spellman, see the *New York Times,* October 10, 1961, p. 23.

[40] Quoted in the *New York Times,* March 6, 1965, p. 1. For family affairs, see the *New York Times,* October 17, 1965, p. 90, and April 6, 1969, p. 58.

[41] Peale is quoted in the *New York Times,* November 25, 1968, p. 19, and Nixon in the *New York Times,* April 28, 1970, p. 47. For Gary Player, see *Time,* 89 (April 21, 1967), p. 57. In letters to the author (May 19, 1969, and June 17, 1969), Prentice-Hall reported that more than 2,505,000 hardbound copies of *The Power of Positive Thinking* had been sold while Fawcett World Library stated that nearly 1,500,000 paperback copies had been sold.

CHAPTER 21

[1] Clyde Kluckhohn, *Mirror for Man* (New York, 1949), p. 235.

[2]*Mme. Millie, Interpretations of Dreams and Fortune Telling by Cards, Dominoes, Dice, Etc.* (Michigan City, Indiana, 1911), p. 3. A point of departure for the subject is Diana Hawthorne, *The Complete Fortune Teller* (New York, 1937). Henry C. Bolton, "Fortune-Telling in America To-Day," *Journal of American Folk-Lore,* 8 (October–December 1895), 299–307, is an outraged report on the subject.

The literature in almost every one of the following fields is immense. Much of it is not slanted for success. The examples selected are not necessarily the most respected experts in each field but rather are representative authors or organizations advocating their techniques for the specific goal of success. How the practitioners in several of these fields operate is discussed in Lee R. Steiner, *Where Do People Take Their Troubles?* (Boston, 1945).

[3] The quotation is from Gertrude A. Lindsay, *Your Hand Inter-*

preter and Your Character Health Vocation Scientific (New York, 1926), p. 27. The finger description is from W. W. De Kerlor, *The Secrets of Your Hands or Palmistry Explained* (New York, 1927), pp. 6, 24–25. An interesting interpretation is Martha Kennedy Brady, *Find Your Fortune in Your Hand* (New York, 1952). For nineteenth-century examples, see Robert A. Campbell, *Mysteries of the Hand Revealed and Explained* (St. Louis, 1879), and *Dick's Mysteries of the Hand or, Palmistry Made Easy* (New York, 1884).

[4] J. MacDonald, *Helps to Succeed or the Secrets of Astrology Revealed* (Binghamton, N. Y., 1923), no pagination. The first quotation is from "Autiobiography" [sic]; the second and third are from "Business and Vocational Astrology."

[5] *Ibid.*, "Preface"; Belle Bart, *Thru the Stars to Success* (East Aurora, N. Y., 1923), pp. 10–11. For other examples of the influence of heavenly bodies on success, see M. M. MacGregor, *Astrology* (Philadelphia, 1904); Senor Amor or David E. Campbell, *The New X-Ray of Life or Secret of Success* (New York, 1923); Anthony Trupo (pseud. Norvell), *You and the Stars* (Hollywood, Calif., 1940); and Erica Ingram-Moore (pseud. June Marsden), *Follow Your Stars to Success* (Los Angeles, 1956). The impact of New Thought on astrology is reflected in Grace Ellery Williams, *How to Know Your Future Business Psychology and Mysteries Interpreted* (New York, 1925).

[6] Paolo Milano, ed., *The Portable Dante* (New York, 1927), p. 106. The reference is to *The Divine Comedy*, "Inferno," Canto XX, Laurence Binyon translation.

James Mars Langham did not present as success literature his astrological works of the 1930s about planetary effects on stock market prices. The same holds true for the sunspot interpretation of stock market prices which kindled some interest in the 1930s. The sunspot interpretation might seem to be a natural gimmick for success writers to exploit, but a review of sunspot books and articles indicates that they ignored it.

Shakespeare was also disenchanted with astrology (*King Lear,* I, ii), but as a fortunetelling device it was in the ascent during the 1960s and early 1970s.

[7] Louis Williams, *Character Reading Made Easy* (Washington, 1904), p. 70; George E. Mellen, *Modern Foresight in Home Life, Social Life, Business Life* (Chicago, 1917). Melvina Hanson, *Mental Development* (Seattle, 1913), bathes phrenology in the effulgence of New Thought. For phrenology and success in the nineteenth century, see John Cowan, *Self-Help in the Attainment of Perfection of Character and Success in Life with a Phrenological and Physiological Chart* (New York, 1870); Prof. William Windsor, *Lectures* (Santa Ana, Calif., 1889). Phrenology at its height in the 1830s and 1840s is described in John Davies, *Phrenology: Fad and Science* (New Heaven, 1955). An interesting, readable introduction to phrenology, physiognomy, graphology, numerology, and kindred ologies and ognomies is Frederick Meier, *Character Reading for Fun and Popularity* (Philadelphia, 1945).

[8] Dean Bryden, *Your Face Is Your Fortune* (New York, 1928), pp. 73–74.

[9] Robert James Botkin, *Face Value* (Denver, Colo., 1947), pp. 192, 62. See also the works of Katherine M. H. Blackford and Harry H. Balkin. Prior to the 1930s, examples of the use of physiognomy to analyze other people, as well as oneself, are Gordon J. Hargrave, *The Right Way of Sizing Up People at Sight* (Chicago, 1920, 1921), vols. 2 and 10; and Elsie L. Benedict and Ralph P. Benedict, *How to Realize Your Personality* (East Aurora, N. Y., 1921).

[10] A. Henry Silver, *What Handwriting Reveals* (New York, 1929), p. 104. Nadya Olyanova, *What Does Your Handwriting Reveal?* (New York, 1929); Paul E. Jackman, et al., *Success Through Handwriting* (Oakland, Calif., 1936); M. N. Bunker, *What Handwriting Tells You about Yourself, Your Friends and Famous People* (Cleveland and New York, 1951). Julia Seton Sears, *Grapho-Psychology* (Boston, 1907), frequently loses graphology in New Thought metaphysics. The respect of two serious psychologists for graphological insights into personality is indicated in Gordon W. Allport and Philip E. Vernon, *Studies in Expressive Movement* (New York, 1933).

[11] Mary MacFadden and Emile Gauvreau, *Dumbbells and Carrot Strips: The Story of Bernarr MacFadden* (New York, 1953), is a merciless, and frequently hilarious, peek behind the scenes. The quotation is from p. 246. Clement Wood, *Bernarr MacFadden: A Study in Success* (New York, 1929), is rhapsodic. Bernarr MacFadden, *How Success Is Won* (New York, 1904), is based on the character ethic of hard work and determination, but the emphasis on the means is heavily weighted in favor of a healthy body and mind and clean habits. What MacFadden calls "true success" is building a strong, beautiful body. A bit more space and enthusiasm than the average success book is devoted to the sections on anti-materialism. It is surprising that *How Success Is Won* should even qualify as a success book, since it was adapted from editorials in two lurid, muckraking magazines, which he edited, entitled *The Cry for Justice* (1902–1903) and *Fair Play* (1903). MacFadden called for control, but not destruction, of the trusts. Bernarr MacFadden, *Eating for Health and Strength* (New York, 1921), is the dietary approach. For an analysis of MacFadden on success, see Clement Wood, *Bernarr MacFadden: A Study in Success*, pp. 261–268.

To put MacFadden, and the strongmen, in some kind of perspective, see D. B. Van Dalen, et al., *A World History of Physical Education* (New York, 1953).

[12] "For you! A Different and Better Way to Muscular Power!" advertisement of Siegmund Breitbart, Inc., in *Psychology,* 3 (September 1924), 61.

[13] "Pull Away from the Crowd of Weaklings!" advertisement of Charles Atlas in *Psychology,* 3 (September 1924), 71. For eight strongmen, not all of whom advocated body-building specifically for material success, however, see the advertisements in *Physical Culture,* 55 (January 1926). Alois P. Swoboda, *Conscious Evolution* (New York, 1921),

very involved and very cryptic, located the source of power for success in "Conscious Energy, Proto Energy, and Gyric Energy." For the Charles Atlas mail course several decades later, see the *New York Times,* January 10, 1959, p. 12. For an example of physical activity as a means to success, see the advertisement for Exercycle ("Are You the Next Man Up . . . or Out?") in the *New York Times Magazine,* October 16, 1960, p. 125.

[14] "A Failure—He Doesn't Know It—but Faulty Lubrication Is to Blame," advertisement of Pecano Manufacturing Co. in *Psychology,* 12 (January 1929), 15. For other examples of nut fascination, see the advertisements for pecan nuts, and the cereal food, Grape-Nuts, which is not made of nuts, but wheat and malted barley, in *Physical Culture,* 55 (January 1926), 3, 154. A success book based on the character ethic which stresses proper food and diet and attentive body care is [George Callahan] *Health and Life* (n.p. [1921]). The role of nerves in success is explained in E. L. Lehman, *New Nerves and Success* (Camden, N. J., 1928).

[15] *Encyclopaedia Britannica* s.v. "Memory" and "Mnemonics"; *Who Was Who* s.v. "Ennever, William Joseph." Pelmanism developed over the years into a course which trained other parts of the mind, e.g., the will and the subconscious. See The Pelman Institute of America, Inc., *Mind and Memory* (New York, 1920).

The Society of Applied Psychology, *The Trained Memory: Being the Fourth of a Series of Twelve Volumes on the Applications of Psychology to the Problems of Personal and Business Efficiency* (San Francisco, 1914), pp. 73, 81–82.

[16] Brendan Byrne, *Three Weeks to a Better Memory* (Philadelphia, 1951), p. 158. See also Arthur R. Robinson, *Memory and the Executive Mind* (Chicago, 1912), and Allan L. Fletcher, *How to Train and Improve Your Memory* (Garden City, N. Y., 1948).

[17] "I Knew You'd Make Good!" advertisement of the International Correspondence Schools in *American Magazine,* 94 (September 1922), 87. "How to Succeed While You're Still Young," advertisement of the Alexander Hamilton Institute, *House Beautiful,* 99 (October 1957), 7. In this general area, "speed reading" courses, which became increasingly popular throughout the 1960s, might also be included when they were sold with an appeal to success.

[18] The quotations are from advertisements in *Time,* 71 (February 3, 1958), 78, and 70 (August 19, 1957), 84.

[19] Johnson O'Connor, "Vocabulary and Success," *Atlantic Monthly,* 153 (February 1934), 160, 161, 163, 166. For a more extensive development, see Johnson O'Connor, *Psychometrics* (Cambridge, Mass., 1934), and *Unsolved Business Problems* (Hoboken, N. J., 1940), especially p. 123 which claims to be able to predict success by vocabulary testing. For an unfavorable evaluation of vocabulary building, see Rudolf Flesch, *How to Make Sense* (New York, 1954), pp. 67–84.

[20] The sales statistics, rounded to the nearest 100,000, are from

Alice Payne Hackett, *70 Years of Best Sellers, 1895–1965* (New York, 1967), pp. 17, 33, 42, 79.

[21] Wilfred Funk and Norman Lewis, *30 Days to a More Powerful Vocabulary* (New York, 1942), pp. 3, 4, 5, 7. See also Wilfred Funk, *Six Weeks to Words of Power* (New York, 1953), and *The Way to Vocabulary Power and Culture* (New York, 1946), esp. pp. 1–7 and 427–429.

[22] Alex F. Osborn, *Applied Imagination* (New York, 1953, 1957), pp. 26, 248–249, 27. Biographical information is in a letter to the author from Alex F. Osborn, dated September 16, 1957. Osborn died in 1966 at the age of seventy-seven.

[23] The second and last quotations are from *ibid.*, pp. 2 and 22. The rest are from Alex Osborn, *Your Creative Power* (New York, 1948), pp. 4, 18, 19, 27, 24.

[24] Alex Osborn, *Applied Imagination*, p. 334.

[25] *Ibid.*, pp. 28, 80.

[26] *Ibid.*, p. 84.

[27] Quoted *ibid.*, p. 84.

[28] *Ibid.*, p. 236.

[29] Quoted *ibid.*, p. 4. Alex Osborn, *How to Think Up* (New York, 1942), is an early exploration by the author into the subject. Osborn's books are repetitious, but see also *Wake Up Your Mind* (New York, 1952). Robert P. Crawford, *The Techniques of Creative Thinking* (New York, 1954), sees the process of creation as the shifting of attributes from one thing to another. For other sources, see the works, specifically about success by creative thinking, of Edward Wortley (pseud. for Alfred Hepper), Ray Josephs, and James D. Woolf and Charles B. Roth as joint authors.

For works of various types relating to creative thinking, see the references following each chapter in Alex Osborn, *Applied Imagination;* and A Student Research Group, Manufacturing Course, Class of 1955, Harvard Graduate School of Business Administration, *Imagination: Undeveloped Resource* (n.p., 1955). Magazine articles which contain useful information are Perrin Stryker, "Can Executives Be Taught to Think?" *Fortune,* 47 (May 1953), 138ff.; "Brainstormer," *Time,* 64 (August 16, 1954), 80–82; "Brainstorming," *Time,* 69 (February 18, 1957), 90; and Bill Davidson, "How to Think Your Way to the Top," *Collier's,* 135 (February 4, 1955), 26ff. A critical opinion of group ideation is expressed in Bernard S. Benson, "Let's Toss This Idea Up . . ." *Fortune,* 56 (October 1957), 145–146.

Manuals and books on specific executive skills and management training frequently contain chapters on the other half of problem solving, i.e. decision-making.

The Creative Education Foundation, founded by Osborn and now located in Buffalo, N. Y., makes available on request a list of materials relating to creative thinking. There has been serious research, of course, on the nature of creativity, e.g., the factors involved in releasing as opposed to producing creativity. In recent years the Creative Education Foundation has been working on techniques involving deferred judgment of the individual as opposed to deferred judgment of the brainstorming group.

[30] Benger is quoted in Alex F. Osborn, *Applied Imagination,* p. 71. The second quotation is on p. 243.

CHAPTER 22

[1] Most of the dilemmas have intentionally been cast in extreme alternatives for purposes of clarity.

[2] Rev. J. O. Bentall, Ph.D., "Why I Am a Christian Socialist," *Arena,* 37 (June 1907), 601. For a biographical reference to Bentall, see "A Leading Clergyman Embraces Christian Socialism," *Arena,* 37 (March 1907), 307.

[3] *Ibid.,* pp. 601–604.

The Christian Socialists reached their peak influence in the 1890s and 1900s. They were the radical left wing of the Protestant Social Gospel movement and the right wing of the Socialist cause. The Social Gospel and Christian Socialism are examined in Nelson R. Burr, *A Critical Bibliography of Religion in America* (Princeton, N. J., 1961), bound in two volumes; Charles Howard Hopkins, *The Rise of the Social Gospel in American Protestantism, 1865–1915* (New Haven, Conn., 1940); and Henry F. May, *Protestant Churches and Industrial America* (New York, 1949). Christian Socialism specifically is the subject of James Dombrowski, *The Early Days of Christian Socialism in America* (New York, 1936); and Robert T. Handy, "Christianity and Socialism in America, 1900–1920," *Church History,* 21 (March 1952), 39–54. An interesting argument from a non-Socialist viewpoint is Gerald D. Heuver, *The Teachings of Jesus Concerning Wealth* (Chicago, 1903).

[4] Robert J. McCracken, "A Sermon: America's Unpardonable Sin," *Church Monthly,* 31 (October 1957), 1–6. McCracken's pastorate at Riverside was from 1946 to 1967. His sermon has been chosen as an example of one tradition, and no suggestion is implied that in other sermons or writings he did not follow a different tradition. See, for example, his *Putting Faith to Work* (New York, 1960), p. 165. McCracken's message is also presented as neither typical of a post-World War II Protestant sermon nor unique to that period but representative of one theological tradition. For this tradition presented in a different form, see the Rev. Robert O. Kevin, S.T.D., "Idolatry of Great Wealth a Hindrance to Salvation," *Philadelphia Inquirer,* January 31, 1953, p. 5, a nationally syndicated Sunday school lesson prepared by the Division of Religious education, National Council of Churches of Christ in the U.S.A.

For secondary authorities who touch upon this dilemma, see Richard D. Lambert, ed., "Religion in American Society," *Annals,* 332 (November 1960), 1–155; Edward C. Bursk, ed., *Business and Religion* (New York, 1959); Robert L. Heilbroner, *The Quest for Wealth* (New York, 1956); Gerhard Lenski, *The Religious Factor* (Garden City, N. Y.,

1961); the Federal Council of Churches' series on ethics and economic life, especially Marquis W. Childs and Douglass Cater, *Ethics in a Business Society* (New York, 1954); Chard Powers Smith, *Yankees and God* (New York, 1954); and Will Herberg, *Protestant-Catholic-Jew* (Garden City, N. Y., 1955).

⁵ Quoted in Kenneth Chorley, "Introduction," in Lee H. Bristol, Jr., *Westminster Choir College* (Princeton, N. J., 1965), p. 7.

⁶ Ralph Waldo Emerson, "Ode" (inscribed to W. H. Channing), and "Wealth," in *The Complete Essays and Other Writings of Ralph Waldo Emerson* (New York, 1940), pp. 770, 699. See also Lyman Abbott's statement in *How to Succeed* (New York, 1882), p. v.

⁷ Cotton Mather, *A Christian at His Calling* (Boston, 1701).

⁸ Clifford Odets, *Golden Boy* (New York, 1937), pp. 76, 213, 214.

⁹ Theodore Dreiser, *Sister Carrie* (1900) (New York, 1917), p. 554.

¹⁰ The first quotation in this discussion of John P. Marquand is from *Sincerely, Willis Wayde* (Boston, 1955), p. 240; the second and third are from *Point of No Return* (Boston, 1949), p. 557. In the play, also entitled *Point of No Return* and adapted by Paul Osborn from the novel, Charles achieves a measure of independent dignity by refusing the suggestion of the bank president to join a more fashionable country club. The independent gesture, by no means an empty one within the context of the drama, destroys a good bit of what Marquand was trying to say in the novel. Paul Osborn, *Point of No Return* (New York, 1952), p. 180.

¹¹ Arthur Miller, *Death of a Salesman* (New York, 1949), pp. 73, 76, 56.

¹² *Ibid.,* p. 65.

¹³ *Ibid.,* p. 138.

¹⁴ The first quotation is from Arthur Miller, "Introduction to the Collected Plays," in *Arthur Miller's Collected Plays* (New York, 1957), p. 28; the second is from John McCarten's review of the movie version of *Death of a Salesman* in *New Yorker,* 27 (December 22, 1951), 70. For the English response, see Ivor Brown, "As London Sees Willy Loman" *New York Times Magazine,* August 28, 1949, pp. 11ff., "Letters," *New York Times Magazine,* September 11, 1949, p. 6; T. C. Worsley, "Poetry without Words," *New Statesman and Nation,* 38 (August 6, 1949), 146–147; Peter Fleming, review of the play in *Spectator,* 183 (August 5, 1949), 173.

¹⁵ *Ibid.,* p. 139.

¹⁶ Max Lerner, "Notes on Literature and American Civilization," *American Quarterly,* 11 (Summer 1959) (Supplement), 223. Without changing the meaning, the verb "is" has been added as the fourth word in the quotation.

¹⁷ *The New York 1950–1955 Album* (New York, 1955), unnumbered pages. For a stinging rebuke of advertising with traditional arguments, see Arnold J. Toynbee, *The Continuing Effect of the American Revolution* (Williamsburg, Virginia, 1961)

CHAPTER 23

[1] Gunnar Myrdal, *An American Dilemma* (New York, 1944), p. 13; Harold Laski, *The American Democracy* (New York, 1948), p. 51. See also Alexis de Tocqueville, *Democracy in America* (New York, 1945), I, 296–297, and Richard M. Huber, "A Theory of American Studies," *American Studies: Essays on Theory and Method,* ed. Robert Meredith (Columbus, Ohio, 1968), pp. 3–13.

[2] For Aurora, see Charles Nordhoff, *The Communistic Societies of the United States* (1874) (New York, 1875), and Robert J. Hendricks, Bethel and Aurora (New York, 1933). An ideal commonwealth projected into the future is revealed in Edward Bellamy, *Looking Backward: 2000–1887* (1888) (Boston and New York, 1898).

[3] Liberal is used throughout this chapter in its twentieth-century meaning and is usually synonymous with reformer. The approach in this chapter is primarily topical rather than chronological.

[4] Among those critics, liberal or radical, who did attack success writers with a political intent was the Socialist, W. J. Ghent. Ghent called success literature " 'dope books' " and classified Orison Swett Marden as an "innocent corrupter of youth." W. J. Ghent, "To the Seekers of Success," *Independent,* 69 (September 1, 1910), 452.

[5] Lester Frank Ward, "Broadening the Way to Success," *Forum,* 2 (December 1886), 340, 343, 345, 346, 350. Another criticism of the value of 'obstacles,' is expressed in Grover Cleveland, *The Self-Made Man in American Life* (New York, 1897). For success, "the result of cruel internecine warfare," interpreted with Social Darwinist overtones, see Titus Munson Coan, M.D., "Successful People," *Galaxy,* 11 (February 1871), 219–228.

[6] Quoted in C. Vann Woodward, *Tom Watson: Agrarian Rebel* (New York, 1938), p. 217.

[7] Woodrow Wilson, *The New Freedom* (New York, 1913), pp. 14–15.
Mobility and opportunity should not be considered political safety valves. While sluggish rates of mobility and shrinking opportunity can lead to political disturbances, it is possible that swifter rates of mobility and expanding opportunity can also result in political unrest.

[8] [Franklin D. Roosevelt] *The Public Papers and Addresses of Franklin D. Roosevelt* (New York, 1938), I, 750.

[9] Pitirim Sorokin, "American Millionaires and Multi-Millionaires," *Journal of Social Forces,* 3 (May 1925), 635 (italics omitted); F. W. Taussig and C. S. Joslyn, *American Business Leaders* (New York, 1932), pp. 234, 264.

[10] Robert S. Lynd and Helen Merrell Lynd, *Middletown in Transition* (New York, 1937), p. 471; Clyde Kluckhohn, *Mirror for Man* (New York, 1949), p. 255; Robert K. Merton, *Social Theory and Social Structure* (Glencoe, Illinois, 1949), p. 380, n. 20; William Miller, "The Recruitment of the American Business Elite," *Quarterly Journal of Eco-*

nomics, 64 (May 1950), 243; Frances W. Gregory and Irene D. Neu, "The American Industrial Elite in the 1870s: Their Social Origins," in William Miller, ed., *Men in Business* (Cambridge, Mass., 1952), p. 204.

[11] C. Wright Mills, *White Collar* (New York, 1951), p. 284; W. Lloyd Warner, *American Life* (Chicago, Illinois, 1953), p. 107; J. O. Hertzler, "Some Tendencies toward a Closed Class System in the United States," *Social Forces,* 30 (March 1952), 314.

The sociological popularizer, Vance Packard, was telling the American people during the Eisenhower years that "status is crystallizing. The boundaries between the various layers are becoming more rigid." Vance Packard, *The Status Seekers* (New York, 1959), p. 306.

C. Wright Mills, "The American Business Elite: A Collective Portrait," *Journal of Economic History,* Supplement 5 (December 1945), using data in the *Dictionary of American Biography,* concluded that "the best time during the history of the United States for the poor boy ambitious for high business success to have been born was around the year 1835."

[12] Seymour Martin Lipset and Reinhard Bendix, *Social Mobility in Industrial Society* (Berkeley and Los Angeles, 1959). There was no assertion, however, that variations did not exist with respect to the rates of elite mobility. The conservative response to these findings is detailed later in this chapter.

[13] Quoted in brochure on Leonard E. Read from the Foundation for Economic Education, Inc., Irvington-on-Hudson, N.Y.; Henry J. Kaiser, *Imagine Your Future* (Oakland, Calif., n.d.), p. 20; Fidelity-Philadelphia Trust Company, *Fidelity Bulletin,* 4 (November 1957), 2.

[14] *New York Times,* May 18, 1966, p. 64. Relevant autobiographies are too numerous to cite, but for a general listing, which begins with the colonial period, see Ruth Crandall, "Autobiographies of Businessmen: Titles Collected from 1950 to 1958," *Explorations in Entrepreneurial History,* 10 (April 1958), 154–161.

Profiles of successful men in the post-World War II decades are contained in Osborn Elliott, *Men at the Top* (New York, 1959); Isadore Barmash, *The Self-Made Man* (New York, 1969); and Kenneth Lamott, *The Moneymakers* (Boston, 1969).

[15] Harold Gray, "Little Orphan Annie," *Philadelphia Inquirer,* June 12, 1955, no page number. Annie and Daddy Warbucks were not hard-hearted, but were personally very charitable towards the needy. It was government 'hand-outs' they objected to. For background and a discussion, see Lyle W. Shannon, "The Opinions of Little Orphan Annie and Her Friends," *Public Opinion Quarterly,* 18 (Summer 1954), 169–179, and James A. Kehl, "Defender of the Faith: Orphan Annie and the Conservative Tradition," *South Atlantic Quarterly,* 59 (Spring 1960), 192–203.

[16] David M. Potter, *People of Plenty* (Chicago, 1954), p. 119.

[17] Excerpts from the *Iron Age* editorial in *Literary Digest,* 101 (June 29, 1929), 9. For observations on luck, see John T. Flynn, "Luck

in Business," *Harpers,* 154 (May 1927), 757–765; Robert K. Merton, *Social Theory and Social Structure* (Glencoe, Illinois, 1949), pp. 138–140; Robin M. Williams, Jr., *American Society* (New York, 1951), p. 135.

[18] Louis Stern, "Article XXX," in *The Problem of Success for Young Men and How to Solve it* (New York, 1903), p. 246; J. Paul Getty, "You Can Make a Million Today," *Playboy,* 8 (June 1961), 47.

Arthur M. Louis, "America's Centimillionaires," *Fortune,* 77 (May 1968), 156, reports that Getty and Howard Hughes are the richest men in America with anywhere from one to one and a half billion dollars. Getty is an American but lives in England.

[19] G. Keith Funston, "Remarks at Trinity College Convocation," Hartford, Conn., November 10, 1955 (in mimeograph). The correct quotation from Warner is "advance and achieve success," but Funston's recording does not change the meaning. For the source, see the discussion of Warner in the previous chapter of this study. The closing quotation in this paragraph is from W. Lloyd Warner and James C. Abegglen, *Occupational Mobility in American Business and Industry* (Minneapolis, 1955), p. 35.

[20] Stephan Thernstrom, *Poverty and Progress: Social Mobility in a Nineteenth Century City* (Cambridge, Mass., 1964), p. 270.

In an earlier section of this chapter, I have condensed the thesis of Lipset and Bendix as precisely as possible. But there is no doubt that the spirit of their work pushes their thesis hard to its limits and that they delighted in discovering in this area of research "discrepancies between scientific facts and popular images of reality" (p. 38, n. 47). They call their conclusion "startling" that "the overall pattern of social mobility appears to be much the same in the industrial societies of various Western countries" (p. 13). Seymour Martin Lipset and Reinhard Bendix, *Social Mobility in Industrial Society* (Berkeley and Los Angeles, 1959).

For methodological difficulties in establishing comparative rates of intergenerational occupational mobility, e.g., similarities and differences assumed from non-comparable data, see Harold L. Wilensky, "Measures and Effects of Social Mobility," in *Social Structure and Mobility in Economic Development,* eds. Neil J. Smelser and Seymour Martin Lipset (Chicago, 1966), pp. 98–105, and Celia S. Heller, ed., *Structured Social Inequality* (New York, 1969), pp. 312–313.

The following social scientists offer points of comparison to the critics of the success idea's description of mobility, opportunity, and the American class structure presented in an earlier section of this chapter: Gideon Sjoberg, "Are Social Classes in America Becoming More Rigid?," *American Sociological Review,* 16 (December 1951), 775–783; William Petersen, "Is America Still the Land of Opportunity?," *Commentary,* 16 (November 1953), 477–486; Mabel Newcomer, *The Big Business Executive* (New York, 1955); Elton F. Jackson and Harry J. Crockett, Jr., "Occupational Mobility in the United States: A Point Estimate and Trend Comparison," *American Sociological Review,* 29 (February 1964), 5–15; Peter M. Blau and Otis Dudley Duncan, *The American Occupational Structure* (New York, 1967); Stephan Thernstrom, "Urbanization, Migration, and Social Mobility in Late Nineteenth-Century America," in *Towards a New Past: Dissenting Essays in American History,* ed. Barton J. Bernstein (New York, 1968), pp. 158–175.

Fresh and interesting approaches to social origins and mobility in historical perspective are Stephan Thernstrom and Richard Sennett eds., *Nineteenth-Century Cities: Essays in the New Urban History* (New Haven, Conn., 1969); Stephan Thernstrom, "Notes on the Historical Study of Social Mobility," *Comparative Studies in Society and History,* 10 (January 1968), 162–172; P. M. G. Harris, "The Social Origins of American Leaders: The Demographic Foundations," *Perspectives in American History,* 3 (1969), 159–344; and Daniel Scott Smith, "Cyclical, Secular, and Structural Change in American Elite Composition," *Perspectives in American History,* 4 (1970), 351–374.

The issue of occupational, propertied, and social mobility raised interesting complexities. For example, increased income may improve an individual's standard of living, but not necessarily his differential success in relation to other white Americans. An expanding economy may enable the son to do better than the father occupationally because the percentage of higher-status white-collar jobs is increasing while the proportion of lower-status manual occupations is declining. Indeed, in the post-World War II decades, white-collar workers did not reproduce themselves in sufficient numbers to fill the increasing number of white-collar jobs available. If the jobs were to be filled at all, they had to be filled by the sons of blue-collar workers.

[21] The first quotation is from a speech by Nevins and is quoted in Edward N. Saveth, "What Historians Teach about Business," *Fortune,* 45 (April 1952), 118; the second quotation is from Allan Nevins, "Should American History be Rewritten?," *Saturday Review,* 37 (February 6, 1954), 48. In response to the question, Nevins took the affirmative and Matthew Josephson the negative position.

[22] "Throwing New Light on the Businessman," *Business Week,* no. 1180 (April 12, 1952), 86ff.; [Congressman] Paul Shafer, " 'Politics' Favorite 'Villain,' " *U.S.A.: The Magazine of American Affairs,* 1 (May, 1952), 62ff.; Edward N. Saveth, "Exit 'Robber Baron & Co.,' " *New York Times Book Review,* July 4, 1954, pp. 6ff.; F. A. Hayek, ed., *Capitalism and the Historians* (Chicago, 1954); Hal Bridges, "The Robber Baron Concept in American History," *Business History Review,* 32 (Spring 1958), 1–13; Allan Nevins, *John D. Rockefeller: The Heroic Age of American Enterprise* (New York, 1940), 2 vols., and " 'A Set of Mere Money-Getters'?" *American Heritage,* 14 (June 1963), 50ff.; Louis M. Hacker, *American Capitalism* (Princeton, N. J., 1957), and *The World of Andrew Carnegie, 1865–1901* (Philadelphia, 1968).

For disenchanted views of the revisionist position, see David Chalmers, "From Robber Barons to Industrial Statesmen: Standard Oil and the Business Historian," *American Journal of Economics and Sociology,* 20 (October 1960), 47–58, and A. S. Eisenstadt, "The World of Andrew Carnegie, 1865–1901: The Odyssey of Louis M. Hacker," *Labor History,* 10 (Spring 1969), 250–273.

[23] Quoted in the *New York Times,* December 14, 1963, p. 19.

²⁴ H. L. Mencken, *A Mencken Chrestomathy* (New York, 1949), p. 13; Arnold J. Toynbee, *A Study of History* (New York, 1957), p. 339 (D. C. Somervell abridgement of volumes VII–X); Lucien Romier, *Who Will Be Master: Europe or America?* (New York, 1928), p. 186; *Brief Facts About Rotary* (Evanston, Illinois, 1961), p. 2.

Adam Smith's restraints on self-interest are discussed in H. M. Robertson, *The Adam Smith Tradition* (London, 1950).

²⁵ Henry R. Luce, "The Reformation of the World's Economics," *Fortune,* 41 (February 1950), 62.

²⁶ Lawrence Fertig, *Prosperity Through Freedom* (Chicago, 1961), p. 66; Earl Bunting, *Be Glad You're a* Real *Liberal,* pamphlet issued by the National Association of Manufacturers, New York, no date.

²⁷ Crawford H. Greenewalt, "What Kind of Incentives?" Speech before the Illinois State Chamber of Commerce, Chicago, Illinois, October 19, 1951, p. 7.

One might ask, if service is a motivation for success, why are any other inducements necessary? The conservative response might be that the inner motivation towards service needs the indispensable addition of external incentives (e.g. money) for the fullest inducement toward effort.

How incentives actually operate in business, and which ones are the most powerful, has engaged the attention of numerous behavioral scientists. The Brookings Institution, for example, discovered that the progressive income tax was insignificant in diminishing work effort among high-income individuals. (Robin Barlow et al., *Economic Behavior of the Affluent* [Washington, D. C., 1966], pp. 129–150.) Our concern here is limited to ideology and its political implications. It is obvious, however, that American Motors Chairman Richard E. Cross is seeing the issue as more than money when he observes that top executives are motivated because "they like business—the power and the thrust and the action." (Quoted in Patricia Korenvaes, "Wanted: $50,000-a-Year Men," *Dun's Review,* 85 [February, 1965], 103.)

²⁸ The 1954 quotation of Wilson is cited in his obituary, *New York Times,* September 27, 1961, p. 37. Wilson's more famous quotation, expressing the identity of interests argument, was ". . . what was good for our country was good for General Motors, and vice versa." Wilson's original statement was garbled. The correct quotation, given here, is in *Hearings Before the Committee on Armed Services, United States Senate, Eighty-Third Congress, First Session on Nominee Designates,* January 15, 1953 (Washington, D.C., 1953), p. 26.

²⁹ Paul L. Poirot, "Human Rights Are More Important Than Property Rights," *Clichés of Socialism,* Number 13, The Foundation for Economic Education, Inc., Irvington-On-Hudson, N. Y., no date.

³⁰ The conservative also feared the power of government to coerce. It was the word "compel" in J. O. Bentall's Christian Socialism which sounded the death knell of liberty. "Socialism . . . would compel every able-bodied individual to produce his share of the necessaries of life. . . ."

Rev. J. O. Bentall, Ph.D., "Why I Am a Christian Socialist," *Arena,* 37 (June 1907), 603–604.

CHAPTER 24

[1] Charles Francis Adams, *An Autobiography* (Boston and New York, 1916), p. 190; [Henry Adams] *The Education of Henry Adams* (Boston, 1918), p. 348. A comma has been omitted after "upwards."

[2] Thomas Colley Grattan, *Civilized America* (London, 1859), II, 320; Ian Maclaren, "The Shadow on American Life: An Impression of a Recent Visit," *Outlook,* 63 (September 9, 1899), 117. Grattan checked the sweep of his generalization by suggesting that it should be accepted with reservations.

[3] Henry James, ed., *The Letters of William James* (Boston, Mass., 1920), II, 260; Roosevelt is quoted in Matthew Josephson, *The President Makers* (New York, 1940), p. 142. In the Roosevelt quotation I have omitted a comma after "instance."

[4] James Russell Lowell, *Literary Essays* (Boston and New York, 1890), II, 292–293.

[5] Edgar Lee Masters, *Spoon River Anthology* (1915) (New York, 1924), p. 123.

[6] Edwin Arlington Robinson, "Miniver Cheevy" (1910) in *Collected Poems* (New York, 1937), p. 348.

[7] Oliver Wendell Holmes, *The Autocrat of the Breakfast-Table* (Boston and New York, 1893), pp. 28, 29, 32, 33, 34.

[8] Robert A. Kavesh, *Businessmen in Fiction: The Capitalist and Executive in American Novels* (Amos Tuck School of Business Administration, Dartmouth College, Hanover, New Hampshire, 1955), p. 1; Charlotte Georgi, *The Businessman in the Novel* (University of North Carolina Library, Chapel Hill, North Carolina, 1959), p. 7. See also John Chamberlain, "The Businessman in Fiction," *Fortune,* 38 (November 1948), 134ff.

[9] George Bernard Shaw, *Pygmalion* (New York, 1939), p. 84 (Act V), quoted in Howard R. Smith, "The American Businessman in the American Novel," *Southern Economic Journal,* 25 (January 1959), 268. Consider, by way of illustration, the generally disparaging image of the psychiatrist in novels. Charles Winick, "The Psychiatrist in Fiction," *Journal of Nervous and Mental Disease,* 136 (January 1963), 43–57.

[10] Sinclair Lewis, *Arrowsmith* (New York, 1925); Irving Howe, *Sherwood Anderson* (New York, 1951), pp. 46–49; Howard Mumford Jones and Walter B. Rideout, eds., *Letters of Sherwood Anderson* (Boston, 1953), p. viii.

[11] In addition to the works cited above, the following are particularly relevant to the businessman in American fiction: Walter Fuller Taylor, *The Economic Novel in America* (Chapel Hill, North Carolina, 1942); Kenneth S. Lynn, *The Dream of Success* (Boston, 1955), and "Authors in Search of the Businessman," *Harvard Business Review,* 34

(September–October 1956), 116–124; Albert Van Nostrand, *The Denatured Novel* (Indianapolis and New York, 1960); A. N. Barnett, *The Image of the Businessman in America: A Selection of Books and Articles of the Decade, 1948–1958* (Lafayette, Indiana, 1958); Blanche Housman Gelfant, *The American City Novel* (Norman, Oklahoma, 1954); J. D. Glover, *The Attack on Big Business* (Boston, Massachusetts, 1954); Daniel Seligman, "The 'Business Novel' Fad," *Fortune*, 60 (August 1959), 104ff.; William G. Scott, "The Novelists' Picture of Management and Manager," *Personnel Administration*, 22 (January–February 1959), 9ff.; William J. Newman, "Subtopia in America or, the Businessman at Work and Play," *Twentieth Century*, 161 (May 1957), 419–434; Howard Mumford Jones, "Looking Around," *Harvard Business Review*, 31 (January–February 1953), 133ff.; Leo Cherne, "The Businessman in America: The Writer and the Entrepreneur," *Saturday Review*, 35 (January 19, 1952), 10ff.; Van R. Halsey, "Fiction and the Businessman: Society through All Its Literature," *American Quarterly*, 11 (Fall 1959), 391–402; "The Management Pattern: The Fiction-Eye View of Business," *Business Week*, 1467 (October 12, 1957), 187; Thomas Munro, "The Failure Story: A Study of Contemporary Pessimism," *Journal of Aesthetics and Art Criticism*, 17 (December 1958), 143–168, and "The Failure Story: An Evaluation," *op. cit.*, 17 (March 1959), 362–387; Robert P. Falk, "From Poor Richard to the Man in the Gray Flannel Suit: A Literary Portrait of the Businessman," *California Management Review*, 1 (Summer 1959), 1–14; William Van O'Connor, "The Novel as a Social Document," *American Quarterly*, 4 (Summer 1952), 169–175; James J. Clark and Robert H. Woodward, eds., *Success in America* (Belmont, California, 1966); Henry Nash Smith, "The Search for a Capitalist Hero," in *The Business Establishment*, ed. Earl F. Cheit (New York, 1964), pp. 77–112; John Lydenberg, "Mobilizing Our Novelists," *American Quarterly*, 4 (Spring 1952), 35–48; Robie Macauley, " 'Let Me Tell You about the Rich . . .'," *Kenyon Review*, 27 (Autumn 1965), 645–671; Jan W. Dietrichson, *The Image of Money in the American Novel of the Gilded Age* (New York, 1969).

For a denunciation of Mammon by poets in the last quarter of the nineteenth century, see Robert H. Walker, *The Poet and the Gilded Age* (Philadelphia, 1963), pp. 221–235.

[12] Frank Norris, *The Octopus* (1901) (New York, 1928), II, 285.

[13] John Steinbeck, *The Grapes of Wrath* (New York, 1939), pp. 42, 43, 44, 45.

[14] Theodore Dreiser, *The Financier* (New York, 1927), pp. 4, 5, 6.

[15] Budd Schulberg, *What Makes Sammy Run?* (New York, 1941), pp. 238, 249.

[16] Arthur Miller, *All My Sons* (1947) in *Arthur Miller's Collected Plays* (New York, 1957), p. 124 (Act 3).

[17] Harold Stearns, *America and the Young Intellectual* (New York, 1921), pp. 11–12. The estrangement of the intellectual during the McCarthyism period of the 1950s was of a different kind than the 1920s. Perceptive studies of the American intellectual are Merle Curti,

American Paradox: The Conflict of Thought and Action (New Brunswick, N. J., 1956); "Anti-Intellectualism in the United States," *Journal of Social Issues*, 11 (1955), No. 3, pp. 1–62, especially William E. Leuchtenburg, "Anti-Intellectualism: An Historical Perspective," pp. 8–17; Merle Curti, "Intellectuals and Other People," *American Historical Review*, 50 (January 1955), 259–282; Thomas P. Neill, "The Social Function of the Intellectual," *Thought*, 32 (Summer 1957), 199–223; Seymour Martin Lipset, "The Egghead Looks at Himself," *New York Times*, November 17, 1957, pp. 22ff., and "The Real Status of American Intellectuals" in George B. de Huszar, ed., *The Intellectuals* (Glencoe, Ill.), pp. 510–516; Richard Hofstadter, *Anti-Intellectualism in American Life* (New York, 1963); Lewis A. Coser, *Men of Ideas* (New York, 1965); J. Rogers Hollingsworth, "American Anti-Intellectualism," *South Atlantic Quarterly*, 63 (Summer 1964), 267–274. Philip Rieff, ed., *On Intellectuals* (Garden City, N. Y., 1969).

[18] Van Wyck Brooks, "America's Coming-of-Age" (1915), in *Three Essays on America* (New York, 1934), pp. 78–79. C. P. Snow, *The Two Cultures and the Scientific Revolution* (Cambridge, England, 1959).

[19] Sinclair Lewis, *Babbitt* (New York, 1922), pp. 2, 69, 242, 114, 125. This is the Random House Modern Library edition.

[20] *Ibid.*, p. 401.

To call someone a Babbitt is to accuse him of being "a self-satisfied person who conforms readily to conventional, middle-class ideas and ideals, esp. of business and material success," according to *The Random House Dictionary of the English Language*, s.v. "Babbitt." Babbitt has been badly used as his name passed into the language, for he was neither "self-satisfied" nor did he conform "readily."

[21] *Ibid.*, p. 101. See also pp. 139, 182–186, 391.

[22] William H. Whyte, Jr., *The Organization Man* (New York, 1956). Among some observers of the American scene, especially during the latter part of the Eisenhower 1950s, the concern over conformity mounted to hysteria. Conformity was felt to be expressed in gray flannel suits, the suburbanality of look-alike houses, corporate security, an apathetic younger generation, enslavement to advertising, inferior intellectual tastes, and resignation to an occupational treadmill. An increased interest in conformity does not necessarily indicate an increase in conformity, of course, but only an increase in those conditions which make a concern for conformity fashionable.

[23] Gustave de Beaumont, *Marie, or Slavery in the United States* (Stanford, California, 1958), pp. 111, 105; Thomas Colley Grattan, *Civilized America* (London, 1859), I, 190.

[24] This study has emphasized the anti-intellectual tone of the success idea, but the high-status sensations that American professors take pleasure in when they travel through Europe should not be attributed entirely to the lesser forces of anti-intellectualism in Europe but to the greater forces of egalitarianism in America. Europeans show deference to anyone with education, breeding, or wealth, from businessmen to intellectuals.

At the same time the intellectual in Europe no doubt was held in higher esteem compared to the businessman than the intellectual in America compared to the businessman.

[25] Lewis B. Monroe, *The Practical Speller* (Philadelphia, 1875), p. 144. Italics added.

[26] Quoted in *Time*, 85 (April 16, 1965), 51.

[27] Of course when the federal government subsidizes farmers or ailing industries, it helps decide who will be a success. And the increasing power of the Pentagon in recent decades has frequently been commented upon. But from both a cross-cultural and potential comparison, the point about government restraint in certain value areas, I think, is fair.

[28] Crosby is quoted in the *New York Times*, January 13, 1965, p. 73.

[29] The quotation is from Newton Minow, "The Vast Wasteland," an address before the 39th Annual Convention of the National Association of Broadcasters in Washington, D.C., on May 9, 1961, and is reprinted in Newton Minow (Lawrence Laurent, ed.), *Equal Time: The Private Broadcaster and the Public Interest* (New York, 1964), pp. 48–64. The quotation is from p. 53.

[30] Since a democracy also consists of the protection of minority rights, alternate forms of instruction and entertainment must be available, e.g., UHF and public television, FM radio, motion pictures, and, of course, books.

[31] Winston S. Churchill, "A Speech to the House of Commons, 11 November 1947," *Europe Unite: Speeches 1947 and 1948* (Boston, 1950), p. 200. As in the previous dilemmas, the alternatives and consequences are presented in the extreme.

CHAPTER 25

[1] Erich Fromm, *The Sane Society* (New York, 1955), p. 207, and *The Art of Loving* (1956) (New York: Bantam edition, 1963), pp. 73, 72. See also August Heckscher, *The Public Happiness* (New York, 1962), p. vi.

[2] Alexis de Tocqueville, *Democracy in America* (New York: Bradley edition, 1945), II, 136, 139.

[3] Dr. Thomas L. Nichols, *Forty Years of American Life* (London, 1864), I, 401–408. A recent discussion with references to earlier articles about Nichols is Philip Gleason, "From Free-Love to Catholicism: Dr. and Mrs. Thomas L. Nichols at Yellow Springs," *Ohio Historical Quarterly*, 70 (October 1961), 283–307.

[4] The first two quotations are from Sigmund Freud, *Civilization and Its Discontents* (1930) (London, 1951), pp. 46, 123. See also Sigmund Freud, *The Origins of Psycho-analysis* (New York, 1954), p. 244; and Karl Menninger, *Man Against Himself* (New York, 1938), pp. 41–42.

[5] Vocational guidance literature and professional counselors, mostly by implication, are critical of general success books. Vocational guidance attempts to be scientific rather than inspirational, ponders individual differences rather than self-help generalizations, seeks a relationship

between level of potential and level of aspiration, and stresses self-satisfaction as well as progress in the job.

Useful studies for understanding the theory and practice of vocational guidance are: Henry Borow, ed., *Man in a World at Work* (Boston, 1964); Donald E. Super, *The Psychology of Careers* (New York, 1957); Anne Roe, *The Psychology of Occupations* (New York, 1956); Donald E. Super and John O. Crites, *Appraising Vocational Fitness* (New York, 1962); Newell Brown, *After College What?* (New York, 1968); and John M. Brewer, *History of Vocational Guidance* (New York, 1942).

⁶ Norman Podhoretz, *Making It* (1967) (New York, 1969), p. 4 (Bantam edition).

⁷ This discussion emphasizes the conflict between the individual and the culture rather than the individual's repressed instinctual drives. The following have been particularly useful: Karen Horney, *The Neurotic Personality of Our Time* (New York, 1937), *Our Inner Conflicts* (New York, 1945), and *Neurosis and Human Growth* (New York, 1950); Erich Fromm, *Man for Himself* (New York, 1947); Rollo May, *The Meaning of Anxiety* (New York, 1950), and *Man's Search for Himself* (New York, 1953); Abram Kardiner, et al., *The Psychological Frontiers of Society* (New York, 1945); Hans Selye, *The Stress of Life* (New York, 1956); Maurice R. Stein, Arthur J. Vidich, and David Manning White, eds., *Identity and Anxiety* (Glencoe, Illinois); Robert S. Lynd, *Knowledge for What?* (Princeton, New Jersey, 1939); Gerald Gurin, Joseph Veroff, and Sheila Feld, *Americans View Their Mental Health* (New York, 1960); T. W. Adorno, et al., *The Authoritarian Personality* (New York, 1950); Lawrence K. Frank, *Society As the Patient* (New Brunswick, New Jersey, 1948); Karl A. Menninger, *Man Against Himself* (New York, 1938); Robin M. Williams, Jr., *American Society* (New York, 1951); Max Lerner, *America As a Civilization* (New York, 1957); Ephraim Harold Mizruchi, *Success and Opportunity: A Study of Anomie* (New York, 1964); David Riesman, in collaboration with Reuel Denney and Nathan Glazer, *The Lonely Crowd* (New Haven, Connecticut, 1950); Margaret Halsey, *The Folks at Home* (New York, 1952); Esther Milner, *The Failure of Success* (New York, 1959); Ludwig von Mises, *The Anti-Capitalistic Mentality* (Princeton, New Jersey, 1956); Richard E. Gordon, Katherine K. Gordon, and Max Gunther, *The Split-Level Trap* (New York, 1961); Claude C. Bowman, "Loneliness and Social Change," *American Journal of Psychiatry*, 112 (September 1955), 194–198; Arnold W. Green, "Why Americans Feel Insecure," *Commentary*, 6 (July 1948), 18–28; "The Executive Ulcer," *Fortune*, 49 (April 1954), 143ff.; Richard Hofstadter, "The Pseudo-Conservative Revolt," *American Scholar*, 24 (Winter 1954–55), 9–27; Robert J. Kleiner and Seymour Parker, "Goal-Striving, Social Status, and Mental Disorder: A Research Review," *American Sociological Review*, 28 (April 1963), 182–203.

⁸ Cartoon by hoff, *New Yorker*, 27 (November 17, 1951), 45.

⁹ Horace Gregory, "Effron Siminsky's Afterdinner Speech," in *Medusa in Gramercy Park* (New York, 1961), p. 15.

[10] Somebody once observed that money isn't everything—but it's way ahead of anything else in second place. Or, money can't buy happiness—but it helps. There is very little empirical evidence on the relationship of money and happiness. Higher income does bring greater happiness, according to Gerald Gurin, Joseph Veroff, and Sheila Feld, *Americans View Their Mental Health* (New York, 1960), pp. 215–218. George Gallup, *The Miracle Ahead* (New York, 1964), pp. 182–185, states that money makes little difference once a certain level is reached. These social scientists would be the first to recognize that it makes a difference how and when the money is acquired and the relative increasing or decreasing amount of it at any particular stage of an individual's life.

Norman M. Bradburn and David Caplovitz, *Reports on Happiness* (Chicago, 1965), in their exploratory probe into happiness, limited to individual participation in the environment, concluded that happiness is the relative balance between positive and negative feelings. A person is more likely to be happy if he is involved in things which contribute to the development of positive feelings and unhappy if subjected to forces which arouse negative feelings. For factors conducive to job satisfaction and dissatisfaction, see Frederick Herzberg, *Work and the Nature of Man* (Cleveland and New York, 1966).

Useful discussions of happiness, not cited elsewhere in this chapter, are R. M. MacIver, *The Pursuit of Happiness* (New York, 1955); Howard Mumford Jones, *The Pursuit of Happiness* (Cambridge, Mass., 1953); [*Life*], "A Guide to Your *Life* Round Table on the Pursuit of Happiness" (New York, 1948); Hadley Cantril, "A Study of Aspirations," *Scientific American*, 208 (February 1963), 3–7; Hadley Cantril and Lloyd A. Free, "Hopes and Fears for Self and Country," *American Behavioral Scientist*, 6 (October 1962), 1–31; Lloyd A. Free and Hadley Cantril, *The Political Beliefs of Americans* (New Brunswick, N. J., 1967), pp. 96–101; Ralph Ross and Ernest Van Den Haag, *The Fabric of Society* (New York, 1957), pp. 190–191; "Happiness" in *The Great Ideas: A Syntopicon of Great Books of the Western World*, eds. Mortimer J. Adler and William Gorman (Chicago, 1952), I, 684–710; Charles Edward Trinkaus, Jr., *Adversity's Noblemen: The Italian Humanists on Happiness* (New York, 1940); Arthur M. Schlesinger, "The Lost Meaning of 'The Pursuit of Happiness,'" *William and Mary Quarterly*, 21 (July 1964), 325–327; Henry Steele Commager, "The Pursuit of Happiness," *Diogenes*, 49 (Spring 1965), 40–65.

[11] Immanuel Kant, *Critique of Pure Reason* (1781), trans. F. Max Müller (New York, 1896), p. 647. For Kant on duty in relation to happiness, see V. McGill, *The Idea of Happiness* (New York, 1967), pp. 91–118.

[12] See Gerald Gurin, Joseph Veroff, and Sheila Feld, *Americans View Their Mental Health* (New York, 1960), pp. xvii–xviii, 143–174.

[13] George Jean Nathan and H. L. Mencken, *The American Credo* (New York, 1921), pp. 29–30. Italics added.

[14] Quoted in *Time*, 75 (June 20, 1960), 18.

[15] Oliver Wendell Holmes, Jr., *Speeches* (Boston, 1918), p. 96.

[16] "Justice Jailed in Theft, 'Kept up with Joneses,'" *Philadelphia Inquirer,* October 3, 1951, p. 33.

[17] The phrase "white-collar crime" is used in this discussion to encompass both the kind of crime as well as the type of person who commits it.

The following works are useful in connecting crime and ethics to the success complex: Robert K. Merton, *Social Theory and Social Structure* (Glencoe, Illinois, 1949); Edwin H. Sutherland and Donald R. Cressey, *Principles of Criminology* (Philadelphia, 1955); Clyde B. Vedder, Samuel Koenig, and Robert E. Clark, eds., *Criminology: A Book of Readings* (New York, 1953); Frank Tannenbaum, *Crime and the Community* (Boston, 1938); Donald R. Taft, *Criminology* (New York, 1942); Edwin H. Sutherland, *White Collar Crime* (New York, 1949); Frank Gibney, *The Operators* (New York, 1960); Daniel Bell, *The End of Ideology* (Glencoe, Illinois, 1960); Blair Bolles, *How to Get Rich in Washington* (New York, 1952); Max Lerner, *America As a Civilization* (New York, 1957); Eric F. Goldman, *The Crucial Decade —And After: America, 1945–1960* (New York, 1961); William Attwood, "The Age of Payola," *Look,* 24 (March 29, 1960), 34ff.; Charles Frankel, "Is It Just TV—or Most of Us?," *New York Times Magazine,* November 15, 1959, pp. 15ff.; Gilbert Geis, ed., *White-Collar Criminal* (New York, 1968); Norman Jaspan with Hillel Black, *The Thief in the White Collar* (Philadelphia and New York, 1960); Walter Goodman, *All Honorable Men: Corruption and Compromise in American Life* (Boston, 1963); Margaret Halsey, *The Pseudo-Ethic* (New York, 1963); Raymond C. Baumhart, S.J., "How Ethical Are Businessmen?," *Harvard Business Review,* 39 (July–August 1961), 6ff.; Fred J. Cook, *The Corrupted Land* (New York, 1966); J. Robert Moskin, *Morality in America* (New York, 1966); James C. Charlesworth, ed., "Ethics in America: Norms and Deviations," *Annals of the American Academy of Political and Social Science,* 363 (January 1966), 1–136.

[18] The President of the United States in 1964 defined the Great Society as a place where leisure is "not a feared cause of boredom and restlessness." Lyndon B. Johnson, "Toward the Great Society," *My Hope for America* (New York, 1964), p. 51. For the occasion at the University of Michigan where these words were spoken, see *Newsweek,* 63 (June 1, 1964), 16.

[19] Mark Twain, *The Adventures of Tom Sawyer* (New York, 1904), p. 33. The word "that" has been omitted.

[20] Studies, not cited elsewhere in these chapters on leisure, which have been useful are: Sigmund Nosow and William H. Form, eds., *Man, Work, and Society* (New York, 1962); Eric Larrabee and Rolf Meyersohn, eds., *Mass Leisure* (Glencoe, Ill., 1958); John Brooks, ed., *The One and the Many: The Individual in the Modern World* (New York, 1962); Arnold W. Green, *Recreation, Leisure, and Politics* (New York, 1964); Max Gunther, *The Weekenders* (Philadelphia, 1964); George A. Lundberg et al., *Leisure: A Suburban Study* (New York, 1934); Sloan Wilson, "Happy Idle Hours Become a Rat Race," *Life,*

47 (December 18, 1959), 118ff.; Bruce Bliven, "Using Our Leisure Is No Easy Job," *New York Times Magazine*, April 26, 1964, pp. 18ff.; Wilbert E. Moore, *Man, Time, and Society* (New York, 1963); John M. Blum, "Exegesis of the Gospel of Work: Success and Satisfaction in Recent American Culture," in *Trends in Modern Society*, ed. Clarence Morris (Philadelphia, 1962), pp. 17–36. Published after this section was written, Staffan B. Linder, *The Harried Leisure Class* (New York, 1970), examines in detail increasing scarcity of time in an affluent society.

[21] One historical change, of course, is that in some of these jobs one started making money later (because of educational preparation) and quit earlier (because of forced retirement) than in the nineteenth century.

A thoughtful report is Harold L. Wilensky, "The Uneven Distribution of Leisure: The Impact of Economic Growth on 'Free Time,'" *Social Problems*, 9 (Summer 1961), 32–56.

[22] August Heckscher and Sebastian de Grazia, "Problems in Review: Executive Leisure," *Harvard Business Review*, 37 (July–August 1959), 6ff. See also, "1,700 Top Executives," *Fortune*, 60 (November 1959), 138ff., and Robin Barlow, Harvey E. Brazer, and James N. Morgan, *Economic Behavior of the Affluent* (Washington, D. C., 1966), pp. 134–136.

[23] See Harold L. Wilensky, "Mass Society and Mass Culture: Interdependence or Independence?," *American Sociological Review*, 29 (April 1964), 173–197.

[24] Quoted in Charles E. Silberman, "The Money Left Over for the Good Life," *Fortune*, 60 (November 1959), 137; Arnold W. Green, *Recreation, Leisure, and Politics* (New York, 1964), p. 168.

[25] The policemen's statistic is cited in the *New York Times*, October 17, 1960, p. 54. A follow-up story is in the *New York Times*, January 24, 1966, p. 19.

During the 1960s, to choose a specific decade, the oft-quoted government statistic about moonlighting is misleadingly low. Male moonlighters, in the age group from twenty-five to sixty-four years, were supposed to be 7% of all persons employed, according to Harvey R. Hamel and Forrest A. Bogan, "Special Labor Force Report: Multiple Jobholders in May 1964," a reprint from the *Monthly Labor Review*, March 1965, with additional tables, designated as Reprint No. 2458 of the Bureau of Labor Statistics, United States Department of Labor. The percentage figure of 7% does not include those who failed to confess their moonlighting when questioned, and there were powerful reasons for remaining discreet. Labor unions frowned on multiple jobholding, and increased declared income meant increased taxes. A meaningful percentage figure would also require that the total number of people in those occupations be excluded which do not generally supply candidates for moonlighting.

Particularly useful on moonlighting are Harold L. Wilensky, "The Moonlighter: A Product of Relative Deprivation," *Industrial Relations*, 3 (October 1963), 105–124; Sebastian de Grazia, *Of Time, Work, and*

Leisure (New York, 1962), pp. 70–72; R. H. Bergmann, "Moonlighting and the American Dream," *Nation*, 193 (July 1, 1961), 3–5; Theodore Irwin, "Making Ends Meet—By Moonlight," *New York Times Magazine*, April 3, 1966, pp. 73ff.

For a new look at the 36-hour work week of Akron rubber employees, see the report on John Dieter's doctoral dissertation in "Akron Moonlighters: A Special Breed," *Business Week*, No. 1840 (December 5, 1964), 68–70.

A consequence of the consecration of work was the attribution of immorality to idleness. But work was more than a moral avoidance of leisure, as well as a source of livelihood. Nancy C. Morse and Robert S. Weiss, "The Function and Meaning of Work and the Job," *American Sociological Review*, 20 (April 1955), 191–198, concluded that work, for the typical man in a middle-class occupation, meant to have a purpose in life, to realize a sense of accomplishment, and to express himself. For the typical man in a working-class occupation, work meant to have something to do.

[26] U.S. Department of Labor, *Handbook of Labor Statistics 1969* (Washington, D. C., 1969), p. 32.

[27] Werner Sombart, "Study of the Historical Development and Evolution of the American Proletariat," *International Socialist Review*, 6 (September 1905), 133, translated by A. M. Simons.

[28] Van Wyck Brooks, "America's Coming-of-Age" (1915), in *Three Essays on America* (New York, 1934), pp. 24–25, 33.

[29] Henry David Thoreau, *Walden; or, Life in the Woods* (1854) (New York, 1948), p. 74, the Rinehart edition with introduction by Norman Holmes Pearson. A good sketch of Thoreau's life is Carl Bode's introduction to *The Portable Thoreau* (New York, 1947), pp. 1–27, the Viking Press edition.

[30] Henry David Thoreau, *Walden*, pp. 5, 3, 74, 10, 19, 28, 77.

[31] *Ibid.*, pp. 24, 26, 75, 29.

[32] *Ibid.*, pp. 72, 76, 274, 75, 181, 272.

[33] I am of the school of historians which believes that basic values are slow to change in a society. Once the charter and structure is set, fundamental values have an enduring quality. With that caveat in mind, I have called this dissenting group the New Romantics and the movement the New Romanticism because I think we have here something far more significant in the history of American values than simply, at the moment, Indian beads and long hair. My analysis, however, pretends to be no more than an introduction to the movement.

[34] Henry Ward Beecher, *Lectures to Young Men* (1844) (Boston and New York, 1846), p. 44; John Cotton, *Christ the Fountaine of Life* (London, 1651), p. 119. I have changed the word "himseife" in Cotton's text to "himself," because it is an obvious misspelling. William Wordsworth, "The Tables Turned," *The Poetical Works of William Wordsworth* (London, 1849), V, 6.

[35] James Terry White, "Not by Bread Alone" (after Hippocrates),

Century, 74 (August 1907), 519. The poem is an adaptation of a Persian theme.

[36] Alden B. Hoag, "A Dissent from Despair," *New York Times Magazine,* April 5, 1964, p. 114; Robert H. Hamill, "Machine: Promise or Threat?," p. 5, a mimeographed revision of an address reported in the *New York Times,* March 2, 1965, p. 28.

For national goals, see C. D. Jackson, publisher, "The Aim of *Life,*" *Life,* 50 (June 2, 1961), 1, and the series on national goals beginning in the issue of May 23, 1960. Many of the essays were published in [*Life*], *The National Purpose* (New York, 1960). See also Report of the President's Commission on National Goals, *Goals for Americans* (New York, 1960), and United States Air Force Academy, *National Goals: Challenges for the Sixties* (n.p., 1961). Max Ways, "Finding the American Direction," *Fortune,* 82 (October 1970), 70ff., is yet another example of a first-class journalist working through hard questions.

[37] Quoted in Ezra Sampson, *Brief Remarker on the Ways of Man* (New York, 1818), p. 32.

[38] The word "loses" has been changed to "lose" in this quotation. The American philosophy of Boosterism was constructed on the cheerful view that growth was synonymous with progress. Beginning with intensity in the late 1960s, this position was challenged by ecological activists who were concerned less with the GNP and more with Gross National Pollution.

CHAPTER 26

[1] The quotation, in which apostrophes have been omitted, is from Robert Graves, *Mammon and the Black Goddess* (New York, 1965), p. 3. For an expression of true success, see Caroline M. Huber, *As I See Politics* (Philadelphia [1952]), pp. 86–88.

[2] John D. Rockefeller, Jr., "Letters to the Editor: Caruso and John D. Rockefeller," *Listener,* 52 (September 30, 1954), 529, unequivocally denies that his father suffered from poor digestion or a bad stomach. Edwin Arlington Robinson, "Richard Cory," in *Collected Poems of Edwin Arlington Robinson* (New York, 1961), p. 82.

[3] Franklin P. Adams, "The Rich Man," *Tobogganing on Parnassus* (New York, 1911), p. 30. Cf. Emily Dickinson's "Success is counted sweetest/By those who ne'er succeed. . . ." (Thomas H. Johnson, ed., *The Poems of Emily Dickinson* [Cambridge, Mass., 1955], p. 53.)

The attitude that the poor are generally happier than the rich is revealed in an informal poll in Theodore Caplow, "Editor's Introduction," *The Cause of Wealth,* by Jean Fourastié (Glencoe, Illinois, 1960), p. 8.

[4] For a discussion of Marx and materialism, see Clinton Rossiter, *Marxism: The View from America* (New York, 1960), pp. 32ff.

[5] Believing that honesty is not always connected with success differs, however, from believing that dishonesty is a prime requisite for success

or that most successful people are dishonest. The ambivalent feelings of the former are productive for an industrial society while the latter convictions are counterproductive.

[6] William Shakespeare, *Julius Caesar,* II, i, 21–27.

[7] Ralph Waldo Emerson, "American Civilization," *Miscellanies,* in *Emerson's Complete Works* (Cambridge, Mass., 1883), XI, 279. The Lincoln quotation is from the Second Annual Message, December 1, 1862.

[1] Samuel McChord Crothers, "That History Should Be Readable," *The Gentle Reader* (Boston and New York, 1903), p. 172. A comma has been added after "dogs."

FOREWORD
TO THE 1987 EDITION

REFERENCES

[1] Adam Smith, *Wealth of Nations,* (London, 1776), I, 17. The quotation, which often varies in wording when cited, is here taken from a reprint of the original 1776 edition. A comma after "baker" has been omitted for purposes of clarity.

The paperback edition of *The American Idea of Success* has been reprinted faithfully from the first edition, with the exception of a few minor corrections, mostly typographical changes.

[2] T.S. Eliot, "The Dry Salvages, *Four Quartets,* in *The Complete Poems and Plays,* 1909-1950 (New York, 1952), p. 133.

[3] The quotations are from Daniel Goleman, "The Strange Agony of Success" *New York Times,* August 24, 1986, Sect. 3, p. 1; The Higher Education Research Institute, Graduate School of Education, University of California, Los Angeles, *The American Freshman: National Norms for Fall 1985* (Los Angeles, 1985), p. 2. The numbers have been rounded from 43.5, 71.2, 82.9, and 43.3 percent; John Gross, "Critic's Notebook: Writing about the Rich, in Revival, Gains Name," *New York Times,* March 31, 1986, p. C17.

The return to Establishment values was reported as early as 1973 in Robert D. McFadden, "Establishment Values Rule on Campus," *New York Times,* April 23, 1973, p. 26. Norman Podhoretz, "My Turn: The Return to Success," *Newsweek,* 90 (August 29, 1977), 11, is a thoughtful comment. For representative viewpoints, see Lawrence D. Maloney, "Success! The Chase is Back in Style Again," *U.S. News & World Report,* 95 (October 3, 1983), 60 ff, and James A. Michener, "You Can Call the 1980's 'The Ugly Decade,'" *New York Times,* January 1, 1987, p. 27.

Historians are always trying to instill some tidiness into the messiness of history. A benchmark for the healing of the generations might be the Bicentennial of the Declaration of Independence, July 1976. Evening fireworks in communities across the nation by at least that date symbolized celebrations of harmony rather than explosions of protest.

[4] The designation "'me' generation" is often and incorrectly attributed to the journalist Tom Wolfe. Tom Wolfe, "The Me Decade and the Third Great Awakening," *New West,* 1 (August 30, 1976), 27 ff, used the designation to refer to a decade, not a generation: "...the 1970's, a period that will come to be known as the Me Decade." Participants in the characteristics of that decade, as Wolfe saw it, were not necessarily of a generation but from all age groups. Commentators nailed the Baby Boomers with the rebuke.

By the mid-1980's the "'me' generation" had broadened beyond a decade or a generation to include anyone of apparently any age who is selfish. See, for example, William Safire, "Essay: Face Down in the Mud," *New York Times,* December 22, 1986, p. A23, and Nadine Brozan, "Colleges Encourage Student Volunteers," *New York Times,* January 14, 1987, pp. C1 ff.

[5] The individual-centering emphasis is detailed in a larger study interpreting American society through the dynamics of major trends.

INDEX

Abbott, Jacob, 86
Abbott, Lyman, 85–90, 465, 529
Abegglen, James C., 482, 532
Aberdeenshire, Scotland, 213
Abingdon Press, 316
Achievement, used synonymously
    with success, 460
Adams, Charles Francis, 402, 403
Adams, Franklin P., 450, 513
Adams, Henry, 403
Adler, Alfred, 179, 235
Adler, Mortimer J., 540
Adorno, T. W., 539
Advertising:
    as institutionalization of the per-
        sonality ethic, 377–379
    television and the social democ-
        racy dilemma, 420–422
Advertising Federation of America,
    511
Albert, Ethel M., 481
Aldridge, Alfred Owen, 463
Alexander, Franz, 482
Alexander Hamilton Institute, 349,
    504
Alger, Horatio, Jr., 43–50, 51, 61,
    148, 167, 199, 213, 280, 323
Allen, Abel Leighton, 486
Allen, Frederick Lewis, 186, 497
Allen, Hervey, 466
Allen, James, 235
Allen, Josie, 138
Allen, Leighton, 483
Allport, Gordon W., 525
Aluminum Company of America,
    355

Ambition to succeed, causes of,
    107–122, 186–190
American Academy of Dramatic
    Arts, 233
American Efficiency Foundation, 220
American Magazine, 213, 215
American Motors, 534
American Schools and Colleges
    Association, 43
American Telephone and Telegraph
    Company, 207
Amherst College, 199
Amor, Senor, 524
AMORC, The Rosicrucian Order,
    520
Amory, Cleveland, 473
Andover Theological Seminary, 148
Anti-intellectualism, expression of in
    success literature (*see* summaries
    of character, mind power,
    personality ethics)
Apple, R. W., Jr., 460
Appleseed, Johnny, 21
Appleton, William, 473
Arabian Nights, 50
Aram, Genevieve V., 495, 497
Aristotle, 20
Armour & Company, 232
Arnold, Matthew, 309
Aronson, Sidney H., 467
Arthur, Timothy Shay, 28–30
Astor, John Jacob, 50, 425
Atkins, Gaius Glenn, 493
Atkinson, John W., 481
Atkinson, William Walker, 483, 484,
    485, 486, 488, 495, 503

Atlantic Monthly, 285, 350
Atlas, Charles, 346, 347
Attwood, William, 541
Auden, W. H., 293
Aurora, Oregon, 381
Australia, 133
Avary, Myrta Lockett, 490

Babbitt, 414, 415, 443
Bach, Marcus, 516
Bacharach, Bert, 507
Bacheller, Irving, 187, 188
Bagehot, Walter, 8
Bailyn, Bernard, 481
Balch, David A., 475
Balkin, Harry H., 525
Baltimore, Maryland, 29, 234
Barker, Raymond Charles, 520
Barlow, Robin, 534, 542
Barmash, Isadore, 531
Barnett, A. N., 536
Barnhart, Clarence L., 513
Barnum, P. T., 26, 72
Barrymore, John, 26
Bart, Belle, 524
Barton, Bruce, 196–209, 212, 215,
    223, 352, 412, 413
Barton, William Eleazar, 196, 197
Baruch, Bernard, 44
Bates, Ernest Sutherland, 484
Batten, Barton, Durstine & Osborn,
    196, 201, 352
Baudouin, Charles, 483
Baumhart, Raymond C., 541
Baxter, Richard, 14
Bayard, Senator, 200
Bayley, Abner, 489, 490
Beard, Charles, 245, 385, 466, 481
Beard, Mary, 245, 466
Bedner, Robert R., 498
Beecher, Henry Ward, 25–28, 86, 443
Beery, Ray C., 508
Behrend, Genevieve, 495
Behrman, S. N., 470
Bell, Daniel, 541
Bell, Whitfield J., Jr., 464
Bellamy, Edward, 530
Bellwald, A. M., 485
Belton, Missouri, 250
Beltone Hearing-Aid Company, 252
Bender, James, 263, 267
Bendix, Reinhard, 388, 389, 460,
    470, 478, 482, 532
Benedict, Elsie L., 525
Benedict, Ralph P., 525

Benger, Ernest, 355
Benson, Bernard S., 527
Bentall, J. O., 358–361, 381, 534,
    535
Berelson, Bernard, 482
Bergmann, R. H., 543
Berkeley, George, 130
Berkeley, Rhode Island, 319
Berle, Adolf A., Jr., 197
Bernstein, Barton J., 533
Bertelson, David, 467
Bestor, Arthur E., 513
Bettger, Frank, 256–258, 503
Bierce, Ambrose, 138
Binghamton, New York, 342
Binyon, Laurence, 524
Bishop, Robert L., 498
"Bitch-Goddess SUCCESS," 403
Bjerregaard, C. H. A., 485
Björkman, Frances Maule, 493
Black, Hillel, 541
Blackford, Katherine M. H., 525
Blackstock, Walter, 490
Blaine, James G., 57
Blake, Eugene Carson, 335, 522
Blake, Robert R., 481
Blanton, Smiley, 321, 518, 519, 523
Blau, Peter M., 532
Bliven, Bruce, 542
Blum, John M., 542
Boatfield, Helen C., 463
Bobbs-Merrill, 126
Bode, Carl, 466, 543
Bolles, Blair, 541
Bolton, Henry C., 523
Bond, Frederick Clifton, 520
Bonnell, John Sutherland, 331
Borow, Henry, 539
Boston, Massachusetts, 45, 53, 149,
    232, 445
Boston University, 148, 149, 273,
    319, 445
Botkin, Robert James, 525
Bourne, Randolph, 252
Bowersville, Ohio, 317
Bowman, Claude C., 539
Boyden, Albert G., 54
Bradburn, Norman M., 540
Braden, Charles S., 483, 484, 516
Brady, Martha Kennedy, 524
Brazer, Harvey E., 542
Breit, Harvey, 262, 518, 522
Breitbart, Siegmund, 346
Bremner, Robert S., 477
Bressler, Marvin, 513

Brewer, John M., 539
Brewster, Massachusetts, 45
Bridge, James H., 473
Bridges, Hal, 533
Briggs, Asa, 488
Bristol, Claude, 296–302
Brogan, D. W., 113
Bromberg, Walter, 485
Bronx, New York, 352
Brookings Institution, 534
Brooklyn, New York, 64, 319, 322
Brooks, George W., 480
Brooks, John, 512, 541
Brooks, Van Wyck, 413, 543, 537
Brophy, Loire, 511
Brown, Arthur W., 489, 490
Brown, Henry Harrison, 172, 488
Brown, Ira V., 476
Brown, Ivor, 529
Brown, Newell, 539
Brown, Norman O., 480
Brown, William Burlie, 467
Brown University, 51, 66, 73
Brunet, Paul Martin, 520
Brutus, 274
Bryan, William Jennings, 35, 203
Bryant & Stratton Business College,
    40
Bryden, Dean, 525
Bryson, Lyman, 467
Buck, Solon J., 467
Buffalo, New York, 527
Bunker, M. N., 494, 525
Bunting, Earl, 398
Burdin, L. Gray, 506
Burke, Marylin C., 505
Burkmar, Lucius, 128
Burma, 94
Burns, George, and Gracie Allen,
    245
Burr, Agnes Rush, 471
Burr, Nelson R., 462, 493, 528
Bursk, Edward C., 528
Bury, Professor, 404
Business Week, 536
Butter, Richard, 511
Byrne, Brendan, 526

Caldwell, Erskine, 466
California, 53, 138, 144
Callahan, George, 526
Calvin, John, 24, 444
Cambridge, Massachusetts, 80
Cambridge Institute, 306
Campbell, David E., 524

Campbell, Robert A., 524
Canby, Henry Seidel, 35
Cantril, Hadley, 540
Cape Cod, Massachusetts, 45
Caplovitz, David, 540
Caplow, Theodore, 544
Career Institute of Chicago, Illinois,
    503
Carlton, Frank T., 515
Carnegie, Andrew, 30, 66–71, 74,
    104, 150, 199, 216, 395, 404,
    490, 517
Carnegie, Dale (Dale Carnagey), x,
    94, 95, 226–251, 257, 259–262,
    265, 272, 278, 288, 291, 292,
    508, 510
Carnegie, Dorothy, 245
Carson, Gerald, 503
Case, Robert Ormond, 471
Case, Victoria, 471
Cassese, Mr., 439
Casson, Herbert N., 501
Cate, Curtis, 522
Cater, Douglass, 529
Catholic Digest, 521
Cawelti, John G., 470
Chalmers, David, 533
Chamberlain, John, 535
Chambers, Clarke A., 479
Champney, Freeman, 475
Chapman, Charles C., 502
Character ethic (see Success, idea of)
Charlesworth, James C., 541
Chase, Stuart, 186
Chautauqua, 57, 232
Cheit, Earl F., 536
Cherne, Leo, 536
Chesterfield, Earl of, 227, 228
Chicago, 117, 149, 314
Chicago, University of, 77, 394
Child-rearing, 117–123
Childs, George William, 53
Childs, Marquis W., 529
China, 88
Chorley, Kenneth, 529
Christian Capitalism, 361
Christian Herald, 153
Christian Socialism, 358–360, 381
Chubbuck, Emily, 477
Churchill, Winston, 422
Cincinnati, Ohio, 132
Civil War, 30–36
Claflin, Horace Brigham, 53
Clark, James J., 536
Clark, John, 45

Clark, Robert E., 541
Clarke, Alfred C., 482
Clay, Henry, 102
Clemenko, Harold B., 504, 506
Cleveland, Ohio, 183
Cleveland, Grover, 530
Cleveland Heater Company, The, 508
Clews, Henry, 35, 473
Clifton, John L., 464
Close, Charles W., 486, 488, 495
Clymer, R. Swinburne, 520
Coan, Titus Munson, 530
Cochran, Thomas C., 66, 466, 497, 500
Cody, Sherwin, 229, 252
Cohen, I. Bernard, 463
Coleridge, Samuel Taylor, 130
Collier, P. F., & Son Co., 503
Columbus, Ohio, 318
Commager, Henry Steele, 465, 493, 540
Concord, Massachusetts, 441
Conformity, 415, 416
Connolly, M., 488–490, 492
Consensus, with respect to shared values, 380–381
Conversation Studies, 507
Conwell, Russell Herman, 55–61, 95, 235
Cook, Fred J., 541
Cooke, Morris L., 218
Cooley, Charles Horton, 116
Coolidge, Calvin, 200, 203
Cooper, Horace, 434
Cooper, Peter, 50, 53, 99
Cooper Union, 40
Copernicus, 122
Coriat, Isador H., 485
Copley, Frank B., 502
Copley, John Singleton, 418
Cornell Club, New York City, 249
Cornerstone Library, 514
Coser, Rose Laub, 481
Cotton, Ethel, 252
Cotton, John, 443, 478
Coué, Émile, 177, 181–185, 295, 306, 412
Cowan, John, 524
Cowley, Malcolm, 469
"Coy mistress," 9
Crafts, Wilbur F., 62–64
Crandall, Ruth, 531
Crawford, Robert P., 352, 527

Creative Education Foundation, The, 352
Cressey, Donald R., 541
Crime, 434–436
Crites, John O., 539
Crocker, Thomas S., 45
Crockett, Harry J., Jr., 478, 481, 532
Crosby, Bing, 420
Crosby, W. C., 471
Cross, Richard E., 534
Crothers, Samuel McChord, 459
Crouse, Russel, 48
Crowell, Thomas Y., 254, 255
Cuber, John F., 460
Cunningham, Raymond J., 485
Curti, Merle, 465, 477, 536, 537
Curwood, James Oliver, 164
Czechoslovakia, 164

Daddy Warbucks, 391, 392
Daily Graphic (New York), 138
Daily Worker, 391
Dale Carnegie Alumni Association, Inc., 247
Dale Carnegie Course in Effective Speaking, Leadership Training, and Human Relations, 245, 247, 248, 251
Dale and Dorothy Carnegie Courses for Women, 245
D'Andrade, Roy, 481
Daniels, George, 82, 475
Dante, 343
Darrah, Estelle M., 468
Darrow, Whitney, Jr., 287
Darwin, 122, 308
Darwin, Charles, 64, 87
Darwinism (see Social Darwinism)
Davidson, Bill, 527
Davies, John, 524
Deardorff, Neva R., 477
de Beaumont, Gustave, 537
de Grazia, Sebastian, 542
de Huszar, George B., 537
de Kerlor, W. W., 524
Demos, John, 461
Dempsey, Jack, 187
Denney, Reuel, 509, 539
Denver, Colorado, 278
Depew, Chauncey M., 473
Destler, Chester M., 472
de Tocqueville, Alexis, 424, 530
Detroit, Michigan, 276
Detroit Journal, 319

Developing nations (*see* Puritan-
    Protestantism)
De Vries, Peter, ix, 508
Dewey, Thomas E., 238, 322
Dichter, Ernest, 507
Dickinson, Emily, 544
Dieter, John, 543
Dietrichson, Jan W., 536
Dilman, Louis, 464
Dingle, Edwin John, 520
Dinitz, Simon, 482
Dionysus, 97
Doherty, William T., 499
Dombrowski, James, 476, 528
Donne, John, 516
Doolittle, Eliza, 138
Doolittle, Liza, 407
Dorfman, Joseph, 462
Dornbusch, Sanford M., 483
Dostoyevsky, Fyodor, 9
Doty, Roy A., 511
Douglas, Lloyd, 316
Drama (*see* Novelists, playwrights,
    and poets)
Dreier, Thomas, 494
Dreiser, Theodore, 153, 370, 410
Dresser, Horatio W., 483–486,
    494
Drew, Daniel, 99
Drucker, Peter F., 512
Drury, Horace B., 501
Duffy, Ben, 498
Dukette, Eugene R., 495
Duke University, 300, 302
Dulles, John Foster, 197
Dunbar, Aldis, 485
Dun & Bradstreet, 8, 47
Duncan, Otis Dudley, 532
Dunninger, Joseph, 299, 300
Du Pont, 355, 399
Durante, Jimmy, 289
Dutton, L. S., 465
Dynes, Russell R., 482

East Aurora, New York, 81
Eastman, George, 240
Eckardt, A. Roy, 522
Economists, 385–389, 393–396
Eddy, Mary Baker, 129, 169
Edes, Grace Williamson, 469
Edgartown, Massachusetts, 51
Edgeworth, Maria, 465
Edison, Thomas, 158
Education, attitude of success
    literature toward (*see* summaries

Education (*continued*):
    of character, mind power, and
    personality ethics)
Edwards, Alba M., 511
Edwards, Jonathan, 146
Efficiency movement, 218–221
Efron, Edith, 513
Egalitarianism, 415–423
Einstein, Albert, 4
Eisenhower, Dwight, 246, 273, 330,
    331, 399, 537
Eisenstadt, A. S., 533
Eisenstadt, S. N., 478
Eldridge, Mrs. Curtis, 469
Eliot, Dr., 229
Eliot, T. S., 413
Elizabeth, Queen, 14
Elliott, Osborn, 531
Ellis, Evelyn, 482
Ellsworth, Paul, 494
Elson, Ruth Miller, 476
Emerson, Ralph Waldo, 111, 130,
    198, 321, 367, 457
Emmanuel Movement, 485
England, 14, 15, 30, 40, 69, 133, 181,
    213, 262, 436
England, Queen of, 39
Ennever, W. J., 348
Esenwein, J. Berg, 505
Ethel Cotton Course in Conversation,
    The, 507
Etiquette manuals, 227
Evans, Miss, 153
Evans, Warren Felt, 129

Fadiman, Clifton, 470
Fairbanks, Douglas, 187
Falk, Robert, 470, 536
Fame, as a part of success, 1–9,
    288–290
Family, 117–123, 285
Fan Club Hollywood News, 289
Farber, Maurice L., 482
Farley, James, 237, 259
Father Divine, 311
Faulkner, Harold U., 497, 500
Faulkner, William, 466
Faust, 369
Fay, Bernard, 463
Feather, Norman T., 481
Federal Council of the Churches of
    Christ in America, 484
Feld, Sheila, 478, 539, 540
Fenichel, Otto, 115
Ferenczi, S., 115

Ferguson, Charles W., 483, 516
Fertig, Lawrence, 398
Fidelity-Philadelphia Trust
    Company, 531
Field, Marshall, 158
Filene, Edward, 223
Filler, Louis, 490
Fillmore, Charles, 311–313, 521
Fillmore, Lowell, 516
Fillmore, Myrtle, 311–313
Financial and Commercial Chronicle,
    214
Fineman, Helene H., 463
Fiore, Jordan D., 470
Firestone, Harvey S., 391
Firestone, Raymond C., 391
Fishwick, Marshall W., 468
Fiske, Charles, 203
Fitzgerald, F. Scott, 8
Fleming, Peter, 529
Flesch, Rudolf, 526
Fletcher, Allan L., 526
Flint, Maurice, 316
Florida, 149
Flynn, John T., 531
Forbes, B. C. (Bertie Charles),
    212–218
Ford, Henry, 36, 104, 126, 177, 186,
    207, 223, 270, 276, 395
Ford, Paul L., 464
Forest Hills, New York, 244
Form, William H., 459, 541
Fortune, 272, 284, 290, 397, 512
Fosdick, Raymond B., 477
Foster Correspondence Schools, 178
Foster, O. D., 501
Foundation for Christian Living, 315
Foundation for Economic Education,
    Inc., 534
Fourastié, Jean, 544
Fowler, Nathaniel C., 62
Fox, Emmet, 125
France, 16, 112, 133, 181, 297, 309
Frank, Lawrence K., 539
Frankel, Charles, 541
Franklin, Benjamin, x, 15–22, 52, 53,
    79, 95, 98, 140, 160, 161, 228,
    468, 512
Free, Lloyd A., 540
Freedley, Edwin T., 36–38
Freeman, James Dillet, 516
French, E. Geoffrey, 478
French, Warren G., 466
Freud, Sigmund, 115, 122, 168, 179,
    238, 308, 321, 425

Fromm, Erich, 108, 424, 509, 513,
    514, 539
Frontier, 42
Frost, Robert, 418
Fuller, Edmund, 522
Fulton, Miss, 169
Funk, Charles E., 497
Funk, Wilfred, 351
Funk & Wagnalls, 252, 351
Funston, G. Keith, 393

Gable, Clark, 235
Gabriel, Ralph H., 477
Galantiere, Lewis, 512
Galbraith, John Kenneth, 395, 512
Gallup, George, 521, 540
Gantt, Henry L., 218
Gauvreau, Emile, 525
Garcia, General, 82–85
Garden City, Long Island, 247
Gardner, Ralph, 45, 469, 470
Garfield, James A., 39, 49, 52, 57,
    318
Gay, Robert M., 493
Gaynor, Janet, 126
Gehring, Mary Louise, 472
Geis, Gilbert, 541
Gelfant, Blanche Housman, 536
General Motors, 399
Georgi, Charlotte, 407
Germain, Walter M., 302
Germany, 112
Getty, J. Paul, 393
Ghent, W. J., 472, 530
Gibney, Frank, 541
Gilbreth, Frank B., 219
Ginzberg, Eli, 460
Girard, Stephen, 150
Glazer, Nathan, 509, 539
Gleason, Philip, 538
Glen Cove, Long Island, 154
Glover, J. D., 536
Godfrey, Arthur, 331
Golden Gate, 137
Goldman, Eric F., 500, 512, 541
Good Housekeeping, 45
Goodman, Walter, 541
Gordon, Arthur, 518, 519, 521–523
Gordon, Frances L., 520
Gordon, Katherine K., 539
Gordon, Richard E., 539
Gorer, Geoffrey, 116, 477
Gorman, William, 540
Gospel of Wealth (*see* Andrew
    Carnegie)

Gould, George M., 485
Gould, Jay, 141
Gow, Charles R., 504
Grace, Daddy, 310
Grady, Henry W., 32
Grafe, Louis M., 269, 270
Graff, Henry F., 465, 467
Graham, Billy, 330, 336
Graham, Lee, 263, 267
Grant, Ulysses S., 52, 57
Grattan, Thomas Colley, 403, 417
Grape-Nuts, 526
Graves, Robert, 499
Gray, Harold, 391
Great man interpretation of history,
    102
Greeley, Andrew M., 478
Greeley, Horace, 40, 41
Green, Arnold, 439, 509, 514, 539,
    541
Green, Robert W., 478
Greene, Theodore P., 468
Greenewalt, Crawford H., 399, 512
Greenstein, Fred I., 468
Greenwich Village, 413
Gregory, Frances W., 388
Gregory, Horace, 428
Griswold, A. Whitney, 463, 483, 485
Grolier Club, 469
Gross National Product, 445–447
Gruber, Frank, 45, 469, 470
Guernsey, Welburn M., 503
Guest, Edgar, 201
Guggenheim, 104
Guideposts, 315
Gunther, Max, 539, 541
Gurin, Gerald, 478, 539, 540

Haber, Samuel, 502
Haber, Ralph Norman, 481
Hacker, Louis M., 533
Hackett, Alice Payne, 316, 483, 484,
    492, 497, 499, 506, 508, 517,
    521, 527
Haddock, Frank, 494, 495
Hagen, Everett S., 481
Hallinan, Charles, 169–172
Halsey, Margaret, 539, 541
Halsey, Van R., 536
Hamill, Robert, 445
Hamilton, Alexander, 24
Hamilton College, 352
Hamlet, 261
Handlin, Oscar, 460
Handy, Robert T., 528

Hanford, Edgar C., 515
Hanna, A. J., 497
Hanson, Melvina, 524
Happiness, 1, 424–434, 445–447,
    448–453
Happy Thought Coffee House, 133
Hargrave, Gordon J., 525
Harper's, 285
Harriman, Margaret Case, 504, 506
Harrington, Alan, 509
Harrington, S. A., 194, 195
Harris, P. M. G., 533
Harris, William B., 511
Harrison, William Henry, 34
Hart, Hornell, 302–307, 515, 521
Hart, James D., 466, 484, 487, 489
Harte, Bret, 138
Harvard Business Review, 273
Harvard Graduate School of
    Business Administration, 527
Harvard Medical School, 148
Harvard University, 45, 46, 51, 80,
    265, 441
Havemann, Ernest, 512
Haverstick, John, 514
Hawthorn Books, 302
Hawthorne, Diana, 523
Hawthorne, Nathaniel, 21
Hayek, F. A., 533
Hayes, Rutherford B., 57
Hayward, John, 516
Hearst, 80, 212
Heaven, 203
Hecht, Ben, 8
Heckscher, August, 542
Hegel, Georg W. F., 130
Heilbroner, Robert L., 528
Heller, Celia S., 532
Hemingway, Ernest, 412
Henderlider, Clair R., 519
Henderson, C. R., 474
Hendrick, B. J., 473
Hendricks, Robert J., 530
Hepner, Harry Walker, 482
Heraclitus, 123
Herberg, Will, 529
Heroes, 21, 30–36, 101–103, 158,
    186, 187, 288–290
Hertzler, J. O., 388
Herzberg, Frederick, 540
Heuver, Gerald D., 528
Hibben, Paxton, 465
Hiestand, Dale L., 460
Higgins, Henry, 138, 407
Hill, James J., 395, 404, 472

Hill, Napoleon, 314, 520
Hillis, Newell Dwight, 474
Hinton, Edward M., 488
Historians, 385, 386, 395
Hoag, Alden B., 445
hoff, 539
Hofstadter, Richard, 65, 537, 539
Holbrook, Stewart H., 475
Holland, Norman N., 470
Hollingshead, August B., 6
Hollywood, 421
Hollingsworth, J. Rogers, 537
Holmes, Ernest, 125, 483, 484, 491,
    520
Holmes, Fenwicke L., 495
Holmes, Mary S., 464
Holmes, Oliver Wendell, Sr., 173,
    406, 407
Holmes, Oliver Wendell, Jr., 434
Holyoke, Massachusetts, 173
Honesty, attitude of success literature
    toward (see summaries of
    character, mind power, and
    personality ethics)
Honolulu, Hawaii, 133
Hook, Sydney, 481
Hoover, Herbert, 186, 210, 211
Hopkins, Charles Howard, 476, 528
Horney, Karen, 113, 482, 539
Hoschouer, William I., 516
Hoshor, John, 516
Houghton Mifflin, 153
Hovenden, Thomas, 117
Howe, Irving, 535
Howell, William Dean, 408
Hubbard, Elbert, 79–85, 235, 497
Huber, Caroline M., 544
Huber, J. Y., 472
Hudson, Winthrop S., 462
Hudson River, 413
Hughes, Everett, 513
Hughes, Howard, 532
Human Engineering Laboratory, 350
Hume, Hugo, 483
Humphrey, Lucius, 520
Hunt, Edward E., 501
Hunt, Freeman, 36–38, 95
Hutchins, Robert, 197
Hutchinson, Paul, 522
Huth, John F., Jr., 490

Ideal Toy Co., 331
Idols of Entertainment, 288–290
Incentive, conservative use of in
    ideology, 397–399

Independent Efficiency Service, 219
India, 130
Industrialism, importance of values
    in, 94, 95
Industrial Revolution in nineteenth
    century, 30–36
Images of Aspiration, 36, 288
Inge, William Ralph, 496
Ingram, K. C., 508, 510
Ingram-Moore, Erica, 524
International Correspondence
    Schools, 232, 349
International New Thought Alliance,
    132, 311, 515
Iron Age, 531
Irwin, Theodore, 543

Jackman, Paul E., 525
Jackson, C. D., 544
Jackson, Elton F., 532
James, Henry, 8, 408, 535
James, William, 125, 168, 178, 235,
    237, 238, 321, 403, 485, 493
Jamison, A. Leland, 493
Janet, Pierre, 485
Janney, J. Elliott, 511
Japan, 150
Jaspan, Norman, 541
Jefferson, Thomas, 21, 35
Jensen, P. A., 485
Jews, 381
John XXIII, Pope, 3
Johnson, Benjamin, 494
Johnson, E. A. J., 461
Johnson, Helen, 514
Johnson, Horace, 514
Johnson, Lyndon, 339, 541
Johnson, Thomas H., 544
Jones, Bobby, 187
Jones, Ernest, 480
Jones, Howard Mumford, 462, 535,
    536, 540
Jones, John G., 504
Josephine, 278
Josephs, Ray, 527
Josephson, Matthew, 467, 475, 533,
    535
Joslyn, C. S., 387
Journal of Commerce, 214
Journal of Social Issues, 537
Jung, 179
Justification for success, expressed
    in success literature (see
    summaries of character, mind
    power and personality ethics)

Kaemmerling, Effie (Barnhurst), 132
Kaiser, Henry J., 390
Kant, Immanuel, 130, 429
Kardiner, Abram, 480, 539
Kaufman, Herbert, 501
Kaufman, William, 114
Kavesh, Robert A., 407
"Keeping up with the Joneses," 187–189
Kehl, James A., 531
Keller, Suzanne, 460, 481
Kemper, Theodore D., 482
Kenkel, William F., 460
Kennedy, John F., 8, 339
Kentucky, 153
Kennedy, Joseph P., 8
Ketcham, Ralph L., 463
Kevin, Robert O., 528
Kinsey report, 330
Kirk, G. S., 482
Kleiner, Robert J., 539
Klopsch, Louis, 153
Kluckhohn, Clyde, 34, 341, 387
Kluckhohn, Florence R., 34
Knight, James A., 115
Knox, George H., 502
Knox, James S., 508
Koenig, Samuel, 541
Kolko, Gabriel, 478
Korea, 331
Korenvaes, Patricia, 534
Krooss, Herman E., 502
Kyne, Peter B., 191, 192

Labaree, Leonard W., 463, 464
Lagaren, Eugene Victor, 179
Lambert, Richard D., 528
Landone, Brown, 495, 520
Langham, James Mars, 524
Langhorne, Pennsylvania, 434
Larrabee, Eric, 541
Larrabee, Harold A., 464
Larson, Cedric A., 460
Larson, Christian D., 494
LaSalle Extension University, 349
Laski, Harold J., 2, 16, 35, 186, 530
Lathem, Maude Allison, 483, 484
Latimer, Hugh, 14
Latimer, J. V. D., 495
Laurie, Piper, 331
Lauterbach, Albert, 482, 511
Lawrence, William, 90, 476
Lazarsfeld, Paul F., 509
League of Nations, 258
Lee, Everett S., 479

Lee, Henry, 506
Lee, Robert E., 39
Lee's Summit, Missouri, 311
Lehman, E. L., 526
Leisure, 436–447
Lenski, Gerhard E., 460, 479, 528
Lerner, Max, 107, 376, 460, 539, 541
LeSourd, Howard M., 517, 519
Lestchinsky, A., 483
Leterman, Elmer G., 508
Leuchtenburg, William E., 537
Lever Brothers, 230
Levin, Harry T., 475
Levittown, 284
Lewis, H. Spencer, 520
Lewis, Norman, 351
Lewis, Sinclair, 26, 261, 262, 291, 408, 414, 415, 494
Liberace, Wladziu Valentino, 296
Liebman, Joshua Loth, 162
Life, 540
Lincoln, Abraham, 36, 39, 49, 50, 52, 244, 457
Lindbergh, Anne Morrow, 293, 294
Lindsay, Gertrude A., 523
Lindsay, Howard, 233
Lindsey, Ben, 150
Lipset, Seymour Martin, 388, 389, 460, 467, 478, 482, 509, 521, 532, 537
Literary Digest, 531
Littell, Robert, 181
Little Orphan Annie, 391, 392
Lloyd, Henry Demarest, 85
London, Jack, 164
London, 7, 133, 138, 181, 261, 348, 374
Longfellow, Henry Wadsworth, 95
Longgood, William, 506
Look, 315, 518
Lord, Everett W., 502
Los Angeles, California, 492
Louis, Arthur M., 532
Lowell, James Russell, 404
Lowenthal, Leo, 509
Lowrey, Frederick C., 154
Loyalties, multiple, 380
Luce, Henry, 197
Luck, 392, 393
(See also summaries of character, mind power, and personality ethics)
Lundberg, George A., 541
Lurton, Douglas, 265
Lydenberg, John, 536

Lynd, Helen Merrell, 387
Lynd, Robert S., 387, 539
Lynn, Kenneth S., 459, 535

Macauley, Robie, 536
McCalls, 45
McCarten, John, 280, 374
McClelland, David, 119, 479
McCloskey, Robert Green, 473
McClure, H. H., 189
McComb, Samuel, 485
McCormick, Cyrus H., 395
McCracken, Robert J., 365, 366
McCutchins, General Luther, 148
MacDonald, Jeremiah, 342
McEvoy, J. P., 506
MacFadden, Bernarr, 346
MacFadden, Mary, 525
McGill, V., 540
McGinley, Phyllis, 465
MacGrail, Joseph F., 491
MacGregor, M. M., 524
McGuffey Readers, 286, 287
McGuffey, William H., 23–25
MacIver, R. M., 540
McKinley, William, 82, 150, 318
Mack, Walter S., Jr., 44
Maclaren, Ian, 403
MacLelland, Bruce (pseud. Joseph
    Erwin Tuttle), 495
McLemore, Ethel Ward, 513
McPherson, Aimee Semple, 310
McWilliams, Carey, 520
Madame Millie, 342
Madison, James, 105
Madison Avenue, 201, 277, 352
Magoun, F. Alexander, 504
Main, Jackson Turner, 460
Maine, 238
Man, nature of, 136, 167, 168, 238,
    253, 444
Manhattan, 201
Marconi, 235
Marden, Charles F., 502
Marden, Orison Swett, 145–164, 370,
    475, 493, 530
Markham, Edwin, 85, 173
Marquand, J. P., 8, 371
Marshall, John, 24
Martin, Alfred W., 484, 485, 493
Martin, Eva, 487, 488
Marts, Arnaud C., 477
Marx, Karl, 79, 452
Maryville, Missouri, 231
Massachusetts, 51, 55

Massachusetts General Court, 51
Massachusetts Institute of
    Technology, 230
Masters, Edgar Lee, 405
Materialism, 96–99, 451, 452
Mather, Cotton, 11–14, 18, 21, 95,
    98, 368, 443
May, Henry F., 528
May, Rollo, 93, 514, 539
Mayer, Albert J., 478
Mayer, F. E., 483
Mayes, Herbert, 45
Mead, Frank S., 518, 521
Mead, Margaret, 118
Mead, Shepherd, 509
Means, Richard L., 478
Meier, Frederick, 524
Mellen, George E., 524
Mellon, Andrew, 186
Mellon Foundation, 104
Mencken, H. L., 112, 164, 396, 430
Menninger, Karl, 538, 539
Menninger, William C., 273
Meredith, Robert, 530
Merton, Robert K., 387, 479, 481,
    532, 541
Merz, Charles, 497
Messer, Alfred, 121
Meyer, Adolph E., 504
Meyer, Donald, 483, 522
Meyersohn, Rolf, 541
Michaelsen, Robert S., 461, 462
Michener, James, ix
Midas, King, 97
Middle Ages, 11, 107
Middletown, 387
Mikado, 83
Milano, Paolo, 524
Miles, Richard D., 463
Miller, Arthur, 9, 372–375, 411
Miller, Clyde R., 507
Miller, Douglas T., 460
Miller, Helen Hill, 513
Miller, Joaquin, 138
Miller, Perry, 462
Miller, William, 66, 387, 477, 497,
    500, 512
Miller, William Lee, 323, 522
Mills, C. Wright, 388, 460, 509, 511,
    512
Mills, Donald L., 459
Milner, Esther, 539
Mind power ethic (*see* Success, idea
    of)
Minnich, Harvey C., 465

Minow, Newton, 421
Missouri, 236, 246
Mitchell, Margaret, 466
Mizruchi, Ephraim Harold, 479, 481, 539
Mobility (*see* Opportunity)
Models of Devotion, 36, 288
Modern Screen, 331
Momand, Arthur "Pop," 188, 189
Money, nature of, 114–117
Monroe, Lewis B., 538
Monroe, Marilyn, 4
Moonlighting, 436–440
Moore, Wilbert E., 466, 542
Morgan, James N., 542
Morgan, John J. B., 503, 504
Morgan, Pierpont, 404
Morison, Samuel Eliot, 471
Morris, Clarence, 542
Morris, (Mrs.) Monia C., 504
Morris, William, 81
Morrow, Dwight W., 186
Morse, Nancy C., 543
Mosely Educational Commission to the United States of America, 477
Mosier, Richard D., 464, 465
Moskin, J. Robert, 541
Mothers, importance of:
in need for achievement, 117–122
in success literature (*see* summaries of character, mind power)
Mott, Frank Luther, 469, 488, 490, 503, 504
Mouton, Jane S., 481
Mueller, Ernst, 480
Mulford, Prentice, 136–144, 165, 487, 488, 490
Müller, Max, 540
Munro, Thomas, 536
Munsey, Frank, 149
Murphy, Joseph, 515
Murphy, R. C., Jr., 522
Murray, Arthur and Kathryn, 245
Muzzey, 23
Myers, Harry, 504
Myrdal, Gunnar, 107, 330, 380, 381
Myth, 93, 94, 101, 448–453 (*See also* Self-made man)

Napoleon, 278
Napoleon Hill Institute, The, 517
Nash, Gary B., 460

Nathan, George Jean, 430
National Association of Manufacturers, 398
National goals, 544
Nebraska, 148, 232
Nebraska, University of, 352
Neill, Thomas P., 537
Neu, Irene D., 388
Nevins, Allan, 395, 466, 474, 475
New England, 43, 56, 86, 128, 197
New England Primer, 23
New Hampshire, 146, 148, 154
New Jersey, 139
New Republic, 181
New Romantics, 443, 444
New Success, 154
New Thought (*see* Mind power ethic)
New York American, 214
New York City, 7, 38, 45, 46, 51, 86, 137, 139, 214, 233, 314, 319, 320, 322
Patrolmen's Benevolent Association, 439
New York Curb Exchange, 260
New York Life Insurance Company, 206, 207
NewYork Stock Exchange, 393
New York Times, 144, 316
New York Tribune, 40, 41
New York University, 86
New Yorker, 287, 374, 377, 428
Newcomer, Mabel, 532
Newman, William J., 536
Newsboys' Lodging House, 46
Nichols, Lewis, 518
Nichols, Thomas, 116, 425
Niebuhr, Reinhold, 330, 336
Nietzsche, Friedrich, 9
Nisbet, Robert A., 516
Nixon, Richard M., 339
Nordhoff, Charles, 530
Norris, Frank, 409
Nosow, Sigmund, 459, 541
Notre Dame University, 278
Novelists, playwrights, and poets, as critical interpreters of success, 369–376, 407–453, 448–453
Nunn, Clyde Z., 481
Nureyev, 419
Nye, Russel B., 470

Oates, Wayne E., 522
Oberlin Theological Seminary, 196
O'Connor, Johnson, 350

O'Connor, William Van, 536
Odets, Clifford, 369
Ohio Wesleyan, 318, 319
Olyanova, Nadya, 525
Opportunity, 380–402
  (*See also* summaries of character,
    mind power, and personality
    ethics)
Oregon, 172
Osborn, Alex F., 352–356
Osborn, Paul, 529
Otis, John Hancock, 405
Overstreet, H. A., 235, 242
Oxford, 67, 68

Packard, S. S., 468
Packard, Vance, 531
Packard Motor Car Company, 233
Paine, Tom, 79
Paris, 7, 153
Parker, Seymour, 539
Park Forest, Illinois, 284
Parkyn, Herbert A., 180
Parsons, Talcott, 478, 479
Parton, James, 468
Patterson, Charles Brodie, 484
Patterson, Grove, 319
Patterson, Mary Baker, 129
Pavlov, Ivan P., 168
Pawling, New York, 315, 322, 339
Payne, Paul Calvin, 522
Peale, Leonard, 319
Peale, Norman Vincent, x, 125, 162,
    295, 314–340, 367
Peale, Robert, 319
Peale, Ruth (Ruth Stafford), 320,
    322–324, 337, 339
Pearson, Norman Holmes, 543
Peary, Robert E., 404
Pecano, 347
Peirce, Charles, 71
Pelman Institute, 348
Pennsylvania, 247
Penn, William, 13, 14
Pepsodent Co., 503
Perkins, George W., 206, 207
Perkins, William, 14
Perry, Bliss, 33
Perry, Ralph Barton, 2, 34
Personality ethic (*see* Success, idea
    of)
Persons, Frederick T., 498
Persons, Stow, 462, 472
Peters, William, 522
Petersen, William, 532

Peterson, A. Everett, 468
Philadelphia, Pennsylvania, 13, 16,
    19, 29, 53, 56, 59, 61, 310
Pickford, Mary, 187, 236
Pierce, Bessie Louise, 500
Piercy, Josephine K., 461
Pierson, George W., 479
Playboy, 393
Player, Gary, 340
Podhoretz, Norman, 427
Poe, Edgar Allan, 29
Poetry (*see* Novelists, playwrights,
    and poets)
Poirot, Paul L., 400
Poland, 164
Pompeian Laboratories, 503
Poole, Allan P., 495
Poor Richard, 17, 20, 160, 161, 228
    280
Popplestone, Charles Edward, 520
Populism, 380–386
Post, Emily, 184
Potter, David, 392, 467, 511
Potter, Stephen, 262
Powers, Melvin, 515
Prentice-Hall, 254, 296, 302, 316,
    317, 518, 523
Presley, Elvis, 289
Presthus, Robert, 482
Priestly, J. B., 493
Pringle, Henry, 47, 466
Pringle, Katherine, 47
Productivity (*see* Puritan-
    Protestantism)
Progressivism, 380–386
  (*See also* Lyman Abbott)
Protestant Council of the City of
    New York, 339
Psycho-Phone Company, 179, 180
Publishers' Weekly, 126
Purinton, Edward Earle, 219–221,
    486
Puritan-Protestantism and
    productivity, 11–20, 90–110,
    367, 368, 448–457

Quakers, 13–15
Quimby, George A., 484
Quimby, Phineas P., 124, 128–130

Rackham, H., 464
Randall, John Herman, 484
Rand Daily Mail (Johannesburg),
    213

Rapson, Richard L., 481
Raven, J. E., 482
Rea, Gardner, 287
Read, Leonard E., 390
Reader's Digest, 351
Reavis, L. U., 468
Redford, P. J., 510
Regardie, Israel, 484, 516
Reissman, Leonard, 460
Religion, 'return to,' in late 1940s
    and 1950s, 330–335, 364–366
Renaissance and Reformation, 11
Reubens, Beatrice G., 460
Reynolds, Quentin, 469
Rhine, J. B., 300
Rhodes, James Ford, 404
Rice, Louis A., 508
Rich, Wilmer Shields, 477
Rideout, Walter B., 535
Ridpath, 56
Rieff, Philip, 537
Riesman, David, 509, 511, 513, 539
Riley, James Whitcomb, 233
Riley, Woodbridge, 494
Rischin, Moses, 470
Roback, A. A., 292
Robbins, Tennessee, 196
Robinson, Arthur R., 526
Robinson, Edwin Arlington, 405, 450
Robinson, Henry Morton, 497
Rockefeller, John D., Sr., 74–78, 79,
    104, 156, 216, 269, 395, 450,
    472, 490
Rockefeller, John D., Jr., 66, 73,
    544
Roe, Anne, 539
Roethlisberger, F. J., 511
Rogers, Will, 258
Role conflict, 357
Roman republic, 445
Romier, Lucien, 189, 534
Roosevelt, Franklin, 202, 234, 250,
    384, 391, 398
Roosevelt, Theodore, 86, 383, 404
Rosen, Bernard, 119, 478, 481
Rosenwald, Julius, 393
Ross, Irwin, 517, 519, 522
Ross, Ralph, 460, 540
Rossiter, Clinton, 544
Rotary, 223, 324
Roth, Charles, 259, 507, 527
Rousseau, Jean Jacques, 444
Rovere, Richard H., 476, 477
Rowan, Andrew S., 82
Roycroft Shops, 81

Rural origins, importance of, in
    success literature (*see* summaries
    of character, mind power and
    personality ethics)
Russell, Anna, 337
Russell, Jane, 331
Ruth, Babe, 187

Sag Harbor, Long Island, 137
St. Augustine, 26
St. Francis College, 266
St. Louis Cardinals, 256
Sampson, Ezra, 445
Samson, Verne L., 471
Samuelsson, Kurt, 478
Sanford, Charles L., 463
San Francisco, 137, 138, 144, 172
Sarnoff, David, 44
Saveth, Edward N., 482, 533
Schlesinger, Arthur M., 461, 503,
    540
Schneider, Herbert W., 463
Schneider, Louis, 483
Schoeffler, Edmund H., 483
Schoonmaker, Edwin D., 502
Schoonmaker, (Mrs.) Florence, 505
Schulberg, Budd, 410, 411
Schwab, Charles, 156, 158, 236, 244,
    248, 260, 266
Scientific management, 218–221
Scopes trial, 64, 203
Scotland, 30, 67
Scott, William G., 536
Scranton, Pennsylvania, 178
Sea Breeze, Florida, 134
Sears, Julia Seton, 525
Sears, Roebuck and Company, 393
Seelye, John, 469
Seine River, 413
Seldes, George, 196
Seldes, Gilbert, 483
Self-made man, 20, 21, 30–36, 43–44,
    101–103, 380–457
Seligman, Daniel, 508, 536
Sellers, Charles Grier, Jr., 467
Selye, Hans, 539
Sennett, Richard, 533
Service, concept of, 395–397
    (*See also* summaries of
        character, mind power, and
        personality ethics)
Seton, Julia, 494
Shackleton, Robert, 471
Shafer, Boyd C., 479
Shafer, Paul, 533

Shakespeare, William, 52, 53, 103, 261, 452, 524
Shannon, Lyle W., 531
Shaplen, Robert, 466
Sharp, Harry, 478
Shaw, George Bernard, 112, 407
Shay, Felix, 475
Sheen, Fulton J., 330
Sheepshead Bay, Long Island, 137
Sheldon, Charles M., 203
Shepperson, Wilbur S., 461
Sherman, Harold, 515
Sherman, William T., 318
Sherrod, Julian, 497
Sherwin Cody School of English, 229, 507
Sherwood, Robert E., 498
Shimkin, Leon, 234
Shir-Cliff, Bernard W., 337
Shurtleff, Harold R., 470, 471
Siddall, John, 199, 215
Siegfried, Andre, 224
Silent Unity, 311
Silberman, Charles E., 542
Silver, A. Henry, 525
Simon, Leila, 132
Simon & Schuster, 234, 504
Simons, A. M., 543
Simpson, Mary Elizabeth, 520
Sjoberg, Gideon, 532
Sklare, Marshall, 482
Slichter, Sumner H., 501
Small, Collie, 504, 506
Smelser, Neil J., 532
Smiles, Samuel, 147, 149
Smith, Adam, 29, 111, 224, 277, 397
Smith, Chard Powers, 529
Smith, Daniel Scott, 533
Smith, Henry Nash, 469, 536
Smith, Howard R., 535
Smith, John, 461
Smith, Lillian, 466
Smith, Matthew Hale, 38, 97, 477
Smith, James Ward, 493
Smyth, Albert H., 462, 503, 512
Snow, C. P., 413, 537
Social class interpretation, 6–8, 33–36, 112, 113, 402–407, 418, 419
Social Darwinism, 64–74, 99, 151, 159, 221, 222, 476
Social Science Research Council, 481
Sociologists, 385–389, 393–396
Socrates, 242

Solomon, 21, 368, 457
Sombart, Werner, 440, 462, 477
Sorokin, Pitirim, 387
Soule, George, 500
South, ix, 30–36
South Africa, 213, 215
South Dakota, 232
South Natick, Massachusetts, 46
Soviet Russia, 447
Spain, 164
Spellman, Cardinal, 339
Spencer, Herbert, 66, 473
Spender, J. A., 497, 502
Spengler, Joseph J., 65, 66
Sperry, Willard L., 484, 493
Spiller, Robert E., 463, 475, 487
Spock, Benjamin, 287
Sprague, Jesse Rainsford, 499
Spykman, Nicholas M., 479
Stanford Institute, 515
Stanford, Leland, 53
Stanton, Frank N., 509
Starr, Harris E., 465, 466
State Normal School, Warrensburg, Missouri (now called Central Missouri State College), 232
State Temperance Alliance, 51
Stearns, Harold, 412, 536
Steffens, Lincoln, 116
Stein, Maurice R., 539
Steiner, Gary A., 482
Steiner, Lee R., 523
Steinbeck, John, 409, 410
Steinhardt, William B., 260
Stern, Louis, 393
Stetson, John B., 81
Stevens, George, 504
Stevenson, Adlai, 338
Stewardship of wealth, 395, 396
    (See also summaries of character, mind power, and personality ethics)
Stewart, Alexander, 53
Stoddard, Charles Warren, 487
Stone, W. Clement, 517
Stowe, Harriet Beecher, 25
Stratton, Clarence, 507
Strodtbeck, Fred L., 482
Strong, Elder, 146
Stryker, Perrin, 272, 511, 512, 527
Success:
    ambivalence toward, 448–453
    causes for ambition toward, 107–122, 186–190
    and child-rearing, 117–123

Success (*continued*):
and crime, 434–436
critics and consequences of,
357–457
cultural definition of, 1–9,
448–453
business and non-business, 1–9
institutional or professional, 3–
5
popular and critical, 5, 6
for women, 5
dilemmas:
character ethic dilemma of
material success vs. 'true
success,' 362–376
summary, 453, 454
justification dilemma of self-
giving vs. self-seeking,
357–368
summary, 453
national security dilemma of
individual self-fulfillment
vs. national power, 424–447
summary, 456, 457
personality ethic dilemma of
hypocrisy vs. sincerity,
376–379
summary, 454, 455
political dilemma of freedom
vs. equality, 380–402
summary, 455
social democracy dilemma of
freedom vs. authority,
402–423
summary, 455, 456
and gout, 480
and happiness, 1, 424–434,
445–447
idea of, in England, 14–16, 488
idea of character ethic:
in seventeenth century, 10–15
in eighteenth century, 15–22
1830s to 1910s, 21–106,
summary, 93–106
1910s and 1920s, 186–225
summary, 190, 191, 194, 195,
221–225
idea of:
conservative use of, 79, 85,
389–401
expressed in a variety of forms,
42, 43, 50–53, 55, 58, 62,
79, 145, 172, 195, 215, 218,
234–237, 254, 272, 324
liberal response to, 380–393

Success (*continued*):
idea of mind power ethic:
1880s to 1920s, 124–185
summary, 155–163, 175–185
reasons for its appeal,
165–172, 175–178, 184
since the 1930s, 294–340
reasons for its appeal,
307–310
summary, 295, 325 330,
332–335, 340
not unique to America, 14, 15
idea of personality ethic:
since the 1930s, 226–294
summary, 239–244, 264–271
causes of shift to, 272–288
summary, 288
psychological consequences
of, 290–294
political implications and
consequences of, 102–106,
158–160, 210–212, 264,
380–402
and leisure, 436–447
miscellaneous techniques for:
astrology, 342, 343
body-building and dietetics, 346,
347
brainstorming, 352–356
correspondence courses, 348,
349
fortunetelling, 341, 342
graphology, 343, 345
memory, 347, 348
palmistry, 342
phrenology, 343, 344
physiognomy, 343–345
vocabulary building, 349–351
patrician response to, 402–407
personal definition of, 448–453
psychic distress as consequence of,
424–447
(*See also* novelists, playwrights,
and poets)
Success, 153
Sugrue, Thomas, 515
Sullivan, Mark, 465
Sullivan, Vincent, 279, 280
Super, Donald E., 511, 539
Sutherland, Edwin H., 541
Sutherland, George, 210
Swift, Tom, 44
Swoboda, Alois, 525
Syracuse, New York, 320, 322
Syracuse, University of, 320

Taft, Donald R., 541
Taft, Robert A., 273
Talleyrand, 116
Tannenbaum, Frank, 541
Tarkington, Booth, 408
Taste leadership, 417–423
Tauber, Maurice F., 471, 472
Taussig, F. W., 387
Tawney, R. H., 464
Taylor, Frederick W., 218, 220
Taylor, Harrison B., 506
Taylor, Walter Fuller, 535
Tebbel, John, 469
Teener, James W., 516
Telepathy, 299
Television, as illustration of social
    democracy dilemma, 420–422
Temple University, 56
Texas, 253, 338
Thayer, Mary Van Rensselaer, 512
Thayer, William M., 502
Thayer, William Makepeace, 50–55,
    61, 151, 161
Thernstrom, Stephan, 394, 460, 479,
    532, 533
Thomas, Lowell, 234, 237, 322, 504
Thomas, Norman, 197
Thomases, Jerome, 468
Thompson, C. Bertrand, 501
Thompson, S. C., 508
Thoreau, Henry David, 441–443, 543
Thrift, in post–World War II dec-
    ades, 280–282
Thrupp, Sylvia L., 477
Thurber, James, 309, 509
Tin-pan Alley, 331
Tolles, Frederick B., 462
Towne, Elizabeth, 172–175, 488, 495,
    497
Towne, William, 173, 495, 497
Toynbee, Arnold, 396, 529
Tragedy, as defined by its own cul-
    ture, 374
Tressler, Irving D., 262
Trine, Ralph Waldo, 126, 165, 493
Trinkaus, Charles Edward, Jr., 540
Truman, Harry, 246
Trupo, Anthony, 524
Tulsa, Oklahoma, 245
Turkin, H. Y., 508
Turkington, Grace A., 500
Twain, Mark, 138, 164, 258, 436

Uncle Juvinell (Morrison Heady),
    471

Underhill, Evelyn, 493
Unitarian Society of Brewster, 45
U.S. Air Force Academy, 544
U.S. Department of Labor, 542, 543
Unity School of Christianity, 311–
    313
U Nu, 476

Vail, Theodore N., 207
Valentino, Rudolf, 187
Value multiplier effect, 94
Van Baalen, Jan Karel, 516
Van Dalen, D. B., 525
Van Den Haag, Ernest, 460, 540
Van Doren, Carl, 463, 464
Van Dyke, John C., 6
Van Epps, Mr., 169–171
Van Fossen, Irene, 487
Van Loon, Hendrik Willem, 184
Van Nostrand, Albert, 536
Veblen, Thorstein, 85, 467, 478, 480
Vedder, Clyde B., 541
Vermont, 200
Vernon, Philip E., 525
Veroff, Joseph, 539, 540
Victoria, Queen, 30, 126
Vidich, Arthur J., 539
Vocational guidance, 538, 539
Vogt, Evon Z., 481
Vollmer, Howard M., 459
von Mises, Ludwig, 539

Waite, Arthur Edward, 487
Wald, Robert M., 511
Walden Pond, 441, 442
Waldorf-Astoria Hotel, 214
Wales, Prince of, 126
Walker, Franklin, 486, 487
Walker, Robert H., 536
Wall Street, 38, 102, 274, 385, 413
Wall Street Journal, 349
Wallace, DeWitt, 197
Wallace, Edgar, 213
Wallach, Ira, 508, 522
Waller, George M., 462
Wanamaker, John, 158
Ward, John William, 467
Ward, Lester Frank, 382, 383, 467,
    480
Warfel, Harry, 461, 465
Warner, Samuel J., 122
Warner, W. Lloyd, 388, 393, 394, 482
Warner, William, 495
Washington, George, 21, 36, 39, 52,
    288

Washington, D.C., 7, 102
Watson, E. M. D., 506
Watson, Tom, 383
Wattles, Wallace D., 494
Wax, Murray, 463
Wax, Rosalie, 463
Ways, Max, 544
Weaver, Edward E., 485
Webb, Ewing T., 503, 504
Webb, Joseph S., 242
Webb, Sidney and Beatrice, 245
Weber, Julius A., 516
Weber, Max, 22, 463, 464, 478
Webster, Daniel, 24, 49, 50
Webster, Noah, 23
Wecter, Dixon, 468
Wee Wisdom, 311
Weigel, Gustave, 522
Weiss, Robert S., 543
Wells, H. G., 184, 403
Welsh, Frank M., 520
Werner, Gertrude, 500
Wesley, John, 64, 474, 475
West, Georgiana Tree, 516
Westinghouse, George, 395
Wetherill, Richard W., 508
Whalen, Grover, 44
Whalen, Richard J., 461
Whalen, Robert G., 480
Wharton, Edith, 8
Wheeler, Elmer ("Mr. Sizzle"), 253, 254, 260, 268, 269, 508, 510
White, Bouck, 499
White, Eugene E., 519
White, David Manning, 539
White, James Terry, 444
Whiting, John W. M., 481
Whitman, Walt, 157
Whitney, Eli, 395
Whitney, Ethel, 494
Whittier, John Greenleaf, 487
Who's Who in America, 5
Whyte, William H., Jr., 284, 416, 512, 513
Wilcox, Ella Wheeler, 173
Wilensky, Harold L., 532, 542
Williams, Albert N., 522
Williams, Charles D., 474
Williams, Grace Ellery, 524

Williams, J. Paul, 516
Williams, John K., 520
Williams, Louis, 524
Williams, Orlo, 496
Williams, Robin M., Jr., 466, 512, 532, 539
Williams, Tennessee, 466
Williams, William Ellis Bellis Meyrick, 495
Willkie, Wendell, 201
Wilmans, Helen, 134, 488, 493
Wilson, Charles E., 399
Wilson, Everett B., 508
Wilson, Sloan, 541
Wilson, Woodrow, 112, 197, 258, 383, 384
Winchell, Walter, 278
Windsor, William, 524
Winick, Charles, 535
Wisconsin, University of, 199
Wissler, Richard H., 471
Wizard, 137
Women, cultural definition of success for, 5
Wood, Clement, 525
Wood, Henry, 486
Woodbridge, William W., 192–194
Woodbury, Clarence, 516, 518, 519
Woodward, C. Vann, 32, 466, 530
Woodward, Robert H., 536
Wohl, R. Richard, 470
Woolf, James D., 527
Worcester, Elwood, 485
Wordsworth, William, 130, 444
Worsley, T. C., 529
Wortley, Edward (pseud. for Alfred Hepper), 527
Wright, Louis B., 461–463
Wright, Richard, 466
Wright, Sylvia B., 508
Wyllie, Irvin G., 463, 472, 477

Young, Filson, 493
Young, Malcolm O., 497
Young Men's Christian Association, 233, 234, 247

Zavalloni, Marisa, 481
Zinn, Howard, 467

PUSHCART